2ND EDITION

THE ECONOMICS OF
EUROPEAN INTEGRATION

RICHARD BALDWIN   CHARLES WYPLOSZ

2ND EDITION

THE ECONOMICS OF EUROPEAN INTEGRATION

RICHARD BALDWIN   CHARLES WYPLOSZ

The **McGraw·Hill** Companies

London   Boston   Burr Ridge, IL   Dubuque, IA   Madison, WI   New York
San Francisco   St. Louis   Bangkok   Bogotá   Caracas   Kuala Lumpur   Lisbon
Madrid   Mexico City   Milan   Montreal   New Delhi   Santiago   Seoul   Singapore
Sydney   Taipei   Toronto

The Economics of European Integration
Second Edition
Richard Baldwin and Charles Wyplosz
ISBN 10: 0-077-111192
ISBN 13: 9780077111199

Published by McGraw-Hill Education
Shoppenhangers Road
Maidenhead
Berkshire
SL6 2QL
Telephone: 44 (0) 1628 502 500
Fax: 44 (0) 1628 770 224
Website: www.mcgraw-hill.co.uk

British Library Cataloguing in Publication Data
A catalogue record for this book is available from the British Library

Library of Congress Cataloging-in-Publication Data
The Library of Congress data for this book has been applied for from the Library of Congress

Acquisitions Editor: Kirsty Reade
Development Editor: Hannah Cooper
Senior Production Editor: Beverley Shields
Marketing Manager: Marca Wosoba

Text Design by Hard Lines
Cover design by Ego Creative Ltd
Printed and bound in Spain by Mateu Cromo, Madrid

First Edition published in 2004 by McGraw-Hill Education

ISBN 10: 0-077-111192
ISBN 13: 9780077111199

DEDICATION

For Sarah, Ted, Julia and Nick.

R.B.

In memory of my parents, whose sufferings inspired my yearning for a Europe at peace, and who taught me the pleasure of learning.

C.W.

Brief Table of Contents

Detailed Table of Contents

Preface

European integration keeps amazing its supporters and critics alike. No other region has displayed similar willingness to jettison important components of sovereignty in pursuit of shared, yet thoroughly imprecise, goals. And, in its own peculiar way, European integration keeps forging ahead at a pace that is too fast for some and too slow for others. No one would deny, though, that the transformation of the past half century is spectacular – a clean break with centuries of intra-European warfare. This integration is clearly important for the 500 or so million Europeans it directly affects, but since Europe accounts for one-quarter of the world economy, half of world trade and one-third of world capital markets, European integration also affects the lives of most non-Europeans.

A subtle interplay of strictly economic and much broader, high-minded goals has driven European integration forward along political, cultural and economic dimensions. The goal of this book is to provide an accessible presentation of the facts, theories and controversies that are necessary to understand this process. Our approach is rooted deeply in economic principles for the simple reason that economic integration has been the vanguard since the Organization for European Economic Cooperation was founded in 1948. Yet economics is not enough; historical, political and cultural factors are brought into the picture when necessary.

What this book is

This is a textbook for courses on European economic integration. Its emphasis is on economics, covering both the microeconomics and macroeconomics of European integration. Understanding European economic integration, however, requires much more than economics, so the book also covers the essential aspects of European history, institutions, laws, politics and policies.

The book is written at a level that should be accessible to second- and third-year undergraduates in economics as well as advanced undergraduates and graduate students in business and in international affairs, European studies and political science. Some knowledge of economics is needed to absorb all the material with ease – a first-year course in the principles of economics should suffice – but the book is self-contained in that it reviews all essential economics behind the analysis. Diligent students should therefore be able to master the material without any formal economics background.

What is in this book

The book is organized into five parts: essential background (Part I), the microeconomics of European integration (Part II), microeconomic policies (Part III), monetary integration (Part IV) and macroeconomic policies (Part V).

Part I presents the essential background for studying European integration.

★ An overview of the post-Second World War historical development of European integration is presented in Chapter 1, which will probably be useful to all students. Even students who are familiar with the main events should profit from this chapter since it stresses, wherever possible, the economic and political economy logic behind the events.

★ A concise presentation of the indispensable background information necessary for the study of European integration is presented in Chapter 2. This includes key facts concerning European economies and a brief review of the EU's legal system and principles. Chapter 2 also presents information on the vital EU institutions and the EU's legislative processes as well as the main features of the EU budget.

★ Chapter 3 presents an economic framework for thinking about EU institutions. The first part explains how the 'theory of fiscal federalism' can be used to consider the appropriateness of the allocation of powers between EU institutions and EU Member States. The second part explains how economic reasoning – game theory in particular – can be used to analyse EU decision-making procedures for their decision-making efficiency as well as their implications for the distribution of power among EU members. While these are not classic topics in the study of European integration, they are essential to understanding the current challenges facing the EU, such as the Constitutional Treaty and the 2004 enlargement.

Part II presents the critical microeconomics of European integration.

★ An introduction to the fundamental methods of trade policy analysis is presented in Chapter 4. The chapter introduces basic supply and demand analysis in an open economy, the key economic welfare concepts of consumer and producer surplus, and uses these to study the simple economics of tariff protection.

★ An in-depth analysis of European preferential trade liberalization is given in Chapter 5. The focus is on how the formation of a customs union or free trade area affects people, companies and governments inside and outside the integrating nations.

★ A thorough study of how the market-expanding aspects of European integration affects the efficiency of European firms is presented in Chapter 6. The main line of reasoning explains how integration in the presence of scale economies and imperfect competition can produce fewer, bigger and more efficient firms facing more effective competition from each other.

★ Chapter 7 gives a detailed study of the growth effects of European integration. The emphasis is on the economic logic linking European integration to medium-run and long-run growth effects. Neoclassical and endogenous growth theory are covered, as are the basic facts and empirical evidence.

★ The new Chapter 8 deals with the labour markets. It recalls the basics of labour economics in order to explain unemployment and develop the notion that social requirements may have seriously negative effects in terms of jobs, wages and growth. The chapter uses these insights to study the effects of integration. It deals with many controversial issues such as social dumping and migration, trying hard to stay above the fray by presenting economic analysis as one logic, not the only one. This chapter synthesizes material from the first edition's Chapters 7 and 17, but it also includes some new material that should allow it to be taught as a single lecture.

Part III covers the main EU policies.

★ Chapter 9 looks at the Common Agricultural Policy (CAP), presenting the economics and facts that are essential for understanding its effects. The chapter takes particular care to examine the economic forces behind recent CAP reform in the light of international trade negotiations (the Doha Round) and the 2004 enlargement.

★ Chapter 10 presents the economics that link European integration to the location of economic activities. This includes a presentation of the main facts on how the location of economic activity has shifted both within nations and between nations. To organize thinking about these facts – and to understand how EU regional policy might affect it – the chapter presents the locations effects of integration in the light of neoclassical theories (Heckscher–Ohlin) as well as the so-called new economic geography. The chapter also presents the main features of the EU's regional policy and considers the implications of the 2004 enlargement.

★ Chapter 11 covers the basic elements of the EU's competition policy and state aid policy (EU jargon for subsidies). Instead of just describing the policies, the chapter motivates and explains them by introducing the basic economic logic of anti-competitive practices. It also presents several cases that illustrate the difficulties of applying simple economics to the complex world of international business.

★ Chapter 12 addresses EU trade policy, i.e. its commercial polices with the rest of the world. While trade policy is not as central to the EU as, say, the CAP and cohesion policies are, it is important. The EU is the world's biggest trader, and trade policy is probably the only EU 'foreign policy' that is consistently effective. The chapter covers EU trade policy by presenting the basic facts on EU trade, covering the EU's institutional arrangements as concerns trade policy, and finally summarizing the EU's policies towards its various trade partners.

Part IV is where macroeconomics starts. It lays the ground for the analysis of monetary integration.

★ Chapter 13 returns to Europe's history, this time from the monetary angle. It recalls ancient times when Europe was a de facto monetary union under the gold standard, whose adjustment mechanism is now back at work. The disastrous inter-war period encapsulates all the policy mistakes that today's policy makers are determined to avoid. The chapter closes by showing how the European Monetary System (EMS) paved the way to the adoption of a single currency.

★ Chapter 14 takes a step sideways. It deals with a very general question: the choice of an exchange rate regime. It presents a summary of the basic macroeconomic principles needed to grasp the significance of exchange rate regimes. It then explains how to assess the desirability of each of the main arrangements, including the two-corner strategy that underlies Europe's shift to the euro, while explaining why others have chosen to stay out.

★ Chapter 15 deals with the European Monetary System, the now defunct first version and the new version, with already six member countries, which is a required step towards monetary union membership. It shows that the successes of the EMS have provided a powerful incentive to go further and create a single currency, while its shortcomings have made the adoption of the euro look like the least bad of all options.

Part V provides a detailed analysis of the monetary union before turning to two issues central to the macroeconomic functioning of the monetary union.

★ Chapter 16 presents the optimum currency area theory that helps to understand the main costs and benefits from sharing a common currency. The theory does not provide a black-and-white answer; rather it develops a set of economic, political and institutional criteria to evaluate the costs and the benefits of forming a monetary union. In addition, the costs and benefits may be endogenous. Europe fulfils some criteria but not others, which explains the unending debates on the merits of the European monetary union.

★ The main features of the European monetary union are laid out in Chapter 17. This includes a description and an analysis of the institutions created by the Maastricht Treaty. It explains the importance attached to price stability and the measures adopted to achieve this objective. The chapter also provides a review of the first years of the euro, assessing the performance of the ECB, including the democratic accountability gap.

★ Fiscal policy is the last national macroeconomic instrument remaining once national monetary policy has been lost. Chapter 18 looks at the Stability and Growth Pact, designed to deliver enough budgetary discipline not to endanger the overriding price stability objective. As we suggested on the first edition, the Pact had serious shortcomings, and they have now forced a revision. The revision and the events that made it necessary are presented, along with doubts about the chosen solution. We emphasize the economic and political difficulties inherent to preserving the last national macroeconomic instrument while ensuring fiscal discipline.

★ The last chapter deals with the financial markets. The financial services industry is being transformed by the Single European Act 1986 and by the adoption of a single currency. Chapter 19 starts with a review of what makes this industry special and then introduces the microeconomics of capital integration. This makes it possible to interpret the changes that have taken place and those that have not yet materialized. Financial markets are also important for monetary policy effectiveness, raising delicate questions: Is the single monetary policy symmetrically affecting member countries? How are financial institutions regulated and supervised? The chapter also examines whether the euro is becoming a worldwide currency, alongside the US dollar.

How to use this book

The book is suitable for a one-semester course that aims at covering both the microeconomics and the macroeconomics of European integration. If the course is long enough, the book can be used sequentially; this is how we teach, and it works well.

Shorter courses may focus on the trade and competition aspects; they can use only Parts I to III. Conversely, a course dealing only with the macroeconomic aspects can use Parts IV and V, and finish with Chapter 8 (which does not really require the previous microeconomic material).

Eclectic courses that focus on theory and cover trade, competition and macroeconomics, can use only Chapters 1 to 8 and 14 to 17. Eclectic courses oriented towards policy issues can use, with some additional lecturing if the students are not familiar with basic theory, Chapters 1, 2, 8 to 12, and 15 to 19. In general, all chapters are self-contained but, inevitably, they often refer to results and facts presented elsewhere.

Each chapter includes self-assessment questions designed to help the students check how well they master the material, and essay questions which can be given as assignments. We also provide additional readings; most of them are easily accessible to undergraduate students though, occasionally, when we did not find adequate references, we point to more advanced material. Students may find some of these readings rewarding.

The second edition continues with our tradition of providing many internet links that should allow students and lecturers alike to get the latest information on the EU's many fast-developing areas. In the new millennium, the internet is an excellent way to stimulate students' interest by bringing classroom teaching to real issues they see every day in the media. While lecturers have long used reference to print and broadcast media for the same purpose, the links we provide go well beyond journalist treatments in a way that allows students to realize the usefulness of the basics they have learned from the text.

Foreword to the second edition

Things move fast in Europe. Since we completed work on the first edition, ten new countries have joined the EU. Two more, Bulgaria and Romania, have signed Accession Treaties and are slated to join in 2007, or 2008 at the latest, and membership negotiations have been opened with Croatia and Turkey.

Meanwhile, the European Convention had approved the draft of the Constitution and the ratification process had started, until it met an ugly 'suspension' when the French and the Dutch people decided to reject it. Add to that the difficulties faced by the Stability and Growth Pact, including an unprecedented censoring of the Council by the Court of Justice of the European Communities, and a feeling of crisis begins to emerge. Has the EU enlarged too fast, as some claim? Or has it forgotten to deepen appropriately to make it possible to enlarge smoothly, as we believe? Are the referenda in two of the founding members of the Community, where the pro-European sentiment remains deep, a signal that the long-mentioned but systematically ignored democratic deficit is a serious issue that will force a rethinking of the institutions put in place nearly fifty years ago?

Although the fast pace of changes makes European integration an exciting field of study, a by-product is that dedicated textbooks are quickly outdated. We have been posting comments and classroom material on the book's dedicated website (http://mcgraw-hill.co.uk/he/ promotions/baldwinandwyplosz/), but that is not good enough.

The second edition reflects all these recent developments and includes updates of all our tables, figures and boxes (thanks to the many of you who sent us comments and suggestions). This edition also includes three new chapters. Following the many requests for more on the EU's competition and trade policies, Chapters 11 and 12, respectively, deal with these two issues. Again following suggestions from readers and reviewers, we unified our treatment of labour markets that was spread between the micro and macro parts in the first edition. The result is our new Chapter 8. Similarly, we merged the micro and macro treatments of capital market integration in a thoroughly revised Chapter 19. Many more changes have been introduced,

mostly the result of our efforts to make the text as reader-friendly and clear as possible.

There is one frequent suggestion that we have not followed – that of adding a chapter on the new and future EU members. One reason is that the 2004 enlargement has now brought in the majority of the formerly planned economy countries. We chose instead to discuss the effects of enlargement, and soon monetary union, on the old and new member countries. Another reason is that, since the first edition, we do not wish to produce 'country studies'. Instead, we present facts and figures for member countries as we develop new ideas. Whenever possible, we have enlarged our tables and figures to include the new members, as well as the future members; comparable data, however, are often not yet available.

As we worked on this new edition, a key concern has been not to lengthen the book too much; we believe that students deserve to be offered a compact treatment, and we see it as our challenge to combine completeness and concision. We tried to take out as much as we added. We are keen to hear back from teachers and students.

Acknowledgements

We are indebted to a number of colleagues for their suggestions and help. In particular, in addition to anonymous referees, we wish to thank Antonio Barbosa, Michael Burda, Ivar Bredesen, Menzie Chinn, Rikard Forslid, Ivar Bredesen, Elena Kolokolova, Samuel Leiser, Henry Overman, Volker Pabst, Armin Riess, Frederic Robert-Nicoud, Horst Siebert and Joachim Tomaschett for catching errors, making useful suggestions or both. We are also grateful to Kirsty Reade and Caroline Prodger at McGraw-Hill, who encouraged us to undertake this new edition and who have organized a panel of readers, and to Hannah Cooper, the Development Editor, who worked hard to produce a high-quality book. We remain responsible for any errors, of course.

Publisher's acknowledgement

The publishers would like to thank the following reviewers for their comments at various stages in the text's development:

Rikard Forslid – Stockholm University
Philipp Schröder – Aarhus University
Niels-Henrik Topp – University of Copenhagen
Sébastien Wälti – Trinity College, Dublin
Peter Holmes – University of Sussex
Morten Skak – University of Southern Denmark
Steven Brakman – Groningen University
Simon Broome – Maynooth University
Malcolm Sawyer – University of Leeds
Michael Ambrosi – Trier University

Yontem Somnez – University of Sheffield
Peter Macmillan – University of St Andrews

Guided Tour

Each part opens with an **introduction** to the key ideas to be considered within the part.

Each chapter commences with an **introduction** to the topic to be covered and indicates the ideas and concepts that will be presented on the following pages.

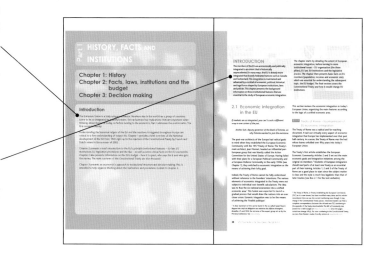

Maps and **diagrams** are provided throughout the text to show geographically the impact of changes in EU integration across the continent.

Boxes throughout the text provide further examples and explanations of key facts, events or economic ideas relating to the European Union.

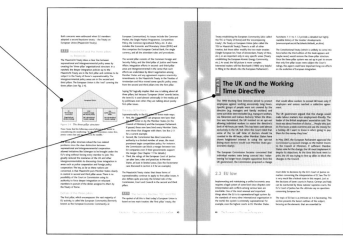

Clear presentation of **economic models** aids the interpretation of economic curves and graphs, with extra notes and explanations where appropriate.

Tables throughout the chapters provide relevant statistics and current data about the European Union and its member states.

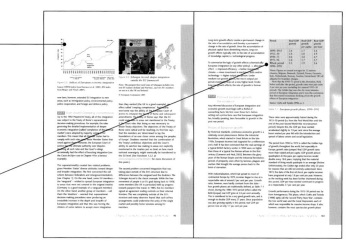

Summaries at the end of each chapter recap the ideas introduced in the preceding pages and emphasize key findings.

Self-assessment questions test comprehension of the economic concepts and facts featured in the chapter.

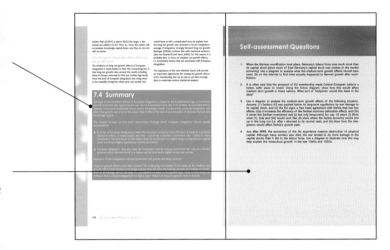

Essay questions offer practice examples for exams or assessment, encouraging students to write full answers that explore ideas in more detail.

Further reading, websites and **references** provide direction for research around the topics covered in the chapter.

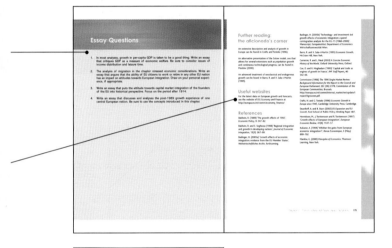

Annex sections offer further economic explanations, data or background information. The appendices enable further study to complement the chapter, covering more advanced concepts and providing greater detail.

Teaching and Learning Resources

Visit www.mcgraw-hill.co.uk/textbooks/baldwinandwyplosz today

Online Learning Centre (OLC)

After completing each chapter, log on to the supporting Online Learning Centre website. Take advantage of the study tools offered to reinforce the material you have read in the text, and to develop your knowledge of marketing in a fun and effective way.

Resources for students include:

- PowerPoint slides for use as lecture presentations and course handouts, with graphs, diagrams and data for manipulation and editing
- Lecturer's manual with suggestions for further sources and reading
- Further tutorial and essay questions for class and for student assessments
- Artwork from the book for use in class or lecture presentations

Students will also be able to access the following supplementary resources:

- Useful web links for EU studies and links to new articles, institutions and news
- Updates of new information, articles, news and features about the EU to ensure the continued currency of the book for lecturers and students

To explore the full range of supplements, visit the Online Learning Centre at www.mcgraw-hill.co.uk/textbooks/baldwinandwyplosz.

Lecturers: Customize Content for your Courses using the McGraw-Hill Primis Content Centre

Now it's incredibly easy to create a flexible, customized solution for your course, using content from both US and European McGraw-Hill Education textbooks, content from our Professional list including Harvard Business Press titles, as well as a selection of over 9000 cases from Harvard, Insead and Darden. In addition, we can incorporate your own material and course notes.

For more information, please contact your local rep who will discuss the right delivery options for your custom publication – including printed readers, e-books and CD-ROMs. To see what McGraw-Hill content you can choose from, visit www.primisonline.com.

Study skills

Open University Press publishes guides to study, research and exam skills to help undergraduate and postgraduate students through their university studies.

Visit www.openup.co.uk/ss to see the full selection of study skills titles, and get a £2 discount by entering the promotional code **study** when buying online.

HISTORY, FACTS AND INSTITUTIONS

Chapter 1: History
Chapter 2: Facts, laws, institutions and the budget
Chapter 3: Decision making

Introduction

The European Union is a truly unique endeavour. Nowhere else in the world has a group of countries come to be so integrated by peaceful means. This uniqueness has implications that are important when thinking about the EU of today, so before turning to the economics, Part I addresses the preliminaries. The first concerns history.

Understanding the historical origins of the EU and the reactions it triggered throughout Europe are critical to a firm understanding of today's EU. Chapter 1 provides a brief overview of the historical development of the EU from 1945 right up to the rejection of the Constitutional Treaty by French and Dutch voters in the summer of 2005.

Chapter 2 presents a brief introduction to the EU's principle institutional features – EU law, EU institutions, EU legislative procedures and the like – as well as some critical facts on the EU economies. Chapter 2 also presents information on the EU's budget – how it is spent, who pays for it and who gets the money. The main contents of the Constitutional Treaty are also discussed.

Chapter 3 presents an economist's approach to institutional structure and decision making. This is intended to help organize thinking about the institutions and procedures studied in Chapter 2.

And what is the plight to which Europe has been reduced? ... over wide areas a vast quivering mass of tormented, hungry, care-worn and bewildered human beings gape at the ruins of their cities and their homes, and scan the dark horizons for the approach of some new peril, tyranny or terror. ... That is all that Europeans, grouped in so many ancient states and nations ... have got by tearing each other to pieces and spreading havoc far and wide.

Yet all the while there is a remedy. ... It is to re-create the European Family, or as much of it as we can, and to provide it with a structure under which it can dwell in peace, in safety and in freedom. We must build a kind of United States of Europe.

Winston Churchill, Zurich, 19 September 1946

Chapter

1 History

INTRODUCTION

Understanding Europe's economic integration requires a good notion of the problems faced and the solutions adopted in the past. Moreover, searching for clear-cut historical patterns is always useful. Such patterns, if they do exist, direct one's attention to critical issues that are likely to arise in the future. This chapter presents the main events in European economic integration in chronological order, stressing, wherever possible, the economic and political economy logic behind the events.

1.1 Early post-war period

In 1945, a family standing almost anywhere in Europe found themselves in a nation which was, or had recently been: (a) ruled by a brutal fascist dictator, (b) occupied by a foreign army or (c) both. As a direct result of these governmental failures, tens of millions of Europeans were dead and Europe's economy lay in ruins. Worse yet, the Second World War was not an isolated historical event. If the parents were middle-aged, it would have been their second experience of colossal death and destruction; the Second World War started just two decades after the cataclysm of the First World War (1914–18). Indeed, the Second World War was the fourth time in 130 years that France and Germany had been at the core of increasingly horrifying wars.

Figure 1.1: *London 1944 and Dresden 1945*

Source: National Maritime Museum, London, and Germany History Museum (DHM), Berlin.

1.1.1 A climate for radical change

In 1945, it was plain to all that something was desperately wrong with the way Europe governed itself. Minds were open to radical changes.

It is almost impossible for students born in the 1970s and later to connect emotionally with the misery and hardship that was commonplace in Europe circa 1945. Yet to do so is essential to the study of European economics. One simply cannot understand European integration without comprehending the mindset of Europeans in the late 1940s.

See for yourself

The miracle of the web now allows students to see photos, watch videos, read original documents and listen to speeches from the time. One of the best sites for all European documents is the Luxembourg-based Centre Virtuel de la Connaissance sur l'Europe. Its excellent and well-organized website is at http://www.ena.lu. Germany History Museum also provides some powerful photos and videos focusing mainly on Germany's experience. It is at http://www.dhm.de/lemo/html/Nachkriegsjahre/DasEndeAlsAnfang/.

War toll

Table 1.1 shows some figures on the death and destruction in the Second World War. In western Europe, the war killed about 8 million people, with Germans accounting for three-quarters of this total. In central and eastern Europe over 9 million perished, of which 6.3 million were Poles. The Soviet Union alone lost over 20 million people. The fact that much of the killing was deliberate genocide made it even more horrifying (see the site www.jewishvirtuallibrary.org for information on the Holocaust).

The scale of this devastation is the key to understanding the post-1945 drive for European integration, but it may be difficult to imagine the mindset in 1945. To put it in perspective, note that the terrible attacks in the USA on 11 September 2001 resulted in about 3000 deaths. This event radically altered many people's and many governments' perception of the world. To approach the death toll during the war in western and central Europe, it would have taken two '11 September' attacks on every single day between 1938 and 1945, and this excludes the 20 million-plus people who perished in the Union of Soviet Socialist Republics (USSR).

The war also caused enormous economic damage. Figures are difficult to find for central and eastern Europe, but the estimates for western Europe are staggering, as the table shows. The war cost Germany and Italy four decades or more of growth and put Austrian and French gross domestic products (GDPs) back to nineteenth-century levels.

Country	Death toll	The economic setback: pre-war year when GDP equalled that of 1945
Austria	525 000	1886
Belgium	82 750	1924
Denmark	4 259	1936
Finland	79 000	1938
France	505 750	1891
Germany	6 363 000	1908
Italy	355 500	1909
Netherlands	250 000	1912
Norway	10 250	1937
Sweden	0	(a)
Switzerland	0	(a)
UK	325 000	(a)

(a) GDP grew during the Second World War.

Source: GDP data from Crafts and Toniolo (1996), p. 4, death toll from http://encarta.msn.com.

Table 1.1: *Death and destruction in the Second World War*

Refugees, hunger and political instability

The economic, political and humanitarian situation in Europe was dire in the years 1945 to 1947, especially in Germany. While the western economies picked up in 1946, much of Europe's infrastructure, industry and housing lay in ruins. Food production in 1946 was low and the 1946–47 winter was especially harsh. Hunger was widespread and food was rationed in most European nations up to the mid-1950s. At times, rations fell to just 900 calories per day in some parts of Germany (2000 calories per day is the standard today). Many Europeans in these years were dependent on humanitarian aid, in

much the same way that people in war-torn African nations are today. The UN Relief and Rehabilitation Administration (UNRRA) spent nearly US$4 billion on emergency food and medical aid, helped to return about 7 million displaced persons, and provided camps for about 1 million refugees who did not want to be repatriated.

Politically, western Europe suffered governmental and constitutional crises. General de Gaulle resigned as president of the provisional government in 1946 over a disagreement on France's new constitution. Italy and Belgium saw bitter internal conflicts over their monarchy. Italy abolished its monarchy in a referendum in which the communists were accused of manipulation. In Belgium, the return of the king sparked riots.

1.1.2 The prime question and guiding ideologies

The horror and revulsion arising from this devastation pushed one question to the forefront in the mid-1940s: How can Europe avoid another war? The solutions offered depended on beliefs about the causes of the war. Three schools of thought were in evidence:

★ The first evoked the time-honoured response of blaming the war on the loser, Germany in this case. The clearest manifestation was contained in a plan, put forth by US Treasury Secretary Henry Morgenthau in 1944, which sought to avoid future European wars by stripping Germany of its industry and converting it into 'a country primarily agricultural and pastoral in character'.

This reproduced the thinking that guided post-First World War arrangements in Europe. That war was blamed on Germany and the victors were rewarded with territorial gains and financial reparations, resulting in a cycle of recovery and national rivalry that led to the Second World War.

★ The second school, Marxism–Leninism, blamed capitalism for most of the world's evils, including both world wars. This belief suggested that communism was the solution.

★ The third blamed destructive nationalism for the war, the solution being tighter integration of all European nations. While calls for a united Europe were heard after the 1914–18 war and during the 1939–45 war, the school's most famous post-war statement was the 1946 'United States of Europe' speech by Winston Churchill (you can listen to it at http://www.ena.lu).

The European integration solution ultimately prevailed, but this outcome was far from clear in the 1940s. Most

European nations were either struggling to re-establish their governments and economies, or were under direct military occupation. Germany and Austria were divided into US, UK, French and Soviet zones. Soviet troops occupied all of central and eastern Europe. In western Europe, 1945 and 1946 passed with hardly any progress towards the establishment of a post-war architecture. West European governments' limited governance capacities were overloaded by the dismal humanitarian situation.

Things moved more rapidly in eastern Europe. The Soviet Union had already begun to implement its vision of a new Europe, during the war. Communism was imposed on the previously independent nations of Estonia, Latvia and Lithuania, and by 1948 communist parties had been pushed to power in every Soviet-occupied country. Communists took power in Albania and Yugoslavia, and were gaining strength in Greece. The communist point of view was also shared by many in western Europe. In the parliamentary elections of 1946, communists won 19 per cent of the vote in Italy and 29 per cent in France.

1.1.3 Emergence of a divided Europe: the Cold War

America and Britain categorically rejected the Soviet's world vision. Their wartime alliance with the USSR unravelled and the Allies-versus-Axis confrontation was replaced by an East–West confrontation, called the Cold War. The USA and Britain concluded by 1947 that an economically strong Germany would be essential to the defence of liberal democracy in western Europe. They merged the British and US zones into 'Bizonia' (September 1947), and France, which had originally favoured the Morgenthau Plan, added its zone in 1948. Germany drew up a constitution in 1948 under the leadership of Konrad Adenauer (see Box 1.1).

In reaction to western moves towards creating a German government in their zones, the USSR escalated harassment of western travel to Berlin. Ultimately, the Soviets imposed the famous Berlin blockade on 24 June 1948 and the western powers countered with the equally famous 'Berlin air bridge' (see http://www.ena.lu for details and photos). In May 1949, the Federal Republic of Germany (informally known as West Germany) was established. The new government agreed to make a military contribution to the western defence effort.

In short, the Soviets' aggressive implementation of their solution triggered a western reaction that narrowed the

Figure 1.2: *The four-way division of Germany*

Source: www.TrumanLibrary.org.

competing ideologies into two schools with an 'iron curtain' between them. East of the iron curtain, the post-war architecture was based on communism and one-party politics. To the west, it was built on multi-party democracy, the social market economy and European integration.

The merger of the French, US and UK zones was a defining moment in Europe. Tentative and ideologically based support for European integration came to be strongly reinforced by western European nations pursuing their own interests. French leaders saw the Franco-German integration as a way of counterbalancing US–UK influence on the Continent, while at the same time assuring that a reindustrialized Germany would become an economic partner rather than a military adversary. The UK and the USA supported European integration as the best way to counter the spread of communism in Europe. German leaders embraced European integration as the surest route to re-establishing Germany as a 'normal' nation (Germany was recognized as an independent nation only in 1955). Italian leaders also welcomed European integration, which provided them with an ideological counterbalance to communism and helped them to close the door on Italy's fascist past.

1.1.4 First steps: the OEEC and EPU

From the economic history perspective, the most important result of the western European effort to resist communism was the so-called Marshall Plan and the Organization for European Economic Cooperation (OEEC). In reaction to the dire economic conditions in Europe and the attendant threat that communists might come to power in Greece, Italy and France, US Secretary of State (i.e. Foreign Minister) George Marshall announced that the USA would give financial assistance to all European nations 'west of the Urals', if they could agree to a joint programme for economic reconstruction.

Konrad Adenauer (1876–1967)

Born to a family of modest means, he rose to become Mayor of Cologne, a post he was stripped of by the Nazis in 1933. He was President of the 1948 Parliamentary Council that drew up Germany's constitution ('Basic Law') before becoming the first Chancellor (i.e. Prime Minister) of Germany – an office he held from 1949 to 1963. Under his leadership, Germany regained its sovereignty, joined the European Economic Community and NATO, and evolved into a cornerstone of western European democracy and economic strength. Adenauer was a key promoter of close Franco-German cooperation and of Germany's social welfare system.

© European Community 2005

Almost immediately, European nations gathered in Paris to study Marshall's proposal (the USSR and the central and eastern European countries eventually withdrew and never received Marshall Plan funds). The conference was intended to determine the amount of aid required and, at US insistence, to create a permanent organization in which Europeans would cooperate in their mutual economic recovery. A joint programme and organization were duly developed by the Europeans. The US Congress, which was initially reluctant, funded the Marshall Plan in April 1948 after the communist takeover in Czechoslovakia.

The new organization, the Organization for European Economic Cooperation (OEEC) was established in 1948 with an initial membership consisting of 13 of what was until recently the EU15 (Finland was under Soviet pressure to stay neutral and Spain was under Franco's dictatorship) plus Norway, Iceland, Switzerland, Turkey and the US–UK zone of the Free Territory of Trieste until it was merged with Italy. Germany was still under occupation, but representatives from the Western Zones participated. From 1948 to 1952, Marshall Plan aid amounted to US$12 billion, with half of this going to the UK, France and West Germany. The Soviet bloc's counterpart to the OEEC, the Council for Mutual Economic Assistance (CMEA), was set up in 1949.

The OEEC divided American aid among its members (see Box 1.2), but a far more important role, as far as

European history is concerned, was the OEEC's mandate to advance European economic integration. It did this by reducing intra-European trade barriers and improving the intra-European system of payments by establishing the European Payments Union (EPU) – see Box 1.3. In 1949, the USA demanded that the OEEC make greater efforts to bring about direct European economic integration, especially intra-OEEC trade liberalization. Up to this point, Marshall Plan money was mainly used to finance European countries' dollar deficits in the EPU. In reaction to US pressure, the OEEC nations agreed to remove quantitative restrictions on private imports. While this had limited scope (at the time much of intra-European trade was conducted by government-controlled corporations), 60 per cent of private intra-European trade was freed action by 1950 thanks to OEEC, with this figure rising to 89 per cent in 1959. The OEEC's trade liberalization was important in at least two ways:

★ The liberalization fostered a rapid growth of trade and incomes. As the figures in Table 1.2 show, the 1950s were marked by a remarkable increase in GDP and the export of manufactured goods, at least on the Continent.

★ The thinking of policy makers was profoundly affected by the fact that industrial output grew at historically unprecedented rates even as European trade was being liberalized.

In the decades following the First World War, especially during the 1930s, economic growth had been viewed as a competition between nations – a competition in which

The Organization for European Economic Cooperation (OEEC)

The OEEC's members formed the Council of the Organization, which ruled on the basis of intergovernmental decision making (unanimity). It was chaired by high-profile figures of the era (Paul-Henri Spaak, Paul van Zeeland, Dirk Strikker, Anthony Eden, Richard Heathcoat Amory). The OEEC's importance waned in 1952 as Marshall Plan aid ended and the focus of American spending shifted to more explicitly military ends in the form of the North Atlantic Treaty Organization (NATO). In 1961, the OEEC was transformed into the Organization for Economic Cooperation and Development (OECD).

Source: Based on the OECD's website, www.oecd.org.

	GDP growth (% p.a.)	Manufacturing export growth (% p.a.)
Germany (West)	7.8	19.7
Italy	5.0	9.2
Netherlands	4.3	11.7
UK	2.0	1.8
France	4.4	3.8

Source: Milward (1992), Table 4.1.

Table 1.2: *Western European trade and output growth in manufactures, 1950–58*

trade barriers played the central role. In the 1940s and 1950s, by contrast, west European economic integration seemed to enhance the growth of all nations; intra-European imports and exports expanded even more rapidly than output. Europe's leaders came to view European integration as an idea that made as much sense economically as it did politically. Economists at the time explained the export–income growth nexus by arguing that exports promoted savings and investment, thus allowing capacity and output to surge without raising inflation (Lamfalussy, 1963). All this prepared the stage for deeper integration. As Milward (1992) put it: 'The proposals for trade liberalisation and customs unions that were made fell therefore on to a receptive soil.'

1.1.5 The drive for deeper integration

While the OEEC succeeded in economic terms, some OEEC members found it too weak and too limited to bring about the deeper integration that they felt was necessary to avoid future wars and restore economic strength. The Cold War lent urgency to this drive. With East–West tensions rising steadily, Germany would not only have to be allowed to regain its industrial might, it would have to rearm in order to counter the threat of Soviet territorial aggression. Since many Europeans, including many Germans, were still uncomfortable with the idea of a Germany that was both economically and militarily strong, integrating Germany into a supranational Europe seemed a natural way forward.

1.2 Two strands of European integration: federalism and intergovernmentalism

While it was clear by the late 1940s that European integration would be the foundation of western Europe's post-war architecture, a serious schism immediately emerged over the role of nation-states. Even today, this schism defines the debate over European integration, so it is worth considering the origins of the two positions.

★ Some Europeans felt that national sovereignty and the nation-state constituted a fragile system prone to warfare. Since time immemorial, European states had been engaged in intermittent struggles for dominance – struggles that typically involved the invasion of other European nations. As the efficiency of killing rose along with industrialization, the cost of these struggles was magnified to the point where there could be no winners. To these thinkers, even democracy was insufficient to prevent horrifying wars. Hitler, after all, gained his first hold on power through

The European Payments Union (EPU), July 1950 to December 1958

Most European nations were bankrupt after 1945, so trade was generally conducted on the basis of bilateral agreements, often involving barter. The EPU multilateralized these bilateral deals. Each month, EPU members added up the deficits and surpluses in their bilateral trade accounts with other EPU members. These were offset against each other so that each nation remained with an overall surplus or deficit with respect to the EPU. The great advantage of this was that since nations no longer owed money to each other directly, the debt-based incentives for importing from or exporting to a particular partner vanished. As a consequence, it was easy to loosen the web of bilateral trade restrictions that had been set up in the early post-war years. In its first year, the EPU removed all discriminatory trade measures among EPU members. EPU/OEEC membership also fostered overall trade liberalization via its Code of Liberalization. This required members to lower trade barriers progressively by 25 per cent of their initial levels. During this time intra-European trade boomed, more than doubling in the EPU's lifetime (1950–58); imports from North America grew by only 50 per cent. The trade surplus with the USA allowed European national central banks to accumulate substantial dollar reserves. This restored their financial stability and fostered trade liberalization by undermining balance-of-payments justifications for import restrictions. By 1958, the financial position of EPU members was strong enough to allow them to restore the convertibility of their currencies (prior to this, the currencies were unconvertible, e.g. it was illegal for private citizens to exchange French francs for dollars or Deutschmarks without government permission).

Source: This box is based largely on Eichengreen and de Macedo (2001).

democratic means. To prevent another cycle of recovery and national rivalry that might lead to a third world war, nations should be embedded in a *federalist* structure – a supranational organization embodied with some of the powers that had traditionally been exercised exclusively by nations.

★ Other Europeans, led by the UK, continued to view nation-states as the most effective and most stable form of government. To them, European integration should take the form of closer cooperation – especially closer economic cooperation – conducted strictly on an *intergovernmental* basis, i.e. all power would remain in the hands of national officials and any cooperation would have to be agreed unanimously by all participants.

Not surprisingly, the federalist school was the more popular in nations that experienced the greatest failures of governance – failures measured in terms of wartime death and destruction. Nations that had experienced land combat and extensive death and destruction were naturally open to radical changes in the way Europe was governed; they were suspicious of nationalism and of fully independent nation-states. This group included Belgium, the Netherlands, Luxembourg, France, Austria, Germany and Italy.

People who lived in nations whose governments somehow managed to avoid foreign occupation and/or catastrophic loss of life tended to maintain their traditional faith in the nation-state. This included the UK, Denmark, Norway and Iceland, as well as the neutrals: Ireland, Sweden and Switzerland. Spain and Portugal remained under fascist dictators until the 1970s.

1.2.1 Two early extremes: Council of Europe and the ECSC

Intergovernmentalism initially dominated the post-war architecture. In part, this was simply a matter of timing. The only major European nation with a truly effective democratic government from 1945 to 1947 was the UK and it was a firm believer in the primacy of the nation-state. The first three organizations – the OEEC, the Council of Europe and the Court of Human Rights – followed the intergovernmental tradition. The OEEC was strictly intergovernmental (see Box 1.2), and the 1948 Congress of Europe, chaired by Winston Churchill in the

Hague, established two intergovernmental structures: the Council of Europe (1949) and the Court of Human Rights (1950).

The first big federalist step came only in 1952 with the implementation of the Schuman Plan inspired by the 'father of European integration', Jean Monnet, but promoted by French Foreign Minister Robert Schuman (see Box 1.4). Schuman proposed that France and Germany should place their coal and steel sectors under the control of a supranational authority. This was a radical federalist move since coal and steel were viewed as the 'commanding heights' of an industrial economy at the time and crucial to a nation's military and industrial strength. Schuman explicitly justified his plan as a means of rendering future Franco-German wars materially impossible. Other European nations were invited to join this European Coal and Steel Community (ECSC), and Belgium, Luxembourg, the Netherlands and Italy actually did. This created a group of nations known simply as 'the Six' – a group that has been the driving force behind European integration ever since. See Box 1.4.

Country	Back-on-track year (year GDP attained highest pre-1939 level)	Reconstruction growth (growth rate during reconstruction years, 1945 to back-on-track year) (%)
Austria	1951	15.2
Belgium	1948	6.0
Denmark	1946	13.5
Finland	1945	n.a.
France	1949	19.0
Germany	1951	13.5
Italy	1950	11.2
Netherlands	1947	39.8
Norway	1946	9.7

Source: Crafts and Toniolo (1996), p. 4.

Table 1.3: *Post-Second World War reconstruction*

Box 1.4 Robert Schuman (1886–1963) and Jean Monnet (1888–1979)

Robert Schuman

© European Community 2005

Born in Luxembourg, Schuman studied and worked in Germany until the end of the First World War. He became French when Alsace-Lorraine reverted to France in 1918. He held several positions in the post-war French governments, including Finance Minister, Premier and Foreign Minister. Schuman provided the political push for the European Coal and Steel Community, which most consider to be the wellspring for the European Union. He was also the first President of the European Parliament (1958–60).

Jean Monnet, born in Cognac in 1888, was a brilliant organizer and as such helped to organize Allied military supply operations in the First and Second World

Jean Monnet

© European Community 2005

Wars. Near the end of the Second World War he joined Charles de Gaulle's provisional Free French government, and was responsible for the 'Monnet Plan', which is credited with helping France's post-war industrialization. Monnet was a convinced Europeanist and led the European movement in the 1950s and 1960s. Monnet, who is sometimes called the 'father of European integration', was the intellect behind the idea of the ECSC and the first President of its 'High Authority' (precursor of the European Commission) from 1952 to 1955. He continued to push for the European Economic Community and the European Atomic Energy Community (Euratom). He died in 1979.

Box 1.5

The European Coal and Steel Community (ECSC)

European Commission

France and Germany launched the ECSC initiative, inviting other nations to place their coal and steel sectors under its supranational authority. Since coal and steel were considered the backbone of a modern industrial economy at the time, most nations declined. The ECSC's structure submerged the role of nation-states to an extent that seems unimaginable from today's perspective. It still represents the 'high water mark' of European federalism. Crucial decisions concerning such issues as pricing, trade and production in the then-critical coal and steel sectors were placed in the hand of the 'High Authority'. This body, the forerunner of today's European Commission, consisted of officials appointed by the six Member States. The High Authority's decisions, some made by majority voting, were subject to limited control by Member State governments. For more on the ECSC, see Spierenburg and Poidevin (1994).

The photo depicts the symbolic opening of the ECSC as a train bearing the flags of the Six crosses a border with coal and steel.

By the time the Schuman Plan had been implemented and the ECSC was running, Europe was a very different place from what it had been in 1945. The year was 1952 and Cold War tensions were high, and rising. Economically, things continued to get better. As Table 1.3 shows, the Six had managed to get their economies back on track, having experienced miraculous growth.

1.2.2 Federalist track: the Treaty of Rome

The ECSC was a success, not so much as a solution to the thorny problems of Europe's coal and steel sectors, but rather as a training scheme for European integration. It showed that the Six could cooperate in a federal structure. The Six as a whole, but especially Germany, continued to grow spectacularly, while East–West tensions continued to mount. This combination made German rearmament essential.

In 1955, Germany joined western Europe's main defence organization, the North Atlantic Treaty Organization (NATO), and began to rearm in earnest. This triggered a reaction from the Soviet bloc: the USSR and the central and eastern European nations formed the Warsaw Pact to counter NATO. It also brought back the question of deeper European integration. By 1955, it had become clear that coal and steel were no longer the 'commanding heights' of Europe's economy in economic or military terms. The ECSC might not be enough to ensure that another Franco-German war remained unthinkable;

European leaders turned their minds to broader economic integration. Having failed to move directly to political or military integration (see Box 1.6), the natural way forward was broader economic integration.

Jean Monnet formed a high-powered pressure group – bluntly called the Action Committee for the United States of Europe – whose membership included leading figures from all the main political parties in each of the Six. The group's aim was nothing less than to merge European nation-states into a supranational organization along the lines of the ECSC but much broader in scope.

Foreign Ministers of the Six met in Messina in Sicily in June 1955 to start a process that soon led to the signing, on 25 March 1957, of two treaties in Rome: the first created the European Atomic Energy Community (Euratom); the second created the European Economic Community (EEC). Because the EEC eventually became much more important than Euratom, the term 'Treaty of Rome' is used to refer to the EEC treaty. The Treaty of Rome was quickly ratified by the six national parliaments and the EEC came into existence in January 1958. (The institutions of the ECSC, the EEC and Euratom were merged into the 'European Communities', or EC, in 1965.) The Treaties of Rome were drafted by the Spaak Committee working from July 1955 to April 1956. The British partook in preliminary meetings of Committee, but dropped out in October 1955. Jean Monnet and others felt the UK was trying to sabotage the Six's federalist initiatives.

Box 1.6

Failed integration, EDC and EPC

Encouraged by the rapid acceptance of the ECSC, Jean Monnet pressed ahead with even more ambitious plans for European unity. In the first years of the 1950s, leaders from the Six worked out plans for a supranational organization concerning defence – the European Defence Community (EDC) – as well as for deep political integration – the European Political Community (EPC). This remarkable enthusiasm for supranationality ultimately failed when the French parliament rejected the EDC. The EPC plans were subsequently abandoned.

It is worth stressing just how revolutionary the ECSC, EDC and EPC proposals were by today's standards. European governments nowadays baulk at pooling their sovereignty over comparatively trivial issues such as air traffic control; the goal of political union among 25 EU members seems quixotic. In most non-European nations, advocating such massive transfers of sovereignty to supranational bodies would be unthinkable; in the USA it might even be considered treasonous. In the shadow of the death and destruction of the Second World War, it was, by contrast, mainstream thinking.

The Treaty of Rome committed the Six to extraordinarily deep economic integration. In addition to forming a customs union (removing all tariffs on intra-EEC trade and adopting a common tariff on imports from non-member nations – see Box 1.7), it promised free labour mobility, capital market integration, free trade in services and a range of common policies, some of which were to be implemented by the supranational European Commission. The Treaty also set up a series of supranational institutions such as the European Parliamentary Assembly (forerunner of the European Parliament) and the European Court of Justice (see Chapter 2).

Figure 1.3: *Messina Conference and signing of the Treaty of Rome*

Left photo: Conference of Messina – the Foreign Ministers of the Six (left to right: Johan Beyen, Gaetano Martino, Joseph Bech, Antoine Pinay, Walter Hallstein, Paul-Henri Spaak). *Right photo*: Signing of the treaties establishing the EEC and Euratom in Rome.

Source: Audiovisual Library of the European Commission.

1.2.3 Intergovernmental track: from OEEC to EFTA

Formation of the EEC introduced an important new element into European economic integration. Hereto trade liberalization in Europe had been orchestrated by the OEEC with nations liberalizing on a non-discriminatory basis. The EEC, however, promised to go much further, removing *all* trade barriers, but this time on a discriminatory, i.e. preferential, basis. Imports from non-member nations would not benefit from the opening. Moreover, the Six were committed to adopting a common tariff against all imports from non-member nations. The other eleven OEEC members were left on the sidelines. Fearing the discrimination and marginalization that might occur if they faced the EEC bilaterally, seven of these 'outsiders' reacted by forming

their own bloc in 1960, the European Free Trade Association (EFTA) – see Box 1.8. This coordinated response was greatly facilitated by the UK's leadership. By the early 1970s, all western European nations had forsaken bilateralism except Ireland, which was in a monetary union with its major trading partner, the UK. Greece and Turkey both applied for associate EEC membership almost as soon as the Treaty of Rome was signed, and Spain signed a preferential trade agreement with the EEC in 1970 and another with EFTA in 1979.

Box 1.7

Formation of the EEC customs union and EFTA

The nascent EEC spent much of its first year of life setting up its administrative machinery in Brussels and developing an integration programme. It started with the most concrete part of the Treaty's ambitious integration scheme, the customs union.

According to the Treaty, the elimination of intra-EEC tariffs was to take place in three stages of four years each: January 1958 to December 1961, January 1962 to December 1965 and January 1966 to December 1969. The possibility of a three-year delay was foreseen, so the maximum liberalization period was 15 years. As it turned out, no extra time was needed. Intra-EEC import quotas were abolished ahead of schedule in 1961 and tariffs were zero by July 1968, 18 months ahead of schedule.

Why was the EEC able to achieve its ambitious Common Market a year and a half early? The formation of the customs union coincided with a period of unprecedented economic prosperity and this largely offset the political and economic costs of liberalization-induced restructuring. Indeed, during this so-called golden age of growth, 1950–73, European unemployment averaged only 2.5 per cent and incomes either doubled, as in France, Belgium and the Netherlands, or tripled, as in Germany and Italy.

The new Common External Tariff (CET) applied by all EEC members was set at the simple arithmetic average of the Six's pre-EEC tariffs. Typically this meant that France and Italy lowered their external tariffs and the Benelux nations raised theirs. Germany's tariffs were approximately at the average to begin with. Under Treaty of Rome rules, the tariff revenue was paid directly to the European Commission. This avoided discussions over a 'fair' division of the revenue (e.g. Dutch authorities collected the CET in Rotterdam even though Rotterdam was the port of entry for many German imports from the USA).

Box 1.8

Formation of EFTA

The Stockholm Convention – EFTA's founding document – committed the EFTA nations (EFTAns) to removing tariffs on trade among themselves in tandem with the EEC's schedule, and EFTA matched the EEC's accelerated tariff-cutting. Importantly, EFTA was a free trade area, not a customs union, so external trade policy did not have to be decided in common. This was important if supranational decision making was to be avoided and it allowed the UK to maintain its preferential tariffs with the Commonwealth. Trade in agricultural goods was excluded from EFTA's liberalization.

1.2.4 Two non-overlapping circles: Common Market and EFTA

The 1960s saw the trade liberalization promised by the Treaty of Rome and the Stockholm Convention (EFTA's founding document) come to fruition. By the late 1960s, trade arrangements in western Europe could be described as two non-overlapping circles. This is depicted schematically in Fig. 1.4.

The lowering of intra-EEC trade barriers had an immediate and dramatic impact on trade patterns. During the formation of the customs union (CU), the EEC's share in its own trade rose from about 30 per cent to almost 50 per cent. At the same time, the share of EEC imports coming from six other major European nations remained almost unchanged, falling from 8 per cent to 7 per cent.

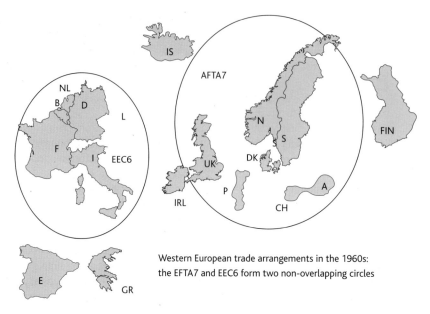

Western European trade arrangements in the 1960s:
the EFTA7 and EEC6 form two non-overlapping circles

B = Belgium, NL = Netherlands, D = Germany, L = Luxembourg, F = France, I = Italy, E = Spain, GR = Greece,
IS = Iceland, IRL = Ireland, UK = United Kingdom, P = Portugal, N = Norway, DK = Denmark, S = Sweden,
CH = Switzerland, A = Austria, FIN = Finland

Figure 1.4: *Europe of two non-overlapping circles*

Source: Baldwin (1994).

1.3 Evolution to two concentric circles: domino effect part I

In the early 1960s, EFTA-based and EEC-based firms had roughly equal access to each other's markets (the preferential liberalization had only just begun). However, as the barriers began to fall within the EEC and within EFTA (but not between the groups), discriminatory effects appeared. This discrimination meant lost profit opportunities for exporters in both groups. Importantly, the relative economic weight and economic performance of the two circles was far from equal. The GDP of the six EEC nations was more than twice that of the seven EFTA nations and was growing faster. Thus the EEC club was far more attractive to exporters than the EFTA club. Accordingly, the progressive reduction of within-group barriers generated new political economy forces in favour of EEC enlargement, but how did discriminatory liberalization create these forces for inclusion?

Discriminatory liberalization is studied in depth in Chapter 5, but the idea behind these new political economy forces can be illustrated with an anecdote. Two

campers in Yellowstone National Park, who have just settled down in their tent, hear the roar of a hungry grizzly bear very close by. One camper sits up and starts putting on his running shoes. The other camper says: 'Are you crazy? You can't outrun a bear!' The first camper, who continues tying his laces, replies: 'Oh, I don't have to outrun the bear. I just have to outrun you.' When it comes to outrunning bears and succeeding in business, relative competitiveness is the key to success. A firm is harmed by anything that helps its rivals.

In the case at hand, closer EEC integration diminished the relative competitiveness of non-EEC firms in EEC markets, thereby harming their sales and profits. Of course, the same happened to EEC firms in EFTA, but given the EEC's much greater economic size, pressures on EFTA members (EFTAns) to adjust were much greater than those on EEC nations. This effect helps explain why preferential integration among some nations can change the political economy attitudes of excluded nations. This is what Baldwin (1994, 1995) calls the 'domino theory' of regional integration: the preferential lowering of some trade barriers creates new pressures for outsiders to join the trade bloc and as the trade bloc gets bigger, the pressure to join grows. As history would have it, the UK government was the first to react to the pressure.

1.3.1 First enlargement and EEC–EFTA free trade agreements

In 1961, the UK – the nation that had so thoroughly distained the federalist track in the 1950s – applied for EEC membership. There are many reasons for this about-turn. In 1955, the UK half expected the EEC to fail as the EDC and EPC had, but once it was clear that the EEC was working, UK industries faced rising discrimination in Europe's largest and fastest growing markets. The UK government had to react; EFTA was not a substitute for free trade access to the EEC6 markets.

The UK's unilateral decision tipped over more dominos. If the UK was to jump from EFTA to the EEC, the remaining EFTANs would face discrimination in an even larger market (since the EEC is a custom union, the UK would have had to reimpose tariffs on imports from other EFTANs). This possibility led other nations to change their attitude towards membership. In this case, Ireland, Denmark and Norway quickly followed the UK's unilateral move. The other EFTANs did not apply for political reasons such as neutrality (Austria, Finland, Sweden and Switzerland), lack of democracy (Portugal), or because they were not heavily dependent on the EEC market (Iceland).

While Germany was broadly in favour of UK membership, France was opposed to it (see Fig. 1.5). In a renowned January 1963 press conference, French President Charles de Gaulle (see Box 1.9) said *non* to this first enlargement attempt (you can hear it on www.ena.lu). The four EFTANs reapplied in 1967 and de Gaulle issued another famous *non*; but after he retired, the applications were reactivated by invitation from the EEC. After many delays, membership for the four was granted in 1973. At that time, Norway's citizens refused EEC membership in a referendum.

Charles de Gaulle (1890–1970)

Deutsches Historisches Museum (DHM), Berlin

Charles André Marie Joseph de Gaulle was born in Lille into a family that was comfortably well off (his father was a professor of literature and history). He was educated in the St Cyr Military Academy and thereafter began his army career. Twice wounded in the First World War, he was eventually captured by German forces and held as a prisoner of war despite his best efforts to escape (he made five attempts). He was a colonel when the Second World War broke out, but was rapidly promoted to brigadier general (the youngest general in the French Army at age 49). De Gaulle was strongly opposed to the French surrender in June 1940 (after just two weeks of combat) and broadcast his renowned 'Appeal of June 18' from London: 'France has lost a battle, but France has not lost the war.' His appeal won over leaders in some of the French Overseas Territories and he created the Free French Movement, which provided an alternative to the collaborationist Vichy Republic lead by Marshal Petain.

After the war, de Gaulle was elected to head the provisional government which organized elections and launched a plan to modernize and industrialize the French economy. He resigned in 1946, frustrated by the dominance of the Parliament in the new Constitution (he wanted more power for the presidency). He returned to power in 1958 in a crisis atmosphere.

De Gaulle, like Adenauer (see Profile Box 1.1), was a strong proponent of Franco-German cooperation, but he was only a reluctant Europeanist. He had always objected to supranational organizations, including the ECSC, but France had already adopted the Treaty of Rome before he came back to power. In 1966, he orchestrated the 'empty chair' policy that essentially eviscerated much of the supranationality in the Treaty of Rome. De Gaulle dominated French political life until he resigned again in 1969. He died the following year.

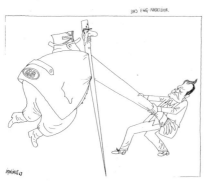

Figure 1.5: *German Chancellor Willy Brandt trying to get the UK into the EEC past the objections of French President Charles de Gaulle*

Source: www.ena.lu.

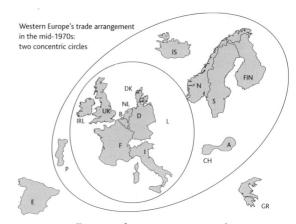

Figure 1.6: *Europe of two concentric circles*

Note: See Fig. 1.4, p. 14, for abbreviations and source.

The impending departure of four EFTAns to the EEC was anticipated well in advance and triggered a secondary domino effect. The 1973 EEC enlargement meant a swelling of the EEC markets and a shrinking of the EFTA markets. Firms based in the remaining EFTA states would suffer a disadvantage (compared with their EEC-based rivals) in more markets and enjoy an advantage (over their EEC-based rivals) in fewer markets. Accordingly, EFTA industries pushed their governments to redress this situation. The result was a set of bilateral free trade agreements (FTAs) between each remaining EFTAn and the EEC, which took effect when the UK and company acceded to the EEC.

Notice that this change of heart does need some explaining. The stance of, say, Sweden towards an FTA with the then-EEC was a matter of top-level political calculation. It may seem strange, therefore, that the calculations of Sweden's political elite led them to sign an FTA in 1972 when they had not found it politically expedient to sign one in the preceding decades. The explanation, of course, is that tighter integration among a nation's trade partners (in this case between the UK, Denmark and Ireland and the EEC) alters the economic landscape facing Swedish exporters. This reshaping of the economic landscape gets translated into a new political landscape. Such forces are in operation today. The 2004 enlargement stimulates demand for free trade with nations on the EU25's new eastern border.

The upshot of all this was that by the mid-1970s trade arrangements in western Europe had evolved from non-overlapping circles into two concentric circles. This is shown schematically in Fig. 1.6. The outer circle, which encompassed both EFTA and EEC nations, represents a

'virtual' free trade area for industrial products, formed by concatenation of the Treaty of Rome (for intra-EEC trade), EFTA's charter, the Stockholm Convention (for intra-EFTA trade) and individual bilateral FTAs between each EFTAn and the EEC (for EEC–EFTA trade). The inner circle was the EEC. These countries were much more thoroughly integrated, even in the mid-1970s.

1.4 Euro-pessimism

Although the customs union was implemented smoothly and ahead of schedule, European integration stagnated soon after its completion. The Community was rocked by a series of political crises in the 1960s soon to be followed by economic shocks in the early 1970s. This led to a period of 'Euro-pessimism' that lasted from the first enlargement in 1973 through to 1985.

1.4.1 Political shocks

The spectacularly good economic performance of Europe's economies in the 1950s and 1960s – teamed with the manifest success of European economic integration – went a long way to restoring the confidence of Europeans in their governments' ability to govern (Milward, 1984). So much so that some nations began to regret the promises of deep integration they made in the Treaty of Rome. At the head of this pro-national sovereignty charge was French President Charles de Gaulle.

The issue came to a head as the final stage in the Treaty of Rome's transition period approached (1 January 1966). At this stage the voting procedures in the EEC's key decision-making body, the Council of Ministers, was scheduled to switch to a particular kind of majority voting (see 'qualified majority voting' in Chapter 2). For de Gaulle, the objectionable part of majority voting was that France might have to accept a majority-backed policy even if France had voted against it. In the end, de Gaulle forced the other EEC members to accept his point of view in the so-called Luxembourg Compromise (see Box 1.10); henceforth, unanimity was the typical rule in EEC decision-making procedures. The insistence on consensus radically reduced the EEC's ability to make decisions (see Chapter 3 on decision-making efficiency) and the problem only got worse as the EEC expanded to nine member states in 1973.

These conflicts came after opposition to federalism had caused the failure of an earlier attempt at deeper political integration. The 1961 EEC summit in Bonn formed a committee – the Fouchet Committee – to propose a plan for political union. Fouchet's plan, which was heavily influenced by de Gaulle's opposition to supranationality, rested on scrupulous respect for national sovereignty. The plan failed for a number of reasons, one of which was a fear among some EU members that it would undermine the existing supranational aspect of the Community (see Factsheet 1.1.2 on www.europarl.eu.int for further details).

Although the Luxembourg Compromise had no legal force, it had an enormous impact. It meant that unanimity was the de facto rule for almost everything. Almost all progress on deeper economic integration was blocked until majority voting was restored in the Single European Act 1986. The compromise in full reads: 'Where, in the case of decisions which may be taken by a majority vote on a proposal from the Commission, very important interests of one or more partners are at stake, the Members of the Council will endeavour, within a reasonable time, to reach solutions which can be adopted by all the Members of the Council while respecting their mutual interests and those of the Community, in accordance with Article 2 of the Treaty.' See Factsheet 1.3.6 on www.europarl.eu.int for further details.

1.4.2 Failure of monetary integration

In the late 1960s, the USA began to run an irresponsible monetary policy – in essence printing money to pay for the Vietnam War. Since all major currencies were linked to the dollar at the time (via the global fixed exchange rate system called Bretton Woods), US inflation was more or less automatically translated into rising inflation in Europe and elsewhere. The political pressures that arose led to the gradual breakdown, between 1971 and 1973, of the global fixed exchange rate system (see Chapter 13 for details).

Box 1.10 The 'empty chair' policy and the Luxembourg Compromise

De Gaulle, who had always opposed supranationality in European integration, challenged the principle in 1966. The test case came when France opposed a range of Commission proposals, which included measures for financing the Common Agricultural Policy. France stopped attending the main Community meetings (the 'empty chair' policy) and threatened to withdraw from the EEC. This marked the end of the post-war climate for radical change, but not the end of the EEC. In exchange for its return to the Council of Ministers, France demanded a political agreement – the Luxembourg Compromise – that de facto over-turned the Treaty of Rome's majority voting provisions whenever a Member State announced that it felt that 'very important interests' were at stake.

Crise de la chaise vide, 1965

© European Community 2005

Figure 1.7: *Euro-pessimism*

Copyright Finn Skovgaard 2001, 2004. Used with permission.
skovgaard.org – skovgaard-europe.com.

Exchange rate stability was widely viewed as a critical factor supporting the rapid post-war growth in trade and international investment and the rising prosperity these brought. The EEC sought ways of restoring exchange rate stability among members. Drawing on studies undertaken in the 1960s, the Werner Committee laid out a step-by-step approach to monetary union. This was adopted in 1971, with the goal being nothing less than full monetary union by 1980.

The economic environment for this new European monetary arrangement could not have been worse. Months after it was launched, the Yom Kippur War in the Middle East triggered an Arab oil boycott of western states. The resulting sharp rise in oil prices had a ruinous economic impact on western Europe. Just as inflationary tendencies were heating up from US actions, the oil shock severely dampened economic activity in Europe and all of its global trading partners. Most European nations adopted expansionary monetary and fiscal policies to compensate for the economic downturn and these further fuelled inflation. The resulting falling income levels and rising inflation rates came to be known as 'stagflation'. Just as the world was recovering from the 1973 oil shock, the Iranian Revolution produced a second massive oil price hike in 1979, aggravating stagflation. A debilitating series of exchange rate crises – which stemmed directly from these massive external shocks – condemned to failure this first post-war attempt at European monetary integration.

1.4.3 Failure of deeper trade integration

Even as tariff barriers were being phased out, Europeans began to erect new trade barriers among themselves.

These new barriers consisted of detailed technical regulations and standards, which had the effect of fragmenting the European markets. While these policies, called 'technical barriers to trade' (TBTs), undoubtedly inhibited intra-European trade, their announced goal was to protect consumers. Indeed, EEC leaders recognized the trade-inhibiting effects of TBTs from the start in 1957. Article 100 of the EU's founding Treaty requires 'approximation' (Euro-speak for harmonization) of national regulations for the 'proper functioning of the common market'.

The EU first systematically took up the removal of technical barriers in 1969 with its General Programme. This launched what came to be called the 'traditional' or 'old' approach to TBT liberalization. The approach adopted relied on detailed technical regulations for single products or groups of products implemented by unanimously agreed directives. Since unanimity was required, this approach failed. Harmonization proceeded much more slowly than the development of new national barriers. For example, ten years were required to adopt a directive on gas containers made of unalloyed steel, and nine and a half years was the average delay for the fifteen directives adopted en masse in 1984. In the meantime, Member States were implementing thousands of technical standards and regulations each year.

Stagflation teamed with the failure of the initiatives for deeper monetary and trade integration created a gloom over the 'European construction'. Many inside and outside Europe suspected that the ideals that had driven European integration since the late 1940s were dying or dead.

1.4.4 Bright spots

There were some bright spots in European integration during this period. Spain, Portugal and Greece all adopted democratic governments, thus rendering them suitable for EEC membership. Greece joined in 1981, followed by the Iberians in 1986. The European Monetary System (EMS), which had good success in stabilizing intra-EEC exchange rates, started operation in 1978. Moreover, the EEC put its financing on a firm footing with two budget treaties, one in 1970 and one in 1975 (see Chapter 2 for further details). The institutions of the three communities (ESCS, Euratom and EEC) were rationalized by the Merger Treaty (1965) and the EU Parliament was directly elected for the first time in 1979 (previously, its members came from the members' national parliaments).

In the USA and Europe, central bankers decided to fight inflation (which had reached double-digit figures in most industrial nations) the old-fashioned way: by inducing a long, hard recession. Between 1981 and 1983, growth was negative or only slightly positive in most of Europe. While inflation rates did decline, this was at the cost of a significant increase in unemployment. Starting in 1984, economic growth recovered. Political attitudes also changed – in particular, a deepened belief in market economics began to spread throughout the industrialized world. US President Ronald Reagan and British Prime Minister Margaret Thatcher are often cited as being in the vanguard, but even the socialist French President François Mitterrand adopted a favourable attitude towards market-based solutions. While there are many causes for this philosophical shift, the fact that highly interventionist policies had failed to prevent ten years of poor economic performance is surely one of the most important.

1.5 Deeper circles and domino effect part II: the Single Market Programme and the EEA

This favourable economic climate was matched with the arrival of a talented promoter of European integration, Jacques Delors (see Box 1.11). Delors, who was appointed to the presidency of the European Commission in 1985, was devoted to the idea of kick-starting European integration. To this end, he pushed a programme that would complete the internal market. He dubbed this the Single Market Programme, although it was often referred to as the Internal Market Programme,

the 1992 Programme, or EC92 for short. It was framed by Lord Cockfield's 1985 White Paper which listed 300 measures necessary to transform the Common Market into the single market. By July 1987, all Member States had adopted the Single European Act, which is the Community legislation that implemented the single market measures (along with many other changes).

1.5.1 The Single Market Programme: EC92

In 1985, EU firms enjoyed duty-free access to each other's markets; however, they certainly did not enjoy free trade. Intra-EC trade was shackled by a long list of trade-inhibiting barriers such as differing technical standards and industrial regulations, capital controls, preferential public procurement, administrative and frontier formalities, value added tax (VAT) and excise tax rate differences and differing transport regulations, to mention just a few. Although the vast majority of these policies seem negligible individually, the confluence of their effects served to substantially restrict intra-Community trade.

Indeed, many of these barriers were introduced in the 1970s as European nations increasingly adopted standards and regulations that were aimed at protecting consumers and the environment. The free movement of goods was also restricted by practices of national and local governments, such as biased purchasing patterns, exclusive production or service rights, and production subsidies to national champions. Likewise, the free movement of services – which was guaranteed in principle by the Treaty of Rome – was far from being a reality, again largely because of national prudential and safety regulations. Service providers were typically required to possess local certification and the requirements for such certification often varied across nations. Moreover, the certification process was often controlled or influenced by the national service providers who had an economic interest in excluding foreign competitors via this certification process.

The key changes in the Single Market Programme were intended to reinforce the 'four freedoms' (free movement of goods, services, people and capital) that had already been promised by the Treaty of Rome. The concrete steps were:

Goods trade liberalization
★ Streamlining or elimination of border formalities.
★ Harmonization of VAT rates within wide bands.
★ Liberalization of government procurement.
★ Harmonization and mutual recognition of technical standards in production, packaging and marketing.

Factor trade liberalization
★ Removal of all capital controls.
★ Increase in capital market integration.
★ Liberalization of cross-border, market-entry policies, including mutual recognition of approval by national regulatory agencies.

The Single European Act also implemented important institutional changes. To clear the decision-making log-jam that had held up similar integration initiatives in the 1970s, EC92 included a major change in the EU's decision-making procedures. Decisions concerning single market issues would be adopted on the basis of majority voting instead of on a basis of unanimity (see Chapter 2 for a discussion of EU decision-making procedures). This change in voting procedures was part of the so-called new approach to TBT liberalization.

Focus on capital mobility

Without a doubt the most novel aspect of the Single Market Programme was its focus on capital mobility; other features can be viewed as deepening or extending integration initiatives already agreed. Some EU members had unilaterally liberalized capital mobility prior to EC92, but substantial pan-EU liberalization came only in the second half of the 1980s with a series of EC92 directives. The opening was completed in 1988 by a directive that ruled out all remaining restrictions on capital movements among EU residents. The definitive system was codified in the Maastricht Treaty.

It is possible to think of the Single Market Programme's liberalization of capital flows as unleashing a process that eventually lead to the creation of the euro (see Chapter 14 for a detailed explanation of the logic linking exchange rate regime choices and capital mobility).

1.5.2 The European Economic Area (EEA) and the fourth enlargement

Since the Single European Act promised much tighter economic integration among EU members, non-EU nations again found themselves threatened by the discriminatory effects of integration in the EU. As in the 1960s and early 1970s, this triggered a domino effect as EFTA firms prompted their governments to offset the discrimination by seeking closer ties to the EU.

In the late 1980s, EFTAn governments had decided that they must react to the single market. Several considered applying for EU membership (Austria actually did), while others considered bilateral negotiations. Jacques Delors forced the decision in January 1989 by proposing the EEA agreement (initially called the European Economic Space agreement). The final version of this agreement is highly complex, but, for our purposes, it can be thought of as extending the single market to EFTA economies, apart from agriculture and the common external tariff.

Given the political economy forces described above, it is easy to understand why the EFTAns would want to participate in the single market. There are, however, two aspects of the EEA that are truly extraordinary. First, the EEA seemed, from some perspectives, to be unbalanced in terms of the rights and obligations of EFTAns when it comes to future EEC legislation. In essence, it forces the EFTAns to accept future EU legislation concerning the single market, without formal input into the formation of these new laws. Second, the EEA created a good deal of supranationality among the EFTAns. This supranationality was extraordinary for two reasons. First, the EU imposed this supranationality on the EFTAns in order to simplify the task of keeping the single market homogeneous. Second, the EFTAns had resisted such supranational authority since the end of the war, so it is astounding that they now said they would accept it.

As it turned out, virtually none of the EFTAns were willing to live with the EEA as it was negotiated. By the end of negotiations on the EEA, Austria, Finland, Sweden, Norway and Switzerland had put in EU membership applications. For these countries, the EEA was a transitional arrangement. Swiss voters rejected that EEA in December 1992, in effect freezing their EU application. Accession talks with the four EFTAns were successful, so the EEA now consists of the EU25 on the one hand, with Norway, Liechtenstein and Iceland on the other (Norway's voters again rejected EU membership in a referendum).

Of course, the membership bids of Sweden, Switzerland, Finland and Austria would have been unthinkable in the old Cold War environment. From 1989, the East–West political division of Europe crumbled and then vanished. These profound political changes, which allowed Sweden, Finland and Austria to join the EU, had far more dramatic implications for the central and eastern European nations – the topic to which we turn next.

1.6 Communism's creeping failure and spectacular collapse

The division of Europe into communist and capitalist camps was cemented, quite literally, in 1961 by the construction of the Berlin Wall. While living standards were not too dissimilar to begin with, by the 1980s, western European living standards were far higher than those in eastern Europe and the USSR. Quite simply, the West's economic system (free markets and an extensive social welfare system), when teamed up with its political system (multi-party democracy and freedom of the press), provided far greater benefits to its citizens than did the East's system of planned economies and one-party rule.

This 'creeping failure' of communism was soon apparent to the central and eastern European countries (CEECs). Soviet leaders, however, repeatedly thwarted reform efforts in the CEECs via constant economic pressure and occasional military intervention. By the 1980s, the inadequacy of the Soviet's economic system forced changes inside the USSR itself. The USSR adopted a policy of timid pro-market reforms (*perestroika*) and a policy of openness (*glasnost*), which involved a marked reduction in internal repression and diminished intervention in the affairs of the Soviet republics and Soviet-bloc nations.

As far as European integration was concerned, the Soviet foreign policy changes were critical. Pro-democracy forces in the CEECs, which had been repeatedly put down by military force hereto, found little resistance from Moscow in the late 1980s. The first breach came in June 1989 when the Polish labour movement, Solidarity,

Figure 1.8: *The Berlin Wall circa 1980*

Source: http://community.webshots.com.

forced the communist government to accept free parliamentary elections. The communists lost and the first democratic government in the Soviet bloc took power. Moscow rapidly established ties with the new Polish government.

Moscow's hands-off approach to the Polish election triggered a chain of events over the next two years that revolutionized European affairs. Pro-reform elements inside the Hungarian Communist Party pressed for democratic elections, and, more dramatically, Hungary opened its border with Austria. Thousands of East Germans reacted by moving to West Germany via Hungary and Austria. This set off mass protests against communist repression in East Germany, protests that culminated in the opening of the border between East and West Germany. On 9 November 1989, thousands of West and East Berlin citizens converged on the Berlin Wall with pickaxes and sledgehammers to dismantle that symbol of a divided Europe. By the end of 1989, democratic forces were in control in Poland, Hungary, Czechoslovakia and East Germany. In 1990, East and West Germany formed a unified Germany and three Soviet republics – Estonia, Latvia and Lithuania – declared their independence from the USSR. By the end of 1991, the Soviet Union itself broke up, putting a definitive end to its interference in central and eastern Europe. The European Union reacted swiftly to this 'geopolitical earthquake' by providing emergency aid and loans to the fledgling democracies.

Figure 1.9: *Solidarity movement and fall of the Berlin Wall*

Source: Polish Maritime Museum and www.berlin-wall.org.

1.6.1 German unification, Maastricht and the euro

The political earthquake caused by the falling of the wall also yielded substantial changes within the EU. With the Berlin Wall gone, unification of the western and eastern parts of Germany was the natural next step, but a unified Germany would be a behemoth. With 80 million citizens and 30 per cent of Europe's output, Germany would be much larger than France, the UK or Italy. This raised many fears, ranging from a disturbed political balance in the EU to the unlikely, but still scary, spectre of German militarism. Many Europeans, both within and outside Germany, felt that Germany would be best unified in conjunction with a big increase in the forces tying EU members together.

Riding on his success with the single market, Jacques Delors seized this moment to propose a radical increase in European economic integration: the formation of a monetary union, a step that many thought would eventually lead to political integration. The idea was quickly championed by French President François Mitterrand and German Chancellor Helmut Kohl. After extensive negotiations, the EU committed itself to a target of forming a monetary union by 1999 and adopting a single currency by 2002 (see Chapter 14). This commitment was made in the Maastricht Treaty.

The Maastricht Treaty is covered in depth in Chapter 14, but for purposes of this chapter it is important to note that the Maastricht Treaty – formally known as the Treaty on European Union – embodied the most profound deepening of European integration since the Treaty of Rome. In addition to committing members to a transfer of national sovereignty over monetary power to a supranational body (the European Central Bank), and abandonment of their national currencies for the euro, the Treaty:

★ created EU citizenship; this included the right to move to and live in any EU state (the Treaty of Rome only guaranteed the right to work in any Member State), and to vote in European and local elections in any Member State;

★ locked in the free movement of capital;

★ strengthened EU cooperation in non-economic areas, including security and defence policy as well as law enforcement, criminal justice, civil judicial matters, and asylum and immigration policies;

★ enshrined the principle of subsidiarity that was meant to control the transfer of responsibilities from Member States to the EU;

★ strengthened the European Parliament's power over EU legislation.

★ introduced the Social Chapter which expanded the EU's social dimension by introducing policies on workers' health and safety, workplace conditions, equal pay and the consultation of employees.

The Maastricht Treaty had great difficulties with ratification. The UK insisted on a formal opt-out from the common currency (the idea was that all other members would have to adopt the euro once they met the criteria) and from the Social Chapter. Even with these provisos, Euros-sceptics from his own party nearly brought down British Prime Minister John Major's Conservative government during the UK parliamentary ratification vote. Danish voters narrowly rejected the Treaty in a referendum, but reversed their decision in a second referendum after Denmark was granted opt-outs on the single currency and defence matters. French President François Mitterrand put the Treaty to a referendum expecting a massive 'yes' vote that would bolster the Treaty's prospects (referenda are not mandatory in France). As history would have it, the French yes vote amounted to only 51.4 per cent. The Treaty was challenged as unconstitutional in the Germany's High Court, but was ultimately judged to be compatible with Germany's constitution. The Treaty came into force in November 1993.

1.7 Reuniting eastern and western Europe

Given that almost every other nation in the area had free trade access to the enormous EU market, free trade agreements with the EU were a commercial necessity for the newly free CEECs. Their strategic goal, however, was EU and NATO membership. In the early days, CEEC leaders felt unsure that the new situation was permanent. If things went wrong in Russia and the iron curtain re-descended, each CEEC wanted to be sure that the curtain would, this time, come down east of its border.

1.7.1 First steps: the Europe Agreements

It was thus for both geopolitical and economic reasons that all CEECs expressed their intention to join the European Union. The EU, by contrast, was initially reluctant. Instead of acknowledging the CEECs' interests in membership, the EU signed Association Agreements, commonly known as Europe Agreements, with Poland, Hungary and Czechoslovakia in 1991. Europe Agreements for other CEECs followed in time, and by 1994 the EU had such deals with Romania, Bulgaria, Albania, Estonia, Latvia and Lithuania. Throughout the early 1990s, EFTA quickly negotiated bilateral free trade agreements with each CEEC that had a Europe Agreement with the EU.

Some CEECs also signed trade arrangements among themselves, the most important being the 1991 Central European Free Trade Agreement that initially promoted trade liberalization among Czechoslovakia, Hungary and Poland. It was subsequently extended to include both successor states to Czechoslovakia as well as Slovenia, Bulgaria and Romania.

The Europe Agreements established bilateral free trade between the EU and each individual CEEC. They committed the EU to removing tariffs and quantitative restrictions on most industrial products by the end of 1994. Substantial EU protection remained for a group of 'sensitive' industrial products, including some textiles, some coal and steel products, and almost all agricultural trade. Beyond the removal of tariffs on most industrial goods, a further goal was to make progress towards 'realizing between them the other economic freedoms on which the Community is based'. The adoption of EU laws and practices (competition policy, harmonized standards, and so on) helped the CEECs to establish functioning market economies faster than they could have done on their own.

The Europe Agreements stopped short of offering EU membership, reflecting the profound ambivalence that many in the west initially had towards EU membership for the CEECs. For instance, slow action of the parliaments of EU Member States meant that the Europe Agreements signed with Hungary and Poland in December 1991 entered into force only in February 1994. Most of the hesitation was due to the nature of the economies of the CEECs. The CEECs were (and still are) poor, populous and agrarian. Since the EU spends 80 per cent of its budget on farms and poor regions, eastern enlargement was viewed as a threat to special-interest groups in the EU15.

1.7.2 Copenhagen to Copenhagen: from 1993 accession criteria to EU membership

The EU officially ended its hesitancy concerning full east–west integration in June 1993. The European Council decided at its Copenhagen summit that 'the associated countries in Central and Eastern Europe that so desire shall become members of the European Union'. This was the first time the EU leaders explicitly sanctioned membership for the CEECs. The Council also defined what has come to be known as the Copenhagen Criteria for EU membership, which continue to be applied today to pre-accession nations such as Croatia and

Turkey. Quoting the summit's final document (known as the Presidency Conclusions in EU jargon):

Membership requires that the candidate country has achieved stability of institutions guaranteeing democracy, the rule of law, human rights and respect for, and protection of, minorities, the existence of a functioning market economy as well as the capacity to cope with competitive pressure and market forces within the Union. Membership presupposes the candidate's ability to take on the obligations of membership including adherence to the aims of political, economic and monetary union.

Nine years later, the European Council met again in Copenhagen to finish the enlargement process. As the Presidency Conclusions of the 12–13 December 2002 meeting state:

Today marks an unprecedented and historic milestone in completing this process with the conclusion of accession negotiations with Cyprus, the Czech Republic, Estonia, Hungary, Latvia, Lithuania, Malta, Poland, the Slovak Republic and Slovenia. The Union now looks forward to welcoming these States as members from 1 May 2004. This achievement testifies to the common determination of the peoples of Europe to come together in a Union that has become the driving force for peace, democracy, stability and prosperity on our continent.

The timing, May 2004, was aimed at allowing the new members to participate in the elections for the European Parliament and in the formation of the new European Commission.

1.8 Preparing for eastern enlargement: Treaties of Amsterdam and Nice

Once the EU15 leaders had confirmed that the CEECs would eventually become EU members, it became clear that EU institutions and procedures would have to be reformed. Structures designed for six members were groaning under the weight of fifteen. Adding between five and ten newcomers would surely bring down the house. In 1996, the EU started a treaty-writing exercise – called an intergovernmental conference (IGC) in EU jargon – that produced the Treaty of Amsterdam in 1997.

1.8.1 Treaty of Amsterdam: cleaning up the Maastricht Treaty

While the ambitions for the Treaty of Amsterdam were high, the IGC failed to produce agreement on reform of the main institutions. The IGC did not end in failure. It produced a treaty that is best thought of as a tidying up of the Maastricht Treaty. The substantive additions included a more substantial role for the EU in social policy (UK Prime Minister Tony Blair cancelled the British opt-out). The powers of the European Parliament were modestly boosted, and the notion of flexible integration, so-called closer cooperation, was introduced (see Chapter 2 for details).

The key enlargement-related reform issues (adjusting voting rules in the Council of Ministers, the number of EU Commissioners, composition of the EU Parliament, among others) were not settled. Rather, EU leaders agreed to a list of issues that had to be solved before the enlargement – the so-called Amsterdam leftovers – and then agreed to launch a new IGC in 2000.

1.8.2 Treaty of Nice: failed attempt to reform EU institutions

After the year-long preparation of the IGC 2000, EU leaders met in the French city of Nice in December 2000 to wrap up a new treaty that was to adjust EU institutions to the impending enlargement. At 4 o'clock in the morning, after the longest EU summit in history, EU leaders announced political agreement on a new treaty. The leaders did not have legal texts in front of them in Nice, so the political agreement was followed by two months of post-summit negotiations. The final treaty text was signed on 26 February 2001.

The Treaty of Nice was not a success. The critical Amsterdam leftover issues – the size and composition of the Commission, extension of majority voting in the Council of Ministers, and reform of Council voting rules – were not fully solved. On Commission reform, the Treaty adopted a temporary, makeshift reform – temporary since it applies only until the 27th member has joined; and makeshift since a long-term solution was not agreed. On the extension of qualified voting issue, the Treaty was basically a house-cleaning exercise with little or no change in the areas to be subject to majority voting. On Council decision-making reform, the Treaty of Nice actually made things worse. Under the chairmanship of Jacques Chirac, EU leaders abandoned the months of preparatory work and, with little more than hurried, late-night staff work and their political instincts to guide them, they adopted a complex system. Subsequent analysis showed that the Nice Treaty voting rules actually made it more difficult for the enlarged EU to act (see Chapter 3). Decision-making efficiency in the EU27 would have been greater with no reform at all. The Treaty also shifted power to large nations in a major way.

The Treaty of Nice, which came into force in 2003, had some trouble with ratification but not nearly as much as the Maastricht Treaty. Although the Treaty implied important redistribution of power among EU members, most electorates were convinced by the argument that the eastern enlargement was worth it. Eastern enlargement would be a historic achievement that would fulfil the aspirations of 100 million Europeans who chose freedom, democracy and markets. It would ensure political and economic stability in Europe by burying the last remnants of pre-1945 Europe that had fostered intolerance, destructive nationalism and war. The Irish referendum delivered a narrow 'no' vote, but after all of the other fourteen EU members had ratified the Treaty and Ireland was granted a number of assurances on Irish neutrality, Irish voters approved the document in a second vote.

Despite the difficult negotiations, EU leaders at the Nice summit knew that the Treaty was incomplete. As part of the final political deal on the Treaty, they agreed to commit themselves to another IGC in 2004 in order to complete the reform process. This 'Declaration on the Future of the Union' highlighted four themes:

Figure 1.10: *The Irish 'no' to the Treaty of Nice*

Note: Sinn Féin opposed the Treaty of Nice, but most political parties supported it. Irish voters reversed themselves after EU assurances on military issues.

Photo: www.sinnfein.ie.

★ defining a more precise division of powers between the EU and its members;
★ clarifying the status of the Charter of Fundamental Rights proclaimed in Nice;
★ making the treaties easier to understand without changing their meaning;
★ defining the role of national parliaments in the European institutions.

There was no mention of the need for an EU constitution.

1.8.3 The 2004 enlargement and the Constitutional Treaty

One year after Nice, the European Council in Laeken adopted the 'Declaration on the Future of the European Union', which started a process leading to a new treaty.[1] Such treaties had in the past been negotiated among EU members in the course of an IGC. In light of the difficult Nice summit talks, the Laeken Council decided to try a novel working method. It convened the 'Convention on the Future of Europe', which came to be known as the European Convention. This was a gathering of representatives from Member State governments, the national parliaments, the European Parliament, the Commission, and the candidate countries. As its Laeken Declaration name suggests, the Convention was supposed to study the fundamental questions that enlargement posed for the future of Europe and to define various solutions. The output of the Convention was then to be taken as a point of departure for standard intergovernmental negotiations at an IGC.

The Laeken Declaration, 15 December 2001

The Laeken Declaration contains a long list of questions that the Convention was supposed to consider. The 56 questions were grouped into the main themes of the Nice Declaration, but Laeken included two crucial novelties.
★ The Declaration implicitly admits that the Nice reforms were insufficient by considering 'how we can improve the efficiency of decision-making and the workings of the institutions in a Union of some thirty Member States', despite the fact that this was the main goal of the Treaty of Nice, and EU leaders had asserted that the Nice reforms were sufficient. In effect, they asked the Convention to consider reforming the Nice reforms, even before those reforms had been implemented (most Treaty

[1] The Declarations are on http://europa.int.eu; use a search engine such as Google to search for the specific Declaration.

of Nice changes took effect only with the eastern enlargement).

★ While the Nice Declaration made no mention of a constitution, the word does appear in the Laeken Declaration. The Laeken Declaration did not instruct the Convention to write a constitution, but it did include a section entitled 'Towards a Constitution for European citizens'. As part of the Laeken Declaration's list of questions, it states in the context of simplification theme: 'The question ultimately arises as to whether this simplification and reorganisation might not lead in the long run to the adoption of a constitutional text in the Union. What might the basic features of such a constitution be? The values which the Union cherishes, the fundamental rights and obligations of its citizens, the relationship between Member States in the Union?'

The European Convention, February 2002 to July 2003

The European Convention was run by former French President Valéry Giscard d'Estaing with the assistance of two vice-chairmen (see Fig. 1.11). It started slowly, and many early observers expected its large size and ill-defined objectives to result in a muddled outcome. However, by mid-2002, President Giscard d'Estaing had managed to redefine the Convention's purpose. The 'Convention on the Future of Europe' set up by Laeken was transformed into a constitution-writing convention. The new goal was to present the EU heads of state and

Figure 1.11: *The European Convention was run by its presidium*

Note: Presidential podium at the plenary session debate on institutional questions, January 2003. From the left, Jean-Luc Dehaene (Vice-Chairman, Belgium), Giuliano Amato (Vice-Chairman, Italy) and Valéry Giscard d'Estaing (Chairman, France).

© European Community 2005

government with a fully written constitution. From that point forward, the tone of the Convention changed and EU Member States started sending heavyweight politicians in place of low-level representatives. All arguments over the need for a constitution were dropped; discussion turned instead to its content.

The chairman, Valéry Giscard d'Estaing, was firmly in charge. The Convention's decision-making procedure involved no voting by representatives and indeed no standard democratic procedure of any kind. The Convention was to adopt its recommendations by 'consensus', with Giscard d'Estaing defining when a consensus existed. The representatives of the candidate countries participated fully in the debate, but their voices were not allowed to prevent a consensus among the representatives of the EU15.

Chairman Giscard d'Estaing had enormous control over the debate and final control over the actual text. One professor of political science who studied the Convention process closely, George Tsebelis, noted that Giscard 'expanded the authority of the Convention, and shaped the document that it produced. By eliminating votes, he enabled the presidium and the secretariat (which means himself) to summarize the debates. By stretching the concept of agenda in order to place issues in the debate, by using time limits as a way of limiting possible opponents from making proposals, by selecting the staff members himself, and taking them away from every possible source of opposition he was able to shape the document in a very efficient way. ... This is one of the reasons that the process is encountering significant problems for ratification' (Tsebelis, 2005).

The draft framework that Giscard d'Estaing presented in October 2002 was fleshed out into a draft that was presented to the June 2003 European Council meeting. Leaders of EU15 leaders accepted the draft as a starting point for the IGC.

The IGC's failure and the Irish compromise

The IGC that considered the draft Constitutional Treaty started in October 2003. Differences that had been papered over by the Convention's unusual decision-making procedure re-emerged. The most contentious issues were the same ones that caused trouble for the IGCs of the Treaties of Amsterdam and Nice: institutional reforms, especially of the Council of Ministers, voting and representation on the European Commission. The final draft produced by the Italian presidency was rejected by the European Council in December 2003. Although several members had problems with many parts of the

Figure 1.12: *Toast at the Convention's last plenary session, 13 June 2003*

Source: European Commission.

draft, the final hold-up was the voting rules which greatly reduced the voting power of Spain and Poland (compared with the Treaty of Nice rules) and greatly increased the voting power of Germany (see Chapter 3). The voting question had not been discussed openly in the Convention since Chairman Giscard d'Estaing did not set up a working group on this critical issue.

Given this failure, enlargement proceeded without agreement on the draft Constitution, so the next European Council to consider the Treaty consisted of 25 members. Importantly, the Spanish Prime Minister José María Anzar, who so forcefully opposed the new voting rules in December 2003, lost his national election, and the new Prime Minister, José Luis Zapatero, proved more flexible on the voting issue. This, combined with skilful diplomacy by the Irish presidency, permitted a grudging and difficult but ultimately unanimous acceptance of the Irish presidency's draft of the Constitution at the June 2004 summit of EU25 leaders.

Ratification difficulties

EU Treaties must be part of each Member State's law, so they must be ratified by each and every member according to each member's own constitutional requirements. In many EU nations, this involves a vote by the national parliament. In others, it involves a referendum. For a variety of reasons, four EU nations that would normally have ratified by parliamentary vote opted for referenda.

Early in the IGC process, British Prime Minister Tony Blair declared that the UK would put the Treaty to a referendum. This served his domestic political interest in that it removed the issue from the 2005 general election

(British voters could reject the Constitution without rejecting Blair who supported it). But it also strengthened Britain's hand in the negotiations. Britain could credibly claim that any Treaty that was too integrationist would be rejected by UK voters. Soon afterwards, French President Jacques Chirac also announced that he would put the Treaty to a popular vote. Again this served his domestic political aims (the opposition Socialists were deeply divided over the Constitution and a referendum was expected to damage their cohesion before the 2007 presidential election). It was also viewed as a necessary counterweight to the 'ultimatum' created by the British referendum. The Dutch referendum was called for by the Dutch parliament – and this against the wishes of the Christian Democrats, the biggest government coalition party. The Dutch referendum was to be the first ever held in the Netherlands since it became a parliamentary democracy in 1848. The vote was not to be legally binding, although all parties agreed to respect the outcome. Likewise, Luxembourg scheduled a consultative referendum – its first since 1936 – which its parliament promised to respect.

French and Dutch voters rejected the Constitutional Treaty by a wide margin in mid-2005. These two 'no' votes posed a very different problem from the Danish and Irish no's to the Maastricht and Nice Treaties. France and the Netherlands are founding members and their citizens are considered solid supporters of the European ideal. The number of 'no' voters was also quite different. In the first Irish poll on the Treaty of Nice, less than 1 million people voted and only 530 000 said no. In the French plebiscite, 29 million voters cast ballots, with 15.5 million saying no. In the Netherlands, the 61.5 per cent 'no' vote meant 4.7 million Dutch rejected the Treaty. While EU leaders could 'work around' 530 000 'no'

Figure 1.13: *Posters for the French Constitutional Treaty referendum*

Source: Audiovisual Library of the European Commission.

sayers, it is hard to ignore 20 million 'no' voters. In July, Luxembourg held a consultative vote on the Treaty in which 56.5 per cent of 221 000 voters said yes; Luxembourg's parliament had already approved the Constitution two weeks in advance of the referendum. The only other referendum held was in Spain, where 10.8 million out of 14 million voters said yes in February 2005.

In reaction to the Dutch and French votes, EU leaders decided to suspend the formal ratification timetable, notably its deadline of November 2006. Since the Constitutional Treaty can enter into force only if it is approved by France and the Netherlands, most observers believe that the Constitutional Treaty will never become law. The future course of action remained undefined as this edition went to print.

1.9 Summary

It is impossible to summarize fifty years of European integration in a few paragraphs. However, it is possible to highlight the main events and lessons as far as the economics of European integration are concerned.

European integration has always been driven by political factors, ranging from a desire to prevent another European war to a desire to share the fruit of integration with the newly democratic nations in central and eastern Europe. Yet, while the goals were always political, the means were always economic.

There have been basically three big increases in European economic integration:

★ Formation of the customs union from 1958 to 1968 eliminated tariffs and quotas on intra-EU trade.
★ The Single Market Programme implemented between 1986 and 1992 (although elements are still being implemented today) eliminated many non-tariff barriers and liberalized capital flows within the EU.
★ The Economic and Monetary Union melded together the currencies of most EU members.

Each of these steps towards deeper integration – but especially the customs union and the Single Market Programme – engendered discriminatory effects that triggered reactions in the non-member nations. Just as the knocking down of one domino triggers a chain reaction that leads to the fall of all dominos, the discriminatory effects of EU integration have created a powerful gravitational force that has progressively drawn all but the most reluctant Europeans into the EU. If there is a lesson to draw from this for the future, it is that the 2004 enlargement is likely to greatly magnify the pro-EU membership forces in the nations further east and south.

Self-assessment questions

1. Draw a diagram (or diagrams) that graphically shows the major steps in European economic integration along with dates and the names of the countries involved. Be sure to explicitly discuss the removal of various barriers to the movement of goods, labour and capital.

2. Draw a diagram like Fig. 1-6 to show the current state of trade arrangements in Europe, including all European nations west of the Urals.

3. Make a list of all the EU treaties (with dates) and provide a brief (10 words or less) explanation of each treaty's major contribution to European integration.

4. Make a list of the dates of the major stages in the Common Agricultural Policy and its reforms (see http://europa.eu.int/comm/agriculture/index_en.htm for details).

5. Make a list of the dates of the major stages in the EU structural spending programmes (see http://europa.eu.int/comm/regional_policy/index_en.htm for details).

6. What were the main challenges posed by eastern enlargement of the EU and how was the Treaty of Nice meant to address these challenges?

7. Some European integration experts subscribe to the so-called bicycle theory of integration, which asserts that European integration must continually move forward to prevent it from 'falling over', i.e. breaking down. List a sequence of events from 1958 to 1992 that lend support to the theory.

8. Explain how Cold War politics accelerated European integration in some ways but hindered it in others, such as geographic expansion of the EU.

9. Explain when and by which means the organization that is known as the European Union has changed names since its inception in 1958.

10. Make a table showing the dates of all changes in EU and EFTA membership.

Essay questions

1. What role has the Council of Europe, which is a non-EU institution, played in pan-European integration?

2. How important was the USA's role in promoting European integration? Do you think Europe would have formed the EEC, or something like it, if the USA had not made the creation of the OEEC a condition for aid?

3. Describe the evolution of the various British governments' attitudes towards European integration in the 1945 to 1975 period. In the early years, Labour opposed membership whereas Conservatives supported it, but recently the roles have reversed. Why do you think this is so?

4. Provide an explanation for why only six of the EU15 nations joined in 1957. You should list specific reasons for each non-member.

5. Write an essay on the work towards deeper European integration that was done in the context of the OEEC. Why did this fail?

6. Write an essay on whether Charles de Gaulle promoted or hindered European integration. [Chapter 8 of Urwin (1995) is a good place to start.]

7. Why did the EPC and EDC plans fail whereas the ECSC succeeded?

Further reading: the aficionado's corner

For a good, general description of the development of European integration see:
Urwin, D. (1995) *The Community of Europe*, Longman, London.

Two books that challenge the traditional view that federalist idealism was important in the development of Europe are:
Milward, A. (1992) *The European Rescue of the Nation-State*, Cambridge University Press, Cambridge.
Moravcsik, A. (1998) *The Choice for Europe: Social Purpose and State Power from Messina to Maastricht*, Cornell University Press, Ithaca.

A detailed description of post-war growth can be found in:
Crafts, N. and G. Toniolo (1996) *Economic Growth in Europe since 1945*, Cambridge University Press, Cambridge.

Useful websites

The European Parliament's factsheets provide an excellent, authoritative and succinct coverage of many historical institutions, policies and debates. For example, the website has pages on the historical development of the Parliament's role, on historical enlargements and on every Treaty. See http://www.europarl.eu.int/factsheets/default_en.htm.

The EU's 'Easy Reading Corner' is not very well organized and the search engine is useless (instead try Google with site: europe.eu.int added to your keyword), but it has a lot of material and will eventually lead you to very detailed information on any topic concerning the EU. Many brochures are oversimplified and not much use to students at the level of this textbook. See http://europa.eu.int/comm/publications/index_en.htm.

A good glossary can be found at http://europa.eu.int/abc/eurojargon/index_en.htm.

Details on specific treaties (including handy summaries) can be found at http://europa.eu.int/abc/treaties_en.htm.

For Marxist–Leninist thinking on capitalism, imperialism and war, see the tract by Leon Trotsky at http://www.marxists.org/archive/trotsky/works/1939/1939-lenin.htm.

The Truman Library website http://www.trumanlibrary.org/teacher/berlin.htm is a good source for early post-war background documents online.

The Centre Virtuel de la Connaissance sur l'Europe provides a complete and well-organized website for documents, photos, videos and so forth on virtually every aspect of European integration at http://www.ena.lu.

Germany History Museum's (DHM) provides photos and videos of Germany's wartime experience at http://www.dhm.de/lemo/html/Nachkriegsjahre/DasEndeAlsAnfang/.

References

Baldwin, R. (1994) *Towards an Integrated Europe*, CEPR, London. Freely downloadable from http://heiwww.unige.ch/~Baldwin/papers.htm.

Baldwin, R. (1995) 'A domino theory of regionalism', in R. Baldwin, P. Haaparanta and J. Kiander (eds) *Expanding European Regionalism: The EU's New Members*, Cambridge University Press, Cambridge.

Crafts, N. and G. Toniolo (1996) *Economic Growth in Europe since 1945*, Cambridge University Press, Cambridge.

Eichengreen, B. and J.B. de Macedo (2001) 'The European Payments Union: history and implications for the evolution of the International Financial Architecture', in A. Lamfalussy, B. Snoy and J. Wilson (eds) *Fragility of the International Financial System*, PIE–Peter Lang, Brussels.

Lamfalussy, A. (1963) *The UK and the Six: An Essay on Economic Growth in Western Europe*, Macmillan, London.

Milward, A. (1984) *The European Rescue of the Nation-State: 1945–51*, Routledge, London.

Milward, A. (1992) *The European Rescue of the Nation-State*, Cambridge University Press, Cambridge.

Spierenburg, D. and R. Poidevin (1994) *The History of the European Coal and Steel Community*, Weidenfeld & Nicolson, London.

Tsebelis, G. (2005) 'Agenda setting in the EU Constitution: from the Giscard Plan to the final document', Working Paper, Domestic Structures and European Integration project, http://dosei.dhv-speyer.de/dosei_start.htm.

Urwin, D. (1995) *The Community of Europe*, Longman, London.

Chronology from 1948 to 2005

Year	Date	Event	Explanation
1948	16 Apr.	OEEC	Organization for European Economic Cooperation (OEEC) established
1950	9 May	Schuman Plan	French Foreign Minister Robert Schuman proposes the establishment of the European Coal and Steel Community (ECSC). Schuman was inspired by Jean Monnet's vision of building Europe step by step. 9 May is celebrated as the Day of Europe
1952	1 Jan.	ECSC	The ECSC is established for 50 years; expired 23 July 2002
1952	27 May	EDC	The Six sign the Treaty establishing the European Defence Community (EDC). The project fails as the French National Assembly rejects the Treaty in 1954
1953	9 Mar.	EPC	A plan for the European Political Community (EPC) is published
1957	25 Mar.	EEC	The Six sign treaties in Rome establishing the European Economic Community (EEC) and the European Atomic Energy Community (Euratom). EEC begins 1 January 1958
1959	21 July	EFTA	European Free Trade Association (EFTA) is established by the Stockholm Convention among Austria, Denmark, Norway, Portugal, Sweden, Switzerland and the UK. EFTA begins on 3 May 1960
1962	1 Jan.	CAP	Common Agricultural Policy starts
1968	1 July	CU completed	Customs union is completed within the EEC and a common external tariff is established
1969	1–2 Dec.	Failed monetary integration launched	At the Hague summit, EC leaders agree to establish a single market, to accelerate integration, and to introduce Economic and Monetary Union by 1980
1972	22 July	EC–EFTA FTAs	Free trade agreements (FTAs) signed with Austria, Iceland, Portugal, Sweden and Switzerland
1973	1 Jan.	First enlargement	The Six become the Nine as Denmark, Ireland and the UK join the EC. Accession treaties were signed on 22 January 1972. EEC signs free trade agreements with Norway (May) and Finland (October)
1974	9–10 Dec.	European Council formalized	At Paris summit, EC leaders agree to meet regularly as a European Council
1978	6–7 July	EMS founded	Bremen European Council establishes the European Monetary System (EMS) and the European currency unit (ECU)
1981	1 Jan.	2nd enlargement	Greece joins
1985	14 June	EC92 White Paper	Commission presents the Cockfield White Paper on the completion of the single market (blueprint for economics in Single European Act)

continued

Year	Date	Event	Explanation
1986	1 Jan.	3rd enlargement	Spain and Portugal join
1986	17, 28 Feb.		Single European Act is signed. Treaty enters into force on 1 July 1987
1990	1 July	EMU stage 1	First stage of Economic and Monetary Union (EMU) begins
1990	10 Oct.	Germany unites	Germany is united as the former German Democratic Republic Länder join the EEC
1991		First Europe Agreements	EC signs Europe Agreements with Poland, Hungary and Czechoslovakia; Europe Agreements for other CEECs signed by 1995
1992	7 Feb.	Maastricht Treaty	Treaty on European Union is signed in Maastricht, creating the EU. Treaty enters into force 1 November 1993 after a difficult ratification process in Denmark
1992	2 May		EC and EFTA sign an agreement establishing the European Economic Area (EEA)
1993	21–22 June	CEECs can join when ready	EU leaders decide CEECs with Europe Agreements can join when they meet the Copenhagen Criteria
1994	1 Jan.	EMU stage 2	The second stage of EMU begins
1994	9–10 Dec.		Essen European Council agrees strategy on eastern enlargement
1995	1 Jan.	4th enlargement	Austria, Finland and Sweden join the EU
1997	2 Oct.	Treaty of Amsterdam	Treaty of Amsterdam is signed; comes into force 1 May 1999
1998	1–2 May	The euro	EU leaders decide 11 to join eurozone (Austria, Belgium, Finland, France, Germany, Ireland, Italy, Luxembourg, the Netherlands, Portugal and Spain)
1998	1 June	ECB	The European Central Bank (ECB) is established
1999	1 Jan.	EMU stage 3	Euro becomes a currency in its own right; only electronic currency until January 2002
2000	7–9 Dec.	Treaty of Nice	Treaty of Nice is signed; comes into force on 1 February 2003 after a difficult ratification process in Ireland
2002	1 Jan.	Euro cash	Euro notes and coins circulate
2002	Feb.	European Convention	Following Laeken Declaration (15 December 2001), the Convention starts.
2003	20 June	Draft Constitution	EU leaders accept Giscard d'Estaing's draft Constitution as starting point for IGC
2003	Oct.	Constitutional IGC	The IGC begins under Italian presidency
2003	13 Dec.	Draft Treaty rejected	European Council fails to adopt the Italian draft of the Treaty; IGC continues
2004	1 May	Eastern enlargement	Ten new members join (Poland, Hungary, Slovakia, Czech Republic, Slovenia, Estonia, Latvia, Lithuania, Malta and Cyprus)

continued

Year	Date	Event	Explanation
2004	18 June	Constitutional Treaty signed	EU heads of state and government sign the Constitutional Treaty. Ratification begins
2005	30 May	French reject Constitution	French referendum on Constitution results in 55% 'no' with 69% participation
2005	1 June	Dutch reject Constitution	62% of Dutch voters reject Constitution; turnout was 63%
2005	17 June	Ratification suspended	EU leaders decided to suspend the November 2006 deadline for ratifying the Constitution. Each Member State decides whether to continue ratification process

Source: These chronologies are based on the excellent and succinct chronology on the website of the 1999 Finnish presidency of the EU (http://presidency.finland.fi/doc/eu/eu_5chro.htm), and the extremely detailed chronology on the European Commission's website (http://europa.eu.int/abc/history/index_en.htm).

> In the infancy of societies, the chiefs of the state shape its institutions; later the institutions shape the chiefs of state.
>
> *Baron de Montesquieu*

Chapter 2

Facts, law, institutions and the budget

INTRODUCTION

The members of the EU are economically and politically integrated to an extent that is historically unprecedented. In many ways, the EU is already more integrated than loosely federated nations such as Canada and Switzerland. This integration is maintained and advanced by a cocktail of economic, political, historical and legal forces shaped by European institutions, laws and policies. This chapter presents the background information on these institutional features that are essential to the study of European economic integration.

The chapter starts by detailing the extent of European economic integration, before turning to more institutional issues – EU organization (the three pillars), EU law, EU institutions and the legislative process. The chapter then presents basic facts on EU members (population, incomes and economic size), which are essential for understanding the subsequent topic, the EU budget. The final section covers the Constitutional Treaty and how it would change EU institutions.

2.1 Economic integration in the EU

If markets are so integrated, you can't cook a different soup in one corner of the pot.

> *Andres Sutt, deputy governor of the Bank of Estonia, on why Estonia wanted to join the eurozone*

The post-war architects of Europe had radical goals in mind when they established the European Economic Community with the 1957 Treaty of Rome. The Treaty's main architect, Jean Monnet, headed an influential pan-European group that was bluntly called the Action Committee for the United States of Europe. Having failed with their plans for a European Political Community and a European Defence Community in the early 1950s (see Chapter 1), they switched to economic integration as the means of achieving their lofty goal.

Indeed, the Treaty of Rome cannot be fully understood without reference to the founders' intentions. The various elements of economics integrated in the Treaty were not subject to individual cost–benefit calculations. The idea was to fuse the six national economies into a unified economic area.[1] This fusion was expected to launch a gradual process that would draw the nations into an ever closer union. Economic integration was to be the means of achieving the 'finalité politique'.

This section reviews the economic integration in today's European Union, organizing the main features according to the logic of a unified economic area.

2.1.1 Treaty of Rome – fountainhead of EU economic integration

The Treaty of Rome was a radical and far-reaching document. It laid out virtually every aspect of economic integration that Europe has implemented over the past half-century. In a sense, the Treaty of Rome was the bud whose leaves unfolded over fifty years into today's European Union.

The Treaty's first article establishes the European Economic Community. Articles 2 and 3 set out the main economic goals and integration initiatives among the original six members.[2] Students of European integration should read parts of at least one Treaty as an essential part of their training. Articles 1, 2 and 3 of the Treaty of Rome are a good place to start since the subject matter is clear and the style is much less legalistic than that of later treaties (see Box 2.1 for the text verbatim).

---

[1] A clear statement of this can be found in the so-called Spaak Report, *Rapport des chefs de délégation aux ministres des Affaires étrangères, Bruxelles, 21 avril 1956*, the outcome of the expert group set up by the Messina Conference. See www.ena.lu.

[2] The Treaty of Rome, or Treaty establishing the European Community (TEC) as it is now known, has been modified many times and its articles renumbered. Here we use the current numbering even though it may change if the Constitutional Treaty passes. Interested readers can find a complete correspondence between the old and new TEC numbering in the appendix of the freely downloadable *The ABC of Community Law* (search for it with Google on http://europa.eu.int/ since the pages sometimes change URLs). For new numbering in the Constitutional Treaty, see Jens-Peter Bonde's reader-friendly version at www.bonde.com.

Articles 1, 2 and 3 of the Treaty of Rome

ARTICLE 1. By this Treaty, the High Contracting Parties establish among themselves a EUROPEAN ECONOMIC COMMUNITY.

ARTICLE 2. The Community shall have as its task, by establishing a common market and progressively approximating the economic policies of Member States, to promote throughout the Community a harmonious development of economic activities, a continuous and balanced expansion, an increase in stability, an accelerated raising of the standard of living and closer relations between the States belonging to it.

ARTICLE 3. For the purposes set out in Article 2, the activities of the Community shall include, as provided in this Treaty and in accordance with the timetable set out therein:

(a) the elimination, as between Member States, of customs duties and of quantitative restrictions on the import and export of goods, and of all other measures having equivalent effect;

(b) the establishment of a common customs tariff and of a common commercial policy towards third countries;

(c) the abolition, as between Member States, of obstacles to freedom of movement for persons, services and capita;

(d) the adoption of a common policy in the sphere of agriculture;

(e) the adoption of a common policy in the sphere of transport;

(f) the institution of a system ensuring that competition in the common market is not distorted;

(g) the application of procedures by which the economic policies of Member States can be coordinated and disequilibria in their balances of payments remedied;

(h) the approximation of the laws of Member States to the extent required for the proper functioning of the common market;

(i) the creation of a European Social Fund in order to improve employment opportunities for workers and to contribute to the raising of their standard of living;

(j) the establishment of a European Investment Bank to facilitate the economic expansion of the Community by opening up fresh resources;

(k) the association of the overseas countries and territories in order to increase trade and to promote jointly economic and social development.

Note: Articles 2 and 3 of the current version of the Treaty of Rome, more formally known as the Treaty establishing the European Community (TEC), are quite similar. Article 2 includes a number of new goals (environment protection, etc.) and Article 3 includes some new activities (strengthening of consumer protection, etc.). You can download a scanned version of the original and current, i.e. consolidated, version from http://europa.eu.int/eur-lex/lex/en/treaties/index.htm

2.1.2 How to create a unified economic area

As far as economics goes, the Treaty of Rome's intention was to create a unified economic area. An area where firms and consumers located anywhere in the area would have equal opportunities to sell or buy goods throughout the area. An area where owners of labour and capital would be free to employ their resources in any economic activity anywhere in the area. The steps necessary to establish this are presented below, along with references to the relevant articles in the current consolidated version of the Treaty of Rome (formally known as the Treaty establishing the European Community, or TEC for short).

Free trade in goods

The most obvious requirement is to remove trade barriers. Article 3a removes all tariffs and quantitative restrictions among members, thus establishing a free trade area for all goods. Tariffs and quotas, however, are not the only means of discriminating against foreign goods and services. Throughout the ages, governments have proved wonderfully imaginative in developing tariff-like and quota-like barriers against foreign goods and services. To remove such 'non-tariff' barriers, and to prevent new non-tariff barriers from offsetting the tariff liberalization, the Treaty rules out all measures that act like tariffs or quotas (in Article 3a).

Common trade policy with the rest of the world

Trade can never be truly free among nations if those nations do not harmonize their trade policy towards non-members. If members have different external tariffs, trade among the Six would have to be closely controlled to prevent 'trade deflection', i.e. imports from non-members pouring into the area through the member with the lowest external tariff. Since such controls would themselves be barriers to intra-EU trade, Article 3b requires the Six to adopt a 'common commercial policy', in other words, identical restrictions on imports from non-members. With these in place, every member can be sure that any product that is physically inside the EU has paid the common tariff and met any common restrictions on, for example, health and safety standards. Tariffs are one of the most important restrictions on external trade, so a common commercial policy with respect to tariffs is referred to with the special name 'customs union'.

Ensuring undistorted competition

Even a customs union is not enough to create a unified economic area. Trade liberalization can be offset by public and private measures that operate inside the borders of EU members. For example, French companies might make a deal whereby they buy only from each other. The Treaty therefore calls for a system ensuring that competition in the area is undistorted (in Article 3g). This general principle is fleshed out in a series of articles that: (i) prohibit trade-distorting subsidies to national producers, (ii) create a common competition policy, (iii) harmonize national laws that affect the operation of the common market, and (iv) harmonize some national taxes. Why are all of these necessary to ensure undistorted competition?

★ *State aids prohibited*. Perhaps the most obvious distortions to competition stem from production subsidies or other forms of government assistance granted to producers located in a particular nation. Such subsidies (called 'state aid' in EU jargon) allow firms to sell their goods cheaper and/or allow uncompetitive firms to stay in business. Both effects put unsubsidized firms in other nations at a disadvantage. Most forms of state aid are prohibited by the Treaty, although a list of exceptions is specified.

★ *Anti-competitive behaviour*. Discrimination from a private agreement operating within a Member State – e.g. a cartel or exclusive purchasing deal – can distort competition. The Treaty prohibits any agreement that prevents, restricts or distorts competition in the area. The focus is on restrictive business practices and abuse of a dominant position (see Chapter 11). Restrictive business practices include a host of unfair practices undertaken by private or state-owned firms. For example, the Treaty explicitly outlaws: price-fixing agreements; controls on production, marketing, R&D or investment; and allocation of exclusive territories to firms in order to reduce competition. The Treaty also requires government monopolies of a commercial character to avoid discrimination based on the nationality of suppliers or customers.

★ *Approximation of laws (EU jargon for harmonize)*. Another source of discrimination stems from product standards and regulations since these can have a dramatic impact on competition and indirectly favour national firms. Moreover, since many product standards are highly technical, so national firms are typically involved in writing a nation's rules. These firms, quite naturally, advise the government to adopt rules that discriminate in favour of their products.

★ *Taxes*. Taxes applied inside Member States can distort competition directly or indirectly by benefiting national firms. On countering this type of discrimination, the Treaty is weak, requiring only that the Commission consider how taxes can be harmonized in the interest of the common market. Of course, if a particular tax provision clearly benefits a well-identified firm or sector within one Member State, then it could be considered as a subsidy and thus directly forbidden.

Unrestricted trade in services

Right from the Treaty of Rome, the principle of freedom of movement of services was embraced, although fleshing this into reality has been hard. Services are provided by people, and governments have to regulate the qualifications of service providers (e.g. medical doctors). The problem has been to separate prudential regulation of qualifications from protectionist restrictions. Box 2.2 provides the example of ski instructors where the roles of protecting consumers and protecting French ski instructors is thoroughly intermingled.

Box 2.2

British ski instructors arrested on French slopes

To flesh out the free movement of people and services, the EU adopted a general system for the recognition of professional education and training in 1992. This ensured that people who got their training in one EU nation could get a job in another EU nation without having to redo their training. The system is based on the principle of mutual trust. If a Briton who has the diploma necessary to teach skiing in Britain wants to teach in France, then France should recognize the British diploma since it should trust the British government's ability to certify ski teachers, just as Britain trusts France to certify its doctors.

French ski-instructor training, however, is difficult, and good jobs are relatively scarce in mountainous regions, so the French government faced pressure to protect the jobs of its ski instructors. Indeed, France used to arrest ski instructors teaching in France without a French diploma. Pressure from the European Commission forced France to justify this practice by asking for an exception from the general system for five jobs: ski instructors, high-altitude mountain guides, diving instructors, parachuting instructors and potholing instructors. French authorities claimed that due to the dangerous nature of the activities concerned, they should have the right to require prospective instructors to pass a test (based on French standards). The effect of such a test could, of course, be equivalent to forcing people to redo their training in France.

The Commission's decision was to allow France to impose the test for two more years, but to cease the practice thereafter. An independent website for snowboarding fans wrote the following in 2004: 'EU nationals won't need a visa to work in France, however, France is the worst country in the world to get a job as a snowboard instructor. The authorities are very protective of their own. If you're caught teaching on the slopes and don't hold the French ski instructor's certificate, you will be arrested and jailed. However, more mundane forms of work such as bar work are permitted' (www.worldsnowboardguide.com).

Figure 2.1: *Ski instructors and the free movement of services*

Labour and capital market integration

If it works properly, a customs union with undistorted competition allows firms and consumers to buy and sell goods throughout the area without facing discrimination based on nationality. This is sufficient to create a unified economic area as far as the trade in goods is concerned. It is not, however, sufficient to fuse national economies into a unified economic area. Accomplishing this also requires integration of capital and labour markets.

Article 3c extends integration to factor markets by instituting a common employment and investment area. It does this by abolishing barriers to the free movement of workers and capital. The basic principles of labour and capital mobility are elaborated in subsequent articles. For instance, the freedom of movement for workers means the elimination of any form of discrimination based on nationality regarding hiring, firing, pay and work conditions. The Treaty also explicitly allows workers to travel freely in search of work.

As for capital mobility, the Treaty focuses on two types of freedom. The first is the right of any Community firm to set up in another Member State. These 'rights of establishment' are essential to integration in sectors with high 'natural' trade barriers, e.g. in sectors such as insurance and banking, where a physical presence in the local market is critical to doing business. The second type concerns financial capital, and here the Treaty goes deep. It states that all restrictions on capital flows (e.g. cross-border investments in stocks and bonds, and direct investment in productive assets by multinationals) shall be abolished. It applies the same to current payments related to capital flows (e.g. the payment of interest and repatriation of profits). Very little capital-market liberalization, however, was undertaken until the 1980s since the Treaty provided an important loophole. It allowed capital market restrictions when capital movements create disturbances in the functioning of a Member State's capital market. Moreover, it did not set a timetable for this liberalization. Capital market liberalization only became a reality thirty years later with the Single European Act and the Maastricht Treaty.

Exchange rate and macroeconomic coordination

Fixed exchange rates were the norm when the Treaty of Rome was written, and throughout the late 1940s and 1950s nations occasionally found that the level of their fixed exchange rate induced their citizens to purchase a value of foreign products and assets that exceeded foreigners' purchases of domestic goods and assets. Such situations, known as balance of payments crises, historically led to many policies – such as tariffs, quotas and competitive devaluations – that would be disruptive in a unified economic area. To avoid such disruptions, the Treaty of Rome called for mechanisms for coordinating members' macroeconomic policies and for fixing balance of payments crises. This seed in the Treaty of Rome eventually sprouted into the euro, the Stability Pact and the European Central Bank. See Chapters 13 and 17 for details.

Common policy in agriculture

From a logical point of view, it might seem that a unified economic area could treat trade in agricultural goods the same way as it treats trade in services and manufactured goods. From a political point of view, however, agriculture is very different from the manufacturing and service industries and the EU has explicitly recognized this right from the beginning.

In the 1950s, Europe's farm sector was far more important economically than it is today. In many European nations, 20 per cent or more of all workers were employed in the sector. Moreover, national policies in the sector were very important and very different across nations. In reaction to the great economic and social turmoil of the 1920s and 1930s, most European nations had adopted highly interventionist policies in

agriculture. These typically involved price controls teamed with trade barriers (Milward, 1992). Moreover, in the 1950s, the competitiveness of the Six's farm sectors differed massively. French and Dutch farmers were far more competitive than German farmers. If the Six were to form a truly integrated economic area, trade in farm goods would have to be included. However, the sharp differences in farm competitiveness among the Six would have meant that free trade would have massively negative effects on many farmers, although, as usual with free trade, the winners would have won more than the losers would have lost.

These simple facts prevented the writers of the Treaty of Rome from including more than the barest sketch of a common farm policy. They did manage to agree on the goals, general principles and a two-year deadline for establishing the common policy. The Common Agricultural Policy came into effect in 1962 (see Chapter 9).

2.1.3 Omitted integration: social policies

The Treaty of Rome was enormously ambitious with respect to economic integration, but it was noticeably silent on the harmonization of social policies (the set of rules that directly affects labour costs such as wage policies, working hours and conditions, and social benefits). Subsequent treaties have not pushed social integration anywhere near as deep as economic integration. This section considers the economic and political logic behind this omission.

The difficult politics of social harmonization

Social harmonization is very difficult politically for at least two reasons. First, nations – even nations as similar as the original six members of the EEC – held very different opinions on what types of social policies should be dictated by the government. Moreover, social policies very directly and very continuously touch citizens' lives, so these opinions are strongly held; much more strongly than, for example, opinions on the common external tariff or the elimination of intra-EEC quotas. The second reason concerns the difficulty of viewing social harmonization as an exchange of concessions.

With tariffs, all Six lower their tariffs against each other's goods. Although the tariffs might not have been identical to start with, there is a certain balance to the notion that we eliminate our tariffs and they eliminate theirs. With social policy, harmonization tends to be viewed as either an upward harmonization (e.g. all adopt a 35-hour working week) or a downward harmonization (e.g. all have to allow shops to open on Sundays). Since social policies in each nation are the outcome of a finely balanced political equilibrium, changes that are 'imposed' by the EU are easy to characterize as undue interference by foreigners, rather than as a two-way exchange. For instance, it would be hard to view as 'balanced' a demand that Germans allow Sunday shopping in the name of social policy harmonization. The same could be said if France were forbidden to impose the 35-hour working week in the name of European integration.

In addition to social harmonization being significantly more difficult politically than economic integration, there are economic arguments suggesting that it is not necessary.

The economics: two schools of thought

Does European economic integration demand harmonization of social policies? This question has been the subject of an intense debate for decades. It arose when the Benelux nations formed their customs union in 1947, when the OEEC was established in 1948, when the European Coal and Steel Community was created in 1953, and when the Treaty of Rome was negotiated.

From the very beginning of this debate there have been two schools of thought. One school of thought – the harmonize-before-liberalizing school – holds that international differences in wages and social conditions provide an 'unfair' advantage to countries with more laissez-faire social policies. In contrast, the no-need-to-harmonize school argues that wages and social policies are reflections of productivity differences and social preferences – differences that wages adjustments will counter. This school rejects calls for harmonization and notes that, in any case, social policies tend to converge as all nations get richer.

The harmonize-before-you-liberalize school is easier to explain. If nations initially have very different social policies, then lowering trade barriers will give nations with low social standards an unbalanced advantage, assuming that exchange rates and wages do not adjust.

The other school of thought (i.e. the school whose ideas prevailed in the Treaty of Rome) points out that wages do adjust. The economics of this is explained in depth in Chapter 8, but here it is in a nutshell. Roughly speaking, firms hire workers up to the point where the total cost of employing workers equals the value they create for the company. As far as the firm is concerned, it is not important whether the cost of the worker stems from a social policy or from wages paid directly to the worker. Different nations have different productivity levels and this is why wages can differ. Now if one nation has more expensive social policies, the workers in that nation will end up taking home (in the form of wages) a lower share of the value they create for the firm. The reason is that the firm pays the costs of the social policy out of the value that workers themselves create for the firm. In short, French workers in our example would be implicitly trading off lower take-home pay for workplace rules that made their lives better. This line of thinking requires an understanding of how markets work, so it is less easily grasped.

2.1.4 Quantifying European economic integration

Recent research by economic historians permits us to quantify the progress of economic integration in Europe. A careful reading of the timing with which various policies were implemented allows the economic historian to quantify (somewhat subjectively) the extent of integration. The indices developed by two different groups are shown in Fig. 2.2. Although the two indices differ in details, they show that European economic integration has been a 'work in progress' for half a century. The DFFM index, which has finer detail on EU integration, clearly shows the main phases:

★ Customs union formation, 1958–68
★ Euro-pessimism, 1973–86
★ Single market, 1986–92
★ EMU, 1993–2001

The BN index makes the useful point that European economic integration started well before the Treaty of Rome. The OEEC produced important trade and payments liberalizations across Europe before 1958 and the ECSC produced deep integration in the coal and steel sectors of the Six (see Chapter 1 for details).

2.2 EU organizational structure: three pillars and a roof

The integration described above did not occur overnight. The decades since 1958 produced a steady stream of new EU laws. Most of these strengthened integration in areas where integration had already begun. Some of the

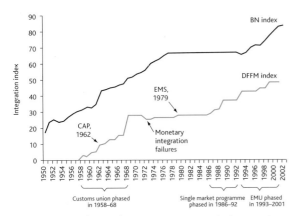

Figure 2.2: *Indices of European economic integration*

Source: DFFM index from Dorrucci *et al.* (2003); BN index from Berger and Nitsch (2005).

Figure 2.3: *Schengen Accord, deeper integration outside the EU framework*

Note: The passport-free travel zone of Schengen includes two non-EU nations (Iceland and Norway), and two EU members are not in it (the UK and Ireland).

© European Community 2005

new laws, however, extended EU integration to new areas, such as immigration policy, environmental policy, police cooperation, and foreign and defence policy.

2.2.1 Ever closer? Creeping competences

Up to the 1992 Maastricht Treaty, all of this integration was subject to the Treaty of Rome's supranational decision-making procedures. For example, the rules governing the detailed implementation of deeper economic integration (called 'completion of the internal market') were adopted by majority voting of EU members. This meant that all Member States had to comply with such rules, even those Member States that voted against them. Moreover, the European Court of Justice was the ultimate authority over disputes involving all such rules and the Court's rulings occasionally had the effect of boosting integration (see the *Cassis de Dijon* case in Chapter 4 for a famous example).

This supranationality created two related problems, given Member States' diverse attitudes toward deeper and broader integration. The first concerned the old schism between federalists and intergovernmentalists (see Chapter 1). On the one hand, some EU members – the 'vanguard' – wished to spread European integration to areas that were not covered in the original treaties (Germany is a good example of a vanguard member). On the other hand, another group of members – call them the 'doubters' – worried that supranational decision-making procedures were producing an irresistible increase in the depth and breadth of European integration and that this was forcing the citizens of some nations to accept more integration

than they wanted (the UK is a good example), an effect called 'creeping competences'. Particularly worrisome was the ability of the European Court of Justice to interpret the Treaty of Rome and subsequent amendments. The Treaty of Rome says that the EC could make laws in areas not mentioned in the Treaty, if the Court rules that doing so was necessary to attain Treaty objectives. The objectives of the Treaty of Rome were radical and far-reaching; its first line says that the members are 'determined to lay the foundations of an ever closer union among the peoples of Europe'. Doubters worried that the combination of the Treaty's ambitious objectives and the Court's ability to sanction law making in areas not explicitly mentioned in the treaties put no limit on how much national sovereignty might eventually be transferred to the EU level. (See Factsheet 1.2.2. at www.europarl.eu.int/factsheets/ for more discussion of this point.)

The second problem concerned integration that was taking place outside of the EU's structure due to differences between the vanguard and the doubters. The Schengen Accord is the classic example. While the free movement of people is an EU goal dating back to 1958, some members (the UK in particular) held up progress towards passport-free travel. In 1985, five EU members signed an agreement ending controls on their internal frontiers. This was completely outside of the EU's structure and many observers feared that such ad hoc arrangements could undermine the unity of the single market and possibly foster tensions among EU members.

Both concerns were addressed when EU members adopted a second keystone treaty – the Treaty on European Union (Maastricht Treaty).

2.2.2 Maastricht and the three pillars as firebreaks

The Maastricht Treaty drew a clear line between supranational and intergovernmental policy areas by creating the 'three-pillar' organizational structure. In a nutshell, the deeper integration policies up to the Maastricht Treaty are in the first pillar and continue to be subject to the Treaty of Rome's supranationality. The intergovernmental policy areas are in the second and third pillars. The European Union is the 'roof' covering the three pillars (see Fig. 2.4).

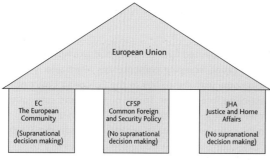

Figure 2.4: *The three-pillar structure*

Note: Some find the following cynical phrase to be useful in remembering the numbering: 'In the EU, economics comes first, justice comes last and security is in the middle.'

The three-pillar structure solved the two related problems since the clear distinction between supranational and intergovernmental cooperation allowed initiatives like Schengen to be brought under the EU's wing without forcing every member to join. This greatly reduced the resistance of the UK and other intergovernmentalists to discussing closer integration in areas such as police cooperation and foreign policy cooperation. The key, as far as these nations are concerned, is that Maastricht puts Member States clearly in control in second- and third-pillar areas. There is no possibility of the Court or Commission using its authority to force deeper integration on reluctant members in pursuit of the duties assigned to them by the Treaty of Rome.

Details of the three pillars

The first pillar, which encompasses the vast majority of EU activity, is called the European Community (formerly known as the European Economic Community, or European Communities). Its issues include the Common Market, the Single Market Programme, Competition Policy, the Common Agricultural Policy, etc. It also includes the Economic and Monetary Union (EMU) and thus comprises the European Central Bank, the single currency, and all the attendant rules and procedures.

The second pillar consists of the Common Foreign and Security Policy, and the third pillar of Justice and Home Affairs. Integration efforts in second- and third-pillar areas are intergovernmental in the sense that such efforts are undertaken by direct negotiation among Member States and any agreement requires unanimity. Amendments to the Maastricht Treaty in the Treaties of Amsterdam and Nice moved some specific policy areas from the second and third pillars into the first pillar.

Saying 'EU' logically implies that one is talking about all three pillars, but because 'European Union' sounds better, the term EU is used almost universally in the media and by politicians even when they are talking about purely first-pillar issues.

The key distinctions

Supranationality in the EU arises in three main ways:
- ★ First, the Commission can propose new laws that are then voted on by the Member States (in the Council of Ministers) and the European Parliament. If passed, these new laws bind every Member State, even those that disagree with them. See Box 2.3 for a current example.
- ★ Second, the Commission has direct executive authority in a limited number of areas, the most prominent being competition policy. For instance, the Commission can block a merger between two EU companies even if their governments support the merger. (See Chapter 11 for details.)
- ★ Third, the rulings of the European Court of Justice can alter laws, rules and practices in Member States, at least in limited areas. (See the *Factortame* case discussed in section 2.3 for an example.)

The Maastricht Treaty states that these forms of supranationality continue to apply to first-pillar issues. It also defines quite precisely the limited role of the Commission, Court and Council in the second and third pillars.

2.2.3 The two key treaties: TEC and TEU

The upshot of all this is that today's European Union is based on two main treaties: the 'first pillar' treaty, the

Treaty establishing the European Community (also called the TEC or Treaty of Rome) and the 'encompassing treaty', the Treaty on European Union (also called the TEU or Maastricht Treaty). There is a raft of other treaties, but these either modify the two main treaties (Single European Act, Treaty of Amsterdam, Treaty of Nice, etc.), or are important only in very specific areas (Treaty establishing the European Atomic Energy Community, etc.). As usual, the full picture is more complex. Interested readers will find Borchardt (1999) very helpful in filling in the details. Also the European Parliament's Factsheets 1.1.1 to 1.1.3 provide a detailed but highly readable history of the treaties' developments (www.europarl.eu.int/factsheets/default_en.htm).

The Constitutional Treaty (which is unlikely to come into force before the third edition of this book appears and maybe never) would remove the three-pillar structure. Since the three-pillar system was set up in part to ensure that only first-pillar issues were subject to the Court's rulings, this aspect could have important long-run effects on the evolution of European integration.

2.3 EU law

Implementing and maintaining a unified economic area requires a legal system of some kind since disputes over interpretation and conflicts among various laws are inevitable. One of the most unusual and important things about the EU is its supranational legal system. By the standards of every other international organization in the world, this system is extremely supranational. For example, even the highest courts in EU Member States must defer to decisions by the EU's Court of Justice on matters concerning the interpretation of EC law. The EU is very much like a federal state in this respect. Just as the decisions of lower courts in France, Germany and Italy can be overturned by those nations' supreme courts, the EU's Court of Justice has the ultimate say on questions concerning European law.

The topic of EU law is as intricate as it is fascinating. This section presents the barest outlines of the subject, focusing on the elements that are essential for understanding the decision-making process in particular,

---

Box 2.3 The UK and the Working Time Directive

The 1993 Working Time Directive aimed to protect employees against working excessively long hours. Specific groups of people were not covered by the directive (e.g. managers and family workers) and some activities were excluded (e.g. transport workers, sea fishermen and trainee doctors). When the directive was formulated, the UK insisted on an opt-out allowing individual workers to waive the directive's limit of 48 hours per week. This has been used almost exclusively in the UK, but when the Court ruled that some of the 'on call' time of doctors should be counted in the 48 hours, other Member States have shown heightened interest in using the opt-out (hiring more doctors would cost Member State governments dearly).

The European Commission became concerned that individual workers were being coerced into 'volunteering' for longer hours. Despite opposition from the UK government, the Commission proposed a change that would allow workers to exceed 48 hours only if employers and unions reached a collective agreement.

The UK government argued that the change would make labour markets less employment-friendly. The leader of the British employers' association said: 'The issue was about freedom of choice. ... People who just do five hours a week overtime and use the money for a holiday. All I want to know is who's going to pay them for the money they lose.'

In May 2005, the European Parliament approved the Commission's proposed change, so the matter moves to the Council of Ministers. If sufficient Member States vote for the change, the UK must implement it despite its objections. At the time this book went to print, the UK was trying to line up allies to block the changes in the Council.

and the economics of European integration more generally. Note that this section is largely based on the freely downloadable book by Borchardt (1999), *The ABC of Community Law* (use a search engine such as Google to find it on http://europa.eu.int/ since the Commission occasionally reorganizes its website). Note on notation: in legal matters, it is important to distinguish between the European Community (first pillar) and the European Union (all three pillars together), so in this section we use EU and EC to mean different things.

2.3.1 'Sources' of EU law

Where did the EU's legal system come from? The legal systems of most democratic nations are based on a constitution. At the time this book went to press, the EU did not have a constitution, and in any case, the legal principles in the European Constitutional Treaty merely codify principles that have been in place for decades. So where did these principles come from? As is true of so many things in the EU, a complete answer to this question would fill a book or two, but the short answer can be given in a few paragraphs. Again, history provides the best organizing principle for the answer. We start with the Treaty of Rome.

The Treaty of Rome commits Member States to a series of general economic and political goals. It also contains a number of highly specific commitments, e.g. on equal pay for men and women. The Treaty transfers important elements of national sovereignty to the European level, for example after 1958, Member States no longer had the right to control their trade policy individually. The Treaty was meant to be a dynamic and adaptive agreement, so it also created ways of making new laws and modifying old ones. Most importantly for the subject at hand, it established a Court to adjudicate the disputes and questions of interpretations that were bound to arise.

The Treaty was not very specific when it came to setting up the legal system. The Treaty establishes the Court of Justice and states that its general task is to 'ensure observance of law and justice in the interpretation and application of this Treaty' (Article164 in the original Treaty). It then goes on to define the Court's composition and to assign the Court a few specific tasks. For example, the Commission can take a Member State before the Court for non-compliance with Treaty obligations, and the Court was charged with interpreting the Treaty.

The Treaty was not specific enough to deal with the

Figure 2.5: *Working session of the Court of Justice*

Source: European Parliament.

many issues that came before the Court. The Court reacted to the lack of specificity in the Treaty by creating the Community's legal system via case law. That is to say, it used decisions relating to particular cases to establish general principles of the EC legal system.

In short, the Treaty of Rome is the wellspring of EC law. The Treaty created the Court and the Court created the EC legal system. EC law is now an enormous mass of laws, rules and practices that have been established by Treaties (primary law), EU laws (secondary law) and decisions of the Court (case law). See Box 2.4 for further details on the types of secondary legislation.

2.3.2 EC legal system: main principles

Since the EC legal system was not created by any single document, its principles have never been officially proclaimed. The 'principles' of EC law are thus general patterns that various jurists have discerned from the thousands of pages of primary, secondary and case law, and different jurists list different principles. Three principles that always are mentioned are 'direct effect', 'primacy of EC law', and 'autonomy' of the EC legal system. These were first established in two landmark cases in 1963 and 1964 (see Box 2.5).

'Direct effect'

'Direct effect' is simple to define: it means that a treaty provisions or other forms of EU law such as directives can create rights which EU citizens can rely upon when they go before their domestic courts. This is radical. It means that EC laws must be enforced by Member States' courts just as if the law had been passed by the national parliament. A good example is the case of a Sabena air stewardess (as they called female flight attendants in the 1970s) who claimed that she was paid less and had to

Box 2.4

Secondary legislation: 'Acts of Community Law'

There are five main types of EU legislation other than the Treaties.

A *regulation* applies to all Member States, companies, authorities and citizens. Regulations apply as they are written, i.e. they are not transposed into other laws or provisions. They apply immediately upon coming into force.

A *directive* may apply to any number of Member States. However, directives only set out the result to be achieved. The Member States decide for themselves, within a prescribed timeframe, what needs to

be done to comply with the conditions set out in the directive. For instance, one Member State may have to introduce new legislation, whereas another may not need to take any action at all if it already meets the requirements set out in the directive.

A *decision* is a legislative act that applies to a specific Member State, company or citizen.

Recommendations and *opinions* are two other types of legislative instruments. They are not legally binding.

Box 2.5

Two cases that established the EC legal system

The EC legal system was not explicitly established in any treaty, so the Court used some early cases to establish three key principles. Since these principles arose in the course of real-world cases, it can be difficult to distinguish precisely among the three principles in the two cases.

Van Gend & Loos v Netherlands, 1963

In this case, the Dutch company Van Gend & Loos brought an action against its own government for imposing an import duty on a chemical product from Germany which was higher than duties on an earlier shipment. The company claimed that this violated the Treaty of Rome's prohibition on tariff hikes on intra-EC trade. The Dutch court suspended the case and asked the EC Court to clarify. The EC Court ruled that the company could rely on provisions in the treaties when arguing against the Dutch government before a Dutch court.

Plainly, this case has an element of direct effect and

primacy. The Dutch government had one rule – the higher tariff rate – whereas the Treaty of Rome had another (no increase allowed). The EC Court said the Treaty provision trumped the national provision. Moreover, the EC Court said that the Dutch court should consider the Treaty directly rather than, for example, the Dutch parliament's transposition of the Treaty's principles into Dutch law. In effect, the Court said that the Treaty was Dutch law as far as the Dutch court was to be concerned. This was new since, normally, a national court can consider only national law when judging a case.

The European Court also took the opportunity to write down its thoughts on the fundamental nature of the EC legal system. In its *Van Gend & Loos v Netherlands* decision, it wrote: 'The Community constitutes a new legal order of international law for the benefit of which the States have limited their sovereign rights, albeit within limited fields, and the subjects of which comprise not only Member States but also their nationals.'

continued

Costa v ENEL, 1964 decision by the European Court of Justice

The next year, the Court expanded its view of the EC legal system in a case involving a dispute over one euro! In 1962, Italy nationalized its electricity grid and grouped it under a national electricity board (ENEL). Mr Flaminio Costa, a shareholder of one nationalized company, felt he had been unjustly deprived of his dividend and so refused to pay his electricity bill for two thousand lira. The non-payment matter came before an arbitration court in Milan but since Mr Costa argued that the nationalization violated EC law, the Milan court asked the European Court to interpret various aspects of the Treaty of Rome.

The Court took the opportunity to go way beyond the question at hand. In its judgement, the Court stated the principle of autonomy and direct effect:

> By contrast with ordinary international treaties, the EEC Treaty has created its own legal system which ... became an integral part of the legal systems of the Member States and which their courts are bound to apply.

Member States have limited their sovereign rights, albeit within limited fields, and have thus created a body of law which binds both their nationals and themselves.

Relying on the logic of what the Treaty of Rome implied – at least implicitly – the Court established the principle of primacy:

> [T]he law stemming from the Treaty, an independent source of law, could not, because of its special and original nature, be overridden by domestic legal provisions, however framed, without being deprived of its character as Community law and without the legal basis of the Community itself being called into question. The transfer by the States from their domestic legal system to the Community legal system of the rights and obligations arising under the Treaty carries with it a permanent limitation of their sovereign rights, against which a subsequent unilateral act incompatible with the concept of the Community cannot prevail.

The Court's justification was that if EC law were not supreme, the objectives of the Treaty could not be met: 'The executive force of Community law cannot vary from one State to another in deference to subsequent domestic laws, without jeopardising the attainment of the objectives of the Treaty.'

retire earlier than male flight attendants. Although this was not a violation of Belgian law at the time, the EC Court ruled in 1976 that the Treaty of Rome (which provides for equality of pay between the sexes) had the force of law in Belgium, or in legalese it had direct effect. The stewardess won the case.

The principle of direct effect is quite unique. For example, when New Zealand ratifies the Kyoto Protocol, it is agreeing to certain obligations, but New Zealand courts ignore these obligations unless they are implemented by a law passed by the New Zealand parliament. Even more unusual is that this direct effect notion applies to EU laws passed by majority voting, e.g. directives. This means that even if a Member State government votes against a particular law, that law automatically has the force of law, so its national courts must treat the EU law as if it were a national law. Importantly, there are complex conditions for a treaty provision to have direct

effect, so not everything in every treaty is automatically enforceable in Member States.

The logical necessity of this principle is straightforward. If laws agreed in Brussels could be ignored in any Member State, the EU would fall into shambles. Each member would be tempted only to implement the EU laws it liked. This would, for example, make it impossible to create a single market or to ensure the free movement of workers.

Primacy of EC law

The principle of the primacy of EC law, which means that Community law has the final say, is not in the Treaty of Rome and indeed appears explicitly for the first time only in the Constitutional Treaty. It is, nonetheless, a principle that is now generally accepted by all EU members. It has repeatedly been used to overturn Member State laws.

One classic example of this is the 1991 *Factortame* case which confirmed the supremacy of EC law over UK law. The UK's Merchant Shipping Act 1988 had the effect of forbidding a Spanish fishing company called Factortame from fishing in UK waters. Factortame asserted in UK courts that this violated EC law, and asked the UK court to suspend the Merchant Shipping Act until the EC Court could rule on the matter (this often takes a couple of years). Under UK law, no British court can suspend an Act of Parliament. The EC Court ruled that under EC law, which was supreme to UK law, a national court could suspend laws which contravened EC law. Subsequently, the highest UK court did strike down the Merchant Fishing Act.

The logical necessity of this principle is just as clear as that of direct effect. Simplifying for clarity's sake, 'direct effect' says that EC laws are automatically laws in every Member State. Primacy says that when EC law and national, regional or local laws conflict, the EC law is what must be enforced.

Autonomy

Most European nations have several layers of courts, local, regional and national. The lower courts, however, do not exist independently of the higher courts, and often the higher courts depend upon the lower courts (e.g. in some nations, the high court can rule only after the case has been tried at a lower level). The EC legal system, however, is entirely independent of the Member States' legal systems according to the principle of autonomy.

2.4 The 'Big-5' institutions

There are many EU agencies, bodies and committees, but one can achieve a very good understanding of how the EU works knowing only the 'Big-5': the Council of the European Union (often called by its old name, the Council of Ministers), the European Council, the European Commission, the European Parliament and the European Court of Justice. (There are many more institutions; interested students should see http://europa.eu.int/institutions/index_en.htm.)

The Constitutional Treaty would change the Big-5 in important ways, but since the Constitution is a long way from coming into force, we present the current facts on the Big-5, grouping together the Constitution's changes for all five in a separate section.

2.4.1 Council of the European Union

The Council of the European Union – also known as the Council of Ministers or 'the Council' for short – is the EU's main decision-making body. Almost every piece of legislation is subject to approval by the Council. The Council consists of one representative from each EU member. The national representatives must be authorized to commit their governments to Council decisions, so Council members are the government ministers responsible for the relevant area – the finance ministers on budget issues, agriculture ministers on farm issues, etc. The Council is the institution where Member States' governments assert their influence most directly.

Since all EU governments are elected (democracy is a must for membership) and the Council members represent their governments, the Council is the ultimate point of democratic control over EU actions and law making.

The main task of the Council is to adopt new EU laws (directives, regulations, rules, etc.). Most of these laws concern measures necessary to implement the treaties, but they also include measures concerning the EU budget and international agreements involving the EU. The Council also is tasked with coordinating the general economic policies of the Member States in the context of the Economic and Monetary Union (EMU). The famous 3 per cent deficit rule, which has caused Germany and France so much trouble in recent years, is part of this coordination effort. On most issues, passing new laws also requires approval of the European Parliament, so on these issues, the Council's legislative power is shared with the Parliament.

Figure 2.6: *Meeting of the Council of Ministers in Brussels*

© European Community 2005

Figure 2.7: *Artemis Joint Combined Military Support Base, Entebbe*

Source: Council of the European Union.

In addition to these first-pillar tasks, the Council takes the decisions pertaining to Common Foreign and Security Policies and measures pertaining to police and judicial cooperation in criminal matters. To the average European, these are some of the most visible actions of the Council. For example, the EU launched a peacekeeping operation in the Democratic Republic of Congo (Artemis) in accordance with a United Nations Resolution asking for the deployment of an interim emergency multinational force in Bunia (a region in the Congo). The EU force, working closely with the United Nations Mission, sought to stabilize security conditions and to improve the humanitarian situation. France led the mission.

The Council has two main decision-making rules. On the most important issues – such as Treaty changes, the accession of new members and setting the multi-year budget plan – Council decisions are by unanimity. On most issues (about 80 per cent of all Council decisions), the Council decides on the basis of what is known as 'qualified majority voting' (QMV). These rules are extremely important for understanding how Europe works, so they are the subject of extensive analysis in Chapter 3.

Presidency of the EU

One EU member holds the presidency, with this office rotating among EU members every six months. The Council of Ministers is chaired by the presiding member and generally meets in Brussels (April, June and October meetings are held in Luxembourg). (For more details see the Council's website at http://ue.eu.int). Although the Council is a single institution, it follows the somewhat confusing practice of using different names to describe

the Council according to the matters being discussed. For example, when the Council addresses EMU matters, it is called the Economic and Financial Affairs Council, or ECOFIN to insiders.

2.4.2 The European Council

The European Council consists of the leaders of each EU member plus the President of the European Commission – the EU phraseology is the 'heads of state and government'. The European Council provides broad guidelines for EU policy and thrashes out the final compromises necessary to conclude the most sensitive aspects of EU business, including reforms of the major EU policies, the EU's multi-year budget plan, Treaty changes, and the final terms of enlargements. This body is by far the most influential institution because its members are the leaders of their respective nations.

The European Council is chaired by the country that has the presidency of the EU. This position can be powerful since it gives the President some power to set the agenda. However, since the Council operates on a basis of consensus, the agenda-setting power can be quite limited.

The European Council meets at least twice a year (in June and December), but meets more frequently when the EU faces major political problems. The highest-profile meetings are those held at the end of each six-month term of the EU presidency. These June and December meetings are important media events – the one aspect of the EU that almost every European has seen on television. The reason for this is that the European Council's decisions determine all of the EU's major moves. For example, the bitter budget battle between the UK and France occurred at the June 2005 summit and the decision to adopt the Constitutional Treaty was made at the June 2004 summit. One particularly historic Council meeting was the 2002 Copenhagen summit at which the ten central and eastern European nations were admitted to the EU (see Fig. 2.8).

The most important decisions of each presidency are contained in a document known as the Conclusions of the Presidency, which is published at the end of each European Council meeting. For example, the decision to accept the ten new members in the 2004 enlargement was announced in the Conclusions released after the December 2002 European Council in Copenhagen. All recent Conclusions are on the Council's website (http://ue.eu.int/).

One peculiarity of the EU is that the European Council has

Figure 2.8: *Group photo with the soon-to-be new members of the EU*

Source: Council of the European Union.

no formal role in EU law making even though it is the most influential body in the process. The political decisions of the European Council have to be translated into law following the standard legislative procedures that we review below. These procedures involve the Commission, the Council of Ministers and, in most areas, the European Parliament.

Confusingly, the European Council and the Council of Ministers are often both called 'the Council'. Moreover, the Council of Ministers and the European Council should also not be confused with the Council of Europe (an international organization entirely unrelated to the EU).

For years, the Council met in the country that had the rotating presidency of the EU. Since 2004, however, all summits are held in Brussels.

2.4.3 The European Commission

The European Commission is at the heart of the EU's institutional structure. It is the main driving force behind deeper and wider European integration. This body, which is based in Brussels, has three main roles:
★ to propose legislation to the Council and Parliament;
★ to administer and implement EU policies;
★ to provide surveillance and enforcement of EU law in coordination with the European Court.

As part of its third role, the Commission is considered to be the 'guardian of the treaties', i.e. the body that is ultimately charged with ensuring that the treaties are implemented and enforced.

The Commission also represents the EU at some international negotiations, such as those relating to trade and cooperation with non-member nations. The Commission's negotiating stances at such meetings are closely monitored by EU members.

Commissioners and the Commission's composition

Before the 2004 enlargement, the European Commission was made up of one Commissioner from each EU member, with an extra Commissioner from the Big-5 nations in the EU15 (Germany, the UK, France, Italy and Spain). This included the President (Romano Prodi up to 2005), two Vice-Presidents and 17 other Commissioners. In the enlarged Union, each nation has one Commissioner since, in an attempt to keep Commission to a manageable size, the big nations agreed to give up their extra Commissioner in the Treaty of Nice. The current Commission, which is presided by former Portuguese Prime Minister José Manuel Barroso, has 25 Commissioners (see Fig. 2.9).

Commissioners are in effect chosen by their national governments, but the choices are subject to political agreement by other members. The Commission as a whole, and the Commission President individually, must also be approved by the European Parliament. Note, however, that Commissioners are not supposed to act as national representatives. They should not accept or seek instruction from their country's government. In practice, Commissioners are generally quite independent of their home governments, but since they have typically held high political office in their home nations, they are naturally sensitive to issues that are of particular concern in their home nations. This ensures that all decisive national sensitivities are heard in Commission deliberations.

Figure 2.9: *The 25-member Barroso Commission*

Note: See http://europa.eu.int/comm/commission_barroso/index_en.htm for notes on each Commissioner.

Source: European Commission.

Commissioners, including the President of the Commission, are appointed all together and serve for five years. This is why people often refer to each Commission by the President's name, e.g. the Prodi Commission or the Santer Commission. The appointments are made just after European Parliamentary elections and take effect in January of the following year. The Barroso Commission's term ends in January 2009.

The Commission has a great deal of independence in practice and often takes views that differ substantially from those of the Member States, the Council and the Parliament. However, it is ultimately answerable to the European Parliament since the Parliament can dismiss the Commission as a whole by adopting a motion of censure. Although this has never happened, a censure motion was almost passed in 1999, triggering a sequence of events that ended in mass resignation of the Commission led by President Jacques Santer (the Prodi Commission's predecessor).

Each politically appointed Commissioner is in charge of a specific area of EU policy. In particular, each runs what can be thought of as the EU equivalent of a national ministry. These 'ministries', called Directorates General or DGs in EU jargon, employ a relatively modest number of international civil servants. The Commission as a whole employs about 17 000, which is fewer than the number of people who work for the city of Vienna. Just as in national ministries, Commission officials tend to provide most of the expertise necessary to administer and analyse the EU's complex network of policies since the Commissioners themselves are typically generalists.

Legislative powers

The Commission's main duty is to prepare proposals for new EU decisions. These range from a new directive on minimum elevator safety standards, to reform of the Common Agricultural Policy (CAP). Neither the Council nor the Parliament can adopt legislation until the Commission presents its proposals, except under extraordinary procedures. This monopoly on the 'right to initiate' makes the Commission the gatekeeper of EU integration. It also allows the Commission to occasionally become the driving force behind deeper or broader integration. This was especially true under the two Delors Commissions that served from 1985 to 1994.

Commission proposals are usually based on general guidelines established by the Council of Ministers, the European Council, the Parliament or the treaties. A proposal is prepared by the relevant Directorate-General

in collaboration with other DGs concerned. In exercising this power of initiative, the Commission consults a broad range of EU actors, including national governments, the European Parliament, national administrations, professional groups and trade unions. This complex consultation process is known in EU jargon as 'comitology'.

Executive powers

The Commission is the executive in all of the EU's endeavours, but its power is most obvious in competition policy. Chapter 13 explains in more detail how the Commission has the power to block mergers, to fine corporations for unfair practices and to insist that EU members remove or modify subsidy to their firms. The Commission also has substantial latitude in administering the Common Agricultural Policy, including the right to impose fines on members that violate CAP rules.

One of the key responsibilities of the Commission is to manage the EU budget subject to supervision by a specialized institution called the EU Court of Auditors. For example, while the Council decided the programme-by-programme allocation of funds in the EU's current multi-year budget ('Financial Perspective' in EU jargon), it was the Commission that decided the year-by-year indicative allocation of Structural Funds across members.

Decision making

The Commission decides, in principle, on the basis of a simple majority. The 'in principle' proviso is necessary because the Commission makes almost all of its decision on the basis of consensus. The reason is that the Commission usually has to get its actions approved by the Council and/or the Parliament, so unless the proposal gains the approval of a substantial majority of the Commissioners, it is likely to fail in the Council and/or Parliament.

2.4.4 The European Parliament

The European Parliament has two main tasks:
★ sharing legislative powers with the Council of Ministers and the Commission;
★ overseeing all EU institutions, but especially the Commission.

The Parliament, on its own initiative, has also begun to act as the 'conscience' of the EU, for example condemning various nations for human rights violations via non-binding resolutions.

Organization

The European Parliament (EP) has 732 members who are directly elected by EU citizens in special elections organized in each Member State. The number of Members of European Parliament (MEPs) per nation varies with population, but the number of MEPs per million EU citizens is much higher for small nations than for large. For example, in the 1999–2004 Parliament, Luxembourg had 6 MEPs and Germany had 99, despite the fact that Germany's population is about 160 times that of Luxembourg.

MEPs are supposed to represent their local constituencies, but the Parliament's organization has evolved along classic European political lines rather than along national lines (Noury and Roland, 2002). The EP election campaigns are generally run by each nation's main political parties, and MEPs are generally associated with a particular national political party. Although this means that over one hundred parties are represented in the EP, fragmentation is avoided because many of these parties have formed political groups. As in most EU Member States, two main political groups – the centre-left and the centre-right – account for two-thirds of the seats and tend to dominate the Parliament's activity. The centre-left grouping in the EP is called the Party of European Socialists; the centre-right group is called the European People's Party.

National delegations of MEPs do not sit together. As in most parliaments, the European Parliament's physical, left-to-right seating arrangement reflects the left-to-right ideology of the MEPs. In the 1999–2004 Parliament, the left flank was occupied by the radical left (communist, former communist, extreme left parties and the Nordic Green Left parties). Continuing left to right, the next is the Party of the European Socialists, the Greens and allies (e.g. regional parties from Spain), the European Liberal Democrat and Reformists group and the European People's Party. On the far right flank are the Euro-sceptic Gaullists and other rightist groups. Details on the size and national composition of the European Parliament can be found on www.europarl.eu.int. These party groups have their own internal structure, including chairs, secretariats, staffs, and 'whips' who keep track of attendance and voting behaviour. The political groups receive budgets from the Parliament.

Statistical analysis of MEPs' voting patterns shows that they vote more along party lines than they do along country lines. Indeed, cohesion within European political groupings is comparable to that in the US Congress,

Figure 2.10: *Debate in the European Parliament*

Source: European Commission.

whereas cohesion of country delegations is significantly lower and is declining, as Noury and Roland (2002) show.

Location

The Parliament is not located in Brussels, the centre of EU decision making, but in Strasbourg owing to France's dogged insistence that it remain in France (the Parliament's predecessor in the European Coal and Steel Community, the Common Assembly, was located there to be near the heart of the coal and steel sectors). Equally determined insistence by Luxembourg has kept the Parliament's secretariat in Luxembourg. Since Brussels is where most of the political action occurs, and is also the location of most of the institutions that the Parliament is supposed to supervise, the Parliament also has offices in Brussels (this is where the various Parliamentary committees meet). The staffs of the Parliament's political groups work in Brussels. It is not clear how much this geographic dispersion hinders the Parliament's effectiveness, but the time and money wasted on shipping documents and people among three locations occasionally produces negative media attention. This shifting location may also help to account for the fact that many MEPs do not attend all sessions. In the third Parliament, an average of 17.6 per cent of the MEPs were absent and 35.5 per cent were physically present but did not vote; this improved in the fourth Parliament where the respective figures were 16.8 per cent and 21.6 per cent (Noury and Roland, 2002).

Democratic control

The Parliament and the Council are the primary democratic controls over the EU's activities. The MEPs are directly elected by EU citizens, so European Parliamentary elections are, in principle, a way for Europeans to have their voices heard on European issues.

In practice, however, European Parliamentary elections are often dominated by standard left-versus-right issues rather than by EU issues. Indeed, European Parliamentary elections are sometimes influenced by pure national concerns, with the voters using the elections as a way of expressing disapproval or approval of the incumbent national government's performance. Moreover, in many Member States, participation in European Parliamentary elections tends to be fairly modest. By contrast, the elections by which national governments are chosen see a much greater level of turnout by the electorate.

2.4.5 European Court of Justice

In the EU, as in every other organization in the world, laws and decisions are open to interpretation and this frequently leads to disputes that cannot be settled by negotiation. The role of the European Court of Justice (ECJ, or sometimes known as the EU Court or EC Court) is to settle these disputes, especially disputes between Member States, between the EU and Member States, between EU institutions, and between individuals and the EU. As discussed above, the EU Court is the highest authority on the application of EU law.

As a result of this power, the Court has had a major impact on European integration. For example, its ruling in the 1970s on non-tariff barriers triggered a sequence of events that eventually led to the Single European Act of 1986 (see Chapter 4 for details). The Court has also been important in defining the relations between the Member States and the EU, and in the legal protection of individuals (EU citizens can take cases directly to the EU Court without going through their governments).

The European Court of Justice, which is located in Luxembourg, consists of one judge from each Member State. Judges are appointed by common accord of the Member States' governments and serve for six years. The Court also has eight advocates-general whose job it is to help the judges by constructing 'reasoned submissions' that suggest what conclusions the judges might take. The Court reaches its decisions by majority voting. The Court of First Instance was set up in the late 1980s to help the EU Court with its ever growing workload.

2.5 Legislative processes

As mentioned, the European Commission has a near monopoly on initiating the EU decision-making process. It is in charge of writing proposed legislation, although it

Figure 2.11: *Headquarters of the European Court of Justice in Luxembourg*

© European Commission 2005

naturally consults widely when doing so. The next step is to present the proposal to the Council for approval. Most EU legislation also requires the European Parliament's approval, although the exact procedure depends upon the issue concerned. (The treaties specify which procedure must be used in which areas.)

The main procedure, called the codecision procedure, gives the Parliament equal standing with the Council. This procedure is used for about 80 per cent of EU legislation, including that dealing with the free movement of workers, creation of the single market, research and technological development, the environment, consumer protection, education, culture and public health.

The codecision procedure is highly complex, but simplifying for clarity's sake, it starts with a proposal from the Commission and then goes through two readings by the Council and the Parliament. Passing the act requires a 'yes' vote from the Council and Parliament. The Council decides by qualified majority whereas the Parliament decides by a simple majority. If the Council and Parliament disagree after the second reading, a conciliation procedure is started. If this does not produce agreement, the act is dropped. For details see Box 2.6.

The other common legislative procedures include:
★ The *consultation procedure*. This is used for a few issues – e.g. the Common Agricultural Policy's periodic price fixing agreements – where the Member States wish to keep tight control over politically sensitive decisions. Under this procedure, the Parliament must give its opinion before the Council adopts a Commission proposal. Such opinions, when they have any influence, are

Box 2.6

The codecision procedure

The procedure starts with a Commission proposal. The Parliament then gives its 'opinion', i.e. evaluates the proposal and suggests desired amendments, by simple majority. After seeing the Parliament's opinion, the Council adopts a 'common position' by a qualified majority, except in the fields of culture, freedom of movement, social security and coordination of the rules for carrying on a profession, which are subject to a unanimous vote. The Parliament then receives the Council's common position and has three months in which to take a decision. If the Parliament expressly approves it, or takes no action by the deadline, the act is adopted immediately. If an absolute majority of Parliament's Members rejects the common position, the process stops, and the act is not adopted. If a majority of MEPs adopts amendments to the common position, these are first put to the Commission for its opinion and then returned to the Council. The Council votes by a qualified majority on Parliament's amendments, although it takes a unanimous vote to accept amendments that have been given a negative opinion by the Commission. The act is adopted if the Council approves all Parliament's amendments no later than three months after receiving them. Otherwise the Conciliation Committee is convened within six weeks.

The Conciliation Committee consists of an equal number of Council and Parliament representatives, assisted by the Commission. It considers the common position on the basis of Parliament's amendments and has six weeks to draft a joint text. The procedure stops and the act is not adopted unless the Committee approves the joint text by the deadline. If it does so, the joint text goes back to the Council and Parliament for approval. The Council and Parliament have six weeks to approve it. The Council acts by a qualified majority and the Parliament by an absolute majority of the votes cast. The act is adopted if Council and Parliament approve the joint text. If either of the institutions has not approved it by the deadline the procedure stops and the act is not adopted.

---

intended to influence the Council or to shape the Commission's proposal.

★ The *assent procedure* is another procedure in which the Parliament plays a subsidiary role. For example, on decisions concerning enlargement, international agreements, sanctioning Member States and the coordination of the Structural Funds, the Parliament can veto, but cannot amend, a proposal made by the Commission and adopted by the Council.

★ The *cooperation procedure* is a historical hangover from the Parliament's gradual increase in power. Specifically, before the codecision procedure was introduced in the Maastricht Treaty, the cooperation procedure was the one that granted the most power to the Parliament. It is best thought of as a codecision procedure in which the Parliament's power to amend the proposal is less explicit. Also, the Council can overrule a Parliamentary rejection by voting unanimously.

2.5.1 Enhanced cooperation

The tension between the 'vanguard' members, who wish to broaden the scope of EU activities, and the 'doubters', who do not, led to the introduction of a new type of integration process called 'closer cooperation' in the Treaty of Amsterdam and 'enhanced cooperation' in the Treaty of Nice. The process allows subgroups of EU members to cooperate on specific areas while still keeping the cooperation under the general framework of the EU.

Subgroups of Member States have long engaged in closer intergovernmental cooperation. What the Treaty of Amsterdam did by creating closer cooperation was to allow such subgroups to proceed while at the same time keeping them under some form of EU discipline and coordination.

However, the conditions for starting new closer cooperations were so strict that no new closer cooperation was established under the Amsterdam rules. The Treaty of Nice made it easier to start such subgroups and relabelled them 'enhanced cooperation arrangements' (ECAs). Although this form of integration has not yet been used, it may come to play a much more important role in the light of the 2004 enlargement. The point is that the diversity of members' preferences for integration will become even more diverse, so subsets of members may well find that starting an ECA is the only way to get things done. See Baldwin *et al.* (2001) for an analysis of this possibility.

There are potentially serious risks involved in integration led by such clubs-within-the-club schemes. For instance, we may see calls for an ECA with respect to tighter police and intelligence cooperation, especially in relation to terrorism and organized crime. Given the uneven quality of governments in the new Member States, the ECA may seek to exclude nations whose intelligence services are not up to standard. This, of course, would be divisive. Allowing a separation of members into groups risks fragmenting the EU politically. Moreover, ECAs could result in an erosion of existing integration, and in so far as ECAs create diversity in integration, they might erode the consistency of European economic and social integration.

Another example can be found in the meeting of finance ministers of the eurozone nations. Just before the standard Council of Ministers meeting for finance ministers (ECOFIN), the eurozone nations gather to discuss issues. Since these twelve constitute a substantial majority in terms of voting power, the non-eurozone nations can sometimes feel that decisions have been sewn up in advance by the eurozone-12.

To guard against these twin risks, the Treaty of Nice gives the Commission a central role in the decision to create and enlarge any enhanced cooperation. Specifically, the Commission can veto ECAs covering deeper economic integration (i.e. first-pillar areas) and it controls subsequent membership enlargements of these. In other areas, the Commission has a strong voice in the process of setting up and expanding ECAs, but less so in the Security and Foreign Policy area (second pillar) than in Justice and Home Affairs areas (third pillar). It can also be the administrator of such groups.

2.6 Some important facts

EU nations are very different, one from another. This simple fact is the source of a large share of EU's problems, so it is important to understand the detail. This section covers the facts on populations, incomes and economic size.

2.6.1 Populations and incomes

There about 460 million EU citizens, a figure that is substantially larger than the corresponding US and Japanese figures (290 and 130 million, respectively).

The EU25 nations and the 'candidate countries' (Bulgaria and Romania scheduled to join in 2007 or 2008, and Turkey) vary enormously in terms of populations, as the lower panel Fig. 2.12 shows. The differences are easier to remember when the nations are grouped into big, medium, small and tiny – where these categories are established by comparison with the population of well-known cities.

★ The 'big' nations are defined here as having 35 million people or more – clearly more people than even the largest city in the world (Mexico City's population is about 20 million). In the EU25 there are six of these – Germany, the UK, France, Italy, Spain and Poland. Germany is substantially larger than the others, more than twice the size of the smallest in the group. The total population of the 'Big-6' accounts for about three-quarters of the

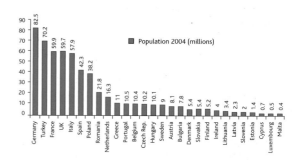

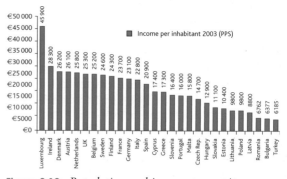

Figure 2.12: *Population and income per capita*

Note: PPS stands for 'purchase power standard'; it is a measure that corrects euro incomes for national price-level differences (e.g. many goods are cheaper in poor nations, so a euro goes further in, say, Latvia, than it does in Germany).

Source: European Commission.

460 million people in the EU25 nations. Turkey, with whom the EU started membership negotiations in October 2005, has over 70 million inhabitants. This exceeds the population of all EU nations except Germany, and given the projected decline in German population and rapid population growth in Turkey, the ordering is likely to be reversed within ten years.

★ The 'medium' nations are defined as having populations between 8 and 11 million, something like that of a really big city, say Paris and its surroundings. There are eight medium nations: seven in the EU25 (Greece, Portugal, Belgium, the Czech Republic, Hungary, Sweden and Austria) and soon-to-join Bulgaria.

★ The 'small' nations have populations along the lines of a big city, ranging from Barcelona (4 million) to Lyons (1.4 million). These are Denmark, Slovakia, Finland, Ireland, Lithuania, Latvia, Slovenia and Estonia.

★ The 'tiny' nations have populations that are smaller than those of a small city like Genoa. The list is Cyprus, Luxembourg and Malta.

★ The only nations that fall between these categories are the Netherlands, with its 16 million people, and Romania, with its 21.8 million.

Incomes

The average income level of the people in these nations also varies enormously. Again, it is useful to classify the nations into three categories: high, medium and low. Luxembourg is in a super-rich class by itself; Luxembourgers are about twice as rich as the French and Swedes. One explanation for this is that Luxembourg is, economically speaking, a medium-sized city and incomes in cities tend to be quite high.

The high-income category – defined as incomes above the EU25 average of €21 400 in 2003 – includes ten of the EU25 nations (Ireland, Denmark, Austria, the Netherlands, the UK, Belgium, Sweden, Finland, France, Germany and Italy in order of decreasing incomes).

In the medium-income category – from €10 000 to €21 000 – there are three relatively poor EU15 members (Spain, Greece and Portugal), and seven new members (Cyprus, Slovenia, Malta, the Czech Republic, Hungary, Slovakia and Estonia).

Defining low-income nations as those with per capita incomes less than €10 000, there are six of these: Lithuania, Poland, Latvia, Romania, Bulgaria and Turkey.

2.6.2 Size of EU economies

The economic size distribution of European economies is also very uneven, measuring economic size with total gross domestic product (GDP). As Fig. 2.13 shows, just six nations, the 'Big-5' (Germany, the UK, France, Italy and Spain) and the Netherlands, account for more than 80 per cent of the GDP of the whole EU25. The other nations are small, tiny or minuscule, using the following definitions:

★ 'Small' is an economy that accounts for between 1 and 3 per cent of the EU25's output. These are Sweden, Belgium, Austria, Denmark, Poland, Finland, Greece, Portugal and Ireland.

★ 'Tiny' is one that accounts for less than 1 per cent of the total. These are the Czech Republic, Hungary, Slovakia, Luxembourg, Slovenia, Lithuania and Cyprus.

★ 'Minuscule' as one that accounts for less than 0.1 per cent of the EU25's GDP: Latvia, Estonia and Malta are the nations in this category.

Figure 2.13 also shows that the 2004 enlargement had very little impact on the overall size of the EU economy; the ten newcomers' economies amount to only about

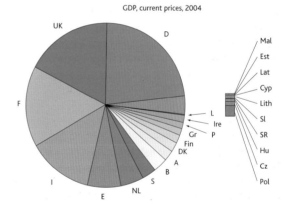

Figure 2.13: *Size distribution of EU25 economies*

Note: Data for 2004, not adjusted for national cost of living differences since we are interested in the relative size of economies rather than individual income levels.

'Big nations': Germany (D), the UK (UK), France (F), Italy (I), Spain (E) and the Netherlands (NL). 'Small nations' (1–3% of total EU25 GDP): Sweden (S), Belgium (B), Austria (A), Denmark (DK), Poland (PL), Finland (Fin), Greece (Gr), Portugal (P) and Ireland (Ire). 'Tiny nations' (0.1–1.0%): Czech Republic (Cz), Hungary (Hu), Slovak Republic (SR), Luxembourg (L), Slovenia (Sl), Lithuania (Lith) and Cyprus (Cyp). 'Minuscule nations' (less than 0.1%): Latvia (Lat), Estonia (Est) and Malta (Mal).

Source: Eurostat website (a great new development – you can download data).

5 per cent of the EU15's GDP, with Poland alone accounting for about half of this 5 per cent.

2.7 The budget

The EU budget is the source of a great deal of both solidarity and tension among EU members, so a full understanding of the EU requires some knowledge of the budget. This section looks at the following questions in order. What is the money spent on? Where does it come from? Who gets the most? What is the budget process?

2.7.1 Expenditure

Total EU spending is now about €100 billion. While this sounds like a lot to most people, it is really fairly small – only about 1 per cent of total EU25 GDP – just €240 per EU citizen. The first priority is to study how this money is spent. We look first at spending by area and then spending by EU member.

Expenditure by area

As with so many things in Europe, understanding EU spending in all its detail would take a lifetime, but understanding the basics takes just a few minutes. Starting at the broadest level, the EU spends its money on:

★ agriculture;
★ poor regions;
★ other things.

Agriculture takes up about half the budget (47 per cent in 2005) and poor regions take about one-third (31 per cent, but one should add the compensation figure and much of the pre-accession aid to this figure). The rest is split among many different uses. Spending on agriculture and poor regions is so important that this book includes separate chapters dealing with each, so we do not go into further detail here (see Chapter 9 on agriculture and Chapter 10 on poor regions). Figure 2.14 shows spending priorities graphically for 2005.

At a slightly finer level of analysis, we break the 'other things' category into four areas:

★ *Other internal policies (7 per cent of budget)*. Here 'other' means other than agriculture and poor regions. As the name suggests, this category is very diverse and includes spending on research and development (R&D), on trans-European transport, energy and telecommunications networks, on

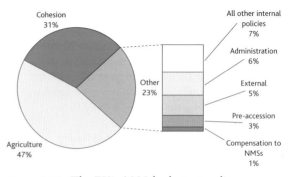

Figure 2.14: *The EU's 2005 budget: spending*

Note: For details on 'Agriculture' see Chapter 9. 'Cohesion' refers to spending on disadvantaged regions. 'All other internal policies' include R&D, energy and transportation, etc. 'External' refers to spending outside the EU on development aid, etc. 'Pre-accession' is spending on nations that are candidates for membership (especially Bulgaria, Romania and Turkey). 'Compensation for NMS' is money earmarked for the new Member States (NMSs) so that they are not net contributors.

Source: General Budget of the EU for the Financial Year 2005: the figures, European Commission.

training and student mobility, the environment, culture, information and communication, etc.
★ *External action (5 per cent of budget)*. This money is spent mainly on humanitarian aid, food aid and development assistance in non-member countries throughout the world. Small amounts are also spent on the Middle East peace process, the reconstruction of Kosovo, the European initiative for democracy and human rights worldwide, international fisheries agreements, and the Common Foreign and Security Policy.
★ *Administration (6 per cent of budget)*. This concerns the cost of running the European Commission, the European Court of Justice and all other European institutions. Taken together, they employ surprisingly few people (about 30 000).
★ *Pre-accession aid (3 per cent of budget)*. This money goes to modernizing agriculture, establishing transport and environmental structures, and to improving government administrations in nations on the road to membership.

Historical development of EU spending by area

The EU's spending priorities and the level of spending has changed dramatically since its inception in 1958. This is shown graphically in Fig. 2.15.

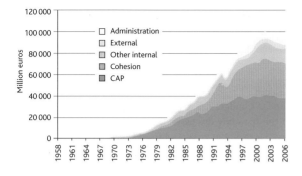

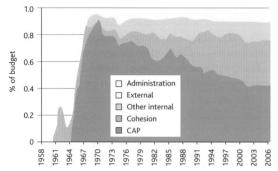

Figure 2.15: *The EU budget spending, 1958–2006*

Source: 1958–99 from *The Community Budget: The Facts in Figures*. European Commission, 2000; 2000–06 from the *Financial Perspective* 2000–2006; both downloadable from http://europa.eu.int.budget.

As the top panel shows, the budget grew rapidly, but started at a very low level (just 0.08 per cent of the EEC6's GDP). EU spending was negligible until the late 1960s, amounting to less than €10 per EU citizen. This changed as the cost of the Common Agricultural Policy (CAP) started to rise rapidly in the 1960s and cohesion spending started to rise in the 1980s. From the early 1970s to the early 1990s, the budget grew steadily as a proportion of EU GDP, starting from about 0.8 per cent and rising to 1.2 per cent by 1993. Since the 1994 enlargement, the budget as a share of GDP has remained quite stable at about 1 per cent. (The share of GDP figures are not shown in Fig. 2.15.)

The lower panel of Fig. 2.15 depicts the spending by area in shares to illustrate how the EU's budget priorities have changed over the past half-century. Until 1965, the budget, tiny as it was, was spent mainly on administration (this was the period when all the European institutions were set up and the customs union was being implemented). CAP spending began in 1965 and soon dominated the budget. For almost a decade, farm spending regularly took 80 per cent or more of

total expenditures; at its peak in 1970, it made up 92 per cent of the budget!

From the date of the first enlargement, 1973, cohesion spending began to grow in importance, pushing down agriculture's share in the process. Indeed, the sum of the shares of these two big-ticket items has remained remarkably steady, ranging between 80 and 85 per cent of the budget. In a very real sense, we can think of cohesion spending as steadily crowding out CAP spending over the past three decades.

2.7.2 Expenditure by member

By far the most important benefit from EU membership is economic integration. By comparison, the financial transfers involved in EU spending are minor. Remember the whole budget is only about 1 per cent of EU GDP and the net contributions (payments to the EU minus payments from the EU) are never greater than 0.1 per cent. Be this as it may, it is interesting to see which members receive the largest shares of EU spending. As the very public failure of the EU to reach agreement on the next long-term budget in June 2005 shows, money matters.

The amount of EU spending varies quite a lot across members, both in terms of the total amount and its nature, as the top panel of Fig. 2.16 shows. In 2003, Spain was the number one recipient with France close behind. Most of the French receipts came from the CAP, whereas cohesion spending was the most important source for Spain. The post-enlargement figures including the new member states were not available when this book went to press.

The figures, however, are entirely different when we look at receipts per capita (see bottom panel of the figure). By far the largest receiver per capita is Luxembourg (€2 359 per person) which sounds like a lot, but since incomes are so high in the Grand Duchy – about twice the EU average at over €50 000 per year in 2003 – this EU spending does not have as large an impact as one might think. The Irish are also very large per-capita recipients – about €700 per person – but even this is only one-third of what the lucky Luxembourgers get. The EU average is €216 per person, which means that Finland, France, Spain, Denmark, Portugal, Belgium, Greece, Ireland and Luxembourg are all above-average recipients.

Because the per-capita numbers for Luxembourg are so high (and Luxembourg is the richest member by a long

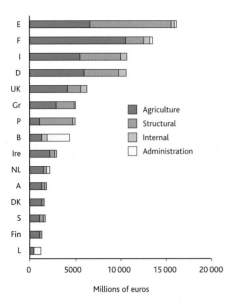

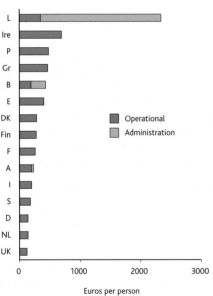

Figure 2.16: *The EU spending by member, by type and per capita, 2003*

Source: 'Allocation of 2003 EU operating expenditure by Member State', European Commission, downloadable from http://europa.eu.int.

way), a political agreement by the European Council directed the European Commission to calculate receipts excluding administrative expenditures. These figures – called 'operational allocated expenditures' – are shown by the dark bars in the bottom panel of Fig. 2.16.

Readers may find the figures in the bottom panel rather strange. Why should rich nations like Luxembourg, Belgium,

Denmark, Finland and France be above-average recipients of EU spending? The answer, which lies in the nature of the EU's decision-making process, is pursued in depth in Chapter 3.

2.7.3 Revenue

The EU's budget must, by law, be balanced every year. All of the spending discussed above must be financed each year by revenues collected from EU members or carried over from previous years.

Up to 1970, the EEC's budget was financed by annual contributions from the members. A pair of treaties in the 1970s and a handful of landmark decisions by the European Council established the system we have today in which there are four main sources of revenue (see Box 2.7 for details). According to the EU treaties, the Union is legally entitled to this revenue, so it is known as 'own resources' in EU jargon.

There are four main types of these own resources and Fig. 2.17 shows how their relative importance has varied over the years. Two of the four have long been used, and indeed in the early days of the Union they were sufficient to finance all payments. These 'traditional own resources' are:

★ *Tariff revenue stemming from the Common External Tariff.* Although trade within the EU is tariff-free, tariffs are imposed on imports from non-member nations. This money accrues to the EU rather than to any particular member.

★ *Agricultural levies.* These are tariffs on agricultural goods that are imported from non-member countries. Conceptually, these are the same as the previous categories (they are both taxes on imports from third nations), but are viewed as distinct since the levies are not formally part of the Common External Tariff. Historically, the level of these tariffs has fluctuated widely according to market conditions (they were part of the CAP's price support mechanism; see Chapter 9).

The importance of these two revenue items has fallen over the years to the point where they are no longer major items (together they make up only one-seventh of the revenue needs). This reduced importance stems from the way that the level of the Common External Tariff has been steadily lowered in the course of World Trade Organization (WTO) rounds (e.g. the 1986–94 Uruguay Round). Moreover, EU enlargement and the signing of free trade agreements with non-members mean that a very large fraction of EU imports from non-members are duty free. The level of the agricultural levies has also been reduced in the context of CAP reform. The third and fourth types of 'own resources' provide most of the money. They are:

Milestones in the EU budget procedure

1958–70. The EU's budget was financed by contributions from its members.

April 1970. The Luxembourg European Council. The 'own resources' system is introduced. These included customs duties, agricultural levies (i.e. variable tariffs), and a share of VAT revenue collected by EU members. The treaty of July 1975 refined and reinforced the system, establishing the European Court of Auditors to oversee the budget and giving the European Parliament the formal right of rejection over annual budgets.

1975–87. This period was marked by sharp disputes over the budget contributions and ever expanding CAP spending. The UK's Margaret Thatcher in particular complained repeatedly about the UK's position as the largest net contributor.

1984. The Fontainebleau European Council. The VAT-based revenue source was increased and the UK was awarded its famous 'rebate'.

1988. Delors I package. This reform established the basis of the current revenue and spending system. It introduced a fourth 'own resource' based on members' GNPs, established an overall ceiling on EU revenue as a percentage of the EU's GNP, and started reducing the role of VAT-based revenue. The package, decided at the Brussels European Council in June, also established the EU's multi-year budgeting process whereby a Financial Perspective sets out the evolution of EU spending by broad categories. Substantively, the financial perspective adopted provided for a major reorientation of EU spending from the CAP to cohesion spending; cohesion spending was doubled and CAP spending growth was capped.

1992. Delors II package. The Edinburgh agreement of December 1992 increased the revenue ceiling slightly to 1.27 per cent and further reduced the role of VAT-based revenue. It also adopted a new Financial Perspective for 1993–99 which amplified the shift of EU spending priorities away from the CAP and towards cohesion.

1999. Agenda 2000 package. The Berlin European Council adopted the 2000–06 Financial Perspective. There were no major changes on the revenue side and the only major change on the spending side was the creation of a new broad category, 'pre-accession expenditures', meant to finance programmes in central and eastern European nations and provide a reserve to cover the cost of any enlargements in this period.

Source: The material in this box was drawn from *The Community Budget: The Facts in Figures*, European Commission, 2000. Also see *Financing the EU: Commission Report on the Operation of the Own Resource System*, 1998, especially Annex 1. Both from http://europa.eu.int/budget/.

★ *VAT resource.* As is often the case when it comes to tax matters, the reality is quite complex, but it is best thought of as a 1 per cent value added tax. The importance of this resource has declined and is set to decline further.
★ *GNP based.* This revenue is a tax based on the GNP of EU members. It is used to top up any revenue shortfall and thus ensures that the EU never runs a deficit.

The other revenue sources – labelled 'miscellaneous' in Fig. 2.17 – have been relatively unimportant since 1977. They include items such as taxes paid by employees of European institutions (they do not pay national taxes), fines, and surpluses carried over from previous years. Until the 1970s' budget treaties came fully into effect, 'miscellaneous' revenue included direct member contributions, which were a crucial source of funding in the early years.

Budget contribution by member

On the contribution side, EU funding amounts to basically 1 per cent of each member's GDP. Some observers find this anomalous since taxation in most nations, especially in Europe, is progressive, i.e. the tax rate that an individual pays rises with his or her income level.

The precise figures are shown in Fig. 2.18. Here we see that the contributions as a share of GDP do not vary much from the median figure of 0.9 per cent. The highest figure in 1999 was 0.99 per cent (for Greece and Ireland). The lowest figure was the UK's 0.61 per cent due to the UK rebate (see below for more on the rebate). The

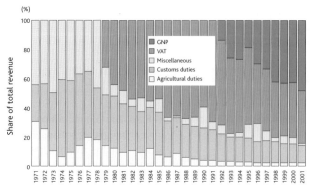

Figure 2.17: *Historical sources of EU funding, 1971–2001*

Source: *The Community Budget: The Facts in Figures*, European Commission, 2000; downloadable from http://europa.eu.int/budget/.

precise contribution rate varies from year to year by Member State owing to the complexities of the system.

For comparison, the nations are ordered by increasing income (the line in the figure shows the national GDP per capita). The income figures here are not corrected for prices, so the per-capita GDP figures are not measures of material standards of living. For example, the prices of many goods and especially services are systematically higher in, say, Denmark than they are in Portugal. Because of this, the figures overstate the purchasing power of

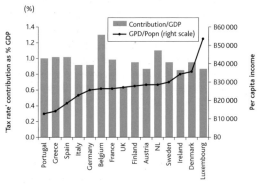

Figure 2.18: *Contribution versus GDP by EU members, 2003*

Notes: (1) The contributions are net of the UK rebate and include the Netherlands' usually large payment of tariffs (Rotterdam is the port of entry for non-EU imports for many EU members, so the Common External Tariff is often paid to the Dutch government even when the goods are headed for, say, Germany).

(2) Some budget items, such as reserves held over from previous years, cannot be allocated by member, so the total of contributions from members is less than the total budget.

Source: 'Allocation of 2003 EU operating expenditure by Member State', European Commission; downloadable from http://europa.eu.int.

Danes versus Portuguese. This is intentional. When nations set tax rates they do not adjust for price differences. For example, despite the fact that living in a city is systematically more expensive than living in the countryside, national income tax rates are based on income per capita, or income per family without price adjustments. What the line shows is that there is basically no correlation between national income levels and the national 'tax rates', i.e. the contribution as a share of GDP.

Figures for the new members are unavailable at the time of going to press; 2003 was the most recent year available.

2.7.4 Net contribution by member

Putting together the receipts by member and the contributions by member allows us to show the net financial contributions in Fig. 2.19. Seven of the EU15 are net contributors (they pay more to the budget than they receive from it), with Germany being by far the largest. Indeed, in 1999, Germany's net contribution was larger than that of all the other net contributors put together. Other net contributors are the UK, the Netherlands, Sweden, Austria, Italy (in 1999, but not in 2000) and Finland. The net recipients, those with negative net contributions, are led by Spain, Greece and Portugal, followed by Belgium, Luxembourg, France and Denmark.

Note that the net transfers are much smaller than the overall budget. In other words, most of the EU budget can be thought of as staying inside each nation. France paid €12.5 billion to the budget and received €13.1 billion from it in 1999, so we can think of the French government as spending €12.5 billion on EU programmes that directly benefit its own citizens, with Brussels sending only €0.6 billion to Paris to add to this. Even for the biggest contributor, Germany, most of its payment can be thought of as being spent on

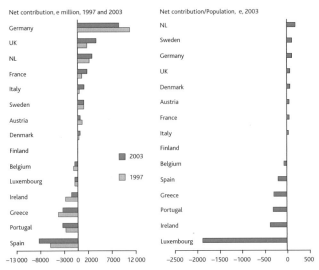

Figure 2.19: *Net financial contribution by EU members*

Source: European Commission for budget data and Eurostat for population data.

Germans. Of the €18.9 billion that the German government gave to Brussels, €10 billion was spent on Germans.

The UK rebate

The basics of the EU spending and contributions were set in 1970, prior to the UK's entry. When the UK joined in 1973 it faced a situation in which it funded a disproportionate share of the EU budget while receiving a less than proportionate share of EU spending. The UK's agricultural situation was the cause of both imbalances. The British agricultural sector was a relatively small share of its economy compared with the agricultural sectors of other members, so the UK got little of the EU's spending on agriculture (which accounted for three-quarters of the budget at the time). The UK also imported a larger share of its food from non-member nations. Since the import taxes charged on such imports are turned over to the EU budget, the UK faced a situation where it was a large net contributor to the budget.

According to some, the 1970 funding system was intentionally aimed at disfavouring the UK once it entered (the UK's application was first made in 1961 and renewed in 1967). For example, Peet and Ussher (1999) state: 'To an extent the original Own Resources Decision, adopted before Britain joined, was deliberately skewed to Britain's disadvantage.' The budgetary imbalance worsened as CAP spending continued to rise and when a new source of EU funding was added in 1979 – the levy on value added tax (VAT) income.

After years of dispute and complaints from the UK over this imbalance, EU leaders decided at their June 1984

meeting in Fontainebleau to give the UK back part of its contribution. The basic principle was that the UK should be rebated around two-thirds of its net contribution. The EU treats the UK rebates as a negative contribution even though one can think of the UK rebate as EU spending (Mrs Thatcher, being a hard core conservative, preferred a tax cut to a spending increase). Consequently, the agreed formula explicitly allocates the cost of this rebate among the other EU members, making the UK rebate a continual source of contention. This is unusual since, for example, Spain is a big recipient of cohesion spending, but it is not obvious which other members are paying for it. The process that led up to the UK 'rebate debate' is cloaked in folklore and usually described in colourful terms – see Box 2.8.

2.7.5 Budget process

The EU's annual budget is guided primarily by a medium-term agreement on spending priorities, called Financial Perspectives. The current Financial Perspective sets out broad spending guidelines for the annual budgets from 2000 to 2006. Since the Financial Perspective is adopted by all the institutions involved in budgeting (the Commission, the European Parliament and the Council), its existence reduces dispute over each annual budget.

The procedure for drawing up the annual budget (as laid down in the treaties) calls for the Commission to prepare a preliminary draft budget. The Commission's draft is presented to the Council for amendments and adoption. Once it has passed the Council, the budget goes to the European Parliament which has some power to amend it.

Box 2.8

Lady Thatcher's 'hand bagging' and the UK rebate

The British perspective on the budget is succinctly put by Peet and Ussher (1999): 'The European budgetary picture after 1973 was simple enough: the Germans and British would pay, but everybody else would benefit. Thanks partly to residual war-guilt, and also to their relative wealth, the Germans were prepared to live with this. But Britain, relatively low down Europe's prosperity league, was never likely to.' The UK government that negotiated membership in 1971, and the one that renegotiated it in 1973, worried about Britain's position as EU paymaster but did little to redress it. For a while, the net contribution was limited by annual adjustments, but such an approach was unsatisfactory to the new government of Margaret Thatcher.

As Peet and Ussher describe it: 'Her performance at the Dublin summit in December 1979 has become legendary. The patrician Valéry Giscard d'Estaing and the haughty Helmut Schmidt were horrified by her vulgar insistence on getting "my money back". But as she continued to bang the table at subsequent summits, they and their successors were forced to offer a British rebate: first of all a series of cash sums, but by 1984 a permanent mechanism known as an abatement, which reimbursed 66 per cent of the difference between the British contribution to VAT-based revenue and the amount of EU expenditure in the UK.'

Newspapers described the event in more flamboyant terms, asserting that the rebate was won through Thatcher's handbag diplomacy. 'The former British prime minister, now Lady Thatcher, is remembered for slamming her handbag on the table and yelling at the other leaders, "I want my money!"' (Barry James, *International Herald Tribune*, 8 October 1998).

The exact procedure for calculating the rebate is complex and results in a fairly wide fluctuation in the UK's net contribution.

For more information, see Annex 4 of reports_en.htm at http://europa.eu.int/comm/budget/agenda2000/.

According to the treaties, the Parliament cannot touch 'compulsory' expenditures (basically agriculture spending), which account for about 40 per cent of the budget, but it can amend the rest. After two readings in the Council and the Parliament, it is the European Parliament which adopts the final budget, and its President who signs it. This formal procedure has been augmented by inter-institutional arrangements between the Parliament, the Council and the Commission that are meant to improve cooperation. For more information see 'The budget of the EU: How is your money spent?' at http://europa.eu.int.

The 2007–13 Financial Perspective

At the time this edition went to press, the European Council was still arguing over the next seven-year budget plan. The failure to agree this plan at the June 2005 summit was viewed by some as a tremendous failure. However, the current seven-year plan was signed just months before it came into effect (in May 1999, taking effect in January 2000). The current plan expires in December 2006, so if a new plan is decided, then early 2006 is the most likely date. Importantly, the 2000–06 plan contains a fallback option. If a new seven-year plan cannot be agreed, the current agreement states that the current spending framework is to be extended mechanically.

2.8 The Constitutional Treaty

The Constitutional Treaty, formally the Treaty establishing a Constitution for Europe, was signed by EU leaders in Rome on 29 October 2004. The Constitution takes effect only if it is ratified by all EU members. French and Dutch voters rejected it in mid-2005 (see Chapter 1), so it seems unlikely that the Treaty will take effect in coming years, if ever.

This section reviews the main changes implied by the Constitution. The changes are important even if the Treaty is abandoned. Many of the changes, especially those reflecting the desire to 'bring the EU closer to the people', can be implemented without a new treaty and so probably will be put into place in coming years. Others represent changes that are absolutely necessary, for example reforming the Council's voting rules; these are likely to be enacted in the future, somehow or other.

2.8.1 Basic constraints

The Constitutional Treaty is an awkward document – 350 pages of legalese and intricate cross references to articles that cross-reference other articles.[3] It fails almost completely in its assigned task of simplification. It is probably fair to say that most law professors, even those specializing in European law, do not really understand the Treaty as a whole or its full implications for Europe.

This outcome, however unfortunate, was unavoidable. The EU cannot have a constitution that looks like a constitution in the traditional sense of the word, i.e. a succinct statement of goals and a description of the allocation of power among decision-making institutions amounting to less than, say, 20 pages. The problem turns on legal logic. A constitution in the standard sense of the word would create a new level of European law. The existing treaties are now the highest level of law, with directives and the like forming secondary law. The new top level of law would pose a threat to legal certainty throughout the EU legal system since one could never be sure when a judicial interpretation of ambiguities between the Constitution and other treaties might alter existing law. The Conventioneers realized this almost immediately. A real constitution, they concluded, 'might well prove a permanent source of conflict' (CONV 250/02, quoted in Norman, 2005, p. 64).

In short, legal logic tells us that a constitution is the easiest way to arrange the affairs of an organization like the EU, but such a constitution would have had to have been written at the beginning. Legal logic tells us that writing a constitution (in the standard meaning of the word) is basically impossible for an organization that has been making laws for fifty years without one.

This is why the Constitutional Treaty had to be so long, so complex and so legalist. It had to include every existing treaty, protocol and annex so as to keep all the 'primary law' at the same level. By one estimate, only about one-fifth of the Constitution contains new or substantially amended articles.[4] This is also why it had to repeal all the existing treaties.

---

[3] Serious students of European integration should at least skim the Constitutional Treaty; see the Commission's excellent site http://europa.eu.int/scadplus/constitution/index_en.htm for the full text and extensive commentary and perspective.

[4] 'Guide to the New Constitutional Treaty', The Federal Trust for education and research, a 60-year-old British think-tank that 'studies the interactions between regional, national, European and global levels of government'. Much of the section is based on this article.

2.8.2 Basic structure of the Constitution

The Constitution begins with a short preamble. The real substance is contained in four parts. These parts are divided into titles which are divided into chapters which are divided into sections and finally into individual articles. Articles are numbered consecutively, 1 to 448, but are usually preceded by the part number. For example, Article II-104, which gives EU citizens the right to petition the European Parliament, can be found in Part II.

The four Parts are outlined below.

Part I: Principles

This is the key part of the Treaty, the part that all students should read. It is a statement of the principles on which the EU's legal and political order is based. Its titles:
- ★ define the goals of the Union;
- ★ define fundamental rights and citizenship of the Union;
- ★ list the areas in which Members States have fully or partially transferred sovereignty to the EU (areas of 'exclusive' or 'shared' competences in EU jargon), and set out the principles of subsidiarity and proportionality;[5]
- ★ explain the EU's institutions, their powers and interrelationships;
- ★ detail the EU's legal instruments and the procedures for adopting them (this basically codifies existing procedures, but reduces the number of instruments).

Part II: Charter of Fundamental Rights

Part II contains the Charter of Fundamental Rights of the Union. This was agreed in the Treaty of Nice, but the Constitution makes it binding on all members. Part II also contains guarantees that the Charter applies only to the institutions and to the Member States when they are implementing EU law. It states explicitly that the Charter does not transfer new powers to the European Union. This messy political compromise helped to overcome the UK government's objections to making the Charter legally binding.

Part III: Policies and Decision-making Details

Part III is the longest, and the hardest to read. It incorporates most of the Rome and Maastricht Treaty articles as modified by subsequent treaties. Particularly important is Article II-396 since this sets out the 'Ordinary Legislative Procedure', i.e. the standard way of making new laws, which, roughly speaking, is the same as the existing codecision procedure.

---

[5] These mean the EU should act only to the extent that action by individual members is insufficient to accomplish the goal at hand; see Chapter 3.

Part IV: General and Final Provisions

Part IV defines the procedures for ratification and amendment of the Constitution. One innovation is that it foresees future treaty reforms as starting with a convention, but ending, as before, with an intergovernmental conference (IGC).

The Constitution ends with a Final Act that gives an overview of the protocols and declarations. Protocols have the same legal status as main Treaty articles, but declarations have no legal value apart from facilitating future interpretations of articles and protocols.

2.8.3 Institutional changes

The Constitution is the third 'scene' in the EU's institutional reform 'play' (Amsterdam and Nice were scenes one and two). It contains important but not radical changes for the Big-5 institutions. The largest changes by far are for the Commission.

Commission

Fierce debate surrounded the Commission reform proposals. Almost everyone realized that a Commission with too many members would be ineffective, but who should sacrifice the right to have a Commissioner? Small members – who view the Commission as an important protector of their rights – felt a Commissioner was critical. Given the skewed size distribution of EU members (see section 2.6), large members felt it essential that there be a Commissioner from each of the six big members who together account for three-quarters of the EU's population.

The compromise was to stick with the Nice Treaty's one-per-member up to 2014, after which the number is capped at two-thirds the number of EU members, with Commissioners rotating equally among Member States. The rotation system is not specified and it might never occur, even if the Constitution takes effect. By 2014, the Commission would have had almost a decade of working with 25-plus members. Critically, the Constitution grants the European Council the power to change the number of Commissioners with a unanimous vote (i.e. without a new treaty), so the Council might well decide to stick with the one-per-member rule.

Council of Ministers

Little change here in terms of organization, except that some Council meetings will be held in public. This is one of the many public relations (PR) changes in the Constitution. The Council, of course, could decide to meet in public with or without a Treaty change, but bundling such 'openness' and 'closer to the people' changes with the changes that really do require a Treaty change was viewed as good PR – a way of showing that the Constitutional Treaty was meant to bring the EU closer to the people.

The big changes are in the Council's voting rules and in the creation of the European Minister for Foreign Affairs.

Voting

From 2009, the Council has a new majority voting rule, a so-called double majority rule where approval requires a 'yes' vote from members representing at least 65 per cent of the EU's population and at least 55 per cent of Member States. This is widely viewed as essential to guarding the EU's ability to act (see Chapter 3).

This was the most fiercely contested issue in the IGC – the issue over which Spain and Poland vetoed the Italian presidency's draft of the Constitutional Treaty in December 2003 (see Chapter 1). The Constitution's voting rules change the power of various Member States as given by the Nice Treaty rules. For example, they substantially raise Germany's power and substantially lower that of Poland and Spain (see Chapter 3). The compromise was to stick with the Treaty of Nice rules until 2009.

European Minister for Foreign Affairs

One of the most important institutional innovations is the creation of a Minister for Foreign Affairs for the EU. This would almost surely boost the EU's role in world affairs. The new Foreign Minister would conduct Common Foreign and Security Policy (CFSP, i.e. the old third pillar), including European Security and Defence Policy (ESDP). The new minister would represent the EU on CFSP issues, conduct political dialogue with third nations, and express the EU's position in international organizations and at international conferences. This would be an extremely high-profile position – at least as prominent (if not as powerful) as the President of the European Commission, European Parliament and European Council.

Currently, responsibility for the CFSP is split between the High Representative for the CFSP (Javier Solana) who sits with the Council of Ministers, and the European Commission's External Relations Commissioner. Neither currently has much power and each plays, at best, a coordinating function. The new position merges the two posts (so the EU Foreign Minister would sit on both the Council and the Commission). Importantly, the new minister would have the power of initiative in the Council. The Council would still act on a basis of unanimity on most critical CFSP issues – especially military and defence matters – so the Member States remain firmly in charge. But the power of initiative can matter a great deal. Many initiatives are suppressed by backdoor pressure from reluctant Member States who do not want to say no in public.

European Council

The Constitution makes only one big change here. Up to now, European Council meetings were chaired by the nation holding the EU presidency, which rotates every six months. The Constitution creates a new post, European Council President, to boost stability and coherence of the European Council's work. The President will be elected by members of the European Council for a two and a half year term, renewable once. The election is decided on the basis of qualified majority voting. Again, this post has little direct power since the European Council must approve issues unanimously (by 'consensus'), but the President's 'agenda-setting' power could prove to be important (see Chapter 3). The chair of the Council of Ministers, by contrast, continues to rotate. Since nothing the European Council decides can come into law without passing through the Council of Ministers, rotation of the Council of Ministers' chair dampens the power of the President of the European Council.

European Parliament

The Constitution implies few changes here. The Parliament's powers of EU legislation have been incrementally boosted by every treaty since the Single European Act 1986, and the Constitutional Treaty is no exception. The Parliament gets an equal say in a few more areas, most notably on the annual budget (up to now, the Parliament could not vote on CAP spending since Member States feared that the Parliament would cut or redirect the monies). Also, the number of Members of European Parliament (MEPs) is capped at 750. The allocation of these among members is to be decided before the standing Parliament's term ends in 2008.

European Court

There are no major organizational changes for the Court. However, since the Constitution eliminates the three-pillar structure of the EU, the Constitution substantially widens the range of issues on which the Court should ensure that the law is observed. Article III-376 explicitly says the Court has no jurisdiction over Common Foreign and Security Policy. Such explicit exclusions, however, were not provided for either second-pillar issues or the Social Charter.

Role of national parliaments

One of the closer-to-the-people elements of the Constitutional Treaty is a commitment by the Commission to send all legislative proposals to the national parliaments who can, in turn, complain to the European Parliament, Council and Commission if they feel the proposal violates the principle of subsidiarity. If one-third of the national parliaments share this belief, the Commission would have to review its proposal.

This is another of the public relations changes made by the Treaty. Currently, the Commission consults with all Member States before making a proposal (after all, the Member States will have to vote on it in the Council), and the Member State governments almost always have a majority in their national parliaments. Thus the fact that the proposal would be formally sent to national parliaments changes little. In fact, the proposal can be downloaded from the web even now. Moreover, the objections of national parliaments have no real legal force under the Constitution. The Commission is supposed only to 'review' its proposal. This is one of the first changes likely to be implemented even without the Constitution.

2.8.4 Legislative processes

The changes in the legislative processes are mainly cosmetic. The Constitution relabels what is the codecision procedure into the 'Ordinary Legislative Procedure'. It eliminates a number of minor legislative procedures that are holdovers from the increasing powers of the European Parliament (Member States have sought to limit that Parliament's power by creating special procedures on sensitive issues). This would make it a little easier to understand the EU, but will change little in practice.

The one big change concerns a new process of modifying the Constitution itself. EU leaders understood that negotiating and ratifying new treaties in a Union of 25-plus members would be extremely difficult. This would have had the effect of slowing, or stopping, the broadening of EU powers to new areas, such as social policy and foreign policy. To avoid this, the Constitution contains 'passerelle' clauses that allow the European Council to change its own decision-making rule from unanimity to the Ordinary Legislative Procedure.[6] (More on this below.)

---

[6] 'Passerelle' is often translated as 'bridge' in English, but it would be better described as an 'overpass', like the aerial walkway between two buildings, since the provision allows EU leaders to avoid the 'busy traffic' of negotiating, signing and ratifying a new treaty.

2.8.5 EU law

The Constitution implies few changes in EU law; however, it codifies existing principles, such as direct effect, primacy and autonomy (see section 2.3).

2.8.6 Motivations and uncertainty

How did the EU Constitution come about? EU leaders never directly asked the Convention to write a constitution: not in the Nice Declaration that set the stage for a new treaty, nor in the Laeken Declaration that set up the Convention, nor in any of the half dozen Conclusions of the Presidency which discussed the Convention's progress. This was due to disagreement among EU members themselves.

The 'federalists' among EU members, such as Belgium and Germany, thought a constitution was a natural destination for the long road to building an ever closer union among the peoples of Europe. More importantly, they felt it was critical to maintaining momentum towards deeper integration in a grouping of more than 25 extremely diverse nations. The 'intergovernmentalists', such as the UK and Denmark, felt that a constitution would be a step too far. The full answer must wait the judgement of history, but the most likely answer is contained in the title of one of the first books on the Constitution, *The Accidental Constitution* by Peter Norman, a journalist for the *Financial Times*. Somehow the Constitution got started, and from then on opposing it was a sure way of reducing a nation's influence over the final document, so everyone supported it.

Given this lack of consensus on the need for a constitution, there was never a clear mandate for what the constitution should accomplish. The result was a lack of major, bold initiatives and an abundance of subtle changes that might or might not have far-reaching effects. This uncertainty allowed the highly federalist former Belgian Prime Minister to declare in June 2004 that 'This constitution marks the passage of the European Union from socio-economic Europe under Maastricht to a more political Europe which will need to be further fleshed out in the years ahead. This is a step along the road.' While British Prime Minister Tony Blair told the House of Commons that the Constitution put clear limits on the degree to which further British sovereignty could be transferred to the EU, and Irish Prime Minister Bertie Ahern said: 'It is not a super state; it's not a federal state. It's about a group of nations, a group of peoples working to a Constitution.'

The subtle, unpredictable changes fall into two categories, the EU's power to extend its own powers, and extension of the EU Court's jurisdiction to new issues.

The power to extend its EU powers: the passerelle and flexibility clauses

The Constitution has two novel provisions that make it possible to broaden EU supranationality without subjecting the changes to national referenda or national parliamentary ratification procedures. First, the passerelle clause (Article 444) would grant the European Council the power to change the law-making procedure from unanimity (intergovernmental) to majority voting (supranational) in many policy areas. Doing this would require unanimous agreement of the European Council. The Constitution also allows any national parliament to veto the switch, and the European Parliament must also approve. However, the leaders on the European Council include all the leaders of national parliaments, and the European Parliament gains power under majority voting, so two additional conditions are unlikely to act as constraints.

For example, under both the current treaties and the Constitutional Treaty, EU laws on corporate taxation must be decided by unanimous vote in the Council of Ministers. Under current practices, this could be changed only with a new treaty that would have to be ratified by all members. Under the Constitution, a unanimous vote by the European Council can change this, making all future laws on corporate taxation subject to majority voting (Ordinary Legislative Procedure). A key effect of these provisions would be to avoid national referenda on initiatives that extend EU supranationality to new areas. Note that the passerelles are one-way; they do not allow EU leaders to switch a policy area from majority voting to unanimity, so they can only deepen EU integration.

This is one of the main reasons why proponents of an ever deeper EU (the German government and the European Commission, for example) are strongly in favour of the Constitution. It is also why opponents of an ever deeper EU (the *Economist* magazine and UK Conservatives, for example) are strongly against it.

The flexibility clause is the second provision. Article I-18 grants the EU the authority to give itself the power necessary to attain its objectives, even if that power is not granted by the Constitution. This clause exists in the Treaty of Rome and was the source of 'creeping competence' and the main reason the Maastricht Treaty set up the pillar structure. However, under the current system, the pillars limit the flexibility clause to first-pillar issues (basically economic integration). The Constitution would apply to every area mentioned in the Constitution, except those where it is explicitly excluded, notably defence policy and the Charter of Fundamental Rights.

In truth, no one can know what the full implications of the passerelle and flexibility clauses would be. Europhiles have faith that the new powers would be used wisely. Euro-sceptics fear that they would be abused by out-of-touch elites to force through more integration than many EU citizens want.

Extension of the EU Court's jurisdiction

The removal of the pillars and the formal inclusion of the European Council in the EU's institutional framework might or might not have important effects. The crux of the matter is that the Constitution, like any political document, is filled with messy political compromises, but the Court works on the basis of legal logic. More than once in the EU's history, the Court's application of logic has had unforeseen consequences (classic examples of this are the *Costa v ENEL* and *Cassis de Dijon* cases).[7]

The Constitution states that the EU Court 'shall ensure that in the interpretation and application of the

---

[7] One of many hypotheticals runs as follows. The fact that it is called a Constitution and explicitly includes the primacy principle, might, logically speaking, make the EU Constitution supreme to national constitutions. While such a conclusion is far-fetched, it is not extremely far from the reasoning the Court used in *Costa v ENEL* to establish primacy. The Court will eventually have to decide cases where the issue is a conflict between a Member State's constitution and the EU Constitution.

Constitution the law is observed'. Without the pillars explicitly limiting the Court's jurisdiction, the Court gains power over every aspect of EU activity except those where it is explicitly denied, such as the Common Foreign and Security Policy (Article III-376). No one can know what the effect of this will be, especially in the area of social policy.

There are many potential conflicts between the Charter and EU members' social policy laws since the Charter views some workplace issues as fundamental rights. For example, 'protection in the event of unjustified dismissal' (Article II-90) and 'fair and just working conditions' (Article II-91) are framed as fundamental rights. The Constitution says the Charter should not be used to create new laws, but the Court is charged with enforcing the law. What would the Court rule if a British worker complains that some UK law violates her right to working conditions with respect to her health, safety and dignity (Article II-91)? No one can know how the contradictions between the Charter and EU members' national laws would be resolved, but case law could, over time, lead to a significant expansion of EU control of the labour and welfare policies of EU members.

Moreover, the fact that the Constitution makes the European Council an EU institution may give the EU Court some power over the European Council. Currently, the European Council is in essence a voluntary gathering of political leaders that is not directly linked to the EU in the strictest legal sense. This is one of the many ambiguities in the Constitution that would have to be sorted out over time. The EU Court, of course, would be the ultimate arbitrator of such ambiguities, and reversing a Court decision would require a Treaty change.

2.9 Summary

This chapter covered seven very different topics.

Economic integration

The economic integration in the EU was designed to create a unified economic area in which firms and consumers located anywhere in the area would have equal opportunities to sell or buy goods throughout the area, and where owners of labour and capital should be free to employ their resources in any economic activity anywhere in the area. This is implemented via the 'four freedoms': the free movements of goods, services, people and capital.

EU organization

The EU is organized into three pillars. The first pillar (relating to supranational decision making and the authority of supranational institutions such as the Commission and EU Court) encompasses economic integration. The other pillars include areas where EU integration proceeds on an intergovernmental basis. The second and third pillars encompass Home and Judicial Affairs, and the Common Foreign and Security Policy, respectively. Formally, the European Union is the 'roof' covering the three pillars and the European Community (EC) is the first pillar.

Law

The EU is unique in that it has a supranational system of law. That is, on matters pertaining to the European Community, EU law and the EU Court take precedence over Member States' laws and courts. The key principles covered were direct effect, primacy and autonomy.

Institutions and legislative procedures

While there are many EU institutions, only five really matter for most things. These are the European Council, the Council of Ministers, the Commission, the Parliament and the Court. These five institutions work in concert to govern the EU and to pursue deeper and wider European economic integration. Under the main legislative procedure, the 'codecision procedure', the Commission proposes draft laws which have to be approved by the Council of Ministers and the European Parliament before taking effect. Most EU legislation has to be turned into national law by each Member State's parliament.

Facts

A dominant feature of the EU members is their diversity in size and income levels.

Budget

The EU budget is rather small, representing only 1 per cent of the EU's GDP. It is spent mainly on a set of agricultural programmes known as the Common Agricultural Policy (roughly half the budget), and on cohesion (resources destined for poor regions in the EU – roughly a third of the budget). The budget is funded through four complicated mechanisms but the result is that each EU member pays roughly 1 per cent of its GDP to the Commission, regardless of its income level. The distribution of net contributions (receipts minus contributions) by Member States is quite unequal. The biggest net recipients are Luxembourg (the richest member) and the three poorest members (Greece, Portugal and Spain).

Constitutional Treaty

The Constitution is unlikely to come into force in the near future, but a number of its elements are likely to be implemented since many of the changes do not require a Treaty change and others are essential. The Constitution does not include any major increases in integration and its institutional reforms are modest, the main ones being the creation of the EU Foreign Minister, changes in the Council of Ministers' voting rules, and abandonment of the principle that each member should have a European Commissioner. The most significant changes are the elimination of the three pillars and inclusion of new, easier ways of modifying the Constitution in the future.

Self-assessment questions

1. Draw a diagram that summarizes the connections between the Council of Ministers, the European Commission and the European Parliament when it comes to passing laws. Use the example of the codecision procedure.

2. Draw a schematic representation of the steady deepening of EU economic integration.

3. Draw a diagram that shows the main steps (and dates) in the development of the Big-5 EU institutions. (Hint: You may have to turn to the websites referred to in the text to find the dates.)

4. Develop an easy way of remembering the names of all of the EU15 members (e.g. there are 4 big ones, 4 small ones, 4 poor ones and 3 new ones). Do the same for the 10 new-comers who joined in 2004.

5. Explain in 25 words or less the difference between EC law and EU law.

6. List the main sources of EU revenue and the main spending priorities. Explain how each of these has developed over time.

7. Explain why it is important that EU Court rulings cannot be appealed in Member States' courts.

8. Make a table of the major changes to each of the Big-5 institutions implied by the Constitutional Treaty. (Use http://europa.eu.int/scadplus/constitution/index_en.htm to get more details than are provided in the text.)

Essay questions

1. The general term for the way in which the EU institutions interact is the 'Community Method'. Describe what this is and how it has evolved over time.

2. Analyse the reasons why the harmonization of corporate income taxes have not been part of EU integration effects.

3. Describe the historical origins of the European Council and how its role has evolved over time. Be sure to cover the way it is addressed in the draft Constitutional Treaty.

4. The European Parliament has progressively gained strength since the EU's inception. Describe this process and explain the forces driving it forward.

5. Compare the powers of the European Parliament with those of the parliament in your nation.

6. If the EU Court decides on a matter, is there any way that EU leaders can overrule that decision?

7. Find where the key elements of EU law discussed in this chapter are transcribed into the draft Constitutional Treaty. Do you think it is a good idea to have these principles in the Constitution?

8. Download the publication *The Community Budget: The Facts in Figures* (European Commission, 2000), and illustrate the evolution of receipts and payments of your favourite EU member in recent years.

9. Ireland is the only EU member that is a large recipient of both CAP spending and cohesion spending. Did Ireland gain or lose from the shift in EU spending priorities that have, since 1986, reduced the CAP's budget share at the expense of cohesion's share?

10. Compare and contrast the reasons behind the French and Dutch 'no' votes on the Constitutional Treaty.

11. Is the Constitutional Treaty a 'treaty' or a 'constitution'?

12. Did the EU have a constitution before the Constitutional Treaty in the same sense that Britain has a constitution?

13. Write an essay on the main institutional reforms undertaken to prepare the EU for eastern enlargement.

Further reading: the aficionado's corner

For more economic statistics on Europe, see the most recent issue of the *Eurostat Yearbook*. This is well organized and provides directly comparable figures for all EU members. Eurostat, which used to charge for data, now allows free downloads of most data series. Much of the same information can be had for free in the Statistical Appendix of the Commission publication *European Economy* (see http://europa.eu.int/). The OECD also provides an excellent statistical overview in its 'OECD in figures'. You can download the latest issue for free from www.oecd.org.

On EU law, an excellent source is *The ABC of Community Law* by Borchardt. This web-book can be freely downloaded from http://europa.eu.int/eur-lex/en/about/abc/.

Comprehensive information on EU institutions and legislative processes are provided by Hix (1999) and Peterson and Shackleton (2002).

Good sources for further information on the budget are Peet and Ussher (1999), as well as the Commission publication 'The budget of the EU: How is your money spent?'. Downloadable from http://europa.eu.int/budget/.

On the process leading to the Constitutional Treaty, see Peter Norman's *The Accidental Constitution* (EuroComment, Brussels, 2005).

Useful websites

The European Parliament's factsheets provide excellent, authoritative and succinct coverage of EU law, institutions, decision-making procedures and the budget process. These pages are especially useful in that they provide brief accounts of the historical development of various institutional aspects of the EU. See http://www.europarl.eu.int/factsheets/default_en.htm.

The most exhaustive source for information on EU law is the Commission's excellent website at http://europa.eu.int/scadplus/.

References

Baldwin, R., E. Berglof, F. Giavazzi and M. Widgren (2001) *Nice Try: Should the Treaty of Nice be Ratified?*, CEPR, London.

Berger, H. and V. Nitsch (2005) 'Zooming out: the trade effect of the euro in historical perspective'. http://www.wiwiss.fu-berlin.de/files/K6UAD7B/discpaper05_05.pdf.

Borchardt, K.-D. (1999) *The ABC of Community Law*, 5th edn, Office for Official Publications of the European Communities, Luxembourg.

Dorrucci, E., S. Firpo, M. Fratzscher and F.P. Mongelli (2003) 'What lessons for Latin America from European institutional and economic integration?', pp. 171–218 in P. van der Haegen and J. Viñals (eds) *Regional Integration in Europe and Latin America: Monetary and Financial Aspects*, Ashgate, Aldershot.

Hix, S. (1999) *The Political System of the European Union*, Palgrave, London.

Milward, A. (1992) *The European Rescue of the Nation-State*, Cambridge University Press, Cambridge.

Noury, A. and G. Roland (2002) *European Parliament: Should it have more power?*, Economic Policy.

Peet, J. and K. Ussher (1999) *The EU Budget: An Agenda for Reform?*, CER Working Paper, February.

Peterson, J. and M. Shackleton (2002) *The Institutions of the European Union*, Oxford University Press, Oxford.

Norman, P. (2005) *The Accidental Constitution*, EuroComment, Brussels.

> In any moment of decision the best thing you can do is the right thing, the next best thing is the wrong thing, and the worst thing you can do is nothing.
>
> *Theodore Roosevelt*

Chapter

3 Decision making

INTRODUCTION

Chapter 2 described how EU institutions work and how they make their decisions. This chapter presents a framework for thinking about EU decision making at a more abstract and more analytical level. The discussion is organized around two major questions:

★ Who should be in charge of what? That is, which decisions should be taken at the EU level and which should be taken at the national or sub-national levels?

★ Is the EU-level decision-making procedure efficient and legitimate?

In answering these questions we shall examine the EU's practice and develop a number of analytical tools. Moreover, we shall look at reforms of the system, since the 2004 enlargement poses huge difficulties for the EU's decision-making structure. Indeed, one can see the Treaties of Amsterdam and Nice and the Constitutional Treaty as attempts to solve enlargement-related challenges to EU decision making.

3.1 Task allocation and subsidiarity: EU practice and principles

Governments set policies in many areas – everything ranging from the speed limit on local roads and national policy on nuclear weapons to the restrictions on imports of Chinese-made shirts. Not all of these policies are made by the same level of government. Most European nations have at least three levels of government (local, provincial and national), and EU members have a fourth level of government, the EU. Typically, local speed limits are set by the local government, but motorway speed limits are determined at the national level as are questions concerning nuclear arms. Why are various policies set at different levels of government? This is the main question addressed by the first two sections of this chapter.

This section begins by covering the existing EU principles guiding the allocation of policies between the EU and Member States. The section briefly covers the actual allocation of tasks in the EU. The next section presents an analytical framework to organizing thinking about the appropriate allocation of tasks among the various levels of government.

3.1.1 EU practice

Some tasks and decisions are assigned to the EU level, some are shared between the EU and Member States,

and others are set exclusively by national governments. In EU jargon, task allocation is referred to as the question of 'competences'. Areas where the EU alone decides are known as 'Community competences' ('exclusive competences' is the term in the Constitutional Treaty). Tasks where responsibility is shared between the EU and Member States are called 'shared competences', and tasks where national or sub-national governments alone decide are called 'national competences'.

There are some clear examples of national competences, the secondary school curriculum is one; and there are clear examples of Community competences, such as competition policy where the European Commission has the final say on, for example, mergers that affect the European market. However, as is true of so many things in the European Union, the exact dividing lines are unclear. The European Parliament's factsheet on subsidiarity explains:

> The demarcation of the areas of exclusive Community competence continues to be a problem, particularly because it is laid down in the Treaties not by reference to specific fields but by means of a functional description.

The task allocation is further blurred by the fact that the Treaty says that the Community's areas of competence can be extended if necessary to attain Treaty objectives. As Chapter 2 pointed out, the objectives of the Treaty of Rome are enormously ambitious, so this proviso puts a great many tasks in the grey area between Community competence and national competence. Often, the dividing line must be established by the EU Court. As the factsheet notes:

> In a number of decisions stemming from the Treaties, for example, the Court has defined and recognized certain competences (which are not explicitly regulated in the Treaties) as exclusive, but it has not laid down a definitive list of such competences.

Clarifying the allocation of tasks was one of the main jobs that EU leaders assigned to the writers of the Constitutional Treaty. More on this below.

3.1.2 Subsidiarity

To help to reduce the blurriness of the task allocation, the EU formally embraced the so-called subsidiarity principle in the Maastricht Treaty. The word 'subsidiarity' has a distinct meaning in the EU – even though it is not defined exactly (see the subsidiarity factsheet at www.europarl.eu.int/factsheets/default_en.htm for details). Subsidiarity basically means that decisions should be made as close to the people as possible, that the EU should not take action unless doing so is more effective than action taken at national, regional or local level.

The Constitutional Treaty defines subsidiarity as follows:

> Under the principle of subsidiarity, in areas which do not fall within its exclusive competence, the Union shall act only if and insofar as the objectives of the proposed action cannot be sufficiently achieved by the Member States, either at central level or at regional and local level, but can rather, by reason of the scale or effects of the proposed action, be better achieved at Union level.
>
> (Article I-11)

While this definition only becomes law in the unlikely event that the Treaty comes into force, in practice the fact that the definition was approved by all EU Member States suggests that even without Treaty ratification, it will become the functional definition of subsidiarity.

3.1.3 Three pillars

Another step towards clarity came with the EU's three-pillar structure, established by the Maastricht Treaty (see Chapter 2). This explicitly delimited the range of Community competences and shared competences by defining areas (second and third pillars) where the EU would not normally be able to make policy, i.e. where

cooperation would be of the more standard intergovernmental type where all the members have to agree unanimously on any common policy.

To summarize the discussion in Chapter 2, the first pillar (the EC, or Community, pillar) includes policy issues relating to the single market, the free movement of persons, goods, services and capital among EU members, and cooperation in the areas of agricultural, environmental, competition and trade policies. It also encompasses the Economic and Monetary Union (EMU). The second pillar consists of the Common Foreign and Security Policy (CFSP). The third pillar covers Justice and Home Affairs, i.e. police cooperation and criminal matters.

The first pillar is where EU members have allocated decision making to the EU level, in effect transferring parts of their national sovereignty by empowering EU institutions to draw up and interpret laws and regulations. Specifically, the Commission has a monopoly on the right to initiate proposals for new laws. The Council and (usually) the European Parliament decide whether to adopt them, often by majority voting. It is exactly this majority-voting element that tells us that Member States have transferred sovereignty to the EU level. An EU member can be outvoted on a particular law, but it still must accept the adopted policy. In many first-pillar areas, the laws are directly enforceable in member countries and the European Court of Justice can overrule any national court on such matters. The classic example of this is trade policy. When some EU clothing manufacturers complained about a rapid increase in imports of clothing from China in early 2005, the EU reacted by negotiating restrictions with China. These restrictions raise prices in the EU; a good outcome for EU clothing makers, but a bad one for EU clothing consumers. The restrictions apply to all Member States – even those without clothing manufacturers – since external trade policy is a Community competence. As this edition went to press, some Member States were complaining about the restrictions, but they are forced to ask the Commission to act – they cannot unilaterally decide their national import policy.

Although the details are complex, the basic rule in second- and third-pillar areas is that members can pursue cooperation but they do not transfer sovereignty to the EU level. That is, members will not be bound by decisions with which they disagree. This does not mean that they do not cooperate. EU members and even non-members do cooperate in initiatives such as the Schengen Accord.

Figure 3.1: *The EU's three pillars*

First pillar: economic policies. New cars crossing border without passing through customs.

© European Community 2005

Second pillar: foreign and security policy. Javier Solanas (right) with Colin Powell.

© European Community 2005

Third pillar: justice and home affairs. Europol officers facilitate the fight against terrorism.

Europol Annual Report 2004.

As Chapter 2 discussed, the past fifty years have seen a progressively wider range of areas transferred to the EU level. In fact, this outcome – an ever closer union – is what the EU's founders intended. The objectives of the EC Treaty (the Treaty of Rome as modified by subsequent treaties) are hugely ambitious, and the Treaty allows for an expansion of competences to attain these objectives. There are thus no limits as to what tasks the EU should be assigned. In recent years an increasingly wide range of Europeans have questioned whether the EU should continue to expand its list of competences. Recognizing this line of thinking, EU leaders said that one of the tasks of the European Convention was to develop a clearer definition of the 'task allocation' between EU, national and sub-national governments (more on this below).

Constitutional Treaty

The Constitutional Treaty (see Chapter 1 for its prospects and Chapter 2 for a summary of its content) does little to clarify the division of competences between the EU and Member States. The Treaty explicitly codifies the existing division of areas into exclusive, shared and complementary competences, but the descriptions of the policy areas remain vague (see Title III of Part I). The Constitution also restates the 'conferral principle' by which the EU can only act in areas conferred on it by the Constitution; competences not conferred on the EU remain with the Member States. However, the so-called

flexibility clause allows the EU to obtain powers in areas not conferred in the Constitution if doing so is necessary to attain the Treaty's objectives. Moreover, the passerelle clause allows EU leaders to switch from unanimity to majority voting on any issue without having to go through a Treaty revision exercise. In a sense, the Constitution codifies the existing fuzzy division of tasks without substantially clarifying it.

With this admittedly blurry notion of how the EU actually allocates tasks at hand, we turn to an analytical framework that helps us think about the pros and cons of allocating some tasks to the EU level and some to lower levels of government.

3.2 Fiscal federalism and task allocation among government levels

Most would agree that it is appropriate for national authorities to set speed limits on motorways, while municipal authorities set the various speed limits within their city. But why is this task allocation so natural? This section presents a framework for thinking about which is the most appropriate level of government for each type of task. A complete consideration of this question, however, would take us into subjects (political science, sociology, national identity, etc.) that are too far afield for this book. The main line of thinking presented here is called the 'theory of fiscal federalism'. Even though this provides only an incomplete approach to the question, it proves to be a very useful framework for organizing one's thinking about the basic trade-offs.

3.2.1 The basic trade-offs

We focus on five important considerations when thinking about the appropriate allocation of policy making among the various levels of government. The first concerns local diversity.

Diversity and local informational advantages

When people in different nations have very different preferences for a particular type of public service, a centralized decision-making process that results in the choice of a single, one-size-fits-all compromise is likely to produce an outcome that is inferior to the outcome one would observe if the decision making were decentralized. To illustrate this general idea more concretely, we turn to Fig. 3.2. (The figure employs supply and demand analysis and the notion of consumer surplus; see Chapter 4 if you are unfamiliar with this type of reasoning.)

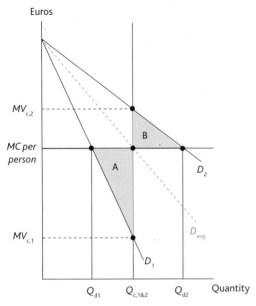

Figure 3.2: *Diversity of preferences and decentralization*

Note: The diagram assumes individuals in each region are identical and the governments are 'benevolent'.

Technical note: the *MC per person* = *MV* criterion is identical to Samuelson's famous sum of *MV* condition since *MC*/*N* = *MV* implies *MC* = *N* * *MV*, where *N* is the number of people in the region.

The figure shows the demand curves for a particular public service. One is for an individual located in region 1 (marked as D_1) and the other for a person in region 2 (marked as D_2). We assume that, for some reason, people in the two regions have different preferences for public services. For example, if we are talking about the density of public bus service, people in region 2 might live in a city where commuting by car is difficult, so they prize bus service more highly than do the people in region 1. These relative preferences can be seen from the fact that D_1 is below D_2; from the consumer surplus analysis in Chapter 4, this means that the marginal value of a slight increase in the density of bus service is lower for individuals in region 1 than it is in region 2.

To start the analysis, we work out the level of bus service that would be provided if the levels were chosen separately by the region 1 and region 2 governments.

The region 1 government would best serve its citizens by choosing the level where a typical region 1 person's

marginal value of a denser bus service (i.e. more buses per day and/or more routes) was just equal to the per-person cost of providing the extra service. In the figure, this optimal level is Q_{d1} for region 1 (the 'd' stands for decentralized and '1' for region 1). Region 2's government would choose a higher level, namely Q_{d2}. (This assumes, for simplicity, that the marginal cost is constant at all levels of service and identical across regions.)

Contrast this with the situation where the policy decision is centralized so that the same level is chosen for both regions. In this case, the central government would look at the average preference for bus services as reflected by the average demand curve, marked D_{avg}. Using the same reasoning as local governments, the optimal average provision is shown by $Q_{c,1\&2}$.

How do these two situations compare in terms of people's welfare? Taking the decentralized choice as the initial situation, the figure shows that people in both regions are made worse off by centralizing the decision. The people in region 1 are forced to pay (via their taxes) for a level of bus service that is too high for their preferences. The loss to a typical region 1 person is given by the triangle A since this measures, for each extra increase in Q, the gap between the marginal value of the denser service and the marginal cost. The marginal value is given by the demand curve D_1 and the marginal cost is given by the *MC per person* line. Region 2 residents also lose, but for them the loss stems from the fact that they would like a denser service than is provided when decision making is centralized. In particular, area B shows their losses since it measures, for each unit reduction of Q, the gap between their marginal value (given by D_2) and the marginal cost (given by *MC per person*).

The conclusion from this analysis is quite intuitive. Choosing a one-size-fits-all policy leads to an inferior outcome when people have diverse preferences.

Of course, it is possible that the central authority could also choose separate Q's for the two regions. But then there is no real reason to centralize the decision. Indeed, there is an argument based on information costs that leads us to think that decentralized decision making would be better in this situation.

Given the way that people find out about things, local authorities are almost surely better informed about local conditions (costs and preferences) than are the national authorities. It might be possible for central authorities to acquire the same information, but doing so would be a waste of resources. The local authorities are already informed, or at least it is likely that they could inform themselves at a lower cost than central authorities. More specifically, suppose it costs X euros more for the central authorities to get the information than it would cost local authorities. Since the decision would be the same in both cases (Q_{d1} and Q_{d2} are chosen), the centralized decision making is worse since taxpayers will have to pay the extra information-gathering cost, X.

Scale economies

The advantage of localized decision making in terms of information efficiency is really quite a robust result. Yet in many situations there are gains from operating at higher scales. For example, in the case of bus services, it seems reasonable to believe that the cost per kilometre of bus service tends to fall as the number of buses gets larger. A large bus company can more easily ensure that the right number of drivers is available, the fixed cost of a maintenance centre can be spread over more buses, and the per-bus cost of administration may fall – at least up to a point – when the bus company is large. Imagine an extreme situation where every bus in, say, Paris is owned and operated by separate companies versus the situation where all the buses are owned by a single company. Surely the latter would be more efficient in terms of costs.

The widespread presence of scale economies in the provision of public services – transport services, medical services, etc. – tends to favour centralisation. To see this point, we refer to Fig. 3.3. The diagram focuses only on the impact of centralization on the typical region 1 individual. In the decentralized situation, the marginal cost per person of a denser bus service is shown by the line marked *MC p.p. (decentralized)*. In the case of centralized service, the marginal cost is lower, namely *MC p.p. (centralized)* owing to scale economies.

The figure shows that there is a trade-off between having the level of service precisely adjusted to local preferences and having a lower service cost due to scale economies. When the decision is local, the optimal provision is – as in Fig. 3.2 – Q_{d1}. When it is centralized, the marginal cost is lower so the intersection of marginal value of the average citizen (D_{avg}) and marginal cost is at $Q_{c,1\&2}$. As before, the level that is optimal for the average citizen is not right for region 1 people, so there is an inefficiency; again, this is measured by a triangle, marked D in Fig. 3.3. This inefficiency, however, is offset by the gain from scale economies. That is, the region 1 person faces a lower marginal cost; the benefit of this is shown by the four-sided area C. (The gain is just like a price

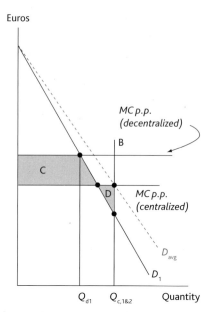

Figure 3.3: *Scale economies and centralization*

reduction in standard consumer surplus analysis; see Chapter 4 for details.)

It appears, from the figure, that the gain from scale economies outweighs the loss from one-size-fits-all decision making. But of course, if the scale economies were less important (i.e. the *MC* fell by less), or preferences were more diverse (i.e. the D_{avg} curve was further from the D_1 curve), then decentralization would be the superior outcome. The analysis for region 2 is quite similar and so it is omitted for the sake of brevity.

To sum up, economies arising from joint decision making tend to favour centralization whereas diversity of preferences and local information advantages favour decentralization.

We turn next to another key issue that arises when the decisions made in one region affect people in other regions. In economics jargon, these are called 'spillovers'.

Spillovers

Many public policy choices involve multi-region effects. National defence is one extreme. The presence of an army almost anywhere in the country deters foreign invasion for the country as a whole, so all the nation's citizens benefit from the army. It would be silly in this case to have taxpayers in each city decide separately on the army's size since, in making their decision, each set of taxpayers is likely to undervalue the nationwide benefit of a slightly bigger army. This is why the size of the army is a decision that is made at the national level in almost every nation. This is an example of what are called 'positive spillovers', i.e. where a slightly higher level of a particular policy or public service in one region benefits citizens in other regions.

A similar line of reasoning works when there are negative spillovers, i.e. when one region's policy has a negative effect on other regions. A good example of this is found in taxation. The value added tax (VAT) rate is set at the national level in all EU nations, but consider why this is so. If the VAT rate were chosen by each region, regions might be tempted to lower their VAT rate in an attempt to lure shoppers. For example, if the VAT in the centre of Frankfurt were 25 per cent, one of the city's suburbs might set its VAT at 15 per cent in order to draw shoppers to its shops. In fact, if this tax undercutting were effective enough, the suburb would actually see its tax collection rise. (If the rate reduction was more than matched by an increase in local sales, the total VAT collected by the suburb would increase.) Of course, if the suburb's tax cutting worked, Frankfurt would probably have to respond by lowering its rate to 15 per cent. In the end, both Frankfurt and the suburb would charge VAT rates below what they would like, but neither would gain shoppers by doing so. This negative spillover is so famous it has a name: 'race to the bottom'. Again, the solution that is adopted by most nations is to set the VAT rate at the national level, but this time it is done to avoid negative spillovers.

As it turns out, cross-border shopping is not much of a problem in most parts of the EU, so there is little incentive to completely harmonize VAT rates at the EU level. The EU does, however, require VAT rates to fall within a wide band so that the maximum difference between VAT rates cannot be massive.

In summary, the existence of important negative or positive spillovers suggests that decisions made locally may be suboptimal for the nation (or EU) as a whole. The very existence of spillovers, however, does not force centralization. First, it may be possible to take account of the spillovers via cooperation among lower-level governments. This does not work for all policies, however, since cooperation is very difficult to sustain when the policies are difficult to observe directly and the spillovers are difficult to quantify. Moreover, even if decentralized cooperation does not work well, one may still resist centralization when there are big differences in preferences. An interesting case study in this sort of fiscal federalism trade-off concerns the EU's different

treatment of general VAT and extra sales taxes on alcohol and tobacco. National preferences within the EU vary enormously when it comes to alcohol and tobacco, so although there is at least as much an argument for partly harmonizing these taxes as there is for harmonizing general VAT rates, the EU has never been able to do so. See Box 3.1 for details.

Democracy as a control mechanism

The analysis up to this point has assumed that governments are only interested in the well-being of their citizens. While there are such perfect public servants in this world, not all government officials and politicians are totally selfless. Indeed, assuming that all politicians are interested in things other than the welfare of their electors it is probably closer to reality than assuming they are all perfect public servants. For example, it is quite common for politicians to systematically favour politically powerful special-interest groups – e.g. granting them tax breaks, subsidies and favourable laws – even when this is bad for the average citizen.

Because of this divergence of interests between voters and decision makers, all European nations have adopted arrangements that check the power of politicians and force governments to stay close to the interest of the people. Democracy is the most powerful of these mechanisms.

Since politicians must win approval of the citizens on a regular basis, they are reluctant to misuse their decision-making power. From this perspective, democracy can be thought of as a control mechanism. The importance of this observation is that it helps to inform the allocation of policy making among levels of government. To understand this, however, we need to think more carefully about how elections discipline politicians.

Although democratic procedures vary across European nations, the following is a stylized version that fits many instances. When a politician runs in an election, the politician or his/her party presents a package of promises to the voters. The voters choose between packages and hope that the winner will actually do what he/she promised (deviations without good reason can be punished in the next election). The fact that issues are packaged together and that voters face a limited range of packages gives politicians some leeway. That is to say, their package does not have to fully represent the best interest of the voters, it only has to be good enough to get the politician elected. This means that parties and

Box 3.1

Beer, cigarettes and VAT harmonization

Since 1 January 1993, EU travellers have been allowed to buy unlimited quantities of alcohol and tobacco (for their own use) in any Member State, and, as long as they pay taxes due in the Member State where they bought the goods, no additional taxes are due when they return home. This has posed some problems for British fiscal authorities since Britain has some of the highest 'sin' taxes in Europe.

While there has been some progress towards the harmonization of excise duties across the EU (incorporated into EC directives adopted on 19 October 1992), this effort consists of establishing specific minimum rates that are quite low. As Commons (2002) notes: 'The sheer variation in duty rates between countries made any closer form of harmonization politically infeasible.' For example, in the UK, beer duty is 34p per pint (5p in France, 3p in Germany and 7p in the Netherlands), duty on a 70 cl bottle of spirits is £5.48 (£2.51 in France and £1.19 in Spain), duty on a 75 cl bottle of wine is £1.16 in the UK (2p in France and 0p in Spain), and the total excise duty on a packet of 20 cigarettes is £2.80 in the UK (£1.22 in France, £1.00 in the Netherlands and 99p in Belgium).

Such differences could, of course, lead to massive tax fraud if, for example, all British publicans stocked up in France, claiming that their truck load of beer was for personal use. To prevent this, the UK sets indicative levels for how much alcohol and tobacco constitutes 'for personal use'. These levels are rather generous: 10 litres of spirits, 20 litres of fortified wine, 90 litres of wine, 110 litres of beer, 200 cigars, 400 cigarillos, 800 cigarettes and 1 kg of smoking tobacco. The problem has become so severe that the UK has begun to seize the vehicles used in this sort of fiscal smuggling – taking over 10 000 vehicles in 2000–01.

Recently, this harsh policy led the Commission to refer the UK to the EU Court. As Frits Bolkestein, European Commissioner for taxation and customs union, said: 'I understand any member state's need to fight fraud but the Commission simply cannot accept penalties that are so disproportionate that they interfere with the rights given to EU consumers by the EU single market to go shopping in other member states. Regrettably, the UK has failed to change its practices, despite our formal request to do so. It is, therefore, time to ask the Court to consider this matter.'

Source: Based on Commons (2002) and
http://www.cec.org.uk.

politicians have room to slip in policies that favour small but influential special-interest groups. Because special-interest groups tend to provide money and other support in election campaigns, skewing the package in favour of these groups tends to increase the likelihood of winning an election.

Given this logic, voters' control over their elected decision makers depends upon the breadth of the package of promises. If democracy consists only of electing national officials once every four or five years, the package of promises must include a vast range of things. This gives politicians and parties a great deal of room to undertake policies that are not in the interest of the general public. By contrast, if the election is for a town mayor, the package will be quite specific and this tends to reduce the room for special-interest politics.

This logic is important. It underpins the basic presumption that decisions should be made at the lowest practical level of government. Or, to put it differently, decisions should be made as close to the voters as possible. As mentioned in the previous chapter, the EU's 'subsidiarity principle' does just this.

Jurisdictional competition

The final element to consider also favours decentralized decision making. It is called 'jurisdictional competition'. Voters can influence the sort of government they live under in two main ways: voice and exit. Voice is what we just discussed: the ability to control politicians and parties by speaking up, in particular by voicing one's opinion at the ballot box. The other way is to leave the jurisdiction that is imposing the policy. This is exit.

While exit is not an option for most voters at the national level, it usually is at the sub-national level. For example, if someone strongly objects to a lack of parks and green areas in a particular town, they could move to a different town. This is called jurisdictional competition since the fact that people can move forces decision makers to pay closer attention to the wishes of the people. By contrast, if all decisions are centralized, voters do not have the exit option. This reduces the pressure on local governments to be efficient in the provision of public services. To put this differently, even if voters rarely move, the fact that they could move if things got bad enough goes some way to ensuring that politicians keep things from going terribly wrong.

To recap, decentralization tends to improve government since it allows (or forces) regions to compete with each other in providing the best value for money in local services. In the marketplace, competition usually improves quality and reduces prices; in local government, competition provides the same sort of benefits.

3.2.2 From theory to practice

The five points discussed in section 3.2.1 provide principles rather than precise guidelines. The situation with respect to particular policies can be extremely complex, making it difficult or impossible to determine the 'correct' level of government for each task. Such debate inevitably turns on personal judgements and so takes us into an area where economists have no particular advantage. Be that as it may, it is interesting to speculate briefly on how our framework helps us to think about the EU's actual allocation of tasks between the EU level and national level.

The one thing that is clear is that subsidiarity is probably a good idea. When in doubt, allocate the task to the lowest practicable level, since higher-level decisions are less subject to democratic control via voice and exit. Going further is trickier.

In the European Union, the main area of centralization has been economic policies (EC pillar), especially policies affecting the single market. As the discussion of the Treaty of Rome in Chapter 2 showed, virtually every policy that directly affects the competitiveness of particular industries is subject to control at the EU level. For example, import taxes, government subsidies (called state aid in EU jargon), exceptional tax benefits, and anti-competitive behaviour by firms are subject to EU-wide rules that are enforceable in the EU Court. The thinking here is that such policies are marked by important and systematic negative spillovers. When one EU nation subsidizes its firms in a particular industry, firms in other EU nations suffer from the artificially intensified competition. As in the tax example above, a likely outcome is a Prisoners' Dilemma – all EU nations end up providing subsidies, but the subsidies cancel each other out. Likewise, each nation might be tempted to introduce idiosyncratic product regulation in an attempt to favour local firms, but the end result would be a highly fragmented European market with too many small firms (see Chapter 6 for an analysis of the economics of this).

The exceptions to centralization in economic policy can also be understood in the light of our five principles. The EU does not attempt to harmonize most social policies or general labour market policies. Nor does it centralize decision making on general taxes such as income taxes and corporate taxes. As explained in Chapter 1, general policies like these do not necessarily affect the competitiveness of particular firms and so are subject to a much lower level of negative spillovers. Moreover, national preferences for such policies are very diverse. In Spain, for example, the primary form of labour market protection for workers is employment protection legislation, i.e. laws that make it difficult to fire workers. Germany relies much more on unemployment benefits. Given this divergence of national preferences, the losses from a one-size-fits-all policy would be likely to outweigh any gains in efficiency or avoidance of negative spillovers. Of course, one can argue with this and it is impossible to settle the argument scientifically. For example, German labour unions insisted that nationalized, one-size-fits-all wage bargaining should also apply to the eastern *Länder* despite the great diversity of economic conditions, and they insisted on the same homogeneity of labour market laws.

Most non-economic policies are decided at the national level. For example, most foreign policy, defence policy, internal security and social policies are made at the national level. Of course, various nations cooperate on some of these policies – a good example is the agreement between France, Germany, Spain and the UK to produce a common military transport plane – but the decision making is allocated to the national level and cooperation is voluntary.

Roughly speaking, first-pillar policies are where there are important spillovers, where national preferences are not too great and common policies tend to benefit from scale economies. The theory of fiscal federalism thus helps us to organize our thinking about why such policies are centralized.

Second-pillar policies – Common Foreign and Security Policies – are marked by enormous scale economies. For example, unifying all of Europe's armies would result in a truly impressive force and allow Europe to develop world-class weapon systems. However, second-pillar policies are also marked by vast differences in national preferences. Some EU members – France and the UK, for example – have a long history of sending their young men to die in foreign lands for various causes. Other EU members – such as Sweden and Ireland – shun almost any sort of armed conflict outside their own borders. Given this diversity of preferences, the gains from scale economies would be more than offset by adopting a one-size-fits-all policy. Because of this, the only common EU policies in these areas are those arrived at by common consent, i.e. by cooperation rather than by centralization.

Third-pillar policies lie somewhere between first- and second-pillar policies, both in terms of the gains from scale economies and in terms of the diversity of preferences.

3.3 Economical view of decision making

The previous sections looked at factors affecting the allocation of tasks between the EU and its Member States. This abstracted from the actual process by which EU-level decisions are made. In other words, we simplified away the question of how decisions are made at the EU level in order to study the issue of which decisions should be made at the EU level.

In this and subsequent sections we reverse this simplification, focusing on the question of how the EU makes decisions. In particular, we shall concentrate on how the decision-making mechanisms affect the EU's ability to act, how they affect the distribution of power among EU nations, and how they affect democratic 'legitimacy'.

Efficiency, power and legitimacy are inherently vague concepts. To make progress, we adopt the tactic of progressive complexity. That is, we start by taking what may seem to be a very shallow view of political actors and their motives. These simplifying assumptions allow us to develop some precise measures of efficiency, legitimacy and national power in EU decision making. The benefit is that these precise measures permit us to

comment on how efficiency and legitimacy have evolved in the EU and how they will evolve with the 2004 enlargement and the Constitutional Treaty, if it ever becomes law.

Before turning to the measures, however, we consider the decision-making rules in detail.

3.3.1 Qualified majority voting

As Chapter 2 pointed out, the EU has several different decision-making procedures; however, about 80 per cent of EU legislation is passed under what is called the 'codecision procedure'. This requires the Council of Ministers to adopt the legislation by a 'qualified majority' and the European Parliament to adopt it by at least a simple majority, i.e. 50 per cent. As part of our simplification, we assume that nations are the only players in the EU's decision-making process. That is, we allow Germans and Italians to differ on a proposal, but we do not consider, for example, a coalition of German and Italian Green parties. A side effect of this simplification is that it makes the European Parliament's role unimportant in efficiency calculations. Box 3.2 explains why.

The Council of Ministers (the Council for short) has two main decision-making rules. On the most important issues, such as Treaty changes, the accession of new members, and setting the multi-year budget plan, Council decisions are by unanimity. On most issues, the Council decides on the basis of qualified majority voting (QMV).

The basic form of the QMV procedure has remained unchanged from its origin in the 1958 Treaty of Rome, although the Constitutional Treaty would, if ratified, change this from 2009. Under QMV, each Member State's minister casts a certain number of votes, with more populous members having more votes, but still many fewer than population-proportionality would suggest. For example, in the EU15, France with its 60 million citizens had 10 votes, whereas Denmark with its 5 million citizens had 3; the total number of votes in the EU15 was 87. The threshold for a winning majority, what is called a 'qualified majority', was 62 votes, so the majority threshold was about 71 per cent ($62 \div 87 = 0.712$).

Various QMV rules

The Treaty of Nice greatly complicated the QMV rules and the Constitutional Treaty abandons it altogether for a radical new voting procedure. However, the Nice Treaty

Box 3.2

Parliament's (non) impact on efficiency

Although the European Parliament's size and national composition has changed over time, this does not affect its passage probability[1] because it uses the simple majority rule. When a body takes its decisions by simple majority, an increase in the number of voters increases the number of ways to win exactly in line with the increase in the number of ways to block (apart from a minor difference arising when switching from even to odd numbers). To see this, note that under the 50 per cent rule any coalition that could block by voting 'no', could win by voting 'yes'. (Brief reflection reveals that the same does not hold for other thresholds, such as the Council's 71 per cent rule.) As a consequence, the passage probability is always 50 per cent. Of course, this fact reveals the simplicity of our efficiency measure.

[1] Passage probability is defined in section 3.3.2 below.

voting rules will govern the Council of Ministers' decision making for the years to come, even if the Constitutional Treaty comes into force. Figure 3.4 illustrates the timing.

★ *May to November 2004.* For a few months after the enlargement, the pre-Treaty of Nice rules applied. Qualified majority voting involved weighted votes and the old majority threshold of 71 per cent to win was kept. The numbers of votes for the incumbent fifteen was unchanged; those for the ten newcomers were a simple interpolation of EU15.

★ *November 2004 to October 2009.* During this period, the Nice Treaty rules apply (due to a last-minute political arrangement that overcame Spanish and Polish resistance to accepting the Constitution's new rules). The Nice Treaty rules are complex. They maintain the basic QMV framework, but add two extra criteria concerning the number of 'yes' voters and the population they represent. Specifically, the vote threshold is 72.2 per cent of the Council votes (232 of the 321 votes), the member threshold is 50 per cent of members (13 members), and the population threshold is 62 per cent of the EU population. Additionally, the Nice rules redistributed votes in a way that heavily favoured the big and near-big members, as Fig. 3.5

shows; Spain and Poland won disproportionate increases.

★ *Constitutional Treaty rules.* From November 2009 onwards, the Constitution's 'double majority' rules will apply (assuming it enters into force). The basic QMV system is abandoned. Instead, a proposal is adopted by the Council only if the Member States voting 'yes' represent at least 55 per cent of the EU members and 65 per cent of the EU population.[1]

3.3.2 EU ability to act: decision-making efficiency

In economics, 'efficiency' usually means an absence of waste. In the EU decision-making context, the word has come to mean 'ability to act'. While 'ability to act' is more specific than efficiency, it is still a long way from operational. For instance, on some issues the EU finds it very easy to make decisions, yet on other issues it has great difficulty in finding a coalition of countries to support a particular law. The perfect measure of efficiency would somehow predict all possible issues, decide how the members would line up into 'yes' and 'no' coalitions, and use this to develop an average measure of how easy it is to get things done in the EU. Such predictions are, of course, impossible given the

Figure 3.4: *Timeline for the various voting rules agreed at June 2004 summit*

[1] A last-minute summit compromise inserted the requirement that at least 15 members vote 'yes', but this is irrelevant; 15 members of 25 is 60 per cent and thus greater than 55 per cent, but by the time these rules take effect, the EU should have 27 members and 55 per cent of 27 is 15 (Bulgaria and Romania are pencilled in for membership in 2007). The 15-member rule will be redundant when it takes effect.

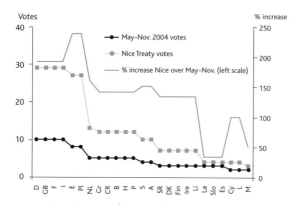

Figure 3.5: *Treaty of Nice and Accession Treaty reweighing of Council votes*

D = Germany, GB = Great Britain, F = France, I = Italy, E = Spain, Pl = Poland, NL = Netherlands, Gr = Greece, CR = Czech Republic, B = Belgium, H = Hungary, P = Portugal, S = Sweden, A = Austria, SR = Slovak Republic, DK = Denmark, Fin = Finland, Ire = Ireland, Li = Lithuania, La = Latvia, Slo = Slovenia, Es = Estonia, Cy = Cyprus, L = Luxembourg, M = Malta.

Source: Accession Treaty, Act of Accession, Article 12.

uncertain and ever changing nature of the challenges facing the EU.

An alternative approach, which we shall study here, sounds strange at first but it is really the best way of thinking systematically about the issue. Rather than trying to predict details of decision making on particular topics, we adopt a 'veil of ignorance'. That is, we focus on a randomly selected issue – random in the sense that no EU member would know whether it would be for or against the proposition.

A quantitative measure of efficiency: passage probability

The specific measure we focus on is called the 'passage probability'. The passage probability measures how easy it is to find a majority given the specific voting rule. Specifically, it is the number of all possible winning coalitions divided by the number of all possible coalitions. If each conceivable coalition is equally likely, the measure tells us the likelihood of approving a randomly selected issue; that is why it is called the passage probability. It works as follows.

Given these simplifications, calculation of the passage probability is straightforward. One uses a computer to calculate all possible coalitions in the Council among EU members. That is to say, it looks at every possible

combination of 'yes' and 'no' voting by EU Member States. Since one can combine nations in many different ways, there are quite a few possible coalitions (in the EU15, for example, there are 32 768 possible coalitions, in the EU25 the number is over 33 million coalitions and in the EU27 it is over 134 million). Next, the computer uses each member's number of votes and the 71 per cent majority threshold to determine how many of these are winning coalitions.

The level of the passage probability is affected by the number of members, the distribution of votes and, above all, by the majority threshold. It is important to note, however, that the exact level of the passage probability is not very important. As Chapter 2 explained, most EU legislation is proposed by the European Commission, and the Commission often refrains from introducing legislation that is unlikely to pass.

Historical efficiency and Treaty of Nice reforms

It is interesting to see how the EU's efficiency has changed over time. Above all, it is interesting to see how the 2004 enlargement will affect the EU's decision-making efficiency.

The five leftmost bars in Fig. 3.6 show the passage probability for qualified majority voting in the historical EUs with 6, 9, 10, 12 and 15 members. These indicate that although efficiency has been declining, past enlargements have only moderately hindered decision-making efficiency. The 1994 enlargement lowered the probability only slightly, from 10 to 8 per cent, and the Iberian expansion lowered it from 14 to 10 per cent. The figures also hide the fact that the Single European Act, which took effect in 1987, greatly boosted efficiency by

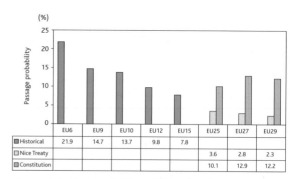

	EU6	EU9	EU10	EU12	EU15	EU25	EU27	EU29
■ Historical	21.9	14.7	13.7	9.8	7.8			
□ Nice Treaty						3.6	2.8	2.3
■ Constitution						10.1	12.9	12.2

Figure 3.6: *Enlarged EU's ability to act*

Notes: The figures show the passage probability which measures the likelihood that a randomly-selected issue would pass in the Council of Ministers.

Source: Authors' calculations.

shifting many more decisions from unanimity to qualified majority voting.

Notice that the 2004 enlargement greatly reduces the passage probability. This is true even with the Nice Treaty voting reforms (which were supposed to maintain the enlarged EU's ability to act). In fact, the Nice Treaty's complex rules made matters slightly worse than they would have been with no reform at all. The results show that accepting in twelve newcomers without reform would dramatically reduce efficiency, cutting the current passage probability by something like one-half, from 7.8 to 3.6 per cent.

This point, which became widely accepted after 2001, was why EU leaders asked the European Convention to reconsider the EU's decision-making rules – the request that eventually led to the Constitution's new double-majority rule for the Council. Note that the decision-making rules in the Parliament and Commission were not viewed as problematic and thus were not reformed by the Constitution.

Cruder efficiency measures: blocking coalition analysis

A second, cruder but more transparent efficiency-measuring tool, i.e. blocking minority analysis, confirms the findings that decision making will get much harder under the Nice Treaty reforms that came into effect in November 2004. Blocking minority analysis considers the ability of a handful of 'likely' coalitions to block decisions. Decisions that require unanimity can be blocked by any nation and this never changes regardless of the number of members. The analysis becomes more interesting when considering qualified majority voting in the Council.

The two coalitions we consider are an alliance of easterners and an alliance of poor nations. How much blocking power would these two coalitions have under the Accession Treaty rules?

Figure 3.7 shows that a coalition of poor nations would easily be able to block any decision in the Council. On the 'number of members' criterion, they will have two more than the fourteen needed to block, and on the votes criterion they will have 80 per cent more votes than they would need to block any proposal. On the population criterion, not even the poor coalition could block, but this does not matter; a measure can be blocked on any of the three thresholds. Once again we conclude that legislating under the Accession Treaty rules (that were first agreed in the Treaty of Nice) will be very difficult.

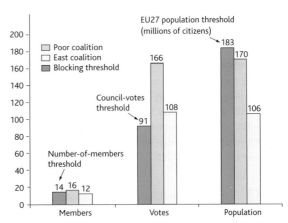

Figure 3.7: *Blocking power of eastern and poor coalitions in the EU27*

Notes: The leftmost bar in each group shows the number necessary to block a QMV decision for the number of members, number of votes and share of population criteria, respectively. The middle bar in each group shows the size of a coalition of all poor nations (the 4 incumbent 'cohesion' nations plus the 12 newcomers) for each of the three ways to block. The rightmost bar shows the size of the eastern coalition (12 newcomers).

Source: Baldwin *et al.* (2001).

3.4 The distribution of power among EU members

The next aspect of EU decision making that we address is the distribution of power among EU members. As with efficiency, there is no perfect measure of power. The tactic we adopt relies on the law of large numbers. That is, we look to see how likely it is that each member's vote is crucial on a randomly-drawn issue. Before turning to the calculations, however, we lay out our specific definition of power.

For our purposes, power means influence, or, more precisely, the ability to influence EU decisions by being in a position to make or break a winning coalition in the Council of Ministers. Of course, no one has absolute power in the EU, so we focus on the likelihood that a Member State will be influential. On some things Germany's vote will be crucial, on others it will be irrelevant, and the same goes for all other members. What determines how likely it is that a particular nation will be influential?

The most direct and intuitive measure of political power is national voting shares in the Council of Ministers.

Under current EU rules, each Member State has a fixed number of votes in the Council of Ministers. Until the 2004 enlargement, 87 Council-of-Minister votes were divided among the 15 EU nations, with large nations receiving more votes than small ones (see Chapter 2 for details). It seems intuitively plausible that nations with more votes are more likely to be influential on average, so the first power measure to try is a nation's share of Council votes. But how can we tell if this power measure captures anything real?

3.4.1 Empirical evidence on power measures' relevance

One cannot measure a nation's power in EU decision making directly, but the exercise of power does leave some 'footprints' in the data. Budget allocations are one manifestation of power that is both observable and quantifiable. To check whether our power measure is useful, we see if it can help to explain the budget allocation puzzles we discussed in Chapter 2.

To understand why our power measure should be related to outward signs of power such as the budgetary spending allocation, we need briefly to review the budget process explained in Chapter 2 and then discuss 'back scratching' and 'horse trading'.

The annual budget must be passed by both the Council of Ministers and the European Parliament (EP). These annual budgets, however, are constrained by medium-term budget plans called Financial Perspectives (the current one covers 2000–06). The Financial Perspectives require unanimity in the Council, but the annual budgets are passed on the basis of qualified majority. For both the Financial Perspectives and the annual budgets, EP decision making is on the basis of a simple majority. As it turns out, the EP does not matter from a national power perspective. This notion is explained in detail in Box 3.3, but the basic notion is based on the different majority thresholds. That is, since the EP's majority threshold (50 per cent) is much lower than the Council's (71 per cent) and the allocation of MEPs per nation in the EP is similar to the allocation of votes per nation in the Council, any coalition of nations that can pass a budget in the Council can also pass it in the Parliament. For this reason, we focus solely on vote shares in the Council of Ministers.

As already pointed out, about 80 per cent of Council decisions are made on the basis of qualified majority voting. Since the Council decides many issues each year, and members do not care dearly about all of them, countries tend to trade their votes on issues that they

view as minor in exchange for support on an issue that they view as major, even if the two issues are totally unrelated. This sort of natural activity is referred to by the colourful names of 'back scratching' and 'horse trading'.

Now that we have discussed the background, we can turn to the main reasoning. Citizens in EU nations, or at least some citizens, benefit when EU money is spent in their district. Successful politicians, responding to the desires of their citizens, use their political clout to direct money homewards. For example, suppose that countries ask for a little 'gift' each time they find themselves in a position that is critical to a winning coalition. In the data, the 'gift' ends up as EU spending, but the actual mechanism could be subtle, say a more favourable treatment in the allocation of EU subsidies to hill farmers, a more generous allocation of milk quotas, or inclusion of reindeer meat in the CAP's price support mechanism. In this light, it seems natural that a country's power measure would equal its expected fraction of all special gifts handed out. If one goes to the cynical extreme and views the whole EU budget as nothing more than a pile of 'gifts', then our power measures should meet the EU's budget allocation perfectly. If high-minded principles such as helping out disadvantaged regions also matter, then the power measure should only partially explain the spending pattern.

As it turns out, Council vote shares go a long way towards solving the 'puzzle' of EU budget allocation discussed in Chapter 2. The horizontal axis in the top panel of Fig. 3.9 plots a measure of the 'bias' in each nation's power per person; specifically, it plots the ratio of each nation's share of Council votes to its share of EU15 population. To understand why this reflects the power bias, suppose a nation has a ratio of exactly 1.0. This would imply that the Council votes per citizen in that nation are exactly equal to the EU15 average. For example, Spain's vote share to population share ratio is 0.9. This means that Spaniards have slightly less than the average number of votes. Greece, on the other hand, has a ratio of 2.6, which means Greeks have 2.6 times more votes per person than the EU average.

The vertical axis plots a measure of the bias in each nation's receipt per capita. Again, to put everything on a common scale, the precise measure we use is the ratio of the nation's share of EU spending to its share of the EU's population. As with the per-capita power measure on the horizontal axis, 1.0 on the vertical axis implies the average receipts per person, taking the EU15 as a whole.

Why Parliamentary reform does not affect national power distributions

Most EU legislation these days must be approved by both the Council and the Parliament. As it turns out, the allocation of seats in the European Parliament does not affect national power, per se. The reason rests on three facts: (i) the national distribution of Council votes and MEP seats is quite similar, as Fig. 3.8 shows; (ii) to pass the Council, a proposal must garner at least 71 per cent of votes; and (iii) to pass the Parliament, a proposal needs to win only half the MEP votes.

To illustrate how these three facts affect the Parliament's power from a purely national perspective, we must cover a few preliminaries. First, we start with a simple assumption: that MEPs act as national representatives and indeed that their votes are controlled directly by national governments (obviously this is false, but going to this extreme helps to build intuition for more realistic cases). Second, recall that we define power as the ability to break a winning coalition, so the question is: Can a nation use the votes of its MEPs to block a coalition that it cannot otherwise block? If the answer is no, then the votes of MEPs do not affect a nation's power, even under the extreme assumption that MEP votes are controlled by governments. And, of course, if national power is not affected by MEP votes when they are directly controlled, then national power is certainly not affected when the MEPs vote by their own conscience. Finally, we assume that each nation's share of Council votes is identical to its share of MEP votes (rather than just similar). Under these assumptions, we can think of the actual procedure as a double-majority system. To pass, a proposal needs to

attract the votes of Member States that have at least 50 per cent of MEP votes, and 71 per cent of Council votes.

Now here is the main point. The first criterion is redundant since the Council vote threshold is higher than the MEP threshold. That is, since the distributions of Council and MEP votes is assumed to be identical, any coalition that has 71 per cent of Council votes will automatically have 71 per cent of MEP votes, which is plainly more than the 50 per cent necessary. Some careful thought and a little mental gymnastics reveal the implications of this for national power: there are no instances when a nation's MEP votes increase its power to block. In every instance where it can block on the basis of MEP votes, it can also block on the basis of Council votes.

Even under a more realistic view of the process, the same conclusion holds. The fact that the distribution of MEP votes is similar to the distribution of Council votes teamed with the fact that the Council threshold is much higher than the Parliament's threshold, means that MEPs' votes could never increase a nation's ability to block, even if the MEPs voted on strictly national lines.

Interestingly, this suggests one indirect reason why the Parliament has tended to form cross-national coalitions. If they acted on purely national lines, MEPs would, on typical issues (i.e. where the national government accurately represents the national view), act as rubber stampers. If they form cross-national coalitions, they may bring something new to the process.

An important caveat to all this is the fact that EU nations are made up of diverse groups. Since some groups are less well represented in their nation's government than they are in the European Parliament (e.g. labour unions when a conservative government is in power), having more seats means that these special-interest groups will have a larger say in EU decision making.

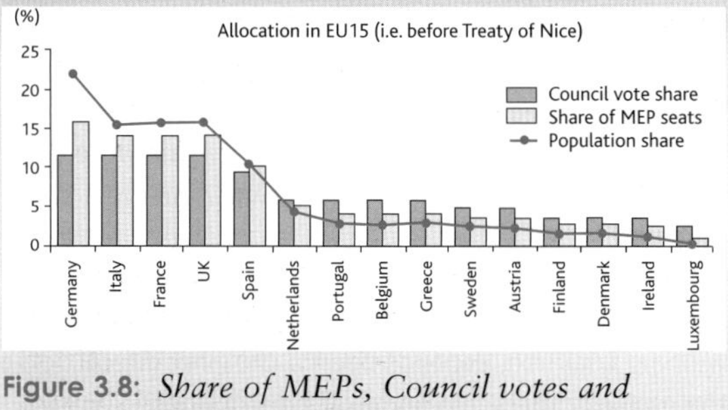

Figure 3.8: *Share of MEPs, Council votes and population in the EU15*

Source: Factsheets on http://www.europarl.eu.int/factsheets/.

For a more detailed analysis, see Bindseil and Hantke (1997).

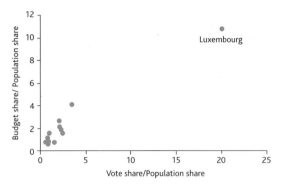

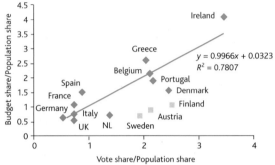

Figure 3.9: *EU15 per-capita vote shares and budget share (average 1995–2000)*

Source: Adapted from Baldwin (1994), Figure 7.2, using European Commission total allocated expenditure data (averaged over 1995 to 2000 to smooth out annual fluctuations).

Each point in the top panel indicates an EU15 member. There are two salient findings here. First, there is a distinct positive relationship between power per person and receipts per person. In other words, it seems as if politicians use their power in the Council of Ministers to direct EU spending towards their home countries. Second, Luxembourg is a real outlier. Luxembourgers have 20 times more votes per person than the EU average and they get almost 11 times more spending per person than the EU average. Because a huge outlier can make it difficult to see what is going on with the others, the bottom panel shows the same figure without Luxembourg.

The bottom panel confirms the positive relation between power and spending, but it also allows us to pick out a few more interesting features. Note that the newest EU members – Austria, Finland and Sweden – are far below the average relationship between power and spending. In other words, given their level of votes per person, the relationship between power and spending that one sees in the older members (the EU12) suggests that they should be getting more EU spending per person. Perhaps

this reflects the fact that these newcomers have not yet learned how to work EU politics in their favour, or maybe they have not had time to do enough 'back scratching'. We can also see that the UK is the nation that receives the least per capita of all EU15 nations. It also has one of the lowest vote ratios, but not the lowest – Germany has that distinction.

Voting weights are a useful rough-and-ready power measure that have the great merit of transparency. Unfortunately, voting weights can give a very misleading depiction of the power distribution.

3.4.2 Vote shares as a power measure: the shortcomings

To illustrate the potential pitfalls of vote weights as a power measure, consider a 'toy model' of the Council. Suppose there are only three countries in this toy model – imaginatively called A, B and C – and they have 40, 40 and 20 votes, respectively. Decisions are based on a simple majority rule (more than 50 per cent to win). If we used voting weights as a measure of power, we would say that countries A and B, each with their 40 votes, were twice as powerful as C with its 20 votes. This is wrong.

With a little reflection you can convince yourself that all three nations are equally powerful in this toy council. The point is that any winning coalition requires two nations, but any two will do. Likewise, any pair of nations can block anything. As a consequence, all three nations are equally powerful in the sense that they are equally likely to make or break a winning coalition.

The level of the majority threshold can also be important for power. For example, continuing with our toy model, raising the majority rule from 50 to 75 per cent would strip nation C of all power. The only winning coalition that C would belong to is the grand coalition A&B&C, but here C would not be able to turn it into a losing one by leaving the coalition. Therefore C's vote can have no influence on the outcome. Again, vote shares in this example would give a very incorrect view of power.

More generally, power, i.e. the ability to make or break a winning coalition, depends upon a complex interaction of the majority threshold and exact distribution of votes. Indeed, the useless-vote situation in which nation C found itself in our second example actually occurred in the early days of the EU (see Box 3.4 for details).

Box 3.4

Luxembourg's useless vote, 1958–73

The 1958 Treaty of Rome laid down the rules for qualified majority voting in the EEC6. The big three – Germany, France and Italy – got 4 votes each, Belgium and the Netherlands got 2 each, and Luxembourg got 1. The minimum threshold for a qualified majority was set at 12 of the 17 votes.

A little thought shows that the Treaty writers did not think hard enough about this. As you can easily confirm, Luxembourg's one vote never matters. Any coalition (group of 'yes' voters) that has enough votes to win can always win with or without Luxembourg. According to formal power measures, this means that Luxembourg had little power over issues decided on a QMV basis. As Felsenthal and Machover (2001) write:

'This didn't matter all that much, because the Treaty of Rome stipulated that QMV would not be used until 1966; and even in 1966–72 it was only used on rare occasions. Still, it seems a bit of a blunder.' All changed from 1973 when the weights were altered to allow for the accession of the UK, Denmark and Ireland. Indeed, since then, Luxembourg's votes have turned out to be crucial in a surprisingly large number of coalitions. Maybe that is why Luxembourg has the highest receipt per capita in the EU despite being the richest nation by far.

Source: This box is based on the excellent web-book by Felsenthal and Machover (2001), which provides a detailed look at voting theory.

Simple counterexamples such as these led to the development of several more sophisticated power indices. We shall focus on the 'Normalized Banzhaf Index'.

3.4.3 Power to break a winning coalition: the Normalized Banzhaf Index

In plain English, the Normalized Banzhaf Index (NBI) gauges how likely it is that a nation finds itself in a position to 'break' a winning coalition on a randomly-selected issue. By way of criticism, note that the set-up behind the NBI provides only a shallow depiction of a real-world voting process. For instance, the questions of who sets the voting agenda, how coalitions are formed and how intensively each country holds its various positions are not considered. In a sense, the equal probability of each coalition occurring and each country switching its vote is meant to deal with this shallowness. The idea is that all of these things would average out over a large number of votes on a broad range of issues. Thus, this measure of power is really a very long-term concept. Another way of looking at it is as a measure of power in the abstract. It tells us how powerful a country is likely to be on a randomly chosen issue. Of course, on particular issues, various countries may be much more or much less powerful.

The calculation of NBI for all EU members is a topic that may fascinate some readers, but it is not essential to our study of EU decision making, so we relegate its description to Box 3.5.

3.4.4 Power shifts from Nice to Constitutional Treaty voting rules

The NBI is a useful tool for understanding many of the struggles among Member States over EU institutional reforms past, present and future. A good example can be found in the switch between the Nice Treaty rules (that are in effect today) and the Constitutional Treaty voting rules that are supposed to come into effect in November 2009, if the Constitution is ratified.

As pointed out in Chapter 1, the Constitutional Treaty had a very hard time getting accepted and much of the difficulty was due to the voting rules in the Council of Ministers. Specifically, the voting rule proposed by Giscard d'Estaing was included in the Italian President's draft presented to the European Council in December 2003. This was rejected for many reasons, but the main sticking point was Spanish and Polish opposition to Giscard's voting rules. To understand the position of the Spaniards and

Box 3.5

Calculating the Normalized Banzhaf Index (NBI)

The mechanical calculation of the NBI is easy to describe and requires nothing more than some patience and a PC with lots of horsepower. To work it out, one asks a computer to look at all possible coalitions (i.e. all conceivable line-ups of 'yes' and 'no' votes) and identify the winning coalitions. Note that listing all possible coalitions is easy to do by hand for low numbers of voters; in a group of 2 voters there are only 4, in a group of 3 there are 8. However, the general formula for the number of all possible coalitions for a group of n voters is 2^n, so determining by hand which coalitions are winners quickly becomes impractical: in the EU15, 32 768 coalitions have to be checked. In the EU27, the number is over 134 million. The computer's next task is to work out all the ways that each winning coalition could be turned into a loser by the defection of a single nation. Finally, the computer calculates the number of times each nation could be a 'deal breaker' as a fraction of the number of times that any country could be a deal breaker. The theory behind this is that the Council decides on a vast array of issues, so the NBI tells us how likely it is that a particular nation will be critical on a randomly selected issue.

For the EU15, it turns out that the theoretically superior power measure (NBI) is not very different from the rough-and-ready national vote-share measure. The measures also are quite similar for the EU27. Readers who distrust sophisticated concepts should find their confidence in the Banzhaf measure bolstered by this similarity – and the same applies to readers who distrust rough-and-ready measures.

If you like this sort of reasoning, see the excellent website, http://powerslave.val.utu.fi, which is devoted to power indices of all types.

Poles, Fig. 3.10 shows the power shifts implied by the proposed new voting rules.

To set the stage, note that Poland and Spain were awarded an enormous increase in their voting power in the 2000 Nice Treaty that took effect in November 2004 (see the top panel). The bottom panel shows that the Constitutional Treaty voting rules will reduce the voting power of Poland and Spain even more than the Treaty of Nice increased it. Given this, it is easy to see why these two nations vetoed the December 2003 draft of the Constitution.

This veto meant that the May 2004 enlargement occurred without agreement on the draft Constitution. Then Ireland took over the EU presidency from Italy and proceeded to negotiate a compromise. What was proposed (the rules actually in the Constitutional Treaty) was almost identical in terms of power shifting to the rules rejected in December 2003, but there was a critical difference. The Spanish Prime Minister José María Anzar, who won the large power increase in Nice (presumably in exchange for some compromise over other issues in the Treaty of Nice) and who had forcefully opposed the new voting rules in December 2003, lost his national election. The new

Spanish Prime Minister, José Luis Zapatero, proved more willing to accept a large reduction in Spanish voting power. Given the absolute necessity of fixing the Nice Treaty rules – as illustrated by the efficiency calculations in Fig. 3.10 – the change in the Spanish government was enough to allow the European Council to accept the Irish presidency's version of the Constitution in June 2004.

It is also interesting to show how both the Treaty of Nice and the Constitutional Treaty change the power distribution between large and small nations. The Treaty of Nice greatly increased the power of large nations, with this gain coming at the expense of the EU's smallest members. The Constitutional Treaty restores some of the power to the smallest states, but provides a huge boost to Germany's power. Since power is measured by shares, and shares must add to 100 per cent, the German and tiny-nation power gains must be paid for by the other members. As the bottom panel of Fig. 3.10 shows, Spain, Poland and the middle-sized EU Member States are the losers from the Constitutional Treaty rules.

Future difficulties

As this edition went to press, the fate of the Constitution looked grim but was not yet certain. One thing, however,

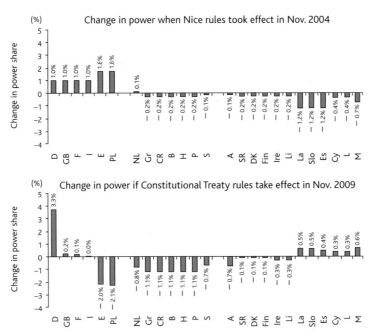

Figure 3.10: *Winners and losers under the Nice rules and Constitution voting rules*

Source: Baldwin and Widgren (2004).

seems quite clear. Whether the Constitution ever comes into effect, the Nice Treaty rules must be fixed in order to restore the enlarged EU's ability to act. This suggests that the topic of voting rules will be in the news in the coming months and years. Although the passage probability and NBI measures are crude, they are likely to prove very useful tools for organizing thinking about these future issues.

3.5 Legitimacy in EU decision making

The EU is a truly unique organization. Nowhere else in the world has so much national sovereignty been transferred to a supranational body. As Chapter 1 pointed out, the massive death and destruction of two world wars is what led the EU's founders to contemplate this transfer, but the continual willingness of the current generation of Europeans to accept it depends upon much more practical considerations. One consideration is the EU's ability to deliver results, but another important consideration is the democratic legitimacy of the EU's decision-making process.

3.5.1 Thinking about democratic legitimacy

What makes a decision-making system legitimate? This is a difficult question so it helps to start with an extreme and obviously illegitimate voting scheme and to think about why it seems illegitimate. Almost every European would view as illegitimate a system that allowed only landowning males the right to vote. Why? Because those without votes would find it unjust. And if the landowning men were forward looking, they would also find it illegitimate since they or their male offspring might one day lose their land. In short, a good way to think about legitimacy is to apply the 'in the other person's shoes' rule. A system is legitimate if all individuals would be happy with any other individual's allocation of voting power, which, if you think about it, requires equality. Equal power per citizen is thus a natural legitimacy principle.

But what constitutes a citizen? In the EU there are two answers: nations and people. The EU is a union of states, so each state is a citizen and should thus have equal voting power. The EU is also a union of people, so people are citizens and so each person should have equal voting power. This makes it impossible to apply the equality principle in a simple manner. Note that there is a more classical way to phrase this same point. Democracy, it has been said, is the tyranny of the majority. To avoid this tyrannical aspect, democracies must have mechanisms that protect the rights and wishes of minorities. Indeed, many nations provide mechanisms for giving disadvantaged groups larger than proportional shares of power, but the starting point for such departures is one vote per person. In the EU, the over-weighting of small nations' votes was one such mechanism. For example, equality of power per person would grant Germany 2000 per cent more power than Ireland; equality per member would grant Luxembourgers 160 times more power per person than Germans. Given the dual-union nature of the EU, neither extreme is legitimate.

Using the Normalized Banzhaf Index described above, we have a very precise (albeit crude) measure of 'power per person' and 'power per nation'. The 'fair' power distribution for the union-of-states view is trivial: in the EU25, each member should get 1/25 of the power. For the union-of-people view, power should be distributed such that each EU citizen has equal power regardless of nationality. As it turns out, the Nice Treaty voting rules favoured the equal-power-per-person view (since it shifted power to big nations). The Constitutional Treaty rules had a less clear-cut impact since they greatly boosted Germany's power but also boosted the power of the EU members with populations below that of a medium-large city.

3.6 Summary

In order just to continue to operate, the EU must make a steady stream of decisions to adjust to the ever changing economic and political landscape. This chapter looked at the EU decision-making process from two perspectives. First, it considered the current EU allocation of 'competences' between the EU-level and national governments of its members. In terms of actual practices and principles, the key points were:

★ Policy making is categorized into: areas where the EU has 'exclusive competence', i.e. where the decision is made only at the EU level; areas where competence is shared; and areas where the EU has no competence, i.e. where decisions are made only at the national or sub-national level.

★ The allocation of policy areas to these three categories is determined by the treaties and decisions of the EU Court of Justice. This allocation, however, is blurred since the treaties do not refer to specific fields; they refer only to areas by functional description. To clarify the allocation, the EU operates on the principle of subsidiarity, which says that unless there is a good reason for allocating a task to the EU level, all tasks should be allocated to national or sub-national governments. The three-pillar structure of the EU also helps to clarify the allocation. First-pillar (Community pillar) issues are under EU competence whereas second- and third-pillar issues are not.

The chapter also presented a framework for thinking about how tasks should be allocated between various levels of government (theory of fiscal federalism). This framework stresses five trade-offs that suggest whether a particular decision should be centralized or not:

★ Diversity and information costs favour decentralized decision making.

★ Scale economies favour centralization.

★ Spillovers, either positive or negative.

★ Democracy as a control device favours decentralization.

★ Jurisdictional competition favours decentralization.

The second part of the chapter considered the EU decision-making process in more detail, focusing on efficiency (i.e. the EU's ability to act), national power shares and democratic legitimacy. These three concepts are inherently vague, but the chapter assumed a series of simplifications that enabled us to present precise measures of all three. Of course, such simplifications mean that the resulting measures provide only shallow measures of efficiency, power and legitimacy, but at least the measures permit a concrete departure point for further discussion. These measures were:

★ *Efficiency*. We measured efficiency by the passage probability, i.e. the likelihood that a randomly selected issue would win a 'yes' vote in the Council of Ministers. We showed that enlargement has continually lowered the EU's passage probability, but that the 2004 enlargement will lower it by a large and unprecedented amount. We also saw that the voting reforms in the Treaty of Nice will make matters worse even though they were intended to maintain decision-making efficiency.

★ *National power distributions*. We showed that the vote shares of small nations far exceed their population shares. Interpreting vote shares as a measure of power, this says that power in the EU is biased towards small nations. We also showed that this allocation of power goes a long way to explain why EU spending patterns may seem strange, i.e. that several rich nations receive above-average receipts per capita. A more sophisticated measure of power, called the Normalized Banzhaf Index, was also presented. This index measures the probability that a given nation will find itself in a position where it can break a winning coalition.

★ *Legitimacy*. This is by far the vaguest of the three concepts. The approach we adopted was to check whether the allocation of votes in the EU's Council of Ministers lines up against two notions of legitimacy. If the EU is viewed as a union-of-people, a natural yardstick is equal power per citizen. If the EU is viewed as a union-of-states, the natural metric is equal power per Member State.

Self-assessment questions

1. List the main trade-offs stressed by the theory of fiscal federalism. Discuss how the tension between negative spillovers and diversity can explain the fact that the EU has adopted only very limited harmonization of social policies.

2. In many European nations, the trend for the past couple of decades has been to decentralize decision making from the national level to the provincial or regional level. How could you explain this trend in terms of the theory of fiscal federalism?

3. Using the actual Council of Minister votes that will come into force after the 2004 enlargement, list five blocking coalitions that you might think of as 'likely'. Do this using the Nice Treaty definition of a qualified majority. Do the same using the qualified majority definition proposed in the Constitutional Treaty.

4. The formal power measure discussed in the chapter assumes that each voter has an equal probability of saying yes or no on a random issue, and that the votes of the various voters are uncorrelated. That is, the likelihood that voter A says yes on a particular issue is unrelated to whether voter B says yes. However, in many situations, the votes of a group of voters will be correlated. For example, poor EU members are all likely to have similar views on issues concerning spending in poor regions. Work out how this correlation changes the distribution of power (defined as likelihood that a particular voter can break a winning coalition). To be concrete, assume that there are five voters (A, B, C, D and E), that each has 20 votes, that the majority rule is 51 per cent, and that A and B always vote the same way.

5. Using the definition of legitimacy proposed in the text (equal power per person), try to determine whether the US Congress is 'legitimate'. Note that the US Congress is bicameral: the Senate and the House of Representatives. In the Senate, each of the 50 states has two Senators, while the number of Representatives per state is proportional to the state's population.

Essay questions

1. Obtain a copy of the Constitutional Treaty and use the theory of fiscal federalism to discuss the appropriateness of the allocation of competences between the EU and Member States.

2. Using the QMV weights in the EEC6 (see Box 3.4), calculate all possible coalitions, i.e. combinations of 'yes' and 'no' votes among the Six. (Hint: There are $2^6 = 64$ of them.) Identify the winning coalitions and find the passage probability.

3. The 2004 enlargement greatly increased the diversity of preferences inside the EU. Use the theory of fiscal federalism to discuss how this change might suggest a different allocation of competences between the EU and the Member States.

4. Discuss how 'enhanced cooperation' agreements (see Chapter 2 for details) fit into the theory of fiscal federalism. Do you think the increase in the diversity of preferences in the EU stemming from the 2004 enlargement will make these agreements more or less attractive to Member States?

5. The Constitutional Treaty produced by the European Convention was first released in draft form in May 2003. Download this draft and compare the Council of Minister's voting scheme to the scheme in the final version in terms of efficiency and legitimacy.

6. Comparing the Nice Treaty's Declaration on the Future of Europe and the Laeken Declaration's list of questions on the allocation of competencies to the Constitutional Treaty's Title III Part I, write an essay on how well the European Convention accomplished its task on the competency issue.

Further reading: the aficionado's corner

More wide-ranging introduction to fiscal federalism applied to the European Union can be found in Dewatripont *et al.* (1995) and Berglof *et al.* (2003). The latter includes a general discussion that applies the theory to the Constitutional Treaty.

For an opinionated view of what decisions should be allocated to the EU, see Alesina and Wacziarg (1999) *Is Europe Going too Far?*, Carnegie-Rochester Conference on Public Policy. Although this contains several factual errors concerning EU law and policies, it contains a highly cogent application of the theory of fiscal federalism to decision making in the EU.

To learn more about formal measures of power and legitimacy, see Felsenthal and Machover (2001). For historical power distributions, see Laruelle and Widgren (1998).

Useful website

Extensive explanation and use of formal voting measures can be found on http://powerslave.val.utu.fi.

References

Baldwin, R. (1994) *Towards an Integrated Europe*, CEPR, London.

Baldwin, R. and M. Widgren (2004) *Council Voting in the Constitutional Treaty: Devil in the Details*, CEPS Policy Brief No. 53. Download from www.ceps.be or www.hei.unige.ch/~baldwin/policy.html.

Baldwin, R. and M. Widgren (2005) The impact of Turkey's membership on EU voting, CEPS Policy Brief No. 62. Download from www.ceps.be or www.hei.unige.ch/~baldwin/policy.html.

Baldwin, R., E. Berglof, F. Giavazzi and M. Widgren (2001) *Nice Try: Should the Treaty of Nice be Ratified?*, CEPR Monitoring European Integration 11, CEPR, London.

Begg, D., J. Crémer, J.-P. Danthine, J. Edwards *et al.* (1993) *Making Sense of Subsidiarity: How Much Centralization for Europe?*, CEPR Monitoring European Integration 4, CEPR, London.

Berglof, E., B. Eichengreen, G. Roland and C. Wyplosz (2003) *Built to Last: A Political Architecture for Europe*, CEPR Monitoring European Integration 12, CEPR, London.

Bindseil, U. and C. Hantke (1997) 'The power distribution in decision making among EU Member States', *European Journal of Political Economy*, 13: 171–85.

Commons (2002) 'Crossborder shopping and smuggling', House of Commons Library, Research Paper 02/40, London.

Dewatripont, M., F. Giavazzi, I. Harden, T. Persson *et al.* (1995) *Flexible Integration: Towards a More Effective and Democratic Europe*, CEPR Monitoring European Integration 6, CEPR, London.

Felsenthal, D. and M. Machover (2001) *Enlargement of the EU and Weighted Voting in the Council of Ministers*, LSE web-book at www.lse.ac.uk.

Laruelle, A. and M. Widgren (1998) 'Is the allocation of voting power among EU Member States fair?', *Public Choice*, 94: 317–39.

Introduction

Learning economics is a bit like learning a language. If you want to read Shakespeare, Zola or Goethe in the original, you start by memorizing simple, rather inane conversations in English, French or German. If you want to understand the full range of microeconomic effects of European integration, you start by working through simple, rather unrealistic cases. Accordingly, the economics in this book is organized by increasing complexity.

We first study the economics of simple trade policy changes in settings that assume away much real-world complexity. Although the simplifying assumptions are frequently spectacularly unrealistic, they allow us to get straight to the core logic of the economic interaction under study. Having got a handle on the core logic, we progressively introduce more realism and more complications. Such an approach may seem circuitous, but it proves an excellent way of tackling difficult problems. The alternative approach – to admit from the start that everything affects everything – often results in muddled thinking.

This book classifies the economic effects of European integration into three broad headings: allocation effects, accumulation effects and location effects.

★ Allocation effects: integration's impact on the sectoral allocation of economic resources.
★ Accumulation effects: integration's impact on the accumulation of economic resources.
★ Location effects: integration's impact on the geographic location of economic activity.

In looking at each of these, we consider the impact on the overall efficiency, prices, quantities, and the distribution of gains and losses across groups within a nation and between nations.

Allocation effects are addressed in Chapters 4 through 6.

★ Chapter 4 introduces essential microeconomic tools.
★ Chapter 5 uses these to study the essential economics of preferential trade liberalization.

The key simplifications in Chapters 4 and 5 are 'perfect competition' and 'constant returns to scale'.

★ Chapter 6 looks at additional effects that arise once one allows for a more realistic framework in which imperfect competition and scale economies are important. The main focus is on how integrating Europe's many small markets can lead to lower prices and more efficient firms.
★ Chapter 7 expands the range of effects by considering growth effects, that is to say, how integration affects a nation's supply of productive factors (especially capital).

Consideration of the economics of location effects is most naturally presented together with the EU's policies aimed at affecting the location of economic activity. For this reason, we postpone consideration of location effects until Chapter 10.

A new chapter, Chapter 8, looks at the economics of Europe's labour markets from both a microeconomic and a macroeconomic perspective.

> Everything should be made as simple as possible, but not simpler.
>
> *Albert Einstein*

Essential microeconomic tools

INTRODUCTION

This chapter presents the tools that we shall need when we begin our study of European economic integration in the next chapter. The tools are simple because we make a series of assumptions that greatly reduce the complexity of economic interactions. The primary simplification in this chapter concerns the behaviour of firms. In particular, all firms are assumed to be 'perfectly competitive', i.e. we assume that firms take as given the prices they observe in the market. Firms, in other words, believe that they have no impact on prices and that they could sell as much as they want at the market price. A good way of thinking about this assumption is to view each firm as so small that it believes that its choice of output has no impact on market prices. This is obviously a very

rough approximation since even medium-sized firms – the Danish producer of Lego toys, or the Dutch brewer of Heineken, for example – realize that the amount they can sell is related to the price they charge.

The second key simplification concerns technology, in particular scale economies. Scale economies refer to the way that average cost falls as the firm produces at higher scales of production. Almost every industry is subject to some sort of falling average cost, so considering them (in Chapter 6) will be important, but a great deal of simplification can be gained by ignoring them. This simplification in turn allows us to master the essentials before adding more complexity in subsequent chapters.

4.1 Preliminaries I: supply and demand diagrams

To assess the economics of European integration it proves convenient to have a simple yet flexible diagram with which to determine the price and volume of imports, as well as the level of domestic consumption and production. The diagram we use – the 'import supply and import demand diagram' – is based on straightforward supply and demand analysis. But to begin from the beginning, we quickly review where demand and supply curves come from. Note that this section assumes that readers have had some exposure to supply and demand analysis; our treatment is intended as a review rather than as an introduction. Readers who find it too brief should consult an introductory economics textbook such as Mankiw (2000).

Those readers with a good background in microeconomics may want to skip this section, moving straight on to the import demand and supply reasoning introduced in section 4.2.

4.1.1 Demand curves and marginal utility

A demand curve shows how much consumers would buy of a particular good at any particular price. Since we assume that consumers' behaviour is driven by a desire

to spend their money in a way that maximizes their material well-being, it is clear that the demand curve is based on a kind of optimization exercise. To see this, the left-hand panel of Fig. 4.1 plots the 'marginal utility' curve for a typical consumer, i.e. the 'happiness' (measured in euros) that a consumer gets from consuming one more unit of the good under study. If we are considering the demand for music CDs, the marginal utility curve shows how much extra joy a consumer gets from having one more CD. Typically the extra joy from an extra CD will depend upon how many CDs the consumer buys per year. For example, if the consumer buys very few CDs a year, say c' in the diagram, the gain from buying an extra one is likely to be pretty high, for example mu' in the diagram. If, however, the consumer buys lots of CDs, the gain from one more is likely to be much lower, as shown by the pair, c'' and mu''.

This marginal utility curve allows us to work out how much the consumer would buy at any given price. Suppose the consumer could buy as many CDs as she likes at the price p^*. How many would she buy? If the consumer is wise, and we assume she is, she will buy CDs up to the point where the last one bought is just barely worth the price. In the diagram, this level of purchase is given by c^* since the marginal benefit (utility) from buying an extra CD exceeds the cost of doing so (the price) for all levels of purchase up to c^*. At this point, the consumer finds that any further CD would not be worth

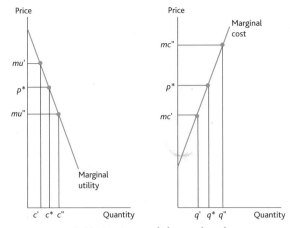

Figure 4.1: *Optimization and demand and supply curves*

the price. For example, the marginal utility from buying $c^* + 1$ CD would be below p^*. As usual, one gets the market demand for CDs by adding all consumers' individual marginal utility curves horizontally (e.g. if the price is p^* and there are 12 000 identical consumers, market demand will be 12 000 times c^*).

A key point to retain from this is that the price that consumers face reflects the marginal utility of consuming a little more.

4.1.2 Supply curves and marginal cost

Derivation of the supply curve follows a similar logic, but here the optimization is done by firms. The right-hand panel of Fig. 4.1 shows the 'marginal cost' curve facing a typical firm (assume that all firms are identical for the sake of simplicity), i.e. the extra cost involved in making one more unit of the good. While the marginal cost of production in the real world often declines with the scale of production, allowing for this involves consideration of scale economies, and these, in turn, introduce a whole range of complicating factors that would merely clutter the analysis at this stage. To keep it simple, we assume that firms are operating at a point where the marginal cost is upward sloping, i.e. that the cost of producing an extra unit rises as the total number of units produced rises. The curve in the diagram shows, for example, that it costs mc' to produce one more unit when the production level (e.g. the number of CDs produced per year) is q'. This is less than the cost, mc'', of producing an extra unit when the firm is producing q'' units per year.

Using this curve we can determine the firm's supply behaviour. Presuming that the firm wants to maximize

profit, the firm will supply the number of goods where the marginal cost just equals the price. For example, if the price is p^*, the firm will want to supply q^* units. Why? If the firm offered one unit less than q^*, it would be missing out on some profit. After all, at that level of output, the price the firm would receive for the good, p^*, exceeds the marginal cost of producing it. Likewise, the firm would not want to supply any more than q^* since, for such a level of output, the marginal cost of producing an extra unit is more than the price received. Again, we get the aggregate supply curve by adding all the firms' individual marginal cost curves horizontally.

A key point here is that under perfect competition the price facing producers reflects the marginal production cost, i.e. the cost of producing one more unit than the firm produces in equilibrium.

4.1.3 Welfare analysis: consumer and producer surplus

Since the demand curve is based on consumers' evaluation of the happiness they get from consuming a good, and the supply curve is based on firms' evaluation of the cost of producing it, the curves can be used to show how consumers and firms are affected by changes in the price. The tools we use, 'consumer surplus' and 'producer surplus', are described below.

Consumers buy up to the point where the marginal utility from the last unit bought just equals the price they pay for it. For all the other units bought, the marginal utility exceeds the price, so the consumer gets what is known as 'consumer surplus' from buying c^* units at price p^* (see Fig. 4.2). How much? For the first unit bought, the marginal unit was mu' but the price paid was only p^*, so the surplus is the area shown by the rectangle **a**. For the second unit, the marginal utility was somewhat lower (not shown in the diagram), so the surplus is lower, specifically it is given by the area **b**. Doing the same for all units shows that buying c^* units at p^* yields a total consumer surplus equal to the sum of all the resulting rectangles. If we take the units to be very finely defined, the triangle defined by the points 1, 2 and 3 gives us the total consumer surplus.

An analogous line of reasoning shows us that the triangle 1, 2, 3 in the right-hand panel gives us a measure of the gain firms get from being able to sell q^* units at a price of p^*. Consider the first unit sold. The marginal cost of producing this unit was mc' but this was sold for p^* so the firm earns a surplus, what we call the 'producer

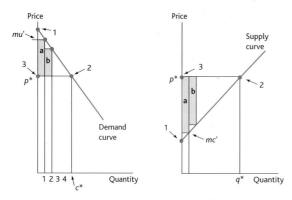

Figure 4.2: *Deriving consumer and producer surplus*

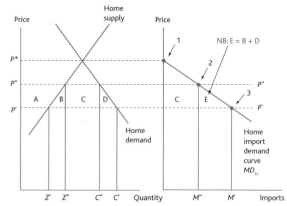

Figure 4.3: *Deriving the import demand curve and welfare changes*

Note: Readers who find these diagrams complicated may benefit from the step-by-step explanations available in the interactive PowerPoint presentation on http://hei.unige.ch/~baldwin/PapersBooks/BW/BW.html (free to download).

surplus', equal to the rectangle **c** in the right panel. Doing the same exercise for each unit sold shows that the total producer surplus is equal to the triangle defined by the points 1, 2 and 3.

If the price changes, the size of the two triangles (consumer surplus and producer surplus) changes. By drawing similar diagrams, you should be able to convince yourself that a price rise increases producer surplus and decreases consumer surplus.

4.2 Preliminaries II: introduction to open economy supply and demand analysis

This section introduces the 'workhorse' diagram in our study of the essential microeconomics of European economic integration: the open economy supply and demand analysis. Readers who have completed a good course in international trade may consider skipping this section and moving straight on to the tariff analysis in section 4.3. The diagram, however, is used throughout this chapter and the next, so even advanced students may wish to review the diagram's foundations; if nothing else, such a review will help with the terminology.

4.2.1 The import demand curve

We first look at where the import demand curve comes from; Fig. 4.3 facilitates the analysis.

The left-hand panel of the diagram depicts a nation's supply and demand curves. If imports were banned for

some reason, the nation would only be able to consume as much as it produced. The normal market interactions would result in a market price of P^* since this is the price where the amount that consumers are willing to buy just matches the amount firms want to produce. Plainly, import demand is zero at P^* (for simplicity, we assume that imported and domestic goods are perfect substitutes). This zero-import point is marked in the right-hand panel as point 1.

How much would the nation import if the price were lower, say P'? The first thing to note is that the import price will fix the domestic price. Since consumers can always import the goods at P', no consumer would pay more than P' for the good. Likewise, there is no reason for domestic firms to charge anything less than P', so P' becomes the domestic price. At price P', consumption demand would be C' and domestic production would be Z'. Since consumers want to buy more of the good at P' than domestic firms are willing to produce, the excess demand would be met by imports. That is to say, imports would be the difference between C' and Z' (in symbols, $M' = C' - Z'$).

What this tells us is that import demand at P' is M'. This point is marked in the right-hand panel of the diagram as point 3. Performing the same exercise for P'' yields point 2, and doing the same for every possible import price yields the import demand curve, i.e. the amount of imports that the nation wants at any given price of imports. The resulting curve is shown as MD_H in the right panel. (For convenience, we often call the nation under study the 'Home' country to distinguish it from its trade partners, what we call the 'Foreign' nations.)

Welfare analysis: MD curves as the marginal benefit of imports

Welfare analysis is simple with this import demand curve. Consider a rise in the import price (i.e. the price faced by Home consumers and producers) from P' to P''. The corresponding equilibrium level of imports drops to M'', since consumption drops to C'' and production rises to Z''. The welfare analysis employed in the left-hand panel involves the notions of consumer and producer surpluses (see section 4.1 for a review of these concepts). Specifically, the price rise from P' to P'' lowers consumer surplus by $A + B + C + D$. The same price rise increases producer surplus by A. The right-hand panel shows how this appears in the import demand diagram. From the left-hand panel, the import price rise means a net loss to the country of $B + C + D$, since the area A cancels out (area A is a gain to Home producers and loss to Home consumers). In the right-hand panel, these changes are shown as areas C and E, where E equals $B + D$.

A powerful perspective: trade volume effects and border price effects

It proves insightful to realize that the MD_H curve shows the marginal benefit of imports to Home. Before explaining why this is so, we show that it is a useful insight. Direct reasoning showed that Home loses areas C and E from a border price rise from P' to P''. Area C is easy to understand. After the price rise, Home pays more for the units it imported at the old price. Area C is the size of this gain. (Say the price rise was €1.2 per unit and M'' was 100; the gain would be €1.2 × 100; geometrically, this is the area C since a rectangle's area is its height times its base.) Understanding area E is where the insight comes in handy. Home reduces its imports at the new price and area E measures how much it loses from the drop in imports. The marginal value of the first lost unit of import is the height of the MD_H curve at M'', but Home had to pay P' for it, so the net loss is the gap between P' and the MD_H curve. If we add up the gaps for all the extra units imported, we get the area E. The jargon terms for these areas are the 'border price effect' (area C), and the 'import volume effect' (area E).

To understand why MD_H is the marginal benefit of imports we use three facts and one bit of logic: (i) the MD_H curve is the difference between the domestic demand curve and the domestic supply curve; (ii) the domestic supply curve is the domestic marginal cost curve, and the domestic demand curve is the domestic

marginal utility curve (see section 4.1 if these points are unfamiliar); and (iii) the difference between domestic marginal utility of consumption and domestic marginal cost of production is the net gain to the nation of producing and consuming one more unit. The logical point is that an extra unit of imports leads to some combination of higher consumption and lower domestic production, and this leads to some combination of higher utility and lower costs; the height of the MD_H curve tells us what that combination is. Or, to put it differently, the nation imports up to the point where the marginal gain from doing so equals the marginal cost. Since the border price is the marginal cost, the border price is also an indication of the marginal benefit of imports.

To see these points in more detail, see the interactive PowerPoint presentations available for free on http://hei.unige.ch/~baldwin/PapersBooks/BW/BW.html.

4.2.2 The import supply curve

Figure 4.4 uses an analogous line of reasoning to derive the import supply schedule. The first thing to keep in mind is that the supply of imports to Home is the supply of exports from foreigners. For simplicity's sake, suppose that there is only one foreign country (simply called 'Foreign' hereafter) and its supply and demand curves look like those in the left-hand panel of the figure.

As with the import demand curve, we start by asking how much Foreign would export for a particular price. For example, how much would it export if the price of its exports was P'? At price P', Foreign firms would produce Z' and Foreign consumers would buy C'. The excess production, equal to $X' = Z' - C'$, would be exported. The fact that Foreign would like to export X' when the

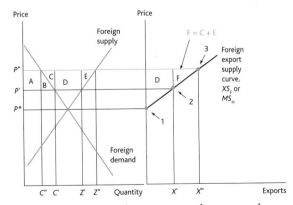

Figure 4.4: *Deriving the export supply curve and welfare changes*

export price is P' is shown in the right-hand panel at point 2. As the price of Foreign exports (i.e. Home's import price) rose, Foreign would be willing to supply a higher level of exports for two reasons: the higher price would (i) induce Foreign firms to produce more and (ii) Foreign consumers to buy less. (Note that, as in the case of import demand, the export price sets the price in Foreign; Foreign firms have no reason to sell for less since they can always export, and competition among Foreign suppliers would prevent any of them from charging Foreign consumers a higher price). For example, the price P'' would bring forth an import supply equal to X'' (this equals $Z'' - C''$); this is shown as point 3 in the right-hand panel. At price P^*, exports are zero. Plotting all such combinations in the right-hand panel produces the export supply curve XS_F. We stress again the simple but critical point that the Foreign export supply is the Home import supply, thus we also label XS_F as MS_H.

Welfare

The left-hand panel of Fig. 4.4 also shows how price changes translate into Foreign welfare changes. If the export price rises from P' to P'', consumers in the exporting country lose by A + B (these letters are not related to those in the previous figure), but the Foreign firms gain producer surplus equal to A + B + C + D + E. The net gain is therefore C + D + E. Using the export supply curve XS_F, we can show the same net welfare change in the right-hand panel as the area D + F. Note that the insight from the MD_H curve extends to the XS_F curve, i.e. the XS_F curve gives the marginal benefit to Foreign of exporting.

This review of import supply and demand was very rapid – probably too rapid for students who have never used such diagrams and probably too long for students who have. For those who find themselves in the first category, there are interactive PowerPoint presentations available on http://hei.unige.ch/~baldwin/PapersBooks/BW/BW.html.

4.2.3 The workhorse diagram: $MD - MS$

The big payoff from having an import supply curve and an import demand curve is that it permits us to find the equilibrium price and quantity of imports. The equilibrium price is found by putting together import demand and supply as shown in the left-hand panel of Fig. 4.5; we drop the 'H' and 'F' subscripts for convenience.

Assuming imports and domestic production are perfect substitutes, the domestic price is set at the point where

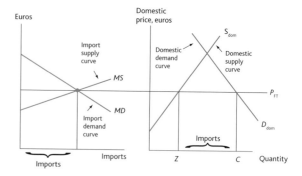

Figure 4.5: *The MD − MS and open economy supply and demand diagrams*

the demand and supply of imports meet, namely P_{FT} (FT stands for free trade). While the import supply and demand diagram, or $MD - MS$ diagram for short, is handy for determining the price and volume of imports, it does not permit us to see the impact of price changes on domestic consumers and firms separately. This is where the right-hand panel becomes useful. In particular, we know that the market clears only when the price is P_{FT}, so we know that Home production equals Z and Home consumption equals C. The equilibrium level of imports may be read off of either panel. In the left-hand panel, it is shown directly; in the right one, it is the difference between domestic consumption and production.

Having explained these basic microeconomic tools, we turn now to using them to study a simple but common real-world problem: the effects of a tax change on imports from all nations.

4.3 MFN tariff analysis

The principle of progressive complexity leads us to take a detour in our drive towards the analysis of preferential trade liberalization in Europe. To introduce the basic method of analysis and gain experience in using the diagrams, we first study the impact of removing the simplest type of trade barrier – a tariff. Although discriminatory liberalization is what happened in Europe, we first look at the non-discriminatory case since it is less complex. For historical reasons, a non-discriminatory tariff is called a 'most favoured nation' tariff, which provides the handy abbreviation, MFN. We also note that all European nations have undertaken substantial MFN tariff liberalizations in the context of World Trade Organization trade negotiations, such as the Uruguay Round, so the analysis has many real-world applications.

4.3.1 Price and quantity effects of a tariff

The first step is to determine how a tariff changes prices and quantities. To be concrete, suppose that the tariff imposed equals T euros per unit.

The first step in finding the post-tariff price is to work out how the tariff changes the *MD–MS* diagram, and here Fig. 4.6 facilitates the analysis. (See section 4.2 if you are unfamiliar with the *MD–MS* diagram.) The right-hand panel of Fig. 4.6 shows the pre-tariff import demand and import supply curves, as *MD* and *MS*, respectively. The left-hand panel shows the foreign export supply curve as *XS*. Note that the vertical axis in the right-hand panel shows the domestic price, whereas the vertical axis in the left-hand panel shows the border price. The difference between the two is simple, but critical (see the note to Fig. 4.6).

A tariff shifts up the MS curve

Imposition of a tariff has no effect on the *MD* curve in the right panel since the *MD* curve tells us how much Home would like to import at any given domestic price. By contrast, imposing a tariff on imports shifts up the *MS* curve by T. The reason is straightforward. After the tariff

is imposed, the domestic price must be higher by T to get Foreign to offer the same quantity as it offered before the tariff. Consider an example. How much would Foreign supply before the tariff if the Home domestic price before the tariff were P_a? The answer, which is given by point 1 on the *MS* curve, is M_a. After the tariff, we get a different answer. To get Foreign to offer M_a after the tariff, the domestic price must be $P_a + T$ so that Foreign sees a border price of P_a.

So far we see that the tariff shifts up the *MS* curve. Now we consider the impact on equilibrium prices and quantities.

The new equilibrium prices and quantities

Even without a diagram, it is intuitively obvious that a tariff (in other words, a tax) raises the domestic price and lowers imports. Why do we need a diagram? The diagram helps us be more specific about this intuition; this specificity allows us to work out how much the nations gain or lose from the tariff. As we shall see, this tells us a great deal about the political economy of trade protection. Returning to our analysis, note that after the tariff, the old import supply curve is no longer valid. The new import supply curve, labelled 'MS with T', is what matters, and the equilibrium price is set at the point where the new import supply curve and the import demand curve cross. As intuition would have it, the new price, marked P' in the diagram, is higher than the pre-tariff price P_{FT} (as already noted, *FT* stands for free trade). Because of the higher domestic price, Home imports are reduced to M' from M_{FT}. To summarize, there are five price and quantity effects of the tariff:

★ The price facing Home firms and consumers (domestic price) rises to P'.
★ The border price (i.e. the price Home pays for imports) falls to $P' - T$; this also means that the price received by Foreigners falls to $P' - T$.
★ The Home import volume falls to M'.

The other two effects cannot be seen in the diagram but are intuitively obvious and could be illustrated explicitly if we included another panel in Fig. 4.6 that resembled the right-hand panel in Fig. 4.5 (this is done later on in Fig. 4.8):

★ Home production rises since Home firms receive a higher price (they see the domestic price since they do not pay the tariffs).
★ Home consumption falls in response to the higher domestic price.

There are also production and consumption effects of the tariff inside the exporting nation. Since the border

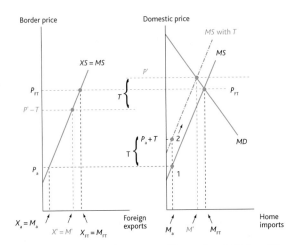

Figure 4.6: *Price and quantity effects of an MFN tariff*

Note: Observe the distinction between the domestic and border prices. The domestic price is the price that domestic consumers pay for the good. The border price is the price foreign producers receive when they sell the good to home. Why can they differ? Because of the tariff (a tariff is nothing more than a tax on imports). When you buy a coffee at a café for, say, €1, the café owner does not get the full €1 because the owner has to pay a tax, called the VAT, on your purchase. As a result, the price that the café owner receives is only 80 cents (the VAT is 20 per cent in this example) even though you pay 100 cents. In exactly the same way, foreigners receive a price (the border price) that equals the domestic price minus the tariff.

price falls, Foreign production drops and Foreign consumption rises. We could see this explicitly if we put a diagram like the left-hand panel of Fig. 4.4 to the left of the diagram in Fig. 4.6.

4.3.2 Welfare effects of a tariff

Having worked out the price and quantity effects, it is simple to calculate the welfare effects of the tariffs, that is to say, who wins, who loses and by how much.

Recall that the *MD* curve comes from optimization by Home consumers and producers, while the $XS = MS$ curve reflects optimization by Foreign consumers and producers. What this means is that we can evaluate the Home welfare effects of the price and quantity changes using only the *MD* curve, and the Foreign welfare effects using only the $XS = MS$ curve, as shown by Fig. 4.7.

We start with the Foreign welfare impact since it is easier. At an intuitive level, we should expect the tariff to harm Foreigners since it means they get a lower price (the border price drops) and they export less. Using the diagram we can quantify these losses. The welfare impact is shown by the areas B and D in the leftmost panel. The area B represents the direct loss from the lower price and D represents the loss from the lower level of sales. As usual, these are the trade price effect (area B) and the trade volume effect (area D).

The diagram also shows the impact of the price change on the welfare of Home residents. Intuitively, it should be clear that Home consumers will lose from the higher domestic price and Home firms will gain from the same, but that the losers will lose more than the gainers will gain since Home consumption exceeds Home

production. The diagram allows us to be more precise about these welfare effects.

As we showed in section 4.1, the loss in the 'private surplus' (i.e. the sum of the changes in consumer surplus and producer surplus) from the price rise from P_{FT} to P' is given by the area A + C in the middle panel. Since a tariff is a tax, the final thing to consider is the impact on Home government revenue. Since Home collects tariff revenue equal to the tariff times the number of units imported, this gain equals the area A + B in the middle panel of Fig. 4.7. Adding together the change in private surplus (minus A and minus C) and the gain in revenue (plus A plus B), the net loss is the area C minus the area B, which we write as B − C for short.

A useful condensation

The first time one works through these welfare calculations, it is useful to separate the Home and Foreign effects using separate diagrams (the left and middle panels in Fig. 4.7). This separation emphasizes the fact that Foreign welfare effects can be derived from the price and quantity changes using only the *XS* curve, and, similarly, the Home welfare effect can be derived from the price and quantity effects using only the *MD* curve. Yet, once one is familiar with the underpinnings of the areas A, B, C and D, it is convenient to condense the analysis into a single diagram, like the right-hand panel in Fig. 4.7.

To summarize, using either the two-panel analysis or the condensed analysis, we find:
★ The tariff reduces Foreign welfare since it means they sell less and receive a lower price. The loss in welfare, measured in euros, equals area B plus area D.
★ The tariff creates private-sector winners and losers (Home firms gain, Home consumers lose), but the losers (consumers) lose more than gainers (firms) gain; the net impact is − A − C.
★ Home collects tariff revenue equal to A + B.
★ The overall Home welfare change, including both revenue and the net private loss, is B − C.
★ The net effect, B − C, may be positive or negative; the relative sizes of B and C depend upon the slopes of the *MD* and *MS* curves and on the size of *T*.
★ The global impact of the tariff, adding Home and Foreign welfare changes together, is definitely negative and equal to the area − C − D.

Before moving on, note that, as in section 4.1, we can trace through the distributional effects of the welfare changes, e.g. the loss to Home consumers and the gains to Home firms, using a diagram that resembles the right-hand panel in Fig. 4.5. This is done in Box 4.1.

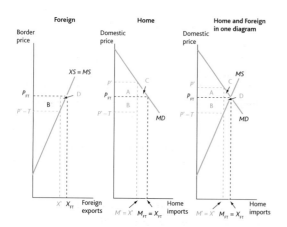

Figure 4.7: *Welfare effects of an MFN tariff*

Home and foreign welfare effects: distributional consequences

The analysis in Fig. 4.7 focused on the overall welfare impact on Home and Foreign. It did not allow us to see the distributional effects of the tariffs, i.e. the impact of the tariff on different groups within Home. Since the politics of an import tariff often depend heavily on the tariff's distributional impact, it is handy to have a diagram where we can see the distributional effects and the overall effects. Figure 4.8, which is based on the open-economic supply and demand diagram, is the diagram that serves this purpose.

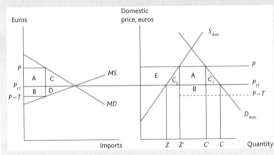

Figure 4.8: *Distributional and overall welfare effects of an MFN tariff*

In both panels of the diagram, the tariff-induced changes in prices and quantities are shown. As noted in the text, the overall private surplus change, that is, the loss to Home consumers minus the gain to Home producers, is minus the areas A and C in the left-hand panel. The right-hand panel allows us to see the producer and consumer surplus components separately. The loss to consumers from the price rise (from P_{FT} to P') is minus the areas $E + C_1 + A + C_2$. The gain to Home producers is the area E. Note that the area C in the left-hand panel equals the sum of the two triangles, C_1 and C_2, in the right-hand panel. The gain in government revenue from the tax on imports is just equal to the area $A + B$.

The gain to producers is, of course, the usual reason that governments impose a tariff: they want to help domestic producers. Despite the fact that this harms domestic consumers, governments often find tariffs to be politically attractive since domestic producers are often better organized politically than are domestic consumers.

4.3.3 Tariffs as a way of taxing foreigners

The result that a tariff might make the Home country better or worse off is worth looking at from a different angle. The two parts of Home's net welfare impact, namely B − C, represent very different kinds of changes:

★ The area B is the 'trade price effect', i.e. the gain from paying less for imports. We can also think of it as the amount of the new tariff revenue that is borne by foreigners. This statement requires some explaining. In the real world, the importing firm pays the whole tariff, so one might think that the importing firm bears the full burden of the import tax. This would be wrong. Part of the burden is passed on to Home residents via higher prices. How much? Well, pre-tariff, the domestic price was P_{FT} and post-tariff it is P', so the difference shows how much of the tariff is passed on to Home residents. Since this price hike applies to a level of imports equal to M', we can say that the share of the tariff revenue borne by Home residents is area A. Using the same logic, we see that some of the tariff

burden is also passed back to Foreign suppliers. The before-versus-after border price gap is P_{FT} minus $(P' − T)$ and this applies to M' units of imports. So area B is a measure of how much of the tariff revenue is borne by foreigners.

★ Area C is the 'trade volume effect', i.e. the impact of lowering imports. Here is the argument. The *MD* curve shows the marginal benefit to Home of importing each unit (see section 4.2 if this reasoning is unfamiliar to you). Given this, the gap between the *MD* curve and P_{FT} gives us a measure of how much Home loses for each unit it ceases to import. The area of the triangle C is simply all the gaps summed from M' to M_{FT}.

To put it differently, area B represents Home's gain from taxing foreigners whereas area C represents an efficiency loss from the tariff.

Given all this, we can say that if *T* raises Home welfare, then it does so only because the tariff allows the Home government to indirectly tax foreigners enough to offset the tariff's inefficiency effects on the Home economy. That is, T causes economic inefficiency at Home but T is also a way of exploiting foreigners. Since the exploitation gains may outweigh the inefficiency effects, Home may gain from imposing a tariff.

4.3.4 Global welfare effects and retaliation

The global welfare impact is simply a matter of summing up effects and it turns out to be negative. The net Home welfare effect is $B - C$. For foreign it is $-B - D$. The global welfare change is thus a loss, namely $-C - D$.

Put this way, the gains from a tariff are clearly suspect. For example, if Home and Foreign were symmetric and both imposed tariffs, both would lose the efficiency triangle C, and the gain to Home of B on imports would be lost to Home on its exports to Foreign. Home would also lose the deadweight triangle D on exports, so the net loss to each of the symmetric nations would be $-C - D$. In short, protection by all nations is worse than a zero-sum game. It is exactly this point that underpins the economics of WTO tariff-cutting negotiations. If only one nation liberalizes, it might lose. If, however, the nation's liberalization is coordinated with its trading partners' liberalization, the zero-sum aspect tends to disappear.

4.4 Types of protection: an economic classification

Tariffs are only one of many types of import barriers that European integration has removed. The first phase of EU integration, 1958–68, focused on tariff removal, but the Single Market Programme that was started in 1986 focused on a much wider range of 'non-tariff barriers'.

While there are several methods of categorizing such barriers, it proves useful to focus on how the barriers affect so-called trade rents. A tariff, for instance, drives a wedge between the Home price and the border price (i.e. the price paid to foreigners). This allows someone (in the tariff case it will be the Home government) to indirectly collect the 'profit' from selling at the high domestic price while buying at the low border price. For historical reasons, economists refer to such profits (area $A + B$ in Fig. 4.9) as 'rents'. When it comes to welfare analysis, we must watch the trade rents closely. For some import barriers, Home residents get the rents, but for others no rents are created, or foreigners get the rents. This distinction is highlighted by distinguishing three

categories of trade barriers: domestically captured rent (DCR) barriers, foreign-captured rent (FCR) barriers and 'frictional' barriers.

4.4.1 DCR barriers

Tariffs form the classic DCR barrier. Here the Home government gets the trade rents. From a Home nationwide welfare perspective, however, it does not really matter whether the government, Home firms or Home consumers earn these rents, as long as the rents are captured domestically. What sorts of barriers other than tariffs would lead to domestically captured rents? Some forms of quotas are DCR barriers. A quota is a quantitative limit on the number of goods that can be imported each year. To control the number of foreign goods entering the country, the government hands out a fixed number of import licences and 'collects' one licence per unit imported. The price and quantity effects of a quota that restricts imports to M' in Fig. 4.9 are identical to the effects of a tariff equal to T. The point is that if imports are limited to M', then the gap between domestic consumption and production can be no more than M', implying that the domestic price must be driven up to P'. Another way to say this is that T is the 'tariff equivalent' of the quota. Now consider the trade rents. With a quota, whoever has the licence can buy the goods at the border price $P' - T$ and resell them in the Home market for P. This earns the licence holders $A + B$. If the government gives the licences to Home residents, then the quota is a DCR barrier. If it gives them to foreigners, the quota is an FCR barrier.

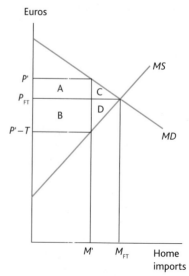

Figure 4.9: *Home welfare effects of import protection*

4.4.2 FCR barriers

A prime example of an FCR barrier is a 'price undertaking', a trade barrier that was commonly imposed against imports from central and eastern Europe before the 2004 enlargement. In these cases, the EU strikes an agreement whereby foreign producers undertake to sell their goods at a price no lower than that agreed. For example, if the agreed level were P' from Fig. 4.9, the price undertaking would have the same price and quantity effects as a tariff T. Importantly, however, the undertaking allows foreign producers, rather than the Home government, to garner the rents $A + B$. Throughout the industrialized world, and in the EU in particular, it is usual for trade barriers to be arranged so that foreigners earn the rents. One reason is that trade rents are used as a kind of gift to soothe foreign companies and governments that are likely to be angered by the imposition of a trade barrier.

A more recent example of an FCR barrier is the EU's restrictions on Chinese clothing exports. The European Commission negotiated limits on how fast Chinese exports to the EU could grow. But since it is the Chinese who control the quantity (via export licences), it is the Chinese who get the trade rents. This was done on purpose to appease the Chinese government. The USA also imposed restraints on Chinese clothing exports but it is the USA that controls the quotas, so the quota rents go to US residents. No wonder the Chinese were happier

about the way the EU reacted. Policy in this area was evolving as this edition went to print; for the latest see http://europa.eu.int/comm/trade/issues/sectoral/index_en.htm and click through 'textile sector'.

Finally, note that an FCR barrier harms national welfare more than does a DCR barrier. Specifically, the welfare cost of an FCR barrier is always negative, i.e. $-A - C$, instead of being ambiguous, i.e. $B - C$. Moreover, the foreign welfare impact is now $A - D$, so an FCR barrier may end up helping foreigners.

4.4.3 Frictional barriers

The main type of trade barrier remaining inside the EU consists of what are sometimes called 'technical barriers to trade' (TBTs). Western European countries often restrict imports by subjecting them to a range of policies that increase the real cost of buying foreign goods. Some examples of TBTs are excessive bureaucratic 'red-tape' restrictions and industrial standards that discriminate against foreign goods. One of the most famous examples is discussed in Box 4.2.

Such barriers raise the cost of imports by increasing the difficulty, and thereby the cost, of selling to the Home market. Nobody gets the rents with such barriers since no rents are created. From the Home perspective,

---

Box 4.2 Cassis de Dijon: a history-making technical barrier to trade

One very common type of frictional barrier concerns health and safety regulations that have the side effect of hindering trade. Perhaps the most famous of these was a German regulation that forbade the importation of certain low-alcohol spirits including the sweet French liqueur, Cassis – used in making the famous white wine drink, Kir. This regulation was challenged before the European Court of Justice as a barrier to trade. When challenged on this regulation, the German government argued that the prohibition was necessary to protect public health (since weak spirits more easily promote alcohol tolerance) and to protect consumers (since consumers might buy weak spirits, thinking they were strong). In 1979, the Court ruled that the measure was not necessary since wide-spread availability of low-alcohol drinks (e.g. beer) in Germany made the prohibition ineffective in furthering public health. It also found that putting the alcohol content on the label was sufficient to protect consumers, so the import ban was not necessary for the protection of consumers. This Court ruling resulted in the frictional barrier being removed. More importantly, it established the basic principle known as 'mutual recognition' whereby goods that are lawfully sold in one EU nation shall be presumed to be safe for sale in all EU nations. Exceptions to this principle require explicit motivation. By the way, the formal name for this Court case is *Rewe-Zentral AG v Bundesmonopolverwaltung für Branntwein*; no wonder it is called *Cassis de Dijon*.

frictional and FCR barriers have identical effects: using the areas in Fig. 4.9, Home loses A + C. From the Foreign perspective, an FCR barrier is superior. Specifically, the Foreign welfare change is A − D for FCR, but −B − D for a frictional barrier.

Since frictional barriers are bad for a nation, one may ask why they are so prevalent. Box 4.3 provides one explanation.

One important class of frictional, i.e. cost-creating, barriers involves industrial and health standards that are chosen at least in part to restrict imports. For example, some countries refuse to accept safety tests that are performed in foreign countries, even in highly industrialized nations. This forces importers to retest their products in the local country. Beyond raising the real cost of imported goods, this sort of barrier delays the introduction of new products. While this clearly harms consumers, home producers may benefit since it may give them time to introduce competing varieties.

Another example involves imposing industrial, health, safety or environmental standards that differ from internationally recognized norms. It is often difficult to know objectively whether an unusual regulation or standard represents a valid public interest concern or whether it is just a protectionist device. In fact, both motives are usually behind the adoption of such measures.

Regardless of why such policies are adopted, they have the effect of protecting home producers or service providers. Home firms design their products with these standards in mind whereas foreign firms, for whom the home market may be relatively unimportant, are unlikely to do so. Bringing imported products into conformity raises the real cost of imports.

For example, all cars sold in Sweden must have wipers for the headlights. While this policy may have some merit as a safety regulation (in the old days Sweden had lots of dusty rural roads), it also has the effect of raising

Box 4.3 Why do frictional barriers arise so often?

Government agencies charged with formulating and enforcing standards are often 'captured' by special-interest groups from the regulated industries. Moreover, the domestic firms that are to be subjected to the standards often play an important role in setting the standards. For example, when regulating a highly technical field such as elevators, the government (who probably does not employ many full-time elevator experts) naturally asks the opinions of domestic firms that produce elevators. With an eye to their foreign competitors, they quite naturally push for standards that raise the cost of imported goods more than the cost of locally produced goods.

An example can be found in the paper industry. Sweden and Finland produce paper mainly from new trees whereas French and German paper producers use a lot of recycled paper and rags. In the early 1990s, the EU was considering a regulation that would require all paper sold in the EU to contain a certain fraction of recycled paper. This sounds like a public interest regulation. However, it would also have had the effect of eliminating the resource-based advantage of Swedish and Finnish firms, much to the joy of French and German firms. In other words, it would have raised the real cost of imports (since the Nordic producers would have had to switch to less efficient techniques). As it turns out, it is not clear which production method is greener. Recycling paper requires lots of chemicals that may be released into the environment, whereas setting up more tree plantations is, well, green – a point that was not raised by French and German paper producers.

Since Finland and Sweden joined the EU, the regulation was not adopted, but this shows the subtle mixing of public interest and protectionism that inevitably arises when nations adopt regulations and standards. Of course nations do need health, safety, environmental and industrial standards, so we cannot eliminate frictional barriers by just abolishing all regulation. This is one of the things tackled by the EU's 1992 programme.

the price of imported cars in Sweden more than it raises the price of Swedish cars. From the drawing board onwards, all models of Volvos and Saabs – and their production facilities – are designed with these headlight wipers in mind. For other car makers, take Renault as an example, the Swedish market is far too small to really matter. The design of Renaults and Renault's mass production facilities are not optimized for the installation of headlight wipers. Consequently, while it is expensive to put headlight wipers on both Swedish and French cars, it is much more so for French cars. This gives the Swedish car makers an edge in Sweden. Similar sorts of barriers give the French an edge in their domestic market.

Such barriers are extremely common (Box 4.3 explores why). In fact, the EU initiated the 1992 Single Market Programme with the express intent of eliminating such barriers via the mutual recognition of product standards (with minimum harmonization).

With the MFN case as background, we are ready to turn, in Chapter 5, to the analysis of discriminatory trade liberalization of the types undertaken in Europe.

4.5 Summary

This chapter presented the essential microeconomic tools for trade policy analysis in the simplified world where we assume there is no imperfect competition and no scale economies. The two most important diagrams are the open-economy supply and demand diagram (right-hand panel of Fig. 4.5), and the *MD–MS* diagram (left-hand panel of Fig. 4.5). The *MD–MS* diagram provides a compact way of working out the impact of import protection on prices, quantities and overall Home and Foreign welfare. The open-economy supply and demand diagram allows us to consider the distributional impact of import protection, i.e. to separate the overall effect into its component effects on Home consumers, Home producers and Home revenue.

The chapter also discussed types of trade barriers in Europe and classified them according to what happens to the trade rents. Under the first type, DCR barriers, the rents go to domestic residents. For FCR barriers, the rents go to foreigners, and with frictional barriers the rents disappear. European integration consisted primarily of removing DCR barriers up until the mid-1970s. Subsequent goods-market liberalization has focused on frictional barriers.

Self-assessment questions

1. Using a diagram like Fig. 4.8, show the full Foreign welfare effects of imposing a Home tariff equal to T, i.e. show the impact on Foreign producers and Foreign consumers separately.

2. In August 2005, EU clothing retailers such as Sweden's H&M complained about the new EU restrictions on imports from China that were imposed after complaints from EU clothing producers based in Italy, France, Spain, Portugal and Greece. Use a diagram like Fig. 4.8 to explain the positions of the various EU interest groups.

3. One way to think about the slope of the MS curve is in terms of the 'size' of the home nation. The idea is that the demand from a very small nation has a very small impact on the world price. For example, Switzerland could probably increase its oil imports by 10 per cent without having any impact on the world oil price. Using a diagram like Fig. 4.7, show that the welfare costs of imposing an MFN tariff are larger for smaller nations, interpreting this in terms of the MS curve's slope. Show that when the MS curve is perfectly flat, the welfare effects are unambiguously negative.

4. Using a diagram like Fig. 4.7, show that a country facing an upward-sloping MS curve can gain – starting from free trade – from imposing a sufficiently small tariff. (Hint: The rectangle gains and triangle losses both increase in size as the tariff gets bigger, but the rectangle gets bigger faster.) Show that any level of a frictional or FCR barrier lowers Home welfare.

5. Using the results from the previous exercise, consider the impact of Home imposing a tariff on Foreign exports and Foreign retaliating with a tariff on Home's exports. Assume that the MS and MD curves for both goods (Home exports to Foreign and Foreign exports to Home) are identical. Starting from a situation where Home and Foreign both impose a tariff of T, show that both unambiguously gain if both remove their tariffs, but one nation might lose if it removed its tariff unilaterally. By the way, this exercise illustrates why nations that are willing to lower their tariffs in the context of a WTO multilateral trade agreement are often not willing to remove their tariffs unilaterally.

6. Using a diagram like Fig. 4.5, show that an import tariff equal to T has exactly the same impact on prices, quantities and welfare as a domestic consumption tax equal to T and a domestic production subsidy equal to T. (Hint: A production subsidy lowers the effective marginal cost of domestic firms and so lowers the domestic supply curve by T.)

7. Using a diagram like Fig. 4.7, show the impact on quantities, prices and welfare when Home has no tariff, but Foreign charges an export tax equal to T.

8. Using a diagram like Fig. 4.5, show the impact on quantities, prices and welfare when Home has no tariff, but Foreign imposes an export quota with a tariff-equivalent of T.

9. Using a diagram like Fig. 4.7, show that the welfare effects of a quota that restricts imports to M' are exactly the same as a tariff equal to T; assume that each quota licence (i.e. the right to import one unit) is sold by the government to the highest bidder.

Essay questions

1. The concepts of consumer surplus, producer surplus and tariff revenue are meant to capture the key welfare effects of trade policy. Discuss two or three aspects of socio-economic well-being that are not captured by these concepts.

2. The welfare analysis in this chapter assumes that governments weigh one euro of consumer surplus and producer surplus equally. Find an account in a newspaper of a real-world trade policy change and summarize the analysis in the article (the basic facts, the points of view report, etc.). Does the newspaper article make it seem as if the government cares equally about consumers and producers?

3. Go on to the European Commission's website and find an example of a frictional barrier that the Commission is trying to remove. Explain what the barrier is, how it is justified by Member States and why it was not removed during the 1992 Single Market Programme. One URL to try is: http://europa.eu.int/comm/internal_market/en/index.htm.

4. Write an essay describing the events that led up to the EU's and USA's imposition of protection against Chinese clothing exports in 2005. Be sure to mention the role of the Uruguay Round agreement on the elimination of the Multifibre Agreement, the surge of exports, the Chinese export tax, and reactions of buyers and makers of clothing in the EU and USA. Use the diagrams developed in this chapter to explain the positons taken by the US, EU and Chinese governments as well as the positions of EU and US buyers and makers of clothing.

Further reading: the aficionado's corner

Every undergraduate textbook on international economics has a chapter on tariff analysis that covers the same material as this chapter. One particularly accessible treatment can be found in Krugman and Obstfeld (2000). For much more on the economics of trade protection, see Vousden (1990).

Useful websites

The World Bank's website provides extensive research on trade policy analysis. This includes many papers on non-discriminatory trade policy but also a very large section on preferential trade arrangements under the heading of 'regionalism'. See www.worldbank.org.

The Commission's website on trade issues can be found at http://europa.eu.int/comm/trade/index_en.htm. It has lots of information on the latest EU trade policy changes.

References

Krugman, P. and M. Obstfeld (2000) *International Economics*, HarperCollins, New York.

Mankiw, G. (2000) *Principles of Economics*, Thomson Learning, New York.

Vousden, N. (1990) *The Economics of Trade Protection*, Cambridge University Press, Cambridge.

> ... the ideas of economists and political philosophers, both when they are right and when they are wrong, are more powerful than is commonly understood. Indeed the world is ruled by little else. Practical men, who believe themselves to be exempt from any intellectual influences, are usually the slaves of some defunct economist.
>
> *John Maynard Keynes, 1935*

5

The essential economics of preferential liberalization

INTRODUCTION

This chapter begins our progressive study of the microeconomics of European integration, focusing on the preferential, i.e. discriminatory, aspects. The discriminatory effects are important since they played a central role in the spread of European integration, as was discussed in Chapter 1. The main goal of this chapter is to provide a framework for analysing the essential economics of preferential liberalization.

5.1 Analysis of unilateral discriminatory liberalization

The non-discriminatory liberalization studied in the previous chapter assumed that Home imposed the same tariff on imports from all nations since all trading partners were lumped into one nation called 'Foreign'. While useful for pedagogical purposes, all European countries, and indeed most countries in the world, maintain different barriers against imports from different nations. Studying such discriminatory liberalization is the topic of the present chapter.

The organization of our study of the economic impact of discriminatory liberalization is directed by the principle of progressive complexity. In this section, we look at what happens when a nation removes its tariff on imports from only one of its trading partners. Of course, European integration has always involved two-way reductions in tariffs (e.g. France and Germany lowered their tariffs against each other's exports at the same time during the 1960s), but we postpone consideration of changes in partner tariffs until the next section for the sake of clarity.

Again, we continue with the last chapter's simplifying assumptions of no imperfect competition and no increasing returns (NICNIR). While these assumptions are both monumentally unrealistic, they are pedagogically convenient (see Box 5.1), and, more importantly, they allow us to study the main economic logic of

---

<table>
<tr><td>**Box 5.1**</td><td># Why use the NICNIR framework?</td></tr>
</table>

There are good reasons for starting our study of the economics of European integration in the highly simplified NICNIR framework.

NICNIR is the simplest framework that allows us to understand the discriminatory effect of preferential liberalization – an effect that plays a central role in understanding the economic forces driving the spread of European integration. In the early 1960s, in the mid-1970s and again in the mid-1980s, EU members embarked on liberalizations that created discriminatory effects that induced non-members to react (see Chapter 1 for details). In the 1960s, the UK reacted by forming a parallel free trade area, the European Free Trade Association (EFTA), and, in the following year, by putting in an application for EU membership. That application received a curt *non* from French President Charles de Gaulle, but when it was renewed and eventually accepted in the early 1970s, the EFTA members that did not follow the UK into the EU reacted by signing FTAs with the enlarged EU. The NICNIR framework allows us to present the core logic behind these reactions in a setting that is as intellectually uncluttered as possible.

Because the NICNIR framework is so simple, it is a good tool for illustrating a variety of effects and for analysing a variety of policies that would be too complex to study in more realistic frameworks – at least too complex for the sort of diagrammatic analysis employed in this book.

discriminatory liberalization without having to invest a lot of time in learning new tools (that is postponed until the next chapter).

Before starting, we note that the theory of preferential liberalization is often taught using an additional simplifying factor called the 'small economy' assumption. While this simplifies the analysis from the perspective of the Home country, it also assumes away the critical impact that preferential liberalization has on excluded nations. Interested readers can find this case in Annex A at the end of the chapter.

5.1.1 The PTA diagram

Consideration of discriminatory liberalization requires at least three countries – at least two integrating nations and at least one excluded nation. Our first task is to extend the workhorse MD–MS diagram from Chapter 4 to allow for two sources of imports. Figure 5.1 shows how.

Free trade equilibrium

The two leftmost panels of Fig. 5.1 show the export supply curves for two individual countries, which we call Partner and Rest of World (RoW) for reasons that will become obvious. To minimize complications, we assume that Partner and RoW are identical; interested readers may want to work out how the diagram and analysis change when the foreign countries are asymmetric.

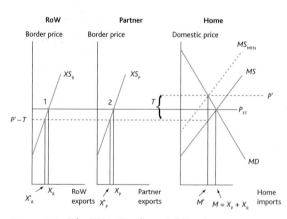

Figure 5.1: *The PTA (Preferential Trade Arrangement) diagram*

Note: Readers who find the diagrams in this section somewhat involved may benefit from the step-by-step explanations available in the interactive PowerPoint presentation that can be freely downloaded from http://hei.unige.ch/~baldwin/PapersBooks/BW.BW.html.

To find the free trade price in equilibrium, we need to find the intersection between the MD curve and the MS curve, as in Chapter 4. But what is the MS curve? Here there are two potential suppliers of imports, so we must aggregate their supply curves. As in standard microeconomics, the total supply of imports to Home is the horizontal sum of the two export supply curves. This summed curve is shown as MS in the right-hand panel (it is flatter than XS_P and XS_R since a given price increase will raise supply from both Partner and RoW). The equilibrium price, when no tariff is imposed, is where MS and MD cross, namely P_{FT}. Total imports are M. To find the imports from both Partner and RoW, we use each supplier's XS curve to see how much would be offered at the price P_{FT}. The answers are given by the points 1 and 2 in the diagram, namely RoW and Partner export X'_P and X'_R, respectively.

MFN tariff with two import suppliers

In order to investigate the impact of removing a tariff on a preferential basis, we need to establish the baseline where a tariff, equal to T, is applied to both nations. To this end, we first work out the effects of Home imposing a tariff of T on both RoW and Partner. As always, the first task is to find how the tariff affects the MS curve. As we saw in Chapter 4, an MFN tariff shifts the MS curve up by T since the domestic price would have to be T higher to elicit the same quantity of imports after the tariff is imposed. The new MS curve is shown in the diagram as the curve marked MS_{MFN}. As before, tariff protection does nothing to the MD curve.

The intersection of MS_{MFN} and MD tells us that the post-tariff equilibrium domestic price for imports is P' and the new import level is M'; with P' as the new domestic price, the new border price is P' − T. At this border price, both import suppliers are willing to supply less, namely X'_R and, X'_P as shown in the diagram.

5.1.2 Price and quantity effects of discriminatory liberalization

What happens when Home removes T but only for imports from Partner, i.e. when Home unilaterally liberalizes on a preferential basis?

The first step in answering this question is, as always, to see how the preferential liberalization alters the MS curve. The new MS curve, which we will call MS_{PTA}, where PTA stands for preferential trade arrangement, is shown in Fig. 5.2.

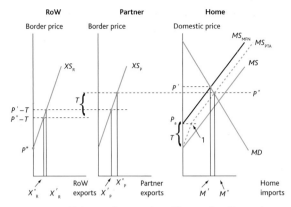

Figure 5.2: *Price and quantity effects of unilateral, discriminatory tariff liberalization*

The position of the MS_{PTA} is quite intuitive. After the preferential tariff liberalization, half of Home's import suppliers get duty-free access; the other half pays T. It seems natural therefore that MS_{PTA} lies between the free-trade and MFN-protection MS curves. In fact, MS_{PTA} is halfway between the import supply curve with no tariffs, namely MS, and the import supply curve with tariffs on all imports, namely MS_{MFN}. One small qualification, however, is necessary, and considering this helps us see how MS_{PTA} is constructed.

The tariff prevents RoW firms from exporting until the domestic price in Home rises above the price marked P_a in Fig. 5.2. The reason is that when Home's domestic price is below P_a, the border price faced by RoW exports is below their zero-supply price (marked as P^* in the diagram). Partner-based firms, by constast, would export when Home's domestic price is slightly below P_a since they face Home's domestic price (not the Home price minus the tariff). As a consequence, Partner firms – but only Partner firms – will supply imports at the domestic price P_a, i.e. up to the point marked 1 in the diagram. Thus the MS_{PTA} curve is Partner's XS curve up to point 1. After that, both foreigners supply imports, so the MS_{PTA} resumes its normal slope.

The domestic price change and conflicting border price changes

The MS_{PTA} and MD curves intersect at P'', so this is the new, post-PTA domestic price. As expected, the new domestic price is lower than the old MFN tariff price since imports from Partner can now enter duty-free.

The impact on the border price is a bit more complex. For Partner-based firms, the liberalization means that they now face Home's domestic price, P', so for them the liberalization means that their border price *rises* from

$P' - T$ to P'' (since they no longer pay the tariff, they get the full price paid by Home consumers). For RoW, however, the border price falls from $P' - T$ to $P'' - T$. One way to think of the RoW border price effect is to note that in order to stay competitive with Partner firms' exports, RoW firms must cut their border price so that Home consumers see the same price for imports from RoW and Partner in the Home market.

Supply switching

Given that Partner firms see a price rise, they increase exports from X'_p to X''_p. RoW exports fall from X'_R to X''_R because their border price has fallen. This combination of higher Partner sales and lower RoW sales is known as the 'supply switching', or 'trade diversion', effect of discriminatory liberalization. Defining it directly, supply switching occurs when a discriminatory liberalization induces the Home nation to switch some of its purchases to import suppliers who benefit from the PTA and away from suppliers based in nations that did not benefit from the PTA.

Did this sort of supply switching occur in Europe? When the EEC eliminated tariffs on a discriminatory basis during the formation of its customs union between 1958 and 1968, Box 5.2 shows that supply switching did occur.

These price and quantity effects may seem strange at first. The preferential tariff cut raises the price that Partner exporters receive but lowers the price faced by RoW exporters. Moreover, Home buys more from the nation whose border price has risen and less from the nation whose border price has fallen. This strangeness is simple to understand. The discriminatory liberalization distorts price signals so that Home consumers are not aware of the fact that Partner goods cost the nation more than RoW goods. To the Home consumer, imports from the two sources cost the same, namely P''.

To summarize, the price and quantity effects are:
★ Home's domestic price falls from P' to P''.
★ The border price falls from $P' - T$ to $P'' - T$ for RoW imports.
★ The border price rises from $P' - T$ to P'' for Partner imports.
★ The RoW exports fall.
★ The Partner exports rise.
★ Total Home imports rise from M' to M''.

Interested readers may want to add a fourth panel to Fig. 5.2 by drawing a standard open economy supply and

Box 5.2

The supply-switching effects of the formation of the EEC customs union

Figure 5.3 shows the trade volume effects that occurred when the EEC6 removed their internal tariffs between 1958 and 1968. In the left-hand panel, the columns show the import shares broken down into intra-EEC6 imports, imports from six other European nations (the ones who joined in the EU's first three enlargements), and the rest of the world.

Note that as the EEC6 share of exports to itself rose from about 30 per cent in 1958 to about 45 per cent in 1968, the share of EEC imports from other nations had to fall. Part of the displacement occurred with respect to imports from other non-EEC European nations. As the dark bars show, the import share from six other western European nations (UK, Ireland, Portugal, Spain, Denmark and Greece) fell during this period by a small amount, from around 9 per cent to 7 per cent. The main displacement came from the rest of the world, mainly imports from the USA. The right-hand panel, however, shows that imports from all sources were in fact growing rapidly. Thus we have to interpret the 'supply switching' as a relative phenomenon. That is, if the customs union had not been formed, imports from non-EEC6 members would have risen even faster.

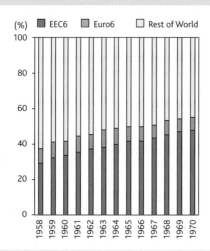 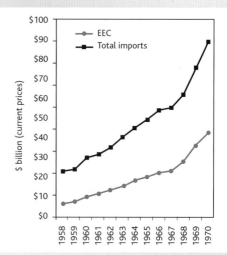

Figure 5.3: *Supply switching and formation of the Common Market, 1958–70*

Note: Left-hand panel shows share of EEC6's imports from the three regions. Euro6 are the six countries that joined the EU by the mid-1980s, the UK, Ireland, Denmark, Spain, Portugal and Greece.

Source: European Commission.

demand figure for Home to the right of the *MD–MS* panel. Doing so allows you to see that Home production falls and Home consumption rises owing to the domestic price drop.

5.1.3 Welfare effects

Showing the welfare implications in the same figure as the price and quantity effects would complicate the diagram too much. Figure 5.4 reproduces Fig. 5.2, omitting unnecessary lines to reduce its 'clutter factor'. All the welfare effects stem from the price and quantity changes, so these are all that we really need to keep track of.

The welfare effects on foreigners are straightforward. Partner gains D since it gets a higher price and sells more. In other words, Partner experiences a positive

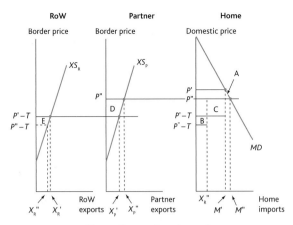

Figure 5.4: *Welfare effects of unilateral discriminatory liberalization*

border price effect and a positive trade volume effect. RoW's losses are E for the reverse reasons; it gets a lower price and sells less (a negative border price effect and a negative trade volume effect).

Home's welfare effects are slightly more complex owing to the two-fold impact on the border price. The direct way of gauging Home's net welfare effect is to use the concepts of trade volume effects and border price effects that were introduced in Chapter 4. This direct approach is also the easiest way to remember the Home welfare effects and it is the easiest way to understand them, so this is what we do in Fig. 5.4. Some readers, however, may benefit from working through the welfare impact using the indirect method of adding up the separate impacts on consumer surplus, producer surplus and tariff revenue (see Box 5.3). The two methods lead to the same answer.

Following the direct analysis, we note that the preferential tariff liberalization has increased imports, and produced two conflicting border price effects. By the usual reasoning (see Chapter 4), the increase in imports raises Home welfare, with the exact measure being the gap between the *MD* curve and *P'* summed over all the extra units imported. This equals the area marked as A in Fig. 5.4.

We turn next to building intuition for the key point: the ambiguity of Home's welfare effect.

The border price effect tells us how much more or less Home is paying for the goods it imported before the PTA.

Box 5.3

Home welfare effects of discriminatory tariff cutting in detail

Here we consider the 'gross' welfare implications of the price and quantity changes derived in Fig. 5.4. To see consumer and producer surplus separately, we put the rightmost panel from Fig. 5.4 in the left-hand panel of Fig. 5.5 and add to it a right panel consisting of a standard open economy supply and demand diagram. (As we are focusing on Home welfare, we shall drop the two Foreign panels.) Turn first to the right-hand panel. The drop in the domestic price from P' to P'' raises consumer surplus by $D + A_2 + A_1 + A_3$, but lowers producer surplus by D (see Chapter 4 if this reasoning is unfamiliar). The net change in the private surplus (i.e. producer and consumer surplus combined) is $A_2 + A_1 + A_3$. The change in tariff revenue is slightly more involved than usual. Originally, the tariff revenue was $A_1 + B_1 + C$ (i.e. $T \times M'$). After the PTA, the tariff revenue is $B_1 + B$ since T is charged only on X''_R. Thus, the change in tariff revenue is $B - A_1 - C$. Adding the private surplus

change and the net revenue change, we find that the net impact on Home is $A_2 + A_1 + A_3 + B - A_1 - C$. Cancelling, this becomes $A_2 + A_3 + B - C$. In Chapter 4 we showed that $A_2 + A_3$ equals A in the left panel, so the net effect is just $A + B - C$ as in Fig. 5.4.

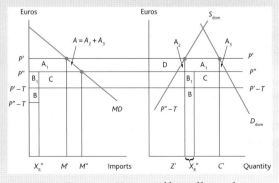

Figure 5.5: *Focus on Home welfare effects of unilateral discriminatory liberalization*

Home imports amounted to M' before the PTA. After the PTA, an amount equal to X''_R comes from RoW and the rest of M', namely $M' - X''_R$, comes from Partner. The goods coming from RoW have fallen in price, so Home gains on these. The exact size of the gain is just the amount of imports affected times the price drop; in the figure this gain equals the area B. The goods coming from Partner have risen in price, so Home experiences a loss. The size of the loss is again the amount of imports affected (namely, $M' - X''_R$) times the price rise, namely the difference between $P' - T$ and P''. Graphically, this is the area C. What about the border price effect on the extra imports, $M'' - M'$? The border price effect does not apply to these units; since Home did not import them to begin with, it does not make sense to talk about how much more or less they cost post-liberalization.

Putting together the trade volume effect and the border price effects, Home's overall welfare change is equal to the areas A plus B minus C. A key point to remember and understand is that this welfare effect may be positive or negative. As drawn, the net welfare impact looks negative. Interested readers should be able to show that discriminatory liberalization will lead to a welfare gain if T is large enough. Moreover, as usual with tax analysis, the slopes of the supply and demand curves also affect the size of the welfare effects.

5.1.4 Intuition for Viner's ambiguity: trade creation and trade diversion

The fact that the Home country might gain or lose from a unilateral preferential liberalization is known as *Viner's ambiguity* since Jacob Viner was the first to crystallize economists' thinking about this ambiguity. The ambiguity is extremely easy to understand at an intuitive level – a point we can make by studying the two words in the term 'discriminatory liberalization'.

Start with the 'liberalization' part. In the NICNIR framework, we know that firms produce up to the point where their marginal cost equals the price they receive, so the price they receive tells us what their marginal cost is (see Chapter 4 if this point is not familiar). Tariffs keep domestic prices above foreign prices, so we know that Home consumers are buying some of their consumption from higher-marginal-cost domestic producers and some from lower-marginal-cost foreign producers. This is plainly inefficient. Home could get more for its money by shifting some purchases from domestic firms to foreign firms. Removing the tariff wedge between domestic firms and Partner-nation firms (this is the liberalization part of

discriminatory liberalization) tends to improve Home's welfare by shifting some purchases from higher-cost Home firms to lower-cost Partner firms.

But because the liberalization is 'discriminatory', a new price wedge appears. The discriminatory tariff means that the border price faced by Partner-nation firms and RoW firms are different. (Partner-based firms see Home's domestic price since they face no tariff, but RoW-based firms face Home's domestic price minus the tariff.) Just as the domestic-versus-foreign wedge led to an inefficient buying pattern to start with, the appearance of the Partner-versus-RoW wedge – a wedge that did not exist before the discriminatory liberalization – leads to a new source of inefficiency. Specifically, it leads Home to buy more from Partner firms (whose costs are now higher) and less from RoW firms (whose costs are now lower). In short, the 'liberalization' part removes one source of inefficiency, but the 'discrimination' part introduces a new one. No wonder, then, that discriminatory liberalization has ambiguous welfare effects.

These points are quite general and flow directly from the powerful set of NICNIR tools developed in the decades following the Second World War. For example, the basic points would apply to an analysis of any 'discriminatory' change in tax rates, say, a reduction in the VAT rate that was applied to some firms but not others. Unhappily, the first post-war economist to carefully illustrate the ambiguous welfare effects of a customs union, Jacob Viner, did not have the benefit of this powerful toolkit. Instead, he invented new terms to describe these two basic effects: 'trade creation' and 'trade diversion'. Since they do capture the basic intuition behind the ambiguity, these terms have become quite standard, so much so that one really cannot talk about preferential liberalization without mentioning them. This is unfortunate since they are slightly misleading (suggesting that trade volumes are the key even though they refer to cost/price changes). They also fail to cover all the effects (e.g. gains from increased imports). For more on the famous 'trade creation, trade diversion' phraseology, see Box 5.4.

5.2 Analysis of a customs union

Until now we have considered only unilateral tariff cuts. European integration, however, involves reciprocal, i.e.

Box 5.4

Terminology in detail: trade creation, trade diversion

If one were to sneak into the bedroom of almost any famous international economist, shake that famous economist awake and shout loudly: 'Free trade area – good or bad?', the first words out of the economist's mouth would surely include 'trade creation and trade diversion'. Indeed, these terms are so influential that one really must know them despite their short-comings.

It should be clear to readers who have worked through the PTA diagram that this terminology fails to capture all welfare effects of discriminatory tariff liberalization, and, as we shall see in section 5.2.3, it is completely useless when it comes to the types of barriers European integration has addressed since the mid-1970s, i.e. non-tariff barriers. One economist who has studied the history of 'customs union theory' suggests that the terms persist since they are 'highly effective tools of focusing policy makers' attention on the ambiguous welfare effects of PTAs' (Panagariya, 1999).

Economists have dealt with the incompleteness of Viner's terms in two ways. Some stretch the original meaning of his terms to cover the full effects in the simplest case where the MS curves are flat (see Annex A at the end of this chapter). Others have introduced new jargon, adding such terms as 'internal versus external trade creation' and 'trade expansion'. All this variance in literary interpretation is possible because Viner did not use diagrams in his book and certainly no maths, so there is some debate over exactly what he meant. The most convincing translation of Viner's words into modern economics was undertaken by Nobel Laureate James Meade in his famous 1955 book *The Theory of Customs Unions*. That book employed a general approach based on the powerful NICNIR toolkit developed by, among others, Paul Samuelson, Kenneth Arrow, James Mirrles and Meade himself. Namely, he breaks down net welfare effects into what we have called trade volume effects and border price effects.

Jacob Viner, 1892–1970

James Meade, 1907–95; Nobel Prize winner 1977

Paul Samuelson, 1915–; Nobel Prize winner in 1970

two-way, preferential liberalizations, so it is important to think through the case of two-way preferential liberalization. In our simple model, that means Home and Partner both set their tariffs to zero on each other's exports.

As it turns out, the study of a customs union is an easy stretch of the unilateral PTA analysis. The main extra insight we get from studying a customs union (a free

trade agreement with a common external tariff) arises from the fact that a customs union (CU) is systematically more favourable for participating countries than are unilateral liberalization schemes since Home exporters gain from Partner tariff cuts.

To keep things simple, we shall look at the formation of a CU between Home and Partner, assuming that all three countries (Home, Partner and RoW) are symmetric initially in all aspects, including the MFN tariff they initially impose on all imports. To do this carefully, we must address the question of the three-nation trade pattern. Again, to streamline the analysis we adopt the simplest combination that permits us to study the issues. This leads us to assume that three goods are traded (goods 1, 2 and 3). Each country produces all three goods, but cost structures are such that each nation exports two of the three goods while importing the remaining one. The trade pattern, shown schematically in Fig. 5.6, entails Home importing good 1 from Partner and RoW, and Partner importing good 2 from Home and RoW.

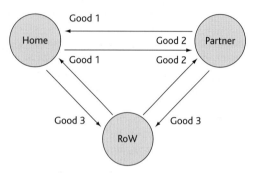

Figure 5.6: *Three-nation trade pattern*

5.2.1 Price and quantity effects

A CU is formed between Home and Partner when Home eliminates T on imports of good 1 from Partner, and Partner eliminates T on imports of good 2 from Home. The tariffs facing RoW exports are not changed, and since Home's and Partner's MFN tariffs were identical to start with, there is no need to harmonize their tariffs towards RoW; T becomes the common external tariff.

We first address the price and quantity effects. Plainly the impact of Home's discriminatory liberalization is exactly the same as the impact shown in Fig. 5.2, so there is no need to repeat it here. The impact of Partner's discriminatory liberalization of imports of good 2 from Home can also be seen using the same diagram. Here is the key point.

A moment's reflection reveals that, given the assumed symmetry of nations, what happens to Home's exports when Partner lowers its barriers is exactly what happened to Partner's exports when Home lowered its barriers. We can, therefore, rely on analysis with which we are already familiar. More specifically, the price of good 2 in Partner falls from P' to P'' (see Fig. 5.2) but

the border price facing Home exporters when they sell good 2 to Partner rises; it rises from $P' - T$ to P''. Nothing happens to domestic prices in RoW (since they did not liberalize), but RoW exporters face a lower border price for its exports to Partner. The trade volume effects are similarly simple. Partner imports rise from M' to M'' and Home exports to Partner rise; using the terminology from Fig. 5.2, Home exports to Partner rise from $X'_p - X''_p$. RoW exports to Partner fall as in Fig. 5.2.

5.2.2 Welfare effects

The welfare effects are also just a matter of adding up effects illustrated above. On Home's import side (i.e. in the market for good 1), Home gains the usual $A + B - C$ in the right panel of Fig. 5.7. On Home's export market (good 2), Home's situation is shown in the left panel, so it gains area D. The welfare effects on Partner are identical to this due to the assumed symmetry of goods and nations.

It is useful to study the welfare effects a bit closer, using Fig. 5.8. This diagram only shows the two liberalizing nations, Home and Partner. To be concrete, suppose this is the market for good 1, which Home imports and Partner exports. The diagram is based on the two rightmost panels of Fig. 5.7 but we have added further detail to the areas. In particular, the trade price loss associated with area C is here split into two parts, C_1 and C_2, for a good reason.

Recall that Home loses $C_1 + C_2$ because the tariff cut raised the price it paid for imports from Partner (from $P' - T$ to P''). The first area, C_1, identifies how much it pays for the units it continues to import from Partner

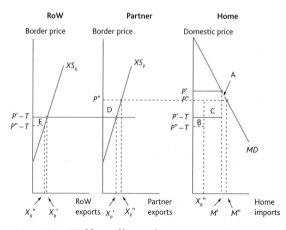

Figure 5.7: *Welfare effects of a customs union*

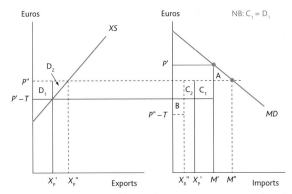

Figure 5.8: *Welfare effects of a customs union in detail*

$(M' - X'_P)$. Home's loss of C_1, however, is exactly matched by a gain to Partner of the same size; the higher price for the X'_P units transfers C_1 from Home to Partner. The key point is that because C_1 is just a transfer between CU members, Home's loss of C_1 on its imports of good 1 will be offset by a gain of $D_1 = C_1$ on its exports of good 2 to Partner. After all, Partner also lowers its tariff against Home exports, so we know that Home will gain an area exactly equal to C_1 in its exports of good 2. In addition, Home will gain D_2 in its export market.

Area C_2 is quite different. It identifies the direct cost of the supply switching (trade diversion), so there is no offset gain on the export side. More specifically, recall that from pre-CU symmetry, we know that RoW exports to Home pre-CU were equal to X'_P. After the CU, RoW exports are X''_R, so the difference, $X'_P - X''_R$, measures the amount of supply switching. This quantity is multiplied by the price change ($P' - T$ to P'') to get the welfare cost of the supply switching.

In summary, using the fact that $D_1 = C_1$, the net gain to Home is $A + B + D_2 - C_2$. This net welfare effect may still be negative, but it is clear that the welfare change from a CU is more positive (or less negative) than the welfare change from a unilateral discriminatory liberalization with Partner.

The losses to RoW from the CU are twice the size of their losses shown in Fig. 5.4, since they lose E both on the exports of good 1 to Home and on their exports of good 2 to Partner. Readers who find this reasoning a bit complex may benefit from the step-by-step explanations in the interactive PowerPoint presentations that can be freely downloaded from http://heiwww.unige/ch/~baldwin/BW/BW.htm.

Second-order terms of trade changes

Lastly, we must consider the indirect or second-round implications of the CU.

RoW experiences a reduction in the value of its exports, yet has not reduced the value of its imports from Home and Partner. While this sort of trade deficit may be sustainable in the short run, eventually RoW must turn the situation around. In the real world, this is usually accomplished by a real depreciation of its currency (or a term of trade worsening if it is in a monetary union). This makes all RoW exports to Home and Partner cheaper and simultaneously makes imports from those two countries more expensive. Both changes have positive welfare implications for the Home and Partner countries; they earn more on their exports to RoW and pay less for their imports from RoW. This is a further negative trade price effect for RoW stemming from general equilibrium effects of the CU between its trading Partners. Such effects, however, are likely to be small.

5.2.3 Frictional barriers:
the 1992 Single Market Programme

Hereto we have dealt with tariff liberalization, which was an important aspect of European integration up to the mid-1970s (see Chapter 1 for details). The next task is to study the economics of frictional barrier liberalization (see Chapter 4 if this terminology is not familiar), the type of liberalization that has dominated European economic integration over the past three decades. Fortunately, the tools we developed while looking at tariff liberalization make this simple.

Price and quantity effects

The removal of frictional barriers was a critical element of the EU's programme to complete the single market by 1992. Although several important aspects of the Single Market Programme (EC92 for short) cannot be understood in the uncomplicated framework used in this chapter, the most basic points can. To keep things simple, suppose that initially all three nations, Home, Partner and RoW, impose a frictional barrier whose tariff equivalent is T (i.e. it drives a wedge equal to T between the border price and the Home price). The specific policy change to be studied is a lowering of T to zero on all trade between Home and Partner with no change in the barriers on RoW–Home or Partner–RoW trade.

The price and quantity effects of the preferential liberalization are similar to those discussed in Fig. 5.2. The only change concerns the border price. With frictional barriers the domestic price is the border price for the importing nation, so the liberalization lowers Home's border price. At the same time, the exporter that benefits from the liberalization receives a higher price for its exports, so the exporter's border price rises.[1] For example, using the Fig. 5.2 terms, the price and quantity effects in the good-1 market are: (i) Home imports of good 1 rise, (ii) the domestic price of good 1 in Home falls from P' to P'', (iii) the border price of good 1 for Partner exporters rises from $P' - T$ to P'', (iv) the border price of good 1 for RoW exporters falls from $P' - T$ to $P'' - T$, and (v) as usual, we get supply switching since Partner exports rise and RoW exports fall.

Welfare effects

The welfare effects on Home are simple. As with tariffs, the change in Home private surplus equals areas $F + A$ in Fig. 5.9. This is not offset by a loss in tariff revenues, as was the case in Fig. 5.4. Removing frictional barriers, even on a preferential basis, always lowers the price that the nation pays for its imports. Although both Partner and RoW exporters see changes in the prices they receive for exports to Home, and this leads to supply switching, this 'trade diversion' has no welfare consequences for Home.

In the good-2 market, where Home is an exporter to Partner, the welfare effect is also positive. Home exporters get a higher price and sell more, so they gain the area $D + D_2$. The overall welfare effect of the FTA is thus $D + D_2 + F + A$.

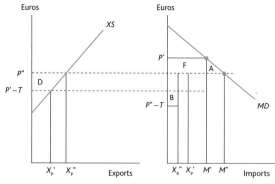

Figure 5.9: *Welfare effects of preferential frictional barrier liberalization*

---

[1] As discussed in Chapter 4, the importer's and exporter's border prices differ with a frictional barrier; the importer's border price is higher than that of the exporter by T.

Non-applicability of trade creation and trade diversion concepts

Notice that Viner's ambiguity has disappeared. With frictional barriers, any kind of liberalization will lead to positive border price effects and positive trade volume effects since the border price equals the domestic price with frictional barriers.

5.3 Customs unions versus free trade agreements

The 1957 Treaty of Rome committed the six original EU members to eliminating all tariffs and quotas on trade among themselves but it also committed them to completely harmonizing their tariffs on imports from non-member nations. In reaction to this customs union, other western European nations formed another trade bloc – known as the European Free Trade Association (EFTA) – in 1960. This was not a customs union, only a free trade area since EFTA members did not adopt a common external tariff.

What are the key differences between a customs union and a free trade area (FTA)? Why did the EEC go for a customs union while EFTA went for an FTA? We address these questions in order, starting with the main economic differences.

5.3.1 Stopping tariff cheats: 'trade deflection' and 'rules of origin'

When tariffs between two nations are zero, yet they charge two different tariffs on imports from third nations, firms have an incentive to cheat on tariffs. Take our three-nation example. If all Home–Partner trade is duty free, yet Home charges a 10 per cent tariff on imports from RoW while Partner charges only a 5 per cent tariff on goods coming from RoW, Home-based buyers of RoW goods would be tempted to import the goods first into Partner (thus paying only a 5 per cent tariff) and then to import them duty free from Partner to Home. To thwart this practice – known as trade deflection – Home and Partner have two choices. They can eliminate the temptation by harmonizing their external tariffs (thus turning their FTA into a customs union), or they can stay with the FTA but restrict duty-free treatment to goods that are actually *made* in Home or Foreign. The set of rules that enforce the latter option are called 'rules of origin'.

One problem with rules of origin, and thus with FTAs, is that it can be difficult to know where a product is made in today's highly globalized markets. Personal computers made in, say, Switzerland will contain components from all over the world. The Swiss company may be doing little more than customized assembly of parts from the USA and Asia. In the extreme, it may be doing nothing more than opening the box of a US-made computer and putting in an instruction manual translated into, say, Norwegian. Should the full value of this computer be given duty-free treatment when it is exported to Norway? (Switzerland and Norway are both EFTA members.)

The costs of rules of origin

For manufactured goods, the basic rule of origin is that a good has to have changed its 'tariff classification' to qualify for duty-free treatment. If the component comes into Switzerland under 'TV and computer monitors', for example, but the good to be exported to Norway is classed as 'Office equipment', then the good is considered Swiss and thus granted duty-free access to Germany. But, for many products, the rules can be much more complex and much more expensive to comply with. Another popular rule requires that some fixed percentage of the product's value-added be done in the exporting nation. Owing to the high cost of compliance with these rules, many non-EU firms who could in principle qualify for duty-free treatment (e.g. Swiss firms) decide instead to pay the EU's CET (Common External Tariff).

An additional problem with rules of origin is that they can end up as hidden protection. Since rules of origin are specified at the product level, they can be difficult for non-experts to evaluate – just as is the case with technical barriers to trade. As a consequence, rules of origin are usually written in consultation with domestic firms who have an incentive to shape the rules into protectionist devices.

One great advantage of a customs union like the EU is that firms do not have to demonstrate the origin of a product before it is allowed to cross an intra-EU border duty free. Any good that is physically in Germany was either made in Germany or paid the CET when it entered. In either case, the good merits duty-free passage into any other EU member without any documentation at all.

The EU has greatly simplified the problem of rules of origin by adopting the Pan-European Cumulation System. See Chapter 12 for details.

5.3.2 Political integration and customs unions

Most preferential trade arrangements in the world are free trade agreements rather than customs unions, like the EU. The reason is simple: political integration. Getting a group of nations to agree on a common external tariff at the launch of a customs union is difficult, but the real problems begin as time passes. For instance, if one member nation believes its industry is being undercut by some non-member nation who is exporting its goods at a price that is below cost (so-called dumping), it may want to impose tariffs to offset the dumping. In a customs union, all nations must agree on every dumping duty since external tariffs must always remain constant. Likewise, nations typically reduce their tariffs in the context of GATT/WTO negotiations. For a customs union, this requires all members to agree on a common negotiating position on every single product.

In practice, keeping the Common External Tariff common requires some integration of decision making. In the EU, the Commission formally has the power to set tariffs on third-nation goods (even though it naturally consults with Member States before doing so), but very few groups of countries are willing to transfer that amount of national sovereignty. As a result, most trade blocs, including EFTA and the North American Free Trade Agreement (NAFTA), are free trade areas rather than customs unions.

Another way to 'solve' the decision-making problem is for the members to let one nation decide everything. This is the case in all the successful customs unions in the world apart from the EU. For example, South Africa is the dominant nation in the Southern African Customs Union (see http://www.dfa.gov.za/for-relations/multilateral/sacu.htm), and Switzerland is the dominant nation in the Swiss–Liechtenstein customs union.

5.4 WTO rules

The world trading system is governed by a set of rules, known as the General Agreement on Tariffs and Trade (GATT), and an organization, known as the World Trade Organization (WTO). The most important guiding principle of the WTO/GATT is non-discrimination in trade policy, i.e. the so-called most favoured nation principle, or MFN for short. This says that nations should, in principle, impose tariffs on a non-discriminatory basis. Of course, all of the preferential liberalization discussed above contradicts this principle, so why is it allowed? As it turns out, the GATT created an explicit loophole for FTAs and customs unions. Allowing this loophole was important for some of the early GATT members since they wished to maintain existing preferential arrangements (especially Great Britain's Commonwealth Preferences).

The loophole, formally known as Article 24, specifically allows preferential liberalization, subject to a few restrictions; the most important of which are:

* free trade agreements and customs unions must completely eliminate tariffs on 'substantially all the trade' among members;
* the phasing out of tariffs must take place within a reasonable period.

Although there are no hard definitions, 'substantially all trade' is usually taken to mean at least 80 per cent of all goods and a 'reasonable period' is taken to be ten years or less.

For a customs union, there is the additional requirement that the common external tariff 'shall not on the whole be higher or more restrictive' than before the customs union. That is, when forming the customs union, the members cannot harmonize the CET to the highest level of any member. In the case of the EEC's customs union formation, external tariff harmonization generally involved a reduction in French and Italian tariffs, a rise in Benelux tariffs and little change in the German tariffs.

5.5 Empirical studies

Modern empirical analyses of European integration go far beyond the NICNIR framework we employed in this chapter. They include effects that we shall study in Chapters 6 and 7. Indeed, no major study of EU economic integration has relied solely on the NICNIR framework since the mid-1980s. There are, however, many examples of empirical studies based on NICNIR reasoning from the 1970s. For example, the UK's entry into the EU elicited a large volume of empirical work in the early 1970s. While economists at the time knew of scale effects and growth effects, they did not have the theoretical tools necessary to handle them. Moreover, few economists had access to computers (PCs became widespread only in the 1980s), so much of the empirical work in the NICNIR framework consisted of what we would today call rough calculations, or 'back of the envelope' methods. The most popular method was to

loosely associate the positive effects of customs union formation with an increase in imports and the negative effects loosely with diverted imports. Since most studies at the time found little or no evidence that the EEC's formation was trade diverting (Balassa, 1975), the general conclusion was that the EEC must have been good for the EEC and not bad for the rest of the world. The main challenge in these studies was to determine what the trade pattern would have been without the EEC – a problem that is more difficult to resolve than one might think since imports from all sources were growing rapidly (see Fig. 5.3).

Since these NICNIR studies are now twenty years out of date, we do not review their findings here (see Artis and Nixson, 2001, for a summary). One thing that is worth discussing is the fact that all empirical studies using the NICNIR framework found that the EEC had a negligible impact on national welfare.

Balassa (1975), for example, concluded that the EU's customs union added only 0.5 per cent to the Six's GDP. This struck most observers as far too low, but such low estimates are inevitable in the NICNIR framework. To understand why, it helps to consider a simple example. Suppose that Home is a small country and removes all tariffs on an MFN basis. As Annex A shows, the welfare impact of this on Home will be *larger* than the welfare impact of any possible free trade area, so we know that the number we shall arrive at will be an overestimate of the true gain. The welfare impact of this is 0.5 times the change in imports times the level of the tariff. In symbols, this is $\Delta W = (\Delta M)(\Delta T)/2$, where Δ means 'the change in' and W stands for welfare, M for imports and T for the tariff. The change in imports is related to the responsiveness of imports to price changes, i.e. Home's import demand elasticity, ε, defined as $(\Delta M/M)/(\Delta P/P)$. In symbols, $\Delta M = \varepsilon(\Delta T)(M/P)$, so the welfare gain as a share of GDP is:

$$\frac{\Delta W}{\text{GDP}} = \frac{\varepsilon(M \times P/\text{GDP})(\Delta TP)^2}{2}$$

A typical, import-demand elasticity is something like 2.0, a typical EEC nation had an import to GDP ratio, i.e. ($M \times P/\text{GDP}$), equal to about 0.2 in the 1960s, and the level of tariffs averaged less than 25 per cent. Taking all this together means that the gains would be 2(0.2)(0.625)/2, which equals just 0.0125 or 1.25 per cent of GDP – and that is an overestimate of the NICNIR effects.

The general point to learn from this back-of-the-envelope calculation is that NICNIR welfare gains just cannot be big. They inevitably involve the multiplication of several fractions and this inevitably produces small numbers. If trade liberalization is to have welfare effects that are big enough to matter, we need to consider scale effects, growth effects and location effects – the subjects of the next chapters.

5.6 Summary

This chapter introduced the graphical methods necessary to study preferential trade liberalization in a NICNIR setting. After going over the preliminaries, we studied the price, quantity and welfare effects of the formation of a customs union. The main technical points are:

★ Formation of a preferential trade arrangement like the EEC's customs union, or EFTA's free trade area, tends to lower domestic prices and raise imports overall, but the discriminatory aspects of these liberalizations also produce supply-switching, that is to say, a switch from non-member supplier to member-based suppliers.

★ The welfare effects of any trade liberalization, including PTA liberalization, can be captured by standard public-finance concepts, which we here call trade volume effects and border price (or trade price) effects.

★ The welfare impact of preferential tariff liberalization is ambiguous for the liberalizing nations; this is called Viner's ambiguity. The deep fundamental reason is that PTAs are discriminatory liberalizations; the liberalization part – what Viner called trade creation – tends to boost economic efficiency, whereas the discrimination part – what Viner called trade diversion – tends to lower it. The impact on excluded nations is always negative.

★ Estimates of the welfare impact of trade liberalization in the NICNIR setting are inevitably very small. This suggests to most observers that one has to look to more complicated frameworks if one is to understand why trade liberalization in general, and European integration in particular, matter.

The bigger lessons from the chapter concern the way in which the economic analysis helps us to understand the trends in, and reactions of other nations to, European integration.

★ The NICNIR framework helped us to study the impact of discriminatory liberalization on outsiders in an intellectually uncluttered setting. This helps us to understand why outsiders always reacted to the deepening and widening of EU integration. As we showed, preferential liberalization definitely harms excluded nations since it leads them to face lower prices for their exports to the customs union and lower export sales. It seems natural, therefore, that the outsiders would react either by forming their own preferential arrangements (as happened in the 1960s with EFTA), or by deepening the integration between the outsiders and the EU (as outsiders did in the 1970s and again in the 1990s), or by joining the EU (as nine formerly outsider western European nations had done by 1994).

Self-assessment questions

The NICNIR was the backbone of 'customs union theory' for years, so quite a number of extensions and provisos were put forth in the NICNIR setting. Some of them are still insightful and the following exercises illustrate the basic points.

1. (Kemp–Wan theorem.) Starting from a situation like that shown in Fig. 5.1, where the three nations are symmetric in everything including the initial MFN tariff T, suppose that Home and Partner form a customs union *and* lower their common tariff against RoW to the point where the new, post-liberalization border price facing RoW exporters is the same as it was before the liberalization, i.e. $P' - T$. Show that this 'Kemp–Wan' adjustment ensures that Home and Partner gain while RoW does not lose from this CU-with-CET-reduction scheme.

2. (Cooper–Massell extended.) We can think of a preferential unilateral liberalization in the following roundabout manner. Home lowers its tariffs to zero on an MFN basis, but then raises it back to T on imports only from RoW. Now suppose that Home faces a flat MS curve for imports from both Partner and RoW (this is the 'small country' case). Moreover, suppose that Partner's MS is somewhat above that of RoW.
    First, work out the welfare effects on Home. (Hint: This is covered in Annex A.)
    Second, show that Home would gain more from a unilateral MFN liberalization than it would from a unilateral preferential liberalization. (Historical note: Taking their NICNIR analysis as definitive, this result led Cooper and Massell to suggest that small countries must join customs unions for political reasons only. You can see that this is only a partial analysis by realizing that a customs union also lowers tariffs facing Home-based exporters.) Try to figure out how Home gains from Partner's removal on Home-to-Partner exports. After doing this, see if you can say definitely whether Home gains more from unilateral free trade, or from joining the customs union. You should also be able to show that the optimal policy for a small nation is to have unilateral free trade *and* to join every FTA that it can.

3. (Large Partner rule of thumb.) Redo the FTA formation exercise from the text assuming that RoW is initially a much smaller trading partner of Home and Partner in the sense that most of Home's imports are from Partner and most of Partner's imports are from Home when all three nations impose the initial MFN tariff, T. Show that the 'net border price effect' (area $B - C_1 - C_2$ in Fig. 5.8) is smaller when RoW is initially a less important trading partner of Home and Partner nations. (Hint: Focus on the Home country and start with a diagram like Fig. 5.1. Keep the vertical intersections of XS_P and XS_R at the same height, but make the XS_R steeper and the XS_P flatter in a way that does not change P'. Our thanks to Jonathan Gage for help with this problem.)

4. (Growth effects and RoW impact.) Suppose that signing an FTA between Home and Partner produces a growth effect that raises their income level and thus shifts their MD curves upwards. Use a diagram like Fig. 5.4 to show how big the upward shift would have to be to ensure that RoW did not lose from the Home–Partner FTA. (In the 1970s,

this was the informal explanation for why the EEC6 formation did not lead to trade diversion.) Can you show the welfare impact of this growth on Home?

5. (Hub and spoke bilateralism.) Using PTA diagrams, show what the price, quantity and welfare effects would be of a hub-and-spoke arrangement among three nations. (Hub-and-spoke means that country 1 signs FTAs with countries 2 and 3, but 2 and 3 do not liberalize trade between them.) Assume that there are *only* frictional barriers in this world, that initially all import barriers have a tariff equivalent of T, and that the FTAs concern only frictional barrier liberalization. Be sure to look at the price, quantity and welfare impact on (i) a typical spoke economy (2 or 3) and (ii) the hub economy.

6. (Sapir, 1992.) Consider a situation where Home and Partner have formed a customs union but have not eliminated frictional barriers between them. Specifically assume that all trade flows among Home, Partner and RoW are subject to frictional trade barriers equal to T' and additionally the tariff on trade between the CU and RoW is equal to T'. Show that eliminating frictional barriers inside the CU might harm welfare since it leads to a reduction in the amount of tariff revenue collected on imports from RoW.

7. Suppose Home has no trade barriers, except anti-dumping measures. These anti-dumping measures take the form of price undertakings, i.e. instead of Home imposing a tariff on RoW and Partner imports, Home requires Partner and RoW firms to charge a high price for their sales to Home. Show the price, quantity and welfare effects of imposing this import price floor (look at all three nations). Next, show the price, quantity and welfare effects of removing the price undertaking (i.e. allowing free trade) only for imports from Partner. Be sure to illustrate the impact on all three nations. (Hint: The price undertaking is a price floor, so it does not act just like a tariff; be very careful in constructing the MS_{PTA} for this situation.)

Essay questions

1. Using the analysis of a customs union in this chapter, explain how the domino theory of integration could explain the fact that virtually all nations in and around western Europe now have or want to have preferential trade arrangements with the EU.

2. Using the economic analysis in this chapter, together with the political economy logic of special-interest groups (well-organized groups often have political weight that is far in excess of their economic weight), explain why the WTO restrictions on customs unions and free trade areas might be a good idea.

3. Using the economic analysis in this chapter and political economy logic, explain why most trade liberalizations are reciprocal rather than unilateral.

4. Some international trade experts believe that formation of the EU's customs union lead to pressures from the USA and Japan for a multilateral tariff-cutting round called the Kennedy Round. Use the economic analysis in this chapter, together with the political economy logic of special interest groups, to explain why this view might make sense. (Hint: US and Japanese exporters are a very powerful special-interest group.)

5. When Bismarck led the drive to unify the many small regions and nation-states of Germany, he used a customs union (*Zollverien*) as both a carrot and a stick to encourage unification. Use the economic analysis in this chapter (especially the impact on RoW) to make sense of this strategy.

Further reading: the aficionado's corner

The modern study of European economic integration began life under the name of 'customs union theory' with Viner (1950). Viner's seminal text triggered a flood of work. At the time, tariffs were the key trade barriers and theorists had few tools for dealing with imperfect competition, so the early literature focused on tariff removals in the NICNIR setting. For a highly readable survey of this literature, see Pomfret (1986). O'Brien (1975) provides a review of pre-Vinerian literature.

Following Viner's theory, which associated welfare effects with changes in trade flows, early empirical studies focused on trade creation and diversion. Surveys of this literature include Mayes (1978), Winters (1987) and Srinivasan *et al.* (1993).

A more extensively graphic presentation of pre- and post-1958 trade flows in Europe can be found in Neal and Berbezat (1998).

Useful websites

While the EU's customs union has been completed for over three decades, some policy issues occasionally arise. See the Commission's website at http://europa.eu.int/comm/taxationcustoms/.

The history of EFTA's free trade area can be found on http://www.efta.int/.

Further information on WTO rules concerning preferential trade arrangements can be found on www.wto.org.

References

Artis, M. and F. Nixson (2001) *The Economics of the European Union*. Oxford University Press, Oxford.

Balassa, B. (1975) 'Trade creation and trade diversion to the European Common Market', in B. Balassa (ed.) *European Economic Integration*, North-Holland, Amsterdam.

Baldwin, R.E. and A. Venables (1995) 'Regional economic integration', in G. Grossman and K. Rogoff (eds) *Handbook of International Economics*, Volume III, North-Holland, Amsterdam.

Cooper, C. and D. Massell (1965) 'Towards a general theory of customs unions in developing countries', *Journal of Political Economy*, 73: 256–83.

Kemp, M. and H. Wan (1976) 'An elementary proposition concerning the formation of customs unions', *Economic Journal*, 6: 95–7.

Mankiw, G. (2000) *Principles of Economics*, Thomson Learning, New York.

Mayes, D. (1978) 'The effects of economic integration on trade', *Journal of Common Market Studies*, XVII (Sept.): 1–25.

Meade, J. (1955) *The Theory of Customs Unions*, North-Holland, Amsterdam.

Neal, L. and D. Berbezat (1998) *The Economics of the European Union and the Economics of Europe*, Oxford University Press, London.

O'Brien, D.P. (1975) 'Classical monetary theory', pp. 140–69 in *The Classical Economists*, Clarendon Press, Oxford.

Panagariya, A. (1999) 'Preferential trade liberalisation: the traditional theory and new developments', University of Maryland mimeo. Download from www.bsos.umd.edu/econ/panagariya/song/surveypt.pdf.

Pomfret, R. (1986) 'The theory of preferential trading arrangements', *Weltwirtschaftliches Archiv*, 122: 439–64.

Sapir, A. (1992) 'Regional integration in Europe', *Economic Journal*, 102 (415): 1491–506.

Srinivasan, T.N., J. Whalley and I. Wooton (1993) 'Measuring the effects of regionalism on trade and welfare', pp. 52–79 in K. Anderson and R. Blackhurst (eds) *Regional Integration and the Global Trading System*, Harvester-Wheatsheaf, London, for the GATT Secretariat.

Viner, J. (1950) *The Customs Union Issue*, Carnegie Endowment for International Peace, New York.

Winters, L.A. (1987) 'Britain in Europe: a survey of quantitative trade studies', *Journal of Common Market Studies*, 25: 315–35.

Annex A

Discriminatory liberalization: small country case

This background appendix presents the classic analysis of unilateral preferential tariff liberalization for the 'small country' case. The so-called small country case means that we make the simplifying assumption that the volume of a nation's imports is unrelated to the price of those imports. In this case, we do not need the import supply and demand diagram discussed above. Rather, we can work directly with a simpler open economy supply and demand diagram.

Figure A5.1, which allows for two potential sources of imports (countries A and B), helps to organize the reasoning. To set the stage, suppose that Home initially imposes a tariff of T on imports from A and B. (Goods produced in the countries A, B and Home are all perfect substitutes.) The Home nation is assumed to face a flat import supply curve from both countries. The idea behind this simplification is that Home is so small that it can buy as much or as little as it wants without affecting the price. Specifically, the import supply curves from A and B are the flat curves at the levels P_A and P_B. We can see that country A producers are more efficient since they can offer the goods at a lower price. That is, importing from A costs Home consumers $P_A + T$, while importing from B costs $P_B + T$. Plainly, all imports initially come from the cheaper supplier, namely A.

Adding together the three sources of supply (Home, A and B), we find the pre-liberalization total supply curve to be TS_1. Because it is the horizontal sum of the Home supply curve and the two import supply curves, it follows the Home supply curve up to $P_A + T$; beyond that it follows A's import supply curve. The equilibrium Home price (i.e. the price facing Home consumers and producers) is $P_A + T$ since this is where total supply meets demand. The border price, namely the price that Home as a country pays for imports, is P_A.

Next we ask what would happen if the tariff were removed on a discriminatory basis? That is to say, if it were removed on imports from only A or only B. Both cases must be considered. We turn now to the price, quantity and welfare effects of the two cases.

A.1 Price and quantity analysis, liberalization with low-cost country

In the first case, the liberalization is applied to Home's current trading partner, namely A. The total supply curve becomes TS_3, so the Home price falls to P_A. Home consumption rises, Home production falls, imports rise and nothing happens to the border price of imports. To summarize:

★ The price in the Home market of both imports and Home import-competing goods falls to P_A.
★ Home production falls from Q_3 to Q_1.
★ Home consumption rises from Q_4 to Q_6.
★ The import volume rises from the difference between Q_3 and Q_4 to the difference between Q_1 and Q_6.
★ The border price (i.e. the price of imported goods before the imposition of the tax) remains unchanged at P_A.

With some thought, it is clear that discriminatory liberalization with the low-cost country has the same impact as an MFN liberalization. After all, both types of liberalization remove the tariff on all imports (the preferential tariff cut leaves the tariff on goods from B, but no imports come from B before or after the liberalization).

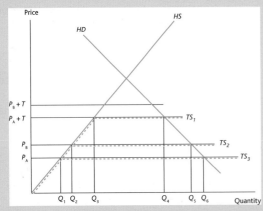

Figure A5.1: *Price and quantity effects of discriminatory liberalization (small nation)*

continued

A.2 Welfare analysis: liberalization with low-cost country

As with the price and quantity analysis, in this case the welfare analysis is identical to that of non-discriminatory liberalization. Home consumer surplus rises and Home producer surplus falls because of the liberalization. Since more units are consumed than produced domestically, the sum of consumer and producer surpluses rises. Part of this gain is offset by a loss in tariff revenue. Using Fig. A5.2 to be more precise:

★ Consumer surplus rises by the sum of all the areas A through J.
★ Producer surplus falls by the area A + E.
★ Government revenue falls by C + H.
★ The net effect is unambiguously positive and equal to (B + F + G) and (D + I + J).

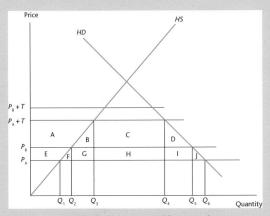

Figure A5.2: *Small country welfare analysis*

A.3 Liberalization with high-cost country: supply switching

The analysis is only slightly trickier when the preferential trade arrangement is signed with the high-cost country.

Graphically, as shown in Fig. A5.1, this results in a total supply curve of TS_2 and a Home price of P_B. Recall that since country B is the high-cost supplier (i.e. P_B is above P_A) nothing was imported from B initially. Granting duty-free access to goods from B artificially changes the relative competitiveness of goods from A and B – at least in the eyes of Home consumers. Goods from B cost P_B whereas goods from A cost $P_A + T$. Quite naturally, Home importers of goods will divert all their import demand from A towards B. We call this the 'supply switching' effect of discriminatory liberalization; it is the first of two elements that arise with discriminatory liberalization but which do not arise with non-discriminatory liberalization. Note, however, that discriminatory liberalization does not always lead to supply switching. It can only do so when it is done with the high-cost country.

The second novel aspect of discriminatory liberalization is the border price impact. That is, as consumers switch from the low-cost source to the high-cost source (country B), the Home border price rises. We call this the 'border price' effect, or the import-price-rising effect. The importance of this price change should be clear: such liberalization will raise the cost of imports to the country as a whole.

To summarize, there are six price and quantity effects:

★ The preferential liberalization increases competition from imports and thereby forces down the Home price of locally made and imported goods to P_B.
★ Consumption rises to Q_5.
★ Some high-cost Home production is replaced by lower cost imports. This amount is equal to $Q_3 - Q_2$.
★ The new Home production level is Q_2.
★ Imports from A are entirely replaced by imports from B and the level of imports rises.
★ The border price rises. That is to say, Home now pays more for its imports (namely P_B) than it did before (namely P_A).

A.4 Welfare analysis: liberalization with high-cost country

When the tariffs come down only on imports from the country that initially sells nothing to Home, the welfare effects turn out to be ambiguous. To summarize using Fig. A5.2, there are three welfare effects of a discriminatory liberalization of a tariff (or any DCR barrier):

★ Home consumers gain the area A + B + C + D.

★ Home producers lose the area A.

★ All tariff revenue is lost. This lowers Home welfare; the change being $-C - H$.

The net effect is $B + D - H$. This may be positive or negative; discriminatory tariff liberalization there-fore has ambiguous welfare effects. This is the so-called Viner ambiguity. Notice that the net welfare impact depends only on the change in the quantity of imports (which rises in this case) and the change in the price of imports (which also rises in this case).

The countries of Europe are too small to give their peoples the prosperity that is now attainable and therefore necessary. They need wider markets.

Jean Monnet, 1943

By its size – the biggest in the world – the single market without frontiers is an invaluable asset to revitalise our businesses and make them more competitive. It is one of the main engines of the European Union.

Jacques Delors, July 1987

Chapter

6

Market size and scale effects

INTRODUCTION

Market size matters. From its inception in the 1950s, an important premise behind European economic integration was the belief that unification of European economies would, by allowing European firms access to a bigger market, make European firms more efficient, and this, in turn, would allow them to lower prices, raise quality and gain competitiveness in external markets.

This chapter explores the economic logic of how European integration can lead to fewer, larger firms operating at a more efficient scale and facing more effective competition. The chapter also considers policy responses to these changes, notably the enforcement of rules that prohibit unfair subsidization of firms and rules restricting anti-competitive behaviour. In the EU, such policies are called, respectively, state aids policy and competition policy.

6.1 Liberalization, defragmentation and industrial restructuring: logic and facts

We start the chapter by explaining the logic that links European integration to industrial restructuring; we then present some facts on mergers and acquisitions (M&As) and the effects on competition.

Europe's national markets are separated by a host of barriers. These included tariffs and quotas until the Common Market was completed in 1968, and tariffs between the EEC and EFTA until the EEC–EFTA free trade agreements were signed in 1974. Yet, even though intra-EU trade has been duty free for over three decades, trade among European nations is not as free as it is within any given nation. Many technical, physical and fiscal barriers still make it easier for companies to sell in their local market than in other EU markets. While most of these barriers seem trivial or even silly when considered in isolation, the confluence of thousands of seemingly small barriers serves to substantially restrict intra-EU trade. As a result, EU firms can often be dominant in their home market while being marginal players in other EU markets (think of the European car market). This situation, known as market fragmentation, reduces competition and this, in turn, raises prices and keeps too many firms in business. Keeping firms in business is not, of course, a bad thing in itself. The problem is that this results in an industrial structure marked by too many inefficient small firms that can get away with charging high prices to cover the cost of their inefficiency. Due to the absence of competition, poor and/or low-quality services and goods may also accompany the high prices (think of the European telephone service before liberalization).

Tearing down these intra-EU barriers defragments the markets and produces extra competition. This 'pro-competitive effect' in turn puts pressure on profits and the market's response is 'merger mania'. That is, the pro-competitive effect squeezes the least efficient firms, prompting an industrial restructuring in which Europe's weaker firms merge or get bought up. In the end, Europe is left with a more efficient industrial structure, with fewer, bigger, more efficient firms competing more effectively with each other. All this means improved material well-being for Europeans as prices fall and output rises. In some industries, restructuring may be accompanied by a sizeable reallocation of employment, as firms cut back on redundant workers and close inefficient plants and offices (a painful process for workers who have to change jobs). In other industries, however, liberalization can unleash a virtuous circle of more competition, lower prices, higher sales and higher employment.

In the remainder of the chapter we work through the logic of what was just presented informally. Schematically, the steps can be summarized as: liberalization → defragmentation → pro-competitive effect → industrial restructuring. The result is fewer, bigger, more efficient firms facing more effective competition from each other.

6.1.1 Some facts

As shown on the left of Fig. 6.1, the number of mergers and acquisitions (M&As) in the EU15 remained at a high

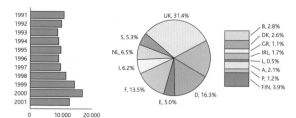

Figure 6.1: *Mergers and acquisitions (M&As) involving EU15 firms, 1991–2001*

Note: The left panel shows the evolution of the number of mergers and acquisitions involving EU15 firms. The right panel shows the distribution of all operations from 1991 to 2001 by Member State.

Source: Data drawn from *European Economy*, Supplement A, No. 12, December 2001; downloadable from http://wuropa.eu.int/comm/economy_finance/publications/supplement_a_en.htm.

steady level of about 10 000 operations per year until 1997, when the number started climbing steadily to a record total of 12 557 operations in 2000. In terms of the total value of deals, however, the EU figure climbed steadily and rapidly from 1991 to 2000, from about €100 billion to €2400 billion. The number and value were lower in 2001, reflecting the slowdown in economic activity, but at over 10 000 operations, it was still a considerable number.

It is interesting to note that much of this M&A activity consists of the mergers of firms within the same Member State, e.g. German firms buying other German firms. Indeed, at the end of the period, about 55 per cent of all operations were of this domestic type. The remaining 45 per cent of the deals involved a non-domestic firm. This 45 per cent is split between operations where one firm was a non-EU firm (24 per cent), where one firm was located in another EU nation (15 per cent) and operations where the counterparty's nationality was not identified (6 per cent).

The right-hand panel of Fig. 6.1 shows the breakdown of firms by Member State. Two points are worth stressing. First, the distribution of M&A operations is quite varied. The big four economies (France, Italy, Germany and the UK) have the most operations; however, except for the UK, these nations' share of M&As activity is much lower than their share of the European economy. Italy, France and Germany together account for only 36 per cent of

the M&As even though their economies account for 59 per cent of the EU15 economy. By contrast, many of the small EU15 members seem to have a share of M&A activity that is systematically higher than their share of the EU15's GDP. This link between domestic market size and the impact of integration on restructuring fits in with the basic logic described above. Stylizing the facts to make the point, we can say that the problem of a too-small market was most severe in the smaller EU members; integration produced the largest changes (large in proportion to their economy) in the smallest members.

The second point comes from the exceptions to this rule. The EU has yet to harmonize rules on takeovers. Despite many years of trying, some members still have restrictive takeover practices that make M&As very difficult, whereas others, such as the UK, have very liberal rules. The implication of this lack of harmonization is that the restructuring effects of integration have been felt very differently in the various Member States.

The sectoral composition of M&A activity (not shown in the figure) is also noteworthy. About two-thirds of all the activity in this period took place in service sectors, especially in banking. However, during the early years of the Single Market Programme (1986–92), the M&A activity was centred on manufacturing, with mergers often occurring in anticipation of liberalization that was scheduled (Commission, 1996). Interested readers can find a wealth of details on the nature of this activity in *European Economy* (2001).

This restructuring increased the level of concentration at the EU level. From 1987 to 1993, the share of the four largest firms in the EU's total market rose from 20.5 to 22.8 per cent, whereas this measure of concentration at the national level fell. In short, defragmentation resulted in fewer firms at the EU level, but more even competition at the national level.

Econometric evidence from Allen *et al.* (1998a) suggests that the Single Market Programme reduced price–cost margins by 4 per cent on average. This impact varied from quite high, e.g. −15 per cent in the office machinery sector, to quite small, e.g. −0.1 per cent in brewing. It is noteworthy that in the auto sector – a sector that was granted a bloc exemption from the Single Market Programme – the price–cost margin actually rose.

6.2 Theoretical preliminaries: monopoly, duopoly and oligopoly

To study the logic of European integration's impact on scale and competition we need a simple yet flexible framework that allows for imperfect competition. The framework we employ below, the BE–COMP diagram, assumes a knowledge of simple imperfect competition models so, by way of preliminaries, we briefly review the simplest forms of imperfect competition: monopoly, duopoly and oligopoly. Advanced readers may want to skip this section and move directly to the *BE–COMP* diagram in section 6.3, but since this section introduces notation and basic concepts, even advanced readers may find it useful.

As usual, we start with the simplest problem, namely the decision faced by a firm that has a monopoly (it was worked out by Joan Robinson in the 1930s; see Box 6.1). The monopoly case is easy because it avoids strategic interactions. When a firm is the only seller of a product, it can choose how much to sell and what price to charge without considering the reaction of other suppliers. The only restraint a monopolist faces is the demand curve. A downward-sloping demand curve is a constraint because it forces the monopolist to confront a trade-off between

price and sales; higher prices mean lower sales. When considering the impact of European integration on imperfectly competitive firms, we need to determine how various policy changes will alter prices and sales. The first step in this direction is to see what determines a monopolist's price and sales in a closed economy. The natural question then is: What is the profit-maximizing level of sales for the monopolist?

An excellent way to proceed is to make a guess at the optimal level, say, Q' in the left-hand panel of Fig. 6.2. Almost surely this initial guess will be wrong, but what we want to know is whether Q' is too low or too high. To this end, we calculate the profit earned when Q' units are sold at the highest obtainable price, namely P'. The answer is A + B, since the total value of sales is price times quantity (area A + B + C) minus cost (area C).

Would profits rise or fall if the firm sold an extra unit? Of course, to sell the extra unit, the firm will have to let its price fall a bit, to P''. The change in profit equals the change in revenue minus the change in cost. Consider first the change in revenue. This has two parts. Selling the extra unit brings in extra revenue (represented by area D + E), but it also depresses the price received for all units sold initially (lowering revenue by an amount equal to area A). The net change in revenue (called marginal revenue) is given by the area D + E minus the area A. The change in cost (called marginal cost) is area E. Plainly, profit only increases if the extra revenue D − A

exceeds the extra cost E. As it is drawn, D − A + E appears to be negative, so marginal revenue is less than marginal cost at Q′ + 1. This means that raising output from Q′ would lower profits; so the initial guess of Q′ turns out to be too high.

To find the profit-maximizing level using this trial-and-error method, we would consider a lower guess, say Q′ − 4 units, and repeat the procedure applied above. At the profit-maximizing level, marginal revenue just equals marginal cost. This level must be optimal since any increase or decrease in sales will lower profit. Increasing sales beyond this point will increase cost more than revenue, whereas decreasing sales would lower revenue more than cost. Both would reduce profit.

The right-hand panel of Fig. 6.2 shows an easier way to find the point where marginal revenue equals marginal cost. The diagram includes a new curve, called the marginal revenue curve. This shows how the marginal revenue (measured in euros) declines as the level of sales rises. (It declines since area A from the left-hand panel gets very small for low levels of sales.) At the sales level marked Q*, marginal revenue just equals marginal cost. The firm charges the most it can at this level of sales, and this is P*. These are the profit-maximizing levels of sales and price.

Lessons

Several deep aspects of imperfect competition come through even in the monopoly case. First, in setting up the problem, we had to assume things about the firm's beliefs concerning the behaviour of other economic agents. In this case, the monopolist is assumed to believe that consumers are price-takers and that the trade-off between prices and sales depended only on the demand curve (rather than, for example, on the reaction of firms in other markets). Second, the critical difference between perfect and imperfect competition comes out clearly. As part of the definition, perfectly competitive firms are assumed to take the price of their output as given (a classic example is a wheat farmer who cannot set his own price; he just sells at the current market price). This means that such firms are assumed to be ignorant of the fact that selling more will depress the market price. In terms of the diagram, perfectly competitive firms ignore the area A, so they maximize profits by selling an amount where price equals marginal cost. Of course, any increase in sales would have some negative impact on price, so it is best to think of perfect competition as a simplifying assumption that is close to true when all firms have market shares that are close to zero. By stepping away from this simplification, imperfect competition allows firms to explicitly consider the price-depressing effect – area A – when deciding how much to sell.

6.2.1 Duopolist as monopolist on residual demand curve

The monopoly case is instructive, but not very realistic – most European firms face some competition. Taking account of this, however, brings us up against the strategic considerations discussed above. The convention we adopt to sort out this interaction is the so-called Cournot–Nash equilibrium that won John Nash a Nobel Prize (see Box 6.2). That is, we assume that each firm acts as if the other firms' outputs are fixed. The equilibrium we are interested in is where each firm's expectations of the other firms' outputs turn out to be correct, i.e. no one is fooled. This no-one-fooled notion proves to be somewhat difficult to comprehend in the abstract but, as we shall see below, it is easy in specific applications.

The residual demand curve shortcut

Since firms take as given the sales of other firms, the only constraint facing a typical firm is the demand curve shifted to the left by the amount of sales of all other firms. In other words, each firm believes it is a monopolist on the shifted demand curve (we called the shifted demand curve the 'residual demand curve'). This realization is handy since it means that we can directly apply the solution technique from the monopolist's problem; the only change is that we calculate the marginal revenue curve based on the residual demand curve instead of the demand curve.

This trick is shown in Fig. 6.3 for a competition between two firms producing the same good – a situation that economists call 'duopoly'. For simplicity, we assume that the firms have the same marginal cost curves. Taking firm

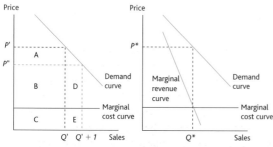

Figure 6.2: *Monopoly profit maximization graphically*

Box 6.2

John Nash (1928–)

www.nobel.se

Early work on imperfect competition (see Profile Box 6.1) was hampered by the problem of strategic interactions among firms. The 'Nash equilibrium' was the concept that cleared away confusions and opened the door to thousands of books and articles on imperfect competition.

has attracted an unusual amount of public attention. Since Nash's path-breaking publications have been interspersed with periods of paranoid schizophrenia, Hollywood found it easy to cast him in the cherished stereotype of a mad genius, making his life the subject of a big-budget movie entitled *A Beautiful Mind* in 2001. The basis of the Nash equilibrium concept was his 1950 article entitled 'Non-cooperative games'. Just 27 pages long, it earned him the Nobel Prize in economics in 1994. An autobiographical account of his life is on http://www.nobel.se/economics/laureates/1994/index.html.

The brilliant but troubled creator of the Nash equilibrium concept is a mathematician whose career

2's sales as given at Q_2, firm 1 has a monopoly on the residual demand curve labelled RD_1. Firm 1's optimal output in this case is x'_1 (since at point A_1, the residual marginal revenue curve, RMR_1, crosses the marginal cost curve MC). The right-hand panel shows the same sort of analysis for firm 2. Taking firm 1's output as fixed at Q_1, firm 2's optimal output is x'_2.

Note that the situation in Fig. 6.3 is not an equilibrium. To highlight the importance of the difference between expected and actual outcomes, the diagram shows the solutions of the two firms when their expectations about the other firm's output do not match the reality. The consistent-expectations outcome, i.e. the Nash equilibrium, is shown in Fig. 6.4, but we first consider why Fig. 6.3 is not an equilibrium.

As drawn, x'_1 and x'_2 are not a Cournot–Nash equilibrium since the firms' actual output levels do not match expectations; firm 1 produces x'_1, which is greater than what firm 2 expected (namely, Q_1), and likewise, firm 2 produces x'_2, which is greater than what firm 1 expected (namely, Q_2). We can also see the problem by observing that the implied prices are not equal. If x'_1 and x'_2 were actually produced by the firms, then firms would not be able to charge the prices they expected to charge. In other words, this is not an equilibrium because the outcome is not consistent with expectations.

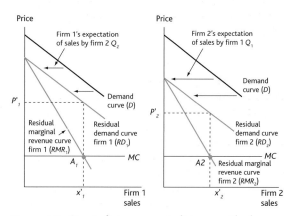

Figure 6.3: *Duopolist as monopolist on residual demand: example of a non-equilibrium*

Finding the expectations consistent equilibrium

How do we find the expectation-consistent set of outputs? The easiest way is to use the assumed symmetry of firms. In the symmetric equilibrium, each firm will sell the same amount. With this fact in mind, a little thought reveals that the residual demand curve facing each firm must be half of the overall demand curve. This situation is shown in the left-hand panel of Fig. 6.4 for a duopoly. Some facts to note are that: (i) the

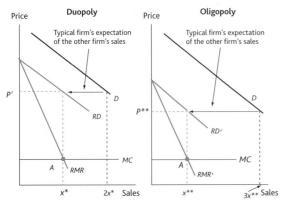

Figure 6.4: *Duopoly and oligopoly: expectation-consistent outputs*

optimal output for a typical firm is x^*, given by the intersection of *RMR* and *MC*; (ii) the total sales to the market are $2x^*$ and at this level of sales the overall market price (given by the demand curve, *D*) is consistent with the price each firm expects to receive given the residual demand curve, *RD*; and (iii) the output of the identical firms are equal in equilibrium.

6.2.2 Oligopoly: Cournot–Nash for an arbitrary number of firms

While allowing for two firms was more realistic than allowing for only one firm, studying the impact of European integration on mergers and acquisitions requires us to allow for an arbitrary number of firms. In economists' jargon, this situation is called an oligopoly. As it turns out, this situation is straightforward to deal with when firms are symmetric. The right-hand panel of Fig. 6.4 shows the argument for the case of three firms.

As more firms are competing in the market (here we consider three instead of two), the residual demand curve facing each one shifts inwards, so the residual marginal revenue curve also shifts inwards; the new curves are shown in the right-hand panel as RD' and RMR'. The implications of this shift for prices is clear. The new $RMR = MC$ point occurs at a lower level of per-firm output and this implies a lower price. In equilibrium (i.e. where outcomes match expectations), each of the three firms produces an identical amount, identified as x^{**} in the diagram, and charges an identical price, p^{**}.

Given that we have worked through the 1, 2 and 3 firm cases, readers should be able to see what would happen

as the number of firms continues to rise. Each increase in the number of competitors will shift inwards the *RD* curve facing each one of them. This will inevitably lead to lower prices and lower output per firm.

Of course, this analysis is just formalizing what most readers would expect. If one adds more competitors to a market, prices will fall along with the market share of each firm. As is so often the case, the brilliant concepts are simple.

6.3 The *BE–COMP* diagram in a closed economy

To study the impact of European integration on firm size and efficiency, the number of firms, prices, output and the like, it is useful to have a diagram in which all of these things are determined. The presentation of this diagram, which actually consists of three sub-diagrams, is the first order of business. To keep things simple, we begin with the case of a closed economy. Advanced readers may find the mathematical appendix to this chapter helpful in understanding the diagrams (freely downloadable from www.hei.unige.ch/~baldwin/PapersBooks/.).

The heart of the *BE–COMP* diagram is the sub-diagram in which the number of firms and the profit-maximizing price–cost margin are determined. As usual, the equilibrium will be the intersection of two curves, the *BE* curve and the *COMP* curve. We start by presenting the *COMP* curve.

6.3.1 The COMP curve

It is easy to understand that imperfectly competitive firms charge a price that exceeds their marginal cost; they do so in order to maximize profit. But how wide is the gap between price and marginal cost, and how does it vary with the number of competitors? These questions are answered by the *COMP* curve.

If there is only one firm, the price–cost gap – what we call the 'mark-up' of price over marginal cost – will equal the mark-up that a monopolist would charge. If there are more firms competing in the market, competition will force each firm to charge a lower mark-up. We summarize this 'competition-side' relationship between the mark-up and the number of firms as the '*COMP* curve' shown in Fig. 6.5. It is

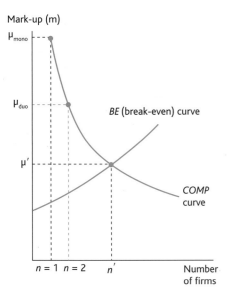

Mark-up (m)

μ_{mono}

μ_{duo}

BE (break-even) curve

μ'

COMP curve

$n = 1$ $n = 2$ n' Number of firms

Figure 6.5: *The COMP and BE curves*

downward sloping since competition drives the mark-up down as the number of competitors rises, as explained above. We denote the mark-up with the Greek letter μ, pronounced mu, since 'mu' is a convenient abbreviation for mark-up. We call it the *COMP* curve since the size of the mark-up is an indicator of how competitive the market is.

While this intuitive connection between price and marginal cost may suffice for some readers, extra insight is gained by considering the derivation of the *COMP* curve in more detail. This is done in Box 6.3.

6.3.2 The break-even (BE) curve

The mark-up and number of firms are related in another way, summarized by the *BE* curve.

When a sector is marked by increasing returns to scale, there is only room for a certain number of firms in a market of a given size. Intuitively, more firms will be able to survive if the price is far above marginal cost, i.e. if the mark-up is high. The curve that captures this relationship is called the break-even curve, or zero-profit curve (*BE* curve, for short) in Fig. 6.5. It has a positive (upward) slope since more firms can break even when the mark-up is high. That is to say, taking the mark-up as given, the *BE* curve shows the number of firms that can earn enough to cover their fixed cost, which might be the cost of setting up a factory, for example.

Again, this intuitive presentation of the *BE* curve will suffice for many readers, but might well raise questions in the minds of more advanced readers. These questions are addressed in Box 6.4.

6.3.3 Equilibrium prices, output and firm size

It is important to note that firms are not always on the *BE* curve since they can earn above-normal or below-normal profits for a while. In the long run, however, firms can enter or exit the market, so the number of firms rises or falls until the typical firm earns just enough to cover its fixed cost. By contrast, firms are always on the *COMP* curve since firms can change prices quickly in response to any change in the number of firms.

With this in mind, we are ready to work out the equilibrium mark-up, number of firms, price and firm size in a closed economy using Fig. 6.8. The right-hand panel combines the *BE* curve with the *COMP* curve. The intersection of the two defines the equilibrium mark-up and long-run number of firms. More specifically, the *COMP* curve tells us that firms would charge a mark-up of μ' when there are n' firms in the market, and the *BE* curve tells us that n' firms could break even when the mark-up is μ'. The equilibrium price is, by definition of the mark-up, just the equilibrium mark-up plus the marginal cost, *MC*. Using the *MC* curve from the left-hand panel, we see that the equilibrium price is p' (this equals μ' plus *MC*). The middle panel shows the demand curve and this allows us to see that the total level of consumption implied by the equilibrium price is C'.

The left-hand panel helps us to find the equilibrium firm size, i.e. sales per firm, which we denote as x'. This sub-diagram shows the average and marginal cost curves of a typical firm. As a little reflection reveals, a typical firm's total profit is zero when price equals average cost (when price equals average cost, total revenue equals total cost). Since we know that total profits are zero at the equilibrium and we know the price is p', it must be that the equilibrium firm size is x' since this is where the firm's size implies an average cost equal to p'.

In summary, Fig. 6.8 lets us determine the equilibrium number of firms, mark-up, price, total consumption and firm size all in one diagram. With this in hand, we are now ready to study how European integration has sparked a wave of industrial restructuring.

Box 6.3

COMP curve in detail

Consider how the profit-maximizing mark-up changes when the number of firms increases. To keep the reasoning concrete, consider an increase from one firm (the monopoly case) to two firms (the duopoly case). The solid lines in the left-hand panel of Fig. 6.6 show the usual problem for a monopolist, with the demand curve marked as D and the marginal revenue curve marked as MR. (See section 6.2, if you are not familiar with the monopolist case.) The profit-maximizing output, x_{mono}, is indicated by the point A, i.e. the intersection of marginal cost (marked as MC in the diagram) and marginal revenue (marked as MR in the diagram). The firm charges the most it can for the level of sales x_{mono}, i.e. p'. The price–marginal-cost mark-up (called the mark-up for short) equals $p' - MC$, as shown. We can also see the size of operating profit (i.e. profit without considering fixed cost) in the diagram since it is, by definition, just the monopolist mark-up times the monopoly level of sales x_{mono}. In the diagram this is shown by the area of the box marked by the points p', A', A and MC.

When a second firm competes in this market, we have a duopoly rather than a monopoly. To solve this, we adopt the standard Cournot–Nash approach of assuming that each firm takes as given the output of the other firm(s). Practically speaking, this means that each firm acts as if it were a monopolist on the 'residual demand curve', i.e. the demand curve shifted to the left by the amount of other firms' sales (marked as RD in the diagram). The exact equilibrium price and output are found by identifying the intersection of the residual marginal revenue curve (RMR) and the marginal cost curve; again, firms charge the highest possible price for this level of sales, namely p''. In drawing the diagram, we have supposed that the two firms have identical marginal cost curves (for simplicity), so the outcome of the competition will be that each firm sells an equal amount. You can verify that p'' is the price that the full demand curve, D, says would result if two times x_{duo} were sold.

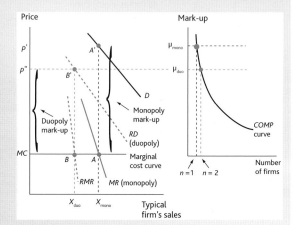

Figure 6.6: *Impact of more firms on prices and price–cost mark-ups*

The net result of adding a firm is that the price drops from p' to p'' and thus lowers the equilibrium mark-up. We also note that more competition lowers the level of sales per firm, although the sum of sales of the two competing firms exceeds the sales of a monopolist. Finally, note that adding in more firms lowers each firm's operating profit since it reduces the mark-up and sales per firm. The duopoly operating profit is the duopoly mark-up times x_{duo}; this is shown by the area p'', B', B, MC in the diagram.

Here we have looked only at the switch from one to two firms, but it should be clear that continuing to add in more firms would produce a similar result. As the number of firms rose, the residual demand curve facing each firm would shift inwards, resulting in a lower price, lower level of output per firm and, most importantly, in a lower price–cost margin, i.e. a lower mark-up. In the extreme, an infinite number of firms would push the price down to marginal cost, eliminating the price–cost margin and all operating profits; each firm would be infinitely small (this is why perfectly competitive firms are sometimes called atomistic).

Box 6.4

Derivation of the *BE* curve

While the positive link between mark-up and the break-even number of firms is quite intuitive, it is useful to study the relationship more closely. To keep the reasoning as easy as possible we consider the simplest form of increasing returns to scale, namely a situation where the typical firm faces a flat marginal cost curve and a fixed cost of operating. The fixed cost could represent, for example, the cost of building a factory, establishing a brand name or training workers. This combination of fixed cost and flat marginal cost implies increasing returns since the typical firm's average cost falls as its scale of production rises, as is shown in the left-hand panel of Fig. 6.7.

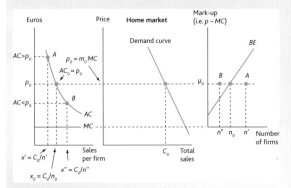

Figure 6.7: *The BE curve in detail*

If a firm is to survive in this situation, it must earn enough on its sales to cover its fixed cost. The amount it earns on sales is called its 'operating profit', and this is simply the mark-up times the level of sales. For example, if the mark-up (i.e. price minus marginal cost) is €200 and each firm sells 20 000 units, then the operating profit per firm will be €4 million. As we shall see, this simple connection between the mark-up, sales and operating profit makes it quite easy to figure out the number of firms that can break even at any given mark-up.

Since all firms are identical in this example, a given mark-up implies that the price will also be given, specifically it will equal the mark-up plus marginal cost. For example, if the mark-up is μ_0 as in Fig. 6.7, then the price will be $p_0 = \mu_0 + MC$. At this price, the demand curve tells us that the level of total sales will

be C_0. Finally, we again use the symmetry of firms to work out the level of sales per firm; this will be total sales divided by the number of firms, which, in symbols, is C_0/n. To see how many firms can break even when the mark-up is μ_0, we turn to the left-hand panel in the diagram. With a little thought, you should be able to see that a firm will make zero total profit (i.e. operating profit plus the fixed cost) when its average cost exactly equals the price. Using the average cost curve, marked as AC in the left-hand panel, we see that the typical firm's average cost equals price when the sales of the typical firm equals x_0. Because we know that sales per firm will be C_0/n, we can work out the number of firms where the sales per firm just equal x_0. In symbols, the break-even number of firms, call this n_0, is where C_0/n_0 equals x_0.

It is instructive to consider what would happen if the mark-up were μ_0 but there were more than n_0 firms, say n' firms, in the market. In this case, the sales per firm would be lower than x_0, namely $x' = C_0/n'$, so the typical firm's average cost would be higher and this means that the average cost of a typical firm would exceed the price. Plainly, such a situation is not sustainable since all the firms would be losing money (earning operating profits that were too low to allow them to cover their fixed cost). This case is shown by point A in the left-hand panel of the diagram. The same point A can be shown in the right-hand panel as the combination of the mark-up μ_0 and n'; we know that at this point, firms are not covering their fixed cost, so there would be a tendency for some firms to exit the industry. In the real world this sort of 'exit' takes the form of mergers or bankruptcies. The opposite case of too few firms is shown in the right- and left-hand panels as point B; here firms' average cost is below the price and so all are making pure profits (i.e. their operating profits exceed the fixed cost). Such a situation would encourage more firms to enter the market.

To work out all the points on the *BE* curve, we would go through a similar analysis for every given level of the mark-up. The logic presented above, however, makes it clear that the result would be an upward-sloping *BE* curve.

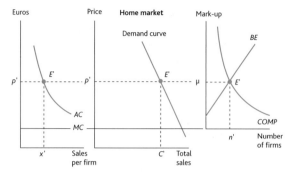

Figure 6.8: *Prices, output and equilibrium firm size in a closed economy*

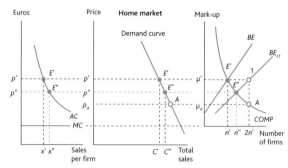

Figure 6.9: *Prices, output and equilibrium firm size with integration*

Note: Readers who find these diagrams complicated may benefit from the interactive PowerPoint presentations on http://heiwww.unige.ch/~Baldwin/BW/BW.htm.

6.4 The impact of European liberalization

European integration has involved a gradual reduction of trade barriers. The basic economic effects of this gradual reduction can, however, be illustrated more simply by considering a much more drastic liberalization: taking a completely closed economy and making it a completely open economy. To keep things simple, we suppose that there are only two nations, Home and Partner, and that these nations are identical. Since they are identical, we could trace through the effects looking at either market, but we focus on Home's market for convenience.

6.4.1 No-trade-to-free-trade liberalization

The immediate impact of the no-trade-to-free-trade liberalization is to provide each firm with a second market of the same size and to double the number of competitors in each market. How does this change the outcome?

The competition aspect of the liberalization is simple to trace out. The increased number of competitors in each market makes competition tougher. In reaction, the typical firm will lower its mark-up in each market to point A in Fig. 6.9.

The doubling of the market size facing each firm also has an important effect. The liberalization adds a new market for each firm, so it makes sense that more firms will be able to survive. To see how many more firms can survive,

we work out the impact of the liberalization on the *BE* curve. As it turns out, the liberalization shifts the *BE* curve to the right, specifically to BE_{FT}, as shown in the diagram. Why? Shifting *BE* to the right means that at any given mark-up more firms can break even. This is true since as the market size increases the sales per firm increase, thus providing a higher operating profit per firm at any given level of the mark-up.

The size of the rightward shift is determined without difficulty. If there were no change in the mark-up (there will be in the new equilibrium, but ignore this for the moment), then double the number of firms could break even since each firm would be selling the same number of units. In other words, the new *BE* curve must pass through the point marked 1 in the diagram; at point 1, the mark-up is μ', the number of firms is $2n'$, and logic tells us that this combination of μ and n would result in all firms breaking even. Point 1, however, is merely an intellectual landmark used to determine how far out the *BE* curve shifts. It is not where the economy would be right after liberalization since the mark-up would immediately be pushed down to μA.

Because the increase in competition would immediately push down the mark-up to μA, the two newly integrated markets will initially be at a point that is below the *BE* curve. We know that all firms will be losing money at point *A* since the actual mark-up (μA) is less than what would be needed to have all $2n'$ firms break even. Now, this loss of profit is not a problem in the short run since firms need only to break even in the long run. Indeed, the profit losses are what would trigger the process of industrial restructuring that will eventually reduce the number of firms.

The corresponding effect on prices is shown in the middle diagram as the move from E' to A and then to E''. Before explaining this, observe that the middle panel shows the demand curve for Home only, so the no-trade-to-free-trade liberalization does not shift the demand curve. The Foreign market has an identical demand, but since exactly the same thing goes on in Foreign, we omit the Foreign demand curve to reduce the diagram's complexity.

As mentioned above, the initial impact of the extra competition ($2n'$ firms selling to the Home market instead of n') pushes the equilibrium mark-up down to μA, so the price falls to pA. Thus during this industrial restructuring phase, price would rise to p'' (from pA), but this rise does not take the price all the way back to its pre-liberalization level of p'.

The impact of this combination of extra competition and industrial restructuring on a typical firm is shown in the left-hand panel. As prices are falling, firms that remain in the market increase their efficiency, i.e. lower their average costs, by spreading their fixed cost over a larger number of sales. Indeed, since price equalled average cost before the liberalization and in the long run after liberalization, we know that the price drop is exactly equal to the efficiency gain. In the left-hand panel, this is shown as a move from E' to E''. Increasing returns to scale are the root of this efficiency gain. As the equilibrium scale of a typical firm rises from x' to x'', average costs fall.

To summarize, the no-trade-to-free-trade liberalization results in fewer, larger firms. The resulting scale economies lower average cost and thus make these firms more efficient. The extra competition ensures that these savings are passed on to lower prices. It is useful to think of the integration as leading to two steps.

Step 1. Short term: defragmentation and the pro-competitive effect (from E' to A)
We start with the short-term impact, that is to say, the impact before the number of firms can adjust. Before the liberalization, each market was extremely fragmented in the sense that firms in each nation had a local market share of $1/n'$ and a zero share in the other market. After the liberalization, the market share of each firm is the same in each market, namely $n'/2$. This elimination of market fragmentation has a pro-competitive effect, which is defined as a decrease in the price–cost mark-up. This is shown in the right-hand panel of Fig. 6.9 as a move from E' to A. The short-term impact on prices and sales can be seen in the middle panel as a drop from p' to pA.

Step 2. Long term: industrial restructuring and scale effects (A to E'')

Point A is not a long-term equilibrium since the operating profit earned by a typical firm is insufficient to cover the fixed cost. We see this by noting that point A is below the BE curve and this tells us that the mark-up is too low to allow $2n'$ firms to break even. To restore a normal level of profitability, the overall number of firms has to fall from $2n'$ to n''. In Europe, this process typically occurs via mergers and buyouts, but in some cases the number of firms is reduced by bankruptcies. As this industrial consolidation occurs, the economy moves from point A to point E''. During this process, firms enlarge their market shares, the mark-up rises somewhat and profitability is restored.

Welfare effects

The welfare effects of this liberalization are quite straightforward. The four-sided area marked by p', p'', E' and E'' in the middle panel of Fig. 6.9 corresponds to the gain in Home consumer surplus. As usual, this gain can be broken down into the gain to consumers of paying a lower price for the units they bought prior to the liberalization, and the gains from buying more (C'' versus C'). Note that the exact same gain occurs in the Foreign market (not shown in the diagram).

As it turns out, this four-sided region, labelled **A** in Figure 6.10, is Home's long-term welfare gain because there is no offsetting loss to producers and there was no tariff revenue to begin with. Firms made zero profits before liberalization and they earn zero profits after liberalization. Note, however, that this long-term calculation ignores the medium-term adjustment costs. These costs, which stem from the industrial restructuring, can be politically very important. Indeed, many governments attempt to thwart the restructuring by adopting a variety of policies such as industrial subsidies and various anti-merger and anti-acquisition policies (discussed in Chapter 11). We should also note that the welfare gains shown can be rather substantial.

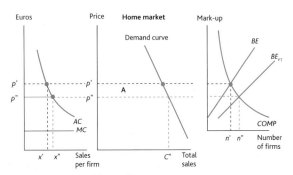

Figure 6.10: *Welfare effects*

Roughly speaking, the percentage gain in real GDP equals the share of the economy affected (industry in the EU, for instance, accounts for about 30 per cent of output) times the percentage drop in price.

6.4.2 Slow and fast adjustments

The discussion above has shown that the integration initially leads to big price reductions and large profit losses. These profit losses are eliminated as the number of firms falls and profits are restored to normal levels. During this industrial restructuring process, prices rise slightly. This sequence of steps – sometimes called industry 'consolidation' or 'shake-out' – is relevant to some industries, for example, air travel. Here Europe's liberalization has resulted in large profit losses for many European airlines and big price reductions for consumers. At first, airlines were reluctant to merge – largely because most airlines were government-owned and their governments were willing to use taxpayer euros to cover the losses. More recently, however, European airlines are rationalizing their costs by forming cooperative alliances. While the actual number of firms has not yet fallen, the number of planes flying a particular route is reduced. For example, before the two firms went bankrupt, cooperation between Swiss Air and Sabena, the Belgian national airline, meant that instead of having two planes flying the Geneva–Brussels route (one Swiss Air and one Sabena), only one plane flew. Nevertheless, Swiss Air called it a Swiss Air flight and Sabena called it a Sabena flight. Such 'code-sharing' arrangements are a way of achieving scale economies without actually eliminating a national carrier. Interestingly, both airlines eventually went bankrupt but the Swiss and Belgian governments stepped in to create replacement airlines, Swiss and SN Brussels Airlines.

In other industries, firms anticipate the increased competition and undertake the mergers and acquisitions quickly enough to avoid big losses. European banking is an example. The introduction of the euro and continuing liberalization of the banking sector mean that European banks will have to become fewer and bigger in order to break even. However, instead of waiting for profit losses to become intolerable, banks have launched a record-breaking series of mergers and acquisitions. In terms of Fig. 6.9, this would look like a move from E' directly to E''.

6.4.3 Empirical evidence

There is ample empirical evidence that European industry is marked by fewer, bigger, more efficient firms since the Single Market Programme. For example, the 1996 Single Market Review by the European Commission presents several studies illustrating these trends (see Commission, 1996, for a brief review of this multi-volume study). Unfortunately, there is little direct evidence in Europe that it was caused by market integration, although this is what most economists believe is the obvious explanation. More direct evidence linking market size with efficiency and competition can be found in Campbell and Hopenhayn (2002). The authors study the impact of market size on the size distribution of firms in retail industries across 225 US cities. In every industry examined, establishments were larger in larger cities. The authors conclude that their results support the notion that competition is tougher in larger markets and this accounts for the link between firm size and market size.

6.5 Summary

Three main points have been made in this chapter:

★ One very obvious impact of European integration has been to face individual European firms with a bigger 'home' market. This produces a chain reaction that leads to fewer, bigger, more efficient firms that face more effective competition from each other. Understanding the economic logic driving this chain reaction is the main goal of this chapter. This logic can be summarized as follows. Integration defragments Europe's markets in the sense that it removes the privileged position of national firms in their national markets. As a result, all firms face more competition from other firms in their national market, but at the same time they have better access to the other EU markets. This general increase in competition puts downward pressure on price–cost mark-ups, prices and profits. The profit squeeze results in industrial restructuring, a process by which the total number of firms in Europe falls. The lower price and lower number of firms means that the average firm becomes larger and this, in turn, allows firms to better exploit economies of scale. This efficiency increase, in turn, permits the firms to break even despite the lower prices.

★ The industrial restructuring is often politically painful since it may result in lay-offs and the closure of inefficient plants. Governments often attempt to offset this political pain by providing state aid to their national firms. Such state aid can be viewed as unfair, and the perception of unfairness threatens to undermine EU members' interest in integration. To avoid these problems, the founders of the EU established rules that prohibit state aid that distorts competition. The Commission is charged with enforcing these rules. These rules are covered in Chapter 11.

★ Industrial restructuring raises another problem that led the EU's founders to set out another set of rules. As integration proceeds and the number of firms falls, the temptation for firms to collude may increase. To avoid this, the EU has strict rules on anti-competitive practices. The EU also screens mergers to ensure that the merger will enhance efficiency. Again, the Commission is charged with enforcing these rules. These rules are covered in Chapter 11.

Self-assessment questions

1. Suppose that liberalization occurs as in section 6.4 and the result is a pro-competitive effect, but instead of merging or restructuring, all firms are bought by their national governments to allow the firms to continue operating. What will be the impact of this on prices and government revenues? Now that the governments are the owners, will they have an incentive to continue with liberalization? Can you imagine why this might favour firms located in nations with big, rich governments?

2. Use a three-panel diagram, like Fig. 6.8, to show how the number of firms, mark-up and firm size would change in a closed economy if the demand for the particular good rose, i.e. the demand curve shifted outwards.

3. Using your findings from Question 2, you should be able to consider the impact of a no-trade-to-free-trade integration between a large and a small nation, where size is defined by the position of the demand curve (the demand curve in the large nation will be further out than the demand curve in the small nation). To do this, you will need two of the three-panelled diagrams of the Fig. 6.8 type to show the pre-integration situation. Then use a three-panelled diagram of the Fig. 6.9 type to show what happens to prices, firm size and the number of firms in the integrated economy. Note that you will want to show both demand curves in the middle panel. As usual, assume that all firms have the same marginal cost. What does this analysis tell you about how integration affects firms in small nations versus large nations?

4. Consider a sequence of EU 'enlargements' where each enlargement involves a no-trade-to-free-trade addition of one more member. Specifically, suppose there are three initially identical economies, each of which looks like the one described in section 6.3. Initially, all nations are closed to trade. Now, consider a no-trade-to-free-trade integration between two of the nations (just as in section 6.4). Then consider a no-trade-to-free-trade integration of a third nation. (Hint: The second step will be very much like the integration between unequal-sized economies explored in Question 3.) Calculate how much the third nation gains from joining and compare it with how much the existing two-nation bloc gains from the third nation's membership. Who gains more in proportion to size: the incumbents or the entrant?

Essay questions

1. When the Single Market Programme was launched in the mid-1980s, European leaders asserted that it would improve the competitiveness of European firms *vis-à-vis* US firms. Explain how one can make sense of this assertion by extending the reasoning in this chapter.

2. Has the strategy of defragmenting Europe's markets worked in the sense of promoting bigger, more efficient firms facing more effective competition? Choose an industry, for example telecoms, chemicals, pharmaceuticals or autos, and compare the evaluation of the EU industry with that of the US or Japan. You can find information on these and many more industries at the Commission website http://europa.eu.int/comm/enterprise/index_en.htm. Search the site with Google to find specific information on specific sectors.

3. Some EU members allow their companies to engage in 'anti-takeover' practices. Discuss how differences in EU members' laws concerning these practices might be viewed as unfair when EU industry is being transformed by a wave of mergers and acquisitions.

4. Write an essay on the historical role of the scale economies argument played in the economic case for deeper European integration. Start with the Spaak Report (see www.ena.lu) and the Cockfield Report, *Completing the Internal Market*, White Paper, COM (85) 310 final (you can find it in French, *Livre blanc sur l'achèvement du marché intérieur* on www.ena.lu under the subject 'The Delors White Paper').

Further reading:
the aficionado's corner

Consideration of imperfect competition and scale effects was made possible in the 1980s with development of the so-called new trade theory (Helpman and Krugman, 1985, 1989). The new theory was naturally applied to analysis of the Single Market Programme when it was first discussed in the mid-1980s. Many of the classic studies are contained in Winters (1992). Baldwin and Venables (1995) provides a synthetic, graduate-level survey of this literature.

An alternative presentation of the theory and a thorough empirical evaluation is provided by Allen *et al.* (1998b).

Useful websites

A large number of evaluations of the single market, most of which employ ICIR frameworks, can be found on http://europa.eu.int/comm/economy_finance/publications/; the document *The Internal Market: 10 Years without Frontiers* is especially useful. This site also posts the annual *State Aids Report*, which provides the latest data on subsidies.

References

Allen, C., M. Gasiorek and M.A.M. Smith (1998a) 'The competition effects of the single market', *Economic Policy*, London; downloadable from www.economicpolicy.org.

Allen, C., M. Gasiorek and M. A. M. Smith (1998b) 'European single market: how the programme has fostered competition', *Economic Policy*, 441–86.

Baldwin, R. and A. Venables (1995) 'Regional economic integration', in G. Grossman and K. Rogoff (eds) *Handbook of International Economics*, North-Holland, New York.

Campbell, J. and H. Hopenhayn (2002) *Market Size Matters*, NBER Working Paper 9113, Cambridge, Mass.

Commission (1996) *The 1996 Single Market Review: Background Information for the Report to the Council and European Parliament*, Commission Staff Working Paper, Brussels. Download from http://europa.eu.int/comm/internal_market/en/update/impact/index.htm.

European Economy (2001) Supplement A, No. 12, December. Download from http://europa.eu.int/comm/economy_finance/publications/supplement_a_en.htm.

Helpman, E. and P. Krugman (1985) *Market Structure and Foreign Trade: Increasing Returns, Imperfect Competition and the International Economy*, MIT Press, Cambridge, Mass.

Helpman, E. and P. Krugman (1989) *Trade Policy and Market Structure*, MIT Press, Cambridge, Mass.

Winters, L.A. (1992) *Trade Flows and Trade Policies after '1992'*, Cambridge University Press, Cambridge.

The Union has today set itself a new strategic goal for the next decade: to become the most competitive and dynamic knowledge-based economy in the world capable of sustainable economic growth with more and better jobs and greater social cohesion.

Presidency Conclusions, Lisbon European Council, March 2000

Growth effects and factor market integration

7.1 The logic of growth and the facts

7.1.1 The logic of growth: medium-run and long-run effects

7.1.2 Post-war European growth: the evidence

7.1.3 Are growth and European integration related?

7.2 Medium-run growth effects: induced capital formation with Solow's analysis

7.2.1 Solow diagram

7.2.2 Liberalization, allocation effects and the medium-run growth bonus

7.2.3 Other medium-run growth effects: changes in the investment rate

7.2.4 Evidence from the 'poor four'

7.3 Long-run growth effects: faster knowledge creation and absorption

7.3.1 Solow-like diagram with long-run growth

7.4 Summary

INTRODUCTION

The two previous chapters looked at 'allocation effects' of European integration, i.e. the impact on the efficiency with which economic resources within nations are allocated across economic activities. Allocation effects are one-off in the sense that a single policy change leads to a single reallocation of resources. European leaders, however, have long emphasized a different type of economic effect: the growth effect. Growth effects operate in a way that is fundamentally different from allocation effects; they operate by changing the rate at which new factors of production – mainly capital – are accumulated, hence the name 'accumulation effects'.

Factor market integration is another channel by which European integration can change the supply of productive factors within EU members. Under EU rules, citizens of any EU nation may work in any other EU nation. Similar rules guarantee the free movement of capital, so this aspect of European integration can, in principle, alter the amount of productive factors employed in any given EU member. Or, to put it differently, capital and labour movements can look like an allocation-of-resources effect from the EU perspective, but like an accumulation effect from the national perspective. This chapter therefore also studies the economics of factor market integration.

7.1 The logic of growth and the facts

The link between European integration and growth rests on the logic of growth. The logic of growth is simple but widely misunderstood, so before looking at the facts, we briefly present the logic of growth in words.

7.1.1 The logic of growth: medium-run and long-run effects

Economic growth means producing more and more every year. Per-capita growth means an annual rise in the output per person. In most western European nations, output per capita rises at between 1 and 3 per cent per year in normal times. How does this happen?

If a nation's workers are to produce more goods and services year after year, the economy must provide workers with more 'tools' year after year. Here 'tools' is meant in the broadest possible sense – what economists call capital. Three categories of capital must be distinguished:

★ physical capital (machines, etc.);
★ human capital (skills, training, experience, etc.);
★ knowledge capital (technology).

Given this necessity, the rate of output growth is hitched straight to the rate of physical, human and knowledge capital accumulation. Most capital accumulation is intentional and is called investment. Accordingly, we can say that European integration affects growth mainly via its effect on investment in human capital, physical capital and knowledge capital. The qualification 'mainly' is necessary since integration may unintentionally affect accumulation, for instance by speeding the international dissemination of technological progress (this is especially important in central European nations).

Growth effects fall naturally into two categories: medium term and long term. An instance of medium-term effects is 'induced physical capital formation'. For all the reasons documented in the previous chapters, European integration improves the efficiency with which productive factors are combined to produce output. As a side effect, this heightened efficiency typically makes Europe a better place to invest, so more investment occurs. The result is that the initial efficiency gains from integration are boosted by induced capital formation. While the above-normal capital formation is occurring, the economies experience a medium-term growth effect. This growth effect is only medium term since it will eventually peter out: as the amount of capital per worker rises, the gain from investing in each further unit of capital diminishes. Eventually the gain from investing in an extra unit reaches the cost of doing so and the above-normal capital formation stops. A good example of this is the investment boom that Spain experienced around the time of its accession to the EU.

Long-term growth effects involve a permanent change in the rate of accumulation, and thereby a permanent change in the rate of growth. Since the accumulation of physical capital faces diminishing returns, long-run growth effects typically refer to the rate of accumulation of knowledge capital, i.e. technological progress.

To summarize the logic of growth effects schematically: European integration (or any other policy) → allocation effect → improved efficiency → better investment climate → more investment in machines, skills and/or technology → higher output per person. Under medium-run growth effects, the rise in output per person eventually stops at a new, higher level. Under long-run growth effects, the rate of growth is forever higher.

7.1.2 Post-war European growth: the evidence

Any informed discussion of European integration and economic growth must begin with a fistful of overarching facts. We first cover these facts before setting out a prima facie case that European integration has, broadly speaking, been favourable to growth in the post-war period.

Phases of European growth

By historical standards, continuous economic growth is a relatively recent phenomenon. Before the Industrial Revolution, which started in Great Britain in the late 1700s, European incomes had stagnated for a millennium and a half. It has been estimated that the real earnings of a typical British factory worker in 1850 were no higher than those of a typical free Roman artisan in the first century (Cameron and Neal, 2003). Between the glory years of the Roman Empire and the Industrial Revolution, periods of prosperity were offset by famines, plagues and warfare that brought the average person back to the brink of starvation.

With industrialization, which had spread to most of continental Europe by 1870, incomes began to rise at a respectable rate of around 2 per cent per year. Growth rates, however, were hardly constant from this date – four growth phases are traditionally defined, as Table 7.1 shows. During the 1890–1913 period (often called the *Belle Époque*) real GDP grew at 2.6 per cent annually. This is considered to be a very good growth rate, and is enough to double GDP every 27 years. Since population was also growing rapidly in this period, real GDP per person rose at only 1.7 per cent per year.

Period	Real GDP growth	Real GDP growth per capita	Real GDP growth per hour
1890–1913	2.6	1.7	1.6
1913–50	1.4	1.0	1.9
1950–73	4.6	3.8	4.7
1973–92	2.0	1.7	2.7
Whole period 1890–1992	2.5	1.9	2.6

Notes: Figures are annual averages for 12 nations (Austria, Belgium, Denmark, Finland, France, Germany, Italy, Netherlands, Norway, Sweden, Switzerland, UK) all adjusted for boundary changes.

Note that the 1950–73 perod is the aberration. Both before and after this period, growth rates were just under 2 per cent per year (excluding the unusual 1913–50 period). The Golden Age was also the most intensive period of European integration and it was this correlation that first started economists thinking about the growth effects of European integration.

Source: Crafts and Toniolo (1996), p. 2.

Table 7.1: *European growth phases, 1890–1992*

These rates were approximately halved during the 1913–50 period (i.e. from the First World War until the end of the post-Second World War reconstruction period). Despite this, the GDP per hour worked accelerated slightly to 1.9 per cent since the average hours worked per year fell with the introduction and spread of labour unions and social legislation.

The period from 1950 to 1973 is called the Golden Age of growth; throughout the world, but especially in Europe, growth rates jumped. Real GDP growth rates more than tripled and per-capita GDP growth almost quadrupled. At this pace, per-capita incomes would double every 18.6 years, implying that the material standard of living would quadruple in an average lifetime. Unfortunately, the Golden Age ended after only 23 years for reasons that are still not entirely understood. Since 1973, the date of the first oil shock, per-capita incomes have progressed at only 1.9 per cent per year. However, as the working week has been further shortened during this period, GDP-per-hour-worked continued to progress at a respectable 2.7 per cent per year.

Growth performance during the 1913–50 period was far from homogeneous. This phase, which Crafts and Toniolo (1996) aptly call the 'second Thirty Years' War', contains the two world wars and the Great Depression, each of which was responsible for massive income drops. It also,

	The setback: pre-war year when GDP equalled that of 1945	Back-on-track year: year GDP attained highest pre-war level	Reconstruction: growth rate during reconstruction years (1945 to column 2 year) (%)
Austria	1886	1951	15.2
Belgium	1924	1948	6.0
Denmark	1936	1946	13.5
Finland	1938	1945	n.a.
France	1891	1949	19.0
Germany	1908	1951	13.5
Italy	1909	1950	11.2
Netherlands	1912	1947	39.8
Norway	1937	1946	9.7
Sweden			
Switzerland	These countries actually grew during the Second World War		
UK			

Source: Crafts and Toniolo (1996), p. 4.

Table 7.2: *Growth in the post-Second World War reconstruction phase*

however, contains the most spectacular growth phase that Europe has ever seen, namely the years of reconstruction, 1945–50. Table 7.2 shows various aspects of this 'reconstruction period' for twelve European nations.

The first point (a point we also made in Chapter 1) is that the Second World War caused enormous economic damage. It cost Germany and Italy four decades or more of growth and put Austrian and French GDPs back to nineteenth-century levels. Despite this, recovery was remarkably rapid. By 1951, every European nation was back on the pre-war growth path. This resurgence was due to a short period of truly astonishing growth. All the growth rates were double-digit (except Belgium's); France, for instance, grew at almost 20 per cent per year for four consecutive years, and the Netherlands grew at almost twice that pace for two years. To a large extent, however, this rapid growth is an illusion. It consisted of merely setting back up or repairing production facilities created in earlier years. This also indicates that much of the Second World War drop in GDP was due to the temporary disorganization of Europe's economy rather than to permanent destruction.

7.1.3 Are growth and European integration related?

The prima facie case

The Brothers Grimm tale of the rooster who believes that his crowing makes the sun rise each day should alert us to the dangers of confusing correlation and causality. There is, nonetheless, some general evidence – what might be called prima facie evidence in a court of law – that supports the integration-fosters-growth hypothesis.

The first element of the prima facie case concerns a country-by-country analysis of growth during the 1950–73 period. Recall from Chapter 1 that this period saw rapid integration among European nations. From 1950 to 1958, the main liberalization was common to west European nations, but from 1958 to 1968 the EEC6 integrated much faster than did EFTA members (UK, Sweden, Switzerland, Finland, Norway, Austria, Portugal and Iceland). Table 7.3 shows the growth performance of various OEEC members during this period. Focusing first on the third column, we note that the EEC6 (data for Luxembourg were not available) rose in the GDP per capita rankings. Germany jumped five places, Italy two, while the Netherlands and Belgium slipped slightly. By contrast, the EFTAns lost ground, with the UK and Norway dropping five and four places, respectively, with Sweden and Denmark gaining one, and Austria gaining two.

The non-EEC, non-EFTA nations also lost, especially Ireland, which was tightly linked to EFTA by a bilateral free trade agreement with the UK. Note also that the average growth performance of the EEC members was almost 50 per cent better than that of the EFTAns, although much of this may be explained by a 'catching-up' phenomenon (EEC nations were poorer than EFTAns in 1950 and poorer nations tend to grow more quickly than do rich nations).

What is particularly striking is the performance of the 'big 4' nations, France, Germany, Italy and the UK. The first three were members of the EEC and grew between 1.7 and 2.1 times faster than the UK. Again, catch-up played some role in this, but by 1973 both France and Germany were richer than the UK, so the catch-up roles were reversed by the end of the period. This suggests a correlation between integration and growth since the economic integration in the EEC was much tighter than that of the EFTA during this period.

Of course, not much should be read into such simple correlation, but at the time the UK's laggard growth

	1950 GDP (1990 $)	European rank 1950	Change in rank 1950–73	GDP growth rate 1950–73 (%)
EEC average	**4825**	**8.0**	**+1.2**	**4.2**
Netherlands	5850	5	−1	3.4
Belgium	5346	6	−2	3.5
France	5221	7	+2	4.0
Germany	4281	9	+5	5.0
Italy	3425	13	+2	4.9
EFTA average	**6835**	**3.6**	**−1.4**	**3.0**
Switzerland	8939	1	0	3.1
UK	6847	2	−5	2.4
Sweden	6738	3	+1	3.1
Denmark	6683	4	+1	3.1
Norway	4969	8	−4	3.2
Finland	4131	10	0	4.2
Austria	3731	11	+2	4.9
Others average	**2401**	**14.3**	**−0.3**	**5.2**
Ireland	3518	12	−3	3.1
Spain	2397	14	+1	5.8
Portugal	2132	15	+1	5.6
Greece	1558	16	0	6.2
For comparison USA	9573			2.4
Japan	1873			8.0

Source: Crafts and Toniolo (1996), p. 3.

Table 7.3: *GDP per capita and rankings, 1950 and 1973 (1990 international dollars)*

performance in the face of the Continental growth booms played an important role in shaping British attitudes towards EEC membership. Or, to put it more bluntly, regardless of whether EEC integration was responsible for the EEC6's superior growth performance, political leaders at the time believed there was a connection.

Another line of indicative evidence comes from comparing the before and after growth rates of nations who have joined the EU. The facts are shown in Table 7.4.

Data are available for four enlargements (the 2004 enlargement is too recent). Growth picked up in half the cases (the third and fourth), but slowed in the other half.

However, many things affect growth apart from EU membership. The world experienced serious growth slowdowns during the first oil shock (1973–75) and when OECD central banks decided to fight inflation with restrictive monetary policies (1981–83). One way to partially control for this is to compare the growth rate of the entrants to the average west European growth rate over the same period. We see that all the enlargements have been pro-growth by this rough measure, except Greece's.

The combined GDP of the first entrants (Britain, Denmark and Ireland) was growth much slower than the European average during the five years before accession in 1973, but only slightly less fast in the five years

	West Europe (%)	Britain + Denmark + Ireland (%)	Greece (%)	Spain + Portugal (%)	Finland + Austria + Sweden (%)
Pre-1968–72	18.5	12.5			
Post-1973–77	5.8	4.8			
Pre-1976–80	10.2		9.0		
Post-1981–85	7.4		0.1		
Pre-1981–85	7.4			2.7	
Post-1986–90	16.2			23.0	
Pre-1989–93	3.7				−5.0
Post-1994–98	12.7				12.4

Note: Real GDP in constant prices; 5-year average, not annualized. 'West Europe' is all the nations that eventually ended up in the EU or EFTA, i.e. the EU15 plus Iceland, Norway and Switzerland.

Source: *Penn World*, table, 6.1 (RGDPL), Center for International Comparisons, University of Pennsylvania, http://pwt.econ.upenn.edu/.

Table 7.4: *Growth rates five years before and five years after accession*

following membership (i.e. 18.5 versus 12.5 per cent compared with 5.8 versus 4.8 per cent). For the third and fourth enlargements, the five-year growth rates for the entrants was behind the pan-European average before but ahead of it after they joined. The one exception is that of Greece – a theme that comes out clearly in a closer examination of the data below.

Formal statistical evidence

There are better ways to isolate the impact of integration and growth than simply comparing to the west European growth average. These techniques involve statistical methods – regression analysis – that are standard in the scientific literature on trade and growth. The consensus in this literature is that economic integration is good for income growth, although the exact relationship is not fully understood. The literature on European integration per se is much less developed. A recent pair of papers by Harald Badinger suggests that although there is no long-run (i.e. permanent) boost to growth, tighter European integration does produce a sizeable medium-run growth effect (Badinger 2005a, b).

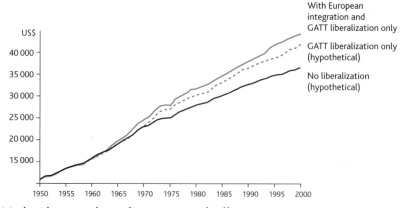

Figure 7.1: *Empirical evidence on the medium-run growth effect*

Note: The top line shows EU income growth. The middle and lower lines show a simulation of how much lower EU income per worker would have been under two hypothetical situations: without European integration (middle) and without any integration (lower). The difference between the middle and top line is Badinger's estimate of the medium-run growth effect.

Source: Badinger (2005a), working paper version.

See also Coe and Moghadam (1993), Italianer (1994) and Henrekson *et al.* (1997) for views on the subject.

The point is illustrated in Figure 7.1. In reality, European integration did occur and this produced the income growth we can observe in the data. To work out the fraction of this income that was due to an integration-induced growth effect, one needs to simulate what income would have been *without* European integration. The difference is the medium-run growth effect.

We turn now to a more careful consideration of *how* integration might affect growth. Establishing such an analytical framework is useful to understanding the growth–integration link, but more importantly, it allows us to make more pointed predictions that can be confronted with the data.

7.2 Medium-run growth effects: induced capital formation with Solow's analysis

Spain's accession to the EU in the mid-1980s was accompanied by an investment boom that raised Spain's GDP growth by several percentage points for a few years. In this section, we consider ways of understanding how EU membership could yield such a medium-term growth bonus.

The key to the medium-term growth bonus is 'induced capital formation'. That is to say, integration induces firms to raise the level of capital per worker employed. For the moment, we focus exclusively on the machine

Box 7.1

Robert Solow (1924–)

Federal Reserve Bank of Minneapolis

Robert Solow, universally known as Bob, is a classic example of the Second World War generation of economists who thought that it was their duty to use their minds to improve the social situation. To this day, he remains engaged in public policy debates, for example taking an active stance against the Iraq War via Eonomists Allied for Arms Reduction.

His most famous contributions to economics, published in the late 1950s, revolutionized thinking about the causes of growth. Before Solow, the dominant thinking was that capital accumulation (the Harrod–Domar model) by itself was the driving force of growth. What Solow showed was that capital accumulation was driven by technological progress, so the ultimate growth driver was technological progress. This simple realization shifted the focus of government's pro-growth policies worldwide from investment in machines to investment in knowledge.

A brilliant and precocious student (he enrolled in Harvard at 16 years old, and started teaching at MIT two years before finishing his PhD), Solow as a professor turned out to be an excellent teacher who devoted inordinate amounts of time to students. He is also famous for being one of the wittiest living economists. A leader of the Keynesian school (which supports active government intervention), Solow criticized his fellow economists with wit and wisdom – economists ranging from interventionists such as John Kenneth Galbraith to arch-conservatives such as Milton Friedman. Solow once wrote that Galbraith's disdain for ordinary consumer goods 'reminds one of the Duchess who, upon acquiring a full appreciation of sex, asked the Duke if it were not perhaps too good for the common people'. Of Milton Friedman, Solow wrote, 'Everything reminds Milton of the money supply. Well, everything reminds me of sex, but I keep it out of the paper.' (See www.minneapolisfed.org for recent examples in an interview.)

Solow was part of President Kennedy's 'Camelot', working from 1961 to 1963 on the Council of Economic Advisers. In 1961, he won the American Economic Association's John Bates Clark Award, given to the best economist under the age of 40. In 1987, he won the Nobel Prize (see his autobiography at www.nobelprize.org).

per worker (i.e. physical-capital to labour) ratio, so the first step is to identify a means of determining the equilibrium capital/labour ratio. The approach we adopt was discovered by Nobel Laureate Robert Solow in the 1950s (see Box 7.1). It assumes that people save and then invest a fixed share of their income.

7.2.1 Solow diagram

To keep things easy, we start by viewing the whole EU as a single, closed economy with fully integrated capital and labour markets and the same technology everywhere.

We begin our study of the logic linking growth and integration by focusing on the connection between GDP-per-worker and capital-per-worker. When a firm provides its workers with more and better equipment, output per worker rises. However, output per worker does not increase in proportion with equipment per worker. To see this, consider the example of the efficiency of your studying and your personal capital/labour ratio. The most primitive method of studying would be to just go to lectures and listen. Buying some paper and pencils would allow you to take notes and this would boost your productivity enormously in terms of both time and quality. Going further, you could buy the book, and again this would boost your productivity (i.e. the effectiveness per hour of studying) but not as much as would the pencils and paper. It would also be nice to have a calculator, a laptop, high-speed connection to the internet at home, and a laser printer of your own.

Each subsequent increase in your 'capital' would boost your effectiveness, but each euro of capital investment would provide progressively lower increases in productivity. As it turns out, this sort of 'diminishing returns' to investment also marks the economy as a whole. Raising the capital/labour ratio in the economy increases output per hour worked, but the rate of increase diminishes as the level of the capital/labour ratio rises.

This sort of less-than-proportional increase in efficiency is portrayed in Fig. 7.2 by the GDP/L curve. This shows that raising the capital/labour ratio (K/L, which is plotted on the horizontal axis) increases output per worker, but a 10 per cent hike in K/L raises GDP/L by less than 10 per cent. This is why the curve is bowed downwards. (Alternatively, think of the curve as rising less rapidly than a straight line.)

The GDP/L curve shows us what output per worker would be for any given K/L, but what will the K/L be? The equilibrium K/L ratio depends upon the inflow and outflow of new capital per worker. The inflow is investment: firms building new factories, buying new trucks, installing new

machines, etc. The outflow is depreciation: factories, trucks and machinery deteriorate or break down with use and must be repaired or replaced. The equilibrium K/L is where the inflow of new investment just balances depreciation of capital. The reason is simple. If the flow of savings exceeds the depreciation of capital, then K/L rises. If depreciation outstrips investment, K/L falls. The next step is to find the inflow and outflow of capital.

Solow simply assumed that people save and invest a constant fraction of their income each year, so the inflow of capital is just a fraction of GDP/L; in the diagram, this constant savings and investment fraction is denoted as s, so the inflow-of-capital curve is marked as s(GDP/L). (In European nations, s is somewhere between 20 and 35 per cent.) The investment-per-worker curve has a shape that is similar to that of the GDP/L curve but it is rotated clockwise since the savings are a fraction of GDP/L. As for depreciation, Solow made an equally simple assumption. He assumed that a constant fraction of capital stock depreciates each year. In the figure, the constant fraction of the capital stock that depreciates each year is denoted with the Greek letter delta, δ. (In Europe, something like 12 per cent of the capital stock depreciates each year.) The depreciation per worker line is shown as $\delta(K/L)$. It is a straight line since the amount of depreciation per worker increases in proportion with the amount of capital per worker.

The important point in the figure is point A, the crossing of the s(GDP/L) curve and the $\delta(K/L)$ line. This occurs at K/L*. At this capital/labour ratio, the inflow of new investment just balances the outflow. For a ratio below K/L* the capital/labour ratio would rise since investment outstrips depreciation. For example, if K/L were K/L$_0$, then

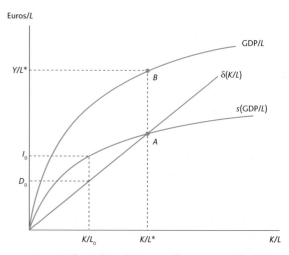

Figure 7.2: *The Solow diagram: determining the equilibrium capital/labour ratio*

the inflow would be I_0 and the outflow would be D_0. Since I_0 is higher than D_0, the amount of new capital per worker installed would be greater than the amount of capital per worker lost to depreciation. Naturally, the capital/labour ratio would rise. With more capital being installed for a ratio higher than this, depreciation surpasses investment, so K/L would fall. The last thing to work out is the output per worker implied by the equilibrium K/L. The answer, which is given by the GDP/L curve at point B, tells us that output per worker in this equilibrium will be Y/L^*.

Although it is not essential to our main line of analysis, we finish our discussion of the Solow diagram with a consideration of long-run growth. The main point that Solow made with his diagram was that the accumulation of capital is not a source of long-run growth. Capital rises up to the point where the K/L ratio reaches its equilibrium value and then stops, unless something changes. To explain the year after year growth we see in the modern world – about 2 per cent per year on average – Solow relied on technological progress. He assumed that technological advances would rotate the GDP/L curve upwards year after year, pulling the s(GDP/L) curve up with it. As can be easily verified in the Solow diagram, such progress will lead to an ever rising output per worker and an ever rising capital/labour ratio. When we look at the growth effects of European integration we shall be referring to growth that is higher than the growth that would have otherwise occurred due to technological progress.

We next use the Solow diagram to study how European integration might boost growth.

7.2.2 Liberalization, allocation effects and the medium-run growth bonus

The verbal logic of growth effects is straightforward. Integration improves the efficiency of the European economy by encouraging a more efficient allocation of European resources. Not surprisingly, this improved efficiency also makes Europe a better place to invest and thus boosts investment beyond what it otherwise would have been. The extra investment means more tools per worker, and this raises the output per worker. As workers get more tools than they would have without integration, output per worker rises faster than it would have done otherwise. To put this differently, integration produces extra growth as the capital/labour ratio approaches its new equilibrium output. This is the medium-run growth bonus introduced by Baldwin (1989). It is medium term since the higher growth disappears once the new equilibrium capital/labour ratio is reached.

Medium-run growth bonus in detail

Figure 7.3 allows us to portray the logic in more detail. The first step is to realize how 'allocation effects' of European integration alter the diagram. For all the reasons presented in Chapters 4–6, European integration has improved the effectiveness with which capital, labour and technology are combined to produce output. To take one concrete example, we saw that integration can lead to fewer, more efficient firms. From the firm-level perspective, this improved efficiency means lower average cost. At the economy-wide perspective, the improved efficiency means that the same amount of capital and labour can produce more output. How can we show this in the Solow diagram?

The positive allocation effect shifts the GDP/L curve to the blue line marked GDP/L' in Fig. 7.3. The new GDP/L curve is the old one rotated up counterclockwise since the improved efficiency means that the economy is able to produce more output, say, 2 per cent more, for any given capital/labour ratio. This is the first step. The impact of the higher efficiency on output is shown by point C. That is, holding the capital/labour ratio constant at K/L^*, output would rise from Y/L^* to Y/L_C. This is not the end of the story, however, since K/L^* is no longer the equilibrium capital/labour ratio. This brings us to the second step.

The shift up in the GDP/L curve to GDP/L' also shifts up the investment curve to s(GDP/L)$'$. After all, the fixed investment rate now applies to higher output and so generates a higher inflow of investment for any given capital/labour ratio. This is shown in the diagram by the blue curve s(GDP/L)$'$. Since the inflow has risen, K/L^* is no longer the equilibrium. At K/L^*, the inflow exceeds the outflow, so the economy's capital/labour ratio begins to rise. The new equilibrium is at the new intersection of the inflow and outflow curves, namely point D, so the new equilibrium capital/labour ratio is K/L'. The rise from K/L^* to K/L' is called 'induced capital formation' and reflects the fact that improved efficiency will tend to stimulate investment.

What are the growth implications? As the capital/labour ratio rises from K/L^* to K/L', output per worker rises from Y/L_C to Y/L'. This is shown in the diagram as the movement from point C to point E. Since the capital stock builds up only slowly, the movement between C and E can take years. The key to the second step is to realize that the rise in output per worker between C and E would show up as faster than normal growth until the economy reaches point E. At that time, the growth rate would return to normal.

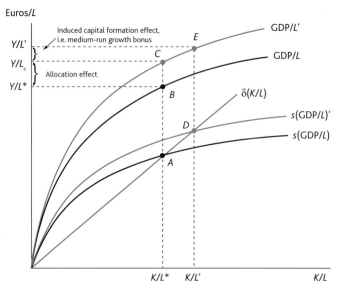

Figure 7.3: *Medium-run growth bonus from European integration*

Source: Baldwin (1989).

Summary in words

In words, the integration-causes-growth mechanism is: integration → improved efficiency → higher GDP/L → higher investment per worker → economy's capital/labour ratio starts to rise towards new, higher equilibrium value → faster growth of output per worker during the transition from the old to the new capital/labour ratio. This is the so-called medium-run growth bonus from European integration.

When it comes to welfare, however, it is important to note that higher output is not a pure welfare gain. In order to invest more, citizens must save more, and this means forgoing consumption today. Consequently, the higher levels of consumption made possible tomorrow by the higher K/L ratio are partly offset by the forgone consumption of today.

7.2.3 Other medium-run growth effects: changes in the investment rate

The Solow diagram relied on an extremely convenient simplifying assumption: a constant investment rate. Unfortunately, taking the investment rate as given severely limits the range of growth effects that we can study. As the introduction pointed out, the basic logic of growth rests on the decision to invest in new physical capital (machines), new human capital (skills), and/or new knowledge capital (innovations). Many growth effects operate by altering the costs and/or benefits of investing and thus by altering the investment *rate*, what we called s

in the diagram. For instance, many people claim that the euro will make it easier, cheaper and safer to invest in Europe. If this turns out to be true, the extra investment would boost growth at least in the medium term, but how would we get this into the Solow framework?

If European integration raises the investment rate from, say, s to s', the inflow of capital curve, namely s(GDP/L) will rotate upwards, as shown in Fig. 7.4. This change would in turn alter the equilibrium capital/labour ratio. Following the logic we considered above, the inflow of capital at the old capital/labour ratio K/L* would exceed the outflow, so the capital stock per worker would rise to the new equilibrium shown by point C in the diagram. As before, the rising K/L would raise output per worker from Y/L* to Y/L' (these Y/L* and Y/L' are unrelated to those in previous figures). During this process, growth would be somewhat higher than it would otherwise have been.

This shows that it is straightforward to illustrate this second type of growth effect in the Solow diagram.

7.2.4 Evidence from the 'poor four'

Western Europe grew rapidly in the post-war period and experienced rapid integration. The problem, however, is that it is very difficult to separate the effects of European integration from the many other factors affecting growth. One natural experiment is to look at what happened to nations that joined the EU. These nations experienced a rather sudden and well-defined increase in economic

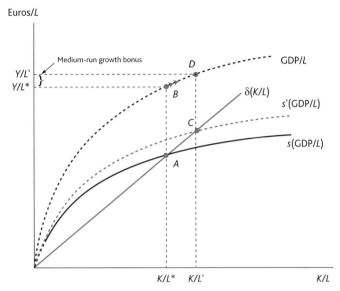

Figure 7.4: *European integration and the investment rate*

integration when they joined. Moreover, we shall study the impact that EU membership had on the four relatively poor entrants that joined the EU between 1960 and 1995: Ireland (in 1973), Greece (in 1981) and Portugal and Spain (in 1986).

The logic sketched out above explains how integration may raise a nation's steady-state capital stock. What sorts of 'footprints' would this leave in the data? First, heightened efficiency makes investment more worthwhile, i.e. it tends to raise the real return to capital. Moreover, this will normally be associated with an increase in the profitability of existing capital and this, in turn, should show up in the average behaviour of the stock market (as long as the stock market reflects a broad sample of firms). An important caveat comes from the fact that liberalization usually harms some firms and sectors even when it is beneficial for the nation as a whole. If the stock market is dominated by, say, state-controlled 'white elephants' that will face increased pressure in a more liberal economy, a drop in the stock market index may accompany the enlargement. Second, the Solow diagram is too simple to distinguish between domestic and foreign investors, but we presume that an improvement in the national investment climate should attract more investment from both sources. These two effects are likely to leave four kinds of 'footprints' in the data:

★ stock market prices should increase;
★ the aggregate investment to GDP ratio should rise;
★ the net direct investment figures should improve;
★ the current account should deteriorate as more foreign capital flows in.

Portugal and Spain

The case that EU membership induced investment-led growth is the strongest for the Iberians. Following restoration of democracy in the mid-1970s, Portugal and Spain applied to the EU in 1977, with membership talks beginning in 1978. The talks proved difficult, so accession occurred only in 1986. Growth in Portugal picked up rapidly and stayed high both during the negotiations and after accession; and between 1977 and 1992, Portugal expanded 13 per cent more than France (the country we have chosen as a 'control'). In Spain, however, growth was worse than that of France until accession. From 1986, it picked up significantly, and between 1986 and 1992 Spain's cumulative growth edge over France amounted to 7.5 per cent, about the same as Portugal's.

As the bottom-left panel of Fig. 7.5 shows, much of this rapid growth was due to a higher rate of physical capital formation. Portugal's investment rate responded strongly and quickly to the combination of democracy and the prospects of EU membership. The importance of membership probably stems from some mixture of reduced uncertainty concerning the nation's stability and the prospects of improved market access. Note, however, that as a member of EFTA, Portugal already had duty-free access to the EU market for industrial goods. The pattern of the Spanish investment rate, in contrast, did not differ significantly from that of our control country until accession actually occurred. At that point, however, the Spanish investment-rate pattern does follow the predictions of integration-induced investment-led growth.

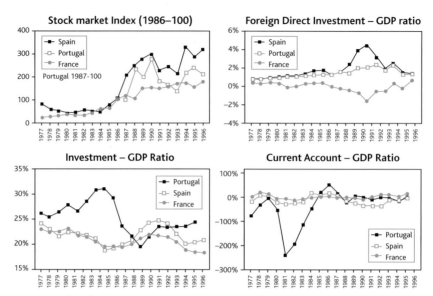

Figure 7.5: *Integration-induced investment in Spain and Portugal*

Source: Baldwin and Seghezza (1998).

The top-left panel of the figure shows the same pattern for the stock market price indices. Spain's index tracked that of France until accession but thereafter showed signs of a significant improvement in the investment climate. Portuguese data are available only from 1987, but clearly show a better-than-average performance in subsequent years. The other two panels display the evidence for net foreign direct investment and the current account. Here the prospect of membership and domestic market-oriented reforms boosted the attractiveness of Spain and Portugal as industrial locations. Note that the boom in Portuguese foreign direct investment came only after accession. Finally, the current account shows that a good portion of high rates of investment in the Iberian peninsula was in effect financed by foreign capital inflows, although foreign capital played a more important role for Portugal prior to accession and for Spain after accession.

Ireland

Ireland's long trek to EU membership shadowed that of the UK. Namely, its first application in 1961 was rejected in 1963; its second application, which it made in 1967, was accepted in 1972.

Ireland was the first poor country to join the EU and is a fairly clear case of integration-induced investment-led growth. Between its accession and 1983, Ireland experienced a cumulative growth differential of 12 percentage points over France (by 1995, the cumulative difference was almost 50 per cent). Figure 7.6 shows data on our four indicators of investment-led growth for the

five years prior to, and ten years after, the Irish accession. As the top-right panel of the figure shows, Ireland's investment rate picked up faster than that of France, once the first oil shock recession ended. The bottom-right panel (current account to GDP ratio) shows that much of the above-normal investment ratio was coming from foreign capital. As far as foreign direct investment is concerned, the top-left panel shows that Ireland's inflow was similar in magnitude and pattern to that of Spain, fluctuating between 1 and 3 per cent of GDP.

Irish stock prices, however, did respond directly to the accession. Part of this may be explained by the composition effect involved in Ireland's growth. Since its accession, Ireland's 'traditional' manufacturing sectors such as textiles, clothing and footwear, have experienced a secular decline, while foreign-owned firms have expanded rapidly. To the extent that the Irish stock market was dominated by the declining traditional sectors – at least in the short run – it is not surprising that the Irish stock prices did not diverge significantly from those of the control nation.

Greece

As in the case of Portugal and Spain, the Greek accession (1981) came just after a period of undemocratic governments. However, unlike the Iberians, Greece continued its pervasive state controls of the economy. These controls prevented the Greek economy from reacting flexibly to any shock, and EU membership turned out to be one such example. Moreover, the poor macroeconomic management of the Greek economy further harmed the

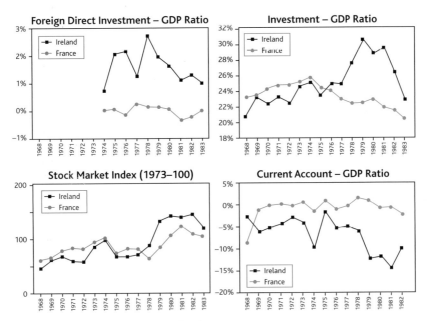

Figure 7.6: *Integration-induced investment in Ireland*

Source: Baldwin and Seghezza (1998).

investment climate. The high and unstable inflation rate provides an example. While most European nations brought inflation down during the 1981–91 period, the Greek inflation rate hardly moved (from 25 per cent in 1981 to 20 per cent in 1991). Moreover, during this period inflation fluctuated greatly, jumping up or down by more than 3 percentage points in a single year in five out of the ten years.

Given this background, it is not surprising that we find no evidence of investment-led growth in Greece. Figure 7.7 shows the Greek numbers for the five years prior to, and ten years subsequent to, accession. None of the figures suggests that EU membership had any impact on our four indicators.

The sharp contrast between the Greek case and the other three tells an important lesson. While integration may improve the investment climate in a nation, this can certainly be offset by other factors.

7.3 Long-run growth effects: faster knowledge creation and absorption

Up to this point we have focused on physical capital. Here we focus on knowledge capital, i.e. technology. Although both technology and machines are capital in the sense that they provide a flow of productive services over time, there is an enormous difference between the two. The most important, for our purposes, concerns diminishing returns. It is easy to see that raising the physical capital is subject to diminishing returns. Is knowledge capital subject to the same effects? The answer is clearly no.

The stock of knowledge per worker has risen steadily at least since the Enlightenment in the seventeenth century. Moreover, even as the knowledge stock rises, there seems to be no tendency for the usefulness of more knowledge to diminish. In the late nineteenth century, at the end of a particularly impressive burst of innovation called, by some, the second industrial revolution, the chief of the US Patent Office made the famously incorrect statement that Congress should close the Patent Office since everything had already been invented. This myopic viewpoint seems humorous exactly because knowledge, by its very nature, does not seem to be subject to the same sort of limits as physical capital.

As we pointed out in section 7.2.1, technological progress shifts the GDP/L curve up in the Solow diagram and this raises output per worker in exactly the same way as we saw in the Fig. 7.3 analysis. In short, we can think of technological progress as an allocative efficiency gain that comes every year, but instead of the gain being

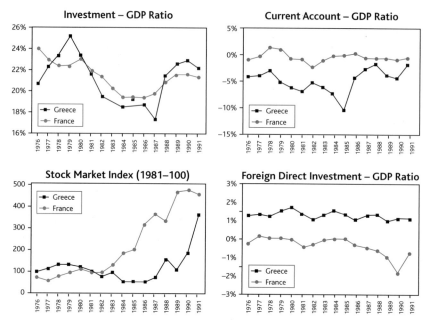

Figure 7.7: *Integration-induced investment in Greece*

Source: Baldwin and Seghezza (1998).

driven by European integration, it is driven by technology.

From this perspective, it is clear that the rate of technological progress is the key to understanding the long-run growth rate. The key point from our perspective is that, in principle, European integration can alter the rate of technological progress.

7.3.1 Solow-like diagram with long-run growth

To study this possibility in closer detail, we draw a Solow-like diagram where we focus on knowledge capital accumulation, rather than physical capital accumulation. The key difference is that knowledge capital does not face diminishing returns, so the GDP/L curve rises in a straight-line fashion with respect to the knowledge-per-worker ratio, referred to as K/L in Fig. 7.8 (note that the K/L here is not the same as K/L in the previous figures; here it is knowledge capital per worker instead of physical capital per worker).

To keep things simple, we continue to assume that each nation invests a constant fraction of its national income in the accumulation of knowledge capital (This rate – referred to as s in the diagram – could be measured by the fraction of a nation's income invested in R&D, i.e. typically something like 3 to 5 per cent in European

nations.) To see how the total investment in new knowledge changes with the knowledge/labour ratio (K/L), we plot $s(GDP/L)$ as before. However, now it is a straight line since the GDP/L curve is a straight line.

We also continue to assume that depreciation is constant in the sense that a given fraction of the national knowledge capital stock 'depreciates' each year. When it comes to knowledge, we usually say the knowledge capital has become obsolete rather than saying it has depreciated, but the wording does not change the logic. In both cases, a certain fraction of the capital becomes worthless every year.

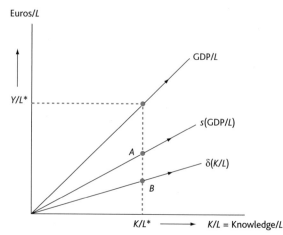

Figure 7.8: *A Solow-like diagram with long-run growth*

As drawn in Fig. 7.8, the investment rate exceeds the depreciation rate at all levels of K/L. For example, at a moment in time when the K/L ratio equals K/L^*, the amount of new knowledge capital per worker that is created is given by point A, while the amount of knowledge per worker that becomes obsolete is B. Since the inflow of new knowledge exceeds the outflow, the knowledge capital stock rises. This is shown by the arrow on the horizontal axis that suggests that K/L will continually rise.

As K/L rises for ever, the output per worker will rise for ever, along with the amount of new knowledge created and the amount of new knowledge that depreciates. These points are shown by the arrows on the GDP/L line, the s(GDP/L) line and the $\delta(K/L)$ line.

The diagram does not let us see directly how fast output per worker is rising, but it is easy to work this out. The further that s(GDP/L) is above $\delta(K/L)$, the larger is the annual net addition to K/L. Thus, as s rises, the nation will accumulate knowledge capital faster, and thus its income will rise faster.

Does European integration affect the long-run growth rate?

The evidence on long-run growth effects of European integration is much harder to find. The overarching fact is that long-run growth rates around the world, including those in Europe, returned to their pre-Golden Age levels. Since the level of European integration was rising more or less steadily during the whole post-war period, one would have to tell a complicated story to explain how the long-run growth rate returned to its pre-integration average, if integration strongly boosted long-run growth. Badinger (2005a) confirms this with statistical evidence (also see Deardorff and Stern, 2002). For this reason, it is probably best to focus on medium-run growth effects, i.e. investment booms that are associated with European integration.

The experience of the new Member States will provide an important opportunity for testing the growth effects of EU membership, but we do not as yet have enough data to undertake serious statistical analysis.

7.4 Summary

The logic of accumulation effects of European integration is based on the fundamental logic of economic growth. A nation's per-capita income can rise on a sustained basis only if its workers are provided with a steadily rising stock of physical, human and/or knowledge capital. Consequently, European integration will affect the growth rate only to the extent that it affects the rate of accumulation of physical, human and knowledge capital.

The chapter focused on two basic mechanisms through which European integration affects capital accumulation.

★ In so far as European integration makes the European economy more efficient, i.e. leads to a positive allocation effect, it raises output, and this – assuming a constant investment rate – leads to more investment. The end result of this higher level of investment is a higher long-run equilibrium capital stock and thus a higher equilibrium income per person.

★ European integration may also raise the investment rate by making investment less risky. As with the previous effect, the end result is a higher capital stock and a higher output per worker.

Examples of this integration-induced investment-led growth are fairly common.

Long-run growth effects were also studied. The underlying mechanism is the same as for medium-run growth effects but, because knowledge capital does not face diminishing returns, an increase in investment in knowledge (R&D) can lead to a permanent increase in the growth rate. There is little empirical evidence that European integration has had a major impact on long-run growth rates in Europe.

Self-assessment questions

1. When the German reunification took place, Germany's labour force rose much more than its capital stock (since much of East Germany's capital stock was useless in the market economy). Use a diagram to analyse what the medium-term growth effects should have been. Go on the internet to find what actually happened to German growth after reunification.

2. It is often said that the prospect of EU membership made Central European nations a better, safer place to invest. Using the Solow diagram, show how this would affect medium-term growth in these nations. What sort of 'footprints' would this leave in the data?

3. Use a diagram to analyse the medium-term growth effects of the following situation. Assume: (1) Serbia's K/L was pushed below its long-term equilibrium by war damage to its capital stock, and (2) the EU signs a free trade agreement with Serbia that has two effects: (2a) it increases the efficiency of the Serbian economy (allocation effect), and (2b) it raises the Serbian investment rate (s) but only temporarily, for, say, 10 years. (i) Show what (1), (2a) and (2b) would look like; (ii) show where the Serbian economy would end up in the long run (i.e. after s returned to its normal rate), and (iii) show how the integration would affect Serbia's growth path.

4. Just after the Second World War, the economics of the Six experience massive destruction of physical capital. Although many workers also died, the war tended to do more damage to the capital stocks than it did to the labour force. Use a diagram to illustrate how this may help explain the 'miraculous growth' in the late 1940s and 1950s.

Essay questions

1. In most analyses, growth in per-capita GDP is taken to be a good thing. Write an essay that critiques GDP as a measure of economic welfare. Be sure to consider issues of income distribution and leisure time.

2. The analysis of migration in the chapter stressed economic considerations. Write an essay that argues that the ability of EU citizens to work or retire in any other EU nation has an impact on attitudes towards European integration. Draw on your personal experience, if appropriate.

3. Write an essay that puts the attitude towards capital market integration of the founders of the EU into historical perspective. Focus on the period after 1914.

4. Write an essay that discusses and analyses the post-1989 growth experience of one central European nation. Be sure to use the concepts introduced in this chapter.

Further reading: the aficionado's corner

An extensive description and analysis of growth in Europe can be found in Crafts and Toniolo (1996).

An alternative presentation of the Solow model, one that allows for several extensions such as population growth and continuous technological progress, can be found in Mankiw (2000).

An advanced treatment of neoclassical and endogenous growth can be found in Barro, R. and X. Sala-i-Martin (1995).

Useful website

For the latest data on European growth and forecasts, see the website of DG Economy and Finance at
http://europa.eu.int/comm/economy_finance/.

References

Baldwin, R. (1989) 'The growth effects of 1992', *Economic Policy*, 9: 247–82.

Baldwin, R. and E. Seghezza (1998) 'Regional integration and growth in developing nations', *Journal of Economic Integration*, 13(3): 367–99.

Badinger, H. (2005a) 'Growth effects of economic integration: evidence from the EU Member States', *Weltwirtschaftliches Archiv*, 1: 50–78.

Badinger, H. (2005b) 'Technology- and investment-led growth effects of economic integration: a panel cointegration analysis for the EU-15 (1960–2000)', Manuscript, Europainstitut, Department of Economics Wirtschaftsuniversität Wien.

Barro, R. and X. Sala-i-Martin (1995) *Economic Growth*, McGraw-Hill, New York.

Cameron, R. and L. Neal (2003) *A Concise Economic History of the World*, Oxford University Press, Oxford.

Coe, D. and R. Moghadam (1993) 'Capital and trade as engines of growth in France', *IMF Staff Papers*, 40: 542–66.

Commission (1996) *The 1996 Single Market Review: Background Information for the Report to the Council and European Parliament*, SEC (96) 2378, Commission of the European Communities, Brussels.
http://europa.eu.int/comm/internal_market/en/update/impact/bgrounen.pdf.

Crafts, N. and G. Toniolo (1996) *Economic Growth in Europe since 1945*, Cambridge University Press, Cambridge.

Deardorff, A. and R. Stern (2002) *EU Expansion and EU Growth*, Ford School of Public Policy, Working Paper 487.

Henrekson, M., J. Torstensson and R. Torstensson (1997) 'Growth effects of European integration', *European Economic Review*, 41(8): 1537–57.

Italianer, A. (1994) 'Whither the gains from European economic integration?', *Revue Economique*, 3 (May): 689–702.

Mankiw, G. (2000) *Principles of Economics*, Thomson Learning, New York.

As the extent of economic integration approaches that of the United States, labour market institutions and labour market outcomes may also begin to resemble their American counterparts. [...] Full and irreversible economic integration may call for harmonization of social and market-market institutions within the European Union.

Giuseppe Bertola (2000)

Economic integration, labour markets and migration

INTRODUCTION

For many Europeans, a good job is an essential element of a good life. Unemployment is therefore a critical political and economic issue throughout Europe. This chapter explores the linkages between jobs and European economic integration, looking at it from both a macro and micro perspective.

The chapter starts by describing the situation of the European labour markets. It shows that in some countries, mainly the larger ones, unemployment is high and labour force participation is low. We next look at a very simple analytical framework that explains the unemployment phenomenon. This framework shows that socially desirable features of the labour market have serious economic costs. Put differently, social protection results in labour market rigidities. With these basics in place the next section, section 8.3, studies the impact of European integration on Europe's labour markets. We argue that economic and labour market integration, as well as monetary union, puts great reliance in labour market flexibility. The combination of rigidities and deepening integration means that either the cost of integration is high or that labour market institutions will need to undergo reforms, as has already been the case in a number of countries. The last section looks at the case of migration. Migration may create hardship for certain groups of native workers, but it does not have to be the case. Here again, labour market flexibility makes it more likely that migration raises welfare for most, if not all, workers.

8.1 European labour markets: a brief overview

Despite important differences from one country to another, the European labour markets are among the most inflexible in the world. The combination of low geographic mobility of workers and high labour market rigidity stands in sharp contrast to the situation in the USA, where workers are highly mobile and markets highly flexible. These features are understood to play an important role in the smooth working of the 'dollar area'.[1] At the heart of this question lies the fact that, compared with economic efficiency, European labour market institutions have long attached considerably more weight to social protection than have their US counterparts.

Labour market institutions have already changed in many countries, partly in response to the massive unemployment of the past thirty years. Figure 8.1 shows that, in the USA, the rate of unemployment increased – a little – and then moved back down. The situation is similar in the UK and in many of the smaller EMU

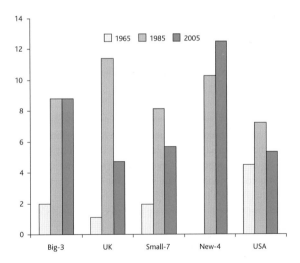

Figure 8.1: *Unemployment rates, 1965–2005*

Note: The Big-3 are France, Germany and Italy. The Small-7 are Austria, Belgium, Denmark, Ireland, the Netherlands, Portugal and Sweden. Finland, which underwent a massive shock in the early 1990s, is kept apart, as is Greece which resembles the Big-3. The New-4 are the Czech Republic, Hungary, Poland and Slovakia; for these countries, the figure reports data for 1995 instead of 1985, when their economies were centrally planned.

Source: *Economic Outlook*, OECD, June 2005.

[1] Chapter 16, especially section 16.3.4, provides the relevant evidence.

member countries. The three large European countries stand apart – unemployment there has gone up and up, never to fall again. Unfortunately, among the new members, many of the central and eastern European countries have even higher rates of unemployment.

Another worrisome indication is that, when they lose jobs, Europeans spend considerably more time finding new employment than do Americans. Table 8.1 shows that, in the Big-3 countries, nearly half of the unemployed workers have been out of work for at least one year. This proportion is significantly higher than in the other European countries, and an order of magnitude greater than the US rate. For some reason, European job markets do not allow people to find jobs as easily as they do in the USA.

Unemployment is but one symptom of a malfunctioning labour market. Another gauge is the participation rate, the proportion of the working-age population which either works or is actively looking for a job (Box 8.1 provides precise definitions of frequently used concepts). Figure 8.2 displays both indicators. It shows that where the rate of unemployment is high, participation tends to be low. In these countries, large segments of the population of working age do not work, sometimes because they are unemployed, but more often because they are simply not trying to find work. This concerns, for example, 38 per cent of working-age Italians. So, what do they do?

Some of them may work in the black market or be involved in criminal activities, but the majority simply stay home, perhaps taking care of the family, but often being discouraged or not even interested in finding a job. Some young people pursue studies for lack of better alternatives, while many older people have been offered early retirement. Still others prefer to cash in welfare

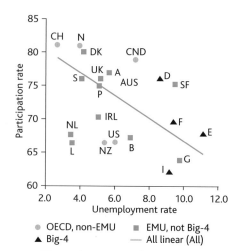

Figure 8.2: *Unemployment and participation in 2003*

Source: *Economic Outlook*, OECD, June 2005.

payments, unemployment benefits or, in some cases, permanent disability benefits. In the end, most European countries devote considerable efforts towards educating their children and preparing them for a successful adult life, but they fail to provide them with rewarding job opportunities. This massive waste of resources reveals severe rigidities in the labour markets.

A broad-brush interpretation, to be explained and refined in the following sections, goes as follows. The flexible US labour markets have been able to recover easily from adverse shocks that regularly hit the world (the oil shocks of the 1970s and 1980s, the bursting of the high-tech bubble in the early 1990s). Labour markets in the smaller EMU countries and the UK were quite inflexible, so the shocks led to a strong rise in unemployment, but successful reforms in the 1990s resulted in sharp improvements. The Big-4 (France, Germany, Italy and Spain) started with inflexible labour markets, implemented modest, if any, reforms, and still face very high unemployment. Box 8.2 presents the reforms conducted by Chancellor Schroeder.

8.2 Microeconomics of labour market rigidities

8.2.1 The simplest framework

If labour markets operated like other markets, there would be no unemployment. Faced with an adverse shock, say a decline in world demand for domestic goods and thus for the workers who help produce them, wages

Country	%	Country	%
France	41.6	Spain	37.7
Germany	51.8	Sweden	18.9
Italy	49.7	Switzerland	33.5
Japan	33.7	UK	21.4
Netherlands	32.5	USA	12.7

[a] Percentage of people unemployed for one year or more.

Source: OECD.

Table 8.1: *Proportion of long-term[a] unemployment, 2004*

Box 8.1

Labour market concepts

The unemployment rate (u) is the ratio of the number (U) of people who declare themselves unemployed (they have no job and are actively looking for one) to the labour force (L), which is the sum of the employed (E) and the unemployed (U):

$$u = \frac{U}{L} \text{ , where } L = E + U$$

The employment rate (e) is the remaining proportion of the labour force, composed of those who hold jobs:

$$e = \frac{E}{L} = 1 - u$$

The labour force is distinct from the working-age population (N), defined conventionally as all valid people between 15 and 65 years old. Thus the working-age population includes those who are employed, those who are unemployed and those who are out of the labour force (O):

$$N = L + O = E + U + O$$

The participation rate (p) is the ratio of the labour force to the working-age population:

$$P = \frac{L}{N} = 1 - \frac{O}{N}$$

How are people counted? This is not an innocuous question. The working-age population N is simply all people between, say, 15 and 60 or 65, except those on disability. Each country has census polls and other formal population-counting procedures. The employed, E, are identified from firms reporting taxes, from various welfare contributions and from surveys. The unemployed, U, are identified either through polls or because they are officially registered as such (the difference matters as each country has its own procedure; the International Labour Office produces harmonized data based on surveys). This leaves those out of the labour force, O, as a residual ($O = N - E - U$). Precision is not the name of the game, just think about the black market which can include 10 or 20 per cent of the working-age population.

An important distinction is between voluntary and involuntary unemployment. In principle, people who do not want to work are classified as out of the labour force (O). In practice, however, things are less clear cut: some people counted in U are really voluntarily unemployed or actually employed, whereas others counted in O are involuntarily unemployed. Three main reasons explain this discrepancy. First, some unemployed people are really working in the black market (they are counted in U whereas they should be in E). Second, being unemployed opens the door to a range of welfare payments, mainly unemployment insurance benefits. It is believed that these benefits enable workers to be choosier and to reject some job offers or to search less than would otherwise be the case; yet, they must identify themselves as involuntarily unemployed either by registering or when polled. Finally, some people who have searched for a job for a long time become discouraged and simply drop out of the labour force (i.e. they are counted in O whereas they really are in U).

Note: These concepts are further defined and explained in International Labour Organization (ILO) publications. See http://www.ilo.org.

would decline. This is illustrated in Fig. 8.3, where employment is measured as total hours worked: the product of the number of people employed and the number of hours that they work. The demand for labour is downward-sloping since an increase in real wages, w (nominal wages W adjusted for the price level P, i.e. $w = W/P$) leads firms to shift to more capital-intensive production processes or to relocate in cheaper countries. The supply of labour is upward-sloping to describe the way better pay induces more workers into the labour force and encourages existing workers to work longer hours.

Box 8.2

Chancellor Schroeder's Agenda 2010

During his election campaign in 1998, Gerhard Schroeder promised to bring unemployment down to 3.5 million people. By the time he ran again in 2002, 4 million people were unemployed. For his third run in 2005, the number is 4.8 billion. Having failed to push any serious reform during his first mandate, he set up a Commission under the chairmanship of Peter Hartz, then Director of Human Resources at Volkswagen, shortly after his re-election in 2002. The Commission's recommendations have been translated into Agenda 2010, a reform programme gradually implemented during Schroeder's mandate, often against strong trade union resistance. The four reform packages, called Hartz I, II, III and IV, include a number of measures designed to make Germany's notoriously inflexible job market more flexible:

★ Hartz I focused on employment agencies, with the creation of the personal service agencies that work under contract from the national Bundes Agentur für Arbeit. The package also allowed for limited-duration contracts for workers aged 52 and over.

★ Hartz II aimed at encouraging unemployed people to return to work. Its most visible and successful component was the creation of 'mini-jobs' and 'midi-jobs', new labour contracts applicable to people who earn less than €800 a month independently of the number of hours worked. Taxes and national insurance payments on these jobs are reduced. The package also offered subsidies to unemployed people who become self-employed (a measure called 'Ich-AG', i.e. Me Ltd).

★ Hartz III and IV included measures designed to make collective dismissals made easier, consolidated many welfare programmes and created special job contracts for new companies. The emphasis was on preventing unemployment insurance from encouraging people to stay unemployed: the duration of the insurance payments was reduced, job search effort was to be monitored and sanctions for turning down job offers were tightened up.

All these measures are known to reduce unemployment eventually, but many of them are slow to produce their effects. They were enacted late and piecemeal, with no visible effect, thus maximizing the political costs and minimizing the economic benefits.

We thank Michael Burda for help with this box.

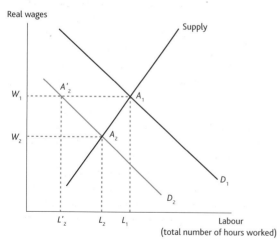

Real wages

Figure 8.3: *Labour market adjustment to an adverse shock*

We start from point A_1, where the real wage is w_1 and unemployment is L_1. Note that where the demand and supply curves intersect, there is no unemployment. All the hours that are offered by workers at w_1 are taken up by employers when the real wage is w_1. Of course, this is unrealistic. To see what is wrong about it, let us still assume that this is the initial situation and consider an adverse shock that suddenly reduces demand for labour. The shock is represented by the leftward shift of the labour demand schedule. If we still insist on looking at the intersection of the demand and supply curves, we move to point A_2. Employment, measured in total hours worked (an issue to which we return below), declines from L_1 to L_2, while real wages decline from w_1 to w_2. This is rather unpleasant, of course, but since we remain on the labour supply curve the drop in employment is voluntary: at this lower wage rate people choose to work shorter hours or just to stop working. We still do not have any involuntary unemployment, i.e. people who want to work and do not find a job.

How, then, can we explain the widespread phenomenon of unemployment? We have to admit that this is not a good description of real labour markets. The goods that are bought and sold on this market are people's time, talent and effort. Quite obviously, these are very special goods, and indeed labour markets are highly organized and regulated. The price of labour, the real wage, is not set like the price of oil or corn, through bidding. It is negotiated, normally through collective negotiations that bring together unions of employers and employees, and set for periods that extend usually to one year or more. In most countries, it is illegal for an employer to cut nominal wages. In addition, there often exists legislation that sets limits to dismissals and mandates compensatory payments. As a result, when the demand for labour declines, firms do not discard labour. Labour relations involve complex, sometimes adversarial, considerations: skills acquired on the job, the reputation of the employers as fair providers of jobs, possibly collective opposition including strikes.

To see how these things actually play out, and simplifying somewhat, consider that, for legal, social or fairness reasons, it is impossible to cut the real wage, which remains at the pre-shock level w_1. In that case, if firms are free to adjust the number of hours they hire (either by firing some workers or by reducing the number of hours worked by each worker), the situation is now described by point A'_2. Employment falls to L'_2, a larger reduction than when wages are flexible. More importantly, perhaps, point A'_2 is no longer on the labour supply curve. This means that some workers do not find any demand for the work that they supply: the distance $A_1A'_2$ represents involuntary unemployment, either people laid off but willing to work, or a forced reduction of hours worked and, therefore, labour income. If real wages are inflexible and tight restrictions exist on firing and hours worked, we could stay at point A_1 with no decline in employment but firms off their demand curve are being hurt. If they are forced to keep on their payrolls more workers than they wish, they face declining profits, possibly losses. If the shock is mild, firms will react by cutting other expenses, chiefly investment in productive capacity, hurting future growth and employment. If the shock is severe and lasting, a number of firms will face bankruptcy, which involves collective labour dismissals, bringing us to point A'_2 through an indirect but dangerous route. Either way, wage rigidity – preventing wage adjustments in order to bring demand and supply to equality – is the simplest and foremost explanation of unemployment. This raises the next question: What

makes labour markets special? In brief, the answer is that labour markets are characterized by some unique economic and social conditions that we now review.

8.2.2 Economic market failures

A number of economic features prevent labour markets from operating as the textbook's perfect-market paradigm. One way or another, they contribute to lasting unemployment by preventing wages to adjust to the level where demand and supply are equal.

★ *The possibility for one side of the market to exercise excessive power.* Dominant employers will set wages too low (as was widely the case a century ago); dominant trade unions will set the wages too high (as in closed-shop firms where trade unions control hiring and working conditions). Rules and legislation are required to prevent dominance of either side. This includes implementing and regulating the negotiation process, which reduces wage flexibility.

★ *Information asymmetry.* Employers cannot monitor work effort and skills, hence how much they should pay each employee, whereas employees cannot determine their own contributions to productivity, hence what their wages should be. As a consequence, wages cannot be set individually. The usual solution is to set industry and national norms that further curtail free competition on the labour market. The result is wage rigidity.

★ *Individual workers are highly vulnerable to uncertainty.* Losing a job is a normal implication of a market economy, but it often leaves affected workers with no viable options. This calls for the adoption and funding of mandatory insurance (unemployment, health, retirement) and for limits on the ability to fire redundant workers. Financing unemployment insurance directly raises the cost of labour, while labour protection rules raise it indirectly.

★ *Human capital.* Many individual skills are acquired on the job. Training benefits society as a whole, if only because a large pool of qualified workers allows all firms to respond efficiently to market needs. Firms have an incentive to train their workers but what if their workers leave? A natural response is to offer higher wages to the better qualified workers and to use the less qualified workers to deal with market fluctuations. The result may be rigid wages for the qualified workers and bouts of unemployment for the less qualified ones.

These characteristics are inherent to the labour market. They all represent a market failure in the sense that they prevent the market from reaching full employment.

8.2.3 Social imperatives

To further complicate matters, economic effectiveness is not the only consideration that drives labour markets. Social considerations also matter a great deal, and apparently more so in Europe than elsewhere, such as in the USA.

★ *Fairness*. People are born different, with varying skills and fortunes. Education opportunities will further aggravate differences in the ability to perform on the labour markets. To varying degrees, societies see these inherited and acquired disparities as unfair. Free and open education is one response, but other measures are required to protect the weaker during their professional lives. This includes minimum wages, social minima, established working conditions (hours, holidays, wage increases, etc.), all of which may keep the real wage above full-employment equilibrium.

★ *Income stability*. Uncertainty and aversion to risk, identified above as sources of economic failure, also include a social concern. Losing a job or becoming too ill to work does not only affect the worker, it also affects his family and the education opportunities of his children. This explains why welfare systems often go beyond the minimum insurance that economic effectiveness would justify.

★ *Job security*. Where unemployment is high, as in some suburban areas, significant segments of the population feel estranged from society. Quite often, the result is a deteriorating quality of life, not to mention increased crime and insecurity. This serious concern is often met by special programmes and subsidies aimed either at restricting firms' ability to dismiss workers or at encouraging hiring.

8.2.4 Labour market institutions: the effects of collective negotiations

We now amend the simple framework presented in section 8.2.1 to illustrate how specific labour market institutions designed to deal with market failures or social imperatives affect the labour market. We focus on the most common of these institutions, collective wage bargaining. Indeed, a distinguishing feature of labour markets is that all job characteristics – wages, contract lengths, working conditions, hiring and firing practices – are usually not set freely between individual employers and employees but are negotiated between employer associations and trade unions, or set by the government.

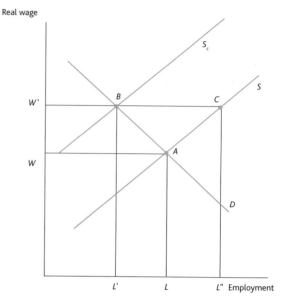

Figure 8.4: *The role of collective negotiations: an illustration*

Point *A* in Fig. 8.4 shows the outcome of the free interplay of individual demand and supply in the labour market in the absence of any rigidity: employment is *L* and the real wage is *w*. Workers resort to a collective representation, call it a trade union for the sake of simplicity, because it allows them to achieve better wages. As any agent with market power – the best-known example of which is monopoly power – the trade union holds back a bit of supply to push up wages. This is shown by the collective supply curve S_c, which lies to the left and above the individual supply curve *S*. The outcome of the negotiation is now represented by point *B*. As collective negotiations raise the real wage to *w'*, firms respond by aiming at production processes that are less labour-intensive and employment declines to *L'*. Note that, at the new, higher wage level *w'*, the amount of labour that workers wish to supply increases to *L"*, corresponding to point *C*. The result is involuntary unemployment represented by the distance *BC*. Unemployment is the natural outcome of the union's effort to boost the well-being of those that have a job. Restricting labour supply implies that not everyone who wants to work at the going wage will find a willing employer. Less employment also implies that output too is reduced; wasting labour resources is economically ineffective.

Why is this feature of labour markets so widespread? The overwhelming majority of workers are employed. Democratically, therefore, they support any institution that delivers higher wages, even at the cost of unemployment. In fact, trade unions also ask for assistance for the unemployed. Unemployment benefits are usually financed, partly at least, through taxes paid for by the employed, who then feel that the outcome is beneficial to them and fair to the unemployed.

8.3 Effects of integration

The EU's single market four freedoms include the movement of goods, services, capital and workers.[2] All four freedoms deeply affect the labour markets. In order to compete in the goods and services markets, producers must fight on all fronts, first and foremost, their production costs. Production costs include three main components:

★ labour costs;
★ the price of equipment;
★ the price of materials.

Both equipment and material costs are largely determined abroad (since domestically produced goods must compete with imports), leaving labour costs, which typically amount to over 50 per cent of total production costs, as a key source of competitiveness. This, in turn, means that the labour force must be used efficiently. That does not mean low wages per se, only that wages must be in line with workers' productivity. Indirectly, therefore, labour markets compete against each other.

8.3.1 The challenge of economic integration

There is no obvious 'first best' solution to the often conflicting economic and social objectives at play in Europe's labour markets. Throughout their political and social histories, different countries have established different labour market institutions to deal with both market failures and social imperatives. These institutions imply various degrees and forms of rigidity, with various effects on productive efficiency and unemployment, as seen above in the first section. How do labour market institutions and economic integration interact? Influences run in both directions.

First, economic integration affects the nature of labour market institutions. These institutions arise from a compromise between economic and social imperatives. As integration affects the economic imperative it alters the institutions. When faced with deep economic

integration, labour market institutions become a strategic characteristic in the quest for competitiveness, i.e. economic effectiveness. The ability of firms to compete across borders on the single market depends on the ability of employers and employees to react adequately to adverse shocks, which, as seen above, may occasionally require reductions in production costs.

Second, the labour market institutions affect integration. Economic integration almost always creates winners and losers, but typically the winners win more than the losers lose. Europeans' willingness to elect leaders who push ever deeper integration hinges critically on their belief that labour market institutions, and the social programmes more broadly, will share the net benefits of integration by dampening the pain felt by the losers. Without these 'safety nets' it is unlikely that broad political support for ever closer economic integration could be maintained in EU nations. In addition, trade integration shifts production patterns. If the labour markets are inflexible, integration may result in job losses with no job gains and possibly even no general economic gain either.

We turn now to fleshing out the logic of the last point – how institutions affect the medium-run effects of deeper integration. We start with the single market and then move on to the impact of the monetary union.

8.3.2 Economics of 'social dumping'

Workers in many EU nations are convinced that competition from the new Member States (NMSs) will force a reduction of the level of social protection that they enjoy today. Wages are much lower in the NMSs (see Table 8.2), and in some NMSs the level of social protection is also considerably laxer than in the EU15. There is nothing new here; it is an old, old concern. It was, for example, the crux of a major debate over the shape of the Treaty of Rome in the 1950s. In the early 1950s, French workers worried that lax social policy in Italy and Germany would undermine French social policy. As history would have it, social protection of workers rose spectacularly throughout western Europe despite (or maybe because of) the deep integration between nations that initially had very different wage and social protection levels.

While the leaders of the six founding nations of the European Union worried about 'social dumping', they decided that harmonization of most social policies was not a necessary component of European integration. The economic logic behind this judgement continues to

---

[2] Chapter 7 deals with the freedom of movement of capital. See the factsheets on www.europarl.eu.int for further details on EU policy and laws concerning the four freedoms.

Country	Index: Germany = 100
Bulgaria	5
Croatia	22
Czech Republic	19
Estonia	13
Hungary	20
Latvia	7
Lithuania	10
Poland	16
Romania	7
Slovakia	15
Slovenia	33

Source: Federation of European Employers (2005).

Table 8.2: *Median weekly private sector earnings, February 2005*

affect EU policy, so it is worth considering in some detail.

Basic economics of wage and non-wage costs of employment

To get a handle on the basic issues, we start by making strong assumptions to radically simplify the range of issues at hand. We add back in some important aspects of reality after having established the basic points.

Taking the example of France, we start by supposing that, as in section 8.2.1, labour markets operate like other markets, so the wage adjusts to make sure that there is no involuntary unemployment. Moreover, to keep things simple, suppose France starts without any social policies and initially is closed to trade. The equilibrium, shown in the left-hand panel of Fig. 8.5, is where the real wage is w and the employment level is L.

Now suppose the French government adopted a whole series of social policies, e.g. limits on working hours, obligatory retirement benefits, maternity leave, sick leave, six weeks of annual holidays, etc. These policies would undoubtedly be good for most workers. Indeed, most Europeans view these as necessities, not luxuries. Yet, however good these policies are for workers and the society at large, such policies are expensive for firms. To be specific, suppose that they raise the cost of employing workers by T euros per week. What happens to wages and employment? The demand schedule shifts vertically down by T, since labour cost has increased by

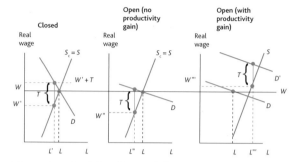

Figure 8.5: *Social policy and distortions*

that amount. The new equilibrium wage paid to workers – this is called the 'take-home' pay – with the general policy will be w'.[3] It is useful to think of the social policy 'tax' being paid partly by consumers (in the form of higher prices) and partly by workers (in the form of lower take-home wages). The firms we consider here are competitive and so cannot bear any part of T; they earn zero profits both before and after T is imposed.

Why does the take-home wage fall when social policies are imposed? Firms hire workers up to the point where the extra value they create for the firm equals the extra cost of employing them (the value of workers is determined primarily by their productivity). This cost includes wage and non-wage costs, such as the cost of social policies. Firms cannot pay higher labour costs if they want to avoid losing money.

Given this iron law of the labour market – firms hire workers up to the point where all-included employment costs equal the workers' value to the firm – everything that raises non-wage labour costs must force down the take-home pay of workers. In essence, the social policies are a way of 'forcing' workers to take part of their remuneration in the form of non-wage 'payment', e.g. four weeks of paid holiday or generous sick leave, instead of in the direct form of take-home pay.

Next, consider the impact of freeing trade in goods between France and other nations. As far as the labour market is concerned, freer trade has two main impacts:

★ As discussed at length in Chapters 4, 5, 6 and 7, trade tends to boost the productivity of an economy. It does this by allowing a nation's capital and labour to be allocated more efficiently. For example, Chapter 6 showed how freer trade produced fewer, larger, more efficient firms that faced more effective competition from each other.

[3] Readers who have had a good course in microeconomics will recognize this as the analysis of the 'incidence' of the 'tax' T.

★ Trade also tends to flatten the demand curve since it heightens the competition between national firms and foreign firms. For example, if real wage costs rise by €100 per week, firms will have to raise prices. The negative impact of higher prices on output, and therefore employment, is greater in the presence of foreign competition. Or, to put it more directly, greater integration of goods markets means that workers in different nations compete more directly with each other.

We begin with the second concern since this is closest to the everyday concerns of many workers in Europe. The middle panel in Fig. 8.5 shows the impact of the flatter demand curve for French labour. The way the diagram is drawn, openness per se would have no impact if there were no social policy. Without the tax T, wage and employment levels would be as in the closed economy case (i.e. w and L). The non-wage costs, i.e. T, however, change things. Since labour demand is now more responsive to total labour costs, the take-home wage of French workers will fall more, to w'' rather than w' when T is imposed. The reason is simple. Greater openness gives consumers a wider range of options; when T is imposed more of it gets paid by workers rather than by consumers. In other words, the greater price sensitivity forces workers to bear more of the burden of the social-policy 'tax'.

The result that greater openness reduces wages flies in the face of Europe's experience. The incomes of European workers have been growing steadily as European markets have become more tightly integrated. Moreover, as discussed in Chapter 7, some of the fastest income growth occurred in the 1960s when European trade integration was proceeding at its fastest pace. How can we explain this? The efficiency-enhancing effects of trade integration is the answer.

The third panel in Fig. 8.5 shows the labour market implications of trade-induced efficiency gains. As productivity rises, the value of workers to firms rises and this shows up as a shift up the demand curve to D'. Now we see that even if trade integration makes the demand curve flatter, the shift up in the labour demand curve more than offsets flattening. In the figure, the take-home wage has rise to w''' and employment has increased to L'''.

Considering unemployment

So far we have put the issue of unemployment to the side by assuming that the labour market clears as in section 8.2.1. To consider unemployment, we allow the 'collective' labour supply curve (S_c) and the individual labour supply curve (S) to differ as in section 8.2.4. This is done in Fig. 8.6, which corresponds to the second panel of Fig. 8.5. The initial position is characterized by unemployment U, with employment L and supply L_s. The social policy distortion reduces employment to L' and supply to L_s'. The effect on unemployment is not clear, however, and this is also the case of the trade-opening effect. If the S_c and S curves are parallel, as drawn here and in Fig. 8.4, the gap between the number of people who would like to work, L_s', and those who are actually hired by firms, L', does not vary with the wage. Consequently, trade integration has no direct impact on unemployment, only on employment.

This result should be intuitive. Unemployment is caused by labour market institutions that prevent wages from matching the number of jobs with the number of job seekers. As long as trade integration, per se, has no clear impact on the labour market institutions, it has no clear impact on unemployment. This lines up with the facts. As we saw above, the tighter integration of European markets has been accompanied by steady or rising unemployment rates in some EU members such as France and Germany, but falling unemployment rates in members such as the UK, Sweden and Spain.

Economics of social dumping

What has all this got to do with social dumping? What we have shown is that the total cost of employing workers – wage and non-wage costs – is tied to the productivity of workers. If governments raise social policy

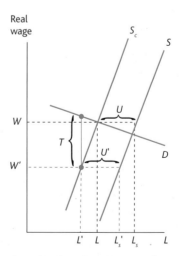

Figure 8.6: *Social policy distortions with involuntary unemployment*

standards, the economy will adjust by lowering employment, raising prices and reducing the wages (of course, nominal wages rarely fall; what would happen is that wages would rise more slowly than productivity for a number of years, as happened in France when the 35-hour week was introduced). When an economy is more open, the wage and employment adjustments tend to be greater, other things equal. Or, to put it more colloquially, the anti-employment effects of social policies are magnified by greater openness.

However, this does not necessarily put pressure on social policies. The key point is that the same mechanism is working in France's trade partners. If the other nations have lower social policy standards then their workers will have higher take-home pay than otherwise, since the foreign firms hire workers up to the point where their total labour cost matches their workers' productivity. If the EU forced the new Member States (NMSs) to raise social protection, the NMS wage would fall to compensate, so social policy harmonization would have little impact on the competitive pressures facing French employers. Turning this around, the logic also tells us that lowering French social policy standards would not boost French competitiveness in anything but the short run.

The upshot of all this should be clear. The logic of competition ties the sum of wage and non-wage costs to workers' productivity. The founders of the EU therefore believed that the division between wage and non-wage costs could be left to the choice of each Member State exactly because this division has only a moderate impact on external competitiveness.

8.3.3 The single market effect

EU integration has progressively deepened the integration of European markets for goods, services, capital and labour while widening integration with successive enlargements. Each of the four freedoms interacts with institutions to determine the medium-run labour market effects.

Trade in goods and services is the easiest. As barriers to trade in goods are lowered, the true competitiveness of various nations' industries is revealed. As pointed out in Chapters 4 and 5, this often involves an output reduction in import-competing sectors and an expansion of export sectors. In terms of the analysis above, this is very much like a shift in the labour demand curve, but at the sectoral level. Where labour markets are flexible, most of the adjustment occurs via wage adjustments. As mentioned above, we see greater wage inequality but

less unemployment. If the nations' general welfare and tax system is working well, this inequality at the workplace will be dampened by rising tax payments by the winners and rising benefits paid to the losers. Where labour markets are rigid, the impact tends to be more unemployment but less inequality in take-home pay.

Theoretically, the free movement of capital can magnify these medium-run labour market effects since firms can react to inflexible labour markets by taking their capital elsewhere when faced by a negative shock. This tends to speed up the pace at which production is relocated across countries in response to deeper integration. On one hand, this allows the expanding sectors to expand more quickly, but on the other hand, it means that the shrinking sectors shrink faster. It is important to note, though, that this is a matter of timing rather than extent. If a nation's firms in a particular sector are uncompetitive, they will reduce employment eventually, one way or the other.

Finally, the free movement of labour tends to mitigate the problem. For example, the ability of East Germans to move to West Germany meant that unemployment was less of a problem than it could have been today.

8.3.4 The monetary union effect: four channels

What effect, if any, will the monetary union have on labour markets? Four main channels have been identified.

Trade integration

The first channel is deeper trade integration, which in turn should affect labour markets, as explained in the previous section. Why should the single currency increase trade? As will be explained in Chapter 16, a monetary union is believed to boost trade for three main reasons:
★ It allows exporters and importers to save on currency exchange costs.
★ It eliminates risk on the evolution of exchange rates.
★ Finally, trivially maybe, it increases transparency as it is possible to make direct price comparisons.

Monetary discipline and wage negotiations

A key ingredient of wage negotiations is the expected rate of inflation. If trade unions expect prices to increase, they insist on higher wages. If employers agree and also expect prices to rise, they go along and increase their own prices, in effect feeding inflation. This then puts pressure on the central bank to accommodate the price increases. The result is a higher rate of inflation than wished for. This is one reason why central banks attach great value to their reputations: if they are known to deliver price stability, wage negotiators will moderate wage increases, which will deliver price stability.

The removal of the 'exchange rate option' changes the situation. When each country had its own currency, trade unions could aim at high wages and expect that any loss in national competitiveness would be compensated for through an exchange rate depreciation. With this option now gone, trade unions understand that unjustified wage increases – in the sense that they exceed productivity gains – will translate into a loss of competitiveness and, therefore, unemployment.

As will be explained in Chapter 17, the adoption of a common currency comes with the establishment of a common central bank, the Eurosystem. This central bank is likely to be less sensitive to national conditions, including the evolution of wages. The expected result is that trade unions will moderate wage claims.

Centralization of negotiations

Section 8.2.4 explains the role of collective labour market negotiations. In a nutshell, the more unions push hard on high wages, the higher is the rate of unemployment and, quite possibly, the greater the loss in terms of GDP. Collective negotiations may take place at three levels:

★ at the plant level;
★ at the industry level, e.g. for all steel or retail trade workers;
★ at the national level, setting base wages for all workers, with particular firms or industries possibly topping up over agreed wages.

When they negotiate at the plant level, workers and their unions are keenly aware that high wage settlements could endanger their firm's competitiveness and result in job losses or, worse, in the firm's bankruptcy. This realization exerts a moderating influence on wage claims. Similarly, when trade unions conduct negotiations at the national level, they can see that the whole economy's competitiveness is at stake, which leads them to be careful about the employment implications of high wages. At the industry level, in contrast, unions feel responsible for neither the entire economy nor any particular firm. They have little incentive to restrain wage claims that apply to all firms that compete against each other.

This reasoning suggests that the adverse employment effect of collective negotiations is more likely to be felt when negotiations are partially coordinated (e.g. occur at the industry level) than when they are either fully uncoordinated or fully coordinated. This conjecture receives some support from Fig. 8.7, which displays the degree of coordination in wage bargaining on the horizontal axis (0 meaning no coordination and 1 full coordination at the national level), and the average employment ratio on the vertical axis. The curve is statistically fitted to represent as best as possible the link between coordination and employment.[4] Of course, many other factors influence the employment ratio so the curve misses most points, but it suggests that the soft belly in the middle is less employment-friendly than either extreme; the fully uncoordinated case emerges as the most conducive to low wages and high employment.

What effect, if any, will the monetary union have on wage negotiations? If we now look at the eurozone as a single economic area, each country becomes a 'regional' unit. In that view national-level negotiations become 'regional-level', and industry-level negotiations only concern firms in a 'region'. De facto, all negotiations are then less coordinated than before, as if all countries were moving to the left in Fig. 8.7, except of course those already at the far left. This implies more wage moderation and more employment for those countries currently in the middle range, which may be good news

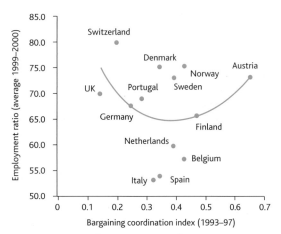

Figure 8.7: *Wage bargaining coordination and employment*

Source: Calmfors (2001) and OECD.

[4] Formally, this is a third-order polynomial trend.

for some, but bad news for those initially to the right and moving towards the centre.

It is too early to know whether wage restraint has increased or not since the launch of the euro. Yet, another question is, how can trade unions react to what is a loss of influence *vis-à-vis* the monetary authority. A natural response to the creation of a unique central bank would be for national trade unions to form pan-European coalitions. If coalitions take place at the industry level, where it could be easiest, the effect in Fig. 8.7 would be a shift towards the middle of the centralization axis, precisely where wage moderation and flexibility are lowest. Box 8.3 looks at one important reason why such a shift has not yet happened and why it is unlikely to happen in the foreseeable future.

The need for flexibility

We already observed that without the inflation and exchange rate option, labour market flexibility becomes the main margin of adjustment in the presence of disturbances. We also observed that, prior to the adoption of the euro, each country found its own delicate equilibrium between often conflicting economic efficiency and social concerns. Will the monetary union challenge the existing equilibria and push them towards more flexibility?

In many ways it has already happened. Several of the smaller countries – the Netherlands, for instance – had made their labour market institutions more conducive to flexibility before the adoption of the euro. The spotlight has moved to the Big-3, whose quite rigid labour

Box 8.3 The national base of trade unions

In contrast to almost any other institution in Europe, including football teams and central banks, trade unions remain organized exclusively along national lines. This stands in sharp contrast with their counterparts (i.e. firms), which are increasingly consolidating across borders. As a result, employers are able to play workers against each other, threatening to move their activities to other countries in order to extract concessions. It would be in the clear interest of employees to match the strategy of employers, so what is holding them? Most likely, the likelihood that trade unions would lose much of their existing power.

In many countries, trade unions effectively control labour negotiations even though they have few active members, as can be seen in Table 8.3. The table's first column displays the proportion of employees whose working conditions are set in collective negotiations where unions represent the employees. By and large, nearly all EU employees are covered by collective negotiations, the exceptions being Ireland, the UK and some of the new Member States. This is the case independently of the unions' representativity, as measured by union density, that is, the percentage of employees who are union members, reported in the second column. The most spectacular case is France, where only 10 per cent of employees are union members but nearly all of them

are covered by negotiations conducted between employers and trade unions. How can that be? The answer is provided in the last column, which indicates the existence of legislation that automatically applies the outcome of collective negotiations to all firms in the same industry. The Nordic countries, where there is no such legislation but where a huge proportion of employees are union members, stand apart. The reason for the apparent popularity of unions in the Nordic countries lies in another piece of legislation which arranges for unions to manage unemployment benefits.

The table illustrates a key feature of European labour market institutions: the influence of trade unions rests on legal arrangements. This feature can be contrasted with the Anglo-Saxon countries (Ireland, the UK and the USA), where no such laws exist and where, accordingly, unions are considerably less influential. Given that their power depends on national legislation, it is understandable that trade unions are highly reluctant to reorganize themselves at the EU level. To do so, they would have to be reassured that they would benefit from similar EU-wide legislation. Since social issues can only be decided at the EU level by majority voting, the unions have good reasons to fear that they would not enjoy a similar privilege, if only because the UK is likely to veto any such move.

continued

continued

Country	Collective bargaining coverage (%)	Union density (%)	Extension laws
Austria	95+	37	Yes
Belgium	90+	56	Yes
Czech Republic	25+	27	n.a.
Denmark	80+	74	No
Finland	90+	76	Yes
France	90+	10	Yes
Germany	68	25	Yes
Hungary	30+	20	Yes
Ireland	n.a.	38	No
Italy	80+	35	Yes
Netherlands	80+	23	Yes
Norway	70+	54	No
Poland	40+	15	Yes
Portugal	80+	24	Yes
Slovakia	50+	36	Yes
Spain	80+	15	Yes
Sweden	90+	79	No
Switzerland	40+	18	Yes
UK	30+	31	No
USA	14	13	No

Source: CESifo–DICE database, 2005.

Table 8.3: *Trade unions in Europe, 2000*

markets are associated with poor performance in terms of both employment and unemployment (see Fig. 8.1). Germany has taken some important but limited steps under the Agenda 2010 and Hartz IV programmes, as has France albeit less systematically. The spotlight is also on many new member countries, which inherited from central planning severely distorted labour markets and have conducted limited reforms. More reforms are likely to follow as the contrast between economic performances in the more and less flexible countries will increasingly put pressure on the latter to emulate the former.

Just listing some of the arrangements that are being challenged is telling of the political difficulties of reform. A more in-depth discussion is presented on the companion website.

★ *Statutory minimum wages.* When they are high enough to protect a significant number of workers, minimum wages discourage firms from hiring people with low skills, typically the less educated, especially the young, and those who used to work in declining industries.

★ *Unemployment insurance.* It is obvious that workers who have become unemployed must be provided with decent means of existence while they look for a new job. This is a form of insurance that exists in virtually all advanced economies. At the same time, evidence has been accumulating that generous and long-lasting unemployment benefits discourage some people from actively searching employment opportunities or encourage them to turn down job offers.

★ *Employment protection*. Most countries limit the ability of employers to dismiss their employees. Employment protection includes measures such as advanced warning periods, mandatory severance pay and penalties, regulations on fixed-term contracts, and sometimes restrictions on the conditions under which workers can be fired. Here again, the social reasons for such measures are clear enough, but the economic costs, especially as a source of rigidity in the face of rapidly changing conditions, are quite significant.

★ *Payroll taxes*. Many welfare programmes, including unemployment and health insurance, are usually financed by taxes levied on wage income. These taxes either make labour more expensive, which reduces demand in Fig. 8.4, or reduce take-home pay, which reduces individual supply in the same figure; more generally there is a mix of both. The result is the same: more involuntary unemployment and less employment. This can trigger a vicious circle: following serious adverse shocks – like the oil shocks of the 1970s and 1980s – unemployment rises, which raises the cost of servicing unemployment benefits, hence the need to raise taxes on a shrinking number of employed workers, which in turn results in more unemployment.

8.4 Migration

The free movement of workers is the cornerstone of EU integration and has been since its inception in the 1950s. This goal of the freedom of movement is both economic and political. Allowing workers to move freely within the Community should enhance economic efficiency by allowing workers to find the jobs that best suit their skills and experience, while simultaneously allowing firms to hire the most appropriate workers. On a political level, the architects of the EU hoped that this sort of mobility would foster mutual understanding among the peoples of Europe. As many readers will know from first-hand experience, the fact that many young Europeans spend some time living, studying or working in other EU nations has had a big impact on the way Europeans view

each other. This section considers European migration. We start with some facts.

8.4.1 Facts

The spectacular growth performance of the EEC economies during the 1940s and 1950s brought about conditions of full employment. After this was achieved, northern European governments and firms sought out foreign labour, and substantial south-to-north migration flows were the result. The turnaround in northern Europe's economic fortunes, starting with the 1973 recession, produced a significant drop in migration, as Fig. 8.8 shows. (In the diagram, negative numbers indicate an outflow of workers; positive numbers an inflow.)

What we see is that southern Europe (Italy, Spain, Portugal and Greece) and south-eastern Europe (mainly Turkey) were the prime sending nations up to the growth slowdown in 1973. The northern European nations (the EEC6 less Italy plus the Nordics and alpine economies) were big receiving nations during the same phase. Migration rates overall were quite modest until the economic recovery began in the early 1980s. At that point, northern Europe regained its appetite for foreign workers, but, and most importantly, the southern European nations, which had been net providers of workers pre-1973, became net importers. Some of this migration involves the return of Spanish, Italian and Portuguese workers, who had emigrated in the pre-1973 period, but it also reflects an increasing inflow of non-European workers from places such as North Africa. Turkey, by contrast, resumed its role as a provider of migrants. In this role, Turkey was joined by central and

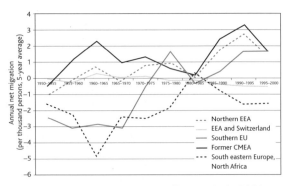

Figure 8.8: *European migration flows, 1950–2000*

Source: Brücker (2002), 'Can international migration solve the problems of European labour markets?' on www.unece.org/ead/sem/sem2002/papers/Brucker.pdf.

eastern European nations who had, by the end of the 1980s, dropped general restrictions on emigration.

Migration within the EU is, in principle, free. Yet, when the EU was expanded in 2004, special provisions were temporarily imposed on the ten new members to limit migration from these countries to the incumbent 15 members. Box 8.4 explains why fears of massive immigration from central and eastern Europe are unjustified. In fact, seven out of ten foreign workers in EU Member States are from non-EU countries. The policies that govern labour flows from non-member nations are entirely national – the EU does not try to impose what might be called a common external migration policy. To put it differently, being part of the EU's common labour market does not seem to matter very much, at least as far as the raw number of workers is concerned.

Table 8.4 shows that the importance of migrants in the various nations' populations varies quite a lot, both within the EU and between EU and non-EU nations. Moreover, being part of a common labour market does

not seem to be the key to determining the origin of migrants. Migrants from EU nations make up a much higher percentage of foreign workers in Norway and Switzerland than they do in France and Germany. This shows that the discriminatory liberalization implied by the free mobility of workers within the EU (i.e. workers from one EU nation are free to work in any other EU nation, but they need special permission to work in non-EU nations such as Norway) is not a dominant factor in determining migration patterns. This contrasts sharply with discriminatory liberalization of goods. As Chapter 7 shows, the composition of imports is strongly influenced by implementation of the customs union.

What this means is that, so far at least, Common Market membership has not boosted international labour movements. There is really no mystery here. In the 1950s and 1960s, nations across north-western Europe were experiencing such rapid growth that industry found itself short of workers. Individual nations responded by facilitating inward migration from many

Box 8.4 Migration from the new Member States

The 2004 enlargement brought millions of new citizens into the European Union. By the time Bulgaria and Romania are in, the number will be about 100 million. Most workers in the new Member States (NMSs) are paid substantially less in their home nations than they would be doing similar jobs in the EU15 due primarily to higher labour productivity in the EU15. The income gap between the east and the west in Europe is approximately 50 per cent when adjusted for higher prices in the west; at current exchange rates, the income gap is even larger. This raised the prospect of massive east–west migration, but this possibility has not become reality. With a few exceptions such as Albania and eastern Germany, the removal of emigration barriers for the people in the former Eastern Bloc produced relatively small outflows. Boeri and Brücker (2005) estimate that cumulative net emigration since 1989 from the NMSs is about 1.1 million people. In part, the moderate nature of these flows reflects the EU15's tight immigration restrictions; most EU15 nations negotiated

long transition periods during which NMS workers cannot move freely into their labour markets. But the low numbers also reflect the fact that central and east Europeans share much of the west European resistance to moving (see Chapter 16).

What will happen when the transitional restrictions end? According to Boeri and Brücker, the mainstream estimate of the long-run migration from the NMSs to the EU15 is of the order of 3–4 per cent of the population of the NMSs, or about 3 million migrants. Some estimates, however, are significantly higher and some are lower. The variance in these estimates can be largely traced back to different econometric estimation procedures. One of the simplest estimation techniques is to look at what happened with north–south income gaps in Europe, which were about as big as the east–west gaps are now. During the 1960s and 1970s, about 3 per cent of the populations of the poor south moved north. Since the 1980s, these flows have been reversed as the migrants have returned home.

	Immigrants as % of population	% immigrants from EU	Share with low education				
			Total population	Nationals	EU foreigners	Non-EU foreigners	Immigrants (millions)
Immigrants are more than 5% of population							
Luxembourg	33	90	55	51	62	42	0.1
Austria	9		29	28	16	51	0.7
Germany	9	25	30	30	36	56	7.3
Belgium	9	63	41	41	n.a.	48	0.9
France	6	37	41	31	65	69	3.6
Immigrants are more than 3% of population							
Denmark	5	21	31	31	28	66	0.2
Netherlands	4	28	28	27	32	60	0.7
UK	4	38	41	41	49	28	2.1
Ireland	3	71	51	52	38	21	0.1
Immigrants are less than 2% of population							
Portugal	2	25	81	81	23	50	0.2
Greece	2	28	50	50	25	37	0.2
Italy	2	15	60	60	30	36	0.9
Finland	1	19	33	33	23	24	0.1
Spain	1	47	62	62	29	37	0.5
EU15	5	31					
Non-EU nations							
Switzerland	19	60					
Norway	4	41					

Source: Adapted from Brücker (2002) 'Can international migration solve the problems of European labour markets?' on www.unece.org/ead/sem/sem2002/papers/Brucker.pdf. **Data on immigrant numbers and source countries from 1998; data on education levels from 1996.**

Table 8.4: *Facts about immigrants in the EU*

different nations. Not surprisingly, nations that wanted to 'import' workers found it easiest to induce migration from nations with low wages and relatively high unemployment. The fact that Spain, Portugal and Greece were not at the time members of the EU did little to hinder the flow of workers into EU members such as Germany. Indeed, German immigration policy in the 1960s was at least as welcoming to Turks and Spaniards as it was to southern Italians. Moreover, nations such as Sweden and the UK, whose industry also experienced labour shortages, managed to attract migrants – including some migrants from EU nations such as Italy – even without being part of the Common Market. In short, the western European policies that fostered the big migration flows in the 1960s were basically unrelated to the policies of the Common Market.

8.4.2 Microeconomics of labour market integration

Labour migration is probably the most contentious aspect of economic integration in Europe. In most Western European nations, popular opinion holds immigrants responsible for high unemployment, abuse of social welfare programmes, street crime and deterioration of neighbourhoods. As a result, a number of explicitly anti-immigration political parties have fared well in elections. How does immigration affect the sending and receiving nations, and who gains and loses from it?

Simplest framework

We start with the simplest analytical framework that allows us to organize our thinking about the economic consequences of labour migration.[5] We start with the case where migration is not allowed between two nations (Home and Foreign) who initially have different wages.

Figure 8.9 shows a situation where workers initially earn better wages in Home than in Foreign. Now allow migration, and labour will tend to flow from Foreign to Home. This will push down wages in Home and thus harm the Home workers while benefiting Home capital owners. The opposite happens in Foreign. As some Foreign labour moves to Home, Foreign wages tend to rise, making the remaining Foreign workers better off and Foreign capital owners worse off. As before, both countries will gain overall, if we add the gains and losses to each nation's capital and labour.[6] This all assumes that there is no unemployment to start with and therefore seems unrealistic; we return to this issue in section 8.4.3 below.

In short, while migration creates winners and losers in both nations, both nations gain from the movement of labour. The reason for this has to do with efficiency. Without migration, the worldwide allocation of productive factors is inefficient. Migration thus improves the overall efficiency of the world economy, and the gains from this are split between Home and Foreign.

Broader interpretation of the results and empirical evidence

The analysis above classifies all productive factors into two categories: capital and labour. It is important to note, however, that for most EU nations we should interpret 'capital' as including 'human capital', i.e. highly educated workers. The reason has to do with the economic notion of 'complementarity' versus 'substitutability'.

Rather than defining these concepts directly, consider the example of how productive factors combine to produce hotel services. Apart from material inputs such as food and bed linen, hotels require unskilled workers (cleaners, etc.), skilled workers (managers, marketing people, etc.) and capital (the building, furniture, etc.). In a country like Norway, unskilled labour is very costly so hotels are very expensive; consequently there are relatively few hotels. If Norway allowed hotels to hire

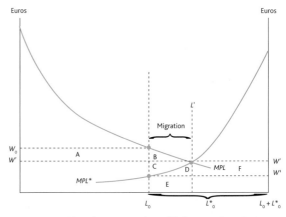

Figure 8.9: *Simple economics of labour migration*

foreign workers at lower wages, some factors would be hurt – the unskilled workers who earned high wages before the immigration – but other factors would be helped. Skilled workers and capital would find that their rewards rise. As the price of hotel rooms fell, the hotel industry would expand, raising the demand for highly skilled workers and capital. In this situation, we say that unskilled workers are complements to skilled workers and capital: demand for skilled workers and capital rises as the supply of unskilled workers increases and their price falls.

The point of this is to put the losses to domestic labour in perspective. As Table 8.4 shows, immigrants often have a skill mix that is very different from that of domestic workers. Most domestic workers can thus be thought of as belonging to 'capital' in the Fig. 8.9 analysis and thus winning from immigration. In France and Germany, for example, immigrants often work at jobs, e.g. in factories, that boost the productivity of native workers in related fields like management, finance, sales and marketing. Indeed, immigrants often fill jobs that no native would take, such as kitchen workers, street sweepers, etc.; this is an extreme form of complementarity in which there are no economic losers in the receiving nation.

Looking more closely at Table 8.4, we see that in some EU nations – especially the poor members like Portugal, Greece, Ireland and Spain – immigrants have higher skill levels (as measured by education) than the average native worker. In these cases, the analysis of immigration is somewhat different. Instead of shifting L from Foreign to Home, migration shifts 'capital'. Graphically this raises the MPL curve in Fig. 8.9 for Home and lowers it for Foreign. The reason is that the presence of more skilled workers tends to raise the productivity of unskilled

---

[5] As it turns out, this framework is just like Fig. 19.2, the diagram we shall use to study capital mobility. We simply reverse the roles of capital and labour in order to study the allocative efficiency effects and distribution effects of labour mobility.

[6] You are invited to refer to Chapter 7 for detailed explanations.

workers. If you want a mental picture of this process, think of American entrepreneurs coming into Ireland and starting businesses that hire Irish workers away from the farm sector. Again, we see that immigration can be a win–win situation for the receiving nation.

Another insight from the notion of complementarity is that of micro-level matching. Some immigration into the EU consists of workers who have very specific skills – computer programming in English, for example – that are lacking in the receiving nation. Since these workers do not compete with native workers, or compete with very few native workers, such immigration is usually less contentious since it creates few losers. This level of matching among countries can proceed to an even lower level. For example, even within a single company, the experiences of workers vary, and free mobility of labour may make it easier to move workers into jobs that best fit their experience. Again, it is entirely possible that everyone gains from such matching.

More generally, immigrants who have skills that are complementary to the skill mix in the receiving nation are typically less likely to create losers in the receiving nation. Close inspection of the numbers in Table 8.3 reveals that, in many EU nations, the skill mix of immigrants from other EU nations tends to be complementary to that of immigrants from non-EU nations. This may help to explain why immigrants from other EU nations tend to generate less controversy than immigrants from outside the EU.

Empirical evidence

So much for the theory. What does the evidence tell us? Given the importance of immigration in the various national debates in Europe, economists have done a great deal of work estimating the impact of migration on the wages of domestic workers. Generally, these studies find that a 1 per cent rise in the supply of workers via migration changes the wages of native workers by between +1 per cent and −1 per cent, with most studies putting the figure in the even narrower range of ±0.3 per cent. There are two key points to take away from these findings. First, it is not obvious that immigration always lowers wages. Since nations tend to let in workers who have skills that are complementary to those of domestic workers, the impact is often positive. Second, whether it is slightly positive or slightly negative, the impact is quite small. Again, this outcome is due in part to the fact that countries tend to restrict the types of labour inflow that would have large negative effects on wages.

8.4.3 Unemployment

Framework

One common belief is that immigrants cause unemployment. To understand the logic of how this might be true we first note that the framework discussed in section 8.4.2 above will not do since it implicitly assumes that all workers get jobs, or more exactly that the market wage rises or falls until firms want to hire all the workers that want jobs. Instead, we use the analytical framework presented in section 8.2.1. The main result from this section is that, if wages were perfectly flexible, the wage rate paid for each hour of work would adjust to match the amount of labour workers were willing to supply to the amount that firms were willing to buy. Put differently, unemployment can be seen as a mismatch between supply and demand in the labour market. Section 8.2 also shows that wages in Europe are not flexible and that the outcome is almost always excess supply (unemployment) rather than excess demand (labour shortage) because national labour market institutions are typically biased in favour of workers who already have jobs.

Point A in Fig. 8.10 represents the situation before immigration is allowed. The level of unemployment is U since collective negotiations restrain the effective labour supply to S_c, lower than the individual supply S. The real wage w is set by the trade union, which trades off some unemployment against higher wages for all those who have a job.

Next, we suppose that some immigrants enter the country. The impact of immigrants is not obvious since we do not know whether immigrants will operate in the labour market in the same way as native workers. To be

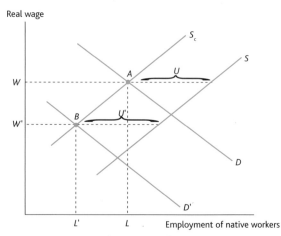

Figure 8.10: *Unemployment and migration*

concrete, consider one extreme, namely that immigrants are willing and able to perform the same jobs as natives but at a wage that is below the union-set wage w. In this extreme case, the impact of migration is to shift the demand curve for native workers to the left. The idea here is that firms first hire cheap immigrants and then turn to the native market to fulfil any remaining demands. The result is that the union-set wage and native employment fall. Two points, however, are worth stressing. First, even in this extreme case – where firms are able to hire immigrants at below market wages – the drop in native employment is less than the number of immigrants. As a consequence, total employment, counting both natives and immigrants, rises. That is, the horizontal shift of the demand curve from D to D', the size of which exactly equals the number of jobs taken by immigrants, is less than the change in equilibrium employment, namely L to L'. This dampening is due to the resulting drop in native wages.

Second, there may be no change in unemployment. Because unemployment is a result of the labour market's structure, immigration will affect unemployment only to the extent that it affects the structure of the labour market. In the particular example shown in the diagram, there is no change in the number of unemployed natives since the drop in wages from w to w' decreases the number of native workers who say they want to work at the going wage by as much as the drop in native employment. If we had drawn the two labour supply curves as converging or diverging instead of parallel, we would have got a different answer. The main point, however, is that if immigration is to affect unemployment, it must do so by altering labour market structure.

Another way to capture the impact of immigration would be to make the other polar assumption that immigrants participate in the labour market in exactly the same way as native workers do. In this case (not shown in the diagram), both the S and S_c curves would shift to the right. The results

would be qualitatively identical to those shown in Fig. 8.10; there would be some drop in the wage and some increase in employment. Since the true impact of immigrants on national labour markets is probably somewhere between these two extremes, it seems reasonable to believe that the standard impact of immigration will be some increase in employment, some decrease in wages and an ambiguous effect on unemployment.

As a final analytical note, observe that, until now, we have been viewing immigrants as substitutes for native workers. If, instead, they are complements, the Fig. 8.10 analysis is reversed. That is, immigration raises the demand for native workers and this results in higher wages, higher employment and an ambiguously favourable impact on unemployment.

Empirical evidence

Again, we turn from theory to evidence. As it turns out, the evidence is mixed. Some studies have found that immigrants increase the chance of unemployment for some groups of workers, but have the opposite effect on other groups of workers. (Think about the complements and substitutes analysis to understand why this might be true.) Other authors find little or no effect of immigration on the risk of being unemployed. In summary, the empirical evidence we have to date does not support the notion that immigration has large, negative effects on European labour markets. As usual, this lack of convincing evidence is due in part to the fact that countries tend to pick and choose their immigrants. While EU members cannot restrict the immigration of other EU nations, this sort of immigration is not very important in those members where certain types of immigration are really important (Germany and France alone account for 11 of the 18 million migrants currently located in the EU). EU members can and do control labour flows from non-EU nations, especially when they would otherwise have large negative effects on employment and/or unemployment.

8.5 Summary

A general feature of European labour markets is that they tend to be inflexible, although the situation differs considerably from one country to another. The worrisome fact is that the three largest eurozone members – France, Germany and Italy – are among those where the labour markets are most rigid and, unsurprisingly, where unemployment is stubbornly high.

A number of economic reasons explain why labour markets do not operate as in the perfect competition paradigm. Power (of employers as well as of workers' unions) plays an important role. Serious information asymmetries render individual wage-setting impossible. Individual workers are highly vulnerable to job losses and need appropriate insurance. Finally, investment in human capital generates significant spillovers. For all these reasons, labour markets require specific institutions that are likely to interfere with economic effectiveness.

Social concerns further explain specific features of labour market institutions. There is limited tolerance for the kind of income inequality that unfettered markets may deliver. Income stability matters not just for the individual workers but for their families as well. Likewise, the lack of job security has widespread consequences for society as a whole. There is no best way of trading off social aims and economic efficiency. As a result, each arrangement is highly controversial, as is any reform proposal.

Trade unions, for instance, have an important role to play in protecting workers from the harshness inherent in economic efficiency and in promoting some degree of equality across wage-earners. At the same time, trade unions have become powerful institutions that protect the interests of their members, the employed – occasionally at the expense of the unemployed.

In general, labour market institutions – minimum wages, unemployment benefits, employment protection legislation – all have a useful role to play, but they do not come without economic costs, and many of these costs are likely to rise as economic integration deepens.

Trade integration affects the labour markets in two ways. It creates winners and losers, which leads trade unions to step in as they wish to use labour institutions to share in the gains; it shifts production patterns, which requires labour market flexibility to avoid job losses.

A particularly influential view is that heightened competition on the goods market translates into competition among labour market institutions, leading to 'social dumping'. An important result is that general social policies do not distort trade, whereas sector-specific policies do. This means that an intensification of competition does not need to put pressure on social policies, at least if they are general. When the labour markets are rigid, there may be some distortions but they are likely to be small as long as the policies that create the rigidities are 'general'.

Competition via migration – the fear that immigrant workers bid down wages – is another popular fear. As the EU provides for the free movement of people, this fear has resurfaced in the wake of the accession of countries from central and eastern Europe where wages and standards of living are much lower than in the western part.

EU integration has progressively deepened the integration of European markets for goods, services, capital and labour while widening integration with successive enlargements. Each of the four freedoms interacts with institutions to determine the medium-run labour market effects.

Trades in goods and services are the easiest. As barriers to trade in goods are lowered, the true competitiveness of various nations' industries are revealed. As pointed out in Chapters 4 and 5, this often involves an output reduction in import-competing sectors and an expansion of export sectors. In terms of the analysis above, this is very much like a shift in the labour demand curve but at the sectoral level. Where labour markets are flexible, most of the adjustment occurs via wage adjustments. As mentioned above, we see greater wage inequality but less unemployment. If the nations' general welfare and tax system is working well, this inequality at the workplace will be dampened by rising tax payments by the winners and rising benefits paid to the losers. Where labour markets are rigid, the impact tends to be more unemployment but less inequality in take-home pay.

In theory, the free movement of capital can magnify these medium-run labour market effects since firms can react to inflexible labour markets by taking their capital elsewhere when faced by a negative shock. This tends to speed up the pace at which production is relocated across countries in response to deeper integration. On one hand, this allows the expanding sectors to expand more quickly, but on the other hand, it means that the shrinking sectors shrink faster. It is important to note, though, that this is a matter of timing rather than extent. If a nation's firms in a particular sector are uncompetitive, they will reduce employment eventually, one way or another.

Does the free movement of labour mitigate the problem? The presumption is correct if the immigrants can be substituted to local workers. If they are complementary – filling up jobs that are not taken by locals or bringing in skills in short supply – immigration raises national incomes in both the emitting and the receiving countries, without creating losers. Observation of intra-European migrations over the past decades suggests that complementarity is more widespread than substitutability. Moreover, the last decade has witnessed large-scale return migration of workers from southern Europe who had settled in northern Europe over previous decades.

The single currency removes the possibility of changing the exchange rate in the face of an adverse disturbance or in case of domestic cost pressure. This is expected to impose more wage restraint on trade unions. An open question is how trade unions may respond to a weakening of their power, e.g. with respect to the European Central Bank. Very different labour market institutions and legislation suggest that trade unions are unlikely to reorganize at the European level.

Migration, in principle, raises economic efficiency and welfare but it is highly controversial, to put it mildly. One reason is that migration is likely to exercise downward pressure on some categories of workers, mostly low-skilled workers. Another reason is that rigid labour markets, which lead to unemployment, are ill-suited to deal with migration. There is little evidence to support the widely held view that migration is a source of serious hardship. There is also little reason to expect large migration flows from the new to the ancient EU members, even if all restrictions are lifted.

Self-assessment questions

1. In Fig. 8.9, explain what areas A to F represent. What is the overall effect of migration? What makes it bigger? Can it ever turn negative?

2. Figure 8.11 depicts the evolution of the unemployment rate in France and in the UK, distinguishing between a trend and deviations from the trend. In the UK, the rate tends to deviate more from its trend than in France. Can you explain this pattern?

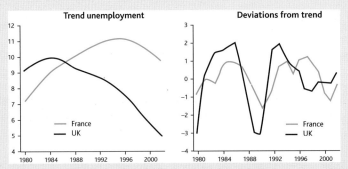

Figure 8.11: *Unemployment rates in France and the UK (% of labour force)*

Source: *Economic Outlook*, OECD, July 2003, and authors' calculations.

3. List the sources of wage rigidities and of employment rigidities.

4. Why can deeper integration make existing labour market institutions ill-suited?

5. Why is it the case that we observe fewer people moving from job to job in those countries where employment protection legislation is strictest?

6. What is the difference between general and specific measures? Why does it matter?

7. In Spain, the rules regarding eligibility to unemployment benefits have changed, disallowing unemployed workers from turning down job offers more than twice. What is the rationale and what could be the effects of this change?

8. Before the EMU, inflation was used to change relative labour costs across industries. How could that work?

Essay questions

1. Why do unemployed workers not underbid wages to get jobs?

2. Some economists predict that the EMU will eventually make labour markets more efficient; others predict the opposite. What is your view, and why?

3. Assume that European trade unions agree to merge. What would be the effect if wage negotiations were conducted at the European level? At the industry level? At the plant level?

4. If we move to similar labour institutions, will governments lose any role in social policies?

5. It is argued – and it is the case in some countries – that the minimum wage should be set at different levels for the young, for the older, for the unskilled or for particular industries. Evaluate this argument.

6. Italy exhibits a 'Mezzogiorno problem'. For decades now, Italy's South has benefited from generous subsidies initially designed to compensate for being less developed than the North. Yet, unemployment in the South is high and growth is slow, while northern Italy is one of the most vibrant economic regions in Europe. How can you interpret this situation and what lessons can you draw for Europe?

7. Evaluate the following statement in the UK Treasury's assessment of eurozone membership. 'It is important to make more progress at the European level, in particular on employment flexibility, trade and the Single Market in financial services. The less progress on flexibility is achieved in the EU, the greater the premium on a high level of flexibility in the UK economy.'

Further reading: the aficionado's corner

For general overviews, see:

Andersen, T.M. (2004) 'The European labour markets: wage norms in Europe – a curse or blessing?', *CESifo Forum*, 5(1): 31–3.

Bean, C., S. Bentolila, G. Bertola and J. Dolado (1998) *Social Europe: One for All?*, CEPR Monitoring European Integration 8, Centre for Economic Policy Research, London.

Bertola, G., F.D. Blau and L.M. Kahn (2002) 'Comparative analysis of labour market outcomes: lessons for the US from international long-run evidence', pp. 159–218 in A. Krueger and R. Solow (eds) *The Roaring Nineties: Can Full Employment be Sustained?*, Russell Sage and Century Foundations, New York.

Federation of European Employers (2005) *Pay in Europe 2005*, CAMC Publications, Oxford.

Freeman, R.B. (2004) 'The European labour markets: are European labour markets as awful as all that?', *CESifo Forum*, 5(1): 34–9.

Nickell, S. (2002) *Unemployment in Europe: Reasons and Remedies*. Available on http://www.cesifo.de.

Phelps, E. and G. Zoega (2004) 'The European labour markets: the search for routes to better economic performance in continental Europe', *CESifo Forum*, 5(1): 3–11.

Pierrard, O. and H.R. Sneessens (2004) 'The European labour markets: aggregate unemployment and relative wage rigidities', *CESifo Forum*, 5(1): 19–23.

Portugal, P. and J.T. Addison (2004) 'The European labour markets: disincentive effects of unemployment benefits on the paths out of unemployment', *CESifo Forum*, 5(1): 24–30.

Puhani, P.A. (2004) 'The European labour markets: differences in labour markets across the Atlantic', *CESifo Forum*, 5(1): 12–18.

Saint-Paul, G. (2000) *The Political Economy of Labour Market Institutions*, Oxford University Press, Oxford.

On the trade-off between economic efficiency and social concerns, see:

Atkinson, A. (1999) *The Economic Consequences on Rolling Back the Welfare State*, MIT Press, Cambridge, Mass.

Bertola, G., J.F. Jimeno, R. Marimon and C. Pissarides (2001) 'Welfare systems and labour markets in Europe: what convergence before and after EMU?', in G. Bertola, T. Boeri and G. Nicoletti (eds) *Welfare and Employment in a United Europe*, MIT Press, Cambridge, Mass.

On trade unions, see:

Calmfors, L., A. Booth, M. Burda, D. Checchi, R. Naylor and J. Visser (2001) 'What do unions do in Europe? Prospects and challenges for union presence and union influence', in T. Boeri, A. Brugiavini and L. Calmfors (eds) *The Role of Unions in the Twenty-first Century*, Oxford University Press, Oxford.

Checci, D. and C. Lucifora (2002) 'Unions and labour market institutions in Europe', *Economic Policy*, 35: 361–408.

On migration, see:

Friedberg, R.M. and J. Hunt (1995) 'The impact of immigrants on host country wages, employment and growth', *Journal of Economic Perspectives*, 9(2): 23–44.

Boeri, T. and H. Brücker (2005) 'Why are Europeans so tough on migrants?', *Economic Policy*, 44, October.

Card, D. (1990) 'The impact of the Mariel boatlift on the Miami labor market', *Industrial Labor Relations Review*, 43(2): 245–57.

Useful websites

Official site relevant to the Lisbon Process: http://europa.eu.int/growthandjobs/index.htm.

The website of the Rodolfo de Benedetti Foundation, dedicated to European labour market issues: http://www.frdb.org.

References

Boeri, T. and H. Brücker (2005) 'Why are Europeans so tough on migrants?', *Economic Policy*, 44, October.

Calmfors, L. (2001) 'Wages and wage-bargaining institutions in the EMU: a survey of the issues', *Empirica*, 28(4): 325–51.

Part III

EU POLICIES

Chapter 9: The Common Agricultural Policy
Chapter 10: Location effects, economic geography and regional policy
Chapter 11: EU competition and state aid policy
Chapter 12: EU trade policy

Introduction

The European Union has hundreds of policies. It would take a lifetime to study them all. But as is true of so much of the EU, less is more when it comes to policy. Studying the main policies in detail provides a much better understanding of the EU than a superficial coverage of all the policies.

The major policies in the EU are the Common Agricultural Policy (CAP) and 'Cohesion' Policy. These two policies, which are actually collections of related programmes and practices, account for 80 per cent of the EU budget. They will also continue to 'be in the headlines' since they are the source of continual friction among EU members. Moreover, the CAP causes a great deal of friction in the World Trade Organization.

The CAP is covered in Chapter 9 and the regional policies in Chapter 10, along with the necessary microeconomics.

There are two new Part-III chapters in this second edition. Chapter 11 looks at the economics and practices of EU competition policy. This is one of the areas in which Member States have delegated a great deal of sovereignty to the EU level. Some of the economics in this chapter were extracted from Chapter 6 of the first edition, but they have been augmented and the description of EU policy is greatly expanded. Chapter 12 looks at EU trade policies with the rest of the world. Again, this is an area where the Member States must make their decisions together since the EU has a common commercial policy with respect to the rest of the world.

> A common agricultural policy that encourages surpluses which 〈 have to be disposed of – again at considerable costs – is no lon〈 acceptable or sustainable. Public expenditure must yield something in return – whether it is the food quality, the preservation of the environment and animal welfare, landscapes, cultural heritage, or enhancing social balance and equity.
>
> *European Commissioner Franz Fischler, 2002*

Chapter 9

The Common Agricultural Policy

9.1 Early days: domestic price supports

9.2 CAP problems

INTRODUCTION

The Common Agricultural Policy (CAP) is a set of policies aimed at raising the farm incomes in the EU. The CAP is problematic. It accounts for about half the EU budget but farmers continue to leave the land. It accounts for many of the quarrels among EU members and between the EU and third nations, yet it is extremely difficult to reform. Given all these problems and its dominant role in the budget, a good understanding of the CAP is essential to the study of European integration. This chapter presents the essential elements and economics of the CAP.

A major CAP reform was announced just as this book went to press. See the Online Learning Centre website for an update on the June 2005 reform package and its implications.

9.1 Early days: domestic price supports

Today's CAP is a massively complex matrix of policies, but it was not always that way. The CAP started life in 1962 as a rather straightforward policy of keeping agricultural prices high and stable. The policy led to a series of problems that triggered a series of reforms. While these reforms addressed some of the CAP's main defects, most of the original problems remain. These facts suggest a natural organization for this chapter. First we study the CAP in its simple form. Then we present the problems that this created and the reforms they triggered. Before closing the chapter with some discussion of the future challenges facing the CAP, we consider the problems that still plague today's CAP.

Farming is different

Most nations treat farming differently. Rich nations tend to support their farmers with subsidies and high prices; poor countries tend to tax their farmers, especially those producing export crops. In Europe, the special treatment of farming began in the 1920s and 1930s (Milward, 1992, Chapter 5). By the 1950s, all six of the original EU members intervened in agricultural markets in an effort to stabilize prices, the main difference being the height at which prices were stabilized.

As Zobbe (2001) says, 'it is easy to see how a CAP based on price support as the main instrument must have looked extremely simple to the decision makers in the early 1960s'. Moreover, there was no question of leaving agriculture out of the EU's design. As Chapter 1 showed, the EU's founders had grand plans for an 'ever closer union among the peoples of Europe', and agriculture accounted for a good fraction of those peoples in the 1950s – about one in five Europeans lived on farms when the Treaty of Rome was written (Zobbe, 2001).

9.1.1 Basic price-floor diagram for a net importer

Standard economic terminology for a 'domestic price support' is a 'price floor', so this is the term we shall employ. Note, however, that the phraseology of the CAP is far more involved since it must capture aspects of reality that we ignore for the sake of clarity (see Box 9.1).

CAP price support jargon

This chapter tries to simplify the CAP to make it understandable to students. It is instructive, however, to take a look at the sorts of complexities that we are glossing over. After reading this box you will understand why many people, even professional economists, view the CAP as 'headache material'.

For historical reasons, the terms used for the price floor vary according to the product (intervention price, guaranteed price, basic price or norm price), as does the exact procedure for setting them. The wheat jargon and procedures, however, serve as a fairly representative model.

Around April of every year, EU farm ministers meet in the Council of Ministers to fix prices for the coming crop year. The first price to set is a theoretical price – the 'target price' – as a guideline for the practical prices. Strange as it may seem, the target price refers to the wholesale price of wheat in Duisburg, Germany, a city on the Ruhr (since this was the locality of shortest supply; see Nevin 1990). The main operational price – the 'intervention price' – is set lower than the target price, typically 12–20 per cent lower. As its name suggests, authorities are committed to 'intervene', i.e. buy unlimited quantities of wheat at the 'intervention price' in any EU member's market. This ensures that no EU market prices fall below the intervention price, so the intervention price is the price floor. Each EU member has its own authority, often a semi-official producers' organization; these 'buyers of last resort' are responsible for storing or otherwise disposing of goods they buy to support the price floor. The funding for this is drawn from the Guarantee section of the EU's European Agricultural Guidance and Guarantee Fund (EAGGF, or FEOGA in French). The second practical price, the 'threshold price' is the minimum price at which wheat can be imported into the EU from third nations. This is set at the target price minus the transport and handling costs for imported wheat arriving at Europe's largest port, Rotterdam, and sold in Duisburg. The threshold price is always above the intervention price so that intervention authorities will not have to spend EU money buying imported wheat at the intervention price. In normal years, the threshold price is far above the world price so the import tariff – the 'variable import levy' – is set so that wheat is never imported below the threshold price. The simplification in Fig. 9.1 assumes that the intervention price and threshold price are the same.

A taste of the CAP's complexity can be had by considering the impact of higher wheat prices. Various grains – wheat, maize, etc. – are somewhat substitutable, especially when they are used to feed farm animals. Because of this, avoiding excessive substitution requires that a high target price for wheat be accompanied by a high price for other grains. Moreover, since feed grain is an important input in milk and meat production, high grain prices would squeeze EU milk and meat producers unless their prices were also raised. Likewise, much of the EU's beef comes from dairy cows that are too old to produce milk efficiently, so higher milk production means more cows and this means a higher supply of beef.

Source: This box is based mainly on Chapter 14 of Nevin (1990).

The EU set (and still sets) price floors for all the major farm products including grains, dairy products, beef, veal and sugar. For most of the CAP's existence, these prices were between 50 and 100 per cent higher than world prices (Molle, 1997, table 11.4). These price floors were enforced by guaranteed, unlimited purchase by CAP authorities at the price floor, but only as a last resort. In the early days of the CAP, the EU was a net importer of most farm products, so it could ensure that supply and demand matched at high prices by manipulating the amount of foreign food that entered the EU market. The manipulation was done with import tariffs, so the best way to understand the early CAP is with a standard open economy supply and demand diagram of the type we considered in Chapter 4.

The economics of the tariffs used to raise EU food prices above the price floor are quite similar to the standard

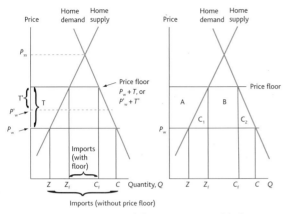

Figure 9.1: *Economics of the CAP's 'variable levies'*

tariff analysis presented in Chapter 4. For convenience, we briefly repeat the analysis here, pointing out the minor differences (the presentation in Chapter 4 provides much more detail and explanation). The goal of these tariffs – called 'variable levies' in the parlance of the CAP – is to ensure that the imported food does not push EU prices below the price floor.

The left-hand panel of Fig. 9.1 helps us to analyse the impact of such a price floor in cases where it is set above the world price (P_w) but below the level where the EU would import no food (in agricultural economics, this level is called the point of 'self-sufficiency', so we mark the level as p_{ss} in the diagram). As we saw in Chapter 4, the domestic price ends up as the world price plus the tariff. The reason is that potential competition from imports (priced at P_w plus the tariff, T) means that no one would pay more than $P_w + T$. And the inability of domestic producers to make enough food to satisfy the demand at $P_w + T$ means that farmers would never accept a price lower than $P_w + T$. At $P_w + T$, domestic production is Z_f while domestic consumption is C_f; the difference between consumption and production equals the level of imports. The subscript 'f' indicates 'floor'.

Price instability is a key feature of food markets, so we need to consider what happens when the world price changes to, say, P_w'. In this case, maintaining its price floor requires the EU to apply a lower tariff. Specifically, it cuts its tariff to T' so that $P_w' + T'$ equals the price floor. Until the practice was abandoned in 1995, variable levies richly deserved their name; they were adjusted *daily* to reflect changes in world market prices. Because of these tariffs, EU agricultural product prices were typically between 50 and 100 per cent above world prices. Note that, from 1995, the EU was forbidden from varying its agricultural tariffs under a WTO agreement called the Uruguay Round.

What is the economic impact of a price floor?
★ The higher price induces EU farmers to produce more.
★ An unintended side effect of the higher price is to discourage food consumption.
★ Since imports exactly equal the gap between EU consumption and production, the first two effects imply that imports of food fall, i.e. they move the EU towards self-sufficiency in food.
★ Since the price floor is enforced by a variable tariff, the EU receives tariff revenue equal to the area B in the right-hand panel.

The food tax and subsidy interpretation

An excellent way of thinking about a price floor supported by a tariff is to view it as an all-in-one package made up of simpler policy measures. The all-in-one package consists of (i) free trade in the presence of (ii) a consumption tax equal to T and (iii) a production subsidy equal to T. Under this thought-experiment package, the consumption tax means that consumers pay the world price plus T (this is exactly equal to the price floor in the left-hand panel of Fig. 9.1) so they consume C_f. EU producers sell at the world price but they also receive the production subsidy T (i.e. they sell all output at the world price but they also get a payment from the government equal to T for each unit of output they sell), so the amount they actually get per unit sold is the price floor, $P_w + T$; given this, they produce Z_f. The consumption tax revenue from this scheme is consumption $C_f \times T$, and the production subsidy payment to farmers is production $Z_f \times T$, so the government's receipt net of its payments is equal to $(C_f - Z_f) \times T$. This is exactly equal to the tariff revenue B.

This way of looking at the price floor is insightful since it makes it quite plain that consumers are the ones who pay for a price floor enforced with a variable levy. Part of what they pay goes to domestic farmers (area A), part of it goes to the EU budget (area B) and part is wasted (areas C_1 and C_2). This interpretation also applies to the analysis of a tariff, and becomes important when we think about the distributional impact of price floors in more detail.

Aggregate welfare effects

The overall welfare effects of the tariff should be familiar from Chapter 4; for convenience, they are briefly reviewed in the right panel of Fig. 9.1. The higher price ($P_w + T$ instead of P_w) means that consumer surplus falls by $A + C_1 + B + C_2$. The first part of this, $A + C_1 + B$, reflects the higher cost consumers pay for the food they continue to consume. The second part, C_2, is what they lose from the tariff-induced drop in consumption. For producers, the gain in producer surplus is equal to area A. As with consumers, we can think of this as consisting of the impact of getting a higher price for the amount they would have produced without the tariff (i.e. Z) plus the gain in producer surplus from the higher sales. Since the EU would be a large importer of food under free trade, the tariffs tend to lower the world price. This effect, not shown in Fig. 9.1 for the sake of simplicity, counts as a welfare improvement for the EU.

This overall welfare analysis lumped all EU farms together, and while this is useful to get started, it hides a very important effect of price floors: the distribution of benefits among farms.

9.1.2 Farm size, efficiency and distribution of farmer benefits

Anyone who has done much travelling in Europe realizes that a 'farm' means different things in different places. A wheat farm in the Parisian basin and a farm on a small Greek island, for example, are very dissimilar. On the Parisian plain, farms tend to be very large and very high tech. They use expensive, high-yield, disease-resistant seeds to boost their 'yield' (food produced per hectare), they apply large quantities of pesticides to control bugs, large quantities of chemical fertilizers to maintain the soil's fertility, and they use massive, labour-saving machines to sow, tend and harvest. In the Greek islands, farming is a lot more traditional. Farms tend to be smaller and agricultural equipment much simpler. As a result, the big French farms are substantially more efficient and very much larger. Moreover, the French farm is likely to be run by a corporation whereas the Greek island farm is likely to be a family farm. As it turns out,

these differences have important implications for the distribution of gains from price floors.

The logic is best illustrated with the help of Fig. 9.2. To keep things simple, suppose there are only two farms in the EU, one large commercial farm and one small family farm (Box 9.2 presents some facts on the actual farm-size distribution). The supply curve of the family farm is shown in the left-hand panel, the supply curve of the commercial farm in the middle panel, and the total supply curve in the right-hand panel. Note that the small (family) farm's supply curve is above the large (commercial) farm's supply curve, reflecting the fact that large farms are typically more efficient. (Remember from Chapter 4 that the supply curve shows marginal cost, so a higher supply curve means that the small farm has higher marginal cost at any level of output.)

The world price is marked as P_w. Note that at this price only the commercial farm would produce anything. The small farm would stop farming, since with free trade the EU price would fall to the world price, which is lower than the small farm's marginal cost of producing. However, with the price floor at $P_w + T$, both farms do produce. Specifically the family farm produces Z_{small} and the large farm produces Z_{big}. Total output is just the sum of the two.

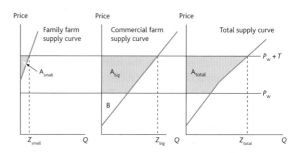

Figure 9.2: *Distribution of gains, big and small farms*

The European Commission published figures on the size distribution of farms. Figures for 1987, which you can download from the internet, show how remarkably skewed the ownership of farmland was in the EU 12 (this got worse with the EU15 and became much worse after the 2004 enlargement, as we shall see below). About

half the EU12 farmland was owned by just 7 per cent of the farmers (obviously this included the big farms). At the small-farm end, about 7 per cent of the EU12's farmland was split among 50 per cent of the farmers.

Source: *The Agricultural Situation in the Community*, European Commission, 1993, table 3.5.4.1.

From Fig. 9.2 we see that the producer surplus generated by the price floor is quite unevenly distributed. The small, low-technology, high-cost family farm earns only A_{small}, whereas the large, modern industrial farm earns A_{big}. This should be intuitively obvious. Since a price floor helps producers in proportion to their production, big producers will benefit more from the policy.

How is this connected with income levels? The benefit from owning a farm is the producer surplus it yields, so the income generated by the small farm is A_{small} and the income for owners of the large farm is $A_{big} + B$, since B measures the producer surplus that the large farm would have without the price floor. Plainly, the owners of big farms tend to be richer than the owners of small farms. This is the main point. *Price floors help all farmers but most of the gains go to large farmers who tend to be richer: after all, they own larger farms.*

This uneven-distribution point is critical – the key to many of the CAP's paradoxes – so it is worth presenting it from another angle. Few readers will be familiar with modern farming, but everyone has been to a food store. Box 9.3 presents an analogy by considering what would happen if CAP-like policies were used to support the owners of European food stores.

How inequitable were CAP benefits?

According to one widely cited estimate by the European Commission concerning the pre-reform CAP, 20 per cent of the farmers got 80 per cent of the benefits of the CAP (European Commission, 1994, p. 27). The basic reason is that about 80 per cent of the farm output comes from the big, efficient farms and a price floor rewards output regardless of farm size.

A little maths reveals the grave implications of this. In 1987, the EU12 had 6.9 million farms and spent €23 billion on the CAP (65 per cent of the EU budget). The 20/80 estimate meant that €18.4 billion was spent on 1.38 million farms, which works out to €13 333 per farm. The remaining 20 per cent of the CAP spending, €4.6 billion, was spread over 5.52 million farms, implying an average of €833 per farm. For 80 per cent of the farms, the CAP's spending was peanuts; little wonder most farmers said the CAP was inadequate and protested vehemently against any cuts in CAP spending. The same numbers also show that the 1.38 million big-farm owners received 52 per cent of the whole EU budget. We do not know exactly how many owners there are per farm, but let us estimate it as one owner per farm. If this estimate is roughly right, over half the budget went to help just 0.4 per cent of the EU population. Worse yet, these owners overwhelmingly tended to be the richer ones (European Commission, 1994, p. 27).

This inequity of the CAP support is worth exploring more carefully in the light of today's CAP, but we postpone this until we work through the problems created by the CAP and its various reforms.

For convenience, the Fig. 9.1 analysis lumps all consumers together, but this aggregation hides an important factor. As it turns out, high food prices hit poor consumers harder than they hit rich consumers. The point is very simple and is best illustrated by thinking of the price floor in terms of the all-in-one policy package described above. In particular, we focus on the food consumption tax part of the package.

Being a necessity, food tends to come first in people's weekly budget. People tend to spend on other items only when they have at least enough to eat. Clearly, rich people have incomes that allow them to buy much more than just food. Poor people, at least in Europe, also tend to buy much more than the 'bare necessities', but the *fraction* of poor people's incomes that is spent on food is higher than that of rich people. This means that the food tax as a fraction of poor people's incomes is higher than it is for rich people.

For example, about 18 per cent of an average French family's total spending is on food and drink, but this average hides a wide dispersion among families (for figures on expenditure shares by nation see www.ers.usda.gov/briefing/EuropeanUnion/). The figure could be doubled for a poor family and halved for a rich family. To be concrete, suppose the poor family spends 30 per cent of its income on food, while the rich family spends 9 per cent. Now consider the impact of raising the price-floor 'tax', by one-third for example. Since prices would be one-third higher, we can say that the average French family would have to spend more on food, roughly 6 per cent more of their total expenditure (one-third of 18 per cent). But for poor families, spending one-third more means raising food's share in the income from 30 per cent to 40 per cent. This would be equivalent to a 10 per cent income tax on the poor family with no price change. For rich families, the one-third higher prices would increase food's share in their budget from 9 per cent to 12 per cent. This would be equivalent to a 3 per cent income tax on the rich family. In this sense, the price floor can be thought of as being paid for by a 'regressive' tax, that is, a tax whose rate is higher for poor families than it is for rich families.

In summary, the distributional consequences of using price floors to support the EU farm sector are quite regressive.

★ The benefits of price supports go mainly to the largest EU farms because large farms produce a lot (and the support is tied to the level of production) and because large farms tend to be more efficient (so their costs are lower). Since the owners of large farms tend to be rich, the benefits of a price floor are systematically biased in favour of large, rich farmers.

★ Since price floors are paid for by consumers (they are the ones that have to pay the higher price), and food tends to be more important in the budget of poor families than it is in the budget of rich families, price floors are in essence paid for by a regressive consumption tax. In short, a price floor has a tendency to redistribute spending power from relatively poor consumer families to relatively rich farmers.

9.2 CAP problems

In its first few years of life, the CAP was a politician's dream. By setting the price floors above the world price, the CAP provided higher prices to farmers, so they were happy. This boost to farm incomes also suited the EU's goal of fostering 'social cohesion' between rural and urban Europe. The higher prices substantially raised food production and this, at the time, was viewed as a good thing. The extra production furthered Europe's goal of reducing its dependence on imported food. Best of all, since the EU continued to import food, the tariffs that supported the price floors generated an important amount of revenue.

The only ones who might have objected were European consumers, since they paid for the policy via higher prices. As it turned out, consumers were also happy about the CAP for three reasons:

★ Average incomes in the 1950s and 1960s rose rapidly – much faster than food prices – so the share of people's income spent on food actually fell, although not as fast as it would have done without the CAP.

★ During the Second World War and its aftermath, food was in short supply and rationed in most European nations. The memory of this, and of the hunger that came with it, was still fresh in people's minds in the early 1960s. More food and lower dependence on food imports seemed like good ideas to most Europeans.

★ Consumers had a great deal of empathy with farmers. As is still the case today, most Europeans viewed agriculture as a form of economic activity unlike others. As former CAP administer Rolf Moehler points out:

At the Stresa Conference in 1958, which laid the basis for the development of the CAP, Ministers of the six original member states stressed the importance of the farming population for social stability. . . . Rural life and thus the farmer had a symbolic value for all those who felt uncomfortable with or hostile to modernisation of society triggered by industrialisation and urbanisation. There was a belief that as the farmer is ensuring the livelihood of society, society has to ensure the farmer's livelihood. In addition he was still representing the good old times, when European countries were basically rural societies.

(Moehler, 1997)

The CAP's honeymoon period, however, was soon to end.

9.2.1 The supply problem

The post-war period saw revolutionary advances in the application of science to agricultural production. This technology allowed farmers to substantially boost their productivity. The new technology involved the development of superior strains of wheat and other main crops, the development of effective pesticides to control insect damage, and herbicides to control weeds. Also, part of this was the development of highly efficient chemical fertilizers and of effective and affordable farm machines that radically reduced the labour needed to sow, tend and harvest. Strange as it may seem today, this chemical- and machine-intensive technology was known as the 'green revolution'.

Since the CAP rewarded output, farmers switched to these new, more intensive farming methods. The result was impressive. As the top panel of Fig. 9.3 shows, EU wheat production rose rapidly in the CAP's first ten years – not because the area planted rose, but because the yield jumped 50 per cent between 1961 and 1971. Similar productivity advances were seen in all the farm products supported by the CAP. As the bottom panel of Fig. 9.3 shows, the EU swung from an importer to an exporter in most farm products between the 1960s and the 1990s.

In most goods, this sort of rapid productivity growth would be a cause for celebration. And the first objective listed in Article 39 of the Treaty of Rome was 'to increase agricultural productivity by promoting technical progress'. But one should be careful about what one wishes; as Benjamin Franklin put it, 'If a man could have half his wishes he would double his troubles.' Rising productivity has been an unrelenting source of problems for the CAP.

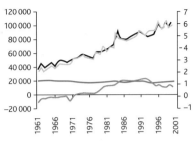

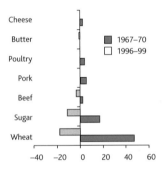

Figure 9.3: *EU wheat production, 1961–2000, and trade balance in other products*

Note: The bottom panel shows EU net exports in key food products.

Source: Data from US Department of Agriculture Economic Research Service, www.ers.usdagov/Briefing/EuropeanUnion/data.htm.

The foundation of the problem is the unresponsiveness of food demand to food prices (how much would the price of bread have to fall to get you to double your consumption?). This unresponsiveness means that productivity gains (a downward shift in the supply curve) normally result in steeply falling prices. World prices for food, for example, have been falling at about 2 per cent per year for decades (European Commission, 1994). Yet EU political leaders did not want EU farmers to see the price of their output fall, so they set EU food prices above the world price. Not surprisingly, supply continued to rise. Indeed, supply rose so much faster than consumption that the EU switched from being a net importer of most agricultural goods to a net exporter of most agricultural goods. For example, the top panel of Fig. 9.3 shows that 1977 was the last year the EU was a net importer of wheat (i.e. had negative exports). The story for other crops is similar, as the bottom panel of Fig. 9.3 shows. This is where the problems began for the CAP's price floor.

Price

$P_{1,SS}$

$P_{2,SS}$

$P_{3,SS}$

$P_{4,SS}$

S_1 S_2 S_3 S_4

a b c d e Price floor

Home demand

Quantity

Figure 9.4: *The green revolution and price floors: EU becomes an exporter*

Figure 9.4 shows this switch from importer to exporter in a simple supply and demand diagram. Technological improvements shifted the supply curve down (recall that the supply curve is marginal cost, so cost-lowering technology shifts the whole curve downwards). When the EU was a food importer, the EU supply curve was something like the one labelled S_1 (the price floor is below the self-sufficiency price $p_{1,ss}$, so demand exceeds supply at the price floor and the excess demand is met by imports). Imports are the difference between consumption at point d and production at point a. Since the price floor did not fall (in fact it rose somewhat relative to the world price but we ignore this in the diagram for simplicity's sake), a technological improvement that shifts the supply curve to S_2 reduces the level of EU food imports (from point d minus point a to point d minus point b). At this point, the EU is still an importer since the new self-sufficiency point, $p_{2,ss}$, is above the price floor. Continual technological innovation – spurred in part by the guarantee that all output can be sold at the high price floor – shifted the supply out to S_3 and then to S_4. Importantly, at S_4 the price floor is above the corresponding self-sufficiency price $p_{4,ss}$, so the EU ceases to import. With S_4 the EU produces more food

than it consumes, i.e. the EU has a surplus of food at the price floor.

EU becomes a major food buyer

When the EU stopped being an importer, it could no longer enforce the price floor with a tariff. Even when tariffs shut off all imports, EU supply exceeded EU demand. In this situation, the EU had to manipulate demand to ensure that supply and demand met at the price floor. In other words, the EU had to act as the 'buyer of last resort' and this meant that the EU became a major buyer of food; in Fig. 9.4, the EU would have to buy a quantity of food equal to e minus d in order to enforce the price floor. This posed two immediate problems: disposal and finance.

9.2.2 Grain, beef and butter mountains: the disposal problem

The EU had no particular use for the food it bought, so it faced the question of what to do with its newly purchased wheat, butter, etc. When the food 'surpluses' first appeared, the EU viewed them as temporary. The main solution was to store the food in the hope that supply in future years would shift back to a point where EU demand exceeded supply at the price floor. If this happened, the EU could meet the excess demand by selling out of storage. Unfortunately, the high prices, guaranteed sales and steady technological progress made investment in agriculture very attractive. The supply curve continued to shift outwards.

The EU continued to buy large quantities of food and the storage facilities continued to fill. The EU found itself the owner of what the media called 'wheat, beef and butter mountains'. As Table 9.1 shows, in 1985 the EU had 18.5 million tonnes of cereals stored. To put the size of this into perspective, this worked out to about 70 kg per EU9 citizen. The result was a serious amount of spoilage, and a major public relations problem (it looks bad to pay high prices for food that is allowed to rot).

	1983	1984	1985	1986	1987	1988	1989	1990
All cereals	4 335	13 927	18 502	14 271	11 748	9 146	11 795	18 729
Butter			1 122	1 188	640	64	820	324
Skimmed milk powder			646	765	240	7	21	354

Source: European Commission (1994), table 19.

Table 9.1: *EU food storage (intervention stocks, 1000 tonnes), 1983–90*

Dumping and
international objections

Exporting was one alternative to storing the surplus food. Because EU prices were above world prices, exporters found themselves buying at a high price and selling at a lower price. To convince traders to do this, the EU had to pay them 'restitution' or 'export refunds' equal to the difference between EU and world prices. 'Dumping' is the standard name given to the practice of exporting goods at a price that is below cost. Under WTO rules for non-food items, this is normally not permitted, especially when the practice is driven by government subsidies. Until the Uruguay Round agreement (see below), however, the WTO placed few restrictions on the dumping of agricultural goods.

What's wrong with the EU driving down the world price of food? As we saw in Chapters 4 and 5, a drop in the world price is a gain for net importers but a loss for net exporters. The EU's dumping infuriated food exporters based outside the EU. The biggest losers from the CAP's dumping were the largest food-exporting nations. In terms of overall volume, this is the so-called Cairns Group (Argentina, Australia, Bolivia, Brazil, Chile, Colombia, Costa Rica, Guatemala, New Zealand, Paraguay, the Philippines, South Africa, Thailand and Uruguay) as well as the USA and Canada. As we shall see below, the objections of these nations to the CAP played a major role in its 1992 reform – and they will surely continue to play a role in the future – so it is worth looking at the economics of this more carefully.

Economics of the CAP's impact on world food markets

Even in the early days, the CAP's price floor policy harmed other nations. By shutting off EU markets to the exports of non-members, the CAP reduced the world price of food as well as reduced the volume of non-members' exports. As the EU's food surplus grew, and the EU started to subsidize its exports, non-members were further harmed.

The economics of this can be seen in Fig. 9.5. The solid lines marked 'MD (no CAP)' and 'MS (no dumping)' show the world import demand (i.e. MD) and import supply (i.e. MS) without the CAP's tariffs and without the CAP's dumping. The price would be $P_{w,0}$ and total food exports would be X_0. In the first stage, the CAP harmed the market by reducing the demand for world imports. That is, the EU was one of the largest importers of food in the world, so the tariff-induced reduction in its demand for imported

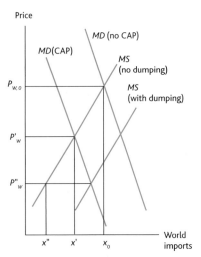

Figure 9.5: *Impact of CAP protection and dumping on world markets*

food shifted the world import demand inwards to MD (CAP). This resulted in lower export prices for non-EU members (the price falls to p'_w) and lower exports (the quantity drops to X'). When the CAP led the EU to become a net exporter, the market was further harmed since these subsidized exporters shifted out the world MS curve to MS (with dumping). Note that the EU pays whatever it takes to sell its surplus on the world market, so the size of the horizontal shift between MS (no dumping) and MS (with dumping) is exactly equal to the amount of food dumped by the EU. This practice further erodes prices (to p''_w) and further reduces non-member exports to X''.

Most countries practise some form of import protection on food, so while the CAP's tariffs were harmful to the world market, they were not viewed as particularly out of line with the rest of the world's practice. The subsidized export of food, however, was more unusual. Additionally, the USA and the EU were, at the time, the only major subsidizers and often engaged in subsidy wars. (We shall study the world-market effects of the current CAP in more detail below.)

Budget troubles

The second immediate difficulty posed by the supply problem was budgetary. Instead of earning money by imposing tariffs, the EU had to dole out large sums from its budget to buy the 'excess' food. As discussed above, the EU sold the food at subsidized prices to get back some of the money spent buying food and to alleviate the storage problem. Some of this subsidized food was sold to non-standard consumers within the EU. For example, one-sixth of the wheat crop in 1969 was rendered unfit for human consumption and sold as animal feed at a subsidized price. However, the major destination for the subsidized sales were foreign markets. This practice of buying high and selling low was not cheap, as Fig. 9.6 shows.

The CAP came into operation in 1962 and did not incur a positive expenditure until 1965. After this, however, its

cost and share of the budget started to grow exponentially, rising from 8 per cent in 1965 to 80 per cent in 1969. The link between the EU farm sector's rapidly rising productivity and the EU budget is explored in greater depth in Box 9.4.

Next we look at one of the most puzzling problems the CAP had at the time: the farm income problem.

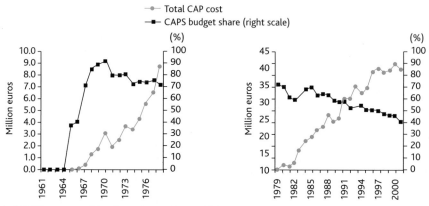

Figure 9.6: *Total CAP costs and budget share, 1961–2000*

Note: The left and right panels have different scales.

Source: Budget data from European Commission (2000).

Box 9.4

The economics linking the supply problem and budget effects

The logic of the supply–budget link underpins all of the CAP reforms that have been adopted and it is likely to rule all future CAP reforms, so we examine it more carefully with the help of Fig. 9.7.

The left-hand panel of the diagram reproduces a simplified version of Fig. 9.4 in showing how techno-logical improvement plus a price floor shifted the EU from a food importer to a food exporter. With S_4 the EU produces more food than it consumes. To support the price floor, the EU must buy a quantity of food equal to the horizontal difference between the point e and the point d. We show this in the right-hand panel as Z_f minus C_f. If the food is destroyed or stored until it spoils, the cost will be the price floor times the volume purchased. If it is exported, the EU will have to pay a subsidy equal to the difference between the price floor and the world price P_w,

namely S'. The cost of this will be $B + C_1 + C_2$ (i.e. the per-unit subsidy S' times the number of units exported).

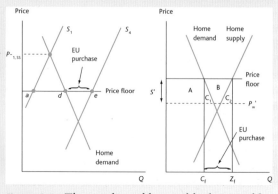

Figure 9.7: *The supply problem and budget troubles*

9.2.5 The farm income problem

Despite its massive budgetary cost and high 'tax' on European food consumers, the CAP failed to bring the reward to farming in line with the incomes of average EU citizens. In 1990, the average income from farming per worker in agriculture averaged less than 40 per cent of the income per worker in the EU12 economy as a whole (European Commission, 1994). While most farm family income was augmented by some non-farm earnings, farming was not a very attractive activity. In addition to occasional demonstrations, farmers showed their discontent with the CAP by 'voting with their feet', i.e. leaving the sector. The number of farms and farmers has declined steadily since the CAP's inception (see Nevin, 1990, table 15.1, for data stretching back to 1958). This is the truest indication that the average EU farmer – who, as we saw above, had a very small farm – found that even with CAP support, farm incomes were not keeping up with those in the rest of the economy. In short, farmers felt that the CAP was not providing them with sufficient support.

This would seem to be a puzzle. How can farming be unattractive to the average farmer despite the CAP's billions? The solution lies in the uneven distribution of CAP benefits. As we showed above, most EU farms get little from the CAP since the lion's share of the support goes to help large farms, most of which are owned by rich people. For example, the Queen of England receives over €1 million a year in CAP support (more on this below).

As if disposal problems, budget troubles, international problems and the farm income problem were not enough, technology's and the CAP's productivity effects transformed the very nature of European agriculture. This created three new problems.

9.2.6 Industrialization of farming: pollution, animal welfare and nostalgia

The policies of the CAP affect two-thirds of the EU's land and the CAP has had a major impact on how the land is used. The resulting change, what might be called 'the industrialization of farming', has occurred throughout the developed world, but its appearance in Europe was fostered and guided by CAP spending. The problem is that industrial farming led to more intensive use of some land and, as the Commission put it: 'This had a negative impact on, amongst other things, the environment, the countryside and the quality of certain products offered to the consumer' (European Commission, 1999). As the

public's interest in environmental concerns reawakened in the 1980s and 1990s, these harmful effects of the CAP eroded public support for the CAP. We consider the environmental effects first.

Negative environmental impact

The EU Court of Auditors produced a highly critical evaluation of the CAP's environmental impact in 2000. It stated:

> Agriculture has become increasingly polarised in recent years, with the intensification of practices in certain regions and abandonment of farming in other areas. This development has created environmental problems: nitrates and other pollution of rivers, lakes and groundwater, including sources of drinking water; erosion, pollution and impoverishment of soil; reduction of wildlife; damage to the atmosphere and to the rural landscape; and abandonment of environmentally beneficial extensive farming in poorer regions.

The basic problem was that the CAP's price support mechanism encouraged farmers to produce more than they otherwise would and the best way to produce more on a farm was to use more chemicals. Box 9.5 provides more detail on the CAP's environmental impact.

Animal welfare and factory farming

Just as science improved the yields of crops, science has also been applied to boost the efficiency with which animal products – meat, eggs, milk, etc. – are produced. Efficiency in this sense typically means producing the most meat at the least cost. Doing so has involved studying the most efficient density of animals, the use of antibiotics to control disease and promote growth, the scientific design of animal feed, and the breeding of higher-yielding, disease-resistant animals. While raising farm productivity, these practices have moved modern farming a very long way from the pastoral scenes still in the minds of many Europeans. As the non-governmental organization, Compassion in World Farming, puts it:

> CAP has encouraged the industrialization of agriculture, giving rise to factory farming practices and widespread animal suffering. Through the CAP, animals have been taken off the land and put into overcrowded buildings, straw-based housing has been replaced with bare concrete or slatted floors and live animals have been transported over much greater distances. The CAP also pays very generous subsidies to dealers who export live cattle from Europe to the Middle East. The long journeys often inflict tremendous suffering on the animals and end in slaughter in far away abattoirs

Box 9.5

The CAP's environmental impact

According to a 2002 report to the British agricultural ministry (JNCC, 2002), the CAP has changed agricultural land use in four ways: specialization, intensification, marginalization and abandonment. To quote the report, these are:

Intensification. Encouraged by the CAP, many farmers have sought to raise yields through increased use of fertilizers and pesticides and higher stocking densities. The associated changes in the way land is managed have led to a decline in the area of semi-natural habitats, populations of associated wildlife species, and the diversity of landscape features. The amount of available land has been increased through the removal of hedges, walls, farm ponds, etc. These changes have allowed easier access for larger machinery, which in turn has reduced farm labour requirements and has led to damaging effects on soil structure and functionality.

Specialization. The CAP has encouraged specialization of particular crops (e.g. cereals, oilseeds and peas/beans) and livestock enterprises (e.g. dairy) as a result of market intervention, particularly high levels of subsidy and quota systems. Such changes have encouraged monocultures with the loss of mixed farming enterprises, and have had impacts on land use, landscape character and biodiversity in these areas.

Marginalization. In areas where land is of poor agricultural quality, traditionally under mixed and low-productivity livestock systems, the low returns from these enterprises have required farmers to seek alternative sources of income or to intensify production methods. These changes have led to the social and economic marginalization of farming.

Abandonment. Parts of Europe with poor infrastructure provision, low economic vitality, declining populations and low agricultural productivity have seen the abandonment of farmed land. These areas are concentrated in southern Member States and France, although in parts of the UK land abandonment has played a part in the switch from farming to forestry.

(JNCC, 2002, p. 3)

Deteriorating water quality due to the application of chemical fertilizers is a problem. Chemical fertilizers, which are necessary to replace the soil's fertility when it is intensively farmed, are a main culprit in the nitrate and phosphate pollution of EU water supplies. Nitrates and phosphates tend to soak through the soil into the groundwater or get into streams and rivers via runoff from fertilized farmland. High levels of these chemicals tend to 'kill' lakes (eutrophication) by overstimulating water plants; this reduces aquatic biodiversity. In extreme cases, nitrogen can be a threat to human health. In some areas where pork and beef production are particularly intensive, animal manure is even more of a problem than agrichemicals.

A second clear-cut problem stems from pesticide use. The CAP encourages its use in the same way as it encourages fertilizer usage. That is, farmers find it profitable to use weedkillers and pesticides to reduce weeds and insect damage in order to increase output. The problem, as the JNCC report says, is that 'high levels of pesticides reduce the biodiversity of on-farm ecosystems, e.g. arable weed communities and farmland birds'. And, pesticides may get into streams through runoff and may drift into adjacent semi-natural habitats, thus damaging plant and animal communities.

where all too often the conditions can only be described as appalling.

(www.ciwf.co.uk).

Some aspects of industrial farming became known to the wider public as the result of two animal diseases:

★ BSE – 'mad cow' disease – which was spread by the practice of processing the carcasses of dead cows (some of which had the disease) into feed that was then given to healthy cows.

★ 'Foot and mouth' disease, in which large numbers of animals were destroyed to mitigate the economic consequences. The disease does not kill the animals but renders them uneconomical. The alternative to culling (killing massive numbers of animals) was vaccination, but this would have made the export of healthy animals very difficult.

Some Europeans reacted strongly against this factory farming as inhumane treatment of animals. While there are some extremists, the concern has become quite mainstream. For instance, 1 million people from all Member States signed a 1991 petition to the European Parliament calling for animals to be given a new status in the Treaty of Rome as sentient beings. In 1994, the Parliament endorsed the petition, and in 1995 it called for the Treaty to be strengthened to make concern for animal welfare one of the fundamental principles of the EU. Indeed, the Maastricht Treaty includes a 'Declaration on the Protection of Animals' and the Treaty of Amsterdam includes a protocol stating that the EU should 'pay full regard to the welfare requirements of animals'. This legal recognition is included in the draft Constitutional Treaty endorsed by EU leaders in June 2003. See Halverson (1987) for further details on factory farming.

The vanishing family farm

The industrialization of European farming has also changed its fundamental character. At the CAP's inception, most European farms were family-run affairs (Zobbe, 2001). As mentioned before, this fact, teamed with the view that rural Europe – family farming in particular – was a key element in the fabric of European societies, was important to the CAP's support among the wider public. Europeans by and large felt that family farmers deserved special treatment on cultural, historical and nostalgic grounds. Many of these family farms, however, were too small to operate efficient farming techniques. Consequently, there has been a steady reduction in the total number of farms, which has changed the nature of EU farming.

As Fig. 9.8 shows, the number of large farms had risen greatly by the end of the 1980s, while the number of small farms had shrunk. Interestingly, the drop in small farms was less marked for really small farms, i.e. farms of less than 5 hectares. Since such farms are unlikely to yield a full-time living, this suggested that a dual structure was emerging in European farming. On one hand, the majority of farms provided only a part-time occupation for the millions of farmers who work on them. On the other hand, a very few large farms provided most of Europe's food and a handsome living

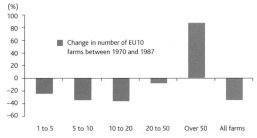

Figure 9.8: *Change in shares of big and very small farms between 1970 and 1987*

Source: Data from *European Commission* (1994), table 12.

for a few hundred thousand farmers. The intermediate-sized farm, whose owners were trying to make a living from farming, found themselves continually on the edge of bankruptcy (European Commission, 1994, p. 53).

The disappearance of the family farm can also be seen in the most recent figures on farmland ownership. According to OECD (2003), less than 60 per cent of EU farmland is owned by the farmer. The same source shows that total farm household income is increasingly coming from off-farm sources. The figures range from around 67 per cent and 75 per cent in the UK and Sweden, respectively, to about 20 per cent in Germany.

9.3 Reforms

As the analysis above shows, all the CAP's biggest problems stemmed from the EU's determination to keep EU domestic prices far above world prices. The most obvious reform solution would have been to reduce these prices. This, however, was not politically feasible.

Although the number of farmers was small – less than 5 per cent of the population – their political power was, and still is, enormous. Large commercial farmers have become used to the extra billions that the high prices brought them. Moreover, they have invested in restructuring their farms and reorienting their operations to focus on the farm goods most heavily supported by the CAP. Small farmers earned much less from the CAP, but without the higher prices many would be driven out of farming altogether. Part of the farmers' disproportionate power stemmed from the fact that average Europeans continued to approve of the CAP's support for farmers.

It is important to note that the EU's special treatment of farmers was not unusual. In the early 1990s, the EU's generosity was only in the middle of the OECD pack. The OECD (1994) reports that the subsidy equivalent per EU farmer was $13 000, less than half the amount for EFTA members (Sweden, Switzerland, Norway, Finland and Austria) and about equal with that of the USA and Japan.

9.3.1 Ad hoc attempts to control supply without lower price floors

Up to the mid-1980s, the primary way of dealing with higher CAP costs was to increase the contribution from the members.

However, when Spain and Portugal joined in 1986, the politics in the Council of Ministers shifted importantly. The CAP did little to help Spanish and Portuguese farmers since their climates prevented them from producing the goods that the CAP supported the most, i.e. dairy, wheat and beef. The newcomers, who were reluctant to see their national contributions to the budget rise year after year in order to subsidize the production of rich north European farmers, teamed up with the two incumbent poor nations (Ireland and Greece) to shift EU spending priorities towards 'structural spending' in poor nations (see Chapter 3 for further details). One option would have been to expand the EU budget to pay for the extra structural spending, but the EU net contributors (especially Germany, Denmark and the UK) opposed this.

This political roadblock posed a reform dilemma: lowering prices was out, but buying all the excess food was too expensive. The EU's first reaction was to try to work around the problem, dealing with the surplus situation without fundamentally changing the price-floor system. As European Commission (1994) puts it, the 1983 to 1991 period were 'years of experimentation'.

The CAP during this period became fantastically complex. Fortunately, most of these experiments have been dropped, so most students of European integration have no need to study their details. What is important is the outcome of these new policies. The CAP's share of the budget began to fall, so the political imperative of shifting resources to poor nations was met. However, the policies failed to address the fundamental oversupply problem. The wheat and butter mountains continued to grow along with subsidized exports, and, despite this, average farm incomes continued to fall relative to the EU-wide average.

The first really big reform was driven by pressure from the EU's trade partners who were fed up with seeing the market for their exports ruined by export subsidies (the USA also subsidized its exports). This reform package, called the MacSharry reforms after the EU Commissioner responsible for it, was the template for all subsequent reforms to date, so it is worth studying in some detail.

9.3.2 MacSharry reforms

In 1986, the world embarked on a set of trade talks (called the Uruguay Round) that were supposed to end after four years. One of the explicit goals was to reduce protectionist farm policies such as those of the USA, the EU and Japan. While earlier world trade talks had repeatedly failed to tackle the issue, the situation in the 1980s was quite different. In particular, instead of opposing agricultural liberalization as it had done in the past, the USA backed liberalization in the Uruguay Round. Moreover, a group of food-exporting countries – called the Cairns Group – steadfastly refused any agreement that did not include important farm trade liberalization. Throughout the talks, the EU declined to agree to any substantial liberalization. When the 'final' meeting came in December 1990, the EU's refusal to liberalize led to a walk-out by the Cairns Group.

This crisis threatened the whole future of the world trading system – an outcome that most EU exporters could not accept (over 80 per cent of EU exports involve industrial goods). EU governments began to face serious pressure from their own industrialists and export-oriented service sectors. In the end, this pressure was sufficient to force a reform of the CAP that was substantial enough to allow a Uruguay Round agreement that was acceptable to the Cairns Group. The reform package, called the MacSharry reforms after the European Agriculture Commissioner, was adopted in mid-1992. The Uruguay Round deal was struck 18 months later.

Decoupling, direct payments, set-asides and price cuts

The main thrust of the MacSharry reforms was to cut the price floors nearly to world prices. To make these acceptable to politically powerful farmers, the MacSharry reforms 'compensated' farmers with cash payments. This is illustrated in Fig. 9.9. The drop in the price floor from 'old price floor' to the 'new price floor' lowers producer surplus by areas A + B. The direct payments to farmers were roughly equal to area A + B. Thus the MacSharry reforms did not substantially lower the cost of the CAP. What it did was shift the nature of the payments. Before, most of the money went to buying and then disposing of excess

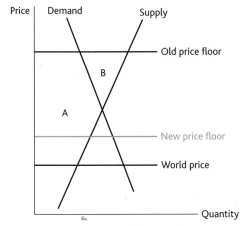

Figure 9.9: *The economics of decoupling payments and production*

food. After, most of the money was handed over directly to farmers.

Another part of the MacSharry reforms that continued the CAP's long history of unbelievable-but-true features was that it paid farmers *not* to grow food. Specifically, to get the direct payment, farmers had to agree to reduce the area they planted by 15 per cent. Similar linkages were created to foster pro-environmental and animal welfare measures. For example, farmers received a premium per animal for keeping the number of cattle per hectare below specified limits.

Note that the politically powerful milk and sugar sectors were not reformed in 1992.

Big farms, big cheques

How much money did each farmer get? Since the idea of these so-called compensatory payments was to offset farmers' income losses, big productive farms got big payments and small farms got small payments. Importantly, the payments were not made to particular farmers; they were tied to the land. This detail had three significant implications.

★ The money was paid to the owner of the farmland regardless of whether the owner was a farmer or not. (This is why the CAP continues to pay money directly to the Queen even today.)

★ The money was paid only if the land was farmed, so the payments were still coupled indirectly to production. This detail meant that some marginal farmland was kept in production in order to collect the compensation cheque.

★ The money continued to be distributed disproportionately to big, rich landowners.

9.3.3 Subsequent reforms

The 1994 Uruguay Round agreement also had important effects on EU farm policies, of which three liberalizing elements stand out. First, variable levies and quantitative import restrictions had to be converted into standard, non-fluctuating tariffs. In the end, the EU subverted the liberalizing intent of this by setting their fixed tariffs at extremely high levels, typically between 40 and 150 per cent. The Uruguay Round, however, insisted that nations allow imports of most products equal to at least 5 per cent of domestic consumption, so some import liberalization did occur. The second element was a reduction of domestic support (i.e. subsidies), but the EU's compensatory payments, however, were not covered by this. The final element was a commitment to gradually reduce the subsidization of exports by between one-fifth and one-third.

An additional element of the Uruguay Round has proved important in recent years. Before, agricultural export subsidies could not be challenged under the same WTO law that covered the export of industrial goods. After the Uruguay Round, farm and industrial exports were treated symmetrically. Brazil recently accused the EU of subsidizing sugar exports and the USA of subsidizing cotton exports. It won both cases in the WTO judicial system. As this book went to print, the European Commission was attempting to reform the CAP's sugar policies to comply with the WTO ruling, but the power of the EU sugar lobby (mainly very large French and German landowners in the North) is resisting. (You can find the details of these cases on the web by typing 'Brazil sugar WTO case' into a search engine such as Google.)

There have been two major CAP reforms since the MacSharry package. Both can be thought of as pushing the basic MacSharry logic even further. Both involved further price cuts that were compensated by direct payments to landowners. The first – Agenda 2000 – came at the March 1999 meeting of the European Council in Berlin. The second came in preparation for the ongoing WTO talks – the so-called Doha Round – where the EU pushed MacSharry-like reforms even further. One subtle change was to decouple the payments even more. Before, a compensatory payment to land on which wheat had been grown was paid only if wheat continued to be grown on the land (the same principle applied to other farm products). After the June 2003 reforms, sometimes called the Fischler reforms after European Agriculture Commissioner Franz Fischler, the payments are made as long as some type of farm good is produced on the land.

The Fischler reforms also linked payment to a wide variety of pro-environmental and animal welfare criteria. A very recent reform of the sugar sector has been forced by Brazil's winning a case against the EU before the WTO's court.

9.4 Evaluation of today's CAP

The CAP remains highly problematic. It continues to consume about half the EU budget yet most farmers complain about the lack of support and many leave the farm sector altogether, often abandoning marginal farmland in the process. The CAP also causes Europe enormous problems in the world trading system since the CAP indirectly harms the livelihoods of some of the world's poorest citizens – small farmers in poor nations – while simultaneously infuriating some of the EU's most powerful trade partners.

This section reviews the CAP's remaining problems, starting with the most important of them.

9.4.1 Farm income and the inequity of CAP support

Income from farming activities did rise sharply just after the MacSharry reforms, but have risen little ever since. Moreover, the gross inequity of the CAP's farm support has also continued. One unintentional merit of the reformed CAP, however, is that it forced Member States to gather extremely detailed information on all their farms (to enforce, for example, the set-aside measures). These new data allow analysts to more accurately gauge who wins and who loses from the CAP.

Recent analysis has pointed out two important problems that help us to solve the 'farm income puzzle' discussed above. First, the figures show quite clearly that most of the CAP's support goes to a narrow minority of farmers whose incomes are far above the average in the farm sector; indeed, many of them are rich by any standard. Second, we can see that only a modest fraction of the CAP's support actually makes it through to EU farmers. We address these points in turn.

Reformed CAP support goes mostly to big, rich farmers

Figures released by the OECD make the point that big, well-off farmers get the most out of the CAP.

Specifically, 25 per cent of the farms get 70 per cent of the support (OECD, 2003). The basic economics of this is easy to understand using the analogy we introduced in Box 9.3, where we thought about applying a CAP-like policy to helping food store owners. Continuing with the analogy, the switch from price support to direct payments based on hectares would be like switching from a subsidy to stores based on sales, to a subsidy based on floor space. Obviously, the hypermarkets would continue to gather up the lion's share of such support. In the case of the CAP, the continued inequity is even more obvious. The size of the direct payments was calculated in such a way as to offset the loss of the price cuts. Since the big rich farmers got most of the gains from high prices in the unreformed CAP, the compensatory direct payments perpetuate the inequality.

The direct payments are made to individuals and corporations, so governments know exactly who gets the CAP cash. Most EU governments are reluctant to reveal this information, fearing a political backlash. The British, Danish and Swedish governments, however, have revealed the list. The facts have turned out to be a public relationship problem for the CAP.

The Queen of England and farm payments

The list of English CAP recipients (the Scottish and Welsh governments refuse to release the information) includes some of the richest people in the realm. The Duke of Westminster, whose net worth is about €7 billion, received about €1 million over two years), the Duke of Marlborough got €1.5 million over the same period, and the Queen and Prince Charles received more than €1.5 million according to the data. The royal family is also a major landowner in Scotland (for which the data are still secret), so this is probably a serious underestimate. Multinational corporations, however, received even more. At the head of the subsidy list is the multinational corporation Tate & Lyle. It received more than ten times what the Queen and Prince Charles got, some €180 million (most of this went to paying for the dumping of sugar on the world market). Nestlé got €30 million.

Overall there were 24 525 names on the list, but one-eighth of the payments went to the top 20 names; half of the money went to the top 2000 recipients. Or, to put it differently, half the money was divided among the 22 500 smallest farms. The share of payments going to the bottom 10 000 recipients was just 13 per cent. (See the *Guardian* newspaper's website for a full list. A similar list can be downloaded for Denmark from www.dicar.dk.)

Government ministers receiving CAP payments

In the Dutch and Danish cases, some scandal has been caused by the fact that the politicians charged with overseeing the CAP are actually receiving some of the money. For example, four of the eighteen Danish ministers or their spouses, including the Agriculture Minister, received CAP money. The biggest scandal to date, however, involved the Dutch Agriculture Minister Cees Veerman. He receives about €190 000 annually in CAP subsidies for the farms he owns.

The scandal was revealed when British Prime Minister Tony Blair suggested a reform of the CAP in the summer of 2005. Dutch Prime Minister Jan Peter Balkenende at first supported Blair, but Veerman threatened to resign in protest if Balkenende backed Blair. According to an *International Herald Tribune* article (19 August 2005), a spokesman for the Dutch Ministry of Agriculture claimed that there was no connection between Veerman's cash receipts and his opposition to CAP reform. One can question this, however, since Veerman referred to his farms as 'my pension' according to a report in the *Guardian*.

This makes it easier to understand why governments have opposed the release of detailed information on who is getting the taxpayers' money. As more EU nations reveal the names of CAP recipients, the pressure to reform the welfare-for-rich-landowners aspects of the CAP is likely to grow. One proposal put forth several times by the European Commission (and rejected by the Council) would put an upper bound on the payment per farm.

Farmers only get about half of the CAP's support

Another problem with the CAP is that a great deal of the money ends up in the hands of people other than farmers. An OECD study in 2003 that examined the actual beneficiaries of the reformed CAP found that much of the support ends up in the pockets of input suppliers such as non-farming landowners and agrichemical firms.

When it comes to direct payments based on hectares, one euro of payment ends up having a minimal impact on the earnings of farm household labour. Since the payments are tied to the land, it is the land price that soaks up most of the subsidy. This is not a problem for farmers who owned their land before the area payments were instituted, but about 40 per cent of EU farmland is not owned by the people who farm it.

The OECD calculates that about 45 cents of every euro of direct payment benefits non-farming landowners instead of farmers. The other major CAP policy – market price support – does even worse. Farmers get only 48 cents of the euro, with 38 cents going to real resource costs and input suppliers.

9.4.2 Environmental impact, animal welfare and family farms

The reformed CAP has started to take account of farming's environmental impact. In particular, the lower prices have reduced the artificial incentives to farm intensively. Moreover, the EU has started to directly address the issue of environmental impact and animal welfare with a series of rules forbidding the worst practices. This progress, however, is probably only the beginning of incorporating green concerns into the CAP. Environmental groups and political parties continue to criticize the reformed CAP for its negative impact on EU landscape, water quality and biodiversity.

Since the reformed CAP continues to provide most of its support to very large EU farms, family farming has continued to decline. Indeed, the farm-size distribution has continued to develop in the 'twin peaks' direction presented in Fig. 9.8. One peak consists of small farms run by part-time farmers, i.e. by farm families whose income depends mainly on non-farm sources. The other peak consists of large and very large farms. The intermediate-sized farms that used to provide a living for a full-time farming family are increasingly being squeezed out of the sector.

9.4.3 Oversupply problems ameliorated

The reform of the CAP – in particular the lowering of the EU price floor towards world prices – solved some of the CAP's problems detailed above.

Lower prices reduced the artificial incentive to produce and at the same time stimulated EU demand. This allowed the EU to sustain the price floors without having to buy and store massive quantities of food. Indeed, for various unanticipated reasons, the world wheat price rose sharply in the late 1990s, pushing the world price above the EU price floor. The result was an impressive drop in the size of the wheat, butter and beef mountains, as the right-hand panel of Fig. 9.10 shows. As the 1992 reforms were instituted, the EU food stocks fell sharply. While there is some evidence that they are starting to pile up again, the overall stock levels are less than half of what they were before the 1992 reform.

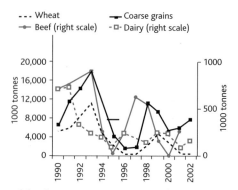

Figure 9.10: *CAP spending 1991 vs 2001 and evolution of food mountains, 1990–2002*

Source: *Agriculture in the EU – Statistics and Economic Information*, European Commission, various issues.

One thing the reform did not remedy was the rising budget cost even though it did change the nature of CAP spending. The overall level of CAP spending continued to rise, but the EU now spends most of the money on direct payments to farmers instead of on buying mountains of food (see the left-hand panel of Fig. 9.10). Agenda 2000 went some way to reducing CAP spending as a fraction of the EU budget, but CAP spending is set to remain at more than two-fifths of the budget for the foreseeable future.

Dumping reduced

Restrictions imposed by the Uruguay Round agreement on agriculture obliged the EU to reduce its dumping of food on world markets. By bringing EU supply quantities and demand quantities closer together, the price-lowering aspects of the MacSharry and Agenda 2000 reforms allowed the EU to meet this commitment while at the same time taming the lowering of its food stocks.

Reduced dumping by rich nations, especially the EU and the USA, did have positive effects on world market prices. EU food dumping, however, continues. In fact, the EU members are now the only rich nations that continue to subsidize food exporters in a major way. Figure 9.11 shows that the EU has been responsible for over 90 per cent of worldwide food dumping in recent years.

The CAP remains one of the most contentious issues in the world trade system.

Dumping food on world markets

The EU dumping practice is very strongly opposed by the world's major food exporters, but its saddest impact is what it does to some of the world's poorest countries. EU sugar exports have been singled out as especially harmful.

The EU and three countries consistently account for over 95% of all export subsidy expenditures. Total global export subsidies (US$ billion)

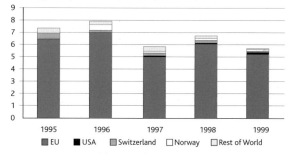

Figure 9.11: *World agricultural export subsidies, 1995–99*

Source: US Department of Agriculture Economic Research Services on http://www.ers.usda.gov/briefing/EuropeanUnion/Policy.

Sugar produced from sugar cane is one of the few products in which really poor tropical nations have a comparative advantage, and sugar is most definitely not one of the EU's comparative advantages. Given that sugar cane cannot grow in most EU nations, sugar in Europe is produced from sugar beet – a crop that can be grown in northern Europe. Although the CAP limits sugar beet production via production quotas, its high sugar prices induce EU farmers to produce far more sugar than they would in a free market. This artificial production, which is protected by high EU tariffs and export subsidies, increases the world supply and thus harms sugar producers in the world's poorest nations. See Box 9.6 for more details on the damage caused by EU sugar exports.

Box 9.6

EU sugar policy and Mozambique

The CAP's sugar policy is one of the oldest and most complex EU policies. EU sugar prices are maintained at about three times the world price, but not for all production. At the high price, many EU farmers would find it profitable to switch to growing sugar beet. EU leaders recognized this impending 'supply problem' from the beginning, so the amount of sugar for which farmers receive the high price is capped. Since the EU produces more sugar than it consumes at the high prices, the EU has to subsidize the export of the excess, but again not for all production. The EU sets a quota for the maximum amount of exports it will subsidize; anything beyond this must be sold at world prices. One more strange thing about EU sugar policy is that it actually *taxes EU farmers* in order to raise the money for the export subsidies. High EU tariffs shut off almost all imports, but again with an exception. The EU allows entry for some imported sugar from its former colonies, the so-called ACP nations (ACP stands for African, Caribbean and Pacific), but the EU must re-export this, with subsidies, since it already produces more sugar than it consumes. Note that more than half of the EU's sugar is grown in Germany and France.

All this manipulation has made the EU the world's largest exporter of white sugar (it accounts for about two-fifths of world white-sugar exports). EU subsidies depress the world price and its tariffs deny other nations the opportunity to sell in the EU market. Taken together, the CAP's sugar policy has a powerfully negative impact on poor countries, especially on poor nation farmers – a group that tends to be the poorest people in poor countries.

By way of illustration, the non-governmental organization Oxfam has highlighted the impact of EU sugar policies on Mozambique (see www.oxfam.org.uk). Its report points out that per-capita income in Mozambique is under €250 per year and two-thirds of the population lives below the poverty line. The 80 per cent of the population that live in rural areas rely mainly on agriculture for their living, with sugar production being the largest source of jobs in the country. Oxfam estimates that Mozambique is one of the lowest-cost producers of sugar in the world, with a production cost under €300 per tonne. Removal of EU sugar tariffs would help Mozambique directly, but even a cessation of export subsidies would be welcome. For example, the EU exports almost 1 million tonnes of sugar to Algeria and Nigeria, nations that would otherwise be natural markets for Mozambique's sugar.

9.5 Future challenges

While CAP reforms have helped to address some of the CAP's problems, EU agriculture is facing two new important challenges: the 2004 enlargement and the new round of WTO talks known as the Doha Development Agenda. The June 2003 reform of the CAP goes some way to meeting these challenges. The reforms, however, are extremely complex, so we do not yet know what their real impact will be. The Online Learning Centre website for this book will post periodic updates as the relevant research emerges. The actual reform adopted and some analysis can be found on the European Commission's website at http://europa.eu.int/comm/agriculture/mtr/index_en.htm.

9.5.1 Enlargement

The 2004 enlargement will have important effects on EU farm markets and EU farm policy. The basic point is simple. The new members are blessed with an abundant quantity of farmland that is well suited to producing the products that the CAP supports most heavily: dairy, beef, wheat and sugar beet. Moreover, a much larger fraction of the newcomers' populations works on the land. Basic facts are shown in Table 9.2.

We see that the 2004 enlargement will bring in almost 4 million new farms – a 50 per cent increase. The number of farmers will rise by even more since the average farm in the newcomers is smaller: 9 hectares as opposed to the EU15 average of 18.7. Since most of the CAP money goes to large farms in rich Member States, the political power of all these new, small EU farmers is likely to accelerate the trimming of payments to landowners.

CAP spending is decided by politicians in the Council of Ministers. Once the newcomers get their voting power in the Council, their farmers are very likely to push hard for a fairer treatment under the CAP. Under the 2002 Copenhagen deal – which was decided without the newcomers – the CAP spending per newcomer farm is just €172. This is so far below the EU15 average of €5000 that political difficulties are inevitable. After all, why should a relatively poor nation like Poland contribute to a budget of which a large part is paid to rich farmers in the rich EU nations? While it might be difficult to alter the CAP in the very near term, the current multi-year budget plan ends in 2006. What comes next was undecided when this edition went to press.

9.5.2 Doha Round

The Doha Round was supposed to finish in 2004. One of the key issues on the table is agriculture, just as in the Uruguay Round. The Cairns Group is again at the forefront of the pro-liberalization forces, but many developing nations are also calling for reform. And just as in the Uruguay Round, agriculture is proving to be one of the stickiest issues. At the time this book went to press, the negotiations had made little progress on farm issues. As mentioned above, however, the 2004 enlargement will totally reorient the balance of political power in the EU's Council of Ministers and this may open the door to substantial CAP revisions before 2006.

	Farmland (m ha.)	Number of farms ('000)	Average farm size (ha.)	Agricultural employment ('000)	Agri. share of employment (%)	Agri. GDP share (%)
Czech Rep.	3.7	54	67	212	4.5	1.1
Estonia	0.8	37	22	37	6.3	2.2
Cyprus	0.1	45	4	17	5.2	3.7
Latvia	1.6	141	10	146	14.6	2.1
Lithuania	2.5	279	9	276	18.7	2.6
Hungary	5.9	773	6	211	5.4	2.7
Malta	0.0	11	1	4	2.5	1.6
Poland	16.1	2178	7	2485	18.2	2.3
Slovenia	0.5	77	6	75	8.4	1.6
Slovakia	2.2	72	30	130	6.0	1.2
NMS10	33.5	3667	9	3593		
EU15	130.0	6766	18.7	6487	4.0	1.6

Note: Number of EU15 farms and average farm size for 2000 reported due to missing data for 2004. Agricultural employment is employment in agriculture, forestry, hunting and fishing (column 5). Part-time farmers who also work off the farm may not be classified as farmers (e.g. there are more holdings in Slovenia than people employed in agriculture).

Source: European Commission (2004), table 2.0.1.2.

Table 9.2: *Basic agricultural facts for 2004 entrants*

9.6 Summary

The CAP started in the 1960s as a way of guaranteeing EU farmers high and stable prices. Because agricultural technology advanced rapidly, and because the high prices encouraged farm investment, EU food production rose rapidly – much faster than EU food demand. As a consequence, the EU switched from being an importer of food to being an exporter of food. This change meant that supporting prices required much more than keeping cheaper foreign food out with high tariffs. The EU had to purchase massive amounts of food – an operation that became very expensive, consuming over 80 per cent of the EU's budget in the 1970s. Since the EU had no use for the food it bought, it disposed of the surplus by storing it or dumping it on the world market. The former was expensive and wasteful; the latter had serious international repercussions since it tended to ruin world markets for farmers outside the EU.

A combination of budget constraints and pressure from EU trade partners forced a major reform of the CAP in the 1990s, the so-called MacSharry reform. This reform lowered the guaranteed prices, and thus reduced the amount of food the EU had to buy, but it compensated farmers for the price cut by providing them with direct payments. This type of price-cut-and-compensate reform was carried further by the Agenda 2000 reforms and the June 2003 reforms.

The economic impact of the CAP is quite unusual at first glance. Despite high prices and massive subsidies, the EU farming population continues to decline because CAP support is distributed in an extraordinarily unequal way. The largest farms, which are typically owned by rich citizens or corporations, receive most of the money, while the small farms get very little. In short, CAP payments to most EU farms are too small to prevent many farmers from quitting. Yet despite the small size of most payments, the total cost of the CAP is huge since payments to big farms are big. The MacSharry and Agenda 2000 reforms did little to change this since the direct payments are related to farm size.

The CAP is headed for very serious reforms in the near future. Despite the reforms to date, the CAP continues to consume half the EU's budget, continues to tax food imports heavily, and continues to subsidize the export of some foods, directly or indirectly. All this means that the EU continues to face serious internal and external pressure to reform the CAP further.

The most likely reform direction will be to completely decouple payments from production and then to turn over the CAP payments to Member States. In this way, the French taxpayers would be free to continue handing millions of euros to large landowners and multinationals without upsetting poor Polish farmers. In the terminology of Chapter 3, the CAP is a classic situation where local information and a lack of scale economies make national decision making the superior choice.

Self-assessment questions

1. In 2003, the world wheat price is above the CAP's target price so the price floor has become a price ceiling. (i) Using a diagram like Fig. 9.1, show how the EU could implement the price ceiling with an export tax. (ii) What are the effects of this in the EU and in the rest of the world (prices, quantities and welfare)?

2. Some developing nations accuse the EU of using technical standards for food (pesticide content, etc.) as a barrier to trade. Suppose they are correct. Use diagrams to show how you would analyse the impact of such protection on EU and RoW welfare. (Hint: See Chapter 4's analysis of frictional barriers.)

3. Before the UK adopted the CAP, it supported its farmers with a system of 'deficiency payments', which is the agri-jargon for production subsidies. Using a diagram like Fig. 9.1, analyse this policy assuming that the import of food was duty free, but the government directly paid farmers the difference between the market price and a target price for each unit of food they produced. Be sure to consider the implications for world prices, UK production and UK imports, as well as the welfare implications for UK farmers, consumers and taxpayers.

4. Suppose that the EU allowed free trade in food and subsidized production on small farms only. Analyse the price, quantity and welfare implications of this policy using a diagram.

5. The text mentions that since direct payments are tied to the land, it is the land price that soaks up most of the subsidy. Use a classic supply and demand diagram to demonstrate this result. (Hint: This is a standard exercise in what is known as the 'incidence of a tax' since a subsidy is just a negative tax.)

6. The European Commission has proposed putting an upper limit on the total direct payment per farm of approximately €300 000. What would be the impact of this on prices, output and the distribution of farm incomes?

Essay questions

1. Compare the EU's agricultural policy with that of the USA. The EU's policy is based on price support plus direct payments. Does the USA have the same system? Which policy provides a higher level of support to farmers? (Hint: The US Department of Agriculture has an excellent website, and the OECD annually publishes a comparison of farm policies.)

2. What sort of CAP reforms are proposed by environmental groups in Europe? Choose one group's policy recommendations and discuss its implications for the overall level of support to the farm sector, its distribution among farmers and its implications for world food markets.

3. Select a particular European nation and investigate the political influence of its farmers. In particular, identify the main farm lobby group(s) and show how they put pressure on politicians to continue the high level of support.

4. What is the overall impact of the EU's CAP on farmers in developing nations. (Hint: The IMF published a study on this issue in its September 2002 *World Economic Outlook*, http://www.imf.org.

5. Using the theory of fiscal federalism presented in Chapter 2, can you argue that agricultural policy should be set at the EU level?

Further reading: the aficionado's corner

A wide-ranging and accessible consideration of the CAP can be found in K. Hathaway and D. Hathaway (eds) (1997) *Searching for Common Ground: European Union Enlargement and Agricultural Policy*, FAO, Rome.

Useful websites

For a non-institutional view of the CAP, and a series of readable and informative essays, see
http://members.tripod.com/~WynGrant/WynGrantCAPpage.html.

The Commission's website http://europa.eu.int/comm/agriculture/ provides a wealth of data and analysis, although much of it is politically constrained to be fairly pro-CAP. The US Department of Agriculture provides even more analysis and tends to be more openly critical of the CAP; the pages of the Economic Research Service are especially informative. See http://www.ers.usda.gov/briefing/EuropeanUnion/PolicyCommon.htm.

Every year, the OECD publishes an excellent report on agricultural policy of all OECD members (this includes the CAP). For the latest figures and exhaustive analysis, see www.oecd.org.

References

ERS (1999) *The EU's CAP: Pressures for Change*, US Department of Agriculture Economic Research Service, International Agriculture and Trade Reports, WRS-99–2. www.ers.usda.gov/publications/wrs992/wrs992.pdf.

European Commission (1994) 'EC agricultural policy for the 21st century', *European Economy, Reports and Studies*, No. 4.

European Commission (1999) *Agriculture, Environment, Rural Development: Facts and Figures. A Challenge for Agriculture*, DG Agriculture, Brussels. http://europa.eu.int/comm/agriculture/envir/report/en/.

European Commission (2000) *The Community Budget: The Facts in Figures*, European Commission, Brussels. http://europa.eu.int/comm/budget/.

European Commission (2004) *Agriculture in the EU – Statistics and Economic Information*, European Commission, Brussels.

Halverson, D. (1987) *Factory Farming: The Experiment that Failed*, Animal Welfare Institute, London.

JNCC (2002) *Environmental Effects of the Common Agricultural Policy and Possible Mitigation Measures*, Report Prepared for the Department for Environment, Food and Rural Affairs by the Joint Nature Conservation Committee. http://www.jncc.gov.uk/.

Milward, A. (1992) *The European Rescue of the Nation-State*, University of California Press, Berkeley.

Moehler, R. (1997) 'The role of agriculture in the economy and society', in K. Hathaway and D. Hathaway (eds) *Searching for Common Ground: European Union Enlargement and Agricultural Policy*, FAO, Rome. www.fao.org/docrep/W7440E/w7440e00.htm.

Molle, W. (1997) *The Economics of European Integration*, Ashgate Press, London.

Nevin, E. (1990) *The Economics of Europe*, Macmillan, London.

OECD (1994) *Agriculture Policies in OECD Countries*, OECD, Paris.

OECD (2003) *Farm Household Income: Issues and Policy Responses*, OECD, Paris.

Zobbe, H. (2001) *The Economic and Historical Foundation of the Common Agricultural Policy in Europe*, working paper, Royal Veterinary and Agricultural University, Copenhagen. www.flec.kvl.dk/kok/ore-seminar/zobbe.pdf.

> ... the Community shall aim at reducing disparities between the levels of development of the various regions and the backwardness of the least favoured regions or islands, including rural areas.
>
> *Treaty Establishing the European Community, 1958*

Chapter 10 — Location effects, economic geography and regional policy

INTRODUCTION

When deeper European economic integration took off in the 1950s, rural Europe was really poor. Electricity and telephones were far from standard in rural households and many were without indoor plumbing. The rapid economic growth that Europe experienced at the time seemed mainly to benefit cities and a few industrial regions. Recognizing this, the founders of the European Union made a concern for rural Europe one of the key goals of European integration, as the quote above makes clear.

The problems of poor regions, however, are not just historical. Even today, there are enormous gaps among EU regions in terms of average incomes, and these differences increased massively with the 2004 enlargement since the per-capita incomes in the central and eastern European nations are far below the EU15 average.

This chapter looks at the facts, theory and policy connecting European integration to the location of economic activity in Europe.

10.1 Europe's economic geography: the facts

Europe is a highly centralized continent as far as economic activity is concerned. The area made up of western Germany, the Benelux nations, north-eastern France and south-eastern England, for example, contains only one-seventh of the EU's land but one-third of its population and half its economic activity, as Table 10.1 shows. This area, which we call the 'EU core' or 'core regions', is the economic centre of Europe. Although distance is continuous, it proves convenient to group other European regions into two groups: 'intermediate' regions and 'peripheral' regions. The peripheral regions have 65 per cent of the land and 40 per cent of the population but only 20 per cent of the economic activity.

Why should anyone care about the location of economic activity? There are, after all, very few people in northern Finland. Why is it a problem that there is also very little economic activity there?

The last three columns in Table 10.1 go a long way to answering this question. As it turns out, the peripheral regions score low on measures of economic performance that directly affect people's well-being. The periphery's unemployment rate is much higher than it is in the core, especially among young workers, and only 20 per cent of the people located in the periphery have above-average incomes, while the figure for core-based people is almost 90 per cent.

Much more detail on the state of the EU's economic and social cohesion can be found in the Cohesion Reports and annual updates (Progress Reports) that are posted on http://europa.eu.int/comm/regional_policy/.

Regions	Land share (%)	Population share (%)	GDP share (%)	Unemployment rate (EU27 = 100)	Youth unemployment rate (EU27 = 100)	Share of population with income above EU27 average (%)
Core	14.0	33.2	47.2	74.0	60.5	88.8
Intermediate	21.1	25.5	31.7	101.0	95.3	70.3
Peripheral	64.9	41.3	21.1	120.8	134.2	18.1

Note: EU27 includes the EU15 and the 10 nations that will join in 2004, plus Bulgaria and Romania. Regions are defined at the NUTS2 level of aggregation; see http://europa.eu.int/comm/regional_policy/ for definitions.

Source: European Commission (2001).

Table 10.1: *Economic activity in the European core and periphery, EU27*

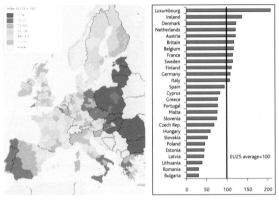

Figure 10.1: *Income disparity in the EU*

Notes: the left-hand panel shows regional GDP per capita adjusted for prices (PPS), the right-hand panel shows the same for national averages; both for 2002.

Source: Third Cohesion Report, European Commission. (Search the European Commission's Regional Policy site http://europa.eu.int/comm/regional_policy with a search engine such as Google since the exact URL can change.)

10.1.1 Geographical income inequality

The distribution of income per person in Europe is very uneven geographically. As the right-hand panel of Fig. 10.1 shows, incomes vary enormously across the continent. Limiting ourselves to the EU25 plus Bulgaria and Romania, which are scheduled to join soon, we see that income gaps are gigantic, ranging from Bulgaria's income which is just 29 per cent of EU25 average to Luxembourg's income which is 207 per cent of the average. Even within the EU15, income differences are huge: the average Dane, for example, earns about twice what Greeks do.

The disparity is even greater when looking at sub-national regions, as the left-hand panel of Fig. 10.1 shows. The richest region in the EU25 is Inner London; its average per-capita income was about €67 000 (adjusted for prices), which is 315 per cent of the EU25 average. The poorest is Lubelskie in Poland, whose average income at €6700 (adjusted for prices) is just 32 per cent of the EU25 average.

Evolution over time: narrower national differences, wider regional differences

While the dispersion of income levels across nations is still very high, the gaps among EU members have been steadily narrowing. The first part of Table 10.2 displays some figures on this, showing that a common measure of income dispersion across EU members (standard deviation of national incomes per capita) fell by 4.4 points between 1983 and 1993. In the remainder of the table the same measure shows that income inequality among nations continues to fall, with smaller drops from 1990 to 1994 and from 1995 to 2000.

The catch-up has been particularly important in the 'cohesion four – Greece, Ireland, Spain and Portugal – with Ireland's growth being downright brilliant. Between 1988 and 2002, the Irish went from an income level that was just 64 per cent of the EU15 average to being the second richest EU nation. Spanish income jumped

	Change in standard deviation across EU nations		
	1983–93	1990–94	1995–2000
EU15	−4.4	−2.7	−1.1
	Change in standard deviation across regions in each nation		
	1983–93	1990–94	1995–2000
Belgium	2.6	0.8	−1.4
Germany		9.5	0.6
excl. new Länder	3.8	1.6	2.0
Greece	1.0	1.5	−0.8
Spain	2.6	1.0	1.3
France	0.9	1.9	0.1
Ireland		0.0	5.1
Italy	1.2	0.7	−1.3
Netherlands	−15.9	0.2	2.0
Austria		0.6	−1.5
Portugal	5.2	0.3	1.4
Finland		−0.8	5.5
Sweden		0.2	8.9
UK	0.6	−1.9	2.7

Note: Important statistical redefinition occurred in 1995. Luxembourg and Denmark report no regional-level data.

Source: 1983 and 1993 data from European Commission (1996); 1990–2000 data from European Commission (2003).

Table 10.2: *Regional income-per-capita disparity by EU member, 1983–2000*

from 73 per cent of the average in 1988 to 82 per cent in 2000. The figures for Portugal were 59 versus 68 per cent, and for Greece 58 versus 70 per cent.

The convergence across nations, however, hides an important trend. Income inequality across regions within EU nations has been rising steadily. The other rows show how a measure of within-nation regional income inequality has changed since 1983. From 1983 to 1993, regional inequality rose in every member with one exception, the Netherlands. The same can be said about the early 1990s, with Finland being the exception. The picture in the end of the 1990s is a little less bleak, since regional income disparities rose in only ten of the thirteen nations on which we have data, but it is still clear that in most Member States, the regional distribution of per-capita income is getting worse. The 2004 enlargement of the Union greatly increased regional income disparity since almost all of the regions in the new Member States have incomes that are at least 25 per cent below the EU25 average, with many regions being 50 per cent or more below the average.

10.1.2 Integration and production specialization

The evidence presented up to this point suggests that European economic integration has had only a modest impact on the location of economic activity as a whole, with the many changes occurring within nations rather than across nations. Lumping all economic activity (i.e. measuring activity by total GDP), however, may hide changes in the composition of economic activity within each nation or region. European integration may have encouraged a clustering of manufacturing by sector rather than by region. To explore this possibility we look at regions' and nations' industrial structures and their evolution. We focus on industry since it is difficult to get comparable data on services.

Figures for European nations

Using a particular measure of specialization – called the Krugman specialization index – we look at how different the industrial structures are in various European nations and how they have evolved. The Krugman index tells us what fraction of manufacturing activity would have to change sector in order to make the particular nation's sector-shares line up with the sector-shares of the average of all other EU15 nations.

The indices for the EU15 are shown in Fig. 10.2. The dark bars show the level of Krugman index for each nation in 1970–73. The light bars show how the index changed from 1970 to 1997. Since almost all the changes are positive, we conclude that the industrial structures of most nations are diverging from the average EU industrial structure. In other words, taking the EU average as our standard, most European nations experienced an increase in the extent to which they specialized in the various manufacturing sectors. The only major exception is that of Spain, whose industrial structure became substantially more similar to the EU average over this period.

How important is this increase in specialization? To take one example, Ireland's index in 1970–73 was 70 per cent, which means that 35 per cent of total production would have to change sector to bring it into line with the rest of the EU. Ireland's index had increased by 8 per cent by 1997, so by 1997, 38 per cent of Ireland's manufacturing would have to change sector to get into line with the EU average. For most EU nations, the change has been fairly mild, of the order of 5 or 10 per cent.

10.1.3 Summary of facts

To summarize, the facts are:

★ Europe's economic activity is highly concentrated geographically at the national level as well as within nations.

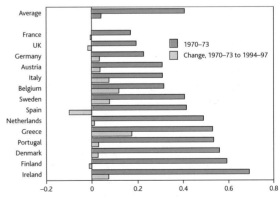

Figure 10.2: *Specialization of European industrial structure, 1970–73 and change 1970–97*

Source: Data from Midelfart-Knarvik and Overman (2002).

- ★ People located in the core enjoy higher incomes and lower unemployment rates.
- ★ While the income equality across nations has narrowed steadily with European integration, the geographic distribution of economic activity within Member States has become more concentrated (taking income per capita as a measure of economic activity per capita).
- ★ As far as specialization is concerned, European integration has been accompanied by only modest relocation of industry among nations, at least when one lumps all forms of manufacturing together.
- ★ The little movement that there has been tends to lean in the direction of manufacturing activities having become more geographically dispersed across nations, not less.
- ★ Most European nations have become more specialized on a sector-by-sector basis.
- ★ At the sub-national level, we see that industry has become more concentrated spatially.

10.2 Theory part I: comparative advantage

We now turn to the economic logic that connects European integration and the location of economic activity, focusing on two aspects in particular: specialization at the international level and agglomeration at the international level.

To keep things simple, we consider each effect in isolation, using a separate framework for each. The first framework focuses on natural differences among European nations, what economists call comparative advantage. The second framework, which is presented in the next section, focuses on the tendency of closer integration to encourage the geographic clustering of economic activity.

10.2.1 Comparative advantage and specialization

An elementary proposition in the theory of international trade is that liberalizing trade raises economic efficiency by allowing the liberalizing nation to concentrate its productive resources in sectors where it has an edge over other nations. The jargon word for the edge is 'comparative advantage'. It accomplishes this by allowing

the nation to import goods that it is relatively inefficient at making in exchange for goods that it is relatively efficient at producing. Or, to use the jargon, trade liberalization allows a nation to specialize in sectors where it has a comparative advantage. This effect of liberalization can have important effects on the location of industry because it encourages sectoral specialization on a nation-by-nation basis. The main purpose of this section is to show how comparative advantage and European economic integration help explain the nation-by-nation specialization illustrated in Fig. 10.2.

An example

To see the basic idea more clearly, think about what Europe would look like without any trade. European nations have different supplies of productive factors – and different types of goods use factors in different proportions – so without trade the output of a nation would be largely determined by its supplies of factors. Focusing on labour supplies, consider the current distribution of labour among EU members, dividing labour into three types: those with little education (less than secondary), those with at least secondary education, and highly educated workers (researchers). To make the numbers comparable, we compute each nation's supply of low-education workers relative to its total supply of workers and compare this to the same ratio calculated for the EU as a whole (EU's supply of low-educated labour to overall labour) – and we do the same for the other two labour types.

The numbers are shown in Fig. 10.3. For example, we see that Portugal's supply of low-education workers (divided by Portugal's total supply of workers) is 83 per cent above the EU average. Germany's is 52 per cent below the EU average. Now consider what this means for the price of a good that uses low-education labour intensively, such as clothing. Without any trade, Germany and Portugal would have to make all their own clothes. Since the factor that is used intensively in clothes production is relatively abundant in Portugal and relatively scarce in Germany, we should expect clothing to be more expensive in Germany than in Portugal.

Now think about what would happen if trade between Germany and Portugal opened up. Since clothes are relatively cheap in Portugal, we would see Portugal exporting clothing to Germany. But what would Germany export to Portugal in exchange? As Fig. 10.3 shows, Germany is relatively abundant in high-education labour. Using the same logic that told us that clothing

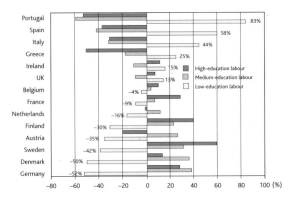

Figure 10.3: *Relative labour endowments in Europe*

Source: Data from Midelfart-Knarvik and Overman (2002).

would be relatively cheap in Portugal without trade, we know that goods that are intensive in their use of high-education labour – for example, pharmaceuticals – would be relatively cheap in Germany. In this highly simplified world with trade between only Portugal and Germany, we would see Portugal exporting clothing (and other goods that are intensive in the use of low-education labour) in exchange for pharmaceuticals (and other goods that are intensive in the use of high-education labour) from Germany.

Germans would get their clothes for less and Portuguese would get their pharmaceuticals for less, so this exchange would be good for both nations (although individual workers might be hurt by the attendant structural adjustment). The key to this 'gain from trade' is the way in which trade allows for a more efficient allocation of production across countries. Instead of each nation having to make everything it consumes, trade allows production to locate in its 'natural' place. In this case, some production of low-education-intensive goods shifts to the nation that is relatively abundant in this type of labour.

Before turning to the main point – the implication of this trade liberalization for the spatial allocation of manufacturing – it is worth stressing the logical necessity of each nation having a comparative advantage in something. The way we defined our measure of relative factor abundance, each nation's labour supplies must either be exactly in line with the EU average (Belgium's is very close to this), or it must be abundant in some types of labour and scarce in other types of labour. Thus without trade, each nation would have some goods that were relatively expensive and some goods that were relatively cheap. This type of comparative advantage,

based on relative factor endowments, is known to economists as Heckscher–Ohlin comparative advantage (it is named after the two Swedish economists who worked out its logic in the 1920s and 1930s).

The spatial implications of Heckscher–Ohlin comparative advantage

How does trade change the geographic pattern of production in this framework? In the example, trade induces an expansion in Portuguese sectors that are intensive in the use of low-education labour. Since the resources needed to expand output in these sectors must come from somewhere, trade also induces a contraction of other Portuguese sectors, in particular the sectors that had relatively high prices without trade, e.g. pharmaceuticals and other goods that are intensive in the use of high-education labour. In the simple example, the mirror-image shift would occur in Germany's industrial structure. If we view this from the international level, the resulting structural changes would look like a shift of clothing production from Germany to Portugal and a shift of the production of pharmaceuticals in the opposite direction. As a result, the industrial structures of both Portugal and Germany would become more specialized.

Of course, European integration is not limited to two nations. Allowing for many nations makes the analysis much more difficult, but it does not change the basic results that freer trade induces nations to specialize in producing products that they are relatively good at and importing products that they are relatively bad at producing. Consequently, trade liberalization of any type – including European economic integration – tends to lead nations to specialize on a nation-by-nation basis. Economic resources get shifted between sectors within each nation and, as a result, it seems as if production is being reallocated sector by sector across nations.

From the point of view of economic geography, this shows up as an increase in national specialization sector by sector. While this is not the only possible explanation for the increased specialization we saw in Fig. 10.2 (more on this below), it provides a very natural way of understanding why European integration was so systematically associated with an increase in specialization by nation.

We turn now to the logic behind the increased concentration of economic activity within European nations.

10.3 Theory part II: agglomeration and the new economic geography

The comparative advantage mechanism just discussed works without any mobility of productive factors across nations. As we shall see in this section, the story can be quite different when productive factors can move across borders and trade is not costless. In particular, a combination of scale economies and trade costs generates forces that encourage geographic clustering of economic activity. This clustering can take two distinct forms:

★ Overall clustering, which results in some areas with lots of economic activity and some areas with almost none.

★ Sectoral clustering, where each sector clusters together in a region, but different sectors cluster in different regions, so all regions end up having some industry.

The economic logic connecting European integration to these clustering outcomes is based on 'agglomeration' forces. Here these concepts are introduced with verbal logic alone. Annex A provides a more rigorous approach based on diagrams.

10.3.1 Agglomeration and dispersion forces in general

To put it simply, an agglomeration force exists when the spatial concentration of economic activity creates forces that encourage further spatial concentration. While this may seem more circular than the straight-line chain of causes and effects usually presented in economics, this circularity is the heart of the subject.

There are many agglomeration forces, but some of them operate only on a very local scale. These explain, for instance, why banks tend to group together in one part of London and dance clubs cluster in another part of the city. While the study of such agglomerations – urban economics – is fascinating, it is not the level of agglomeration that interests us. European policy is concerned with the impact of European integration on agglomeration at the level of regions and nations. As it turns out, the two most important agglomeration forces that operate across great geographic spaces are called demand linkages and cost linkages (also known as backward and forward linkages, respectively).

Backward and forward linkages

To illustrate the circular-causality logic of demand-linked and cost-linked agglomeration forces as simply as possible, we make a couple of bold assumptions. First, we assume that firms will choose one location (see Box 10.1 for the economics behind this assumption). Second, we

---

Box 10.1

How scale economies force manufacturing firms to choose a location

By definition, a firm that is subject to scale economies is one whose average cost, i.e. the per-unit cost, of producing a good falls as the scale of production rises. This means that firms whose production is subject to scale economies will benefit from concentrating production in a single location – think of it as a single factory, rather than setting up a factory near every market. For example, contrast the production of car engines, which is marked by huge scale economies, with the production of cheese, which is economical even at fairly low levels of output. Owing to scale economies, most European car companies make all engines of a particular type in a single factory located somewhere in Europe. The reason is that the per-engine cost of production is much lower in big factories. When it comes to cheese, however, the cost reduction from having a single massive cheese factory would not lower per-kilo production costs by much. For this reason, companies tend to put cheese factories near the milk production rather than ship massive quantities of milk to a massive cheese factory.

assume that there are only two possible locations: a region called North and a region called South.

The demand-linked circular causality rests on market size issues (hence its name). Firms want to locate where they will have good access to a large market in order to reduce trade costs. This is where demand linkages start. Firms want to be in the big market but in moving to the big market they tend to make the big market bigger. For example, the firms directly affect market size since firms buy goods from each other (these are called intermediate inputs). Firms also affect the market size indirectly because workers tend to go where the firms and jobs are located. Since workers tend to spend their salaries locally, they also make the big market bigger. For example, when a firm leaves Dijon to set up in Paris, it makes the Dijon market smaller and the Paris market larger. This is an agglomeration force since spatial concentration (the Dijon-to-Paris move) of economic activity creates forces (the change in market sizes) that encourage further spatial concentration.

Demand-link circular causality describes the way in which firms are attracted to big markets and how their moving to the big market makes the big market bigger.

The cost-linked circular causality works in a similar fashion but involves the cost of production. Most firms buy plenty of inputs, raw materials, machinery and equipment as well as specialized services such as marketing and financial services. Owing to trade costs (and other costs such as information costs that are related to distance), these inputs tend to be cheaper in locations where there are lots of firms making these inputs. Thus the cost linkage works by encouraging firms to locate near their suppliers, but since firms also supply other firms, moving to a low-cost location for intermediates tends to lower the cost of intermediates in that location even further. We call this an agglomeration force since, again, spatial clustering of economic activity creates forces that encourage further clustering.

Cost-linked circular causality describes the way in which firms are attracted to the presence of many suppliers of inputs in the big market and how firms moving to the big market widens the range of supplies and thus makes the big market even more attractive from a cost-of-production point of view.

Dispersion forces

There are, of course, many forces opposing concentration, and these are called 'dispersion' forces

(they favour geographic dispersion of economic activity). For example, land prices and the cost of some forms of labour (mainly unskilled) tend to be higher in built-up areas. This counteracts the agglomeration forces by increasing the attractiveness of less-developed regions. While these congestion-based dispersion forces are important in the real world, we will ignore them for the moment.

The sole dispersion force we consider to begin with is the 'local competition' force. That is, given trade costs and imperfect competition, firms are naturally attracted to markets where they would face few locally-based competitors. In seeking to avoid local competition, firms spread themselves evenly across markets. In this way, local competition tends to disperse economic activity.

The spatial distribution of economic activity in equilibrium depends upon the balance of the pro-concentration (agglomeration) forces and anti-concentration (dispersion) forces. The main question is how European integration affects the equilibrium location of industry.

10.3.2 The locational effects of European integration

European integration affects the balance of agglomeration and dispersion forces in complex ways. Such complexity is important for understanding the real world since, as the facts presented above show, the locational effects of European integration are far from simple. The best way to understand this complex logic, however, is to follow the principle of progressive complexity. We start with a set of simplifying assumptions that allow us to focus on the critical logical relationships. Once we have understood this logic in a simplified setting, we add back in complicating factors.

A very simple analytical framework

To simplify, we start by assuming away all dispersion forces except 'local competition'. We also assume away cost-linked circular causality (by assuming firms buy no intermediate inputs). Finally, we simplify the demand linkage by ignoring the feedback effect of delocation on market size. In our two regions, North and South, the northern region is bigger than the southern region, but the movement of firms from South to North (i.e. delocation) does not change the size difference. This leaves us with only one pro-agglomeration consideration and one pro-dispersion consideration. The pro-agglomeration force is that firms would, all else equal, prefer to locate in the big market in order to save on trade costs, i.e. to be close to more of their customers than they would be if they were located in the small market. The pro-dispersion force is that firms would, all else equal, prefer to be in the market where there are few local competitors and that means locating in the small market.

To study the balance of the agglomeration and dispersion forces, it helps to have a simple diagram. Figure 10.4 serves this purpose. The diagram has the strength of agglomeration and dispersion forces on the vertical axis. The horizontal axis plots the share of all firms that are located in the big, northern region. The agglomeration force line is flat because we assumed away circular causality on the demand side. That is, the attractiveness of the big market to firms does not change as the share of firms located in the big region (North) rises. The dispersion force line, however, is rising since the benefit of staying in the small region rises as more firms move to the northern market. The point is that the difference between the degree of local competition in the North and in the South increases as a higher share of firms move to the North.

The locational equilibrium is shown by point E, but it is instructive to consider why other points are not the equilibrium. For example, consider the point where half the firms are in the North, i.e. $s_n = \frac{1}{2}$. At this division of firms, the strength of the agglomeration force is shown by point A, while the strength of the dispersion force is shown by point B. Plainly, A is greater than B so we know that $s_n = \frac{1}{2}$ cannot be the equilibrium. Moreover, since the agglomeration force is stronger than the dispersion force at $s_n = \frac{1}{2}$, some firms will move from the small South to the big North. In fact, for all levels of s_n below the s_n corresponding to point E, the agglomeration forces are stronger than the dispersion forces. Although it is not shown in the diagram, readers can easily convince themselves that points to the right of point E involve a situation where the dispersion forces are larger than the agglomeration forces so the share of firms in the big region would tend to fall back to point E.

How does reducing trade costs affect the locational equilibrium? The agglomeration force is based on the fact that the northern market is the bigger, and this fact does not change when trade gets freer, so nothing happens to the agglomeration force line. Freer trade, however, has a very direct effect on the dispersion force

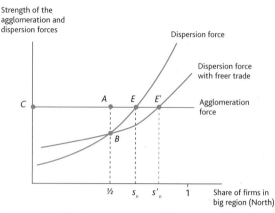

Figure 10.4: *Agglomeration and dispersion forces in a simple diagram*

curve. The source of the dispersion force is that trade costs protect firms located in the small market from competition from firms located in the big market. As trade gets freer, the strength of the dispersion force drops – at least when the share of firms in the big North market is greater than one-half, as is the case when we start at the equilibrium point E. If s_n is less than $\frac{1}{2}$, then most of the firms are in the small South and trade costs are providing relatively more protection to firms in the North. In this case, lowering trade costs raises the degree of competition faced by firms in the North more than it raises it for firms in the South. For this reason, the dispersion force line rotates around the $s_n = \frac{1}{2}$ point. (See Annex A for a more detailed treatment of Fig. 10.4.)

Given that the dispersion force curve rotates clockwise and the agglomeration force curve stays put, the new locational equilibrium is at point E'. Note that this involves a higher share of firms in the big region. In other words, free trade promotes the agglomeration of economic activity in the initially big region.

The simplifying assumptions above made it very easy to study integration's impact on the location of economic activity in Fig. 10.4. While it assumed away many important factors affecting the location of economic activity, it is sufficient for understanding the basic economic logic of how tighter European integration can be expected to favour the location of industry in Europe's core regions. Some readers, however, will want to explore the economics of this in greater depth. Box 10.2 shows how some factors can be included in a modified version of Fig. 10.4. Annex A presents the logic more formally (i.e. using mathematics).

Box 10.2

Considering additional complicating factors

As it turns out, it is not very difficult to add back in a number of complicating factors that we assumed away to start with. For example, we can easily allow for circular causality in the agglomeration force. We do this by drawing the agglomeration force line as upward sloping. If the line slopes upwards, it says that the strength of the agglomeration force rises as a larger share of firms move to the big northern region. Interested readers can redraw the figure allowing the agglomeration force line to rise from point C. It starts as point C since this shows the strength of the agglomeration force when s_n has no effect at all; if moving firms to the North makes the agglomeration force stronger, then the new agglomeration force must be higher than the old line at every point other than $s_n = 0$ (where the new and old lines share a point in common). Interested readers can redraw the diagram allowing for demand-linked circular causality and they will find that any increase in integration has a larger impact on the location of firms. That is, the rise in s_n will be larger when the agglomeration force line is upward sloping.

We can include cost-linked circular causality in the same way. As far as the equilibrium is concerned, the key point is that the big market becomes more attractive as more firms move to the big market. In other words, we can show cost-linked circular causality in the same way as demand-linked circular causality, i.e. with an upward-sloping agglomeration force line.

We can consider other dispersion forces by shifting the dispersion force curve up or twisting it at the ends. For dispersion forces that are not related to the share of firms in the North, the dispersion force curve is shifted up vertically. For example, it could be that the cold, rainy weather in northern Europe is a force that tends to encourage workers and firms to stay in the sunny South. Since the impact of this on location does not depend upon the s_n, we allow for such forces by shifting the curve up. Interested readers can easily check that such a shift will lower the equilibrium s_n. Other dispersion forces, however, are related to s_n. For example, the concentration of firms in Europe's north-east corner drives up the wages of workers in this region. Other things equal, this acts as a dispersion force in that it discourages some southern firms from moving to the core. We can reflect this in the diagram by rotating the dispersion force line anti-clockwise around $s_n = 1/2$. (As before, $s_n = 1/2$ is the rotation point since for $s_n < 1/2$, firms are concentrated in the South, not the North.)

10.4 Theory part III: putting it all together

The facts presented above showed that European integration was accompanied by location effects within nations that are quite different from those between nations. At the highest level of aggregation – adding up all economic activity within each Member State and dividing it by the number of residents – European integration seems to be associated with a greater dispersion of economic activity; this is the same as saying the per-capita GDP figures converged. Within nations, however, the opposite has happened. In most Member States, regional disparities have grown as European integration has deepened. The theory presented above helps us to understand the difference. The key factor is the mobility of capital and labour.

While there are few remaining restrictions on intra-EU labour flows, labourers seldom move across national borders in the EU. Labour mobility between regions within a nation is higher, but still not enormous – as we can see with the huge variation in regional unemployment rates. However, labour mobility has not always been low within nations. The post-war period, for example, saw a massive shift of the population from rural regions to urban regions, and this often involved a move across regional boundaries. Moreover, other productive factors are more mobile; for example, capital and skilled workers are quite mobile between regions within the same nation.

Oversimplifying to make the point, think of all factors as perfectly mobile within nations, but perfectly immobile across nations. In this case, removing barriers to trade allows nations to specialize in the sectors in which they have a comparative advantage. The resulting efficiency gain allows all nations to increase their output. Moreover, deeper aspects of integration, such as foreign direct investment and mobility of students, suggest that European integration would also be accompanied by a convergence of national technology frontiers to the best practice in Europe, with the technological laggards catching up with the technological leaders. Both of these factors would promote a convergence of per-capita incomes across European nations. Importantly, the lack of factor mobility across nations means that agglomeration forces are not dominant at the national level. That is to say, the cycles of circular causality that might lead all economic activity to leave a region have no chance of starting. This conclusion must be modified to allow for sector-specific clusters. Even if productive factors do not move across national boundaries, agglomeration forces operating at the sectoral level could result in nations specializing in particular industries. For example, deeper integration could foster greater geographic clustering of, say, the chemicals industry and the car industry, but in the end each nation ends up with some industry.

By contrast, the much greater mobility of factors within nations permits backward and forward linkages to operate. As one region grows, it becomes attractive to firms for demand reasons and cost reasons, so more firms and more factors move to the region, thereby fuelling further growth.

10.4.1 Regional unemployment

The analysis so far has assumed that wages are flexible enough to ensure full employment of all labour. Since regional unemployment is a serious problem in Europe, we turn to the economic logic connecting delocation and unemployment. As usual, we follow the principle of progressive complexity by starting simple.

If wages were adjusted instantaneously across time and space, we would have no unemployment. The wage rate paid for each hour of work would adjust so that the amount of labour that workers would like to supply at that price just matched the amount that firms would like to 'buy' (hire). In this hypothetical world, the wages would instantaneously jump to the market-clearing level,

i.e. the level where labour supply matches labour demand. Things are not that simple, however.

For many reasons, most European nations have decided to prevent the wage – the price of labour – from jumping around like the price of crude oil or government bonds. (See Chapter 8 for a more formal treatment of unemployment.) All sorts of labour market institutions, ranging from trade unions and unemployment benefits to minimum wages and employment protection legislation, mean that the price of labour is systematically stabilized at a level that exceeds the market-clearing wage level. The direct logical consequence is that workers systematically want to offer more labour at the going wage than firms are willing to hire; this is the definition of unemployment. As in any market, if the price is fixed too high, the amount offered for sale will exceed the amount that is bought.

In most European nations there is a strong spatial element to this price-fixing of labour. Take Germany for example. For many reasons, labour productivity in the eastern *Länder* is lower than it is in the western *Länder*. Thus, firms would only be willing to employ all the eastern labour offered if wages were lower in the east. However, German labour unions have methodically prevented eastern wages from falling to their market-clearing level, either in an attempt to avoid downward pressure on their own wages, or, more charitably, in the spirit of solidarity with the eastern workers who actually do get employed. Whatever the source of regional wage inflexibility, its logical consequence is regional unemployment. Moreover, since firms can leave a region much more easily than workers can, a continual within-nation clustering of economic activity will tend to be associated with high levels of unemployment in the contracting regions and low levels in the expanding regions.

Finally, it should be clear that this sort of mismatch of migration speeds (firms move faster than workers) – teamed with a lack of regional wage flexibility – has the effect of creating an agglomeration force. A little shift of industry raises unemployment in the contracting region and lowers it in the expanding region. Since unemployment is an important factor in workers' migration decisions, the initial shift makes workers more likely to migrate to the expanding region. Such migration, however, changes the relative market sizes in a way that tends to encourage more firms to leave the contracting region. (For a detailed account of geographic clustering of unemployment in Europe, see Overman and Puga, 2001.)

Peripherality and real geography

Our theoretical discussion has intentionally simplified physical geography considerations by working with only two nations, both of which are thought of as points in space. Real-world geography, of course, is much more interesting, and this matters for the location of economic activity. We can use the basic logic of demand-linked agglomeration forces to consider how one can put real geography back into the picture.

As discussed above, firms that want to concentrate production in a single location tend, other things being equal, to locate in a place that minimizes transportation costs. With only two markets, this means locating in the bigger market; but when the economic activity is spread out over real geography, the answer can be less obvious. However, the fact that economic activity is highly concentrated in Europe makes the problem easier. As the map in Fig. 10.1 showed, the core of Europe is fairly compact from a geographic point of view, i.e. it is concentrated in the north-east corner of the continent. This is why it is useful to abstract Europe's geography as consisting of two regions, the core and the periphery, what we called the North and the South in the previous section.

There are many complicating factors, however. For example, despite the Alps forming a wall between northern Italy and the big French, German and UK markets, northern Italy has quite good road access thanks to several tunnels and passes through the mountains.

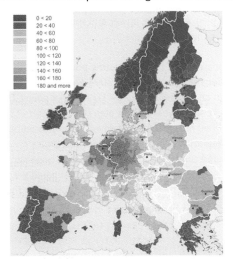

Figure 10.5: *Real geography and market accessibility*

Note: The map is scaled such that 100 equals the average accessibility in the EU27.

Source: Third Cohesion Report, European Commission. Downloadable from http://europa.int.eu.

Economists have a way of taking account of the various real-geography features: it is known as the accessibility index (also called the market potential index). See Fig. 10.5 for a recent example. The accessibility index for each region measures the region's closeness to other regions that have a lot of economic activity. For example, to calculate the accessibility of the region that contains Paris – the Île de France – one calculates how long it would take to get from the centre of Paris to the main urban centre of every other region in the EU (the calculation varies somewhat according to the form of transport used; the map here works with road transportation). Finally, one weights each of these transport times by the destination region's share of the EU's total economic activity. Adding up these weighted times gives us an idea of how close Paris is to the bulk of EU economic activity. Doing the same for every other region gives us an index of accessibility by region.

10.5 EU regional policy

As mentioned in the introduction, a concern for Europe's disadvantaged regions has always been a headline goal of the EU. For the first three and a half decades of the EU's existence, however, the task of helping less-favoured regions was left firmly in the hands of national governments. All European nations, both inside and outside the EU, spent huge sums on rural infrastructure during the 1950s, 1960s and 1970s. They extended their electricity and telephone grids to every city, town, village and farmhouse. They built roads, rail networks and provincial universities in an effort to develop their less-favoured regions. In many cases, modern banking was extended to the rural community via the state-owned PTTs (Post, Telephone and Telegraph).

The EEC, as it was known at the time, did have some programmes for rural regions, but despite real poverty in some members' regions – such as Italy's Mezzogiorno – the level of EU funding was negligible. Structural spending was only 3 per cent of the budget in 1970, rising to only 11 per cent by 1980. To the extent that the EEC was involved in helping rural communities at all, it did so by artificially raising the price of agricultural goods via the Common Agricultural Policy (CAP), as pointed out in Chapter 9. Major EU funding for less-favoured regions would have to wait for a change in Community politics. When the first 'poor' member, Ireland, joined in 1973, a new fund – the European Regional Development Fund (ERDF) – was set up to redistribute money to the poorest regions, but its budget was minor. The situation changed in the 1980s, when the EU admitted three new members:

Greece, Spain and Portugal. These nations were substantially poorer than the incumbent members, and, importantly, their farmers did not produce the goods that the CAP supported most heavily (mainly wheat, sugarbeet, dairy and beef). If these nations were to benefit financially from the EU's budget, EU spending priorities would have to be changed.

As it turned out, the voting power of Spain and Portugal, teamed with the votes of Ireland and Greece, was sufficient to produce a major realignment of EU spending priorities (see Chapter 3 for an analysis of how power politics shapes the EU budget). During the Iberian accession talks, the EU promised to substantially increase spending on poor regions. The official rationale for the increase was the assertion that economic integration implied by the Single European Act 1986 favoured Europe's industrial core (an assertion that fits in perfectly with the economics of agglomeration described in the previous section). As the Commission's website puts it, the policy was 'designed to offset the burden of the single market for southern countries and other less-favoured regions'. Whether it was caused by a new-found concern for less-favoured regions, simple power politics or a combination of the two, the fact is that EU spending on poor regions rose sharply in the mid- to late-1980s, as Fig. 10.6 shows.

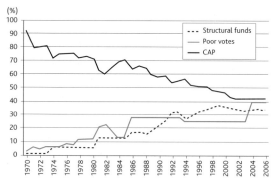

(%)

Figure 10.6: *EU budgetary expenditures, 1965–2006, CAP vs Structural Funds*

Note: The web page www.europarl.eu.int/ factsheets.4_4_1_en.htm provides more detail on the historical development of the EU's regional policy. Poor votes is the vote share of Greece, Ireland, Spain and Portugal in the Council of Ministers up to 2004: afterwards it is the vote shares of Greece, Spain and Portugal plus the ten new members according to the weights assigned in the Treaty of Nice.

Source: 1970–2000 from *The Community Budget: The Facts in Figures* European Commission (2000); 2001–2006 from *Financial Perspective*, 2000–2006; both can be found on http://europa.eu.int/comm/budget/.

When the issue of monetary union was raised in talks leading up to the Maastricht Treaty, the 'Poor-4' again managed to obtain a significant increase in regional spending via the creation of a new fund (the Cohesion Fund) that could be spent only in Greece, Ireland, Spain and Portugal. Again, the justification was that tighter economic integration would favour mostly Europe's industrial core, so peripheral regions should be compensated by a big increase in EU money for poor regions, what is known as 'structural spending' in EU jargon. The practical outcome was that structural spending doubled its share of the EU budget between 1986 and 1993.

10.5.1 Politics and the allocation of EU regional spending

This link between the political power of poor countries and the budget is clear to see in Fig. 10.6. The share of the EU budget going to poor regions rises in tandem with the share of poor countries' votes in the Council of Ministers. Up to the enlargement, when Austria, Finland and Sweden joined, the correlation was remarkably good. Since 1994, however, the connection between poor nations and structural spending has been greatly diluted. Large parts of Finland and Sweden were designated as eligible, and even some Austrian regions, together with all of the former East Germany, were deemed poor. The figure also projects the power of 'poor nations' after the ten new members have joined, and compares this vote share to the budget projections in the EU's long-term budget plan. As we see, power and spending seem set to continue their co-movement.

This apparent link between voting power and budget allocations suggests that the 2004 enlargement will result in an expanding role for EU regional policy. The EU's next seven-year budget plan (for the 2007–13 period) had not yet been approved when this edition went to print, but reports of the various drafts considered suggested a major increase in regional spending in the new Member States compared with what they are due to receive in 2005 and 2006 under the current budget plan.

10.5.2 Instruments, objectives and guiding principles

The EU now spends about one-third of its budget on less-favoured regions. How is this money allocated? As mentioned above, politics plays a role, but the EU does have a set of guidelines, objectives and principles that help to channel the spending to where it will do the most good. Here we just touch upon the main points. (Interested readers can find well-written documentation of all the details on http://europa.eu.int/comm/regional_policy/.)

Importantly, the European Commission has proposed a significant reform of EU regional policy in its July 2005 document *Cohesion Policy in Support of Growth and Jobs: Community Strategic Guidelines, 2007–2013*. This presents the Commission's proposal for reforms that are to be implemented in the context of the 2007–13 budget plan. This Commission proposal is likely to be modified in any eventual agreement on the EU's next long-term budget plan (called 'Financial Perspective' in EU jargon), but the basic elements are likely to survive. See Box 10.3 for a summary. A review of the actual reforms adopted will be posted on the Online Learning Centre website for this book when the details emerge.

The many structural funds

For historical reasons, most EU regional spending is channelled through five 'funds': four Structural Funds and the Cohesion Fund (new funds were often set up to meet new political demands that emerged during the deepening and widening of European integration). Although there are five funds, they are subsumed in an overall strategy aimed at fighting unemployment and stimulating growth in poor regions. While the four Structural Funds can be spent in any qualified EU region, the fifth fund, the Cohesion Fund, directly funds individual environment and transport projects only in Ireland, Greece, Spain and Portugal.

Box 10.3 The Commission's 2005 reform proposal for regional policy

The Commission's proposal for the 2007–13 period is very much a continuation of the reforms that were implemented in the 2000–06 budget plan (the Commission's vision for the 2000–06 budget plan was called Agenda 2000). The Structural Funds and spending priorities developed as ad hoc responses to new political pressures that appeared each time the EU enlarged. In Agenda 2000 and in its current proposal, the Commission has sought to impose greater coherence and to improve the effectiveness with which the money is spent.

The Commission's 2005 proposal seeks improvements in two main areas:

★ Greater strategic coordination of cohesion policy to ensure that EU regional policy priorities are better integrated into national and regional development programmes. To date, little has been achieved in ensuring that the EU's billions spent on cohesion policy work in tandem with other EU policies and with Member States' policies. The Commission seeks to strengthen this coordination.

★ Greater 'ownership' of cohesion policy by local participants. 'Ownership' is a jargon word used in the international financial aid community to mean local control. The aim is to improve the effectiveness of the money by establishing a clearer and more decentralized sharing of responsibilities in areas such as financial management and control. The proposals also create a clearer division of responsibilities between the Commission, Member States and the Parliament. As explained in Chapter 3, the level of government that makes decisions can have a big impact on outcomes. This part of the proposal seeks to push the basic decisions to a lower level. The idea is that if local authorities think of this as 'their' money, they are more likely to spend it wisely.

Because EU regional policy involves so much money (around €30 billion a year), the spending priorities are inevitably subject to hardball politics. We shall see this politics emerge as the 2007–13 budget deal is struck. Agreement on the current plan came just a few months before it was due to take effect, so the most likely date for an agreement is the second half of 2006.

You can find the Commission's proposal at http://europa.eu.int/comm/regional-policy/index_en.htm.

The details of the Structural Funds are only important for experts, but, for the record, the four funds are: the European Regional Development Fund (which finances infrastructure, job-creating investments, local development projects and aid for small firms), the European Social Fund (which helps the unemployed and disadvantaged people to get back to work, mainly by financing training measures and systems of recruitment aid), the Financial Instrument for Fisheries Guidance (which helps to adapt and modernize the fishing industry), and the Guidance Section of the European Agricultural Guidance and Guarantee Fund (which finances rural development measures and aid for farmers, mainly in less-favoured regions).

Spending priorities

What is this money spent on? Although there are many programmes, initiatives and objectives, over 90 per cent is spent on three priority 'objectives':

★ *Objective 1* (about 70 per cent of structural spending). This concerns spending on basic infrastructure and production subsidies in less-developed regions (generally defined as regions whose per-capita GDP is less than 75 per cent of the EU average). In the EU15, there are about fifty Objective 1 regions, which together account for about 20 per cent of the EU population. The type of spending consists of infrastructures (about 40 per cent), of which approximately half is for transport infrastructure, human resources (about 25 per cent), with priority given to employment policies and education and training systems, and aid for the production sectors (about 35 per cent). Virtually all regions in the new Member States are considered Objective 1 regions.
★ *Objective 2* (about 10 per cent of structural spending). This concerns projects in regions whose economies are specialized in declining sectors such as coal mining, fishing and steel production. The spending is supposed to support economic and social 'conversion', i.e. shifting employment and investment to more promising activities; about 18 per cent of the Union's population lives in Objective 2 regions. According to the rules, two-thirds of the population covered by this should come from industrial or urban areas; rural or fisheries-dependent regions account for the remaining one-third.
★ *Objective 3* (about 10 per cent of the funding). This concerns measures aimed at modernizing national systems of training and employment promotion. It covers all EU regions, excluding Objective 1 regions. Eligible measures are broadly defined, e.g. active labour market policies to fight unemployment, the promotion of social inclusion and equal opportunities for men and women, and employability via lifelong education systems.

Eligible regions

Although the rationale of EU regional policy is based upon the notion of rich regions helping the poor regions, politics has ensured that almost every region gets a 'slice of the pie'. As the left-hand panel of Fig. 10.7 shows, most regions in the EU25 are considered less-favoured regions (in the sense of being eligible for structural spending under either Objective 1 or Objective 2). This even includes regions in Luxembourg, which has a national per-capita income that is twice the EU average and five times that of the poorest EU25 member.

The right-hand panel of the figure shows that the actual distribution of Structural Funds is not as bad as the left-hand panel might suggest. It shows the importance of the Structural Funds as a percentage of the receiving region's GDP. Since the peripheral regions have low GDP per capita and they get a lot of the money, the structural spending is much more important for EU periphery regions.

Guiding principles

The Structural Funds are not spent on projects chosen at the European level. The choice of projects and their management are solely the responsibility of the national and regional authorities. The projects, however, are co-financed from both national and Community funds. As a matter of principle – the so-called additionality principle – Community funding should not be used to economize on national funds. This principle is naturally difficult to verify: national budgetary priorities change frequently, so it is hard to know how much the members would have spent if the Community funding were not available.

Besides additionality, the structural spending is characterized by five other basic rules:

★ *Concentration*. The spending should be geographically concentrated.
★ *Programme planning*. Spending should be in the context of broad development programmes that are drawn up by EU members and approved by the Commission.
★ *Partnership*. The Commission, the Member State concerned, the regional and local authorities, industry and labour unions should cooperate in the spending.
★ *Monitoring and evaluation*. The spending should be monitored and evaluated.

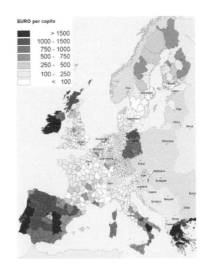

EURO per capita

	> 1500
	1000 - 1500
	750 - 1000
	500 - 750
	250 - 500
	100 - 250
	< 100

Figure 10.7: *The EU's less-favoured regions*

Notes: All the coloured regions in the left map are eligible for Objective 1 or 2 support. The right map shows structural funds received per capita in 1999.

Source: (left panel) *Third Report on Economic and Social Cohesion*, European Commission, 2004; (right panel) '*The territorial effects of structural funds*', Nordregio, www.nordregio.se.

★ *Consistency and complementarity.* The spending should be consistent with the provisions of the treaties and other Community policies such as the single market, the CAP and the Common Fisheries Policy.

10.5.3 Political allocation

As part of its responsibilities within the framework of Structural Funds management, the European Commission takes decisions on the concrete implementation of the regulations. This includes allocating the money by Objective and by EU member. The outcome of the most recent deal is shown in Table 10.3. Note that this is set years in advance.

10.5.4 The impact of eastern enlargement

The EU's regional problem got much harder when the ten new members joined in 2004. With the exception of two tiny nations (Cyprus and Slovenia), all the new entrants have national per-capita incomes that are below that of Greece, the poorest of the EU15. This made about 75 million more people eligible for Objective 1 spending. Moreover, since the newcomers lowered the EU average income substantially, some of the Objective 1 regions in the EU15 found their incomes were pushed above the 75 per cent threshold as the average fell. The Commission has called these 'statistical effect' regions since their incomes are below 75 per cent of the EU15 average but above that of the EU25 average.

The regional policy spending is already locked in up to the end of 2006, so these regions' Objective 1 status has not been affected yet. The actual treatment of these regions will emerge from the political bargaining over the 2007–13 budget plan. The Commission's proposal, however, is to continue to treat them as Objective 1 regions for a transitional period.

It seems clear that the 2004 enlargement will reorient EU spending priorities, just as the entry of Spain and Portugal did. A quick look at what the EU15 leaders decided to allocate to the ten new members reveals the magnitude of the potential problems. At the Copenhagen European Council meeting in 2002, EU leaders set down indicative amounts of aid for each of the ten newcomers. As Fig. 10.8 shows, the average annual allocation for the new Member States is not low compared with the EU15 as a whole, but they are substantially lower than what is allocated to the poor EU members, and much lower than might be expected if the newcomers were treated in the same way as incumbents. How much lower?

The line in the figure shows how cohesion-cash-per-person and per-capita income are related in the EU15 (as usual, Luxembourg's extraordinarily high income makes the country an outlier, so we exclude it when fitting the cash–income line). This 'trend line' has a negative slope as expected, since in the EU15, cohesion-cash-per-person rises as a nation's income falls. The line shows the

Country	Objective 1	Objective 2	Total	Share (%)
Spain	37 744	2553	43 087	23
Italy	21 935	2145	28 484	16
Germany	19 229	2984	28 156	15
Greece	20 961	0	20 961	11
Portugal	16 124	0	19 029	10
UK	5085	2989	15 635	9
France	3254	5437	14 620	8
Ireland	1315	0	3088	2
Netherlands	0	676	2635	1
Sweden	722	354	1908	1
Finland	913	459	1836	1
Belgium	0	368	1829	1
Austria	261	578	1473	1
Denmark	0	156	745	0
Luxembourg	0	34	78	0
EU15	127 543	18 733	183 564	100

Source: *Commisson decision fixing an indicative allocation by Member State of the commitment appropriations for Objective 1 of the Structural Funds for the period 2000 to 2006.* Downloadable from europa.eu.int/comm/regional_policy/sources/slides/Zir_en.ppt.

Table 10.3: *Country allocations in the financial perspective, 2000–06*

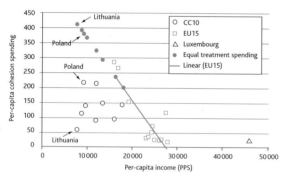

Figure 10.8: *Cohesion spending and income levels, EU15 vs CC10*

Source: European Commission (2001) and authors' calculations.

average relationship. Observe that the promised treatment of every single newcomer is below this line (each entrant is represented by a circle). That is, given how poor they are, the income–cohesion-cash link in the EU15 suggests that they should get much more than the poor nations in the EU15. To illustrate this point, the diagram plots the 'equal treatment' cohesion-cash-per-person that is predicted by the trend line; the predictions are shown with dark dots. Just to illustrate the point,

Lithuania (the poorest of the newcomers) and Poland (the biggest of the newcomers) are identified explicitly. What this projection suggests is that Poland would have received €380 per person under 'equal treatment' instead of just €214. Lithuania would have received €411 instead of the €69 it was allocated.

10.6 Empirical evidence

The chapter has stressed three main determinants of the location of economic activity: regional policy and two purely economic determinants (comparative advantage and agglomeration). We now consider the importance of these three forces.

To evaluate the determinants of industrial location in the EU, researchers try to explain how regional and national shares of various types of manufacturing vary with regional and national characteristics, where it is useful to divide the national characteristics into three broad groups: relative labour supplies, economic geography features and policies affecting industrial location.

For instance, the theory section explained why we should expect nations that have a high share of the

EU's skilled labour also to have a high share of the EU's manufacturing sectors that are relatively intensive in their use of skilled labour. The same link should be expected for relative endowments of other types of labour – low-skilled and medium-skilled workers – and sectors that use these types of labour intensively as well as regional endowments of agricultural land and industries that use agricultural inputs intensively.

The theory section also explained that the spatial allocation of demand affects the location of industry, since sectors where firms tend to concentrate production in a single location (i.e. those marked by important economies of scale) will tend to favour locations that are near large markets. This so-called demand linkage (firms want to be near the demands for their goods) is complemented by so-called supply linkages; that is, firms in sectors that use lots of intermediate inputs will tend to favour locations with concentrations of their suppliers.

Finally, policy can directly encourage the location of particular types of sectors in particular locations and this effect can either amplify or dampen the impact of factor endowments and economic geography factors on the location of industry.

Although the research in this area is limited – owing mainly to a lack of data on the location of manufacturing and regional labour endowments – the results so far suggest that all three factors matter. Interestingly, it seems that labour endowments have become more important in determining location as European economic integration has become tighter. One of the two agglomeration forces, namely supply linkages, seems to be getting stronger, whereas the demand linkage is getting weaker. (See Redding et al., 2001, for a survey of empirical results. This can be downloaded from http://econ.lse.ac.uk/staff/ajv/research_material.html.)

Given that EU regional policy has been operating at a significant level only since the mid-1980s, results on the impact of policy are even more tenuous. The best study in this area, Midelfart-Knarvik and Overman (2002), finds that EU policy has significantly affected the geographic location of industry. In particular, these authors find that EU structural spending did affect the location of high-skilled intensive industries. For an integrated survey of the empirical evidence, see Combes and Overman (2003).

10.7 Summary

Europe's economic activity is highly concentrated geographically at the national level as well as within nations. This is a problem for social cohesion since people located in the 'core' enjoy higher incomes and lower unemployment rates than people elsewhere. European integration seems to have led to a narrowing of income equality across nations but an increase in inequality within nations. Nevertheless, European integration has been accompanied by only modest relocation of industry among nations, but the little movement we have seen has been in the direction of manufacturing activities having become more geographically dispersed, not less, while most European nations have become more specialized on a sector-by-sector basis.

The chapter presents two main theories that could account for these facts. The first – the comparative advantage framework – explains why nations have become more specialized while at the same time income differences have narrowed. The second – based on the so-called new economic geography – focuses on agglomeration forces that account for the way in which tighter economic integration can foster the clustering of economic activities within nations.

The chapter also presents the main outlines of the EU's regional policy. The goal of this policy is to help to disperse economic activity to less-favoured regions. Most of the money is spent on Objective 1 regions that typically have per-capita incomes that are less than 75 per cent of the EU average. The EU spends about one-third of its budget on these policies. The 2004 enlargement will engender enormous changes for the EU's regional policies. All but two of the ten newcomers are poorer than the poorest EU15 member. This will make the poor regions in the incumbent nations look relatively rich, as well as increase the cost of the EU's regional policies.

Self-assessment questions

1. Draw a diagram with the extensions to the agglomeration diagram suggested in Box 10.2.

2. Download the European Commission's proposals for reforming structural spending and compare them with the principles of the system in place up to the end of 2006.

3. The educational level in all EU nations is rising. How would this affect the spatial allocation of production in the Heckscher–Ohlin framework?

Essay questions

1. EU regional policy was reformed in the context of Agenda 2000. What were the major reform themes and how successfully were they implemented?

2. When the ten newcomers joined, some Objective 1 regions became 'statistically' rich. That is, the lowering of the EU average pushed their incomes above the 75 per cent threshold for Objective 1 status. Referring to the two theoretical frameworks discussed in the chapter, do you think it is correct for the EU to remove their Objective 1 status?

3. Many of the ten newcomer members are both very agrarian and very poor. Some of them have agricultural land that is well suited to the production of the products that the CAP supports most. How do you think these nations will vote when the new long-term budget plan is drawn up for the post-2006 period? (Hint: Think about special-interest group politics and the position of farmers in the political life of the newcomer countries.)

4. Using the theory of fiscal federalism presented in Chapter 2, can you argue that regional policy should be set at the EU level?

Further reading: the aficionado's corner

For a more extensive discussion of the facts concerning changes in the location of economic activity in the EU, see Brülhart and Traeger (2003).

Each year, the Commission produces a report on cohesion in the EU. This contains a large number of maps showing things like unemployment, declining population, share of the economy in agriculture, industry and services. It also presents a large number of indicators of social cohesion such as youth unemployment and income distribution.

For an advanced treatment of the new economic geography, see part I of *Economic Geography and Public Policy* by Baldwin *et al.* (2003), freely downloadable from http://heiwww.unige.ch/~baldwin/.

Useful websites

The webpage www.europarl.eu.int/factsheets/4_4_1_en.htm provides a wealth of information on EU regional policy.

The Commission department devoted to regional policy has an extensive website that provides masses of data and several highly readable explanations of EU policy in the area. Search the EU's main site europa.eu.int with Google using the search words 'EU regional policy' to find the site location (it changes occasionally when the Commission reorganises its web pages).

References

Baldwin, R., R. Forslid, P. Martin *et al.* (2003) *Economic Geography and Public Policy*, Princeton University Press, Princeton, NJ.

Brülhart, M. and R. Traeger (2003) *An Account of Geographic Concentration Patterns in Europe*, Cahiers de Recherches Economiques du Département d'Econométrie et d'Economie Politique (DEEP), University of Lausanne. http://www.hec.unil.ch/deep/publications-english/e-cahiers.htm.

Combes, P. and H. Overman (2003) 'The spatial distribution of economic activity in the EU', in J. Thisse and V. Henderson (eds) *Handbook in Urban and Regional Economics,* Volume 4, North-Holland, Amsterdam.

European Commission (1996) *European Cohesion Report* (First Cohesion Report). http://europa.eu.int/comm/regional_policy/sources/docoffic/official/repor_en.htm.

European Commission (2001) *Second Report on Economic and Social Cohesion*, European Commission, Brussels.

European Commission (2003) *Communication from the Commission: Second Progress Report on Economic and Social Cohesion*, COM (2003) 34 final. http://europa.eu.int/scadplus/leg/en/lvb/g24004.htm.

Midelfart-Knarvik, K.-H. and H. Overman (2002) 'Delocation and European integration: Is structural spending justified?', *Economic Policy*, 17(35): 321–59.

Overman, H. and D. Puga (2001) 'Regional unemployment clusters: nearness matters within and across Europe's national borders', *Economic Policy*, 17(34): 115–47.

Redding, S., H. Overman and A. Venables (2001) *The Economic Geography of Trade, Production and Income: A Survey of Empirics*, CEPR Discussion Paper, London.

Annex A

Agglomeration economics more formally

A.1 The agglomeration diagram

This annex provides a formal treatment of the economics behind Fig. 10.4. The underlying model is the so-called FC model (see Baldwin *et al.*, 2003, Chapter 3 for the mathematical details). The model assumes that firms move to the region where they earn the highest profit. Simplifying assumptions in the model imply that a firm's profit is a constant fraction of its sales, so the choice of location boils down to a comparison of sales when the firm is located in the North versus the South. As firms move to the region in which they would have the highest sales, however, they increase competition in that market and reduce competition in the market they left. As a consequence, the migration of firms (sometimes called delocation) evens out the difference in the market. The equilibrium share of firms in the North is determined by the equality of sales in the two markets.

The model assumes that firms are producing differentiated varieties and that competition is of the Dixit–Stiglitz type. In other words, the varieties are all symmetric in terms of demand and each firm takes as given the prices of all other firms. A final implication of Dixit–Stiglitz competition is that all firms charge the same price-to-marginal-cost mark-up. Given these assumptions, and assuming a CES demand function, the sales of a typical South-based firm are:

$$p_j c_j = \frac{p_j^{1-\sigma} E}{n p_i^{1-\sigma} + n^*(p_i^*)^{1-\sigma}} \quad (1)$$

where E is the total expenditure in the northern market on all varieties in the sector, and σ is the elasticity of substitution among varieties (we must assume that $\sigma > 1$ for the model to make sense). The denominator has two terms. The first term reflects the price of locally-made varieties (of which there are n), and the second term reflects the price of imported varieties (of which there are n^*).

Notice that the denominator is a measure of how much competition there is in this market. If prices are very low and/or there are many firms, then the denominator will be very high (recall that $\sigma > 1$ so

$1 - \sigma < 0$) so the sales for a typical firm will be low, i.e. the typical firm will face a lot of competition.

Note that since firms in North and South have the same marginal cost and use the same constant marginal cost, the only difference between the price of local and imported varieties is the trade cost raised to the power $1 - \sigma$. In other words, p_i^*/p_i equals $\sigma 1 - \sigma$, which we relabelled as σ, a mnemonic for the freeness of trade; when $\phi = 0$, trade costs are probative and no trade occurs in this sector. When $\phi = 1$, trade is costless so $p_i^*/p_i = 1$. Using these simplifications and eqn (1), we can write the value of sales of a North-based firm in the northern market as:

$$p_j c_j = \left(\frac{1}{n_w}\right) \frac{E}{s_n + (1 - s_n)\phi} \quad (2)$$

where n_w is the number of varieties in the world (i.e. in North and South) and s_n is the share of these produced in the North.

Using similar calculations, we can calculate the value of sales of a North-based firm in the southern market. Adding the sales of a North-based firm into both the North and South markets, we get that the total sales of a North-based firm are:

$$Sales_{North} = \left(\frac{1}{n_w}\right) \left(\frac{E}{s_n + (1 - s_n)\phi} + \frac{\phi E^*}{\phi s_n + 1 - s_n} \right) \quad (3)$$

where E^* is total expenditure in the southern market. The parallel expression for a South-based firm is:

$$Sales_{South} = \left(\frac{1}{n_w}\right) \left(\frac{\phi E}{s_n + (1 - s_n)\phi} + \frac{E^*}{\phi s_n + 1 - s_n} \right) \quad (4)$$

The equilibrium location of firms – as measured by s_n – is given by the equality of eqns (3) and (4). A little algebraic manipulation shows that this difference equals:

continued

$$Sales_{North} - Sales_{South} = \left(\frac{1-\phi}{n_w}\right)\left(\frac{E}{s_n + (1-s_n)\phi} - \frac{E^*}{\phi s_n + 1 - s_n}\right) \qquad (5)$$

The equilibrium s_n is the one for which this difference is zero. Since $(1 - \sigma)$ is not zero unless trade is cost-less and location has no implication for sales, the condition that characterizes the spatial equilibrium is:

$$\frac{E}{s_n + (1-s_n)\phi} = \frac{E^*}{\phi s_n + 1 - s_n} \qquad (6)$$

This is simple to solve for s_n, but intuition is boosted by rewriting the location condition as:

$$\frac{E}{E^*} = \frac{s_n + (1-s_n)\phi}{\phi s_n + 1 - s_n} \qquad (7)$$

The left-hand side of this equation is what we called the agglomeration force line; notice that it is not affected by either the level of trade freeness, σ, or the actual distribution of firms, s_n. The larger the left-hand side, the more attractive is the North compared with the South since, all else equal, a higher E/E^* means that a typical firm will sell more when located in the North.

The right-hand side is what we called the dispersion force curve. Since the denominators in the demand functions measured the degree of competition in each market, the right-hand side is the ratio of the degrees of competition in the two markets. Namely, it captures the relative 'local competition' effect. This relative effect is affected by the level of trade freeness and the spatial distribution of firms. In particular, for any given level of σ, raising s_n increases the degree of local competition in the northern market and thus makes staying in the South more attractive.

To study the location condition, suppose firms were evenly divided between the regions, i.e. $s_n = \frac{1}{2}$. In this case, the right-hand side would equal 1. Since the northern market is bigger by assumption, the left-hand side is greater than one, so we know that $s_n = \frac{1}{2}$ cannot be an equilibrium. In particular, the bigger northern market would attract firms until the point that s_n rose high enough that the advantage of the bigger North market was offset by the higher degree of competition.

Finally, note that as trade freeness rises, the impact of s_n on the right-hand side gets stronger. Graphically, this means that the dispersion force curve gets flatter as trade gets freer.

A.2 The EE–KK diagram

In the first edition, we included a more complete analysis of agglomeration forces than shown in Fig. 10.4. Here we reproduce the first edition analysis.

The logic of agglomeration and dispersion forces can be illustrated more deeply with a diagram that relates relative market size to the relative number of firms. To make this diagram no more complicated than needed to illustrate the logic, it is helpful to make some sim-plifying assumptions.

We continue to work with only two regions, North and South, which have the same technology and factor sup-plies (this rules out comparative advantage effects). There will also be only two types of productive factors: labour, which is assumed to be immobile across regions (migration flows are quite small in Europe), and capital, which is assumed to be very mobile across regions. In particular, capital flows to the region with the highest rate of return, so in equilibrium the rate of return is equalized across regions (or else all capital is in the high-return region). Each industrial firm requires some capital and some workers to produce its goods and to make counting easy, so we say that each industrial firm needs one unit of capital. This means that a region's share of total capital is identical to the region's share of industrial firms. Furthermore, to start with, we suppose that North and South have half of the total supply of the immobile factor, labour. We rule out cost linkages by assuming that neither sector buys intermediate inputs. Finally, since we want to focus on agglomeration, we assume that the wages paid in this sector are fixed by things going on in the rest of the economy and that the wages in both regions are the same, so there is no wage-related reason for delocating. (This assumption rules out one very important dispersion force, namely the tendency of agglomeration to drive up wage rates in the core region.)

continued

With all these simplifying assumptions spelled out, we turn to a diagrammatic analysis.

The EE curve

We start with the demand linkage, i.e. the relationship between the share of industry in the North and the North's share of expenditure. Suppose industry – and thus capital – were evenly split between North and South. In this case, the two regions would have the same sized markets. Why? Market size depends upon the purchasing power of local consumers. Since there is the same amount of labour in the two regions and the same amount of capital, the regional income levels must be the same and thus the expenditure in each market must be the same. This case can be illustrated in Fig. A10.1 by point A, which is located at the ($\frac{1}{2}$, $\frac{1}{2}$) point. The diagram has s_E (short for 'share of expenditure') on the horizontal axis and this measures the relative market size of North. That is, if s_E is bigger than $\frac{1}{2}$, then North is the bigger market. On the vertical axis is s_K, which shows the share of industry that is in the North (share of industry and share of capital, K, are identical as mentioned above).

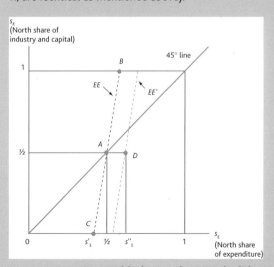

Figure A10.1: *Demand linkages: the EE schedule*

Consider what the North's share of expenditure would be if all industry and thus all capital were in the North. Clearly, s_E would be greater than one-half since North would have half the labour income and all the capital income. But s_E would be less than one, since South still has all the income of its immobile workers (who

would be working only in the service sector). This is shown as point B in the diagram. In a similar fashion, point C shows the North's share of expenditure when all the industry is in the South.

There are three main points to retain:

★ EE is upward sloping since, as North gets a larger share of industry, its market becomes larger relative to that of the South.

★ EE is steeper than the 45° line since the mobile factor makes up only part of total expenditure.

★ As far as the EE line is concerned, the impact of s_K on s_E has nothing to do with trade costs. What matters is how much labour and how much capital is in each region.

The last point to make with this diagram is to consider what happens when South is fundamentally smaller than North, i.e. when, in the initial situation, North has more than half of the immobile factor. It is important to consider this case. Much of the real-world politics of EU regional policy is driven by the fears of small regions and countries.

To consider a situation with one intrinsically small region, we assume that North has more than half the immobile factor. This case is shown as point D, where North's share of expenditure will be more than half because North would have more than half the labour and half of the capital. Likewise, for any given level of s_K, s_E will be higher. Thus the EE curve for the asymmetric size case – marked EE' in the diagram – is to the right of the original EE curve.

The KK curve

The goal of the diagram is to determine both s_E and s_K and to see how these change as trade costs fall. This brings us to the second relationship between the two shares. Capital is mobile between regions and it moves to search out the highest rate of return. To determine the equilibrium division of capital (and thus industry) between regions, we need to calculate the rate of return in each region. In particular, we are interested in seeing how market size and the level of trade costs affect the equilibrium division of industry, where this is defined as the division that equalizes the rate of return across regions for any given distribution of market sizes (i.e. for any given s_E). The combinations of

s_K and s_E that do equalize rates of return make up the KK curve.

To start with, we must discuss the determinants of capital's rate of return. A handy simplification is to suppose that the reward to a unit of capital (which equals the profitability of a single firm, since each firm needs one unit of capital) is proportional to sales. How can this be? Assuming that the profit margin is constant, at, say, 20 per cent, the total profitability of a firm is 20 per cent of sales. This one-to-one relationship between sales and profitability means that the rate of return is equalized between the regions when a typical firm in either region can sell the same amount (sales include both local and export sales).

It seems natural that equalizing the profitability of the two regions would require the North's share of industry to rise as the North's share of expenditure rose. As argued above, firms that must choose one location will tend to prefer a location in the big market, since this would allow them to economize on trade costs. But as more firms move into the big market, competition gets fiercer in the big market and gets weaker in the small market. Consequently, not all firms will move to the big market. The division of industry, i.e. s_K, adjusts to balance the agglomeration forces and dispersion forces.

To better understand this interaction, consider how the KK line would look if there were no trade between the regions, i.e. trade costs were prohibitive. (Although this situation is not very realistic, it provides a useful intellectual landmark.) In particular, what would be the equilibrium division of industry for $s_E = 1/2$? Remember that equalizing the rates of return requires equal sales per firm in the two regions. Since there is no trade in this simple case, equal sales means an equal number of firms in each region, i.e. that $s_K = 1/2$. This is plotted as point A in Fig. A10.2. The same sort of equalize-sales-per-firm reasoning shows that if North has 100 per cent of expenditure then it must also have 100 per cent of firms, and if it has 0 per cent of expenditure, then the equilibrium $s_K = 0$. These points are plotted as B and C, respectively. Repeating the reasoning for any s_E reveals that the equilibrium division without trade would always equal the given s_E. In short, the no-trade KK line coincides with the 45° line between B and C.

But what does KK look like in the more reasonable case when trade is possible but somewhat costly? To find the answer, it is useful to consider in depth why the no-trade KK line had a slope of 1. Start at point A in Fig. A10.2 and increase North's expenditure share by 10 per cent. This automatically reduces South's expenditure share by 10 per cent. If s_K stayed at $1/2$ when s_E was above $1/2$, then the firms in the North would sell more than those in the South and thus earn more. To restore equal profitability, the degree of competition in the North would have to rise by 10 per cent and the degree of competition in the South would have to fall by 10 per cent. Since there is no trade (i.e. total sales consist only of local sales), the 10 per cent increase in competition requires a 10 per cent increase in the number of firms in the North and a 10 per cent reduction in the number of firms in the South.

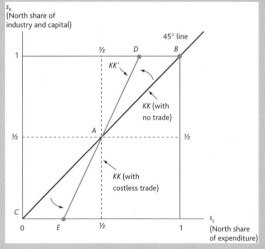

Figure A10.2: *Equalized rates of return for capital: the KK schedule*

This reasoning was simple because there were no exports, i.e. competition was entirely local. Shifting firms from South to North has a more complex impact on the degree of competition when there is trade because each shift in firms changes the degree of competition in both markets. Specifically, if the number of northern firms rises by 10 per cent (by shifting firms from South to North), the degree of competition in the North will not rise by 10 per cent. Why not? The reason is that northern firms now face lower competition in their export market – the southern market – since there are fewer locally-based firms in the South. What this means is that restoring equal sales when there is trade will require the number of North-based firms to rise by more than 10 per cent. This piece of logic is known as the 'home market effect'.

Graphically, the fact that s_K must increase by more than s_E shows up as the KK (with trade) line being steeper than the 45° line. In the diagram this is drawn as KK', which reaches from point E to point D. Of course it passes through point A since equalization of sales-per-firm with $s_E = \frac{1}{2}$ requires that $s_K = \frac{1}{2}$.

How does European integration affect the KK line? As it turns out, lower trade costs make KK steeper. The easiest way to see this is to contrast two extremes: the no-trade extreme, in which case the slope of the KK line is 45° as discussed above, and the costless trade case. When trade is costless, the division of firms between North and South is entirely irrelevant – any division would result in equal earnings per firm since each identical firm would sell the same amount in each region. Graphically, this is the vertical dashed line that extends from $\frac{1}{2}$ to $\frac{1}{2}$ as shown in the diagram. In other words, if the markets were of equal size, then any division of firms would equalize sales. A vertical KK line reflects this since any s_K works for a given s_E.

There are four main points to retain from this discussion of the KK line:

★ The KK curve is upward sloping.
★ It is steeper than the 45° line due to the home market effect (except in the extreme case of no trade).
★ The level of trade costs affects the KK curve. In particular, as trade costs fall from prohibitive levels, KK gets steeper, but since $(\frac{1}{2}, \frac{1}{2})$ is always a point on the KK line, the curve rotates around point A (as indicated by the curved arrows in Fig. A10.2).
★ The share of labour in the two regions has no impact on KK. That is because all that really matters for KK is the share of expenditure, not whether this expenditure comes from labour or from capital spending.

The locational equilibrium

Next we put together the EE and KK curves in Fig. A10.3. The diagram has North as the region with more than half the immobile labour (this is why EE does not pass through the $(\frac{1}{2}, \frac{1}{2})$ point but rather is to the right of it). The intersection of the EE and KK curves, point B, determines the equilibrium division of industry and the relative market sizes. Why?

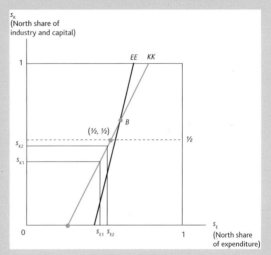

Figure A10.3: *The locational equilibrium*

EE tells us what s_E will be for any given s_K, and KK tells us what s_K will be for any given s_E. At the intersection of the two lines, the rewards to capital are equalized between regions (so there is no pressure for s_K to change) and given this equilibrium s_K, the relative market sizes are given by EE.

It is easy to see that point B is a stable outcome. For instance, suppose that for some reason, we started with s_E equal to $s_{E'}$ 1. Given this level of $s_{E'}$ the KK line tells us that firms would move until s_K were equal to $s_{K'}$ 1. But, if s_K were equal to $s_{K'}$ 1, then EE tells us that s_E would equal $s_{E,1}$. The iterations would continue, with s_K and s_E rising until B is reached.

A.3 The impact of economic integration

Finally, we are ready to consider the impact of deeper European integration on the location of industry with the help of Fig. A10.4. As trade costs fall, KK rotates

continued

anticlockwise to *KK'* and the new equilibrium is *B'*. That is, tighter integration favours concentration of industry in the market that was initially bigger. Indeed, in this very simple model – where competition is the only anti-concentration force – continued lowering of trade costs leads to the 'core–periphery' outcome. That is, a situation where all industry is in the big region (the core) and none is in the small region (the periphery).

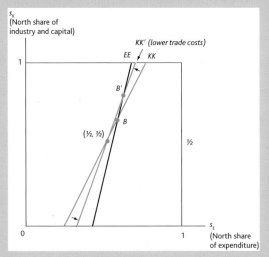

Figure A10.4: *Integration encourages geographic concentration*

A.4 Adding back some elements of reality

In the *EE–KK* diagram, local competition is the only dispersion force, so the model quite easily produces full agglomeration of capital/industry. In the real world, many things, especially land prices, tend to discourage full clustering. That is, as economic activity tends to cluster in, say, Paris, Parisian land prices rise and provincial land prices fall. This geographic change in the relative prices of productive factors tends to prevent all activities from moving to the biggest market.

There are many other dispersion forces. For example, some types of industries are intensive in the use of natural resources that are immobile. Steel production, for example, tends to locate near iron ore mines. Aluminium production, which requires huge inputs of electricity, tends to locate near cheap sources of electricity, like hydroelectric dams and atomic energy plants.

> As European Commissioner for Competition, my aim is to promote
> a fair and free environment for business in Europe. I am working
> for a European Union that is peaceful, prosperous and competitive.
>
> *Neelie Kroes*

11

EU competition and state aid policy

INTRODUCTION

The progressive deepening of European economic integration, together with more general trends such as WTO trade liberalization and globalization, has put European manufacturing and service-sector firms under a great deal of pressure. As discussed in Chapter 6, the long-run outcome of this heightened competitive pressure is typically a newly-shaped industry marked by fewer, bigger, more efficient firms engaged in more effective competition among themselves. However, in the short and medium run, firms may be tempted to collude in order to avoid or postpone industrial restructuring, and Member State governments may be tempted to provide subsidies that delay the necessary but painful restructuring.

The founders of the EU understood that pressures to collude and subsidize would arise in the course of economic integration. They also understood that anticipation of such unfair practices could reduce political support for economic integration in all nations; and 'I will not liberalize since the others are not playing fair' feeling could halt all deeper integration, especially in the sectors where it is most critical, i.e. those marked by substantial scale economies and imperfect competition. To guard against these pressures, the founders wrote into the Treaty of Rome broad prohibitions on private and public policies that distort competition. Of course, the Treaty of Rome has several provisions that have not been followed seriously, and the founders understood that this is frequently the fate of many provisions in many treaties. Yet, the Treaty writers felt that enforcing fair play in the internal market was so important to EU competition policy that it required special institutional arrangements – arrangements that would ensure that political expediency would not hinder the maintenance of a level playing field. To this end, the Treaty grants the European Commission sole power to regulate the EU's competition policy. The Commission's decisions can be overturned by the EU Court but they are not subject to approval by the Council of Ministers or the European Parliament. Of course, the Commission is not a 'Lone Ranger' in such matters. It continuously consults with Member States, especially via their respective competition authorities, but the Commission has the final word on whether mergers are allowed, whether particular business practices are allowed, and whether aid provided by Member States to firms are allowed. We can say that competition policy is one area where the Member States have truly transferred substantial sovereignty to a supranational level.

This chapter opens by providing an introduction to the economics of anti-competitive practices by private firms and subsidies by governments. It then proceeds to discuss the EU's policies.

11.1 The economics of anti-competitive behaviour and state aid

Before looking at how the European Commission regulates unfair business practices, it is important to understand the economics that lead private firms to engage in anti-competitive behaviour and what the effects of this behaviour are on the broader economy.

11.1.1 Allowing collusion in the BE–COMP framework

As EU's single market gets more 'singular' and less fragmented, firms experience greater competition and this forces them to restructure in a way that lowers their costs. Frequently, such adjustments involve waves of mergers and acquisitions. An alternative, however, is for the firms to collude in order to avoid or postpone industrial restructuring. Or, to put it more directly, in many sectors firms face the choice of perishing or engaging in anti-competitive behaviour; some of these firms choose the latter.

While this reaction may be understandable, it is illegal under EU law and economically harmful for Europe as a whole. In a nutshell, allowing collusion among firms can result in too many, too small firms who must charge high prices to compensate for their lack of scale economies. The high prices result in lower demand and production. Thus protecting existing firms can end up reducing the overall level of industrial production. One very clear example was seen in telecoms services. Before liberalization, each European nation had its own monopoly provider, services were expensive since firms were small, and as a result consumers did not spend much on telecommunications. Since liberalization, competition has forced a massive industrial restructuring, a massive increase in the size of firms and a massive reduction in the price of services. The result has been a boom in the amount of telecoms services produced and consumed in Europe.

We illustrate this general point with an extended version of the BE–COMP framework from Chapter 6.

The BE–COMP diagram

The BE–COMP diagram is explained in detail in Chapter 6, and this chapter presumes that the reader has mastered the diagram's logic. Reviewing it briefly, the BE–COMP diagram, shown in Fig. 11.1 , has three panels:

★ The middle panel shows the demand curve facing the sector in a typical nation (the diagram assumes that there are two identical nations).

★ The left-hand panel shows the average and marginal cost curves for a typical firm (all firms are identical). The number of firms, n, adjusts in the long run to eliminate pure profits, so in equilibrium a firm's scale of production must be such that its average cost equals the price.

★ The right-hand panel plots the mark-up (price minus marginal cost) against n. The COMP curve

shows the equilibrium combination of mark-up and number of firms assuming normal (i.e. Cournot) competition (more competitors imply a lower mark-up). The BE (break-even) curve is upward sloping since, as the number of firms rises, the sales per firm falls and so firms would need a higher mark-up in order to cover their fixed costs.

The equilibrium in the three panels identifies the equilibrium number of firms n, mark-up μ, price p, firm size x, and total output/consumption C.

As in Chapter 6, we model European integration as a no-trade-to-free-trade liberalization between two identical nations. While this abstracts from many important aspects of competition, it allows us to present the logic of why European industry faces such systematic pressure to restructure via mergers, acquisitions and closures. The equilibrium with no trade is marked by E'; the one with free trade is marked E''.

There are two immediate and very obvious effects from the no-trade-to-free-trade liberalization: market size and degree of competition. Post-integration, each firm has access to a second market of the same size, and each firm faces twice the number of competitiors. The competition aspect is the simplest to illustrate in Fig. 11.1. The number of firms is now $2n'$, so the typical firm will lower its mark-up in each market to point A – assuming, of course, that firms do not collude (recall that the COMP curve shows the mark-up under normal competition). The market-size effect shifts the BE curve to the right, specifically out to the point marked 1 (see Chapter 6 for a detailed explanation). The extra competition forces mark-ups down to point A, and this pushes prices down to p_A. At this combination of sales per firm and mark-up, all firms begin to lose money

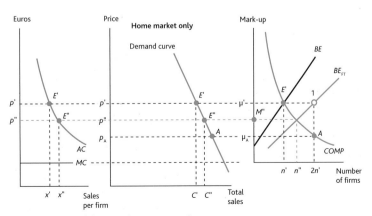

Figure 11.1: *Prices, output and equilibrium firm size with integration*

(i.e. A is below the relevant break-even line, BE_{FT}). This 'profit pressure' forces industrial reorganization (mergers, acquisitions and bankruptcies) that gradually reduces the number of firms to the new long-run equilibrium number, n''. Note that after this long-run 'industry shake-out', firms are bigger and more efficient (the left-hand panel shows that x has increased to x'' and average cost has decreased to p''); they are also facing more effective competition than before the liberalization (the right-hand panel shows that the price–cost margins drop to μ''.

To summarize: deeper European integration boosts the degree of competition and this in turn requires the industry to consolidate so as to achieve a better exploitation of scale economies. Naturally, this consolidation involves the exit of many firms. The classic examples are telecommunications, airlines and autos, where market integration resulted in a wave of mergers.

The key point as far as competition policy is concerned is that deeper European integration will generally be accompanied by a long-run reduction in the number of firms. This is important for two reasons. First, it means that Europe must be even more vigilant to ensure that the fewer bigger firms do not collude. Second, it means that firms may be tempted to engage in anti-competitive practices in order to avoid or delay the industrial restructuring. We turn now to showing what anti-competitive practices look like in the BE–COMP diagram.

Perfect collusion

The COMP curve in Fig. 11.1 assumes that firms do not collude. Both before and after the integration, we assumed that firms engage in 'normal' competition in the sense that each firm decides how much to sell, taking as

given other firms' sales. In other words, firms decide their output individually; they do not collude on output.

This assumption of 'normal' competition is quite reasonable for many industries, but it is not the behaviour that is most profitable for firms in the industry. If firms were allowed to collude, they could raise profits by reducing the amount they sell and raising prices. There are many forms of collusion in the world. The first form of collusion we consider is the simplest form to study. Instead of assuming no collusion on output, we consider the extreme opposite: perfect collusion on output.

If all firms could perfectly coordinate their sales, i.e. if they could act as if they were a single firm, they would limit total sales to the monopoly level. This would allow them to charge the monopoly price and to earn the greatest possible profit from the market. After all, the monopoly price–sales combination is, by definition, the combination that extracts the greatest profit from the market.

The hard part of collusion is finding a way to divide up the monopoly level of sales among the colluding firms. The problem is that because the price is so much higher than marginal cost, each firm would like to sell a little more than its share. To keep things simple, we assume that the firms manage the collusion by allocating an equal share to all firms. This type of behaviour can be illustrated in the BE–COMP diagram with the 'perfect collusion' line shown in Fig. 11.2. This line extends horizontally since it assumes that the mark-up always equals μ_{mono} regardless of the number of firms.

If all firms did charge the monopoly mark-up, then the maximum number of firms that could break even is shown by the point 2. This would involve net entry into this newly liberalized market – an outcome that we

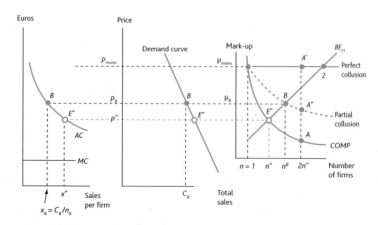

Figure 11.2: *Collusion and industrial restructuring*

rarely observe. Another possibility is that all $2n''$ firms would stay in business, without any new firms entering; this is shown as the point A'.

Partial collusion

Perfect collusion is difficult to maintain since the gains from 'cheating' on other colluders are quite high. To reduce the incentive to cheat, the actual degree of collusion may be milder than perfect collusion; this partial collusion restricts sales of all firms but not all the way back to the monopoly level, so the mark-up is lower than the monopoly mark-up but higher than the *COMP* mark-up. This makes it easier to sustain the collusion since the benefits from cheating are not quite as large. But how much lower would the mark-up be under partial collusion? As it turns out, an understanding of advanced economics is needed to formalize this notion of 'partial collusion', so we do not address it here explicitly (see Mas-Colell *et al.*, 1995, for an advanced treatment). Fortunately, the basic idea can be easily demonstrated in Fig. 11.2.

The curve labelled 'partial collusion' shows a level of collusion where the mark-up is somewhere between the monopoly mark-up and the no-collusion mark-up shown by the *COMP* curve. We do not specify exactly where it lies between the two, but this turns out to be unimportant for the qualitative analysis that we turn to next.

If the $2n'$ firms all engaged in this partial collusion, then the mark-up would be shown by the point A''. In other words, the collusion would partially offset the steeper competition induced by integration. Note, however, that although this mark-up is higher than without collusion (i.e. point A), it is not high enough for all the firms to break even, so in the long run, firms would exit until the outcome moved to point B. Point B is the long-run equilibrium with collusion since nB is the number of firms that can break even, and when there are nB firms, each would charge a mark-up of μB and this would allow them all to break even. What are the economic implications of such collusion?

Long-run economic costs of collusion

The first point is that collusion will not in the end raise firms' profits to above-normal levels. Even with partial collusion, the initial number of firms after liberalization, namely $2n''$, is too high for all of them to break even. Industrial consolidation proceeds as usual, but instead of the zero-profit level being reached when the number of firms has dropped to n'', the process halts at nB, where the *BE* curve and the partial collusion curve meet.

Importantly, and quite naturally, prices are higher with collusion than they would be without collusion (i.e. pB exceeds p''). This also means that total sales are lower with collusion since demand diminishes as the price rises. These two facts, that total sales are lower and that there are more firms, tells us that firms will be smaller under collusion than they would be without collusion (xB as opposed to x''). As the left-hand panel of Fig. 11.2 shows, smaller firms mean higher average cost, i.e. less efficiency. The welfare cost of the collusion is measured by the four-sided area marked by pB, p'', E'' and B.

To summarize: collusion prevents the full benefits of restructuring from occurring. By keeping too many firms in the market, anti-competitive behaviour thwarts part of the industry's adjustment that is the key to the gains from integration.

Having presented a general analysis that suggests why deeper European integration and competition problems tend to go hand in hand, we turn now to considering four types of anti-competitive practice in more detail.

11.1.2 Horizontal anti-competitive practices: cartels and exclusive territories

Firms like to make money. Competition hinders this, so some firms try to limit competition. One age-old way of doing this is to form a cartel with other firms in the industry. For example, one of the best known cartels, the Organization of the Petroleum Exporting Countries (OPEC), has been controlling the international price of crude oil since the early 1970s. A classic example of a cartel in Europe is the vitamins cartel (see Box 11.1).

As Figure 11.3 shows, the economic effects of cartels are rather straightforward (see Chapter 4 if you need a refresher on this sort of economics). The diagram depicts the impact of the price-raising effects of a cartel.

The diagram shows the situation for a particular market, say vitamin C, where the price without the cartel is P. This initial price is shown as being above the average costs (AC), which indicates above-normal profits even before the cartel, but the analysis follows through even if the initial price equals its long-run level, namely AC. When the cartel raises the price to P' by reducing the volume of sales to C', consumer surplus is reduced by the areas A plus B. The cartel's profits rise by the area A minus the area C.

This analysis illustrates the two main problems with cartels: the rip-off effect and the inefficiency effect. First,

Box 11.1

The vitamin cartels

In 2001, the European Commission fined eight companies for their participation in cartels that eliminated competition in the vitamin sector (vitamins A, E, B1, B2, B5, B6, C, D3, biotin, folic acid, beta carotene and carotinoids) for more than ten years. The European vitamins market is worth almost €1 billion a year since, in addition to being sold directly to consumers, vitamins are added to a wide variety of products, such as cereals, biscuits, drinks, animal feed, pharmaceuticals and cosmetics.

The European Commissioner in charge of competition policy at the time, Mario Monti, described the situation as the 'most damaging series of cartels the commission has ever investigated'. Mr Monti said: 'The companies' collusive behaviour enabled them to charge higher prices than if the full forces of competition had been at play, damaging consumers and allowing the companies to pocket illicit profits.'

The firms fixed prices, allocated sales quotas, agreed on and implemented price increases and issued price announcements according to agreed procedures. They also set up a mechanism to monitor and enforce their agreements and participated in regular meetings to implement their plans. This included the establishment of formal structure and hierarchy of different levels of management, often with overlapping membership at the most senior levels to ensure the functioning of the cartels, the exchange of sales values, volume of sales and pricing information on a quarterly or monthly basis at regular meetings, and the preparation, agreement and implementation and monitoring of an annual 'budget' followed by the adjustment of actual sales achieved so as to comply with the quotas allocated.

Under EU law, companies found guilty of antitrust practices can be fined up to 10 per cent of their total annual sales. Hoffman–La Roche of Switzerland received the largest fine (€462 million) for being the cartel ringleader, which also included BASF and Merck (Germany), Aventis SA (France), Solvay Pharmaceuticals (the Netherlands), Daiichi Pharmaceutical, Esai and Takeda Chemical Industries (Japan).

Source: This box is based on information from the European Commission's website; the quotes are from an article dated 21, November 2001 posted on the Guardian Unlimited website, www.guardian.co.uk.

the fact that cartels allow firms to profit at the expense of customers is considered by most people, and by EU law, to be unfair – a rip-off to put it colloquially. Second, the gain to firms is less than the loss to consumers, so the cartel is inefficient from a purely technical point of view. Specifically, the net economic loss is the area B + C. While few Europeans know or care about the efficiency loss, almost all would propose that the rip-off

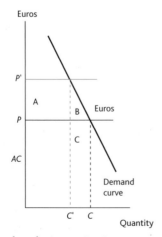
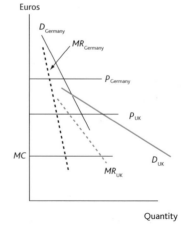

Figure 11.3: *Cartels and exclusive territories*

effect was something their governments should do something about.

Another rather common way of restricting competition is for firms to agree upon so-called exclusive territories. For example, one company would agree to sell only in its local market in exchange for a similar promise by its foreign competitor. One example of this can be found in the market for video games. Nintendo and seven of its official distributors in Europe teamed up in the 1990s to boost profits by dividing up Europe's markets and charging higher prices where consumers had a higher ability to pay. Under this practice, distributors had to prevent games being shipped from their territory to that of another EU market where prices were higher. Independent customers who allowed such sales among territories were punished by being given smaller shipments next time or by being cut off altogether. In this way, these companies managed to maintain big price differences for play consoles and games in various EU markets (e.g. the British enjoyed prices that were 65 per cent cheaper than those faced by Germans and Dutch). The European Commission fined Nintendo and the seven distributors €168 million. (You can find many such examples in the Commission's highly readable document *Competition Policy and the Consumer*.)

Thinking more broadly, it is clear that such practices offset all the goals of European integration, which is exactly why the Treaty of Rome prohibited such behaviour.

The right-hand diagram in Fig. 11.3 shows a situation where a firm would like to charge different prices in the German and UK markets. The diagram shows the two demand curves, with the German curve being steeper. The steepness of a demand curve reflects a 'willingness to pay' since it tells us how much consumption of Nintendo products would drop for a given price increase. The German curve is drawn as steeper to reflect the fact that Germans have fewer options when it comes to consumer electronics and games (owing to the smaller number of people who speak German versus English worldwide, and owing to widespread restrictions on retail outlets in Germany). In this situation, Nintendo would maximize profits by selling the quantities in Germany and the UK that correspond to the intersections of the marginal revenue curves (*MR*) and marginal cost curve (*MC*); see Chapter 6 if this reasoning is unfamiliar.

In an integrated market, independent firms, often called 'traders', could arbitrage the price gap by buying Nintendo goods in the UK and shipping them to Germany. Such shipments – which are known as 'parallel trade' – would lower Nintendo's profits and that of its official distributors. To preserve their profits, Nintendo and its distributors attempted to prevent such trade.

Bullies in the market: abuse of dominant position

Business leaders and stock markets often evaluate a company's performance based on the growth of its market share, so many firms aim to conquer the market. Firms that are lucky or possess excellent products can succeed in establishing a very strong position in their market. This is not a problem if the position reflects superior products and/or efficiency – Google's triumph in the market for search engines could be one example. However, once a firm has a dominant position, it may be tempted to use it to extract extra profits from its suppliers or customers, or it may attempt to arrange the market so as to shield itself from future competitors. According to EU law, such practices, known technically as 'abuse of dominant position', are illegal.

The classic example of this is Microsoft. Most computer users are happy that Microsoft has standardized the basics of personal computing around the world – especially those that move between nations or use more than one machine on a regular basis. In other words, computer operating systems are subject to network externalities. That is, computer operating system software becomes more valuable to each user as more people use it. To understand how and why network externalities work, just think about why the English language has spread so widely and continues to do so: more and more people learn it since so many people speak it. Just as with English, industries characterized by network externalities tend to be marked by a dominant firm, or a handful of firms. In the case of Microsoft, which has dominated the operating system software market for decades, the question is how it came to dominate applications such as Word and Excel. Although it has never been proved in court, many observers believe that the company used frequent updates of its operating system to induce users to drop competing applications (as recently as ten years ago, Microsoft had real competition from rival products such as WordPerfect and Lotus). The details of Windows updates are available to engineers updating Microsoft applications but not to those updating rival applications, so new versions of rival applications often had glitches caused by incompatibilities with the latest version of Windows. Even if a user preferred the other applications, incompatibilities with successive versions of DOS and Windows meant that it was easier to switch to Microsoft's applications than it was to deal with the glitches. Moreover, when competing firms came up with innovative programs, Microsoft typically responded with similar programs and gave them away free. Today, for example, Microsoft charges a high price for Word, where it no longer has any real competitors, but it charges a zero price on software where it has significant rivals, such as on media readers and web browsers.

The European Commission tried to put a stop to such practices by bringing a case against Microsoft in the late 1990s. In 2004, after a long legal battle, the European Commission fined Microsoft €497 million for abusing its dominant position in the market for operating systems for personal computers between 1998 and 2004. The Commission charged Microsoft with withholding information that rivals needed to allow their products to work on consumers' computers, and with forcing consumers to buy their Windows media player bundled with their operating system. According to the Commission's ruling, this had the effect of distorting competition by artificially driving the providers of movies, music and pictures to use the Windows media platform instead of that of its rivals. Microsoft, which earns billions in profits in Europe, has plenty of money for lengthy legal challenges and has appealed the Commission's decision to the European Court of First Instance. If history repeats itself, its rivals will have gone out of business before the matter is settled in court.

A sweeter example of 'abuse of dominance' can be found in the Irish ice cream market, where Unilever handed out freezers to Irish stores free of charge on the condition that they use them only for Unilever goods. The Commission ruled that this restricted Irish consumers' choice and therefore constituted an abuse of Unilever's dominant position.

11.1.3 Merger control

In many European industries, the number of firms is falling as firms merge or buy each other out. This concentration of market power is a natural outcome of European integration, as Fig. 11.1 showed, but it may also produce cartel-like conditions. The basic trade-off can be illustrated with the so-called Williamson diagram in Fig. 11.4.

Consider a merger that allows the merged firms to charge a higher price, but which also allows them to lower average costs by eliminating redundant capacities in marketing, accounting, sales representatives, etc. The price rise is shown in the diagram by the increase in price from P to P' (the diagram assumes that the market was in long-run equilibrium with $P = AC$ to start with). The efficiency gain is shown by the drop in average cost from AC to AC'. The gain to the firm's profitability are strongly positive. Before,

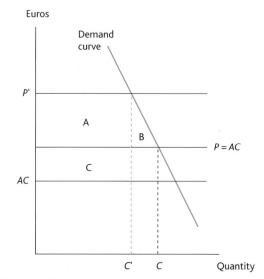

Figure 11.4: *Basic economics of mergers: market power vs efficiency gains*

$P = AC$ meant there were no profits. After, profits are the area A + B. The merger is bad for consumers, however; the price hike implies a loss of consumer surplus equal to the area A + B. The overall gain to society, taking profits and consumer surplus together, is the area C minus the area B, since area A is just a transfer from consumers to firms.

There is a point here that is important for understanding the EU's new rules on mergers. Notice that if entry and exit in the industry are unrestricted, and the remaining firms do not collude, then the long-run outcome of this merger will be to drive the price down to the lower average cost, AC'. This is in essence what happens when the equilibrium shifts from E' to E'' in Fig. 11.1. In this case, the merger-with-efficiency gain is always positive and equal to area A + B. Since entry and exit in most EU industries are fairly unrestricted, there is a presumption that mergers will generally be of the type that boosts efficiency and passes on this efficiency to consumers.

Note that our treatment of competition here is highly simplified. The impact of mergers on pricing and costs can be extremely complicated and highly dependent on the nature of the industry. Examples of such reasoning can be found in the Commission's analysis of actual merger cases on their website http://europa.int.eu/comp/.

11.1.4 State aid

The Fig. 11.1 logic linking integration and industrial restructuring presumes that profit-losing firms would eventually leave the industry – that they would either be bought out by another firm, merged with other firms or go bankrupt. All three of these exit strategies may involve job losses in specific locations or, at the very least, a reorganization that may require workers to change jobs. Since job losses and relocations are painful, governments frequently seek to prevent them. For example, if the firm is government-owned, trade unions may force the government to continue to shore up the money-losing enterprise. If it is privately owned, the government may provide subsidies through direct grants, or through long-term loans that may not be repaid.

What we want to do here is to look at the long-run economics of such subsidies – called 'state aid' in EU jargon – under two distinct scenarios. The first is where all governments provide such support; the second is where only one does.

EU-wide subsidies: thwarting the main source of gains

Start by supposing that both governments provide subsidies that prevent restructuring. To be concrete, we make the additional, more specific assumption that governments make annual payments to all firms exactly equal to their losses. Under this policy, all $2n'$ firms in the Fig. 11.1 analysis will stay in business, but, since firms are not making extraordinary profits, no new firms will enter. The economy, in short, remains at point A owing to the anti-restructuring subsidies.

An insightful way to think about this subsidy policy is as a swap in who pays for the inefficiently small firms. Before integration, prices were high, so consumers paid for the inefficiency. After liberalization, competition drives down the price but this comes at the cost of extra payouts from the national treasuries, so now the taxpayers bear the burden of the industry's inefficiency. Moreover, since all the firms stay in business, integration is prevented from curing the main problem, i.e. the 'too many too small firms' problem. Firms continue to be inefficient since they continue to operate at too small a scale. As a consequence, the subsidies prevent the overall improvement in industry efficiency that was the source of most of the gains discussed in Chapter 6.

Do nations gain from this liberalize-and-subsidize scheme? As it turns out, both nations do gain overall, even counting the cost of the subsidies. We shall show this with a diagram, but before turning to the detailed reasoning, it is instructive to explain the reason for this result. Imperfect competition is inefficient since it leads prices to exceed marginal costs. Recalling from Chapter 4 that the consumer price is a measure of marginal utility,

the fact that price exceeds marginal cost implies that the gain to consumers from an extra unit would exceed the resource cost of providing the unit. In short, society tends to gain from an expansion of output when price exceeds marginal cost. Because of this, policies that increase output tend to improve welfare. In the jargon of public economics, the subsidy is a 'second-best' policy since it reduces the negative effects of market power distortion, even if it does not solve the root of the problem.

Note, however, that this reasoning is very partial. This sort of 'reactive' subsidy turns out to be a very bad idea in the long run. The subsidies are paid to prevent firms from adapting to changed circumstances. While the government may occasionally improve things by preventing change, a culture of reactive interventionism typically results in a stagnant economy. Staying competitive requires industries to change – to adapt to new technologies, to new competitors and to new opportunities. When firms get used to the idea that their governments will keep them in business no matter what, the incentive to innovate and adapt is greatly weakened. Firms with this sort of mindset will soon find themselves far behind the international competition.

Welfare effects of the liberalize-and-subsidize policy

To explain the welfare effects of the liberalize-and-subsidize policy, we refer to Fig. 11.5. The policy we consider freezes the economy at point A in the right and middle panels (this point A corresponds exactly to the point A in Fig. 11.1). We know that the price falls from p' to p_A and consumption rises from C' to C_A. Since the number of firms has not changed but total sales in each market (which must equal total consumption in each market) has increased, we know that the sales of each firm have increased somewhat, as shown in the left-hand panel, from x' to x_A. At this point, firms are losing money, but the government offsets this with a subsidy.

How big will the subsidy be? The easiest way to make this comparison is to adopt a roundabout approach. First, consider the total size of operating profit that the whole Home industry needs to cover all fixed costs before the liberalization. The answer is already in the middle panel. Before the liberalization, the industry broke even by selling a total of C' units at the price p'. The operating profit on this was the area A + B in the middle panel, i.e. the gap between price and marginal cost times the units sold. After the liberalization, the industry's operating profit is area B + C (the new price–cost gap, $p_A - MC$, times the new sales, C_A). The drop in operating profit is thus area C minus area A. The subsidy we are considering would have to exactly offset the loss, so the subsidy would equal area A — C. With these facts established, we turn to the welfare calculation.

The consumer part of the welfare calculation is simple. Consumers see a lower price so consumer surplus rises by the area +A + D. To see the overall welfare effect, we subtract the subsidy, which equals A — C. The net welfare effect is A + D — (A — C), which equals D + C. We know this is right since this area is the gap between price and marginal cost summed over all the extra units consumed. Notice that this is the classic gain from partially redressing a market power distortion.

Only some subsidize: unfair competition

EU members' governments differ over how much they can or want to subsidize loss-making firms. Yet, when only some governments subsidize their firms, the outcome of the restructuring may be unfair in the sense that it gets forced upon the firms in nations that do not subsidize, or that stop subsidizing before the others. The real problem with this is that it may create the impression that European economic integration gives an unfair advantage to some nations' firms.

To examine this problem more closely while keeping the reasoning as simple as possible, we continue with the Fig. 11.1 example of two nations engaged in an extreme no-trade-to-free-trade integration. The integration moves each identical economy from the point E' to A. At A, all firms in both nations are losing money. Now suppose that restructuring takes five years, in the sense that after that time the number of firms has adjusted from $2n'$ to n''. In our simple example, there is no way of telling which of the surviving firms will be Home firms and which will be Foreign firms. Symmetry suggests that half the remaining firms would be Foreign, but nothing in the example ensures that this is the case. This is where subsidies can make a big difference.

To be concrete, suppose that prior to the liberalization there were 10 firms in Home and 10 in Foreign, and that after restructuring there will be 12 firms in total. Furthermore, suppose that Home provides a five-year subsidy to all of its 10 firms, with the size of the subsidy being large enough to offset the liberalization-induced losses. The Foreign government, by contrast, is assumed to pursue a laissez-faire policy, i.e. it allows the market to decide which firms should survive – either because it believes in the market, or because it cannot afford the subsidies. In this situation, it is clear that 8 of the 10 Foreign firms will go out of business, whereas all 10 Home firms will survive. At the end of the five-year period, the Home government no longer needs to subsidize its firms since the exit of eight Foreign firms restores the industry to profitability.

From a purely economic perspective, the Foreign nation might have been the winner, since having firms in our example brings nothing to national welfare (firms earn zero profit in the best of cases). The Home nation's subsidies were merely a waste of taxpayers' money. Two comments are relevant at this stage. First, this sort of conclusion shows that our simple example is actually too simplistic in many ways. For example, we did not consider the cost of workers having to switch jobs and possibly being unemployed for some time. Second, it shows that economics is only part of the picture.

The politics of state aid disciplines: 'I'll play only if the rules are fair'

From a political perspective, the sort of unfair competition just described would be intolerable. Indeed, if trade unions and business groups in Foreign anticipated that this would be the outcome, they might very well block the whole integration exercise. To avoid this sort of resistance to liberalization, the EU establishes very strict rules forbidding such unfair competition. In this sense, one of the most important effects of disciplines on state

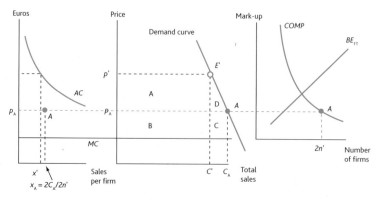

Figure 11.5: *Welfare analysis of a liberalize-and-subsidize policy*

aid is the fact that it allows governments to proceed with painful and politically difficult reforms.

11.2 EU competition policy

Having laid out the basic logic of collusion and subsidies, we turn now to considering EU policy that constrains such behaviour by private actors (anti-competitive practices) and governments (subsidies).

11.2.1 Institutions: the European Commission's power

The EU's founders were fully aware that integrating Europe's market would result in restructuring and that this would produce incentives for private and public actors to resist consolidation. This is very clear, for example, in the 1956 Spaak Report which was the economic blueprint for the Treaty of Rome (*Rapport des chefs de délégation aux ministres des affaires étrangères, Bruxelles, 21 avril 1956*). Moreover, they feared that the perception that some nations might 'cheat' in an effort to shift the burden of consolidation on to others would, in itself, make deeper European integration politically impossible. To ensure that the prevailing attitude was 'I will reform since the rules are fair', instead of 'I cannot reform since other nations will cheat', the Treaty of Rome prohibited any action that prevents, restricts or distorts competition in the common market.

Importantly, the Treaty puts the supranational Commission in charge of enforcing these strictures. Just as European leaders decided to forgo their control over monetary policy (by making central banks independent) since they knew in advance that short-run politics would lead to bad long-run policy, the Treaty of Rome grants a great deal of power on competition policy directly to the European Commission. The idea was that the politicians in the Council of Ministers might not be able to resist the short-run pressure of special-interest groups opposed to the consolidation that is necessary to obtain the long-run gains from European economic integration. In fact, competition policy is probably the area in which the Commission has the greatest unilateral power.

The Commission has considerable powers to investigate suspected abuses of EU competition law, including the right to force companies to hand over documents. Most famously, the Commission has the right to make on-site inspections without prior warning, which the media often called 'dawn raids'. With a court order, the Commission can even inspect the homes of company personnel.

The Commission has the power to prohibit anti-competitive activities. It does this by issuing injunctions against firms. To back up these demands, the Commission has the right to impose fines on firms found guilty of anti-competitive conduct. The fines vary according to severity of the practices, with a maximum of 10 per cent of the offending firm's worldwide turnover. When it comes to subsidies, the Commission has the power to force firms to repay subsidies it deems to be illicit.

Unlike most other areas where the Commission acts, the Commission's decisions are not subject to approval by the Council of Ministers or the European Parliament. The only recourse is through the European Court. This is an area where Member States truly did pool their sovereignty to ensure a better outcome for all.

11.2.2 EU law on anti-competitive behaviour

EU laws on anti-competitive practices are laid out in the Treaty of Rome (formally, the Treaty Establishing the European Community, or EC Treaty for short). Here we review the main provisions, but it is important to note that these give only a hint as to actual policy. EU competition policy has been subject to many decisions of the EU Court and one must master the details of these cases in order to fully understand which practices are prohibited and why. Moreover, the Commission publishes its own administrative guidelines so that firms can more easily determine whether a particular agreement they are contemplating will be permitted by the Commission.

Article 81 of the EC Treaty outright forbids practices that prevent, restrict or distort competition, unless the Commission grants an exemption. This article is clearly written and worth reading in its entirety (see Box 11.2).

Typically, the restrictions in Article 81 are classified as preventing horizontal or vertical anti-competitive agreements. Horizontal agreements are arrangements, like cartels and exclusive territories, upon competitors selling similar goods. Vertical agreements are arrangements between a firm and its suppliers or distributors (e.g. agreements by retailers to charge not less than a certain price, and tie-in arrangements whereby goods are only supplied if the vendor agrees to purchase other products).

The first part of Article 81 is so categorical that it rules out an enormous range of normal business practices, which can in fact be good for the European economy. The final part therefore allows the Commission to grant exemptions to agreements where the benefits outweigh the anti-competitive effects. The Commission does this for individual agreements notified to the Commission for exemption, but it also established the policy of 'block exemptions' that grant permission to broad types of agreements. These exist for technology transfer and R&D agreements. Political pressure has also forced the Commission to grant a block exemption to the anti-competitive practices in the distribution of motor vehicles.

The second major set of policies – restrictions on the abuse of a dominant position – are found in Article 82 of the EC Treaty (see Box 11.3). A dominant position usually depends upon a firm's market share. Abuse is a general term but it includes refusal to supply, unfair prices and conditions, predatory pricing, loyalty rebates, exclusive dealing requirements, and abuse of intellectual property rights.

11.2.3 Control of mergers

The EC Treaty does not contain specific provisions on mergers, but since mergers can affect competition the Treaty requires the Commission to oversee merger activity. The Commission realized that the 1992 programme for the completion of the internal market would produce a flurry of merger activity. To promote transparency and allow firms to better understand whether a particular merger will be allowed, the EU set out explicit rules in Council and Commission Regulations starting in the late 1980s. The current set of regulations is called simply 'Merger Regulation', but it is often referred to by its number, 139/2004. This regulation, which reformed a string of earlier regulations to include new thinking and various EU Court decisions, was introduced in January 2004 and entered into force with the Union's enlargement. The regulation does not stand by itself but rather is one pillar in a merger control edifice that also includes guidelines on the assessment of horizontal mergers, best practice in merger investigations, and on reforms within the Commission.

The Merger Regulation defines anti-competitive behaviour in the following terms: 'A concentration which would significantly impede effective competition, in the common market or in a substantial part of it, in particular by the creation or strengthening of a dominant position, shall be declared incompatible with the

---

Box 11.2

Article 81 (formerly Article 85)

1. The following shall be prohibited as incompatible with the common market: all agreements between undertakings, decisions by associations of under-takings and concerted practices which may affect trade between Member States and which have as their object or effect the prevention, restriction or distortion of competition within the common market, and in particular those which:
   (a) directly or indirectly fix purchase or selling prices or any other trading conditions;
   (b) limit or control production, markets, technical development, or investment;
   (c) share markets or sources of supply;
   (d) apply dissimilar conditions to equivalent transactions with other trading parties, thereby placing them at a competitive disad-vantage;
   (e) make the conclusion of contracts subject to acceptance by the other parties of supplemen-tary obligations which, by their nature or according to commercial usage, have no con-nection with the subject of such contracts.

2. Any agreements or decisions prohibited pursuant to this Article shall be automatically void.

3. The provisions of paragraph 1 may, however, be declared inapplicable in the case of:
   - any agreement or category of agreements between undertakings;
   - any decision or category of decisions by associ-ations of undertakings;
   - any concerted practice or category of concerted practices, which contributes to improving the production or distribution of goods or to pro-moting technical or economic progress, while allowing consumers a fair share of the resulting benefit, and which does not:
   (a) impose on the undertakings concerned restric-tions which are not indispensable to the attainment of these objectives;
   (b) afford such undertakings the possibility of eliminating competition in respect of a sub-stantial part of the products in question.

Article 82 (formerly Article 86)

Any abuse by one or more undertakings of a dominant position within the common market or in a substantial part of it shall be prohibited as incompatible with the common market insofar as it may affect trade between Member States.

Such abuse may, in particular, consist in:
(a) directly or indirectly imposing unfair purchase or selling prices or other unfair trading conditions;

(b) limiting production, markets or technical development to the prejudice of consumers;
(c) applying dissimilar conditions to equivalent transactions with other trading parties, thereby placing them at a competitive disadvantage;
(d) making the conclusion of contracts subject to acceptance by the other parties of supplementary obligations which, by their nature or according to commercial usage, have no connection with the subject of such contracts.

Some merger decision examples

The European pharmaceutical sector has experienced a wave of consolidation and as part of this two mega-mergers were brought to the attention of the European Commission, the Sanofi and Synthélabo link-up and the Pfizer and Pharmacia fusion. The Commission determined that both would lessen competition in certain market segments by limiting the choice of some drugs. The Commission, however, recognized the need for efficiency gains and believed that the mergers could be useful. The outcome was that the Commission allowed the mergers subject to conditions. The firms were required to transfer some of their products to their competitors so as to redress potential anti-competitive effects. For example, Sanofi/Synthélabo sold off certain antibiotics, hypnotics and sedatives.

Another case involved a mainly domestic merger between TotalFina and Elf Aquitaine, which were the main players in the French petroleum sector. The Commission determined that their merger would have allowed the companies to push up costs for independent petrol station operators (e.g. supermarkets) and the combined company would have operated around 60 per cent of the service stations on French motorways. The combined firms would also have been the leading supplier of liquid petroleum gas. The European Commission believed this level of market power would be anti-competitive and agreed to the merger only on the condition that TotalFina/Elf sell off a large proportion of these operations to competitors. For example, it sold 70 motorway service stations in France to competitors.

common market.' Under the new rules, mergers that meet the relevant criteria do not have to be notified to the Commission since they are presumed to be compatible with competition.

The new rules also give a prominent role to national competition authorities and courts, under the European Competition Network which facilitates coordination among EU and national competition authorities and courts.

Box 11.4 describes some examples of Commission rulings in merger cases.

11.2.4 EU policies on state aid

The EU's founders realized that the entire European project would be endangered if EU members felt that other members were taking unfair advantage of the economic integration (see Box 11.5 for an example of unfair

Box 11.5

Subsidies and unfair competition in the energy market

The market for electricity was one of the few markets left largely untouched by the sweeping liberalization of the EU's Single Market Programme between 1986 and 1992. Until the 1990s, the sector was dominated by government-owned or controlled firms, but as part of the general trend towards market-oriented policies, many EU members privatized their state-owned energy monopolies and opened their markets to foreign competition. These moves, however, were not part of a coordinated EU strategy. The resulting difficulties provide an excellent illustration of how important the EU's anti-state-aid policy is to keeping European economic integration on track.

As with much of European industry, the energy sector was, and still is, marked by too many firms which are too small to be truly competitive. As in many other sectors, a process of consolidation and industrial restructuring has begun. Unlike other EU sectors, however, liberalization varies greatly across Member States. France is one of the most closed markets in two senses. It is difficult for foreign firms to supply French customers and the French energy monopoly Electricité de France (EdF) is tightly controlled by the government so it cannot be bought. Moreover, EdF receives various subsidies that give it an advantage in the market.

Other EU members feared that France had embarked on a cynical campaign of ensuring that EdF would be one of the survivors of the industrial restructuring that would inevitably come when energy was eventually liberalized. For example, France consistently opposed full liberalization of energy markets, and when the EU adopted a partial opening measure in which members were bound to open up their energy markets to third-party competition, France delayed passing the necessary laws. The real trouble began when EdF launched an aggressive campaign of

expanding rapidly into the power markets of neighbouring Member States (the UK, Germany, Italy and Spain) while remaining a state-owned monopoly in its home market.

Such expansion would be unremarkable in other sectors, but the perception that EdF's moves were 'unfair' led other EU members to postpone or restrict their own liberalization efforts. For example, in 2001, German Minister for Economic Affairs Werner Müller threatened to prevent the French state-owned power giant EdF from importing electricity into Germany as long as France did not open up its power market to foreign companies. Italy had a similar reaction after EdF began to take over the Italian company Montedison. As Italy's Treasury Minister Vincenzo Visco explained, it was 'unacceptable to let a player with a rigged hand of cards join the game'. The Italian government quickly introduced measures designed to block further takeovers.

To prevent this chain reaction from ruining prospects for liberalization, the Commission launched an investigation in 2002 into EdF's state aid. Following the formal investigation procedure initiated by the Commission on 2 April 2003, the French government agreed to end EdF's unlimited state guarantee by 2005. Mario Monti, the Competition Commissioner at the time, said: 'I welcome the favourable outcome reached in this highly sensitive case.... A competitive situation has for the first time been created for EdF, without distortions due to state aid. The introduction of conditions of fair competition and the correction of past distortions is all the more important in sectors such as energy which are in the process of being liberalised and will enable all the positive effects to be reaped from that liberalisation.'

Source: This box is based mainly on BBC news stories dated 12 June 2001 and 16 October 2002 (see www.bbc.co.uk).

competition in the EU energy market). To prevent this, the 1957 Treaty of Rome bans state aid that provides firms with an unfair advantage and thus distorts competition. Importantly, the EU founders considered this prohibition to be so important that they actually empowered the

supranational European Commission to be in charge of enforcing the prohibition. Indeed, the Commission has the power to force the repayment of illegal state aid, even though the Commission normally has no say over members' individual tax and spending policies.

The EC Treaty prohibits state aid that distorts competition in the EU. The Treaty defines state aid in very broad terms. It can, for instance, take the form of grants, interest relief, tax relief, state guarantee or holding, or the provision by the state of goods and services on preferential terms.

Some state aid, however, is allowed according to the Treaty since subsidies, when used correctly, are an essential instrument in the toolkit of good governance. The permitted exceptions include social policy aid, natural disaster aid and economic development aid to underdeveloped areas. More generally, state aid that is in the general interest of the EU is permitted. For example, the Commission has also adopted a number of block exemption rules that explain which sorts of state aid are indisputable. These include aid to small and medium-sized enterprises, aid for training and aid for employment. More information can be found in DG Competition's highly accessible document *Competition Policy and Consumers*, downloadable from http://europa.eu.int (use a search engine such as Google to find the exact link since the Commission occasionally reshuffles its websites).

A contentious example: airlines in trouble

The Commission is frequently in the headlines over its state aid decisions since these often produce loud protests from firms and/or workers who benefited from any state aid that the DG Competition judges to be illegal. An excellent example concerns the airline industry – an industry where there are clearly too many firms in existence and where the tendency to subsidize is strong. Many European airlines are the national 'flag carrier', and as such are often considered a symbol of national pride.

Consolidation of the European airline industry has been on the cards for years, but the problem was exacerbated by the terrorist attacks of 11 September 2001 in the USA. The ensuing reduction in air travel caused great damage to airlines all around the world and led to calls for massive state aid. To prevent these subsidies from being used as an excuse to put off restructuring, the Commission restricted subsidies to cover only the 'exceptional losses' incurred when transatlantic routes were shut down immediately after 11 September. To date, the Commission has managed to resist the desire of several Member State governments to support their national airlines to the same extent that the US government has supported US airlines.

It is easy to see the logic of the Commission's stance. Low-cost airlines, such as Ryanair and EasyJet, have done well without subsidies. Moreover, artificial support for inefficient national carriers hinders the expansion of low-cost airlines. As Bannerman (2002) puts it:

> No-one will benefit from a return to spiralling subsidies, which damage the industry by encouraging inefficiency. Both consumers and taxpayers would suffer as a result. As for the national carriers, they would probably benefit from some market consolidation, creating fewer, leaner, pan-European airlines – although this process would need monitoring for its competitive effects on key routes. If the airline industry can use the crisis to create more efficient carriers, it will probably be the better for it. But this long-term view cuts little ice with workers who stand to lose their jobs, or with some politicians, for whom a flag carrier is a symbol of national pride. Unfortunately, the benefits of controlling state-aids occur mainly in lower fares and taxes, and are therefore widely diffused among the population. The costs, on the other hand, take the form of job losses, which hurt a small but vocal constituency.

11.3 Summary

Three main points have been made in this chapter.

★ One very obvious impact of European integration has been the creation of a bigger 'home' market for individual European firms. This produces a chain reaction that leads to fewer, bigger, more efficient firms that face more effective competition from each other. The attendant industrial restructuring is often politically painful since it often results in lay-offs and the closure of inefficient plants. Governments often attempt to offset this political pain by providing state aid to their national firms. Such aid can be viewed as unfair, and the perception of unfairness threatens to undermine EU members' interest in integration. To avoid these problems, the founders of the EU established rules that prohibited state aid that distorts competition. The Commission is charged with enforcing these rules.

★ Private firms may also seek to avoid restructuring by engaging in anti-competitive practices, and EU rules prohibit this. Moreover, as integration proceeds and the number of firms falls, the temptation for firms to collude may increase.

★ To help firms avoid this temptation, the EU has strict rules on anti-competitive practices. It also screens mergers to ensure that the merger will enhance efficiency. Again, the Commission is charged with enforcing these rules.

Self-assessment questions

1. Suppose that liberalization occurs as in Fig. 11.1 and the result is a pro-competitive effect, but instead of merging or restructuring, all firms are bought by their national governments to allow the firms to continue operating. What will be the impact of this on prices and government revenues? Now that the governments are the owners, will they have an incentive to continue with liberalization? Can you imagine why this might favour firms located in nations with big, rich governments?

2. Look up a recent state aid case on the Commission's website http://europa.int.eu and explain the economic and legal reasoning behind the Commission's decision using the diagrams in this chapter.

3. Look up a recent abuse of dominant position case (Article 82) on the Commission's website http://europa.int.eu and explain the economic and legal reasoning behind the Commission's decision using the diagrams in this chapter.

4. Look up a recent antitrust case (Article 81) on the Commission's website http://europa.int.eu and explain the economic and legal reasoning behind the Commission's decision using the diagrams in this chapter.

Essay questions

1. When the Single Market Programme was launched in the mid-1980s, European leaders asserted that it would improve the competitiveness of European firms *vis-à-vis* US firms. Explain how one can make sense of this assertion by extending the reasoning in this chapter, and explain why this makes EU competition policy an important part of Europe's external competitiveness.

2. While the case for strengthening European-wide competition policy in tandem with the Single Market Programme is clear, is it obvious that this task should be allocated to the EU level instead of being left in the hands of Member States?

3. Some EU members allow their companies to engage in 'anti-takeover' practices. Discuss how differences in EU members' laws concerning these practices might be viewed as unfair when EU industry is being transformed by a wave of mergers and acquisitions.

4. Read about the EU's Lisbon Strategy and use the reasoning and logic in this chapter to explain the role that EU leaders expected competition policy to play in making the EU the world's most competitive economy by 2010.

Further reading: the aficionado's corner

For a very accessible introduction to EU competition policy, see D. Neven, P. Seabright and M. Nutall (1996) *Fishing for Minnows*, CEPR, London.

Every interested reader should at least skim through the most recent version of the Commission's document, *Competition Policy and the Consumer*. This presents a succinct and authoritative presentation of EU competition policy. It also presents a large number of examples of EU competition policy in action (most of the examples in this chapter are based on these).

Useful website

The website of DG Competition has several highly accessible accounts of EU competition policy and information on recent cases; see http://europa.eu.int/comm/competition/.

References

Bannerman, E. (2002) *The Future of EU Competition Policy*, Centre for European Reform, London. Downloadable from http://www.cer.org.uk/publications/index.html.

Mas-Colell, A., M. Whinston and J.R. Green (1995) *Microeconomic Theory*, Oxford University Press, New York.

The European economy stands or falls on our ability to keep markets open, to open new markets, and to develop new areas where Europe's inventors, investors and entrepreneurs can trade . . .

Peter Mandelson, EU Trade Commissioner

Chapter

12 EU trade policy

INTRODUCTION

The EU is the world's biggest trader. Counting EU exporters within the EU and with third nations, the EU accounts for about 40 per cent of world trade, and its share of trade in services is even greater. Three of the EU25 are individually in the top ten trading nations in the world (Germany, the UK and France). The EU is also a leader in the world trade system, both as a key player in the World Trade Organization (WTO) and as a prolific signer of bilateral trade agreements. While the EU has been one of the staunchest supporters of the WTO's trade rules, many observers view EU trade policy – especially its policy on agricultural goods – as a major obstacle to greater liberalization worldwide. For example, as this edition went to press, disputes over EU agricultural policies were one of the biggest stumbling blocks to the worldwide talks on trade liberalization known as the Doha Round. Other critics claim that EU external trade policy is particularly harmful to the world's poorest nations since the EU puts up its highest barriers against the goods that they are best able to export.

This chapter covers EU trade policy by presenting the basic facts on EU trade, covering the EU's institutional arrangements as concern trade policy, and finally summarizing the EU's policies towards its various trade partners. It is important to note that EU trade policy – like so much about the Union – is mind-numbingly complex. There is a whole army of specialists who do nothing but follow EU trade issues, and most of these have to specialize in a particular area in order to master the detail. Plainly, then, this chapter cannot come even close to surveying all of EU trade policy. Its goal is rather to present the broad outlines and key issues. Readers who wish to find greater detail on a particular trade partner, sector or policy should start with the European Commission's website http://europa.eu.int/comm/trade/.

12.1 Pattern of trade: facts

The EU trades mainly with Europe, especially with itself, as Fig. 12.1 shows. The top diagram shows the share of EU exports that goes to the EU's various partners. The figures include EU sales to non-EU nations as well as exports from one EU nation to another. This gives a perspective on the relative importance of intra-EU trade and external trade. The main points are:

★ Two-thirds of EU25 exports are to other EU25 nations. More than 90 per cent of this is actually among the EU15 trade, since the ten new Member States are fairly small in economic terms.
★ If we add in all the other European nations – EFTA (Switzerland, Norway, Iceland and Liechtenstein), the Commonwealth of Independent States (CIS), Turkey, and all the others (Bulgaria, Romania, Croatia, etc.), the figure rises to three-quarters. In short, three out of four export euros earned by the EU25 are from sales within Europe broadly defined.
★ After Europe, North America and Asia are the EU25's main markets, but each accounts for a little less than one-tenth of EU exports.
★ Africa, Latin America and the Middle East are not very important as EU export destinations; their shares are each less than 3 per cent.

Rounding off to make the numbers easy to remember, we can say that three-quarters of EU exports go to Europe. The remaining quarter is split more or less evenly among three groups of nations: North America, Asia, and all other nations.

The pattern on the import side is very similar, as the bottom diagram shows. The biggest difference lies with Asia since it provides 12 per cent of the EU's imports but absorbs only 7 per cent of EU exports (i.e. the EU runs a trade deficit with Asia). The same is true of the CIS (mainly due to EU imports of Russian oil), but the difference is much smaller. The opposite is true of North America since North America accounts for a larger share of EU exports than of EU imports (i.e. the EU runs a small trade surplus with North America). The EU's trade with the rest of the world is approximately in balance, although it has been in slight surplus in recent years (not shown in the figure).

Again rounding off to make the numbers easy to remember, we can say that three-quarters of EU imports are from Europe, with the fourth quarter split into two more or less even groups of nations: Asia, and all other nations.

It can be useful to take an even closer look by separating out individual nations as in Table 12.1. Just ten nations account for about two-thirds of EU25 *external* trade, but the list is slightly different on the import and export sides. The USA is the number one partner by a very large margin, both as an importer and as an exporter. The next most important market for EU exports is Switzerland, but the Swiss buy only 30 per cent as much as Americans (still this is a big proportion given that there are 7 million Swiss and 300 million Americans). The number two supplier of imports to the EU is China, a partner that is now number three on the EU's export destination list; Chinese trade with the EU has been booming, both imports and exports, so China is set to become the EU's number two partner. Japan, the third economic powerhouse in the world after the USA and the EU, is the number four export destination and number three provider of imports.

The other nations that are big import and export partners of the EU are Russia, Norway, Turkey, Canada and South Korea.

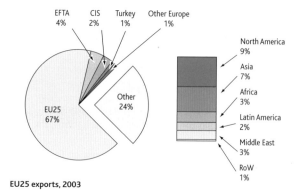

EU25 exports, 2003

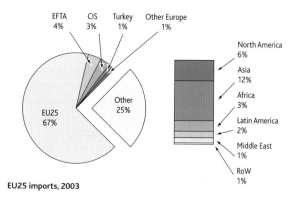

EU25 imports, 2003

Figure 12.1: *EU25 exports and imports by main partner*

Source: Eurostat. The latest data can be downloaded from Eurostat's new user-friendly service at http://europa.eu.int/comm/eurostat/.

	Exports (€ billion)	% of all EU external exports		Imports (€ billion)	% of all EU external imports
USA	226	26	USA	157	17
Switzerland	71	8	China	105	11
China	41	5	Japan	72	8
Japan	41	5	Russia	68	7
Russia	37	4	Switzerland	59	6
Turkey	29	3	Norway	51	5
Norway	28	3	Turkey	26	3
Canada	22	2	South Korea	25	3
Hong Kong	18	2	Taiwan	22	2
Australia	18	2	Brazil	19	2
United Arab Emirates	16	2	Canada	16	2
South Korea	16	2	Malaysia	16	2
Source: Eurostat.					

Table 12.1: *The EU's top ten import and export partners*

12.1.1 Differences among Member States

One of the things that makes EU trade policy a contentious issue is the fact that the various Member States have quite different trade patterns. Some members are landlocked and surrounded by other EU members, whereas others are geographically and/or culturally close to Africa, North America or Latin America. It is not surprising, therefore, that the importance of various trade partners varies quite a lot across the EU25.

Figure 12.2 illustrates this divergence. The reliance of Member States on imports from the various regions is shown by the size of the bars. The leftmost segment shows the share of imports from non-EU Europe. This ranges from about 5 per cent for Luxembourg to almost 80 per cent for Latvia. Geography matters a great deal when it comes to trade partners, so it is not surprising that non-EU Europe, which includes the Ukraine and Russia, plays a big role in the imports for the central European members such as Poland and the Baltic states. The importance of North America varies almost as much. North America's share in Irish external imports is about 40 per cent, whereas for the Baltic states it is 10 per cent or less.

The figure also shows some fairly natural linkages. The Iberians import a large share of their external trade from Latin America and Africa. Africa's is also over 15 per cent for Italy and France.

Asia's role is more constant, although it tends to be larger for members with easy access to the sea, such as the UK, Denmark and Poland.

12.1.2 Composition of EU's external trade

What sorts of goods does the EU25 import and export to and from the rest of the world? As Fig. 12.3 shows, the answer is mainly manufactured goods. The main points from the diagram are:

★ Manufactured goods account for almost 90 per cent of EU exports, with about half of all exports being machinery and transport equipment.
★ On the import side, about two out of every three euros spent on imports goes to buy manufactured goods.
★ Being energy poor, the EU25 is a big importer of fuel; about one in every five euros spent on imports goes to pay for fuel.
★ Other types of goods play a relatively minor part in the EU's trade.

About 5 per cent of EU25 exports to the rest of the world consist of food (more precisely, food, live animals,

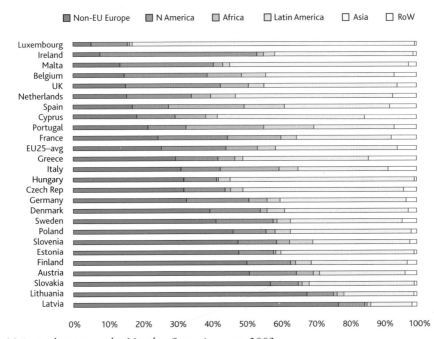

Figure 12.2: *Main trade partners by Member State, imports, 2003*

Source: Eurostat. The latest data can be downloaded from Eurostat's new user-friendly service at http://europa.eu.int/comm/eurostat/.

tobacco and beverages). The EU's imports of such goods account for 6% of all its imports. As the chapter on the CAP (Chapter 9) showed, Europe's trade in agricultural goods is massively distorted by subsidies to EU farmers, subsidies to EU exports, and high barriers against imports. If the CAP were fully liberalized in the direction the Commission is pushing for (see Chapter 9 for details), all trade distortions would be removed and the EU would surely become a net importer of food.

What with whom?

The situation illustrated in Fig. 12.3 aggregates all EU's trade with all partners. This is useful since it gives us an idea of just how dominant manufactured goods are when it comes to EU trade policy, and it provides an important perspective when we turn to EU trade policy where a key fact is that the EU has almost no tariff protection on imported manufactured goods. Moreover, it illustrates quite clearly that agricultural goods play only a minor role in the EU's trade despite the dominance of agriculture in political conflicts both within the EU and with the rest of the world.

The aggregate trade pattern, however, hides a set of facts that are important to understanding the impact of the

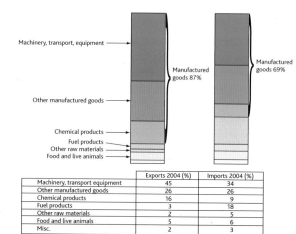

	Exports 2004 (%)	Imports 2004 (%)
Machinery, transport equipment	45	34
Other manufactured goods	26	26
Chemical products	16	9
Fuel products	3	18
Other raw materials	2	5
Food and live animals	5	6
Misc.	2	3

Figure 12.3: *Composition of EU25 imports and exports, aggregate trade*

Source: Eurostat. The latest data can be downloaded from Eurostat's new user-friendly service at http://europa.eu.int/comm/eurostat/.

EU's external trade policy. Simply put, the commodity composition of the EU's *exports* are approximately the same for all of the EU's trade partners, but this is not true for its imports. Figure 12.4 shows the facts.

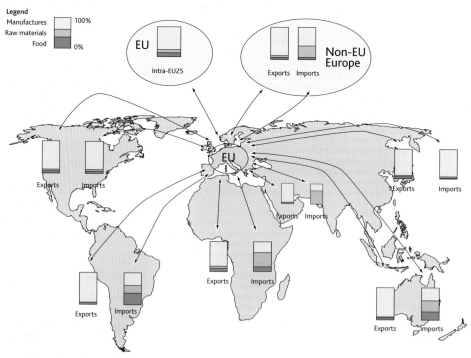

Figure 12.4: *EU25 commodity composition of imports and exports, 2004*

Source: Eurostat. The latest data can be downloaded from Eurostat's new user-friendly service at http://europa.eu.int/comm/eurostat/.

The diagram gathers EU trade partners into eight groups: North America, South America, Africa, Middle East, Asia, the EU25 itself, non-EU Europe, and Oceania (Australia, New Zealand and various Pacific island nations). For each group, the diagram shows two 100 per cent bars (these are basically vertical pie charts). The left-hand bar in each pair shows the percentage of EU exports to the region made up by manufactured goods (top segment), raw materials (middle segment) and food (bottom segment). The right-hand bar in each pair shows the same for EU imports from the region. There is a great deal of information in the diagram, but the main points are:

★ Scanning across the diagram, it is easy to see that all the left-hand bars are quite similar. That is, the shares of manufactures in EU exports to all regions are fairly similar, ranging from 85 per cent to 95 per cent. Things are much more varied, however, on the import side.

★ As might be expected, Europe tends to import a lot of primary goods – food and raw materials, including fuel – from continents that are relatively abundant in natural resources. Raw materials account for over half of EU imports from Africa and the Middle East, with petroleum playing a dominant role in these particular flows.

★ Food is never a dominant import for any of the eight groups (although it is for particular nations, especially small poor nations). The highest shares are for the EU's imports from South America and Oceania (mainly Australia and New Zealand).

★ The EU's import composition from non-EU Europe has a large share of raw materials (about one-third). This group, however, combines two sets of very different nations. On one hand, it includes the nations that sell mostly manufactures to the EU (Switzerland, Bulgaria, Romania, Croatia, etc.). The composition trade with these nations is quite similar to the EU's trade with itself. One the other hand, Russia and Norway are mainly natural resource exporters, with oil and gas dominating their sales to the EU.

12.2 EU institutions for trade policy

Formation of a customs union – which means the elimination of tariffs on intra-EU trade and adoption of a common external tariff – was the EU's first big step towards economic integration. A customs union requires political coordination since trade policy towards third nations is an ever evolving issue. To facilitate this political coordination, the Treaty of Rome granted supranational powers to the EU's institutions as far as external trade policy is concerned. This section reviews the allocation of the powers among the EU institutions.

12.2.1 Trade in goods

Trade policy in today's globalized world touches on a vast array of issues. Correspondingly, EU trade policy is extremely complex since it has to deal with issues ranging from quotas on men's underwear from China, to internet banking, to sugar imports. A good way to tackle this complexity is to start with the most traditional aspects of EU trade policy, i.e. trade in goods.

The Treaty of Rome assigns to the European Commission the task of negotiating trade matters with third nations on behalf of the Member States (Article 133 of the EC Treaty). In practice this means that the EU Trade Commissioner (currently Peter Mandelson) is responsible for conducting trade negotiations. These negotiations are conducted in accordance with specific mandates defined by the Council of Ministers (called Directives for Negotiation). When it comes to very broad and very important trade negotiations, e.g. the WTO's ongoing Doha Round of trade talks, an ad hoc coordination procedure allows Member States to be involved in each phase of the Commission's negotiations.

The Council has the final say on whether to adopt the trade deals negotiated by the Commission. When it comes to agreements involving trade in goods, the Council decides on the basis of qualified majority voting. The European Parliament has no explicit powers regarding the conduct of trade policy in general, but the Commission informs Parliament on a regular basis about developments in European trade policy. The Treaty also puts the Commission in charge of ensuring third countries comply with deals they have struck with the EU. This is why the Commission is always out front in the frequent confrontations between the USA and the EU, e.g. on subsidies to Airbus and Boeing.

12.2.2 Beyond tariffs

In the EU's early days, tariffs were a key trade barrier, so tariffs were the main issue when it came to external trade policy. Indeed, although the Treaty of Rome speaks of the 'Common Commercial Policy' – a name that suggests it should be much more than just tariffs – the wording in the Article provides only a suggestive list, and this basically mentions various forms of tariff protection.

As tariffs have gradually come down through fifty years of multilateral and regional trade negotiations, other barriers have emerged as relatively more important. For example, in the last set of WTO negotiations (the so-called Uruguay Round that lasted from 1986 to 1994), the key negotiating points involved trade-offs in areas far beyond traditional trade in goods. These included: trade in services (e.g. banking and insurance), intellectual property rights (copyrights, patents, etc.) and trade-related measures concerning foreign investment (e.g. policies that require multinationals to buy a certain proportion of their inputs from local suppliers). The Commission found itself in an awkward position with respect to the other major players such as the USA, Japan and Canada, since its formal negotiating mandate included only trade in goods. Moreover, the EU's economy and external trade have reduced their dependence on industrial products; the service sector is now the main source of jobs within the EU and accounts for a large and growing proportion of its trade with nations.

In reaction to these altered circumstances, the Commission has pushed for broader negotiating authority and the Court of Justice has usually backed it by interpreting very broadly the scope of the Common Commercial Policy (as defined by Article 133), at least as far as trade in goods is concerned. (The Court explicitly ruled in 1994 that trade negotiations on services and intellectual property could not be based on Article 133 and so were not part of the EU's exclusive competence on external trade policy.) Nevertheless, the need for a coherent EU stance on external trade – at a minimum, the need for a single chief negotiator – was apparent to all. The Member States have reacted by expanding the Commission authority in various treaties. The 1997 Treaty of Amsterdam took the first tentative steps, and the Treaty of Nice extended the coverage of the common trade policy to the fields of trade in services and the commercial aspects of intellectual property.

Since the Treaty of Nice, agreements on services and intellectual property are decided under the same qualified majority rule as applies to trade in goods. However, it introduces the principle of 'parallelism'. What this means is that decisions relating to the negotiation and conclusion of trade agreements are subject to unanimous voting in the Council if unanimity would be required for the adoption of rules on the same subjects in the context of the single market. For example, unanimity is required on extra-EU immigration issues, but trade agreements very often contain clauses on the free movement of specific types of foreign workers whose physical presence in the

country is a necessary component of free trade in services. To the extent that trade in services, such as banking and insurance, require a local presence, issues surrounding investment, services and free movement of workers are becoming increasingly intertwined. The principle of parallelism determines whether such provisions are subject to unanimity or qualified majority voting.

Changes in the Constitutional Treaty

Although the Constitutional Treaty is unlikely ever to come into force as written (see Chapter 2), many of the hard-fought compromises in the Constitution are likely to re-emerge in other ways. It is important therefore to note that the Constitution extended the EU's authority on external trade matters to include foreign direct investment (Article III-217). Other notable changes included a streamlined decision-making process (although the principle of parallelism is maintained), and an expanded role for the European Parliament.

12.2.3 Anti-dumping and anti-subsidy measures

Under WTO rules, tariff liberalization is a one-way street. Once a nation has lowered its tariff in WTO talks (such talks are often called 'Rounds', the ongoing one being the Doha Round), it is not allowed to put the tariff back up. This principle of 'binding' tariffs applies to the EU's external tariffs (the so-called Common External Tariff, CET). The principle, however, contains some loopholes, the most important of which are anti-dumping and anti-subsidy tariffs.

Dumping is defined as the selling of exports below some normal price. According to WTO rules, a nation, or more broadly speaking, a customs area (i.e. the EU), can impose tariffs on imports if dumping 'causes or threatens material injury to an established industry'. The EU, together with the USA, is one of the world's leading users of such measures, especially in iron and steel, consumer electronics and chemicals.

The European Commission is in charge of investigating dumping complaints. If the Commission finds that: (i) dumping has occurred (this involves intricate and somewhat arbitrary calculations), and (ii) that material injury to EU producers has or might happen, it can impose a provisional duty (that lasts between six and nine months). The Council of Ministers must confirm the Commission's decision before the tariffs become definitive (these stay in place for five years). Sometimes the Commission avoids imposing tariffs by negotiating 'price undertakings' with the exporting nation. These are promises by the exporters to charge a high price for their goods in exchange for suspension or termination of the Commission's anti-dumping investigation. In terms of EU welfare, price undertakings are worse than tariffs since the EU collects no tariff revenue. Nevertheless, price undertakings are often more expedient politically since they are a way of 'bribing' the exporting nation into not complaining too loudly about the EU's new protection. (See Chapter 4 for the economic analysis.)

Since dumping duties, like all tariffs, help producers but harm consumers and firms that buy the goods (see Chapter 4), the Commission often faces a tricky balancing act among Member States. Frequently, the EU producers are concentrated in one or a few Member States whereas there are consumers in every Member State. Typically the former want the Commission to impose dumping duties whereas the latter oppose them. For this reason, the Commission only implements anti-dumping measures when it believes that they are in the broader interest of the EU. For historical and institutional reasons, the EU rarely imposes anti-subsidy duties, preferring to deal with such behaviour as 'below normal' pricing.

Many observers believe that both the EU and the USA employ a cynical manipulation of dumping rules – especially the calculations that determine whether imports have been dumped – in order to provide WTO-consistent protection for sectors whose producers are usually powerful politically. The iron and steel industry and the chemical industry are leading examples.

12.3 EU external trade policy

The EU's external trade policy is extremely complex. For example, the EU has preferential trade agreements with all but nine of the WTO's 148 members. Moreover, each free trade agreement can contain hundreds of pages of exceptions and technical rules, and the EU often has more than one agreement with each of these partners. For example, the EU has a general agreement on trade with Ukraine (a Partnership and Cooperation Agreement), as well as separate sectoral agreements on steel and textiles. On top of this, the EU unilaterally extends duty-free treatment to some Ukrainian exports. Given that the Ukrainian example is typical of the EU's bilateral

agreements with over one hundred nations, it is easy to understand why it would take a lifetime to fully understand EU trade policy.

The best way to a broad understanding of EU external trade policy is by grouping the arrangements into categories. We start with the bouquet of trade arrangements that link the EU with its immediate neighbours. Readers who are interested in one or more of these agreements can find all the details on the European Commission's website; at the end of 2005 the URL was http://europa.eu.int/comm/trade/.

12.3.1 The European Mediterranean trade area

The EU25 encompasses almost all of western Europe and most of central and eastern Europe (Bulgaria and Romania are to join by 2008). The remaining western European nations participate in the single market via the European Economic Area agreement (Norway, Iceland and Liechtenstein) or the EU–Swiss Bilateral Accords. Although there is a multitude of exceptions that matter to specialists, understanding is greatly boosted by thinking of European trade arrangements as being characterized by two concentric circles, the EU and the single market (see Fig. 12.5). That is to say, every nation in the single market circle enjoys the 'four freedoms' with respect to every other nation in the circle. (Trade in food products is generally excluded.) The nations in the EU share even deeper integration in the political, agricultural and several non-economic spheres such as foreign and defence policy.

Euro-Meds

Trade arrangements in Europe go beyond this group of four EFTAns and 27 EU members (counting Bulgaria and Romania). The next most important group of trade links are the Euro-Med Association Agreements that the EU has with ten Mediterranean nations – Morocco, Algeria, Tunisia, Egypt, Israel, the Palestinian Authority, Lebanon, Jordan, Syria and Turkey – a group called the Med-10 for short. These agreements are free trade agreements in that they promise bilateral duty-free trade in industrial goods. They are asymmetric, however, in that the EU had to cut its tariffs to zero faster than did its partners. The EU has already phased out its tariffs on industrial goods and is in the process of gradually lowering trade barriers on most food products. The Med-10 have promised to eliminate their tariffs on EU industrial goods by 2010.

As usual, the full reality is more complicated and these general statements can be subject to endless qualification since each of the ten agreements is slightly different and the EU has multiple agreements with many of the Med-10. Here are several complications that are worth keeping in mind:

★ The EU market can be thought of as the 'hub' in a regional hub and spoke system of trade deals. As Fig. 12.5 shows, the exporters in each of these nations depends heavily on the EU market, whereas each individual nation is negligible for EU exporters. Morocco is a typical case. The EU market accounts for 71 per cent of its exports whereas the Moroccan market accounts for less than 1 per cent of EU external exports. This massive asymmetry in market-dependency gives the EU a great deal of leverage in dealing with these nations.

★ Turkey unilaterally sets its tariffs on industrial imports from third nations at the level of the EU's Common External Tariff, so it can be said to be in a customs union with the EU. Turkey, however, has no voice in the setting of EU external trade policy and this customs union does not apply to trade in agricultural goods.

★ The EFTA nations have signed similar free trade agreements with all the Med-10 in order to ensure that their exporters compete on an equal basis with firms located in the EU (i.e. so EFTA firms face the same tariffs as EU firms do). Indeed, this is true throughout the world: whenever the EU signs a free trade agreement with a new partner, the EFTA nations sign a similar agreement. This creates what might be called a 'virtual free trade area union' between the EU and EFTA nations. Or, to put it in terms of the hub and spoke metaphor, EFTA's practice of shadowing the EU's free trade agreement policy has the effect of making EFTA part of the EU's hub, at least as far as preferential tariffs are concerned. EFTA has pursued this strategy for decades; Turkey has recently followed suit since its customs union with the EU forces it to have the same external trade policy as the EU does.

★ The Euro-Med arrangements are more than free trade agreements since they contain provisions for financial and technical assistance from the EU and they address additional issues such as trade in services and foreign direct investment.

★ Several of the Med-10 are trying to engineer free trade deals among themselves. If they manage to do this, they would create a third concentric circle – a sort of virtual Euro-Med free trade area containing the 27 EU members, 4 EFTAs and Med-10; every industrial firm located in any nation within the circle would have duty-free access to every other market in the circle. As matters now

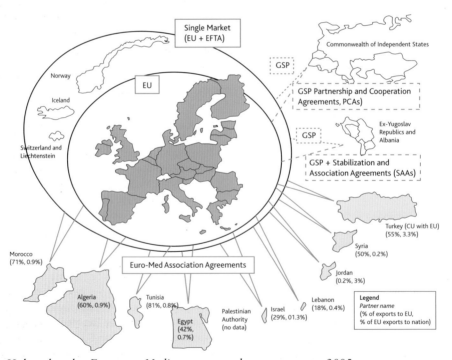

Figure 12.5: *Hub and spoke: European–Mediterranean trade arrangements, 2005*

Source: Authors' simplification of information on http://europa.eu.int/comm/trade/. Adapted from Baldwin (1994).

stand, the 'spoke' economies typically impose relatively high tariffs on each other's industrial exports.

Former Soviet republics and the western Balkans: 'GSP treatment plus'

The EU grants trade preferences to all of the nations of the Commonwealth of Independent States (Russia, Ukraine, Georgia, Belarus, Armenia, Azerbaijan, Kazakhstan, Kyrgyzstan, Moldova and Uzbekistan) under deals called Partnership and Cooperation Agreements (PCAs). These agreements address many matters other than trade. As far as trade is concerned, the deals are asymmetric. The EU has lowered its tariffs on most exports from these nations without requiring that the PCA partners lower theirs. Thus from the trade perspective, the PCAs can be viewed as generous versions of the Generalized System of Preference. (The Generalized System of Preference, or GSP, is a loophole in the WTO's non-discrimination rule that allows rich nations to voluntarily charge lower tariffs on imports from poor nations.) As usual, the EFTAns and Turkey typically mimic the PCAs by extending the same preferences to the PCA nations.

Lastly, we come to the bilateral EU trade deals with Albania and the nations that emerged from the break-up of Yugoslavia, apart from Slovenia which acceded to the EU in 2004. These Stabilization and Association Agreements (SAAs) are best thought of as GSP preferences with additional elements concerning financial assistance, trade in services, etc. Although it is never stated explicitly by the EU, most observers believe the SAAs will eventually lead to EU membership, whereas the PCA nations, for the most part, are unlikely to join the EU in the foreseeable future.

12.3.2 Preferential arrangements with former colonies

Europeans were big colonizers in the nineteenth and twentieth centuries and they still had many colonies right up to the 1960s and 1970s – the UK, France and Belgium in particular. Colonial ties almost always involved important trade relations; usually the 'mother' country's market was the main export destination for the colony's traded goods. When this aberrant system came to an end with the independence movements of the 1960s and 1970s, the former colonists typically wanted to maintain preferential treatment for goods coming from their former colonies. Since the EU is a customs union (i.e. all members must have the same tariffs on

imports from third nations), these pressures came to bear on the EU's external trade policy. In particular, to avoid putting the Common External Tariff (CET) on imports that had long been duty free, the Six signed agreements with many of their former colonies while they were establishing the EU's customs union in the 1960s. These trade deals were asymmetric in the sense that the EU tariffs were set to zero but the poor nations did not remove theirs.

When the UK joined in 1974, these old agreements (Yaoundé Convention and Arusha Agreement) were rolled into a comprehensive policy that was extended to the poor members of the UK's Commonwealth (this way, the UK avoided imposing the CET on these nations' exports). The combined group was labelled the ACP nations since they are located in Africa, the Caribbean and the Pacific; the new agreement was known as the Lomé Convention. This granted duty-free status to all industrial exports and most agricultural exports of ACP nations (with quotas on sensitive items such as sugar and bananas) without requiring the ACP nations to lower their barriers to EU exports.

The Lomé Convention was based on the now discredited belief that such unilateral preferences would help the former colonies to industrialize. Experience has shown that the preferences did not encourage industrialization or growth. Most ACP nations fell further behind while many Asian and Latin American countries enjoyed rapid industrialization, booming exports to the EU and income growth without preferences. When the Lomé Convention came up for renewal in 2000, the EU and the ACP nations agreed to modernize the deal.

The result was the ACP–EU Partnership Agreement, usually referred to as the Cotonou Agreement. This is not a hard-nosed trade agreement to win EU exporters better market access. As with the Euro-Med partners, the EU is a major market for the ACP nations, but the ACP markets are marginal markets for EU exporters. The best way to understand the Cotonou Agreement is to view it as an economic and trade cooperation aimed at fostering development in the ACP nations.

The big change from Lomé was that Cotonou commits the ACP nations to eventually removing their tariffs against EU exports. The idea is that gradually phasing in two-way free trade with the EU is a good way of integrating these developing nations into the world economy and that this is a necessary step towards development in the modern, globalized world. While the Cotonou Agreement lays out principles, the actual trade bargains are struck in bilateral deals known as Economic Partnership Agreements (EPAs). These have been negotiated with all 75 ACP nations (see Table 12.2).

12.3.3 Preferences for poor nations: GSP

As mentioned above, many scholars and policy makers in the 1960s and 1970s believed that rich countries could help poor countries develop by granting unilateral preferential tariff treatment for poor nation industrial exports. This notion was formally brought into world trade rules – i.e. the WTO, or GATT as it was known at the time – in 1971 under the name Generalized System of tariff Preferences, GSP for short. The EU was the first to implement a GSP scheme in 1971 and it now grants GSP preferences to almost every developing nation in the world.

As is true of all aspects of its trade policy, the EU's GSP policy is extremely complex. It helps to categorize the various EU GSP policies into two general groups:
★ General GSP, which is available to all developing nations at the EU's discretion.
★ Super GSP, which involves extra 'generous' EU unilateral preferences for nations that the EU

wishes to encourage for some reason or other. Currently, 'super GSP' is granted to nations that comply with the EU's idea of labour rights, the EU's idea of environmental protection, the EU's idea of combating illegal drugs, and to very poor nations.

The latter group, which is more politely called 'least developed nations', gets the most generous form of GSP preferences – a programme called Everything But Arms, or EBA in EU trade jargon. On paper, EBA grants zero-tariff access to the EU's market for all products from these nations, except arms and munitions. One must say 'on paper' since the goods in which these nations are most competitive are in fact excluded from the deal. Tariffs on bananas, rice and sugar – products where these poor nations could easily expand their EU sales – are to come down only in the future. Moreover, even though all tariffs on these items will be gone by 2009, the export quantities are limited by bilateral quotas. This has led cynical observers of EU trade policy to call EBA the 'Everything But Farms' programme. (Oxfam is particularly pointed in its criticism of EBA and EU trade policy more generally; interested readers may want to consult www.oxfam.org.uk.)

West Africa	Central Africa	East South Africa	Southern Africa	Caribbean	Pacific
Benin	Cameroon	Burundi	Angola	Antigua, Barb.	Cook Is.
Burkina Faso	Central Africa	Comoros	Botswana	Bahamas	Fed. Micron.
Cape Verde Côte d'Ivoire	Chad	Congo (Dem. Rep.)	Lesotho	Barbados	Fiji
Gambia	Congo	Djibouti	Mozambique	Belize	Kiribati
Ghana	Equat. Guinea	Eritrea	Namibia	Dominica	Marshall Is.
Guinea	Gabon	Ethiopia	Swaziland	Dominican Rep.	Nauru
Guinea Biss.	São Tome e Principe	Kenya	Tanzania	Grenada	Niue
		Malawi		Guyana	Palau
Liberia		Mauritius		Haiti	Papua N. G.
Mali		Madagascar		Jamaica	Samoa
Mauritania		Rwanda		St Lucia	Solomon Is.
Niger		Seychelles		St Vincent	Tonga
Nigeria		Sudan		St Ch. and Nevis	Tuvalu
Senegal		Uganda		Surinam	Vanuatu
Sierra Leone		Zambia		Trinidad and Tobago	
Togo		Zimbabwe			

Source: http://europa.eu.int/comm/trade.

Table 12.2: *Regional groups, ACP nations*

Currently, 49 nations qualify for EBA in principle. The list is: Afghanistan, Angola, Bangladesh, Benin, Bhutan, Burkina Faso, Burundi, Cambodia, Cape Verde, Central African Republic, Chad, Comoros, Congo (Democratic Republic), Djibouti, Equatorial Guinea, Eritrea, Ethiopia, Gambia, Guinea, Guinea Bissau, Haiti, Kiribati, Lao PDR, Lesotho, Liberia, Madagascar, Malawi, Maldives, Mali, Mauritania, Mozambique, Myanmar, Nepal, Niger, Rwanda, Samoa, São Tome e Principe, Senegal, Sierra Leone, Solomon Islands, Somalia, Sudan, Tanzania, Togo, Tuvalu, Uganda, Vanuatu, Yemen and Zambia. Note that the EU imposes restrictions on nations it deems to be insufficiently democratic, in violation of international law, or otherwise undesirable.

12.3.4 Non-regional free trade agreements

In recent years, a number of non-European nations have sought out free trade agreements (FTAs) with the EU. The EU is almost always open to FTAs (as long as they exclude agriculture) and so it has signed a number of these deals. In late 2005, when this edition went to press, the list included Mexico, Chile and South Africa. The EU is engaged in FTA negotiations with Mecosul and the Gulf Cooperation Council (Bahrain, Kuwait, Oman, Qatar, Saudi Arabia and United Arab Emirates). The EU announced that it would not pursue any new bilateral FTAs until the ongoing WTO talks, the Doha Round, are concluded.

12.3.5 EU's Common External Tariff

Although the EU has preferential tariffs on imports from all but nine nations in the world, those nine nations account for about one-third of the EU's external trade so the tariff it charges these nations – the CET – matters. The CET also matters since it defines how much of an edge duty-free treatment provides under the EU's preferential trade agreements. If the CET on a product is zero, then acquiring duty-free status via GSP or an FTA is useless for that product.

The EU defines individual tariff rates for about ten thousand products, so we must generalize to get a handle on the EU's tariff policy. The average CET rate is 6.5 per cent but this hides a wide variation. About one-quarter of the rates on all products are set at zero (mostly industrial goods, including electronics), and the average for industrial goods is 4.1 per cent. The average on agricultural imports is just over four times this, namely 16.5 per cent.

Figure 12.6 shows how the CET varies according to a finer disaggregation of products. The dark bars show the average tariff for all goods in the categories listed; the light bars show the maximum tariff in the category. The most obvious fact in the diagram is the enormous difference between agricultural goods and manufactured goods. Owing to the protection imposed by the Common Agricultural Policy, most food imports are subject to high tariffs, with the rate on some dairy goods rising to 210 per cent. The maximum rates on some manufactured goods are still high, but the average rate on manufactures is always below 5 per cent, except for textiles and clothing where the average is 8 per cent.

The fact that the CET is very low on industrial goods goes a long way to explaining why the EU is so ready to

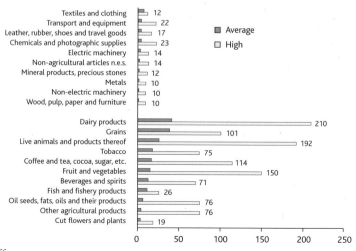

Figure 12.6: *EU tariffs*

Source: WTO, *Trade Policy Review: EU 2004.*

provide duty-free treatment to the industrial exports of its friends. To put it bluntly, granting zero-tariff status to the industrial exports of most nations has very little impact on the EU's market since the non-preferential rates are already very low. Moreover, for the imports where zero-tariffs might matter – the imports from the most highly industrialized non-European nations such as the USA and Japan – the EU is not keen to sign FTAs.

Likewise, the very high tariffs in agriculture show why the EU is reluctant to provide such treatment on agricultural imports.

12.4 Summary

This chapter provided a broad introduction to the immensely complex topic of EU trade policy. It started by presenting facts on the EU's trade pattern. The main points there were:

★ The EU trades mainly with Europe, with itself in particular.

★ The EU is primarily an exporter of manufactured goods.

★ Most EU imports are manufactured goods, although imports of primary goods are important for Africa, the Middle East and Latin America.

The next topic was EU decision making on trade. In a nutshell, the European Commission is in charge of negotiating the EU's external trade policy, but its efforts are directed by mandates from the Council of Ministers and all deals are subject to Council approval. The Parliament has a negligible role.

The last section in the chapter addressed the content of the EU's trade policy. The main points were:

★ Trade arrangements in Europe can be characterized as hub-and-spoke bilateralism. The hub is formed by two concentric circles (the EU, which has the deepest level of integration, and EFTA which participates in the single market apart from agriculture). These circles form a hub around which a network of bilateral agreements are arranged with almost every nation in Europe (broadly defined) and the Mediterranean. These bilateral deals fall into three groups: the Euro-Med agreements, the Stabilization and Association Agreements with western Balkan nations, and the Partnership and Cooperation Agreements with former Soviet republics in the Commonwealth of Independent States.

★ The EU has preferential trade agreements with its former colonies – the so-called ACP nations – that are currently asymmetric (the EU charges zero tariffs but the ACP nations do not), but they are aimed at establishing full two-way free trade agreements in the coming years.

★ The EU grants unilateral preferences of various types to almost all developing nations. These typically include duty-free treatment for industrial exports from these nations, but restrictions on the goods that they could most easily sell to the EU, namely agricultural goods such as sugar.

★ The EU's Common External Tariff (CET) is low on average, but is four times higher on agricultural goods than it is on industrial goods.

Self-assessment questions

1. What is the role of the Member States and the Commission when it comes to external trade policy? Be sure to distinguish between trade in goods and more 'modern' trade issues such as trade in services, trade in intellectual property rights and foreign direct investment.

2. What does the EU buy from and sell to the five continents, Europe, Africa, North America, South America and Asia?

3. What is the most protected good in the EU and which is the least protected good?

4. Why did the EU extend unilateral tariff preferences to former French and Belgian colonies, and why did it extend these to former British colonies in the mid-1970s?

5. Explain the term 'hub-and-spoke bilateralism' as applied to the EU's neighbours in Europe and around the Mediterranean.

Essay questions

1. 'In some sense, the trade policy has been the EU's most effective form of "foreign policy", and indeed up until the Maastricht Treaty it could be considered the EU's only foreign policy.' Write an essay evaluating this statement.

2. 'Some non-governmental organizations (NGOs) claim that the EU only provides developing nations with tariff preferences that are not worth much, either because the developing nations are not competitive in these goods or because the EU's CET is low on these goods so duty-free treatment is not much different from non-preferential treatment.' Write an essay evaluating this statement.

3. Select a particular European trade partner and investigate all the trade agreements the EU has with it and the EU's imports and exports to this nation. You can find trade data on http://europa.eu.int/comm/trade/, and information on trade agreements on the same site (but also check the more general site http://europa.eu.int/comm/world/).

4. Write an essay describing the EU's trade policy in a particular sector, such as steel or textiles.

5. Write an account of the EU's recent troubles with Chinese textile exports. Be sure to explain how this illustrates the allocation of competences and the difficult politics within the EU on trade matters.

Further reading: the aficionado's corner

A very lengthy and complete treatment of the EU's trade policy can be downloaded from the WTO's web site www.wto.org (follow links to the *Trade Policy Reviews*, or use a search engine such as Google with the words EU, Trade Policy Review and WTO). This is an independent review of EU trade policy which includes detailed presentation of its preferential, multilateral and sector policies. This also provides references to many academic studies of the impact of EU policies.

A very sceptical presentation of EU trade policy that includes explicit economic evaluation is Messerlin (2001).

For general information on the WTO, see Hoekman and Kostecki (2001) or the WTO's website www.wto.org.

For more on the EU trade policy with poor nations, see Hinkle and Schiff (2004) and Panagariya (2002). For more on GSP in general, see GAO (1994).

Useful websites

The best general site is the European Commission DG-Trade site http://europa.eu.int/comm/trade/.

For information on preferential trade agreements worldwide, see www.bilaterals.org.

References

Baldwin, R. (1994) *Towards an Integrated Europe*, CEPR, London.

GAO (1994) *Assessment of the Generalized System of Preferences Program*, US General Accounting Office, Washington DC. Downloadable from www.gao.gov.

Hinkle, L. and M. Schiff (2004) Economic Partnership Agreements between Sub-Saharan Africa and the EU: a development perspective, *World Economy*, 27(9): 1321–34.

Hoekman, B. and M. Kostecki (2001) *The Political Economy of the World Trading System*, Oxford, London.

Messerlin, P. (2001) *Measuring the Costs of Protection in Europe: European Commercial Policy in the 2000s*, Institute for International Economics, Washington DC.

Panagariya, A. (2002) 'EU preferential trade policies and developing countries', *World Economy*, 25(10): 1415–32.

Part IV

MONETARY INTEGRATION: HISTORY AND PRINCIPLES

Chapter 13: A monetary history of Europe
Chapter 14: The choice of an exchange rate regime
Chapter 15: The European Monetary System

Introduction

This part lays the ground for the analysis of monetary integration. Chapter 13 quickly reviews Europe's monetary history, showing how the adoption of a single currency follows from previous experiments, some successful, some major failures. It pays particular attention to the old gold standard mechanism because it can be applied to the internal functioning of the monetary union, to the disastrous inter-war period which still haunts policy makers, and to the natural evolution from the European Monetary System to the adoption of a single currency.

Chapter 14 takes up the general question of the choice of an exchange rate regime. It presents a short summary of the basic macroeconomic principles needed to grasp the significance of exchange rate regimes. It describes the various regimes that have been tried, emphasizing their implications for inflation and economic growth. It then explains how to go about assessing the desirability of each of the main arrangements.

Chapter 15 uses these insights to understand and interpret the European Monetary System (EMS). The EMS is partly of historical interest as it has provided some of the structures and incentives needed for the eventual adoption of the single currency. It is also important for the future of monetary integration since it continues to exist in a new version – EMS2 – that all future members of the euro area will have to adopt as an entry pass.

> The civility and internationality prevalent during the age of the gold standard have such charms for us nowadays that it seems almost sacrilege to ask whether these benefits resulted from the gold standard or, instead, coexisted with it by mere coincidence.
>
> *Leland Yeager (1966), p. 264*

13 A monetary history of Europe

INTRODUCTION

This chapter provides an overview of the role and uses of money in Europe (and the world) up to the creation of the monetary union. We start far back in the past, when hundreds of currencies existed in Europe. We next study the gold standard that prevailed until the First World War and was followed by a traumatic inter-war period. The chapter ends with a quick survey of the last half-century, thus providing an introduction to the issues studied in greater detail in the following chapters. The working of the gold standard is not just of historic interest, it also helps in understanding the internal functioning of the monetary union.

13.1 Metallic money

13.1.1 The world as a monetary union

From time immemorial until the end of the nineteenth century, money was metallic (mainly gold and silver) and a bewildering variety of currencies were circulating side by side. Each currency was defined by its content of precious metal and each local lord endeavoured to control the minting of currency in his fiefdom, chiefly because seigniorage was a key source of revenue. When public finances were under pressure, money was frequently debased, i.e. the metallic content was reduced through 'shaving' (rubbing off scraps of metal) or re-minting coins to reduce the precious metal in the alloy. Exchange rates were the relative values of different coins, really measuring the weights of precious metal in each coin. With so many coins circulating in every political jurisdiction, life was not easy:

> The multiplicity and diversity of 'sous' and 'deniers' is such that it would be nearly impossible to assess their precise values, and to sort out these various coins. It would lead to deep confusion which would increase work, trouble and other inconveniences of daily traffic.
>
> (Nicolaus Copernicus, *Monetae Cudendae Ratio;* written in 1556, first published in 1816, quoted by Guggenheim (1973); our translation from French)

It was only during the nineteenth century that people started to identify money and country, a part of the process of building up nation-states.[1] As we will see, the system operated pretty much as a monetary union or, more precisely, the modern monetary union in Europe recreates an old mechanism. This is why the study of the gold standard in section 13.2 is useful.

13.1.2 The first two European monetary unions

By the early nineteenth century, gold and silver coins circulated side by side. The exchange rate between gold and silver fluctuated depending on discoveries. Britain was the first large country to drop silver and adopt the gold standard. On the Continent, bimetallism survived much longer, even though some countries (Germany, the Netherlands, the Scandinavian countries) favoured silver, until gold discoveries in the 1850s resulted in the disappearance of silver money on much of the Continent.[2]

To preserve bimetallism, Belgium, France, Italy and Switzerland formed the Latin European Monetary Union in 1865 – a distant ancestor of today's monetary union. Greece joined in 1868. That effort foundered following the Franco-German war of 1870–71, when the newly established German empire shifted from silver to gold and weakened French finances by imposing war reparations to be paid in gold. When silver discoveries in Nevada depressed the price of silver, the Latin European Monetary Union was abandoned in 1878 and gold became the monetary standard.

The Scandinavian Monetary Union was created in 1873 by Denmark, Norway and Sweden, as part of the

---

[1] Germany and Italy achieved political unification late in that century, and many different currencies still circulated there well into the 1850s. It took Italy two decades after its political unification in 1861 to achieve monetary unification and, when the German Reich was created in 1871, different monetary standards survived until the Bank of Prussia unified German monies.

[2] This is an illustration of Gresham's law, which states that 'bad money drives out good'. If two monies circulate alongside each other (e.g. gold and silver), and one of the currencies becomes overvalued, that currency is hoarded, so that the other, depreciated, currency is the only one that circulates.

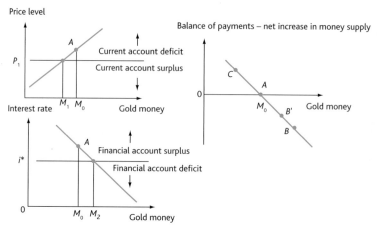

Figure 13.1: *Hume's price–specie mechanism*

'Scandinavianism' movement in support of the symbol of a common krona. These countries' currencies circulated widely in each other's territories. At the outbreak of the First World War, the Scandinavian Monetary Union ceased to exist, and was officially pronounced dead in 1924.

These precedents are merely of historical interest. Currencies were still based on metal so monetary unions amounted to nothing more than harmonized coinage. They were not associated with any trade agreement and, more importantly, there was no common central bank and very little coordination among the national monetary authorities. When external conditions became difficult (the fall of the price of silver in the case of the Latin European Monetary Union, and the dislocations of war in the case of the Scandinavian Monetary Union), each country reacted in its own way to protect its own interests.

13.2 The gold standard

13.2.1 The link between money and the balance of payments: trade flows

The classic gold standard years are conventionally set as the period 1880–1914, followed by largely unsuccessful attempts during the inter-war period to rebuild the system, as explained in section 13.3. A popular mystique attributes great merits to the gold standard – a taste of good old times when things were better and simpler. The truth is less rosy. The gold standard was a period of frequent financial crises, armed conflicts, uneven growth and occasional depressions accompanied by high unemployment and waves of bankruptcies. Even the exchange rates were not very stable.

The working of the gold standard is described by Hume's price–specie mechanism (see Box 13.1). This mechanism is well worth a visit, as it also applies to the working of the EMU. It is based on two familiar macroeconomic principles: the long-run neutrality of money and the effect of money on interest rates.[3]

The neutrality of money states that the rate of inflation is driven by the rate of growth of money, at least in the long run. This is represented in the upper-left panel of Fig. 13.1 by the upward-sloping schedule: more money eventually results in higher domestic prices. Next, in the same panel, we add international competition: if the price of domestic goods P exceeds the price $P*$ of foreign goods, exports decline, imports rise, and the current account worsens.[4] The horizontal line corresponds to the price level P_1 for which exports equal imports and the current account is in equilibrium. Moving upwards, the price level rises and the current account swings into deficit. The area below the horizontal line corresponds to lower prices and current account surpluses. External equilibrium is achieved when the money stock is M_1.

Under the pure gold standard, the stock of money is the quantity of gold held in the country. Where is the gold coming from? Some of it may be dug out from the ground, but Europe has been notoriously poor in that respect and we may as well ignore this source. The rest has to be imported. Some gold may be imported for use in jewellery or production; this is gold-commodity and it is part of the current account. Gold money is different: ignoring for the time being financial flows, gold money is earned through exports and spent on imports. Thus a current account surplus results in an inflow of gold money, the modern-day

[3] Both principles are presented in Chapter 14.

[4] It is the trade balance that changes. It is assumed that the other components of the current account remain unaffected.

Box 13.1

David Hume (1711–76)

National Galleries of Scotland

Born in 1711 to a well-to-do family in Berwickshire, Scotland, Hume has mostly written on philosophy, including the *Principles of Morals* (1751) which founded, among other things, the theory of utility. His works were highly influential even though they were denounced at the time as sceptical and atheistic. His economic thinking, mainly contained in *Political Discourses* (1752), had a large impact on Adam Smith and Thomas Malthus.

equivalent of the accumulation of foreign exchange reserves, the counterpart to a balance of payments surplus.

The downward-sloping schedule in the right-hand panel of Fig. 13.1 summarizes this point; it shows that the higher the stock of money, the more the balance of payment deteriorates. Consider point B, where a high stock of money means high prices and an external deficit: gold is flowing out and the stock of gold money contracts. As this happens, we move to a point such as B' where prices are lower and the deficit is reduced. At B' the deficit is not yet fully eliminated, gold is still flowing out and the money stock keeps contracting, so we continue moving up and to the left until point A is reached. At point A, the price level is just 'right', the balance of payments is in equilibrium and the money stock is stabilized. Obviously, a surplus such as point C will trigger an inflow of money (specie) and an increase in prices, bringing the economy gradually to point A. This link between money and external balance is Hume's price–specie mechanism.

13.2.2 The link between money and the balance of payments: financial flows

The link from the balance of payments to the money stock is instantaneous but prices are rather sticky, so the link from the money supply to the price level takes time. In the shorter run, most of the action takes place in the financial sector, which has been overlooked so far.

The downward supply schedule in the lower part of the left-hand panel of Fig. 13.1 represents a key aspect of the money market: an increase in the stock of money results in a lower interest rate. When the domestic interest rate is below the rate i^* prevailing abroad, it pays to borrow gold at home where interest is low and to ship it abroad for lending at the higher interest rate. The financial account is in equilibrium when the domestic interest rate is the same as it is abroad. Above this line, the financial account is in surplus; below it, it is in deficit. The financial account is balanced when the stock of gold money is M_2. If the stock of gold exceeds M_2, the interest rate is lower than i^*, capital flows out, gold is shipped abroad and the money supply contracts.

Changes in the money supply affect both components of the balance of payments – the current and the financial accounts – in the same direction: a large stock of money means an external deficit because prices rise and an outflow of gold because the interest rate declines. The capital flow route is very fast while the trade route is slower, but both work in the same direction. The right-hand panel of Fig. 13.1 can be reinterpreted as consolidating both routes through the current and financial accounts.

13.2.3 Automaticity: theory and practice

The right-hand panel of Fig. 13.1 shows why balance of payment imbalances are automatically corrected. To the right of point A, money is in excess of M_0 and external deficits automatically translate into outflows of gold, which eventually drive the stock of money back to M_0. To the left of point A, the balance of payments is in surplus and gold inflows raise the stock of money. Note that point A may correspond to imbalances in both the current and capital accounts. For example, as drawn, point A corresponds to a position between M_1 and M_2, where a deficit in the current account exactly matches a capital account surplus.

The automatic return to external balance is the main advantage of the gold standard. A country in deficit, for example, loses gold. As the money supply declines, in the shorter run, the interest rate rises, which attracts capital and partly helps to finance the current account deficit. Over time, money supply stringency creates slack in the economy, growth declines and unemployment rises, which exerts downward pressure on both prices and wages. All markets (financial, goods and labour) work towards eliminating the external imbalance and there is no need for the government to intervene. Note also that there is no monetary policy since the stock of gold money is determined endogenously.

This automaticity depends on the adherence to three principles, known as the 'rules of the game':

* Full gold convertibility at fixed price of banknotes issued by central banks, so that paper money is merely a convenient surrogate for gold.
* Full backing. The central bank holds at least as much gold as it has issued banknotes. In the presence of gold inflows, the central bank prints money; with gold outflows it retires previously created paper money.
* Complete freedom in trade and capital movements, so as not to interfere with the two elements of the adjustment mechanism.

In practice the theory did not work entirely smoothly, for a number of reasons. Bringing prices and wages down can be a long drawn out process involving painful recessions. In addition, the world supply of money was growing along with gold discoveries, while demand for money was driven up by output growth. There was no reason for the two to grow harmoniously together, and when gold discoveries accelerated, so did world inflation (yet it always remained mild by modern standards). When growth outpaced gold production, money was scarce, which led to protracted recessions, and it then became natural to supplement gold money with paper money issued by the central banks. In fact, to make up for the scarcity of gold, privately issued bills of exchange had started to circulate as early as the end of the eighteenth century. That pre-modern form of money acted as a buffer, but it also relaxed the key association between money supply and the balance of payments, and therefore the system's automatism. Governments facing large budget deficits and high public debts, or otherwise politically unable to abide by the tight discipline imposed upon them, chose not to stay in the gold standard. Thus the system was not universal, or even robust.

13.2.4 Lessons from the gold standard

The operation of the European monetary union bears more than a passing resemblance to the gold standard.

The euro replaces gold since national central banks are no longer allowed to issue national currencies and there is no national exchange rate. Within the eurozone, when one country runs a balance of payments surplus, it receives an inflow of euros, and conversely in the case of a deficit. Thus, the Hume mechanism is at work inside the eurozone. In particular, a deficit country can no longer use the exchange rate to re-establish its competitiveness, and adjustment will have to work through prices and wages, which have to increase more slowly than in the rest of the euro area, possibly even to decline. The comparison also means that the same 'rules of the game' must be strictly adhered to if national imbalances are to be automatically corrected. Put differently, tinkering with the rules would destabilize the whole monetary union and the rules are therefore part and parcel of euro area membership.

13.3 The unhappy inter-war period

The gold standard was suspended in 1914 when gold shipping became too dangerous, and the subsequent inter-war period left a bitter taste in Europe that still haunts the Continent. Belligerent countries had emerged exhausted from the First World War, facing huge debts, and over the next thirty years they would never quite fully recover. After the Great Depression, the world monetary leadership shifted to the USA. In many respects, the post-war European economic and political integration represents an effort to rule out any repeat of the inter-war disaster.

13.3.1 The First World War inheritance: from public debts to inflation

Wars are expensive and strain budgets, especially as governments are loath to raise taxes. The two alternatives are either to issue debt or to run the printing press, both of which were used during the First World War. During the war, prices were kept artificially stable through rationing schemes; when prices were freed, the accumulated inflationary pressure burst into the open. Some of the most famous hyperinflations erupted during this period, with Germany, Hungary and Greece facing *monthly* inflation rates of 1000 per cent or more in the early 1920s.

13.3.2 Returning to gold: three case studies

Post-war policy makers were committed to return to the gold standard as soon as practical, but at which exchange rate? Different European countries adopted different

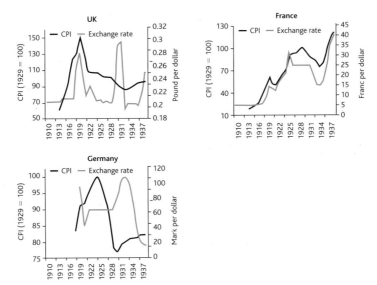

Figure 13.2: *Prices and exchange rates: France, Germany and the UK, 1910–39*

Source: Mitchell (1998).

strategies, which ended up tearing them apart, economically and politically. We look at three prominent cases: the UK, France and Germany.[5]

The UK

The UK, hoping to retain its traditional leadership in international monetary matters, decided to return sterling to the gold standard at its pre-war parity, 'to look the dollar in the face'. The forced appreciation of the pound is shown in Fig. 13.2.[6] This decision has become a landmark policy mistake. Since 1914, prices had increased much more in the UK than in the USA, and returning sterling to its pre-war value resulted in overvaluation. The only solution was to bring prices back down through deflation, a lengthy and painful process. The result was poor growth, a weak current account, and the erosion of trust in sterling, once considered 'as good as gold'. The City of London lost ground to New York's Wall Street.

Both industry and finance were weak so, when the Great Depression followed the crash on Wall Street in 1929, the UK was in no position to deal with yet more hardship. The exchange markets sensed the vulnerability and repeatedly launched speculative attacks on sterling. When, at long last, the Bank of England withdrew from the gold standard in 1931, sterling promptly lost 30 per cent of its value

with respect to gold and the dollar. An ambition was gone, and the price was high: a decade of miserable growth.

France

France, too, initially expected to return to the gold standard at its pre-war parity, but it soon lost control of inflation for several years. The French debt had grown much more than the UK's, and continued to rise at a brisk pace after the war on the premise that Germany's huge war reparations would eventually pick up the bill. When, by 1924, it became clear that Germany would not pay, inflation soared to an annual rate of close to 50 per cent, the franc was attacked and sunk. When inflation was finally stopped in 1926, the franc was stabilized at one-fifth of its pre-war parity.

France officially returned to the gold standard in 1928 but, in contrast to the pound, its exchange rate was now undervalued. Over the next few years, France ran surpluses in its balance of payments and the Banque de France accumulated large reserves. When the Great Depression hit, France escaped relatively unscathed as it was partly protected by its undervalued currency. Its apparently superior health triggered capital inflows, further swelling its gold stock.

Trouble started when sterling's 1931 devaluation was followed by many others including Austria, the Scandinavian countries, Finland, Ireland and Portugal. As a result, France lost its competitiveness. When, under duress, the USA too abandoned the gold standard in 1933 and the dollar was sharply devalued by 40 per cent, the franc overvaluation became unsustainable. France

---

[5] The reasoning implicitly uses the purchasing power parity principle, which is presented in Chapter 14.

[6] The exchange rate is expressed as the number of pounds needed to buy one dollar. A decrease means an appreciation, since fewer pounds are needed to buy one dollar.

and the other countries remaining on the gold standard (Belgium, Luxembourg, Italy, the Netherlands, Poland and Switzerland) formed the Gold Bloc to protect their now overvalued currencies. The Great Depression belatedly hit France, which faced speculative attacks, as had the UK ten years earlier. In the end, the franc was devalued by 42 per cent.

Germany

Germany never considered returning to its pre-war level. Its domestic public debt was huge and massive war reparations had been imposed. As in France, Germany's post-war inflation was high, but in 1922 it slipped out of control.[7] The result was one of history's most violent hyperinflations. A new Deutschmark – worth one million times the old one – was established in 1924 as part of a successful anti-inflation programme. The German economy started to pick up just when it was hit by the Great Depression. Having borrowed heavily abroad, Germany was particularly vulnerable and the Deutschmark soon faced speculative attacks. In 1931, the beleaguered government declared a moratorium on its external debt but did not devalue the Mark. Preservation of the value of the Mark restored in 1924 was seen as essential to dispel the ghosts of hyperinflation.

Having suspended its debt and being committed to an overvalued currency, Germany started to move away from a free trade system. In an attempt to prevent a further haemorrhage of gold, exchange controls were established. Like the franc, the Mark became even more overvalued when more and more countries devalued their own currencies. As the depression deepened, the Nazis came to power. To pull the economy out of depression, they combined public spending with wage and price increases. This further dented external competitiveness and deepened the trade deficit. The Nazi regime's response was to stop the conversion of Marks into gold and foreign currencies and to develop a 'managed trade' system through ever widening state controls on imports and exports. Bilateral barter agreements were worked out with one country after another, in effect allowing Germany to bypass completely the foreign exchange market. Step by step, the Nazis brought all international arrangements (trade and financial) under government control, with a view to protecting the nation's industry and building up a war economy.

13.3.3 Lessons for exchange rate arrangements

For centuries, the world had lived with metallic money. The emergence of paper money – *fiat* money, as it was called, to recognize that the new form of currency was wholly man-made – was a major innovation that radically changed things. It took many decades to understand this innovation and to design appropriate policies. But the learning process was painful. A number of lessons can be learned from this unhappy period:

★ Exchange rate misalignments breed trade barriers. Countries with overvalued currencies suffer from trade deficits and low growth. They soon view surpluses and good growth performance in countries with undervalued currencies as unfair. The next step is protectionism.

★ Rigid adherence to fixed parities hurts. All three countries met deep economic hardship for clinging for too long to an overvalued parity.

★ Piecemeal approaches to exchange rate arrangements do not work. Each country struggled independently, some left the gold standard when others joined, and there were no mutually accepted rules of the game. In that sort of environment, financial markets are highly unstable, which hurts trade.

★ Domestic policy misbehaviour saps fixed exchange rates. France and Germany could not join the gold standard until after they had eliminated budget imbalances and rapid inflation. The UK could not stay on gold because this required excessively tight macroeconomic policies.

★ Fragile systems eventually collapse. The Great Depression was a unique event, but other, milder shocks would have destroyed the inter-war version of the gold standard devoid of accepted rules of the game. The weakness of the inter-war gold standard may well have contributed to the spreading and deepening of the depression.

★ Exchange rate arrangements need a conductor. The pre-war gold standard was managed by the Bank of England and supported by London's financial centre. In the inter-war period, the City could no longer assume that responsibility and Wall Street was not yet ready for it. It is sometimes felt that the world monetary system needs a 'hegemon', a country that dominates the system and sets its rules.

---

[7] This is why pre-hyperinflation prices and exchange rates are not shown in Fig. 13.2.

13.4 The post-war years: fear of the past

13.4.1 Jump-starting Europe after the war

Another lesson from the inter-war period was that peace cannot be long-lasting in the midst of economic turmoil. After the Second World War, there would be no sanctions or war reparations.[8] A new superpower, the USA, was in place and ready to make sure that the world economy, and Europe in particular, would soon resume 'normal' conditions.

Prompted by the emerging Cold War, the Marshall Plan, set up in 1948, provided funds (mostly grants, not loans) to pay for imports from the USA, focusing on goods deemed essential for the recovery from wartime destruction. This aid lessened the pressure on exchange rates and avoided the kind of destructive misalignments that had wrecked the recovery from the First World War. Importantly, war winners and losers alike were part of the programme, avoiding continuing divisions in western Europe.

13.4.2 Bretton Woods as an antidote to the inter-war debacle

When the USA and UK started to plan the Bretton Woods conference towards the end of the Second World War, they were determined to draw on the inter-war lessons. There would be no return to gold, there would be a collective construction with active management of the international monetary system, and exchange rates would be neither set free nor rigidly fixed.

The Bretton Woods system[9] retained gold as the ultimate source of value, but the only currency directly tied to gold was the dollar (at the pre-war parity of $35 per ounce of gold). All the other currencies were defined in terms of the dollar. Exchange rates were 'fixed but adjustable' to avoid both unreasonable adherence to an outdated parity (over- or undervaluation) and an inter-war-type free-for-all.

The system was a collective undertaking with a clear line of command. The International Monetary Fund would wield a carrot and a stick: a carrot in the form of loans, and a stick as enforcer of both discipline and flexibility. It would be formally asked to give its blessing to exchange rate realignments when needed and would provide loans to sustain embattled parties in the face of speculative

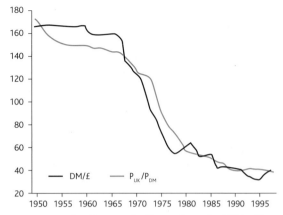

Figure 13.3: *Sterling vs the Deutschmark, 1950–98*

Source: IMF.

attacks. By providing the system's central currency and hosting the IMF in Washington, the USA would be the ultimate economic and political guarantor of the system.

Figure 13.3 shows the evolution of the exchange rate between sterling and the Deutschmark (DM) from 1950 to 1998 when the Deutschmark ceased to exist. The downward trend reflects the long-run tendency of sterling to decline against the Mark. This trend is remarkably well explained by the fact that inflation has been systematically higher in the UK than in Germany, as the darker line, which shows the ratio of German to UK price indices, readily confirms.[10]

13.5 After Bretton Woods: Europe on its own

13.5.1 The collapse of Bretton Woods, the great inflation scare and the Snake

Europe's golden years lasted until the late 1960s when inflation started to rise in a number of countries, partly because of local conditions, partly as a result of the Vietnam War. Staging an increasingly unpopular war, the US authorities allowed for sizeable budget deficits. These budget deficits were partly financed by money, which fuelled inflation and resulted in a loss of competitiveness and continuing external deficits. Inflation also eroded the value of the dollar as a safe standard while the external

---

[8] Not completely, however: German factories were removed to be rebuilt and German patents were confiscated.

[9] The Bretton Woods system is not presented here. For a detailed treatment, see e.g. Burda and Wyplosz (2005).

[10] The figure illustrates the purchasing power parity (PPP) principle presented in Chapter 14. PPP means that the nominal exchange rate E (DM per £) compensates one for one inflation differentials so that the real exchange rate EP_{UK}/P_{DM} is constant; then E and P_{DM}/P_{UK} remain exactly proportional as Fig. 13.3 shows. (Formally: $EP_{UK}/P_{DM} = c$ implies that $E = c\,P_{DM}/P_{UK}$, where c is a constant; in the figure, this constant is set to be 1 on average during the whole period 1950–98.)

deficits, paid for with dollars, raised doubts that the US stock of gold was large enough to back the dollar. Resting now on a wobbly anchor, the Bretton Woods system came under strain when the USA could no longer guarantee the gold value of the dollar. The demise came in two steps.

First, in 1971, the USA 'suspended' the dollar's gold convertibility and devalued by 10 per cent. The move was soon followed by a wave of exchange rate realignments designed to restore order in the system. But the system's credibility was undermined and the currency markets remained jittery, which led to the second decision. In 1973, the 'fixed but adjustable' principle was officially abandoned; each country would now be free to choose its exchange rate regime. This effectively ended the Bretton Woods era.

Europe's early reaction charted the way that would lead to a monetary union three decades later. France and the UK, two high-inflation currencies, had already undergone devaluations in the late 1960s and speculation soon started to tear European currencies apart from each other, as Fig. 13.4 shows. Concerned with the inter-war spectre of over- and undervaluations, the continental countries of Europe promptly resolved to limit exchange rate movements among themselves.

The first response was the 'European Snake', a regional stepped-down version of the Bretton Woods system designed to limit intra-European exchange rate fluctuations (see Box 13.2). But the Snake was not equipped to survive the hectic conditions of the 1970s. Partly as a result of the first oil shock of 1973–74, inflation had become a central preoccupation. However, the determination to combat inflation varied greatly in Europe. Table 13.1 shows that some countries (Germany, the Netherlands and Belgium) succeeded in keeping inflation in check, whereas others (e.g. Italy and the UK) did not. Maintaining exchange rate fixity under such conditions was hopeless and, indeed, several countries had to leave the Snake arrangement. More needed to be done, and the European Monetary System (EMS) was the response.

13.5.2 The European Monetary System

The European Monetary System (EMS) is studied in detail in Chapter 15; here we just look at its historical role. At the heart of the EMS lay the Exchange Rate Mechanism (ERM): a system of jointly managed fixed and adjustable exchange rates backed by mutual support. Formally, all countries that were part of the European Community joined the EMS in 1979, although the UK decided to stay out of the ERM until October 1990. As new countries joined the European Community (later the European Union), EMS membership

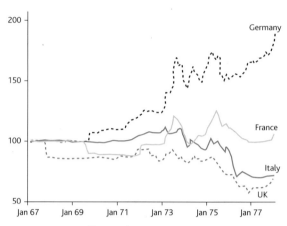

Figure 13.4: *Dollar exchange rates, January 1967–December 1977*

Source: IMF.

widened even though the UK left soon after joining and Sweden declined participation in the ERM (see Table 13.2). When the euro was launched in 1999, the countries that gave up their national currencies left the ERM. A new ERM was then designed and called ERM-2. Among the ten countries that became EU members in 2004, seven have joined ERM-2 alongside Denmark, and the three remaining ones are expected to follow suit.

During the first ten years of the EMS, inflation rates diverged markedly in Europe (Table 13.1). With fixed nominal exchange rates, the result was chronic misalignments. For example, the inflation differential between Germany and Italy averaged more than 10 per cent per year between 1974 and 1982; a fixed parity between the Deutschmark and the lira would have undercut Italy's competitiveness on average by 10 per cent each year, clearly an untenable proposition. Unsurprisingly therefore, realignments were frequent and usually involved several currencies at a time. Between 1979 and 1987, realignment occurred no less than twelve times, once every eight months on average. The implicit rule was to observe inflation rates since the previous realignments and change the parities accordingly.

This process was a bit too transparent, allowing the exchange markets to easily foresee the next realignment and speculate accordingly. As a result, most parity adjustments occurred in the midst of serious market turmoil, calling into question the sustainability of the ERM. The answer was to reduce the inflation differentials. Germany, the largest country with the lowest rate of inflation, naturally became the example to follow. As the other countries undertook to emulate its monetary policy,

The Snake in the tunnel

In 1971, in a last-ditch effort to save the Bretton Woods system, it was decided to widen the margins of fluctuations against the dollar from ±1 per cent to ±2.25 per cent. Non-dollar currencies, such as the Deutschmark (DM) and the franc, would now fluctuate by as much as 9 per cent against each other, as is shown in the upper part of Fig. 13.5. Under the Bretton Woods system, the exchange rates of the French franc and the DM are determined in terms of dollars. Consider the case, represented by both points A, where both currencies are at their opposite extremes with respect to the dollar, the DM is 2.25 per cent above the dollar, and the franc 2.25 per cent below it. As a result, the DM is 4.5 per cent above the franc. At the opposite extremes (points B), the DM is 4.5 per cent below the franc. The total amplitude of these fluctuations is 9 per cent. A number of European countries (the EC members as well as Denmark, Ireland, Norway, the UK and Sweden) felt that this was too wide a margin and decided to maintain their bilateral rates within a common ±2.25 per cent band of fluctuation. This was called the 'Snake in the tunnel' – a colourful representation of their joint movements with respect to the dollar, as shown in the lower part of the figure. Once the Bretton Woods system ended, the tunnel was gone but the EC countries resolved to keep the Snake, i.e. to limit the range of variation of their bilateral exchange rates to a maximum of 4.5 per cent. This led directly to the European Monetary System.

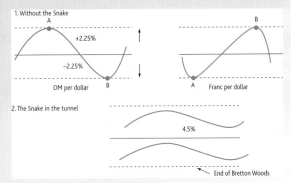

Figure 13.5: *The European Snake (all currencies vs the US dollar)*

	1960	1965	1970	1975	1980	1985	1990	1995	2000
Austria	1.9	4.9	4.4	8.4	6.3	3.2	3.3	2.3	2.4
Belgium	0.3	4.1	3.9	12.8	6.7	4.9	3.5	1.5	2.5
Denmark	1.3	5.5	6.5	9.6	12.3	4.7	2.7	2.1	2.9
Finland	3.2	4.8	2.7	17.8	11.6	5.9	6.1	1.0	3.4
France	4.1	2.7	5.8	11.7	13.5	5.8	3.4	1.8	1.7
Germany	1.5	3.2	3.4	5.9	5.4	2.2	2.7	1.7	1.9
Greece	1.6	3.1	2.9	13.4	24.9	19.3	20.4	8.9	3.2
Ireland	0.5	5.0	8.2	20.9	18.2	5.4	3.3	2.5	5.6
Italy	1.4	4.4	4.8	16.9	21.3	9.2	6.5	5.2	2.5
Netherlands	2.3	5.8	3.7	13.2	6.5	2.2	2.5	1.9	2.5
Portugal	3.0	3.5	4.5	20.4	16.6	19.3	13.4	4.1	2.9
Spain	1.2	13.2	5.8	16.9	15.5	8.8	6.7	4.7	3.4
Sweden	4.1	5.0	7.0	9.8	13.7	7.4	13.5	2.5	0.9
UK	1.0	4.8	6.4	24.2	18.0	6.1	9.5	3.4	2.9

Source: IMF.

Table 13.1: *Inflation rates*

	Joined	Left	Rejoined		Joined
Austria	1995	1999		Cyprus	2005
Belgium	1979	1999		Czech Rep.	
Denmark	1979			Estonia	2004
Finland	1996	1999		Hungary	
France	1979	1999		Latvia	2005
Germany	1979	1999		Lithuania	2004
Greece	1998	1999		Malta	2005
Ireland	1979	1999		Poland	
Italy	1979	1992	1996	Slovakia	2005
Netherlands	1979	1999		Slovenia	2004
Portugal	1992	1999			
Spain	1989	1999			
Sweden					
UK	1990	1992			

Note: Italy, Portugal and Spain initially operated a wider (±6%) band of fluctuation around the central parity than the normal (±2.25%) band. In 1993, the band was widened to ±15%, but Denmark has retained the narrow (±2.25%) band. All other current members of the ERM operate the wide (±15%) band. Luxembourg used the Belgian franc until the euro was created.

Table 13.2: *ERM membership*

the Bundesbank gradually emerged as the centre of the system. After 1986, each country was trying to anchor its currency to the Deutschmark and realignments became rare.

However, inflation did not always decline to German levels and misalignments kept growing. The attempt to hold exchange rates unchanged eventually failed in 1992–93 when a succession of speculative attacks nearly destroyed the EMS. Italy and the UK were forced to leave the ERM, while Ireland, Portugal and Spain had to repeatedly devalue their currencies. France, which had adopted its 'franc fort' policy of shadowing the Deutschmark, adamantly refused to devalue. In order to save the system from further unravelling, the margins of fluctuations were widened to ±15 per cent in 1993.[11] The new ERM had very little of a fixed exchange rate regime left, but the principle of fixed exchange rates remained, keeping alive the prospects of a monetary union.

With the impending launch of the euro and the disappearance of national currencies, the EMS seemed to lose its purpose. Still, since some countries opted not to adopt the euro and other countries were expected to join the EU, the EMS was re-designed and a new ERM-2 was adopted in 1998. It started in 1999 with just one member, Denmark, and has since accepted seven of the ten new EU members, which operate the wide ±15 per cent bands.

13.5.3 The road to and from Maastricht

Monetary union had been in the back of the minds of the signatories of the 1957 Treaty of Rome which established the European Community (the Common Market). Chapter 1 describes the first attempt to do so (the Werner Report that failed), and the second, successful one, the Delors Report.

Why was agreement on a monetary union promptly reached in the late 1980s? As the capital controls that had been in place in most countries since 1945 were dismantled by 1990, unfettered speculative flows could easily overwhelm the central banks. The old ERM was doomed. Convergence to the Bundesbank standard meant that, except for Germany, all countries had in effect lost monetary independence. Replacing the Bundesbank with a common central bank would allow them to recover some influence over monetary policy. Initially, and understandably, reluctant, the German government decided to back the project, mostly on political grounds.

The Delors Report was formally adopted in July 1989 at the Madrid summit. Two intergovernmental conferences were convened to study the creation of an economic and

[11] Germany and the Netherlands independently agreed to keep their bilateral parity within the old ±2.25 per cent margins. Belgium decided on its own to follow the same rule.

	Gold standard	Inter-war	Bretton Woods	EMS	EMU
Long-lasting misalignments must be avoided	✓		✓	✓	
Systems need to be built coherently	✓		✓	✓	✓
Policy misbehaviour must be ruled out					✓
Systems must be robust				✓	✓
Any monetary system needs a conductor	✓		✓	✓	✓

Table 13.3: *Lessons from history*

monetary union and of a political union. Both conferences reported in time for the Council meeting held in Maastricht at the end of 1991. The Maastricht Council decided upon the replacement of the European Community by an economic and political union, the European Union, and included a precise schedule to establish the monetary union.

On 4 January 1999, the exchange rates of eleven countries[12] were 'irrevocably' frozen. The old currencies formally became (odd) fractions of the euro, and the power to conduct monetary policy was transferred from each member country to the European System of Central Banks (ESCB), headquartered in Frankfurt. Ordinary citizens had to wait another three years, until January 2002, to see and touch euro banknotes and coins, but an undertaking that long seemed beyond reach, or even wholly unrealistic, was complete. Europe is the first instance of politically independent countries merging their currencies, reviving among themselves the price–specie mechanics of the gold standard.

13.6 Lessons from history

History never repeats itself, it is said, but the study of historical systems can lead to a number of lessons on how to organize international monetary arrangements. Five of them are summarized in Table 13.3.

★ Misalignments create deep problems, both in the country affected and in its trading partners. They often generate calls for protectionism, and inevitably lead to serious crises. Any good monetary system must have procedures that promptly eliminate misalignments. It was automatic in the gold standard system (Hume's mechanism), and explicit procedures were in place in the Bretton Woods system and the EMS.

★ Piecemeal system building does not work; there is a need for overall coherence. Hume's price–specie mechanism and the associated rules of the game provided for coherence in the gold standard system, while the Bretton Woods system and the EMS were carefully constructed.

★ No system can survive if policy misbehaviour is tolerated. No system, until EMU, was able to impose enough monetary policy discipline.

★ Every monetary system must be ready to cope with a large variety of shocks, ranging from political disturbances to occasional misalignments and policy mistakes. The EMS provided for mutual support, as explained in Chapter 15, and yet failed. The EMU is, so far, untested. It rests on Hume's mechanism, whose automaticity imparts a strong discipline to monetary policy.

★ Someone has to assume responsibility for the smooth working of the system. The UK looked after the gold standard system, and the USA looked after the Bretton Woods system. The EMS and the EMU rely on their own institutions.

[12] Austria, Belgium, Finland, France, Germany, Ireland, Italy, Luxembourg, the Netherlands, Portugal and Spain.

13.7 Summary

For centuries, money was mostly metallic. There was no link between nations and currency, but rather a bewildering and cumbersome variety of currencies that circulated alongside each other. What makes this period worthwhile studying, beyond the historical interest, is that under the gold standard much of the world was in effect operating under a system close to a monetary union. The system was meant to provide for the automatic elimination of payment imbalances through the working of Hume's price–specie mechanism.

Under the price–specie mechanism, a country running a balance of payment surplus accumulates gold money. The interest rate declines, prompting capital outflows; at the same time, prices rise, reducing competitiveness and worsening the current account. Both channels work towards eliminating the surplus. The opposite mechanism works in the case of a payment deficit.

The inter-war period was when paper money definitely replaced metallic money, creating a new situation. Botched attempts to resurrect the gold standard failed, resulting in exchange rate instability. Competitive devaluations were followed by rising protectionism and the disintegration of Europe, economically and politically.

The Bretton Woods system was designed to avoid the disastrous inter-war experience. It was built on a better understanding of paper money and on lessons learned the hard way. In many ways, the Bretton Woods system was the opposite of its predecessors. It relied on clear rules governing a system of fixed but adjustable exchange rates. It established a new international institution, the International Monetary Fund, which was both providing financial support and overseeing national policies. The system was built around the dollar, the new world monetary standard. When the USA failed to live up to its responsibilities, the system collapsed.

Continental Europe's reaction to the demise of the Bretton Woods system was to sever its dependence on the dollar and build up regional exchange rate stability. Lacking a clear rule and coherence, the first attempt (the Snake) failed. The EMS, the second attempt, succeeded despite a chequered history. It gradually led the Member States to latch their currency to the Deutschmark. From there it was a short step to monetary union.

Self-assessment questions

1. Using Fig. 13.1, work out graphically what happens following an initial balance of payments surplus. Why is the capital outflow, prompted by lower interest rates, only partially offsetting financing the current account surplus? Why is there automatic monetary relaxation despite capital outflows?

2. How can the Hume mechanism be applied to the flows of euros within the eurozone?

3. Why did fiscal and monetary indiscipline in the USA lead to the collapse of the Bretton Woods system?

4. How many countries can belong to the new Exchange Rate Mechanism? How many do?

5. Why has the EMS been called a 'greater Deutschmark area'?

6. During the inter-war era, misalignments led to competitive devaluations, which then prompted a tariff war. Explain the links from one step to the next.

Essay questions

1. The inter-war decline of Britain is sometimes imputed to the 1924 return to the gold standard at the overvalued pre-war parity. Explain how and why lasting overvaluation hurts.

2. Proposals to return the world to the gold standard are regularly put forward. Evaluate the pros and the cons of this idea.

3. Drawing lessons from history, determine the EMS's strengths and weaknesses.

4. 'The creation of the European Snake was a sign of US decline in monetary matters.' Comment.

5. Is the EMU robust? Write the cases for and against.

6. Europe's monetary history is sometimes seen as a blueprint for other regions such as Southeast Asia or Latin America. Evaluate what can be replicated and what cannot. In doing so, keep in mind both the political aspects of monetary integration and the evolution of the international financial markets.

Further reading: the aficionado's corner

On the gold standard, recent studies include:
Bordo, M. (1999) *The Gold Standard and Related Regimes*, Cambridge University Press. This book offers a comprehensive and modern analysis of the gold standard and its relevance to today's discussions.
Obstfeld, M. and A. Taylor (2003) 'Sovereign risk, credibility and the gold standard: 1870–1913 versus 1925–31', unpublished paper, University of California at Berkeley. The authors compare the 1914 gold standard with its post-1918 legacy and show that the earlier was more successful and resulted in lower foreign borrowing costs, a sign that risk was perceived as lower. http://repositories.cdlib.org/iber/cider/.

On early efforts at monetary unification:
Bergman, M., S. Gerlach and L. Jonung (1993) 'The rise and fall of the Scandinavian currency union 1873–1920', *European Economic Review*, 37: 507–17.
Bordo, M and Lars Jonung (2000) *Lessons for EMU from the History of Monetary Unions*, Institute of Economic Affairs, London.
Guggenheim, T. (1973) 'Some early views on monetary integration', in H.G. Johnson and A.K. Swoboda (eds) *The Economics of Common Currencies*, Harvard University Press, Cambridge, Mass.
Holtfrerich, C.L. (1993) 'Did monetary unification precede or follow political unification of Germany in the 19th century?', *European Economic Review*, 37: 518–24.

On the need for a hegemon acting as leader of the international monetary system:

Eichengreen, B. (1989) 'Hegemonic stability theories of the international monetary system', in R. Cooper, B. Eichengreen, R. Henning, G. Holtham, G. and R. Putnam (eds) *Can Nations Agree? Issues in International Cooperation*, Brookings Institution, Washington, DC.
Lyons, G. (undated) 'History shows EMU's success may depend on political union', http://www.euro-know.org/articles/rmu.html.
Snidal, D. (1985) 'The limits of hegemonic stability theory', *International Organization*, Autumn.

On the evolution of Europe to the monetary union:
Kenen, P.B. (1995) *Economic and Monetary Union in Europe*, Cambridge University Press, Cambridge.

Useful websites

The European Parliament's factsheet on monetary integration: http://www.europarl.eu.int/factsheets/5_1_0_en.htm.

General resources on monetary history:
http://www.ex.ac.uk/~RDavies/arian/other.html;
http://www.micheloud.com/FXM/MH/Glossary.htm.

References

Burda, M. and C. Wyplosz (2005) *Macroeconomics: A European Text*, 4th edn, Oxford University Press, Oxford.

Mitchell, B.R. (1998) *International Historical Statistics: Europe 1750–1993*, Macmillan, London.

Yeager, L. (1966) *International Monetary Relations*, Harper & Row, New York.

> The grass is always greener on the other side of the parity.
>
> *Jeffrey Frankel (1999)*

14 The choice of an exchange rate regime

INTRODUCTION

What are the reasons for choosing a particular exchange rate regime? To deal with this old but recurring question, this chapter starts by clarifying the link between exchange rate and monetary policies. Two key principles – monetary neutrality and purchasing power parity – bring up the importance of separating out the long run from the short run. The different types of exchange rate regimes are presented next, and their pros and cons examined. The main conclusions are that money and the exchange rate are just two sides of the same coin, and that there is no universally better exchange rate regime, it is all a matter of trade-off.

This chapter – a review of principles often developed in macroeconomics – sets the background for the analyses that follow, and can be skipped by well-trained readers.

14.1 The exchange rate and monetary policy

European monetary integration can be seen as an increasing effort to limit exchange rate fluctuations within the region. Why are most European countries attached to exchange rate stability, to the point of giving up their own currencies? One reason is history; Chapter 13 has shown that many lessons have been drawn from past misfortune. Another reason is economic logic. Chapter 16 looks at the rationale for a common currency, but the euro is just one extreme case of exchange fixity. How do we think about the choice between fixed and flexible exchange rates? This is the issue explored in the present chapter. To start with, it is important to have a clear view of the relationship between money and the exchange rate. This is the subject of this first section.[1]

How money and the exchange rate interact depends on how far in the future we care to look. The long run, a period long enough for the real and monetary spheres to be separated, is easiest. It is characterized by two important results: the neutrality of money and purchasing power parity. In the short run, real and monetary matters interfere, which opens the door to the use of money and the exchange rate to deal with undesirable cyclical fluctuations. Yet, the choice of the exchange rate regime affects the way policies operate.

Fundamentally, money and the exchange rate are just two sides of the same coin.

14.1.1 The long term 1: neutrality of money

A key principle of macroeconomics is that, in the long run, money is *neutral*. Monetary neutrality occurs when the money supply does not affect real variables such as growth, unemployment, wealth, productivity or competitiveness. Instead, increases in the nominal money supply are absorbed by proportional increases in prices.[2]

This principle is illustrated in Fig. 14.1, which shows differences in money growth and inflation between France and Switzerland. Monetary neutrality implies that differences in inflation rates between these two countries should reflect differences in their money growth rates, and France's exchange rate should depreciate *vis-à-vis* the Swiss franc at an equivalent rate. For the moment, we ignore the exchange rate. It is hard to detect any link between inflation and money growth in the first panel, which shows year-to-year changes. Clearly, there is a lot of 'noise' in the short run: money growth is quite volatile while inflation moves more smoothly. The second panel goes some way towards eliminating this noise by plotting five-year moving averages. A pattern clearly emerges, but the association is not perfectly tight. The last panel takes a

---

[1] This section summarizes much of the theory of open economy macroeconomics. Readers familiar with these principles can skim the section. Those who have never studied the theory ought first to understand it. For a complete exposition, see, e.g. Burda and Wyplosz (2005), Chapters 8–13.

[2] Formally, the private sector cares about the real money stock M/P when setting its demand L. The central bank affects the supply of nominal money M. Money market equilibrium implies that $M/P = L$. This condition can be rewritten in rate of growth terms: $\Delta M/M - \Delta P/P = \Delta L/L$. If the demand for real money is constant, we have $\Delta L/L = 0$ so $\Delta P/P = \Delta M/M$, i.e. inflation $\Delta P/P$ is equal to the rate of money growth $\Delta M/M$. If L is changing, e.g. it is increasing because the economy is growing, we still have the result that changes in the rate of money growth affect inflation one for one, given money demand: $\Delta P/P = \Delta M/M - \Delta L/L$.

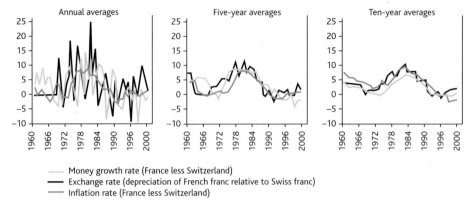

Figure 14.1: *Neutrality principle: France and Switzerland, 1960–2002*

Note: From 1999 onwards, the exchange rate of the French franc is computed by using the exchange rate of the euro.

Source: IMF.

really long-run view by displaying ten-year moving averages. The association is now almost perfect: the French money growth rate usually exceeds the Swiss rate, and this is accompanied by an almost equally high inflation in France. If neutrality is clearly not achieved in the short run, it is valid in the longer run, say five years and more.

Since the neutrality principle carries important implications for European monetary integration, a brief review of the underlying theory may be helpful. Figure 14.2 depicts the standard aggregate demand (*AD*) and aggregate supply (*AS*) schedules.[3] Each schedule explains a fundamental link between the rate of inflation on the vertical axis, and cyclical movements of output around its trend level, conventionally measured by the GDP (gross domestic product) gap on the horizontal axis.

The downward-sloping *AD* schedule represents the fact that inflation erodes the purchasing power of money (and other nominal assets) and therefore discourages consumption by households and investment by firms. The upward-sloping short-term aggregate supply schedule corresponds to a very different mechanism: the setting of prices. Producers of goods and services keep an eye on their competition and costs, including wages. In a recession, demand is weak, the market shrinks and firms attempt to improve their market shares by limiting cost and price increases, while workers, fearful of rising unemployment, accept wage moderation. In the opposite situation, in boom periods, demand is strong so profits can be made by jacking up prices and, as unemployment declines, workers push for higher wages. This explains why the *AS* schedule is upward sloping.

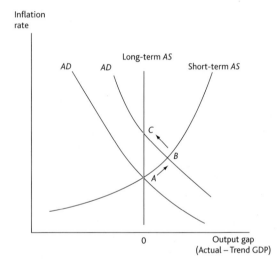

Figure 14.2: *The AS–AD model output gap (Actual − Trend GDP)*

In interpreting the short-term *AS* schedule, we have looked at prices of goods (finished and unfinished) and wages. We now have to consider how they relate to one another in the long run. If good prices (represented by the price index *P*) rise faster than wages (represented by the average wage *W*), the purchasing power of wages (measured as the ratio *W/P*) declines. Sooner or later, workers will want to catch up and will bargain for wage increases. Likewise, if wages rise faster than prices, firms face rising costs and sooner or later will have to raise prices. The long run is precisely the time that it takes for this cat and mouse game to end in a draw, that is, when real wages settle down.[4]

[3] Note that it is the inflation rate that is shown on the vertical axis. The framework is sometimes presented with the price level instead, but the substance of the analysis is not affected.

[4] Real wages rise secularly as productivity allows increases in standards of living. For the sake of simplicity of exposition, we ignore this trend.

14.1.2 The long term 2:
purchasing power parity

Monetary neutrality extends to the exchange rate, a principle known as purchasing power parity (PPP). PPP asserts that the rate of change of the nominal exchange rate between two countries is equal to the difference between the inflation rates in these two countries: the country with more inflation sees its exchange rate depreciate *vis-à-vis* the currency with a lower inflation rate. Since we know that inflation differentials reflect differences in money growth, the evolution of the nominal exchange rate is ultimately driven by relative money growth rates.[5]

We can see how well PPP works by going back to Fig. 14.1. The figure also plots the rate of change of the nominal exchange rate between the French franc (FRF) and the Swiss franc (CHF). This exchange rate is expressed as the number of FRF needed to buy one CHF: when the CHF appreciates *vis-à-vis* the FRF, the exchange rate increases. As before, over the short run, there is no visible link between the exchange rate, money growth and inflation. As the horizon extends to the very long term, things fall nicely into place. The rate of appreciation of the CHF – or, equivalently, the rate of depreciation of the FRF – follows a pattern very similar to those of the money growth and inflation differentials. In brief, why is the CHF typically appreciating *vis-à-vis* the FRF? Because money growth, and therefore inflation, is higher in France than in Switzerland. Table 14.1 confirms that over the period 1960–98 (when the FRF ceased to exist), the average annual rate of appreciation of the CHF *vis-à-vis* the FRF is related to the average difference between inflation in France and in Switzerland. This is PPP.

Average money growth: France less Switzerland	2.0%
Average inflation: France less Switzerland	2.1%
Average appreciation CHF vs FRF	1.0%
Source: IMF.	

Table 14.1: *France vs Switzerland, 1960–98*

An alternative definition of PPP rests on the crucial distinction between the nominal and the real exchange rates. A measure of competitiveness, the real exchange rate is defined as the ratio of domestic to foreign good prices expressed in the same currency. Consider the value of the euro in terms of dollars. The nominal exchange rate (E) is defined as the number of dollars needed to buy 1 euro – for example, 1.1 dollars for 1 euro ($E = 1.1$). The real exchange rate compares the dollar price of a basket of goods made in Europe to the dollar price P^* of a basket of goods made in the USA. To that effect, we need to convert into dollars the basket price of domestic goods in euros P (e.g. $100), and the answer is simply EP (e.g. $110). The real exchange rate λ is the ratio EP/P^*.[6] When the real exchange increases – a real appreciation – domestic goods become more expensive relative to foreign goods; conversely, a real depreciation represents an increased price competitiveness of domestic goods. PPP implies that the real exchange rate is constant since any inflation differential is matched by an equal change in the nominal exchange rate.[7]

From Fig. 14.1, we already know that PPP does not hold in the short run. The nominal exchange rate is seen to be quite volatile while prices are much more stable. This pattern is illustrated in Fig. 14.3, which displays the nominal and real exchange rates between sterling and the Deutschmark. Year-to-year movements in the nominal exchange rate are mirrored in similar but subdued movements in the real exchange rate. Both figures, however, show that PPP is approximately verified in the long run. In Fig. 14.1, long averages reveal that exchange rate changes match the inflation differential and Fig. 14.3 shows that the real exchange moves around a reasonably stable level. Indeed, the five-fold nominal depreciation of the pound since 1950 fails to leave the slightest impression on the real exchange rate.

Thus, like the money neutrality principle of which it is part, PPP is to be understood as a long-run feature. In the short run, the real exchange rate fluctuates, possibly widely, around its long-run real exchange rate level. This long-run level is sometimes called the equilibrium real

---

[5] If E is the exchange rate defined as the foreign price of the domestic currency, and P and P^* are, respectively, the domestic and foreign price levels, PPP can be formally expressed as $\Delta E = \Delta P^*/P^* - \Delta P/P$. The right-hand side is the inflation differential, the foreign inflation rate *less* the domestic inflation rate. It says that our exchange rate appreciates if inflation abroad is higher than inflation at home. The exchange rate depreciates in the opposite case.

[6] It does not matter whether we evaluate prices in euros or in dollars. In the text, we use the foreign currency (the dollar). If we use the euro instead, the domestic currency price of US goods is P^*/E (e.g. if the dollar price is $550, the euro price is €500), and the real exchange rate is still the ratio of these prices: $P/(P^*/E) = EP/P^*$, exactly the same as before.

[7] Formally, the real exchange rate is $\lambda = EP/P^*$. Its rate of change is therefore $\Delta\lambda/\lambda = \Delta E/E + \Delta P/P - \Delta P^*/P^*$. When the real exchange rate λ is constant $\Delta\lambda/\lambda = 0$ and we obtain the PPP condition $\Delta E/E = \Delta P^*/P^* - \Delta P/P$.

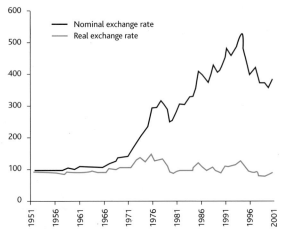

Figure 14.3: *Nominal and real exchange rates (Germany vs UK, 1951–2004)*

Note: The £/DM nominal and real exchange rate indices are set to 100 in 1951. From 1999 onwards, the value of the DM is derived from the evolution of the euro.

Source: IMF.

exchange rate. When the real exchange rate is above equilibrium, it is said to be overvalued, and it is undervalued in the opposite case. Over- and undervaluations are described as misalignments. How long does it take for misalignments to be corrected? Recent studies tend to conclude that the process is very slow. It is generally found that it takes two to four years for the difference between the actual and equilibrium real exchange rate to be halved.

The PPP principle is simple and intuitive. It is a good point to start thinking about the exchange rate over the long run, but it does not hold very precisely nor everywhere and at all times. Not only is it very slow to assert itself but it also suffers from many exceptions. If it works well for countries at similar stages of development, as France and Switzerland or Germany and the UK, it can badly fail in other cases, for well-understood reasons. A key reason, which affects the newer members of the EU, is presented in Box 14.1.

The long-term tendency of the real exchange to return to its equilibrium rate is one aspect of the general principle that, in the long run, real variables are unaffected by nominal variables. Whatever happens to the latter (money growth, nominal depreciation or appreciation, inflation, nominal wages), all real variables tend to return to their trends, and this includes output (real GDP), real wages and real exchange rates. In Fig. 14.2, the neutrality principle is captured by the vertical

long-term aggregate supply schedule. For example, an increase in money growth raises the *AD* schedule to *AD*: starting from point *A*, in the short run the economy moves to point *B*, and will eventually reach point *C*.

14.1.3 The short term

The interest and exchange rate connection when the exchange rate floats freely

We know that money does not have any real long-term effect, but what happens in the short term? An increase in the money supply, for instance, makes credit more abundant. This encourages a decline in interest rates with two main consequences. First, households take advantage of lower interest rates to borrow and spend. Similarly, firms step up investment in productive capacities because bank borrowing is cheaper and because stock prices typically rise when interest rates decline,[8] which makes it more desirable to issue new shares and expand. The result is higher aggregate spending, more GDP growth and a probable decline in unemployment.[9]

Second, investors will move some of their assets out of the country where yields become less appealing. This capital outflow results in a depreciating nominal exchange rate, when it is not pegged. The associated real depreciation represents a gain in competitiveness, exporters sell more and domestically produced goods tend to replace foreign imported goods.

All in all, the effect is expansionary as world (domestic and foreign) demand addressed to domestic goods increases. This is how, in the short run, money is not neutral. The main channels that we have identified are:

★ *The interest rate channel*. More money means lower interest rates, which is an incentive to borrow and spend more.
★ *The credit channel*. More liquidity encourages banks to compete more forcefully in offering loans.
★ *The stock market channel*. Declining interest rates are typically accompanied by higher stock prices. Firms find it interesting to issue shares and invest the proceeds. Households feel wealthier and consume more abundantly.

---

[8] Stock prices are a claim of future firm profits, discounted back to the present at the going interest rate. When interest rates are lower, future earnings are less heavily discounted, and stock prices rise.
[9] The curious reader will observe that more investment leads to more growth – more precisely, to a higher potential GDP – and wonder whether this is a cause of non-neutrality. It could be, although the evidence on this effect is inconclusive.

Box 14.1

The Balassa–Samuelson Effect

PPP works pretty well within the group of advanced economies, including the older members of the EU. However, it is not expected to apply to those new members that have been transiting from planned to market economies. Since 1990, starting with a low income level and poor production capacities of production, the transition economies of eastern and central Europe are catching up on their western neighbours, following the growth process described in Chapter 7. As they build up their production potential and adopt best technologies, they climb up the product quality ladder and produce increasingly more sophisticated products that they can sell at higher prices. As a result, their real exchange rates are on an appreciation trend. This is shown in Table 14.2, which displays the average annual rate of real appreciation over 1993 to 2005 for some of the new EU members. The real appreciation is decomposed into each country's average inflation differential *vis-à-vis* the eurozone and average nominal exchange rate depreciation *vis-à-vis* the euro. All these countries have experienced more inflation than the eurozone. For the real exchange rate to remain constant, they would have had to undergo a nominal depreciation of the same magnitude; in fact, their currencies depreciated by less, even appreciating slightly in the case of the Czech Republic. This phenomenon is called the Balassa–Samuelson effect, after Bela Balassa, a Hungarian economist who taught at Johns Hopkins University in Baltimore and Paul Samuelson from MIT, Nobel Prize winner and father of modern economics. They discovered this phenomenon independently.

Average annual changes *vis-à-vis* the eurozone (%)

	Czech Republic	Hungary	Poland	Slovakia
Real appreciation	4.4	3.4	2.9	3.5
Inflation differential	3.6	10.3	8.7	4.2
Nominal appreciation	0.8	−6.9	−5.8	−0.7

Source: *Economic Outlook*, OECD.

Table 14.2: *The Balassa–Samuelson effect, 1993–2005*

★ *The exchange rate channel*. The nominal depreciation is also a real depreciation and makes domestic goods more competitive.

The resulting expansion, however, fuels inflation. Indeed, in Fig. 14.1, changes in money growth are followed by changes in inflation with a lag of two years or more. Since prices (P) move slowly, a given increase in the nominal stock of money (M) is entirely translated initially into an increase in the purchasing power of money, the real money stock (M/P). Over time, inflation gradually erodes this gain in purchasing power and, eventually, the real money and the real exchange rate return to their initial levels, with no lasting expansionary impact.

The case of a fixed exchange rate

If the exchange rate is fixed (as is the case in the EMS), the situation is radically altered. With gradually rising costs and prices, the real exchange rate appreciates, competitiveness declines and a trade deficit develops.[10] At the same time, lower interest rates worsen the financial account, which exacerbates the balance of payments deficit. Committed to a fixed exchange rate, the central bank must intervene on the exchange market, selling part of its foreign exchange reserves and buying back its own currency. In doing so, the central bank reabsorbs the money it has created, and the money supply shrinks. In fact, to avoid a speculative attack, the money stock will have to return promptly to restore the interest rate to its previous level and bring capital outflows to an end.

The striking implication is that efforts by the central bank to expand its money supply are frustrated by the

---

[10] With E fixed and P rising, the real exchange rate $\lambda = EP/P^*$ rises and domestic goods become more expensive.

need to conduct offsetting foreign exchange market operations in defence of the exchange rate. Monetary policy simply does not work when the exchange rate is fixed. Put differently, monetary policy independence is lost because it is entirely dedicated to the exchange rate commitment. A central bank can control either the money stock or the exchange rate, not both. This is quite obvious when one realizes that the exchange rate is the external price of money: by undertaking to keep this price constant, the central bank is committed to provide whatever amount of money is demanded.[11]

In practice, exchange rates are rarely rigidly fixed, and are usually allowed to move within bands. If the band is narrow (e.g. the 4.5 per cent width in the pre-1993 ERM, see Chapter 13), the room for monetary policy independence is very limited. As the band widens, of course, monetary policy can increasingly be used, but there is then little substantive difference between a fixed exchange rate with wide bands (like the post-1993 ERM, with 30 per cent wide bands) and a floating exchange rate.

An *IS–LM* interpretation

The short-term non-neutrality of money can be described with the *IS–LM* graphical apparatus.[12] The *IS* schedule in Fig. 14.4 describes the goods market equilibrium condition. It is downward sloping because a decline in the interest rate results in more demand and a higher output. The *LM* schedule describes equilibrium in the money market for a given real money supply (*M/P*). An increase in output generates more demand for money and for credit, to which banks respond by raising interest rates, hence the upward slope of the schedule.

An increase in the money supply is captured by a rightward shift of the *LM* schedule. At the initial output level, interest rates are lower (point *B*). Spending gradually expands (as explained in section 14.1.3) and the economy moves from point *B* to point *C* while interest rates start rising, reflecting a stepped-up demand for money and credit.

As long as the interest rate remains low, as at point *C*, capital is likely to flow out – a situation that cannot last very long. What happens next depends on the exchange

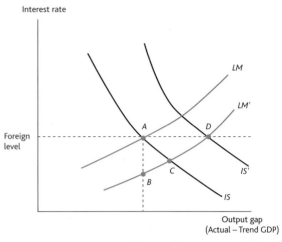

Figure 14.4: *Monetary policy in the IS–LM model*

rate regime. If the exchange rate is freely floating, the capital outflow keeps up the pressure towards depreciation. The continuing improvement in competitiveness is accompanied by rising exports and declining imports, raising demand for domestic goods. This increasing demand pushes the *IS* curve to the right, until it passes through point *D* (position *IS'*,) where the interest rate is back to its initial position and capital flows stop.

If the exchange rate is fixed (as in the ERM), the central bank is bound to intervene on the exchange market. As it does, the money supply shrinks and the *LM* curve starts to move back to the left. This process must continue until the *LM* schedule is back in its original position and the economy is back at point *A*. This establishes the loss of monetary policy independence under a fixed exchange rate regime.

14.1.4 The role of the exchange rate regime on the effects of fiscal policy

The other macroeconomic policy tool is fiscal policy. The *IS–LM* framework can also explain how fiscal policy operates in a small open economy. By changing public spending or taxes, the government affects total spending: raising public expenditures or cutting taxes leads to more demand, which is captured by a rightward shift of the *IS* curve in Fig. 14.5. Unless monetary policy changes, *LM* stays where it is. At the intersection point *B*, output has expanded – the unsurprising effect of an expansionary fiscal policy – but the interest rate has risen. The interest rate increases because the budget deficit has risen and needs financing: the government's borrowing increases upward pressure on the interest rate. In a small open

---

[11] This important result is sometimes described as the 'impossible trinity', which is presented in Chapter 16.

[12] This section can be skipped by readers familiar with this theory, which describes the short run as the period during which prices and wages fail to respond to changing economic conditions. A complete exposition is available, in Burda and Wyplosz (2005), Chapter 10.

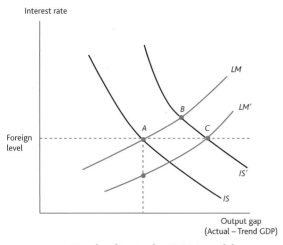

Figure 14.5: *Fiscal policy in the IS-LM model*

We have now seen that, under a fixed exchange rate regime, monetary policy is lost as an independent instrument, but fiscal policy works. Under a flexible exchange rate regime, the opposite occurs: monetary policy is fully available but fiscal policy ceases to be effective. These results, which apply to a small open economy (too small to affect the world interest rate), are summarized in Table 14.3.

	Monetary policy	Fiscal policy
Fixed exchange rate	Ineffective	Effective
Flexible exchange rate	Effective	Ineffective

Table 14.3: *Policy effectiveness and the exchange rate regime*

economy, the interest rate cannot really diverge greatly from the worldwide interest rate. At point *B*, returns on domestic assets are attractive, capital flows in, and what happens next depends crucially on the exchange rate regime.

If the exchange rate is fixed, the central bank finds that the capital inflows create pressure towards appreciation and it must therefore intervene on the foreign exchange market, selling the domestic currency to counteract the pressure exerted by capital inflows. The money supply then rises, the *LM* schedule shifts to the right and we move down the new *IS'* curve. As long as the interest rate is higher than at point *A*, capital keeps flowing in, and the process will stop only when the *LM* schedule has moved all the way to *LM'*, and the economy has reached point *C*.

If the exchange rate is freely floating, the central bank does not intervene on the foreign exchange rate market, it does not change the money supply, and the *LM* schedule does not move. Yet at point *B*, something must give in the face of capital inflows: the exchange rate appreciates. With sticky prices, the nominal appreciation results in a real appreciation, a appreciates loss of external competitiveness and a deterioration of the current account. Demand for domestic goods declines and the *IS* schedule starts shifting to the left. This will continue until the *IS* schedule has returned to its initial position and the economy is back at point *A*. Fiscal policy, therefore, does not work! Its expansionary effect is entirely offset by the contractionary effect of the exchange rate appreciation.

The underlying logic behind these results is both simple and central to the European integration process. Exchange rate policy, i.e. the choice of an exchange rate regime, is simply the same thing as monetary policy. Choosing one fully determines the other. Furthermore, the effect of fiscal policy depends on what the monetary authorities will do. If they are committed to an exchange rate target, they must passively validate the impact of fiscal policy on the financial markets, whereas if they concentrate on monetary policy alone, fiscal policy is frustrated by exchange rate movements.

These results are crucial to an understanding of what a country gives up by forming a monetary union with other countries. It should be clear by now that the answer 'monetary policy is lost' can be misleading. At most, the loss only matters in the short run since monetary policy is neutral in the long run. The real long-term implication of the loss of the monetary instrument is that the inflation rate is no longer established by domestic authorities. This may be highly desirable for inflation-prone countries like Italy, but worrisome for countries like Germany that have traditionally been able to contain inflation. This observation explains many features of the EMU, as is shown in Chapter 17.

These results also indicate that the choice of joining a monetary union cannot be evaluated without considering the alternatives. If the alternative is to let the exchange rate float freely, then there is a serious loss of monetary independence. If the alternative is a fixed exchange rate like the narrow-band ERM, the loss is very limited as the country imports the monetary policy of the country and currency to which it pegs its exchange rate – a point made clear in Chapter 16. Historically, as noted in Chapter 13, most European countries have demonstrated a great reluctance to let their exchange rate float freely. An exception is the UK, which has unsurprisingly displayed little enthusiasm towards EMU.

14.2 The range of exchange rate regimes

The debate regarding the choice of an exchange rate regime is very old, yet it remains as controversial as ever. Fashions come and go, and leave their imprint on history, but, in the end, there is no overwhelming case for any particular regime. The decision involves numerous trade-offs, with the pros and cons playing differently according to circumstances, countries and periods. This section looks at the rainbow of options and reviews some of the evidence; the following section recalls the ongoing debate, focusing on the issues that are most relevant to Europe.

14.2.1 When does the exchange rate regime matter?

Trivial as it may sound, the choice of an exchange rate regime only matters if the exchange rate has real effects. But if monetary policy were fully neutral, even in the short run, it would have no effect other than determining the rate of inflation. The real exchange rate would then never depart from its equilibrium level and the behaviour of the nominal exchange rate would be irrelevant for any practical purpose. Thus we care about the exchange rate regime only to the extent that the real exchange rate is affected by monetary policy, i.e. that money is not neutral in the 'short run'.

From Fig. 14.1, we already know that money is not neutral in the short run, and that the short run is not that short, it extends over a several years. So exchange rate regimes matter. To understand more precisely how, we need to have a good view of why money is not neutral. The theory is that non-neutrality arises because prices and wages move slowly; we say that they are 'sticky'. But are prices and wages really sticky? This is in essence the empirical question that has divided the economics profession at least since 1936, when Keynes launched his famous attack on the 'classics' who were, in

his view, ignoring price and wage stickiness. The debate has not yet fully settled but it is dying down. Figure 14.3 shows that movements in the real exchange rate reflect movements in the nominal exchange rate, thus rejecting neutrality, but one view is that the link is tenuous and short-lived. In that view, neutrality may be an acceptable simplification. Put differently, this view asks whether non-neutralities of the kind seen in Fig. 14.3 are large enough to care about them. If they are not, there is little reason to agonize over the exchange rate regime. For the sake of the argument at least – and also for realism – we assume that prices and wages are sticky enough, and that non-neutralities last long enough, for the exchange rate regime to matter.

14.2.2 What's on the menu?

There are two conventional exchange rate regimes: fixed and flexible. In practice, however, exchange rate regimes come in all sorts of shapes and forms, with many hybrids and a few extremes. In addition, except when the exchange rate is freely floating, all other regimes require choosing a foreign currency to peg to. The main anchors have traditionally been the US dollar and the Deutschmark, now replaced by the euro. An alternative is to adopt a basket of several currencies. This section reviews the various possible arrangements, going from full flexibility to full rigidity.

Freely floating

The simplest regime is when the monetary authorities decline any responsibility for the exchange rate. The rate is then freely determined by the markets and can fluctuate by any amount at any moment. Currently, the US dollar, the euro and the British pound are among the freely floating currencies. What are the drawbacks? One drawback is that the exchange rate can move a lot, which bothers exporters and importers. But the USA and the eurozone are large economies, so exports and imports weigh relatively little – they amount to just above 10 per cent of GDP. The other drawback has been presented in section 14.1.4: fiscal policy may become ineffective. Of course, the other side of the coin is that monetary policy is effective, and monetary policy is a more practical tool than fiscal policy because it can be activated swiftly and has less uncertain effects. In addition, because the USA and the eurozone are large and quite closed, fiscal policy is not fully ineffective.[13] The deal may be less sweet for the UK, a quite open and smaller economy.

---

[13] For large, relatively closed economies, the standard close economy *IS–LM* model offers a good description of the situation.

Managed floating

In small and open economies, the monetary authorities are concerned that a free float results in excessive exchange rate volatility. They display 'fear of floating'. At the same time, for reasons that will become clear below, they may not want to commit themselves to a particular exchange rate, this is 'fear of fixing'. What they wish is to intervene on the exchange markets from time to time, as they see fit. Managed floating, sometimes called dirty floating, is a half-way house between a free float and a peg. Central banks that adopt this strategy buy their own currency when they consider it too weak, and sell it when they see it too strong, but they refrain from pursuing any particular exchange rate target. This also allows them to use fiscal policy if they so wish, and they can do so as long as they accept the implied effect on the exchange rate. Japan is one country that is known to be frequently present on the foreign exchange markets.

Target zones

Target zones imply the choice of a wide range within which the exchange rate is allowed to move *vis-à-vis* its chosen anchor. This leaves some room for manoeuvre for both monetary and fiscal policy. The wider is the band of fluctuation, the more room is available, but also the closer is the regime to a free float. Practically, the central bank must intervene – and lose policy independence – when the exchange rate moves towards the edges of the zone, but it can also intervene at any time it wishes, even if the exchange rate is well within its band of fluctuation. Many central banks actually try to keep the exchange rate close to the midpoint. The authorities can either announce the range, or a midpoint with a tolerance for fluctuations around it, or refrain from stating any precise target and simply be active and enforce its implicit target range, which can be fuzzy. The current ERM (presented in Chapter 15), with a fluctuation band of ±15 per cent around the declared central parity, is an example of a target zone.

Crawling pegs

In a crawling peg regime the authorities declare a central parity and band of fluctuation around it. The characteristic of this regime is that the central parity and the associated maximum and lower levels are allowed to slide regularly: they crawl. The rate of crawl is sometimes pre-announced, sometimes not. The difference between a crawling peg and a target zone is not clear cut, since both involve an acceptable range: margins considered narrow enough to be qualified as a pegged arrangement are typically less than ±5 per cent around the official parity. Many Latin American countries operated crawling

pegs in the 1980s, as did Poland and Russia in the mid-1990s. Figure 14.6 shows the case of Poland; note that the rate of crawl was gradually reduced while the width of the band was progressively widened until the currency was allowed to float freely.

Fixed and adjustable

Fixed exchange rate regimes are characterized by a central parity *vis-à-vis* an anchor currency and a narrow band of fluctuation. The band of fluctuation allows the central bank not to intervene continuously. The parity is adjustable to allow the authorities to modify the parity without changing the regime itself. From 1945 to 1973, fixed and adjustable exchange rates were the rule world wide under the Bretton Woods agreement. The margins were initially set at ±1 per cent until 1971, and then widened to ±2.25 per cent. Between 1979 and 1993, the ERM also operated as a system of fixed and adjustable exchange rates, with a normal ±2.25 per cent band, which was enlarged to ±15 per cent after 1993. The current ERM-2 has retained the latter wide band.

This regime preserves the role of fiscal policy but it restricts the effectiveness of monetary policy. The adjustment option is useful in case of a shock and to deal with an inflation trend that exceeds that of the

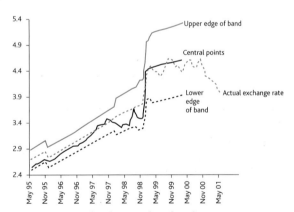

Figure 14.6: *Poland's crawling band, May 1995–March 2000*

Notes: The exchange rate is an index computed by the National Bank, which rises when the currency depreciates. The crawling band was introduced in March 1995 and lasted until April 2000 when the zloty was allowed to float, and soon appreciated. The anchor was a basket index whose composition was occasionally changed (in 1999 it included the euro, with a 55 per cent weight, and the US dollar, with a 45 per cent weight). The vertical scale (zloty per euro) is inverted so that an upward movement represents a nominal appreciation.

Source: National Bank of Poland.

anchor currency and therefore calls for realignments when the real exchange rate has appreciated too far and external competitiveness is eroded.[14] This provides for a limited degree of monetary policy independence – mainly the ability for the inflation rate to differ from that in the anchor currency country.

Currency boards

Currency boards are a tight version of pegged exchange rates. Under a pegged regime, monetary policy has to be wholly dedicated to the exchange rate target but the possibility to devalue or revalue, along with margins of fluctuations, introduce some degree of flexibility that is sometimes misused, mainly to relax monetary policy discipline. Currency boards ensure that monetary policy is entirely dedicated to support the declared parity, with no margin of fluctuation. To that effect, Hume's mechanism (see Chapter 13) is applied: the central bank may only issue domestic money when it acquires foreign exchange reserves, i.e. when the balance of payments is in surplus. In the presence of a deficit, the central bank must spend its foreign exchange reserves to buy back its own currency, which is then retired from circulation, and the money supply shrinks. Monetary policy is entirely passive since the money supply changes automatically as the balance of payments is in surplus or deficit. Fiscal policy, on the other hand, is effective.

Currency boards used to exist in the British empire. They were adopted by a number of Caribbean islands as they became independent, were revived by Hong Kong in 1983, and became more widespread in the 1990s. Countries with weak political institutions, such as Argentina, Bosnia-Herzegovina and Bulgaria, have chosen this rigorous arrangement to put an end to monetary indiscipline and its corollary, raging inflation. Freshly independent from the Soviet Union, with no history of central banking, Estonia and Lithuania have also adopted a currency board arrangement. Argentina's system collapsed in 2002, illustrating the dangers of an inflexible arrangement.

Dollarization/euroization and currency unions

A yet stricter way of pegging a currency is to irrevocably fix the exchange rate, in effect adopting the anchor currency as domestic currency, hence the term 'dollarization' (as in Ecuador, El Salvador, Panama, Liberia)

[14] When the nominal exchange rate E is constant and the domestic price level P rises faster than the foreign one P^*, the real exchange $\lambda = EP/P^*$ rises. A nominal devaluation – a reduction in E – becomes the only way to lower it back to equilibrium.

or 'euroization' (as in Kosovo and Montenegro). With the exception of Panama that did not create its own currency upon becoming independent, the other cases involve small countries with very weak political institutions that were impressed by the demise of the Argentinean currency board and opted therefore for an even stricter arrangement. A special case is the adoption by several countries of the same currency, as in a monetary union. This is of course the case in Europe but is also the case in francophone Africa and in some Caribbean islands (see Box 14.2). Fiscal policy is effective, although the sharing of a common currency may call for some restrictions – an issue discussed in detail in Chapter 18.

14.3 Choices

14.3.1 What drives the choice of an exchange rate regime?

It should be clear by now that the choice of an exchange rate regime is first and foremost a decision about the use of policy instruments. Freely floating exchange rates allow the monetary authorities complete freedom but restrict the use of a fiscal policy. As the degree of fixity rises, i.e. moving down the list above, monetary policy autonomy is increasingly relinquished, but fiscal policy effectiveness is recovered. There is no monetary autonomy left under currency boards and no domestic money under dollarization/euroization. This section therefore reviews the practical usefulness of monetary and fiscal policies. The choice of the exchange regime also affects the way foreign disturbances are transmitted domestically, as explained in Box 14.3.

Monetary policy

Monetary policy can be a useful instrument, and may be used to cushion disturbances that affect the economy, whether of domestic or foreign origin. For example, facing a recession, a monetary policy relaxation can help to speed up the resumption of growth. A key advantage of monetary policy is its flexibility: the central bank can act promptly when it sees the need for action. This flexibility can be a drawback, however, for monetary policy can also be misused. Resorting to the printing press to accommodate budget deficits is a temptation that regularly proves to be too hard to resist. Inflation bias is one reason why some countries decide to tie their own hands and adopt some form of fixity (other reasons are presented in the next chapter). The existence, or the adoption, of good central banking practice enhances the appeal of exchange rate flexibility.

Box 14.2

Monetary unions

The CFA zone was created when the former French colonies reached independence in the 1960s. It includes two unions: the West African Economic and Monetary Union (Benin, Burkina Faso, Côte d'Ivoire, Guinea Bissau, Mali, Niger, Senegal, Togo) and the Central African Economic and Monetary Union (Cameroon, Central African Republic, Chad, Democratic Republic of Congo, Equatorial Guinea, Gabon). These countries never established their own currencies (Mali and Equatorial Guinea did, until they joined the CFA zone in 1985). The two monetary unions are formally independent from each other and each has its own central bank, yet both peg their currency to the French franc at the same rate, devalued by 50 per cent in 1994. They have been pegged to the euro since 1999. The arrangement is special, a legacy of colonial times and based on a guarantee by France, but it is a true, modern monetary union.

The East Caribbean Common Market (Antigua and Barbuda, Dominica, Grenada, St Kitts and Nevis, St Lucia, and St Vincent and the Grenadines) form a monetary union. These are small islands that can hardly be compared to the European monetary union.

Brunei and Singapore also form a currency union.

Other countries have unilaterally adopted a foreign currency and therefore do not actively participate in the running of the central bank. This is the case of Kiribati, Nauru and Tuvalu, which use the Australian dollar; Lesotho, Namibia and Swaziland, which use the South African rand; and Bahamas, Liberia, Marshall Islands, Micronesia, Palau and Panama, which have adopted the US dollar. More recently, Ecuador and San Salvador have also adopted the US dollar since 2001. In Europe, Monaco uses the French franc (now the euro), Liechtenstein the Swiss franc, and San Marino the Italian lira (now the euro). These are not true monetary unions, however, since the centre country is not committed to take into account the interests and viewpoints of its 'satellites', and actually never does.

Fiscal policy

Fiscal policy can also be a useful instrument, but it differs from monetary policy in important respects. It involves considerable politicization as the government must agree with the parliament when it needs to change taxes or spending, although some leeway is permitted in most countries. It is also slow to implement, partly because of the need for political negotiations and partly because spending and tax changes cannot be phased in overnight. These limitations make flexible rates – which preserve the effectiveness of monetary policy – more appealing than fixed rates, which preserve the effectiveness of fiscal policy. Much as monetary policy can be misused, fiscal indiscipline remains a key concern. Indeed, many governments tend to suffer from a budget deficit bias. In this case, the discipline argument favours flexible rates where the incentive to overuse fiscal policy is lessened by its ineffectiveness.

Exchange rate stability

One lesson from Fig. 14.1 is that flexible exchange rates tend to fluctuate considerably, affecting the real exchange rate. Continuous changes in external competitiveness can be disruptive for international trade. For this reason, small, highly integrated economies tend to value some degree of exchange rate fixity.

Ever since the dreadful inter-war period (see Chapter 13), fear of floating has been prevalent among most European countries, especially as they aimed at developing intra-European trade through the Common Market. This is why the ERM was adopted. Once it was in place, many countries started to attach greater importance to the monetary discipline argument, eventually deciding to adopt a common currency (this evolution is documented in Chapter 15).

On the other hand, since the euro area is a large and rather closed economy, the volatility of the euro *vis-à-vis* the rest of the world is not an overwhelming consideration. With a fiercely independent central bank dedicated to monetary discipline, monetary policy is perceived as free from inflation bias and therefore a most useful instrument. This explains why the euro is freely floating. Much the same applies to the USA.

Box 14.3

The insulation properties of exchange rate regimes

The *IS–LM* framework can be used to think about the domestic impact of foreign disturbances. A few cases are briefly presented here.

An increase in worldwide interest rates is shown in panel (a) of Fig. 14.7. The immediate effect is an outflow of capital and a tendency for the exchange rate to depreciate. Under a flexible regime, the central bank does not intervene, and the *LM* schedule does not move. Depreciation improves the current account, which raises demand and moves the *IS* schedule up until it reaches point *C*. Under a fixed exchange rate, the central bank must intervene and buy back its own currency – drawing on its stock of foreign exchange reserves – which moves the *LM* schedule to the left until it reaches point *B*.

An increase in world demand – because of a boom, for example – is shown in panel (b) as a rightward shift of the *IS* schedule to *IS'*. At point *B*, capital inflows tend to push the exchange rate upwards. Under fixed rates, the central bank intervenes, sells money and the *LM* schedule moves rightwards until point *C*. Under flexible rates, the appreciation pushes the *IS* schedule back to the left until we are back at point *A*.

In the end, we see that foreign financial disturbances – a change in the worldwide interest rate – cannot be insulated against, but that the regime deeply affects the outcome in terms of output. A flexible exchange rate insulates the economy from foreign demand disturbances.

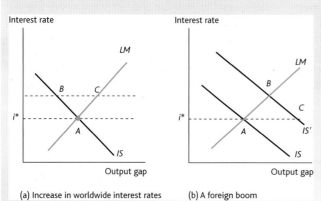

(a) Increase in worldwide interest rates   (b) A foreign boom

Figure 14.7: *Foreign disturbances*

The UK and Sweden have been charting a different course. Being (relatively) small and open, these countries were obvious candidates for a high degree of exchange rate fixity, even for adopting the euro. Both, however, display a high degree of fear of fixing, following a painful experience in the ERM for the UK (see Chapter 15) and with a fixed and adjustable exchange rate regime in the case of Sweden. Both let their currencies float, but they have adopted a regime of inflation targeting which is proving very effective against the inflation bias. Many other countries around the world, from New Zealand – where inflation targeting was invented – to Chile, Brazil, Israel and Thailand, follow the same strategy, accepting potential exchange rate volatility as the price to pay for monetary policy independence.

14.3.2 Fix or float?

Behind the variety of exchange rate arrangements, a central distinction is whether monetary authorities commit themselves to a parity, possibly a range of fluctuation, or whether they reject any responsibility for their exchange rates. Broadly speaking, arrangements from pegs to dollarization belong to the fixed exchange rate category, in contrast to freely or managed floats, with target zones in the middle grey zone.

The case for flexible exchange rates rests on three main considerations:

★ First, real life is full of surprises and disturbances. When shocks occur – national or worldwide recessions, oil shocks, technological change, etc. – prices must be adjusted to avoid the kind of disequilibria that develop into deepening cyclical fluctuations, possibly accompanied by high unemployment and large external imbalances. When prices and wages are sticky, the required adjustments may take far too long and misalignments occur. Flexible exchange rates provide the fast way to adjust relative domestic and foreign costs and prices.

★ Second, exchange rate changes are unavoidably enmeshed with politics. An appreciation or a depreciation affects income distribution[15] and is seen as a judgement on the government's economic know-how. For example, a depreciation is often interpreted, rightly or wrongly, as a signal of government failure. More generally, any sharp change in the exchange rate provides ammunition to political opposition, which can argue that there is something wrong with government policies. Politics rarely mix harmoniously with economics, so removing the exchange rate from the realm of politics may be helpful.

★ Third, the decision to constrain monetary policy is a commitment that is difficult to uphold in each and every circumstance. Failure to abide by the required discipline results in exchange market pressure, which not infrequently leads to bruising currency crises. More worrisome is the fact that the exchange markets themselves occasionally tend to overreact and to display apparently irrational behaviour, provoking unjustified crises.

In the opposite camp, the case for fixed exchange rates emphasizes the tendency of exchange markets to misbehave as well as cases where exchange rate policy is useful.

★ As just noted, destabilizing speculation occurs from time to time. The exchange markets are driven by a short-term financial logic, where information about the future is essential but highly imperfect, giving rise to fads, rumours and herd behaviour which occasionally provokes panic.

★ Even if the exchange market gyrations do not result in panic, they provoke large fluctuations. For international traders and investors, these fluctuations are a source of uncertainty which can hurt trade and foreign direct investment. Box 14.4 provides an example.

★ Harnessing monetary policy to an exchange rate target introduces discipline since foreign exchange markets are likely to immediately sanction inflationary policies by launching speculative attacks.

★ Finally, in case of serious shocks, parity

realignments are possible when the exchange rate is explicitly fixed but adjustable. In the Bretton Woods system, this was seen as an insurance against unexpected events, even though it has often been used as a way of escaping the discipline that a fixed exchange rate regime imposes on monetary policy and especially on inflation.

14.3.3 The two corners

The 1990s was a decade of violent currency crises. Europe's ERM was hit in 1992–93, Latin America followed in 1995–99, then it was Southeast Asia's turn in 1997–98 and Russia in 1998. These countries were operating one form of a peg or another, but very hard peg countries like Hong Kong and Argentina, both with a currency board, escaped the apparently contagious wave. This has made popular the 'two-corner' view according to which the only safe regimes are the extremes ones, free floating or hard pegs like currency boards, monetary unions or dollarization. Hard pegs were seen as impregnable because the central banks have no opportunity to give in to market pressure, even if they wish to do so. Freely floating rates are presumed not to lead to speculative attacks, because there is no peg to attack; like soft pillows, they absorb any blow.

This view is yet another implication of the principles developed in section 14.1.3: either monetary policy is completely free or it is entirely committed to uphold the chosen peg. The intermediate regimes, called soft pegs, attempt to strike a midpoint, combining fear of floating and fear of fixing. They are meant to retain some degree of monetary independence, yet they commit monetary policy to uphold a peg, possibly crawling, possibly within bands of fluctuations. The two-corner view holds that, in the end, soft pegs try to combine irreconcilable objectives and are predestined to fail, possibly badly. This has encouraged a number of countries to leave the middle ground over the 1990s. The two-corner view suffered a serious blow when the Argentinian currency board collapsed in early 2002 and when, a few months later, Brazil faced furious attacks even though its currency was freely floating.

The two-corner fashion has been challenged from a different angle. Most countries announce publicly their chosen exchange regime. However, a close inspection of their actual behaviour tells a different story. Some countries declare that their exchange rate is freely floating, yet they are found to intervene, sometimes heavily, in the foreign exchange market. In fact, they pursue a target zone strategy or they even peg within

[15] An appreciation is good news for consumers, who find imported goods cheaper, but bad news for producers, especially exporters, who must compress profit margins — and maybe even labour costs — to remain competitive. Conversely, a depreciation hurts the consumers and benefits the producers.

Box 14.4

What difference can the exchange rate regime make: France vs the UK

Except for a brief period of ERM membership in 1991–92, the UK has kept its exchange rate floating (at times with some management) since the collapse of the Bretton Woods system. France, on the contrary, has been an enthusiastic, if not always successful, supporter of pegging. Figure 14.8 contrasts the experience of France and Britain between 1980 and 2005. It plots these countries' real exchange rates, measured as their unit labour costs relative to the average in their main trading partners; an increase in the index represents a real appreciation, i.e. a loss of competitiveness.[1] The UK real exchange rate is clearly more volatile than the French rate (the coefficient of variation is 0.14 for the UK, 0.08 for France). Sharp changes in competitiveness hurt exporters and importers. There is mounting evidence that large exchange rate volatility hurts trade. Note that being a 'petro-currency' is one reason advanced by UK authorities to explain why they do not want to tie sterling.

[1] Effective real exchange rates are defined as EW/W*, where W is the unit labour cost (the cost of producing one unit of GDP) at home and W* is the (geometric) average of unit labour costs in main trading partner countries. E is the average of the exchange rates vis-à-vis the same countries, with the same weights.

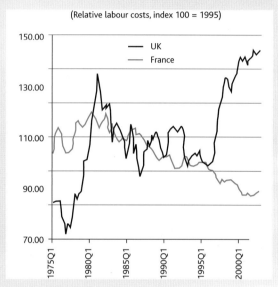

(Relative labour costs, index 100 = 1995)

Figure 14.8: *Real exchange rates of France and the UK, 1980Q1–2005Q1*

Source: *International Financial Statistics*, IMF.

narrow bands. Fear of floating is again present, reflecting deep-seated reluctance to allow exchange rates to fluctuate as much as they would if left to market forces. Other countries declare pegs, with bands, but actually let their exchange rates wander beyond the announced margins. Fear of fixing seems to reflect concerns that resisting market pressure may trigger irresistible speculative attacks.

14.3.4 Regional arrangements

The discussion so far has considered whether a country should attach its currency to another one. This is indeed

how most countries consider the exchange regime choice. A very different possibility is for a number of countries to undertake to peg their exchange rates to each other. This is indeed what has been done in Europe, first through the EMS and then through monetary union. In both cases, the currencies are pegged *vis-à-vis* each other and freely floating *vis-à-vis* all the other currencies. This is an example of a regional arrangement. There are other regional arrangements which, so far, all involve monetary unions, as described in Box 14.2.

14.4 Summary

This chapter examined a very old but still unsettled debate: the choice of an exchange rate regime, to prepare the ground for the study of Europe's particular brand of monetary integration. The first step was to review a number of standard macroeconomic principles. The chapter then looked at the various exchange rate regimes that exist and examined their properties. This then allowed a review of the classic debate of fixed versus flexible exchange rates.

Macroeconomic principles

A key message is that exchange rate and monetary policies are just two sides of the same coin. As a result, some key properties of money extend to the exchange rate, including the distinction between long-run and short-run effects:

★ In the long run, money is neutral. It has no lasting effect on the real side of the economy. It only determines the rate of inflation. Similarly, in the long run, the real exchange rate returns to its equilibrium level. This return involves either changes in the nominal exchange rate, if it is allowed to move, or changes in the inflation rate. The purchasing power parity (PPP) principle asserts that the rate of appreciation is equal to the inflation differential (foreign less domestic).

★ PPP is only verified when the equilibrium exchange rate is approximately constant, which need not always be the case. The Balassa–Samuelson effect identifies one reason why the real exchange rate is not constant: when a country catches up with more developed economies, its equilibrium real exchange rate will be on an appreciation trend.

★ In the short run, money neutrality does not hold, chiefly because prices and wages are sticky. Consequently, monetary policy and nominal exchange rate changes affect the real economy.

Another important result is that the choice of an exchange regime affects the effectiveness of monetary and fiscal policies in small open economies. When the exchange rate is fixed, monetary policy is effectively pledged to the exchange rate target and cannot be used to affect the real side of the economy, even in the short run. When the exchange rate is freely floating, monetary policy independence is recovered, but fiscal policy ceases to be effective because exchange rate changes offset its effect on output.

Exchange rate regimes

'Fixed' or 'floating' are not the only choices. There exist truly floating regimes, but most official free floats are also managed; central banks do intervene on the foreign exchange market, typically to smooth exchange rate fluctuations. Similarly, there are various degrees of fixity. Very hard pegs take the form of currency boards or even the adoption of a foreign currency. Softer pegs allow for realignments and include margins of fluctuations. Crawling pegs let the central parity move on a frequent basis.

Choosing an exchange rate regime

The choice of an exchange rate regime is first and foremost a trade-off among desirable features. There is no universally better regime; each country must consider the various dimensions of the choice and realize that conditions change.

The exchange rate regime involves trading-off the ability to use monetary policy (sometimes to misuse it) against the tendency towards excessive exchange rate volatility. Announced pegs impose some discipline on monetary policy but at the risk of inviting speculative attacks. The main considerations to take into account are the following:

★ A first trade-off concerns the ability to use monetary and fiscal policies, sometimes to misuse them. Monetary policy is flexible and central bank independence can shield it from undesirable political interference. Fiscal policy requires often complex negotiations between different branches of government, a source of lags and politicization.

★ Small open economies value exchange rate stability; large countries are typically rather closed and therefore care less about exchange rate volatility.

★ Announced pegs impose some discipline on monetary policy but at the risk of inviting speculative attacks.

Concern with speculative attacks has popularized the two-corner view. According to this view, only extreme regimes, completely free floats or hard pegs, are viable. This may be so, but the extreme regimes have undesirable properties, so fear of fixing or fear of floating remains a powerful disincentive to heed the two-corner solution recommendation.

Self-assessment questions

1. Section 14.1.3 explains that, when the exchange rate is fixed, a monetary expansion must be completely reversed through exchange market interventions. Why must the real money stock return *exactly* to its initial level?

2. Describe carefully how, following an increase in the supply of money, output initially rises but then returns to its initial level as the price level rises.

3. If the nominal exchange rate appreciates by less than the excess of foreign over domestic inflation, is the real exchange rate appreciating or depreciating?

4. Why are fixed exchange rates believed to impose discipline on monetary policy?

5. Why would the exchange rate regime be irrelevant if money were also neutral in the short run? What would make money neutral in the short run?

6. Redo the analysis of section 14.1.4 assuming that the central bank has a policy of keeping the interest rate unchanged.

7. Why is it asserted that there cannot be speculative attacks against freely floating exchange rates?

8. Using the *IS–LM* framework, study the effect of a sudden increase in the foreign price level. Distinguish between a fixed and a floating exchange rate regime.

9. Why do small open economies tend to favour some degree of exchange rate fixity?

Essay questions

1. The real, not the nominal, exchange rate is what matters for the real side of the economy. Why do central banks not attempt to control the real rather the nominal exchange rate?

2. Why does a fixed exchange rate allow a country to adopt an inflation rate that differs from that in the anchor currency country?

3. Why do many countries display fear of floating? Why do they not correctly report what they do?

4. Dollarization is a good regime only for countries that display a chronic lack of fiscal discipline. Explain and comment.

5. It is often believed that a peg encourages residents (households, firms, banks) to borrow in a foreign currency. Then, if the exchange rate is devalued, many residents face the risk of bankruptcy. Explain and comment.

6. Find out about the behaviour of the exchange rate of Switzerland, a country that is officially floating, *vis-à-vis* the Deutschmark and then the euro. Is this a case of fear of floating? Why?

7. Comment on the following assertion. 'Fixed exchange rate regimes are temporary arrangements.' What is the implication for Europe?

8. Since the late 1990s, the euro/dollar exchange rate has fluctuated by some 50 per cent. Does this invalidate the choice by the USA and the eurozone to let their mutual exchange rate float freely?

Further reading: the aficionado's corner

The following readings present the debate about the choice of exchange rate regimes:
Bordo, M. (2003) 'Exchange rate regime choice in historical perspective', Rutgers University, http://econweb.rutgers.edu/bordo/Thorntonlecture.doc.
Eichengreen, B. (1999) *Toward a New International Financial Architecture: A Practical Post-Asia Agenda*, Institute for International Economics, Washington, DC.
Fischer, S. (2001) 'Exchange rate regimes: is the bipolar view correct?', *Finance and Development*, 38(2): 18–21.
Ghosh, A., A.-M. Gulde and H.C. Wolf (2003) *Exchange Rate Regime: Choices and Consequences*, MIT Press, Cambridge, Mass.

Two studies show the difference between the officially declared regime and what countries actually do:
Levy-Yeyati, E. and F. Sturzenegger (2005) 'Classifying exchange rate regimes: deeds vs. words', *European Economic Review*, 49(6): 1603–35.
Reinhart, C. and K. Rogoff (2002) 'The Modern History of Exchange Rate Arrangements: A Reinterpretation', *Quarterly Journal of Economics*, 119(1): 1–48.

A review of the evidence on purchasing power parity is:
Rogoff, K. (1996) 'The purchasing power parity puzzle', *Journal of Economic Literature*, 34(2): 647–68.

Useful websites

The IMF presents up-to-date evaluations of exchange rate policies: http://www.imf.org.

To find out about the exchange rate regime of a particular country, visit its central bank's website. The list of all central bank websites is at http://www.bis.org/cbanks.htm.

Crises and regimes are debated on Professor Roubini's website at http://www.stern.nyu.edu/globalmacro/.

References

Burda, M. and C. Wyplosz (2005) *Macroeconomics: A European Text*, 4th edn, Oxford University Press, Oxford.

Frankel, J. (1999) *No Single Currency Regime is Right for all Countries at all Times*, NBER Working Paper 7338.

> It was the 1992 EMS crisis that provided the immediate impetus for monetary unification.
>
> *Barry Eichengreen (2002)*

15 The European Monetary System

INTRODUCTION

The European Monetary System (EMS) is not only a bridge between the dollar-centred Bretton Woods system and the monetary union but it is also the entry point for the next waves of countries accessing the EU. The quest for exchange rate stability within Europe required that monetary policies be restricted somehow. Failure to fully recognize this requirement resulted in an agitated history yet, paradoxically, the EMS's shortcomings made the adoption of a single currency seem a natural and desirable step. This in

itself justifies a detailed study. In addition, the EMS did not cease to exist with the launch of the euro; it was adapted and it is taking a new life.

The chapter first presents the rules that govern the EMS. Next, it describes the evolution of the system from a fully symmetric arrangement to what has been called the 'greater Deutschmark area'. The last section presents the changes that followed the speculative crises of 1993 and led to the current EMS.

15.1 The EMS arrangements

The decision to create the EMS was taken in 1978 by German Chancellor Helmut Schmidt and French President Valéry Giscard d'Estaing. They were alarmed by the monetary disorders that had followed the end of the Bretton Woods system and by the inability to sustain the Snake arrangement, described in Chapter 13. In line with a view long held in Europe, they saw large exchange rate movements as a direct threat to the Common Market. They wanted a stronger, more resilient arrangement.

Political sensitivities were important, however. Germany would never take the risk of weakening its star currency, the Deutschmark, while France could not be seen to be playing second fiddle to Germany. Additionally, the smaller countries had to be brought along. Furthermore, the UK was staunchly opposed to a fixed exchange rate regime. The solution came close to squaring the circle. The chosen arrangement was explicitly symmetric, without any currency explicitly put at the centre, and it established a subtle distinction between the European Monetary System (EMS), of which all European Community countries were de facto members, and the Exchange Rate Mechanism (ERM), an optional scheme. The ERM was the only meaningful part of the EMS. It rested on four main elements: a grid of agreed-upon bilateral exchange rates, mutual support, a commitment to joint decision of realignments and the European Currency Unit (ECU).

15.1.1 The ERM's parity grid

All ERM currencies were fixed to each other, with a band of fluctuation of ±2.25 per cent around the central

parity (Italy was initially allowed a margin of fluctuation of ±6 per cent, in recognition of its higher rate of inflation and internal political difficulties). The arrangement was represented by the parity grid, a matrix-like table collecting all pairwise central parities and their associated margins of fluctuations.

The arrangement carried a number of interesting features. First, the system was entirely European, with no reference to the dollar or to gold. Never before had European countries built an exchange rate system standing on its own. Second, the system was fully symmetric: no currency played any special role, in contrast to the dollar in the Bretton Woods system. Third, the responsibility for maintaining each bilateral exchange rate within its margin was explicitly shared by both countries,[1] thus removing the stigma of one weak and one strong currency.

15.1.2 Mutual support

The Snake had failed because the weak currencies had to fend for themselves. In contrast, the ERM included an agreement to automatically provide mutual support. By construction, exchange market pressure would simultaneously hit two countries. For example, the bilateral exchange rate between the Danish krone and the Dutch guilder could be pressed against one of its 2.25 per cent margins where, say, the krone was weak

---

[1] Since all arrangements were bilateral, it would always be the case that the threat to break through a band of fluctuation would simultaneously affect two currencies, a strong one and a weak one.

and the guilder strong. The ERM agreement stipulated that, in this case, the Danish and Dutch central banks were both obliged to intervene on the foreign exchange market. The Dutch would sell guilders to make them more abundant and therefore cheaper, and the Danish central bank would buy krone to raise its value. These interventions could be carried with any currency: for example, the Dutch central bank would sell guilders against US dollars, Deutschmarks, etc., including the krone.

Crucially, in principle, this commitment was *unlimited*. Each concerned central bank was committed to keep intervening as long as its parity *vis-à-vis* any other member currency was pressed against any of its limits. But what if it ran out of ammunition? In the above example, the Dutch central bank could never be in that position since it would be accumulating foreign exchange reserves while selling its own currency, which it could produce in unlimited amounts. The Danish central bank, on the other hand, could run out of foreign exchange reserves, having spent all it had to buy back krone. In that case, the central bank of the Netherlands would also be committed to making a loan to its Danish colleague, allowing for continuing interventions as long as necessary. Other ERM central banks, even if they were not directly involved, could decide to give a helping hand, by also intervening on the foreign exchange markets, buying krone, or lending directly to the Danish central bank.

15.1.3 Joint management of exchange rate realignments

How long should this game be pursued? Clearly, if markets remained unimpressed by the artillery lined up against them, the central banks providing theoretically unlimited support could become concerned that no end was in sight. In that case, the solution would be to throw in the towel, acknowledge the market pressure and realign exchange rates. How was that done?

Allowing any central bank to change its exchange rate as it pleases would have made little contribution to the establishment of a level playing field. The founding fathers of the EMS were concerned that individual countries might try to achieve unfair trade advantage through recurrent devaluations, the infamous beggar-thy-neighbour practice of the inter-war period perceived to have been a source of economic and political disintegration. This is why the ERM stipulated that any change in any bilateral exchange rate had to be jointly decided by all members. The consensus rule implied that, in effect, each country gave up exclusive control of its own exchange rate. Realignments, as the exercise came to be known, turned out to involve tough but ultimately successful bargaining, usually concluded by multiple bilateral parity changes. The history of realignments is shown in Table 15.1.

15.1.4 The ECU

The EMS included the mostly symbolic creation of the European Currency Unit, or ECU. The ECU was a basket of all EMS-country currencies, including those of EC countries that did not participate in the ERM. Each currency entered with a weight meant to represent the country's size and importance in intra-European trade. These weights, which were revised every five years, were initially chosen so that ECU 1 was worth US$ 1. The latest weights are shown in Table 15.2.

Formally, the ECU was designated the official unit of account of the European Community, used for all official transactions and accounts. Yet, any resemblance with a monetary union was then unacceptable. For this reason, it was explicitly designed not to be a currency: there were no physical ECUs and central banks did not carry out transactions in ECUs. The private markets, however,

Dates	24.9.79	30.11.79	22.3.81	5.10.81	22.2.82	14.6.82
No. of currencies involved	2	1	1	2	2	4
Dates	21.3.83	18.5.83	22.7.85	7.4.86	4.8.86	12.1.87
No. of currencies involved	7[a]	7[a]	7[a]	5	1	3
Dates	8.1.90	14.9.92	23.11.92	1.2.93	14.5.93	6.3.95
No. of currencies involved	1	3[b]	2	1	2	2

[a] All ERM currencies realigned.
[b] In addition, two currencies (sterling and lira) leave the ERM.

Table 15.1: *ERM realignments*

	Amount in ECU 1	Weight (%)
Belgian franc	3.43100	8.71
Danish krone	0.19760	2.71
Deutschmark	0.62420	32.68
Dutch guilder	0.21980	10.21
French franc	1.33200	20.79
Greek drachma	1.44000	0.49
Italian lira	151.80000	7.21
Irish punt	0.00855	1.08
Portuguese escudo	1.39300	0.71
Spanish peseta	6.88500	4.24
UK pound sterling	0.08784	11.17

Table 15.2: *The ECU basket*

adopted the ECU and started to issue debt instruments using this unit. Technically and legally, these were currency baskets. When the euro was started on 4 January 1999, it was set to be worth exactly ECU 1 at its first quotation on that day, and the ECU ceased to exist.

15.1.5 Assessment: a flexible and cohesive arrangement

Overall, the EMS was built as a flexible yet cohesive arrangement. It allowed membership *à la carte*, permitting countries unhappy with fixed exchange rate regimes, chiefly the UK, not to join the ERM. Even within the ERM, the margins of fluctuations, normally set at ±2.25 per cent, could be temporarily set at ±6 per cent, an option exercised by Italy from 1979 to 1990, and by Spain and Portugal following their entry in 1989 and 1992, respectively.

On the other hand, the arrangement implied a deep commitment from member central banks. As long as the exchange rate peg was being adhered to, there was little policy independence left, as was explained in Chapter 14. The corresponding principle, the impossible trinity, is presented in Box 15.1. It is formally an implication of the theory presented in section 14.1.3. In addition, the decision to change the exchange rate, the last major remaining degree of monetary policy independence, was removed from national control through the consensus rule explained in section 15.1.3. In return, mutual

Box 15.1 The impossible trinity

The impossible trinity principle holds that the three characteristics listed in the first column below cannot be observed together:

	Early EMS	Late EMS	UK	Netherlands
1. Fixed exchange rate	✓	✓		✓
2. Monetary policy independence	✓		✓	
3. Full capital mobility		✓	✓	✓

It is possible to have any pair at any given moment, however. During the early EMS period, for example, many countries restricted capital movements; they could award themselves some degree of monetary independence even though they were part of the ERM. The UK dismantled its capital controls in the early 1980s and retained monetary policy independence by staying out of the ERM. The Netherlands, which removed its capital controls early, soon tied the guilder rigidly to the Deutschmark, effectively giving up any pretence at monetary policy independence. The trinity proved to be a curse to those countries that were in the ERM and were gradually allowing increased capital mobility, and yet were reluctant to give up the monetary policy instrument. Many of the ERM crises can be directly traced back to failed attempts at breaking this iron law.

support, the agreement that interventions ought to be bilateral, automatic and unlimited, represented an unusually strong collective commitment. Although sterilizations were possible, the arrangement reproduced many of the features of the gold standard, and aimed to achieve a similar degree of robustness (see Chapter 13).

15.2 EMS-1: from divergence to convergence and blow-up

The response to the challenge of the impossible trinity has varied over time. During the first period, which continued until the mid-1980s, ERM members had opted for exchange rate stability and policy independence, with capital controls in place in the devaluation-prone countries. Monetary independence mainly allowed each country to operate with a different inflation rate. As a result, realignments were frequently needed to re-establish competitiveness, an implication of the PPP principle presented in Chapter 14. In a second stage, bringing down inflation became the priority assigned to monetary policy. Within the ERM, it meant that countries with high inflation rates endeavoured to converge to the lowest rate. In effect, monetary policy independence was being surrendered. This is when Germany, the perennial low-inflation country and now the standard to emulate, established its dominance – an evolution that ultimately prompted the next move to monetary union.

15.2.1 The first version of EMS: agreeing to disagree (1979–85)

The EMS was initially conceived to avoid large fluctuations in intra-European real exchange rates. Building a robust ERM was one thing; the constraints implied by the impossible trinity were something else. After the first oil shock of 1973, inflation rates started to diverge markedly, and the second oil shock did nothing to improve the situation. Once committed to a system of fixed but adjustable exchange rates, the ERM countries faced a choice between two strategies. Plan A was to dedicate monetary policies to the exchange pegs. This required similar inflation rates, for any lasting difference would inexorably hurt the competitiveness of high-inflation countries relative to that of low-inflation countries. Plan B was to accept lasting divergences in inflation and adjust the exchange rates as frequently as

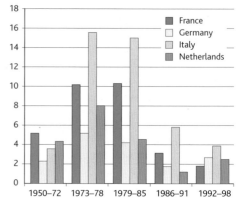

Figure 15.1: *Inflation*

Source: IMF.

needed to avoid competitiveness problems and trade imbalances. As Fig. 15.1 clearly shows, Plan B was chosen in the initial period and Table 15.1 confirms that realignments occurred frequently.

The economic interpretation of this choice is quite straightforward. It is based on the relationship between money and inflation established in Chapter 14. Because, in the long term, inflation depends on money growth, Plan A would have required that all countries adopt similar rates of money growth. However, it was not easy to decide what should be the common inflation rate target. Low inflation is better than high, of course, but money is not neutral in the short term. Aiming at low rates of money growth and inflation would have led to contractionary policies and rising unemployment in high-inflation countries. Conversely, low-inflation countries were unwilling to accept higher rates. France, a country traditionally committed to low unemployment, would not agree to adopt contractionary measures, whereas Germany, a country deeply attached to low inflation, would not countenance any monetary policy relaxation. The inability to resolve this conflict, as well as considerations of national prestige, explains why Plan B was chosen by default.

15.2.2 The second version of EMS: towards a greater Deutschmark area (1986–92)

Plan B did not function without problems, however. Two main difficulties emerged. First, between realignments, high-inflation countries would see their real exchange rate appreciate and, therefore, their trade accounts deteriorate. Inevitably, there would come a time when a remedial nominal depreciation would be needed, and it would have to be agreed upon by all ERM members. Low-inflation countries, which enjoyed a trade surplus, were quite reluctant to allow deep depreciations. The bargaining usually resulted in a depreciation that corrected for the accumulated difference in inflation, but no more. As a result, high-inflation countries were more or less permanently in external deficit while the low-inflation countries exhibited surpluses. This is illustrated in Fig. 15.2, which shows Italy's current account and real exchange rate *vis-à-vis* Germany's (the figure shows the previous year's exchange rate since it takes time to affect the current account). The Italian account's see-saw behaviour closely mirrors the evolution of the real exchange rate: between realignments the real exchange rate appreciates and the current account deteriorates, and devaluations are soon followed by an improvement in the current account.

Another serious problem with Plan B was that realignments were easily foreseen. The precise date could be in doubt – although shrewd observers often correctly identified many of them by looking at the timing of elections and other important political events – but the need to ultimately realign was plain for all to see. Looking at Fig. 15.2, it is quite obvious that the Deutschmark could only be revalued and the lira could only be devalued. To make the bet even easier, the gradually deepening external imbalance unambiguously signalled when this would happen. Speculators did not miss these signals and played what came to be called 'one-way bets': they speculated against the currencies of high-inflation countries and accumulated the currencies of low-inflation countries. As a result, most realignments took place in the midst of acute speculative pressure, hardly the 'island of monetary stability' promised by the founding fathers of the EMS. Plan B quickly exhausted its charms.

A key problem with Plan A had always been the difficulty of agreeing upon a standard in terms of monetary policy. Germany never had any doubt that the Bundesbank had it right but the French (and the Italians, Belgians, etc.) would not easily share this view. By late 1983, France had gone through three humiliating devaluations in just one year, each of which had been preceded by costly speculative attacks. Recently elected President Mitterrand had tried his leftist medicine[2] and it had clearly failed. His Finance Minister, Jacques Delors, convinced him that France ought to 'play the European card'. The strategy of competitive disinflation was born: from now on France would endeavour to replace devaluations with low inflation, hopefully lower even than in Germany. The perennially weak franc would become the 'franc fort'. Monetary policy was redirected towards that overarching objective, eschewing short-term gains from easy money.

Over the following years, all central banks followed suit and emulated the Bundesbank, in effect using the Deutschmark as an anchor. For nearly six years, from early 1987 to September 1992, there was no realignment,[3] as inflation rates gradually declined towards the low German level (Fig. 15.1). During that time, in anticipation of the Single European Act 1992, capital controls were progressively dismantled throughout Europe, and were formally banned as of July 1990. The impossible trinity meant that all central banks had in effect given up their ability to carry out an independent monetary policy. With the Deutschmark serving as anchor, the Bundesbank was the only central bank free to act on its own, which it did with two important consequences: the other countries became eager to move to a monetary union as a way of recovering some influence on their monetary policies, and the EMS exploded.

15.2.3 The crisis of 1992–93

The long period of complete exchange rate stability that followed the adoption of the Deutschmark anchor convinced many that it could last for ever. This proved to be terribly wrong, as the impossible trinity should have

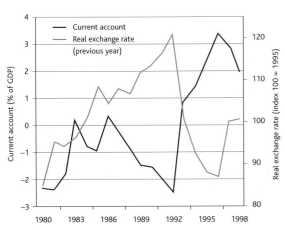

Figure 15.2: *Italy in the EMS*

Source: OECD and IMF.

[2] Soon after his election, Mitterrand relaxed monetary and fiscal policies, significantly raised minimum wages, reduced the working week and proceeded to nationalize several banks and large corporations.
[3] The 1990 realignment (Table 15.1) was not really a realignment. It was merely a technical adjustment prompted by Italy's decision to switch to the narrow ±2.25 per cent band of fluctuation, a consequence of the 'strong lira' policy. It is listed as a realignment because the lira's central parity was brought closer (from 6 per cent to 2.25 per cent) to its weak margin.

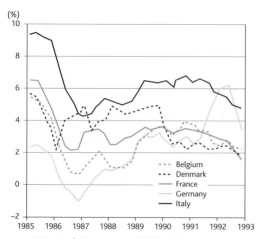

Figure 15.3: *Inflation rates, 1985–93*

Source: IMF.

The chart legend shows:
- - - - Belgium
- - - - Denmark
——— France
——— Germany
——— Italy

forewarned. Trouble accumulated slowly. To start with, the absence of any realignment might have looked good, but inflation rates did not quite fully converge. Figure 15.3 shows that while countries such as Denmark and France indeed moved towards the German inflation rate, others, such as Italy (or Portugal and Spain, not shown in the figure), had failed to get any closer by 1991. For these countries, the fixed exchange rate strategy meant a dangerous loss of competitiveness.

As it turned out, this is when the Berlin Wall collapsed. Germany's unification was a complex operation: taking over an impoverished country of 16 million inhabitants imposed a heavy burden on West Germany's public finances.[4] In addition, to prevent East German workers from moving to the more prosperous west – which they were instantaneously entitled to do as unification occurred – wages were brought up to levels that were inconsistent with the productivity of East German firms. The result was a surge of inflation in Germany, clearly visible in Fig. 15.3. Predictably, the Bundesbank responded by tightening up monetary policy, sharply raising the interest rate.

What could the other ERM members do? One solution would have been to let the Deutschmark appreciate. Blinded by the stability of ERM exchange rates and recent successes in bringing inflation down, and bent on achieving strong currency status, they rejected what they saw as a humiliating depreciation *vis-à-vis* the Deutschmark. This meant that they had to stick with the

strategy of blindly following the Bundesbank and its tight policy imposed by the unification shock. This policy was much too tight for the other ERM members but the Bundesbank, reasonably enough, saw no reason to adjust its stance to the needs of the other countries. Bad luck played its part, too. Outside Germany, the early 1990s were years of slow growth, the wrong time for tight monetary policies. The ERM started to look fallible.

The last stroke came from the EMU project itself. The Maastricht Treaty had been signed in December 1991 and was to be ratified by each member country during 1992. The first country to initiate the ratification process was Denmark, where law mandates that international treaties be submitted to referenda. For a variety of reasons, the Danes voted down the Treaty by a few thousands votes. The Treaty included one provision which stated that it would be void unless ratified by all EU countries. Thus, before the other countries even had a chance to ratify it, the Treaty was technically dead by mid-1992. This alarmed the exchange markets which had bought into the authorities' excessive confidence in both the ERM and the monetary union project. Speculative attacks started immediately, initially targeting Italy (the lira was seriously overvalued by then) and the UK. The UK had finally joined the ERM a year earlier, soon after John Major had replaced Margaret Thatcher as Prime Minister (largely because her opposition to ERM membership appeared anachronistic in the midst of a wave of Euro-optimism), yet the central rate chosen for the pound was seen to be overvalued.

In response to the speculative attacks, the strong currency central banks initially intervened in support of the embattled Banca d'Italia and Bank of England. By mid-September 1992, the attacks had become massive; a frightened Bundesbank decided that truly unlimited interventions were not reasonable and stopped its support. Left to themselves, with foreign exchange reserves falling rapidly, the lira and the pound withdrew from the ERM and the markets concluded that the ERM was considerably more fragile than hitherto admitted. Speculation shifted to the currencies of Ireland, Portugal and Spain, which twice had to be devalued. Contagion then spread to Belgium, Denmark and France, even though inflation in these countries had converged to below the German level and their currencies were not overvalued. By the summer of 1993, huge amounts of reserves had been thrown into the foreign exchange markets and speculation was still going strong. In order to uphold the principle of the ERM, and save face at the same time, the monetary authorities adopted new ultra-large (± 15 per cent) bands of fluctuations. Figure 15.4

---

[4] For an account of the economic challenges, see Begg *et al.* (1990) and Sinn and Sinn (1992).

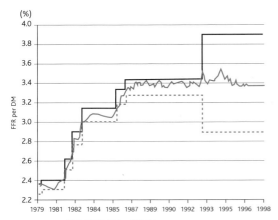

Figure 15.4: *DM/FRF in ERM*

shows the ERM history of the DM/French franc parity. The tight ERM was dead.

It was not only that monetary integration seemed to be a failure, but also bad blood had been spilled, which complicated any reconstruction efforts. The Bundesbank's reneging of the principle of unlimited interventions offended Italy and the UK. After a decade of hesitation, the UK had finally shed its traditional Euro-scepticism and joined the ERM; its forcible departure left a scar that would not heal easily.

15.2.4 The lessons

A number of features of the experience remain controversial. Inflation was successfully reduced among ERM countries. This has been seen as a proof that tying the hands of central banks through an exchange rate peg is the way to get rid of inflation. However, a comparison with non-ERM countries does not indicate that inflation has declined more quickly or less painfully. At the same time, the sharp turnaround of France in 1983 – away from a go-it-alone approach that would have been inflationary – took the form of retaining ERM membership and maintaining exchange rate stability, but these were side benefits of a wider political decision not to turn its back on Europe. A possible interpretation is that, lacking adequate domestic economic and political institutions, an external arrangement like the ERM has a useful substitution role to play.[5] This interpretation also applies to Italy, a country with a history of chronically high inflation, which could explain why, despite the 1993 setback, it has made a major effort to be a founding

[5] A similar argument concerns the Stability and Growth Pact presented in Chapter 18.

member of the euro area. The debate of 2005 about whether Italy would be better off outside the monetary union evokes similar consideration.

On the other hand, a number of lessons seem to be generally accepted:

★ The impossible trinity requires that domestic monetary policy independence be abandoned if the exchange rate is rigidly fixed. This is a tall order when economic conditions differ across countries (Germany was too different as it went through unification).

★ As long as the weaker-currency countries imposed restrictions on capital movements, speculative attacks were manageable. Once full capital mobility was achieved, central banks soon realized that even large stocks of foreign exchange reserves are too small, and that unlimited interventions are practically impossible.

★ In particular, once a speculative attack has started, attempting to defend a parity implies offering the market one-way bets: either the peg is abandoned and the speculators win, or it is upheld and they lose nothing. One-way bets are too good to be turned down: this is why speculative attacks are part-and-parcel of a system of fixed exchange rates in presence of full capital mobility.

★ Consequently, monetary integration with separate currencies is a very risky endeavour, possibly a hopeless quest. Monetary union is one response.

15.3 The EMS re-engineered

15.3.1 A softer ERM

The post-crisis ERM agreed upon in 1993 differed little from a floating exchange rate regime. Bilateral parities could move by 30 per cent, a very wide margin. Unsurprisingly, therefore, the (non)system worked well. Figure 15.4 shows that the DM/FRF fluctuated slightly outside of its earlier narrow ±2.25 per cent range for a few years and then gently converged to its ultimate EMU conversion rate.

One precondition set by the Maastricht Treaty for joining the monetary union is at least two years of ERM membership (the other conditions are presented in Chapter 17). This is why Italy returned to the ERM in 1997, as did two new members of the EU, Austria and Finland. The UK, not interested in joining the monetary union, has not returned and argues that this condition should not be interpreted literally since the wide bands have little practical relevance. This position is supported by Sweden, which has also decided to stay out of the monetary union after joining the EU at the same time as Austria and Finland.

15.3.2 EMS-2

The adoption of the euro in January 1999 has been accompanied by the launch of a new EMS. EMS-2, as it is called, is described in Box 15.2. It incorporates most of the features of its predecessor, yet differs in some key aspects:

★ While EMS-1 was a symmetric system based on a grid of bilateral parities, in EMS-2, parities are defined *vis-à-vis* the euro, which is clearly the centre currency. There is no grid, just a table.

★ The margin of fluctuation is less precisely defined. De facto, the 'standard' band is ±15 per cent as in the latter version of EMS-1, but a narrower band is also possible.

★ Interventions are still automatic and unlimited, but there is a clear signal that the European Central Bank (ECB) may decide to suspend this obligation.

Thus the system is more flexible and less committal than EMS-1, no doubt a consequence of the 1992–93 crisis. In addition, it is *à la carte*, allowing different margins of fluctuation. Two countries joined when EMS-2 came into force, at the same time as the monetary union was launched in January 1999: Greece, with the standard ±15 per cent band, until it joined the monetary union in January 2001, and Denmark, which has adopted the narrow ±2.25 per cent that prevailed in EMS-1. Sweden and the UK have decided to stay out 'for the time being' and continue to argue that ERM membership is not a prerequisite should they wish to join the monetary union.

Box 15.2

The Amsterdam Resolution of the European Council on the establishment of an exchange rate mechanism in the third stage of economic and monetary union (June 1997) – excerpts

'A central rate against the euro will be defined for the currency of each Member State outside the euro area participating in the exchange-rate mechanism. There will be one standard fluctuation band of plus or minus 15 per cent around the central rate. Intervention at the margins will in principle be automatic and unlimited, with very short-term financing available. However, the ECB and the central banks of the other participants could suspend intervention if this were to conflict with their primary objective.'

'On a case-by-case basis, formally agreed fluctuation bands narrower than the standard one and backed up in principle by automatic intervention and financing may be set at the request of the non-euro area Member States concerned.'

'The details of the very short-term financing mechanism will be determined in the agreement between the ECB and the national central banks, broadly on the basis of the present arrangements.'

The full text is available on, for example, the website of the Danish central bank at: http://www.national-banken.dk/nb/nb.nsf/alldocs/Fthe_erm_ii_agreement.

15.3.3 The next wave

Ten countries[6] joined the EU on 1 May 2004, as explained in Chapter 1. Their position regarding the EMS has been stated as follows (Amsterdam Resolution, 1997):[7]

> Participation in the exchange-rate mechanism will be voluntary for the Member States outside the euro area. Nevertheless, Member States with a derogation can be expected to join the mechanism. A Member State which does not participate from the outset in the exchange-rate mechanism may participate at a later date.

This establishes a presumption that they will be asked to join the ERM, but the UK and Swedish examples mean that joining is not an absolute obligation. Table 15.3 shows the situation in December 2005. In addition to Denmark, seven of the ten new Member States are part of the ERM, all with the standard band. However, Estonia and Lithuania had previously adopted a currency board arrangement,[8] which implies an effective 0 per cent band. Several other countries have stated that they intend to practise a narrower band than the standard one, presumably the ±2.25 per cent band. They have stated that it is their intention to join the eurozone as soon as possible, which requires at least two years of ERM membership. It is likely that, when they do, they will convert their currencies into euros at the existing ERM central parities.

Country	Date of ERM membership	Band of fluctuation (%)
Denmark	1 January 1999	± 2.25
Estonia	27 June 2004	± 15
Lithuania	27 June 2004	± 15
Slovenia	27 June 2004	± 15
Cyprus	2 May 2005	± 15
Latvia	2 May 2005	± 15
Malta	2 May 2005	± 15
Slovakia		± 15

Table 15.3: *ERM membership as of December 2005*

[6] Cyprus, the Czech Republic, Estonia, Hungary, Latvia, Lithuania, Malta, Poland, Slovakia and Slovenia.
[7] The text of the Amsterdam resolution, which sets up EMS-2, is available at: http://europa.eu.int/comm/economy_finance/euro/documents/resolution_erm2%20_amsterdam_en.pdf.
[8] Currency boards are explained in Chapter 14.

The three remaining new EU members (the Czech Republic, Hungary and Poland) have so far decided not to join the ERM. There are some good reasons not to join too early. As EU members, they have eliminated all restrictions to capital mobility. According to the impossible trinity, adopting a fixed exchange rate implies the loss of the monetary policy instrument, in effect importing the ECB's policy. In particular, if their inflation

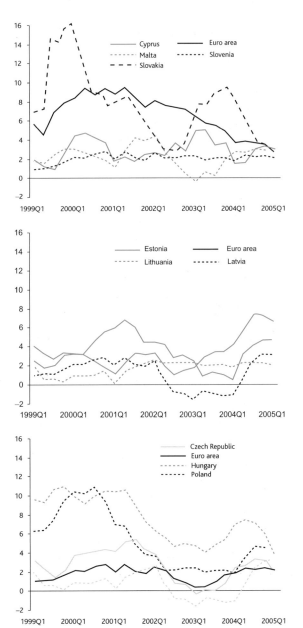

Figure 15.5: *Inflation rates in the new EU members*

Source: IMF.

rates are significantly higher than the eurozone rate, this would imply a very vigorous disinflation policy. It makes sense, therefore, to wait until their inflation rates have converged to the eurozone level. This is especially important in view of the vulnerability to speculative attacks, as discussed in section 15.2.4. The top chart in Fig.15.5 shows that, indeed, three of the ERM members had achieved a high degree of convergence by the time they joined the arrangement. The bottom chart shows that convergence is happening later in the three non-ERM members; presumably, when this pattern is solidified, they will feel ready to join the ERM.

An additional consideration is that admission to the monetary union requires that inflation remains close to the eurozone level.[9] The problem is that the relinquishing of monetary policy implies that the inflation rate is no longer under the control of the central bank, which may jeopardize admission to the monetary union. The middle chart in Fig.15.5 shows the evolution of inflation rates in the Baltic states, two of which have completely given up monetary policy upon adopting a currency board arrangement, and the third one, Latvia, steers its exchange rate very closely as well. Inflation rates have been quite volatile. Besides, the Balassa–Samuelson effect (see Box 14.1) implies that inflation tends to be higher in the fast-growing economies when their exchange rates are fixed.

The upshot is that the ERM membership obligation of the Amsterdam Resolution is not well suited to the new member countries. The wide band of fluctuation offers some room for monetary policy independence, but the experience of previous ERM crises indicates moving too close to the edge could invite speculative attacks. Given the rule, there is no way of avoiding the delicate period of ERM membership, but it is understandable that several countries exert caution.

[9] Chapter 17 presents the entry conditions.

15.4 Summary

The EMS was adopted in 1979 to preserve, as much as possible, exchange rate stability within Europe following the end of the Bretton Woods system. Initially created to shield Europe from international monetary disturbances, it gradually evolved into a state where monetary union appeared the natural next step. A new arrangement has been set up following the adoption of the euro. All EU members are members of the EMS but the active part of the system, the ERM, is optional in the sense that some countries (Denmark and the UK) have a derogation and Sweden is postponing its membership, as are some of the new EU members.

The ERM was based on a grid specifying all bilateral parities and the corresponding margins of fluctuations, normally ± 2.25 per cent. ERM members were committed to jointly defend their bilateral parities, if necessary through unlimited interventions and loans. Realignments were possible, but required the consent of all members. This amounted to a tight and elaborate arrangement.

The EMS went through three phases. During the first period, inflation differed quite widely from one country to another and realignments were frequent. Then, all countries decided to adopt the Bundesbank's low inflation strategy, in effect adopting the Deutschmark as an anchor and avoiding further realignments. Finally, the 1992–93 crisis – which saw two currencies, the Italian lira and the British pound, exit – ended with the adoption of wide margins of ± 15 per cent, allowing the ERM to nominally survive until the launch of the euro.

The 1992–93 crisis provides an example of the impossible trinity. The liberalization of financial markets and the fixity of exchange rates were incompatible with divergent monetary policies. For a while, during the late 1980s, most countries did follow the Bundesbank and achieved low inflation. But when Germany went through its unification shock, the Bundesbank adopted a tight policy stance that was incompatible with the low growth situation in the other ERM member countries.

With the adoption of a single currency, a new EMS was established. EMS-2 differs from EMS-1 mainly in that the euro is now the reference currency and the unlimited intervention obligation no longer exists. As a result, the ERM is asymmetric and its members must rely on their own resources to maintain the declared parities within the standard ± 15 per cent band. EMS-2 remains a prerequisite for joining the euro area.

Seven of the ten new EU members have joined the mechanism. Barring any turmoil, they expect to be admitted into the eurozone after two years of ERM membership. Three others have delayed ERM membership. They may feel that their inflation rates have not yet firmly converged to the eurozone level, or they may be concerned about the constraint on their ability to use monetary policy. With capital free to move, ERM membership may indeed be a risky step.

Self-assessment questions

1. List the similarities and differences between the ERM and the gold standard.

2. How does EMS-2 differ from EMS-1?

3. Why do the UK and Sweden remain outside of the ERM? What about Poland and Hungary?

4. Consider a high-inflation ERM country. Draw the evolution over time of the price level, and the nominal and real exchange rates, allowing for occasional devaluations. Do the same for a low-inflation country that occasionally revalues its nominal exchange rate.

5. Imagine three ERM countries. Compute a fictional parity grid linking their three currencies pairwise.

6. What do we mean by saying the EMS has become a 'Deutschmark area'? How did that happen and could it have been foreseen?

7. How could the ERM countries have reacted to German unification in 1991?

Essay questions

1. Why could the Bundesbank have been concerned about unlimited interventions in EMS-1?

2. Can other groups of countries, e.g. in Asia or Latin America, form a system like the EMS?

3. In retrospect it is claimed that the 1992–93 crisis of the EMS could have been anticipated. Why and why not? Once the crisis started, could Italy and the UK have stayed in the system, and if so under what conditions?

4. Would the Bretton Woods system have survived had it been patterned after the ERM?

5. Contrast the two periods of the EMS: 1979–85 and 1986–92.

6. What lessons do you draw from the 1992–93 wave of speculative attacks? In particular, why did speculators attack some currencies that were obviously not overvalued (the Belgian and French francs, the Danish krone) after other currencies were forced to leave the ERM or to devalue?

7. The EU new members have to operate for at least two years within EMS-2's ERM. What problems can you envision? What alternatives would you suggest?

8. By 1990, the EMS was seen as a major success. Can you provide your own evaluation of the system's performance over the period 1979–90? (You may use any criteria of success that you wish, but be explicit about them.)

Further reading: the aficionado's corner

A very useful description of the EMS is given in Chapter 1 of P. Kenen (1995) *Economic and Monetary Union in Europe*, Cambridge University Press, New York.

On the history of the EMS and its evolution towards EMU, see D. Gros and N. Thygesen (1998) *European Monetary Integration*, 2nd edn, Addison Wesley Longman, London.

A study of the exchange rate regime treatment of accessing countries can be found in D. Begg, B. Eichengreen, L. Halpern, J. von Hagen and C. Wyplosz (2003) *Sustainable Regimes of Capital Movements in Accession Countries*, Policy Paper 10, Centre for Economic Policy Research, London. http://www.cepr.org/pubs/books/PP10.asp.

A Swedish view on the ERM can be found in L. Heikenstein (2003) 'Euro entry before reforms or reforms before euro entry?' http://www.riksbank.se/templates/speech.aspx?id=8544.

A consideration of the choice faced by new members can be found in S. Schadler, P. Drummond, L. Kuijs, Z. Murgasova and R. van Elkan (2005) 'Adopting the euro in central Europe: challenges of the next step in European integration', Occasional Paper 234, IMF, Washington, DC.

Useful website

For a concise summary of the EMS, access the European Parliament's factsheet at http://www.europarl.eu.int/factsheets/5_2_0_en.htm.

References

Begg, D., J.-P. Danthine, F. Giavazzi and C. Wyplosz (1990) *The East, the Deutschmark and EMU*, Monitoring European Integration 1, Centre for Economic Policy Research, London.

Begg, D., B. Eichengreen, L. Halpern, J. von Hagen and C. Wyplosz (2003) *Sustainable Regimes of Capital Movements in Accession Countries*, Policy Paper 10, Centre for Economic Policy Research, London. http://www.cepr.org/pubs/books/PP10.asp.

Eichengreen, B. (2002) *Lessons of the Euro for the Rest of the World*, December. http://emlab.berkeley.edu/users/eichengr/policy.html.

Sinn, G. and H.W. Sinn (1992) *Jumpstart: The Economic Unification of Germany*, MIT Press Cambridge, Mass.

Introduction

This part studies the working of the monetary union, both in theory and in practice.

Chapter 16 presents the optimum currency area theory. This is where we ask the fundamental question: Which countries stand to benefit from sharing the same currency? The theory does not provide a black-and-white answer; rather it develops a set of criteria to evaluate the costs and the benefits of forming a monetary union. Applying these criteria to Europe, we find that some are fulfilled but that others are not. This conclusion illustrates the unending debates on the merits of the European monetary union. It also serves as a warning of where problems may surface, and suggests some answers on how to deal with them.

Chapter 17 describes the European monetary union, its principles and its institutions. The chapter also provides a review of the first years of the euro, its successes and its controversies.

Building a monetary union is not just about launching a new currency and establishing a common central bank. The euro area is a cohesive and complex structure. In addition to removing monetary policy from the national domain, the monetary union sets limits on what governments can do with their fiscal policies, their other macroeconomic policy instrument. The Stability and Growth Pact aims at enforcing fiscal discipline. Why is this part-and-parcel of the monetary union? The issue is highly controversial, as is the particular arrangement that has been adopted. Chapter 18 reviews the situation, including the crisis that occurred in 2003 and how the Pact has been amended in response.

Finally, Chapter 19 looks at the financial markets. One expected benefit from adopting the single currency is to deepen financial integration. It appears that some markets have integrated almost immediately; others remain segmented along national lines. The chapter asks why this has happened and what does this contrasted landscape imply for the working of the union, particularly its monetary policy and its exchange rate.

> The European countries could agree on a common piece of paper,
> ... they could then set up a European monetary authority or
> central bank. ... This is a possible solution, perhaps it is even an
> ideal solution. But it is politically very complicated, almost utopian.
>
> *Robert Mundell (1973)*

Chapter

16 Optimum currency areas

INTRODUCTION

This chapter presents the optimum currency area theory, a systematic way of trying to decide whether it makes sense for a group of countries to abandon their national currencies. Giving up the exchange rate instrument cannot be innocuous, so the question really is, under what conditions is such a step justified? The theory develops a battery of economic and political criteria which recognize that the real economic cost of giving up the exchange rate instrument arises in the presence of asymmetric shocks – shocks that do not affect all currency union member countries. The chapter then examines whether Europe passes these tests. The conclusion is that Europe is not really an optimum currency area, but it does not fail all the tests either. A further consideration is that the reasons that Europe fails some tests may change as a result of the adoption of the euro; Europe may eventually satisfy all or most of the criteria because it now has a single currency.

16.1 The question, the problem and the answer

It is usually taken for granted that each country has its own currency. After all, like the flag or the national anthem, a currency is a symbol of statehood. National heroes or rulers are proudly displayed on coins and banknotes, much as kings, emperors and feudal lords had their faces stamped on gold and silver coins. To be sure, there exist few exceptions to this rule but, until the advent of the euro, these cases were seen as exotic.[1] And yet, it is worth asking whether it makes good *economic* sense for each country to have its currency. If we forget about nations and focus purely on economic relations, how would we redraw the map of the world? This is the question explored in this chapter.

To start with, does the world need more than one currency? Could Zimbabwe, Peru and China share the same currency? Most likely not. At the other extreme, should each city have its own currency, as was sometimes the case a few centuries ago? No, of course not. These answers seem obvious, but exactly why? Box 16.1 presents an example that is suggestive of the issues involved.

16.1.1 Why is a large currency area desirable?

The first step is to understand the benefits from forming a currency area, possibly one that extends beyond national borders. Money is one of humanity's great inventions. Economics textbooks tell you that its key feature is to avoid the 'double coincidence of wants', i.e. barter. With money you buy what you want without bothering about simultaneously selling something. In short, money is useful because it makes commercial and financial transactions immensely easier than barter and also because it is immediately recognized. The more people accept a currency, the more useful it is.[2]

In that sense, the world would benefit from having just one currency that would be accepted everywhere. There would be no need to exchange money when travelling, exporting or importing. Currency exchanges are bothersome – how many unspent foreign coins lie in one of your drawers? Where can I find a place to change money so I can go out to a restaurant tonight? They are costly too; as everyone painfully finds out, selling and buying rates are often 10 per cent or more apart – this is how currency dealers get paid for the service that they provide. In addition, currency transactions are risky as exchange rates fluctuate and seem always to go against you. This is why small currency areas – geographic zones which share the same currency – are clearly not optimum. A currency that is used in a small area is just not very useful.

---

[1] Panama never had its own currency, nor Monaco, San Marino, Liechtenstein and some Pacific islands. Recently, Ecuador and El Salvador have adopted the US dollar.

[2] Technically, money is said to generate network externalities. The theory is developed in Dowd and Greenaway (1993). Network externalities are studied in Chapter 19.

Box 16.1

The case for a Californian dollar

In the late 1980s, something bad happened to the state of California. The Cold War ended shortly after the retirement of President Reagan who had championed the building up of the military and, in particular, massive investments in high-tech equipment. The result was sharp cuts in defence spending. As many of the big weapon-producing firms were based in California, this state suffered a serious blow, which hit at the time of a cyclical downturn in the USA and elsewhere in the world. Figure 16.1 documents the

Growth rates

Figure 16.1: *Growth rates in California and the USA, 1987–2000*

Source: Bureau of Economic Analysis.

impact of these events. The California gross state product declined abruptly, and growth remained negative for three years, a performance far worse than elsewhere in the USA. In fact, by 2003, California had still not recovered the relative position as a percentage of US GDP that it held before the crisis. Hundreds of thousands of jobs were lost. In the mid-1990s, California was the great beneficiary of the information and communications technology revolution. Firms were desperately looking for manpower as they were trying to seize on the apparently unbounded opportunities lying ahead of them.

Now imagine that the state of California had its own currency. A depreciation in the early 1990s would have enhanced the battered state's competitiveness. An appreciation in the late 1990s would have moderated the boom and the accompanying job scarcities that followed when the high-tech mania struck. Sharing the same currency as the rest of the USA certainly increased the size and duration of the imbalances brought about by these two shocks. Yet, no one in California has seriously proposed a monetary secession. Somehow, all Californians consider that belonging to the US dollar currency area provides benefits that far outweigh the costs. The optimum currency area theory's purpose is to explain how and why.

Figure 16.2 symbolically represents this idea. Since the usefulness of a currency grows with the size of the area over which it is being used, its marginal benefit is positive. Yet, it is declining as the area expands because the extra benefit from adding one more country to an already large currency area is smaller than when the initial area was small.

If the marginal benefit is always positive, is the world the optimal currency area? It would be if there did not exist costs. What can these costs be? As a currency area grows larger, it becomes more diverse – in standards of living for instance. If more diversity means more costs when sharing a common currency, the marginal costs are positive and rising with the size of the area. This idea is

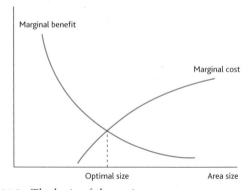

Figure 16.2: *The logic of the optimum currency area theory*

depicted in Fig. 16.2 by the upward-sloping marginal cost schedule. The figure reveals the existence of a trade-off: a large currency area is desirable because it enhances the usefulness of money, but it has drawbacks. The optimal currency area corresponds to a situation when the marginal costs and benefits from sharing the same currency balance each other, as shown in Fig. 16.2. As will become clear, the figure is highly symbolic and there should be no pretence that we can actually draw these schedules.

There are many ways in which diversity matters – some are economic, some are political. Diversity is costly because a common currency requires a single central bank and a single monetary authority is unable to react to each and every local particularity. The optimum currency area (OCA) theory takes the benefits as obvious and aims at identifying more precisely these costs. The basic idea is that diversity translates into asymmetric shocks and that the exchange rate is very useful for dealing with these shocks. The intuition is clearly brought up in Box 16.1.

This section proceeds in three steps. First, it examines asymmetric shocks and their effects. Second, it studies the problems that arise in the presence of asymmetric shocks in a currency area. Finally, it asks how the effects of asymmetric shocks can be mitigated when national exchange rates are no longer available.

16.1.2 Preview: adverse shocks

Imagine that the world demand for a country's exports decline because tastes change or because cheaper alternatives are developed elsewhere. This opens up a hole in the balance of trade. To re-establish its external balance, the country needs to make its exports cheaper. This calls for enhancing competitiveness. One solution would be for prices and wages to decline; but what if they do not? Chapter 14 makes the point that the exchange rate regime matters because prices and wages are sticky. In this case, a depreciation would do the trick if the country has its own currency. If, however, the country is part of a wider currency area, there is no alternative to lowering prices, which requires lower production costs and, hence, lower wages.

The situation is depicted in Fig. 16.3, which relates demand for, and supply of, domestic goods to the real exchange rate, defined as the relative price of domestic to foreign goods ($\lambda = EP/P^*$).[3] The supply of domestic

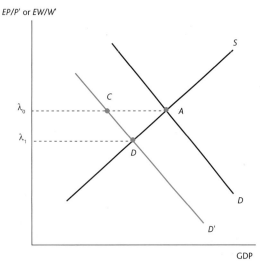

Figure 16.3: *An adverse demand shock*

goods rises as the real exchange rate appreciates because profitability rises at home when some of the production costs are tied to foreign prices (for example, imported machinery and semi-finished goods, oil). Demand declines when the real exchange rate appreciates for the familiar reason that both domestic and foreign customers will shift to cheaper foreign goods.

An alternative way of defining the real exchange rate is in terms of production costs (EW/W^*, where W and W^* are the production costs at home and abroad, each measured in the local currency). Because production costs quickly feed into prices, it matters little whether we use one definition or the other. It will prove helpful to keep in mind that the real exchange rate also represents the evolution of production costs, because production costs are closely associated with labour costs and, therefore, wages.

An adverse demand shock is represented in Fig. 16.3 as the leftward shift of world (domestic and foreign) demand for domestically produced goods, from D to D'. If the nominal exchange rate is allowed to depreciate, or if prices and wages are flexible, the effect will be a shift from point A to point B: output declines and the real exchange rate depreciates from λ_0 to λ_1. This is a painful

---

[3] Real and nominal exchange rates are defined in Chapter 14. Note that in Fig. 14.2 it is the inflation rate that appears on the vertical axis, while here we use the real exchange rate. There is no discrepancy, though: all else being equal, a higher rate of inflation results in an exchange rate appreciation. We use the real exchange rate here to emphasize external competitiveness.

move, of course, but an unavoidable one given the adverse shock.

The outcome is more painful if the exchange rate is fixed and prices and wages are rigid. In that case, the outcome is represented by point C where the output decline is even deeper. At the unchanged real exchange rate λ_0, domestic producers continue to supply the output corresponding to point A, but point C represents the new, lower, demand. The distance AC represents an accumulation of unsold goods. Obviously, domestic firms will not accumulate unsold goods for ever. Something has to give, and this will be cutbacks in production. The recession that sets in implies a rise in unemployment, which should generate incentives to gradually cut prices and wages, eventually bringing the economy to point B. But this is likely to be the outcome of a painful and protracted process.

The example illustrates why exchange rate fixity, when combined with sticky prices and wages, makes an already bad situation worse. The general point is that a monetary union rules out nominal exchange rate changes within the currency area, and yet the real exchange rate of the affected country must be adjusted in the face of an adverse shock. Instead of a simple once-and-for-all change in the nominal exchange rate, the real exchange rate adjustment can only come from changes in prices and wages. If prices and wages are sticky, the adjustment can take time, creating hardship along the way.

16.1.3 Asymmetric shocks

So far we have thought of a country in isolation to set the stage for the study of the key insight from the OCA theory: diversity means that different countries face different shocks. The simplest case is a currency area with two member countries. We call these countries A and B and examine what difference it makes to share or not the same currency. Note carefully that country A has two (nominal and real) exchange rates: one *vis-à-vis* country B and one *vis-à-vis* the rest of the world. The same applies to country B, of course.

If countries A and B are hit by the same adverse shock, we know from the previous section that both have to undergo a real depreciation *vis-à-vis* the rest of the world. If they are similar enough, to a first approximation, there is no need for their bilateral (nominal and real) exchange rate to change. They are in the same boat facing the same headwinds. The situation

is very different, however, in the presence of an asymmetric shock. Assume, for instance, that country A is hit by an adverse shock, but not country B. Country A must now undergo a real depreciation *vis-à-vis* both country B and the rest of the world.

This reasoning shows that the loss of the exchange rate within a currency union is of no consequence as long as all member countries face the same shocks. In the presence of symmetric shocks, the union simply adjusts its common exchange rate *vis-à-vis* the rest of the world and its member countries are as well off as if they had each independently changed their own exchange rate.

With asymmetrical shocks, however, monetary union membership becomes seriously constraining. What happens then? The situation is examined in Fig. 16.4. The vertical axis measures each country's real exchange rate *vis-à-vis* the rest of the world: EP_A/P^* and EP_B/P^*, where P_A and P_B are the price indices in country A and country B, respectively, P^* the price level in the rest of the world, and E is the common currency's exchange rate, initially equal to E_0. Points A in both panels represent the initially balanced situation, with a real exchange rate λ_0, assumed to be the same in both countries: $\lambda_0 = E_0/P_A/P^* = E_0/P_B/P^*$. Prices are assumed to be sticky – otherwise, the exchange rate regime does not matter as we already know from section 16.1.2.

Now let an adverse shock affect country A alone. This is represented in the left-hand panel, which describes country A, as the shift of the demand schedule from D to D'. If country A is not part of a monetary union and can change its own nominal exchange rate, its best course of action is to let it depreciate to E_1 such that the real exchange rate depreciates to $\lambda_1 = E_1/P_A/P^*$, which allows for a new equilibrium at point B. Country B has no reason to change its nominal and real exchange rates, which remain at E_0 and λ_0, respectively. If countries A and B belong to a monetary union, things are very different. If the now-common central bank cares about country A and depreciates the common exchange rate to E_1, with sticky prices both countries share the same real exchange rate λ_1. Figure 16.4 shows that this is not good for country B, which now faces a situation of potentially inflationary excess demand (represented by the distance $B'B''$). Clearly, in the presence of an asymmetric shock, what suits one country hurts the other. This is the fundamental cost of forming a monetary union.

If the union's common external exchange rate floats freely, it will depreciate because of the adverse shock in

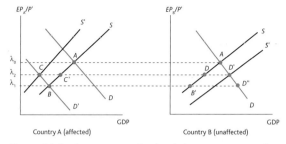

Country A (affected) | Country B (unaffected)

Figure 16.4: *An asymmetric shock in a currency union*

one part of the area, but not all the way to E_1. It will decline to an intermediate level such as E_2, to which corresponds a real exchange rate $\lambda_2 = E_2/P_A/P^* = E_2/P_B/P^*$.[4] The outcome is a combination of excess supply in country A (represented by CC') and excess demand in country B (represented by DD'). Both countries are in disequilibrium. The new exchange rate level is 'correct' on average, but it is still too strong for country A, which is in recession, and too weak for country B, which is overheating. This example illustrates the cost of belonging to a monetary union.

Disequilibria cannot last for ever. What is likely to happen next? The common exchange rate *vis-à-vis* the rest of the world has no reason to change from E_2; it has already done its job of taking into account the average situation in the union. The required adjustment will have to come from prices and wages, in both countries. Country A cannot sell all of its production, so its price level must eventually decline until the real exchange rate depreciates to λ_1, the equilibrium level previously identified. A recession will set in – remember, country A's goods are in excess supply – and unemployment will rise, putting downward pressure on prices and wages. The price of country A's goods will decline until it reaches level P'_A such that $\lambda_1 = E_2 P'_A/P^*$.

Country B is in the opposite situation: facing buoyant demand, the price of its goods will rise to P'_B such that its real exchange rate appreciates back to its equilibrium level, which is the original level $\lambda_0 = E_2 P'_B/P^*$. Recession and disinflation in country A, boom and inflation in country B: these are the costs of operating a monetary union when an asymmetric shock occurs.

---

[4] Where exactly E_2 lies depends on a host of factors, such as the relative size of the two countries and how sensitive is their trade to changes in the real exchange rate.

16.1.4 Symmetric shocks with asymmetric effects

The analysis has focused on asymmetric shocks, but it applies also to the case of symmetric shocks that produce asymmetric effects. There are many reasons why no two countries react in exactly the same way to the same shock. Their differing reactions may be due to their different socio-economic structures, including labour market regulations and traditions, the relative importance of industrial sectors, the role of the financial and banking sectors, the country's external indebtedness, the ability to strike agreements between firms, trade unions and the government, and so on. A good example is the case of a sudden increase in the price of oil and gas. This shock hurts oil- and gas-importing countries but benefits exporting countries, such as the Netherlands, Norway and the UK. It is one reason why the two latter countries have not joined the European monetary union.

Another asymmetry concerns the way monetary policy operates. When a common central bank reacts to a symmetric shock, it is not a foregone conclusion that the effect of its action will be the same throughout the currency union. Differences in the structure of banking and financial markets or in the size of firms – and their ability to borrow – may result in asymmetric effects. Chapter 19 examines this aspect.

When countries are sufficiently different, therefore, symmetric shocks can produce similar effects to asymmetric shocks and the analysis carried out in the previous section fully applies. In particular, the effects can be seen as implying the same situation as the one described in Fig. 16.4. This is why, from here onwards, when reference is made to asymmetric shocks, it also includes the case of symmetric shocks with asymmetric effects.

16.2 The optimum currency area criteria

The key elements of analysis are now in place. Sharing a common currency brings important benefits, but occasional asymmetric shocks may be painful. The issue is one of trading off costs and benefits, as in Fig. 16.2; there is no simple, black-and-white answer to the question of whether it is a good idea to adopt a common currency in a particular area. What the OCA theory does is to propose criteria by which to judge the costs and the desirability of sharing the same currency.

A useful and succinct summary is provided in the British Chancellor of the Exchequer's assessment on UK membership:

> EMU membership could significantly raise UK output and lead to a lasting increase in jobs in the long term. As noted above, the assessment shows that intra-euro area trade has increased strongly in recent years as a result of EMU, perhaps by as much as 3 to 20 per cent; that the UK could enjoy a significant boost to trade with the euro area of up to 50 per cent over 30 years; and that UK national output could rise over a 30-year period by between 5 and 9 per cent.
>
> (*UK Membership and the Single Currency*, HM Treasury, London, June 2003, p. 222)

There are three classic economic criteria and an additional three which are political. The first criterion looks at a way of minimizing the costs of an asymmetric shock within a currency area. The next two economic criteria take a different approach: they aim at identifying which economic areas are likely to be hit by asymmetric shocks infrequently or moderately enough to be of limited concern. The last three criteria deal with political aspects; they ask whether different countries are likely to help each other when faced with asymmetric shocks. This section lists and explains the logic of the OCA criteria; section 16.3 will examine whether they are satisfied in Europe.

16.2.1 Labour mobility (Mundell)

The first criterion was proposed by Robert Mundell (Box 16.2) when he first formulated the notion of an OCA. The idea is that the cost of sharing the same currency would be eliminated if the factors of production, capital and labour were fully mobile across borders. Since it is conventionally assumed that capital is mobile, the real hurdle comes from the lack of labour mobility.

Mundell criterion

Optimum currency areas are those within which people move easily.

The reasoning is illustrated in Fig. 16.4, where the adversely affected country A undergoes unemployment while non-affected country B faces inflationary pressure. Both problems could be solved by a shift of the idle production factors in country A to country B, where they are in short supply. This reallocation is shown as a shift of both countries' supply schedules to S'. At the new

equilibrium exchange rate, country A is at point C and country B is at point D'. What is remarkable is that there is no need for prices and wages to change in either country. Once the factors of production have moved, the currency area's nominal exchange rate E_2 delivers the equilibrium real exchange rate λ_2.

The Mundell criterion thus focuses on labour's willingness to move in response to shocks. This makes good sense: why should unemployment rise in some part of a currency area while, in other parts, firms cannot produce enough to satisfy demand? Yet, as always, things are less simple than they look. A few words of caution are warranted.

First, it is no wonder that actual currency areas generally coincide with nation states. Common culture and language, right and ease of resettling, etc. make labour mobility easier within a country than across borders. Thus a national currency is not just a symbol of statehood, it is usually justified by labour mobility. Across borders, not only do cultural and linguistic differences restrain migration, but institutional barriers further discourage labour mobility. Changes in legislation may make cross-border labour mobility easier and enlarge the size of optimum currency areas and, indeed, this is part of Europe's quest for closer integration.

Second, the goods produced in country A may differ from those produced in country B. It may take quite some time to retrain workers from country A to produce the goods of country B, if at all possible. If the shocks are temporary, it may not be worth the trouble of moving, retraining, etc. Labour mobility is not a panacea, just a factor that mitigates the costs of an asymmetric shock in a currency union.

Finally, labour needs equipment to be productive. What if all equipment is already in use in country B? The usual answer is that capital is mobile, but this view needs to be qualified. Financial capital can move freely and quickly, unless impeded by exchange controls. Installed physical capital (means of production such as plants and equipment) is not mobile. It takes time to build plants and shift the location of economic activities. Closing plants in country A can be done quickly – although social–political resistance may create stumbling blocks – but creating new production facilities in country B may take months, if not years. Even if labour were highly mobile, which it is not, shifting the supply curves as described in Fig. 16.4 may take many years. By then, the asymmetric shock may well have evaporated.

16.2.2 Production diversification (Kenen)

Asymmetric shocks are the source of trouble within a currency area, but how frequent are they, really? If substantial asymmetric shocks happen only rarely, the overall costs are small while the benefits accrue every day. The Kenen criterion takes a first look at this question by asking what the most likely sources of substantial shocks are. Most of the likely shocks can be associated with shifts in spending patterns, which may be a consequence of changing tastes (e.g. German beer consumers find it fashionable to drink wine) or of new technology that brings about new products and makes older ones obsolete (e.g. internet displaces faxes). Such shocks actually occur every day and every year, but most of them are hardly noticed outside the affected industries. To create a problem for a monetary union, a shock must be large and asymmetric.

The countries most likely to be affected by severe shocks are those that have specialized in a narrow range of goods. For example, many of the African countries that are part of the CFA franc zone primarily export a single agricultural product such as coffee or cacao. A decline in the demand for coffee – which may occur because new producers emerge from elsewhere in the world – affects some countries in the CFA franc zone and not others, thus provoking an asymmetric shock. Conversely, a country that produces a wide range of products will be little affected by shocks that concern any particular good because that good weighs relatively little in total production.

This explains the second criterion for an optimum currency area, initially stated by Kenen (Box 16.2): currency area member countries ought to be well diversified and producing similar goods. In that case,

good-specific shocks are likely to be either symmetric or of little aggregate consequence, thus lessening the need for frequent exchange rate adjustments.

Kenen criterion

Countries whose production and exports are widely diversified and of similar structure form an optimum currency area.

16.2.3 Openness (McKinnon)

The next relevant question is whether the exchange rate is a useful tool to deal with an asymmetric shock. If not, little is lost by giving it up. In the analysis of section 16.1, the distinction between 'domestic' and 'foreign' goods refers to where the goods are produced. However, many standard goods, such as paper sheets or electric bulbs, are produced in different countries and are virtually identical. In that case, trade competition will ensure that their prices are the same at home and abroad, or nearly so, and therefore largely independent of the exchange rate. Consequently, changing the exchange rate does not affect competitiveness or, when expressed in domestic currency, prices are not sticky any more and the exchange rate change is no longer an important adjustment tool. This is the basis of the third criterion formulated by McKinnon (Box 16.2). It recognizes that when the economy is small and very open to trade, it has little ability to change the prices of its goods on the international markets. In that case, giving up the exchange rate, that is, not having an independent currency, does not entail much of a loss, at least for moderate shocks.

McKinnon criterion

Countries which are very open to trade and trade heavily with each other form an optimum currency area.

The criterion can be made more precise as follows. When two countries A and B do not share the same currency, they each have their own exchange rate vis-à-vis the rest of the world, E_A and E_B. If they are very open and trade intensively with each other, the distinction between domestic and foreign goods loses much of its significance as competition will equalize the prices of most goods when expressed in the same currency.[5]

[5] This property is known as the law of one price. Despite its name, it is not very well verified in practice. Yet, while deviations from the law of one price are commonplace, the main argument – that exchange rate changes fail to seriously affect their relative prices – remains largely valid.

For example, if the price of country A's domestic goods in domestic currency is P_A, expressed in the rest of the world's currency it is $E_A P_A$, and similarly country B's price is $E_B P_B$. Competition ensures that $E_A P_A = E_B P_B$. Any change of one country's nominal exchange rate, say E_A, must be immediately followed by a change in local currency prices P_A such that the world price level $E_A P_A$ remains unchanged. In effect, P_A and P_B are not sticky any more. In that case, the real exchange rates of both countries vis-à-vis the rest of the world are also equal: $E_A/P_A/P^* = E_B P_B/P^*$. When prices are flexible, creating a currency union by giving up the exchange rate entails no serious loss of policy independence.[6]

16.2.4 Fiscal transfers

An important aspect of the analysis of section 16.1.2 is that country B suffers from the adverse shock that hits country A if they share the same currency. It is therefore in the interest of country B to help alleviate the impact of the shock. One possibility is for country B to financially compensate country A. Such a transfer tends to reduce asymmetric shifts in Fig. 16.4. It mitigates both the recession in country A and the boom in country B, giving time for the shock to disappear if it is temporary, or to work its effects through prices if it is longer lasting. As shocks occur randomly, today's provider of help will be tomorrow's beneficiary. In effect, such transfers work like a common insurance against bad shocks.

Transfer criterion

Countries that agree to compensate each other for adverse shocks form an optimum currency area.

Transfer schemes of this kind exist across regions in every country. Sometimes they are explicit; most often they are implicit. For example, if a particular region suffers an asymmetric shock, then, as income declines, so do tax payments while welfare support – chiefly unemployment benefits – rise. In the net, the region receives transfers from the rest of the country. These transfers are often implicit, part-and-parcel of the redistributive mechanism at work in the country. Some federal countries, such as Germany and Switzerland, operate explicit transfer systems.

[6] Because most goods, nowadays, have little national specificity, a useful distinction is between goods that are traded (exported and imported) and those that are 'non-traded'. Among closely integrated and similar countries, traded goods follow the previous description and their prices differ little. Non-traded goods include many services (e.g. car repair, hairdressing or medical advice) and goods that do not travel easily (e.g. cement that is very heavy or flowers that are perishable). Their prices differ sizeably from one country to another. Openness, then, is better defined as the share of traded goods in total consumption. When this share is high, there are relatively few non-traded goods, and exchange rate changes have relatively small effects.

16.2.5 Homogeneous preferences

Political conditions matter even for symmetric shocks. Section 16.1.2 argues that symmetric shocks do not pose any problem as long as each country reacts in the same way to the shock. But this result assumes that all countries agree on how to deal with each and every possible shock. In practice, however, there rarely exists a 'best way' to deal with a shock. For example, should we be more concerned about inflation or about unemployment? Should we favour the exporters – who wish to have weak exchange rates to buttress competitiveness – or the consumers – who wish to have strong exchange rates to raise their purchasing power? These are trade-offs, which generate the confrontation of opposing interests and are dealt with through the respective influence of political parties, trade unions and lobbies. There is no reason for the resulting decision to be the same across different countries because national preferences are not necessarily homogeneous.

If the currency area member countries do not share the same preferences over such trade-offs, each of them will want the common central bank to pursue different policies. Whatever the central bank chooses to do will be controversial and will leave some, possibly all, countries unhappy. At best, there will be resentment, at worst the currency union may not survive. Box 16.3 shows how this can play in practice.

Homogeneity of preferences criterion

Currency union member countries must share a wide consensus on the way to deal with shocks

Why should preferences differ? A shock, and the way to deal with it, typically has redistributive effects: some groups will lose more than others, and some may even benefit. Each group carries some political weight and will naturally mobilize support in its favour. The collective preference, which shapes the policy response, thus intimately depends on domestic politics, and there is no reason for all the countries of a currency area to share the same balance of political forces. The fifth criterion states that these differences should not be too wide.

16.2.6 Solidarity vs nationalism

The final criterion goes deeper into political considerations. Since none of the previous criteria is likely to be fully satisfied, no currency area is ever optimum. This is even true for individual countries which casually operate as currency areas. One consequence is that shocks, even when symmetric, generate political disagreements as to what the proper response should be. Such disagreements, a familiar feature in any country, may be more pronounced across regional areas if the shocks have asymmetric effect. In individual countries, the eventual resolution of such debates is usually accepted as the cost of living together – the natural consequence of statehood. The outcome is ultimately seen as acceptable because citizens of the same country readily accept some degree of solidarity with one another.

When separate countries contemplate the formation of a currency area, they need to realize that there will be times when there will be disagreements and that these disagreements may follow national lines, especially if the shocks are asymmetric or produce asymmetric effects. For such disagreements to be tolerated, the people that form the currency union must accept that they will be living together and extend their sense of solidarity to the whole union. In short, they must have a shared sense of common destiny that outweighs the nationalist tendencies that would otherwise call for intransigent reactions.

Solidarity criterion

When the common monetary policy gives rise to conflicts of national interests, the countries that form a currency area need to accept the costs in the name of a common destiny.

16.3 Is Europe an optimum currency area?

In principle, the OCA theory should tell us whether it did make sense to establish a monetary union in Europe. As already noted, however, the answer is unlikely to be black and white. The benefits are hard to quantify, as are the six OCA criteria which may be only partly fulfilled. This section distils that rich and unending debate. Box 16.4 reports on the conclusions reached in May 2003 by the British Chancellor of the Exchequer on the basis of five tests inspired by the OCA theory.

16.3.1 Asymmetric shocks

The OCA theory emphasizes the role of asymmetric shocks, so a natural starting point is to ask whether asymmetric shocks happen often enough, and are large enough, to be of serious concern. Of course, we do not know what the future keeps in store. The best that can be done is to assume that the past can be a guide to the future – a poor assumption challenged in section 16.4 – and examine the pre-EMU record. This section looks at the frequency of shocks and how often national

Box 16.3

Will Italy leave the eurozone?

Figure 16.5 shows that growth in Germany and Italy has been constantly slower than in the rest of the eurozone since the common currency came into effect in 1999. There are many reasons for this, but the main one is that these two countries have quite inflexible labour markets, as explained in Chapter 8. Faced with the same problem, that largely pre-dates the advent of the euro, these two countries have reacted differently. Germany's wage moderation contrasts with signifi-

cant increases of production costs in Italy. In addition, the German authorities have started to enact serious labour market reforms, with little progress in Italy.

It may not come as a surprise that, in June 2005, an Italian minister called for his country to leave the euro-zone and re-establish the lira. Most economists consider that such a move would be a disaster for Italy, which has never known as stable prices and low interest rates as those it has enjoyed since it adopted the euro. In addition, given its high public debt, Italy would face much increased debt service costs if, as is nearly certain, its interest rate were to increase significantly after leaving the eurozone. Yet some observers and financial market analysts have become quite jittery and ask whether Italy could indeed leave the monetary union, giving credence to the minister's statement. Interestingly, the minister in question was in charge of labour markets; he may find it easier to reduce employment with an undervalued lira than through unpopular reforms. Of course, Italy's partners would not happily see one EU member play beggar-thy-neighbour inside the single market.

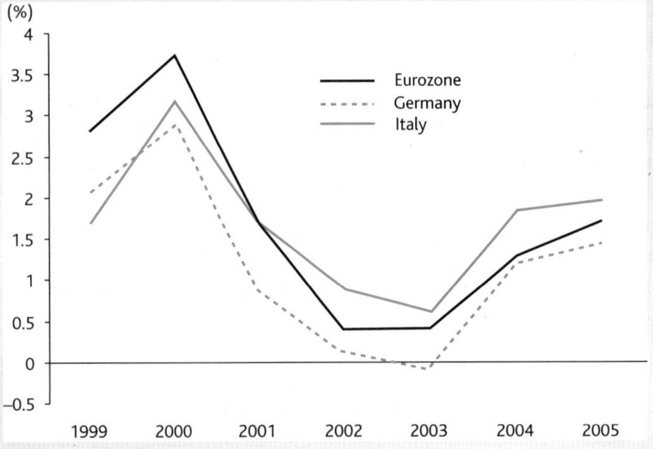

Figure 16.5: *Real GDP growth in Italy and Germany, 1999–2005*
Source: *Economic Outlook*, OECD.

exchange rates have been used to cushion them. If there were only a few shocks, or if the European countries had made little use of their exchange rates, giving up national currencies would be of little importance.

In looking at the record, we have to keep in mind that there are two main reasons for changing the exchange rate. The first, which is the subject of the OCA approach, is the occurrence of asymmetric shocks that are best dealt with through currency realignments. The second is to accommodate inflationary policies, which is ruled out in the EMU as explained in Chapter 17 and must now be ignored.

Figure 16.6 presents a synthetic OCA index computed by asking the following question: Based on past experience, how much would European countries have adjusted their exchange rates *vis-à-vis* the German Deutschmark (taken,

quite reasonably, as the centre currency in Europe) to deal with asymmetric shocks relevant to the three classic economic OCA principles of Mundell, Kenen and McKinnon? The index is larger the more frequent asymmetric shocks have been and, therefore, the more actively the exchange rate should have been used.[7]

---

[7] Technically, the index is computed as: $SD(ER) = -0.09 + 1.46\ SD(\Delta y) + 0.022\ DISSIM - 0.054\ TRADE + 0.012\ SIZE$, where SD stands for standard deviation (a statistical measure of variability), ER the exchange rate *vis-à-vis* the Mark, Δy is the difference between growth in the country and in Germany, a measure of cyclical mismatch meant to capture asymmetric shocks, DISSIM is a measure of the dissimilarity of trade structures meant to capture the Kenen criterion (see section 16.2.2), TRADE is a measure of the intensity of trade with Germany meant to capture the McKinnon criterion, and SIZE is a measure of the country's economic size (its GDP). The particular weights are obtained from a regression analysis. For full details, see Bayoumi and Eichengreen (1997). Recent updates do not produce significant changes.

Box 16.4

Why Britain is not yet ready for the euro

When he was appointed Chancellor of the Exchequer in 1997, Gordon Brown awarded himself a right of veto on the highly political decision of British euro area membership. He announced that he would form his verdict on the basis of five economic tests:

1. *Convergence*. Are business cycles and economic structures compatible so that we and others could live comfortably with euro interest rates on a permanent basis?
2. *Flexibility*. If problems emerge, is there sufficient flexibility to deal with them?
3. *Investment*. Would joining the EMU create better conditions for firms making long-term decisions to invest in the UK?
4. *Financial services*. What impact would entry into the EMU have on the competitive position of the UK's financial services industry, particularly the City's wholesale markets?
5. *Growth, stability and employment*. In summary, will joining the EMU promote higher growth, stability and a lasting increase in jobs?

In May 2003, the Chancellor finally released his first assessment. He found that the convergence and flexibility tests were not met, that the investment and financial services tests were met, and the fifth test would be met when the first two were met. From this he concluded that the UK was not yet ready, adding: 'We will report on progress in the Budget next year. We can then consider the extent of progress and determine whether on the basis of it we make a further Treasury assessment of the five tests which – if positive next year – would allow us at that time to put the issue before the British people in a referendum.'[1]

Two characteristics of this procedure are striking. First, the heavy and explicit use of OCA economic principles. Test 1 deals with the presence of asymmetric shocks, test 2 with the ability to cope with asymmetric shocks, with heavy emphasis on labour markets, while test 3 looks at capital mobility. Test 5 summarizes the OCA approach. Test 4 is specific to the UK's specialization in financial services. Second, the tests are specified in an obviously intended vague way, leaving the Chancellor free to implicitly weigh the political aspects of the undertaking.

[1] *The various documents are available on* www.hm-treasury.gov.uk. *They include a large number of specially commissioned studies that are well worth reading.*

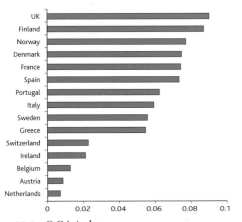

Figure 16.6: *OCA index*

Source: Bayoumi and Eichengreen (1997).

Interestingly, the countries at the top of the list – with the worst OCA index – have decided, initially at least, not to join the EMU, in contrast with those at the bottom. There are a few noteworthy exceptions: Finland, which underwent unusual disturbances in the early 1990s, and Switzerland, which is not a member of the EU. The next sections go into more detail, examining one by one the three classic criteria.

Another aspect of asymmetry noted in section 16.1.3 is the possibility of asymmetric effects of monetary policy. Figure 16.7 shows estimates of the effect, after two years, on GDP (left-hand panel) and prices (right-hand panel) of a 1 percentage point increase in the interest rate. Quite clearly, there are important differences. The reasons for these differences are not well known yet but two of them are often mentioned:

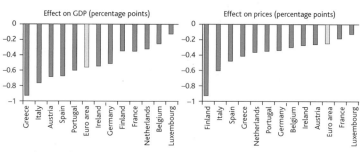

Figure 16.7: *Asymmetric effects of monetary policy*

Source: Angeloni *et al.* (2002).

★ Monetary policy affects spending decisions through the availability and cost of credit by commercial banks. Since national banking structures differ from one country to another, this may explain that monetary policy produces varied effects across the eurozone.

★ Typically, small firms rely more on bank credit than large firms that issue shares and bonds directly on the financial markets, sometimes abroad. In addition, small firms are more easily denied loans during periods of restrictive monetary policy. The relative proportion of small and large firms may be another source of diverse effects of monetary policy.

These features suggest that asymmetry is a concern in the euro area, even though these sharp differences may be erased over time.

16.3.2 Openness

Openness matters in the OCA theory because, in a small open economy, most of the goods produced and consumed are traded on international markets. Accordingly, their prices on the local market are largely independent of local conditions and any change in the value of the currency tends to be promptly passed into domestic prices. When this is the case, exchange rate changes fail to affect the country's competitiveness and are, hence, essentially useless, which is exactly the McKinnon criterion.

Openness is defined as the share of economic activity devoted to international trade. The ratio of exports to GDP measures the proportion of domestic production that is exported. The ratio of imports to GDP measures the proportion of domestic spending that falls on imports. Table 16.1 presents the average of these two ratios for all EU members, for the countries which are negotiating entry and for two large currency areas, Japan and the USA. Most European countries are very open, the more so the smaller they are, which explains why the smaller countries have traditionally been the most enthusiastic supporters

of the monetary union. The ten new member countries, which accessed to the EU in 2004 and will probably join the eurozone by the end of the decade, are also very open, as are the candidate countries. The USA and Japan appear as largely closed, as is the EU as a whole.

A second way to look at openness is to measure how domestic prices respond to exchange rate changes, the pass-through effect. If all prices respond one for one to exchange rate changes, the pass-through is complete and the exchange rate only affects inflation, not competitiveness. Figure 16.8 compares openness (as shown in Table 16.1) and estimates of the short-term pass-through, measured as the impact of exchange rate changes on import prices: for instance, a 0.6 pass-through coefficient means that a 10 per cent depreciation is followed within three months by a 6 per cent increase in import prices. By and large – with some 'strange' results likely to be due to the imprecision of the estimates – the more open the economy, the larger is the

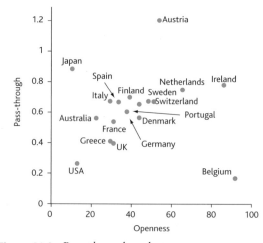

Figure 16.8: *Pass-through and openness*

Source: *European Economy*, 73 (2001), Campa and Goldberg (2002).

Average of ratios of exports and imports to GDP					
Country	%	Country	%	Country	%
Austria	52.3	Cyprus	48.3	Denmark	42.8
Belgium	87.2	Czech Republic	76.0	Sweden	43.9
Finland	35.4	Estonia	92.0	UK	27.9
France	27.2	Hungary	70.1		
Germany	39.9	Latvia	55.0	Bulgaria	65.9
Greece	25.5	Lithuania	56.9	Croatia	54.4
Ireland	72.6	Malta	81.8	Romania	39.3
Italy	27.9	Poland	40.9	Turkey	36.5
Luxembourg	133.3	Slovakia	83.6		
Netherlands	66.4	Slovenia	63.1		
Portugal	36.2			USA	13.8
Spain	29.5	EU25	10.7	Japan	13.5

Source: *European Economy*, Spring 2005.

Table 16.1: *Openness in 2006*

pass-through. Most European countries are characterized by both significant openness and large pass-through coefficients in contrast with the USA and Japan.

The available evidence is quite clear. As far as the McKinnon criterion is concerned, most EU economies qualify for joining a monetary union. They are very open and domestic prices tend to be dominated by the exchange rate. This observation applies very strongly to the smaller countries, less so to the larger ones but certainly more than to many other advanced countries.

16.3.3 Diversification and trade dissimilarity

The Kenen criterion rests on the idea that asymmetric shocks are less likely among countries that share similar production patterns and whose trade is diversified. Figure 16.9 presents an index of dissimilarity of European trade as of end-1995. The index looks at how each country's trade structure differs from the situation in Germany, which serves as a benchmark. The index is based on the decomposition of trade into three classes of goods: agriculture, minerals and manufacturing. Dissimilarity with Germany is highest for Norway and lowest for Austria.

Dissimilarity predicts well that Norway, whose trade is dominated by oil and fish, is not interested in joining the monetary union. It also exposes the case of the Netherlands, quite dependent on natural gas and yet an enthusiastic member of the EMU. This case is a good illustration that the OCA criteria are not absolute, and that they focus on the costs of EMU membership, ignoring the economic and political benefits. The Dutch authorities believe that their economy is far too integrated with the European economy to afford exchange rate fluctuations and wish to be deeply involved in European integration. This is to be contrasted with the cases of Switzerland and the UK, both of which rank well on the dissimilarity index and yet, so far, have remained outside the EMU largely for the broader political reasons presented in sections 16.2.5 and 16.2.6.

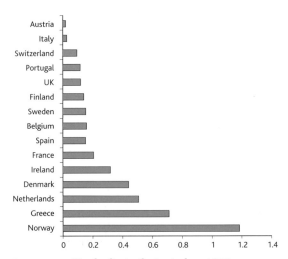

Figure 16.9: *Trade dissimilarity index, 1995*

Note: The index measures the difference of a country's trade structure to that of its partners.

Source: Bayoumi and Eichengreen (1997).

16.3.4 Labour mobility

The OCA theory suggests that labour mobility can go a long way towards alleviating the costs of an asymmetric shock when the exchange rate cannot be adjusted. In this case, labour mobility is about how easily people move in response to economic incentives. Here again, the criterion is a matter of degree. People always move, but to some varying degree, and full mobility is never to be seen. Full labour mobility would occur if people would immediately take advantage of any difference in earnings, and move to where they can earn more. Even such a simple definition is fraught with difficulties. A correct appraisal of 'earnings' must include the following:

★ The cost of moving, possibly including the selling and buying of dwellings.
★ The prospect of becoming unemployed, both in the country of origin and in the country of immigration.
★ Career opportunities, which means not only current but also future earnings.
★ Family career prospects, including the spouse and children and sometimes even more distant relatives.
★ Social benefits including unemployment, health and retirement.
★ Taxation of earnings from both labour and savings.

Labour mobility is also subject to non-economic incentives such as:

★ Cultural differences (language, religion, traditions, possibly racism and xenophobia) in the country considered for immigration.
★ Family and friendship links that can be weakened.
★ Commitment to one's country of origin (nationalism).

For these reasons, labour mobility can only be relative and a natural approach is to proceed by comparison with existing, well-functioning currency areas, such as Canada and the USA. We first compare international migration. Figure 16.10 shows the percentage of the labour force that is foreign-born. Clearly, there is less immigration to European countries than to the USA and Canada, and differences within Europe are wide. In addition, a very small proportion of foreign workers are Europeans (Belgium is a noteworthy exception). Europeans seem to take little advantage of the single market which allows them to work and settle anywhere in the EU.

In fact, Europeans show little movement across regions within their own countries. Figure 16.11 displays the flow of people, as a percentage of the total population, who migrated internally, when each country is spliced into several regions (e.g. 11 regions for Belgium or 12 regions for the UK). It is simply a fact of life that Europeans move

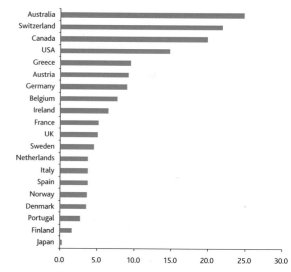

Figure 16.10: *Foreign-born population as a percentage of total population, 1998*

Source: DICE, CESifo.

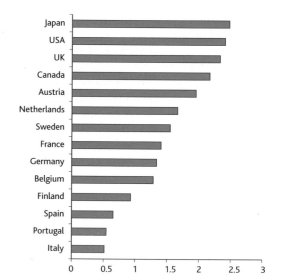

Figure 16.11: *Internal migration across regions as a percentage of total population, 1995*

Source: *Employment Outlook*, OECD, June 2000, p. 53.

only half as often as US citizens.[8] Over the 1990s, 38 per cent of EU citizens changed residence, most of whom (68 per cent) moved within the same town or village and 36 per cent moved to another town in the same region. In Europe, while 21 per cent moved to another region in the

[8] This section draws partly on the final report of the High Level Task Force on Skills and Mobility sponsored by the De Rodolfo de Benedetti Foundation of Bocconi University.

same Member State, only 4.4 per cent moved to another Member State. Even worse for the OCA criterion, Europeans move mainly for personal reasons since professional reasons account for only 5 per cent of moves.

Why do Europeans move so little? There are many reasons, some obvious ones like language and traditions, others less well-appreciated like the fact that housing tends to be more expensive in Europe than in the USA. Other reasons have to do with cracks in the integration process. For instance, moving across countries means switching from one welfare system to another, with serious difficulties regarding health and retirement benefits. In the USA, in contrast, no such difficulty arises when moving from one US state to another.

Europeans, in any event, move relatively little within their own countries, where none of these barriers apply.

Low migration by European nationals could be compensated by immigration from outside the EU.[9] If immigrant workers were to move to where job offers exceed supply, some of the costs of a monetary union would be reduced. Even viewed this way, immigration – a big political issue in Europe – is smaller in Europe than in the USA. In the early 2000s, immigration flows amounted to some 0.3 per cent of the total population in the EU, and to 0.5 per cent in the USA.

In summary, Europe is far from fulfilling the labour mobility criterion. An important implication is that asymmetric shocks, when they occur, are likely to be met

---

Box 16.5 The effects of asymmetric shocks in Europe and the USA

How does Europe's low labour mobility affect the response to an asymmetric shock? A study by Fatás (2000) compares Europe and the USA. Fatás looks at 51 regions in the USA (the 50 states and the District of Columbia) and at 54 regions in Europe (a decomposition of 14 countries, all EU countries with the exception of Luxembourg). He asks what happens when an adverse asymmetric shock occurs, i.e. when it affects just one region. Figure 16.12 shows the result. The figure depicts the joint behaviour of total employment, unemployment and the participation rate in each region (all compared with the overall situation in the USA and Europe, respectively).[1] Obviously, employment declines and, for the same shock size, the effect is quantitatively similar in Europe and in the USA. The difference lies elsewhere. In the USA, most of the drop in employment is met by regional emigration; people move to more fortunate parts of the country. In Europe, instead, most of the drop in employment is met by a fall in the participation rate; people withdraw from the labour force and stay at home. Interestingly, in the long run, in the USA those who leave do not return, and in Europe those who stop working remain inactive.

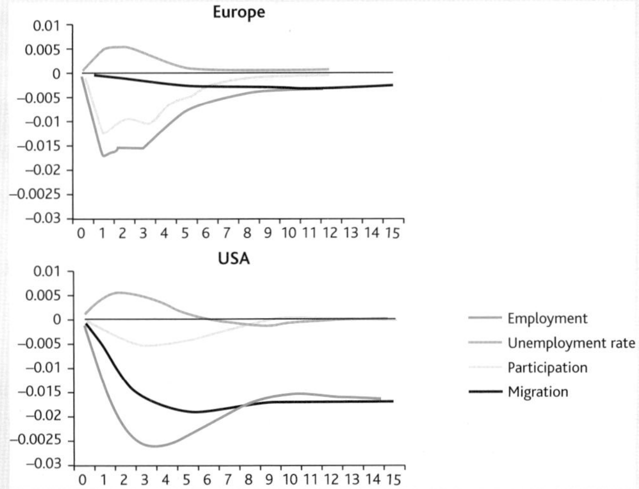

This study corroborates a key element of OCA theory: labour mobility crucially affects the response to asymmetric shocks. The twist is that with low European labour mobility, following an adverse shock, people become unemployed and many others simply give up the hope of working.

Figure 16.12: *Labour market responses*

Source: Fatás (2000).

[1] Box 8.1 provides the definitions of employment, unemployment and participation rates.

---

[9] See Chapter 8 for an analysis of immigration.

by unemployment in countries facing a loss of competitiveness. Box 16.5 reports that, indeed, when asymmetric shocks occur, migration plays a smaller role in Europe than in the USA, with the unfortunate result that employment takes most of the burden.

16.3.5 Fiscal transfers

Countries hit by a temporary adverse shock could receive transfers from better-off countries as compensation for having lost the exchange rate instrument for the common good. Within most countries, seen as currency areas, these transfers are automatic. When adversely hit, a region sees its income decline, at least relatively to the rest of the currency area, and tax payments by its residents decline. At the same time, various welfare payments (unemployment benefits, subsidies to poor people, etc.) rise. In good years, the opposite occurs and the favoured region supports less fortunate regions. In the USA, for instance, it has been estimated that any shortfall of income in a state is compensated by federal transfers that amount to between 10 and 40 per cent of the loss. There is no such system at work in the EU. The EU budget is small, about 1 per cent of GDP, and spent almost entirely on three items: the Commission's operating expenses, the Common Agricultural Policy and the Structural Funds which support the poorer regions irrespective of whether they are hit by shocks. Any transfer system would need a significant increase in the EU budget, which is not likely in the near future.

On this criterion, Europe is definitely not an optimum monetary union.

16.3.6 Homogeneous preferences

Do all countries share similar views about the use of monetary policy? On the basis of past inflation rates (the evidence is reviewed in Chapter 18), this does not seem to be the case. Low-inflation Germany and formerly high-inflation Italy or Greece have very little in common. Similarly, looking at public debts (Chapter 18), there seems a gulf that separates European countries' approaches to fiscal policy. So, is the verdict negative? It may be too early to tell.

Why has the quality of macroeconomic policies been so diverse in Europe? Is it in the genes? Medical research has not yet turned up any clue, but economic research has a lot to say about incentives that policy makers face. Broadly defined, political institutions shape their reactions to various events, and policy-making institutions differ from one country to another. This includes the respective roles of the executive and the

parliament, the number of ideologies of political parties and trade unions, and much more.[10]

The solution has been to accompany integration steps with the setting up of common institutions. In fact, one reason why the inflation-prone countries have been eager to join the monetary union is that it provides for a degree of monetary policy discipline that has been elusive in the past.[11] As far as the single currency is concerned, Chapter 17 shows that a key preoccupation has been to guarantee macroeconomic stability. The European Central Bank is strongly independent and constitutionally committed to price stability. National deficits are bound by an excessive deficit procedure. Still, although all countries are increasingly operating under common institutions, they do not fully share the same views on each and every issue that arises. The result is occasional frictions among governments and a sense of estrangement among some public opinions, which was particularly visible when the Constitution was rejected in the spring of 2005.

We can conclude that there remains some heterogeneity among national preferences. This criterion is only partly fulfilled.

16.3.7 Solidarity vs nationalism

How deep is the European sentiment of solidarity? Put differently, how far are the citizens willing to give up parts of their national sovereignties in the pursuit of the common interest? There is no simple, uncontroversial way to measure the willingness of European citizens. An indication is given in Fig. 16.13 by a public opinion poll; the question was: 'Are you, yourself, for the development towards a European political union?' The poll was conducted in May and June 2005, at the time of the negative referenda in France and the Netherlands, a period of heightened scepticism on European integration. For the whole union, 58 per cent of the answers were positive, balanced by 28 per cent of respondents who opposed such an evolution. The cup is not quite that full, however, since 11 per cent of the respondents did not express a view.[12] Importantly, there are huge differences of opinion from one country to another. Many new member countries are enthusiastic supporters of political integration, while the UK and the Nordic countries – including the new members from the Baltic area – are strongly opposed.

---

[10] The web appendix to Chapter 8 describes the various 'models' in Europe.
[11] This aspect is touched upon in Chapter 15.
[12] An interesting study by Bernd (1999) shows that those who are best informed about the EMU tend to be more positively inclined towards it.

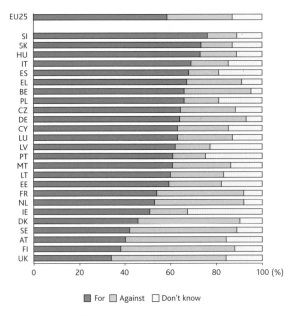

Figure 16.13: *Support to the development towards a European political union*

Source: *Eurobarometer*, 63, July 2005.

Looking around the world, there is no other example of countries that have willingly shared so widely some important components of sovereignty. The national sentiment is still very present, yet it does not fully dominate. Europe may not be scoring very highly on this criterion, but nor is it badly failing.

16.3.8 Is Europe an optimum currency area?

In the end, most European countries do well on openness and diversification, two of the three classic economic OCA criteria, and fail on the third one, labour mobility. Europe also fails on fiscal transfers, with an unclear verdict of the remaining two political criteria. Table 16.2 summarizes this admittedly debatable appraisal. The mixed performance that it reveals can be interpreted in two ways.

Criterion	Satisfied?
Labour mobility	No
Trade openness	Yes
Product diversification	Yes
Fiscal transfers	No
Homogeneity of preferences	Partly
Commonality of destiny	?

Table 16.2: *OCA scorecard*

First, it explains why the single currency project has been and remains so controversial. Neither the supporters nor the opponents have been able to produce an irrefutable case. After all, that was only to be expected as the OCA theory focuses on the costs of forming a monetary union, taking the benefits for granted. Neither the benefits nor the costs can be measured, and the OCA criteria are rarely black and white, entirely satisfied or entirely violated. In the end, the economic case is undecided, and the decision to create the monetary union must rest on political considerations.

Second, the partial fulfilment of the OCA criteria implies that, given that the decision to go ahead has been taken, there will be costs. The OCA theory identifies these costs and suggests two main conclusions: the costs will mainly arise in the labour markets and fiscal transfers will have to be rethought.

16.4 Will Europe become an optimum currency area?

The OCA characteristics of Europe are not frozen. The extent to which the OCA criteria are fulfilled in part reflects history, but the very fact that the single currency exists can change the situation. This section raises an interesting question: Does the existence of the monetary union make Europe increasingly an optimum currency area? One view is that the OCA criteria are endogenous, that they will be increasingly fulfilled over time as citizens and governments learn to live with a common currency.

It is common to contrast Europe with the USA and to conclude that Europe is far from achieving the degree of integration that has been reached across the Atlantic. But one can ask: How would the USA function today had it retained all the different currencies that existed in the nineteenth century? Four main questions arise. First, does a common currency promote further trade integration, the McKinnon criterion? Second, does trade integration lead to more diversification and similarity, the Kenen criterion? Third, how do labour market conditions respond to the loss of the exchange rate, affecting the Mundell criterion? Finally, can Europe-wide transfers be envisioned? We consider these questions in turn.

16.4.1 Effects of a currency union on trade

European policy makers strongly believe that stable exchange rates promote trade integration, which enhances fulfilment of the McKinnon criterion. The reasoning is that exchange rate uncertainty deters trade: why try to sell abroad and take the risk of losses on foreign currency deals? Unfortunately, this is not unambiguously confirmed by the facts. Nor is it necessarily the case from a purely logical viewpoint. To start with, exchange rate movements can lead not only to exchange losses, but to gains as well. Next, traders can insure themselves against currency fluctuations at little cost.[13] On the other hand, no such protection exists for long-term exchanges such as foreign direct investment, an issue taken up in Chapter 19. Thus the removal of long-run uncertainty may encourage firms that were not trading outside of their own countries to consider the eurozone as their new horizon.

There may be other reasons why sharing a common currency encourages trade. As noted in Chapter 8, a common central bank may be less receptive to local pressure for letting inflation rise a little bit when unemployment is high. Knowing that, trade unions may exercise restraint. Wage cost moderation may lead to more competition and more trade. Box 16.6 reviews an ongoing debate on just how big could be the trade effect of the adoption of the euro. The various estimates range from nothing to enormous.

As time passes by, we should be able to observe whether intra-eurozone trade is indeed increasing. Just a few years is not enough to reach safe conclusions. Early evidence, reported in Fig. 16.14, seems to detect a significant effect.[14] Over the decade 1993–2003, bilateral trade flows in Europe have swollen and ebbed as overall economic growth has risen and declined, but trade among the EMU member countries has risen faster and declined less than trade among non-member countries. If confirmed, the evidence suggests that the trade

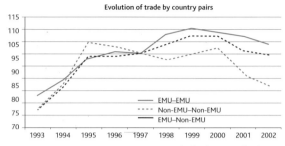

Figure 16.14: *EMU countries' trade before and after monetary union*

Source: Micco *et al.* (2003).

integration criterion, already largely fulfilled within the EMU, will become even more favourable in time.

16.4.2 Effects of trade on specialization

Assuming that adoption of a common currency deepens trade integration, the next question is what effect trade integration may have on diversification, the Kenen criterion. The evidence is open to debate. On one side, it has been argued that trade leads to more specialization as each country or region focuses on its comparative advantage. Trade takes the inter-industry form whereby exports and imports correspond to different goods. This would go against the diversification criterion and makes the monetary union more costly as time goes by. On the other side, it is argued that, among developed countries, integration leads to intra-industry trade: exports and imports include similar goods. Every country produces the whole range of goods, simply with different brands, offering customers more choice. In the process, trade becomes more diversified. The jury is still out, but the evidence accumulated so far seems to support the view that diversification increases with trade integration. In that case, the performance of the EMU with regard to that criterion stands to improve further.

16.4.3 Effects of a currency union on labour markets[15]

European labour mobility is low and few expect it to increase dramatically in the near future. An alternative to mobility is flexibility, and the argument runs as follows. European labour markets are noticeably less flexible than their US counterparts. For example, in the USA, firms are quite free to fire workers when economic conditions worsen, whereas in Europe firing is costly because of

---

[13] Exporters can sell forward the amounts of money that they expect to receive and importers can buy forward the amount of foreign currency that they will need.

[14] Bilateral trade is measured as an index (1997 = 100). For every OECD country, trade is recorded with EMU countries and with non-EMU countries. The EMU–EMU index is the unweighted average of the EMU country's EMU trade indices. The non-EMU–non-EMU index is the unweighted average of the non-EMU country's non-EMU trade indices. The EMU–non-EMU index is the average of all 'cross-group' indices. Nations in the sample: Australia, Austria, Belgium–Luxembourg, Canada, Denmark, Finland, France, Germany, Greece, Iceland, Ireland, Italy, Japan, New Zealand, the Netherlands, Norway, Portugal, Spain, Sweden, Switzerland, the UK and the USA.

[15] This section summarizes Chapter 8.

Box 16.6

The Rose and border effects

Andrew Rose, from the University of California at Berkeley, initially found that trade within a pair of countries that belong to a currency area is three times larger than trade within otherwise similar countries (Rose, 2000). Another approach has been to look at trade in border areas. Engel and Rogers (1996) focused on the border between the USA and Canada. They observe that the prices of the same goods in different cities become more different the further apart are the cities. Their calculations imply that just crossing the border has the same effect as travelling 3000 km within the same country. Further work has shown that among the various reasons why borders matter, the fact that currencies differ plays a powerful role.

These effects are huge, so huge that they are unbelievable. A large literature has explored the robustness of these results. Reviewing the Rose effect, Baldwin (2005) finds an effect of some 50 per cent, and higher for the smaller countries. This is much smaller than initially found, yet it remains a very significant effect.

heavy severance pay and numerous regulations. In addition, US unemployed workers receive less generous welfare support, which encourages them to find and accept another job as soon as possible, sometimes elsewhere in the country, possibly less well paid and in a different activity. Europeans frown on US harshness, but the result is that unemployment is generally higher and longer lasting in Europe.

The question is whether the adoption of a common currency will change that. It is too early to tell, and counter-arguments have been produced. They all revolve around the reason why European labour markets are rigid. In a nutshell, European workers are attached to the high degree of social protection that they have achieved. They understand that this may have costs, in particular in the form of unemployment and low participation rates, but then they insist on welfare programmes which protect the unemployed and those out of the labour force. This all comes at the cost of lower growth, but they consider that economic performance is not an end by itself and ought to be related to fairness, solidarity and quality of life. Will monetary union change that?

One possibility is that the single currency can trigger a virtuous circle. The idea is that the monetary union will increase the costs of the 'European way' and reduce opposition to measures that aim at flexing the labour markets. When each country had its own currency, workers were advocating using monetary policy and the exchange rate to boost the economy. This is now impossible, at least at the national level, and to date there are no pan-European trade unions. In addition, with prices set in euros across the Union, there is increasing transparency in goods markets, which should benefit countries where labour markets are more flexible. Thus, it is believed, economic competition will indirectly lead to competition among the welfare programmes and this will shift the trade-off between economic performance and labour protection.

The opposite, a hardening of labour market rigidities, is possible as well. This possibility is based on increasing emphasis on a 'Social Europe'. Advocates of a high degree of labour protection well understand the risk of competition among the welfare programmes and they have successfully called for the adoption of Union-wide minimum standards. A new title on employment has been incorporated in the Amsterdam Treaty, and the so-called Lisbon Process, adopted in 1999, provides for an annual set of guidelines that each country must implement under its National Action Plan. It is not yet clear whether this process will discourage labour market reforms by stifling competition or, on the contrary, lead to benchmarking (observing what works best) and peer pressure towards more flexibility.

16.4.4 Fiscal transfers

There is at present no political support for established extensive and automatic intra-European transfers, but proposals regularly surface. It has been suggested that a European tax could be established that could support a European unemployment benefit scheme, for example. Some limited funds are disbursed by the European Commission when a country is hard hit by a natural disaster.

It is reasonably certain that, in the not-too-distant future, Europe will have adopted some form of transfer scheme.

16.4.5 Beyond the OCA criteria: politics

We have reached two important conclusions. First, Europe is not exactly an optimum currency area; it does well on some but not all of the criteria. Second, it is not just labour mobility that is insufficient but, more generally, the labour markets that display significant rigidity, especially in the large countries. In these countries, the monetary union may worsen an already painful situation of high unemployment.

It is natural therefore to ask why the European heads of state and governments who gathered in Maastricht in 1991 still decided to take the risk and set up a monetary union. The answer is: politics.[16] Interestingly enough, Harvard economist Martin Feldstein, a sharp critic of the single currency, sees it as a source of conflict:

> Political leaders in Europe seem to be prepared to ignore these adverse consequences because they see EMU as a way of furthering the political agenda of a federalist European political union. . . . The adverse economic effects of EMU and the broader political disagreements will nevertheless induce some countries to ask whether they have made a mistake in joining. Although a sovereign country could in principle withdraw from the EMU, the potential trade sanctions and other pressures on such a country are likely to make membership in EMU irreversible unless there is widespread economic dislocation in Europe or, more generally, a collapse of peaceful coexistence within Europe.

> (Feldstein, 1997, pp. 41–2)

In Feldstein's view, the EMU is not only unjustified on economic grounds (it is not an OCA) but its survival will require a major step towards a federal Europe, including common defence and foreign policies as well as a generalized harmonization of taxation and labour market regulations. Much the same view, that the EMU will trigger a bandwagon of pro-federal moves at the expense of the nation-states, was also harboured by former Prime Minister Margaret Thatcher, and underpinned her staunch opposition to the EMU. In every member country of the Union, a large number of people share this view and adamantly want to preserve the nation-state.

[16] For a detailed discussion, see the exchange between Feldstein and Wyplosz in the symposium published in the *Journal of Economic Perspectives*, 11(4): 3–42, 1997.

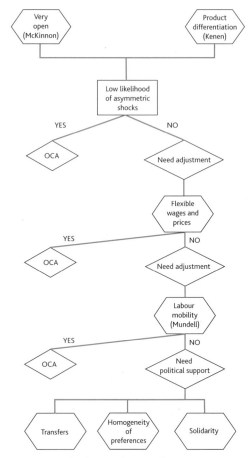

Figure 16.15: *The logic of OCA theory*

Indeed, political considerations have been paramount in launching the euro. It is fair to say that the political leaders who agreed on the monetary union did not think at all in terms of the OCA theory (see Box 16.7). They were largely focusing on the symbolic nature of the undertaking; precisely because money and statehood are intertwined, their intention was to move one step further in the direction of an 'ever closer union'. In that sense, they were upholding a long tradition. Indeed, the fundamental force driving the European integration process from the late 1940s has been the belief that a thousand (or more) years of war has to come to an end and that the solution is ever deeper economic integration. When Europeans have reached a state where economic interests are deeply intertwined, so goes the argument, there will be no incentive to compete other than on the markets, to the benefit of all. At each critical juncture when negotiations become hard, political leaders end up making the concessions needed to produce some sort of agreement, often half-satisfactory, and are prompt to justify it as a step to strengthen peace on the Continent. In this important sense, the Europeans share a sense of common destiny.

Box 16.7

The return of the OCA theory

The negotiators who prepared the Maastricht Treaty did not pay attention to the OCA theory. They were first and foremost heeding the impossible trinity principle, focusing on the need to preserve exchange rate stability in the wake of full capital movement liberalization. They were also concerned that the new currency should be as strong as the Deutschmark, hence the tough entry conditions that are detailed in Chapter 17. Overall they believed that, if the countries allowed into the monetary union had sufficiently converged, and if the new central bank was well protected from political interference, then the undertaking would work.

This view was at variance with many economists' opinion that the OCA criteria were more important and that due account should be paid to the difficulties that would inevitably arise because the Mundell criterion was not satisfied. The authorities are now rediscovering the importance of the OCA theory. In June 2005, for instance, the European Central Bank convened a conference, where both authors of this text were asked to present their views, which paid tribute to the OCA theory and its inventors. The picture shows the panel of the concluding session.

European Central Bank, 17 June 2005. Left to right: Charles Wyplosz, Adam Posen (IIE, Washington), Robert Mundell, Ronald McKinnon, Vitor Gaspar (Bank of Portugal) and Otmar Issing (Chief Economist of the ECB).

16.5 Summary

The OCA theory seeks to determine over what geographic area it is optimal to establish a single currency. The key insight is that the usefulness of money grows with the size of the area but that costs arise when the area becomes too diverse.

Diversity matters mostly because it is a source of asymmetric shocks. If all prices and wages were perfectly flexible, the exchange rate would be economically irrelevant. In the presence of price and wage rigidity, however, the exchange rate can be a powerful instrument to deal with shocks. When the shocks are asymmetric, giving up the exchange rate can be costly. This is why the OCA theory asks what characteristics may either reduce the incidence of asymmetric shocks or take the edge off asymmetric shocks.

The logic of OCA theory is summarized in Fig. 16.15. The first question is whether, over a given geographic area, asymmetric shocks are likely to occur often enough, and strongly enough, to be a serious concern. If the answer is negative, the cost of adopting a common currency is low – even though large asymmetric shocks may occasionally occur. The McKinnon and Kenen criteria provide the answer. The McKinnon criterion says that the exchange rate is of limited use if the countries are very open. The Kenen criterion concludes that countries that produce and trade a wide range of similar goods are unlikely frequently to face asymmetric shocks.

If these criteria are not well satisfied, asymmetric shocks should be expected and the next question is whether the area is well equipped to deal with them. The Mundell criterion says that, in the absence of wage and price flexibility, labour mobility provides a way of cushioning the impact of asymmetric shocks. In the absence of labour mobility, asymmetric shocks will be costly. The next question is whether there is a way of compensating for these shocks.

This last question takes us to the political criteria. An obvious compensation takes the form of financial transfers. Transfers offer an insurance mechanism; a country will receive transfers when adversely hit, and will support other member countries when they face a shock. These transfers can be automatic, via taxes and welfare payments, or explicit, based on sharing rules.

In the presence of asymmetric shocks, the common central bank will have to make hard choices. It must decide how it caters to the varied needs of individual member countries. This is bound to be a controversial decision, which can sap support for the currency area unless a common ground can be designed. Support for the central bank will be more likely if there is broad agreement on its aims, i.e. if policy preferences are reasonably homogeneous, and if there is a sense of solidarity across the currency area, i.e. if the costs are accepted as part of an overall sense that 'we are on the same boat'.

When putting the OCA theory into practice, two issues arise. First, fulfilment of the criteria is not a black-or-white issue. Some criteria can be partly satisfied, others not at all. It is unlikely, therefore, that several independent countries can be identified as forming an optimal currency area. In the end, some judgement must be passed on how to balance the important benefits of a common currency and the potentially severe costs of giving up national monetary policy. Second, a group of countries may not do too well on the OCA criteria, but adopting a common currency may trigger changes that enhance the degree of satisfaction of the criteria. Trade may deepen, product diversification may increase (although some fear that specialization will rather occur), and labour markets can become more flexible (here again, it could go in the opposite direction). Similarly, transfers can be developed and the sharing of a common currency can homogenize preferences and help develop a sense of solidarity. The degree to which the OCA criteria are satisfied could well be endogenous, so that being in a currency union makes it more likely that the criteria are satisfied.

Europe does well on three criteria: openness, diversification and homogeneity of preferences. It does not pass the labour mobility and fiscal transfers conditions. A key question is whether the endogeneity assumption will become verified.

Self-assessment questions

1. In section 16.1.2, it is asserted that the real exchange rate $\lambda = EP/P^*$ can be depreciated either through a depreciation of the nominal exchange rate E or through a change in the price level P. Explain.

2. In the presence of an adverse shock, an alternative to devaluation is to cut imports by raising tariffs. Why is this alternative usually unpalatable?

3. Provide a list of plausible asymmetric shocks. In particular, consider the case of a reduction of the working time hours and investigate its effects using the graphical apparatus in Fig. 16.4.

4. The labour mobility criterion implicitly assumes that the labour force is homogeneous, which is not the case as workers are most often specialized. How should this criterion be refined?

5. Why does a deepening of trade through intra-industry exchanges help with both the diversification (Kenen) and openness (McKinnon) criteria?

6. In Fig. 16.4 an adverse asymmetric shock is met by a depreciation. What does the size of the depreciation depend upon?

7. Why are Europeans less mobile than Americans? Note that low mobility is observed not just across national borders but also within each country. What measures could increase labour mobility in Europe?

8. Why can commercial integration lead to more national or regional specialization? Why can it lead to less specialization?

9. It is sometimes argued that, because the automatic stabilizers are larger in Europe than in the USA, there is less need for automatic transfers. Explain the argument.

Essay questions

1. Could immigration be a solution to the labour immobility problem?

2. Imagine that California is severely hit by a recession in the information technology industry. What would happen if it seceded from the US monetary union and introduced the Californian dollar?

3. You are given the task of designing a transfer system to cope with asymmetric shocks. Consider both how to collect and how to spend these resources.

4. The African countries that make up the CFA zones do not satisfy the classic OCA economic criteria: labour mobility is low, they trade very little with each other and they are specialized in different commodity exports. And yet, the currency union has lasted for 40 years. What can the explanation(s) be?

5. Early evidence is that trade is increasing faster among the EMU countries than among other European non-EMU countries. How can such evidence affect the debate on EMU membership in countries such as Norway, Sweden, Switzerland or the UK?

6. The UK Chancellor of the Exchequer has stated that the UK will join the EMU when five economic tests are passed. These five tests are:

    ★ Are business cycles and economic structures compatible so that we and others could live comfortably with euro interest rates on a permanent basis?

    ★ If problems emerge is there sufficient flexibility to deal with them?

    ★ Would joining the EMU create better conditions for firms making long-term decisions to invest in the UK?

    ★ What impact would entry into the EMU have on the competitive position of the UK's financial services industry, particularly the City's wholesale markets?

    ★ In summary, will joining the EMU promote higher growth, stability and a lasting increase in jobs?

    Evaluate these tests.

7. Write a science fiction story: a severe asymmetric shock occurs and leads to such economic hardship that the European monetary union is dissolved. Carefully explain each step in the process.

8. Write a science fiction story: northern England adopts its own currency.

Further reading: the aficionado's corner

Is Europe an OCA?

When, in 1996, it was trying to decide whether to join the monetary union from its start, the Swedish government appointed a special commission to review the question. The Calmfors Commission came out cautiously approving EMU membership; the government decided to wait and see. Its report has been published as a book that provides a detailed and careful analysis of the pros and cons of monetary union in Europe.
Calmfors, L. et al. (1997) EMU, A Swedish Perspective, Kluwer, Dordrecht.

In May 2003, the UK government released its own study on EMU membership, in fact closely following the OCA criteria. This study represents an excellent way of putting to work the material presented in this chapter. HM Treasury (2003) UK Membership of the Single Currency, HMSO, Norwich. Also available, with additional detailed studies, on: http://www.hm-treasury.gov.uk.

A concise summary of the debates throughout Europe can be found in: Wyplosz, C. (1997) 'EMU: Why and how it might happen', Journal of Economic Perspectives, 11(4): 3–22.

The three classic OCA criteria

Mundell, R. (1961) 'A theory of optimum currency area', American Economic Review, 51: 657–65.
McKinnon, R. (1962) 'Optimum currency areas', American Economic Review, 53: 717–25.
Kenen, P. (1969) 'The theory of optimum currency areas', in R. Mundell and A. Swoboda (eds) Monetary Problems of the International Economy, Chicago University Press, Chicago.

Additional readings

An excellent collection of readings:
De Grauwe, P. (2001) The Political Economy of Monetary Union, Edward Elgar Ltd, Cheltenham.

A detailed review of OCA theory and evidence:
Mongeli, F.P. (2002) New Views on the Optimum Currency Area Theory: What is EMU Telling Us?, Working Paper No. 138, ECB, April. http://www.ecb.int.

The UK analysis of its membership includes a large number of excellent studies:
http://www.hm-treasury.gov.uk.

Trade effect of currency unions

On the Rose effect, see:
Baldwin, R. (2005) 'The euro's trade effect', http://hei.unige.ch/~baldwin.
Glick, R. and A. Rose (2002) 'Does a currency union affect trade? The time series evidence', European Economic Review, 46(6): 1125–51.
Micco, A., E. Stein and G. Ordoñez (2003) 'The currency union effect on trade: early evidence from EMU', Economic Policy, 37: 315–56.
Rose, A. (2000) 'One money, one market: the effects of common currencies on trade', Economic Policy, 30: 7–46.

On the 'border effect', see:
Engel, C. and J. Rogers (1996) 'How wide is the border?', American Economic Review, 86 (December): 1112–25.

Endogeneity vs specialization

The debate on specialization and endogeneity of the OCA criteria has been triggered by the following exchanges:
Frankel, J. and A. Rose (1998) 'The endogeneity of the optimum currency area criteria', Economic Journal, 108 (449): 1009–25.
Glick, R. and A. Rose (2001) Does a currency union affect trade? The time series evidence, NBER Working Paper No. 8396.
Krugman, P. (1993) 'Lessons of Massachusetts for EMU', in F. Torres and F. Giavazzi (eds) Adjustment and Growth in the European Monetary Union, Cambridge University Press, Oxford.

Useful websites

Mundell won the Nobel Memorial Prize partly for his work on currency unions. His website is worth a tour: http://www.columbia.edu/~ram15/i.e./ietoc.html.

Public opinion polls are conducted twice a year on all issues relevant to European affairs and reported on http://europa.eu.int/comm/public_opinion/standard_en.htm.

References

Angeloni, I., A. Kashyap, B. Mojon and D. Terlizzese (2002) Monetary Transmission in the Euro Area: Where Do We Stand?, Working Paper No. 114, ECB, Frankfurt.

Baldwin, R. (2005) 'The Euro's trade effect', http://hei.unige.ch/~baldwin.

Bayoumi, T. and B. Eichengreen (1997) 'Ever closer to heaven? An optimum currency area index for European countries', *European Economic Review*, 41: 761–70.

Bernd, H. (1999) 'Knowledge and attitude towards European monetary union', *Journal of Policy Modelling*, 21(5): 641–51.

Campa, J. and L. Goldberg (2002) *Exchange Rate Pass-through into Import Prices: A Macro or Micro Phenomenon?*, Federal Reserve Bank of New York.

Dowd, K. and D. Greenaway (1993) 'Currency competition, network externalities and switching costs: towards an alternative view of optimun currency areas', *Economic Journal*, 103(420): 1180–9.

Engel, C. and J. Rogers (1996) 'How wide is the border?', *American Economic Review*, 86 (December): 1112–25.

Fatás, A. (2000) 'Intranational migration: business cycles and growth', in E. van Wincoop and G. Hess (eds) *Intranational Macroeconomics*, Cambridge University Press, Cambridge.

Feldstein, M. (1997) 'The political economy of the European Economic and Monetary Union: political sources of an economic liability', *Journal of Economic Perspectives*, 11(4): 23–42.

Micco, A., E. Stein and G. Ordoñez (2003) 'The currency union effect on trade: early evidence from EMU', *Economic Policy*, 37: 315–56.

Mundell, R. (1973) 'A plan for a European currency', in H. Johnson and A. Swoboda (eds) *The Economics of Common Currencies*, George Allen & Unwin, London.

Rose, A. (2000) 'One money, one market: the effects of common currencies on trade', *Economic Policy*, 30: 7–46.

> A normal central bank is a monopolist. Today's Eurosystem is,
> instead, an archipelago of monopolists.
>
> *Tommaso Padoa-Schioppa (Executive Board of the ECB)*

Chapter

17 The European monetary union

INTRODUCTION

The European monetary union did not come as a surprise. It was carefully mapped out in the Maastricht Treaty, which specified how and when the single currency would be launched and laid down a precise set of institutional arrangements, which are presented in section 17.1. Section 17.2 describes how the European Central Bank interacts with the national central banks. The Treaty also prescribes the essential elements of the monetary policy doctrine; section 17.3 explains how these principles are implemented to guarantee price stability. Section 17.4 explains why price stability can only be preserved if the central bank enjoys a high degree of independence and describes how this is done; it also examines the related issue of democratic accountability. The last section reviews the first years of the single currency and discusses the next enlargement of the eurozone.

17.1 The Maastricht Treaty

17.1.1 Main components

The Maastricht Treaty marks the end of a long road – three decades of attempts to achieve a monetary union, summarized in Table 17.1. It was agreed upon in the picturesque Dutch town of Maastricht in December 1991 and ratified by all signatories over the next year and a half in an eventful process recounted in Box 17.1. In many ways, the adoption of the euro has changed the nature of the integration process. At the symbolic level, the official name of the European Community (EC) was changed to European Union (EU) to recognize that the Treaty was not just about economics but also included political considerations. Two new pillars – foreign and defence policies, justice and internal security – were added to the first, economic pillar. The power of the European Parliament was enhanced and it was also agreed to substitute 'qualified majority' for 'unanimity' for Council decisions on a number of issues. Many of these ambitious-looking steps were incomplete, which called for the subsequent treaties of Amsterdam and Nice, and then for the Convention.[1] The monetary union part of the Treaty, however, was fully worked out with the irrevocable decision to adopt a single currency by 1 January 1999. The Treaty described in great detail how the system would work, including the statutes of the European Central Bank (ECB) and the conditions under which monetary union would start.

Towards Maastricht		Between Maastricht and the single currency		The single currency	
1970	Werner Plan	1994	European Monetary Institute (precursor of ECB)	1999	Monetary union starts
1979	European Monetary System starts	1997	Stability and Growth Pact	2001	Greece joins
1989	Delors Committee	1998	Decision on membership	2002	Euro coins and notes introduced
1991	Maastricht Treaty signed	1998	Conversion rates set		
1993	Maastricht Treaty ratified	1998	Creation of ECB		

Table 17.1: *EMU timetable*

---

[1] See Chapter 1 for a survey.

Box 17.1

Ratification of the Maastricht Treaty

Any international treaty must be ratified by the signatories. The ratification procedure varies from one country to another: some countries require a referendum, others must obtain parliament's approval, yet others can decide between these two alternatives.

The first country to undertake ratification of the Maastricht Treaty was Denmark, and it had to be by referendum. The Danish people chose to reject the Treaty by a small margin. A clause stipulated that, to enter into existence, the Treaty must be ratified by all the signatories. Thus the Treaty looked dead before the other countries even had a chance to consider it. Yet, hoping that a legal solution would be found, it was decided to continue with the ratification process.

France offered to be the second country to consider ratification. In the hope of reversing the bad impression created by Denmark's popular rejection, President Mitterrand chose the referendum procedure at a time when polls indicated strong support. As the campaign went on, support gradually eroded. When some polls reported a majority against the Treaty,

fearing a collapse of the whole project, the exchange markets became jittery and speculation gained momentum. In the event, Italy and the UK were ejected from the ERM and several currencies had to be devalued, some of them many times, as described in Chapter 15. Meanwhile the French approved the Treaty by a narrow margin.

The Danes were asked to return to the polls, after the Danish government committed itself to invoke the right not to adopt the single currency, a right included in a special protocol to the Treaty, as is explained below. This time, the Danes approved the Treaty. Just when the road seemed clear, the German Constitutional Court was asked by opponents to decide whether the Treaty was compatible with Germany's constitution. The Court took several months to deliver its opinion, keeping the process hanging. The Court finally decided that the Treaty did not contradict the German constitution. This allowed Germany to ratify the Treaty in late 1993, the last country to do so.

17.1.2 Convergence criteria

When the Treaty was under preparation, the macroeconomic situation differed widely from one country to another. Germany, deeply attached to price stability, was concerned that some countries were not quite ready to adopt the required monetary discipline. It insisted that admission to the monetary union would not be automatic. A selection process was designed to certify which countries had adopted a 'culture of price stability', meaning that they had durably achieved German-style low inflation. In order to join the monetary union, a country has to fulfil the following five convergence criteria, which remain applicable to all future candidate countries.

Inflation

The first criterion deals directly with inflation. To be eligible for monetary union membership, a country's inflation rate should not exceed the average of the three lowest inflation rates achieved by the EU Member States by more than 1.5 percentage points. Figure 17.1 shows

how the 'Club Med' countries of southern Europe managed to bring their inflation rates to within the tolerance margin by 1998. Greece (not shown) failed (actually it did not even try and decided to join later, which it did in 2001).

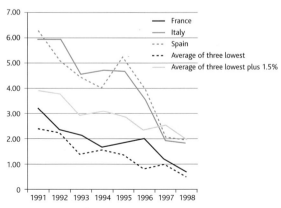

Figure 17.1: *Inflation convergence, 1991–98*

Source: IMF.

Long-term nominal interest rate

An inflation-prone country could possibly squeeze down inflation temporarily, on the last year before admission – for example, by freezing administered prices (electricity, transports) – only to relax the effort afterwards. In order to weed out potential cheaters, a second criterion requires that the long-term interest rate should not exceed the average rates observed in the three lowest inflation rate countries by more than 2 percentage points. The reasoning is shrewd. Long-term interest rates mostly reflect markets' assessment of long-term inflation.[2] Achieving a low long-term interest rate therefore requires convincing naturally sceptical financial markets that inflation would remain low 'for ever'.

ERM membership

The same concern about a superficial conversion to price stability lies behind the third criterion. Here the idea is that a country must have demonstrated its ability to keep its exchange rate tied to its future monetary union partner currencies. The requirement is therefore that every country must have taken part in the ERM for at least two years without having to devalue its currency.[3]

Budget deficit

The three previous criteria require demonstrated low inflation, but it makes sense to eradicate the incentives to tolerate high inflation. Why do some countries end up with high inflation? Inflation is not really desirable, so its acceptance must reflect some deeper problem. Indeed, inflation is typically the result of large budget deficits. The process is well known. As a government borrows to finance its budget deficits, its debt rises. If the process goes on unchecked, eventually the financial markets are likely to ask themselves whether the debts will ever be repaid. Their normal reaction, then, is to stop lending to a highly indebted government. The only alternative to borrowing to finance the deficit is to ask the central bank to run its printing press. This is how continuing budget deficits eventually translate into fast money growth, which ultimately delivers high inflation.

This is why the fourth convergence criterion sets a limit on acceptable budget deficits. But what limit? Here again, German influence prevailed. Germany had long operated a 'golden rule', which specifies that budget deficits are only acceptable if they correspond to public investment spending (on roads, telecommunications and other infrastructures). The idea is that public investment is a source of growth which eventually generates the resources needed to pay for the initial borrowing. The German 'golden rule' considers that public investment typically amounts to some 3 per cent of GDP. Hence the Maastricht Treaty requirement that budget deficits should not exceed 3 per cent of GDP.[4]

Public debt

Much as inflation can be lowered temporarily, deficits can be made to look good on any given year (for example, by shifting public spending and taxes from one year to another). Thus it was decided that a more permanent feature of fiscal discipline ought to be added. The fifth and last criterion mandates a maximum level for the public debt. Here again, the question was: which ceiling? Unimaginatively perhaps, the ceiling was set at 60 per cent of GDP because it was the average debt level when the Maastricht Treaty was being negotiated in 1991. An additional reason was that the 60 per cent debt limit can be seen as compatible with a deficit debt ceiling of 3 per cent as explained in Box 17.2.

However, by definition of an average, some countries had debts in excess of 60 per cent of GDP, and some much larger. In particular, Belgium's public debt stood at some 120 per cent of GDP. Yet, by 1991, Belgium, had overhauled its public finances and was adamant that it was now committed to adhere to a strict budgetary discipline. However, it would take a long time to bring its debt to below 60 per cent.[5] As a founding member of the Common Market in 1957, an enthusiastic European country, and a long advocate of monetary union, Belgium argued that it could not be left out because of past sins now firmly repudiated. At its request, the criterion was couched in prudent terms, calling for a debt to GDP ratio either less than 60 per cent or 'moving in that direction'.

---

[2] This is based on the Fisher principle: nominal interest rate = real interest rate + expected inflation. Since the real interest rate is reasonably constant and set worldwide, the main driving force determining the long-term interest rate is the expected long-term inflation rate. See Box 17.5 for an elaboration.

[3] The exchange rate mechanism is presented in detail in Chapter 14.

[4] This entry condition should be kept distinct from the same limit prescribed by the Stability and Growth Pact, which is studied in Chapter 18. There is a link between the two limits, though: having joined the monetary union, a country is not allowed to let its budget deficits rise again.

[5] By end-2004, the Belgian public debt was 96.6 per cent of GDP.

The arithmetic of deficits and debts

Debts grow out of deficits, but how does the debt/GDP ratio relate to the deficit/GDP ratio? A little arithmetic helps. If total nominal debt at the end of year t is Bt, its increase during the year is $B_t - B_{t-1}$, and this is equal to the annual deficit D_t:

$$B_t - B_{t-1} = Dt \qquad (1)$$

The two fiscal convergence criteria refer not to the debt and deficit levels, but to their ratios to nominal GDP Y, denoted as b_t and d_t, respectively. Divide the previous accounting equality by the current year GDP to get:

$$\frac{B_t - B_{t-1}}{Y_t} = \frac{D_t}{Y_t} \quad \text{or} \quad b_t - \frac{B_{t-1}}{Y_t} = d_t \qquad (2)$$

Then note that $\dfrac{B_{t-1}}{Y_t} = \dfrac{B_{t-1}}{Y_{t-1}}\dfrac{Y_{t-1}}{Y_t} = \dfrac{b_{t-1}}{1 + g_t}$

where $g_t = \dfrac{Y_t - Y_{t-1}}{Y_{t-1}} = \dfrac{Y_t}{Y_{t-1}} - 1$

is the growth rate of GDP in year t. We can rewrite the debt growth eqn (2) as:

$$b_t - b_{t-1} = (1 + g_t)\, d_t - g_t b_t \qquad (3)$$

If the debt to GDP ratio b is to remain constant, we need to have $b_t = b_{t-1}$, which from (3) implies:

$$d_t = \frac{1 + g_t\, b_t}{g_t} \qquad (4)$$

The fiscal convergence criteria sets $d_t = 3$ per cent and $b_t = 60$ per cent. If nominal GDP grows by 5 per cent, eqn (4) is approximately satisfied. The implicit assumption is therefore that real GDP annual growth is about 3 per cent and inflation is 2 per cent, hence a nominal GDP growth rate of 5 per cent.

If the debt level is constant, the debt/GDP ratio declines as the result of GDP growth, the more so the faster nominal GDP grows. This means that some debt increase, and therefore some deficit, is compatible with a constant debt/GDP ratio, and the tolerable deficit is larger the faster nominal GDP grows.

Figure 17.2 shows how deficits and debts looked in 1998, the last year before the launch of the monetary union, which was used to determine which country fulfilled the criteria. All countries managed to bring their deficits below the 3 per cent threshold, sometimes thanks to accounting tricks.[6] Few, however, could report debts below 60 per cent of GDP. In the end, all were saved by the 'Belgian clause'.

17.1.3 Two-speed Europe

An important aspect of the Maastricht Treaty is that it introduced, for the first time, the idea that a major

[6] France privatized part of its state-owned telecommunications corporation, which provided the revenues needed to achieve the deficit target. Italy collected at the end of 1998 some taxes which would normally have been due in early 1999. Even the German government considered selling gold to pay back its debt but backed off as the Bundesbank publicly attacked the idea.

integration move would leave some countries out. Initially, the intention was to protect price stability and not let the inflation wolf enter the den. Then things turned out differently.

Prime Minister Thatcher's Britain was firmly opposed to monetary union. For a while, Thatcher stonewalled the discussions, which went ahead without her. The view in London was that this was a bizarre idea with no future at all, a sort of conventional exercise that no one really intended to bring to fruition. When it realized that the other European countries were in fact serious, the UK found itself cut off from a major negotiation that would powerfully shape Europe's future. Partly because of her unwillingness to engage her partners on the issue, Thatcher was dismissed and replaced by John Major. Unable to scuttle the project, the best he could achieve was to obtain an opt-out clause, which stated that the

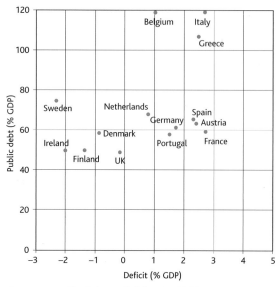

Figure 17.2: *Deficits and debts in 1998*

Source: European Commission.

UK, alone, was not bound to join the monetary union. This further confirmed that Europe could move at different speeds. A similar opt-out clause was given to Denmark after a first rejection of the Treaty by Danish voters (see Box 17.1).

In 1995, Sweden joined the EU. The Swedish authorities made it clear that they were less than enthusiastic towards the monetary union. They asked for an opt-out clause, which was denied. The diplomatic solution was a gentleman's agreement whereby Sweden did not enter the ERM and was therefore disqualified for monetary union membership. De facto, Sweden is treated as Denmark, with the right to decide when to apply for membership to the euro area.

In the end, the monetary union started on time with eleven members. The 'outs' included Greece, which did not meet the convergence criteria, the UK and Denmark, which invoked the opt-out clause, and Sweden. Greece converged later and joined in January 2001.

The story started anew when the EU expanded in 2004 with ten new members: the Czech Republic, Hungary, Poland, Slovakia, Slovenia, Estonia, Latvia, Lithuania, Cyprus and Malta. Some of these countries have long attached their currencies first to the Deutschmark, and then to the euro. Others have let their currencies float freely. As members of the EU, they are supposed to enter the ERM and then fulfil the convergence criteria before joining the monetary union (see section 15.3.3).

17.2 The Eurosystem

17.2.1 N countries, N + 1 central banks

With a single currency there can be only one interest rate, one exchange rate *vis-à-vis* the rest of the world, and therefore one monetary policy. Normally this implies a single central bank, but this is not quite the way the EMU was set up. Each member still comes equipped with its own central bank, the last remaining vestige of lost monetary sovereignty. No matter how daring the founding fathers of the EMU were, they stopped short of merging the national central banks into a single institution, partly for fear of having to dismiss thousands of employees. In fact, as Table 17.2 shows, national central banks have hardly downsized their staff. Paradoxically perhaps, downsizing has been larger in non-euro area central banks.

The solution was inspired by federal states like Germany and the USA where regional central banks coexist with the federal central bank. But the EU is not a federation, and the word 'federation' is highly politically incorrect in Europe. Inevitably, therefore, the chosen structure is complicated. The newly created European Central Bank (ECB) coexists with the national central banks, one of which did not even exist prior to 1999 since Luxembourg, long part of a monetary union with Belgium, only established its own central bank to conform to the new arrangement.

On the other hand, in many respects the euro was meant to be a continuation of Europe's most successful currency, the Deutschmark. The structure of the Bundesbank was used as a blueprint for the monetary union. This inspiration is visible not only in the new institution but also in the policy objective and framework, and in the location of the ECB in Frankfurt, only a few kilometres from the Bundesbank.

17.2.2 The system

The European System of Central Banks (ESCB) is composed of the new, specially created European Central Bank (ECB) and the national central banks (NCBs) of all EU Member States. Since not all EU countries have joined the monetary union, a different term, Eurosystem, has been coined to refer to the ECB and the participating NCBs.[7] The Eurosystem implements the monetary policy of the euro area, as described below. If needed, it also conducts foreign exchange operations, in agreement with

[7] For a full and formal description, see the July 1999 issue of the ECB's *Monthly Bulletin*, pp. 55–63.

	Staff	% change 1997–2002	Staff per million inhabitants		Staff	% change 1997–2002	Staff per million inhabitants
Austria	1153	0.3	143	Ireland	805	29.8	210
Belgium	2316	−14.4	226	Italy	8482	−5.3	146
Finland	708	−8.8	136	Luxembourg	200	51.5	455
France	15 216	−5.9	257	Netherlands	1826	6.1	114
Germany	15 834	−1.3	192	Portugal	1814	0.2	181
Greece	3090	−2.6	308	Spain	3050	−5.5	76
				Denmark	611	5.5	115
ECB	1094	98.9[a]	4	Sweden	501	−24.5	57
Eurosystem	55 588	−2.7	183	UK	2242	−34.6	38

[a]Change relative to the ECB's predecessor, the European Monetary Institute.

Source: Gros and Lannoo (2000), updated by these authors in 2003.

Table 17.2: *Staff in national central banks and the ECB in 2002*

the Finance Ministers of the member countries. It holds and manages the official foreign reserves of the EMU Member States. It monitors the payment systems and it is involved in the prudential supervision of credit institutions and the financial system.

As shown in Fig. 17.3, the ECB is run by an Executive Board of six members, appointed by the heads of state or governments of the countries that have joined the monetary union, following consultation of the European Parliament and the Governing Council of the ESCB. It comprises the six members of the Executive Board and the governors of the NCBs of monetary union Member States. The Governing Council is the key authority deciding on monetary policy. Its decisions are, in principle, taken by majority voting, with each member holding one vote, although it seems to operate by consensus. A transitory body, the General Council, includes the members of the Governing Council and the governors of the NCBs of the countries that have not joined the monetary union. The General Council is in essence fulfilling a liaison role and has no authority.

While decisions are taken by the Governing Council, the ECB plays an important role. Its Chairman presides over the meetings of the Governing Council and reports its decisions at press conferences. The ECB prepares the meetings of the Governing Council and implements its decisions. It also gives instructions to the NCBs to carry out the common monetary policy. An important characteristic of the ECB is that its Executive Board members are not representing any country: they are appointed as individuals, even though the large countries (France, Germany, Italy and Spain) all had a national sitting in the first Board. The first Chairman was Dutch, Wim Duisenberg, and his successor is French, Jean-Claude Trichet, both having previously served as governors of their own NCBs (see Box 17.3). Thus the ECB is of a federal nature while the Eurosystem is a hybrid, partly federal (the ECB) and partly including national institutions (the NCBs).

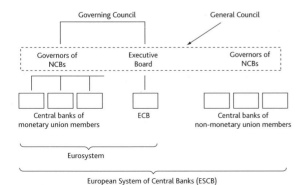

Figure 17.3: *The European system of central banks*

The size of the Governing Council is seen by external observers as a source of difficulty. With 6 + *N* members, where *N* is the number of countries that have joined the monetary union, the Council is large. It will become

Box 17.3

ECB Presidents, 1998–2011

Wim Duisenberg (1998–2003)

www.ecb.int

Wim Duisenberg, the first president of the ECB, was born in 1932. He holds a PhD in economics, worked at the IMF and was professor of macroeconomics at the University of Amsterdam before entering politics in the Labour Party and serving as Minister of Finance. Later on, he joined De Netherlandsche Bank and became its governor in 1982. In 1997, he was appointed President of the European Monetary Institute, in charge of preparing the introduction of the single currency.

Jean-Claude Trichet (2003–11)

www.banque-france-fr

His successor, Jean-Claude Trichet, was also a central bank governor prior to taking over the ECB. Born in 1942, he studied economics and civil engineering before attending the elite Ecole Nationale d'Administration. He capped a distinguished career in the French Finance Ministry by becoming head of the Treasury and, in 1993, Governor of the Banque de France. While at the Treasury, he designed the 'franc fort' policy of disinflation.

larger as new members, possibly ten or more, join the union by the end of the decade, although some change will be introduced to ensure that the decision-making committee's size is, and remains, efficient (see Box 17.4).

17.3 Objectives, instruments and strategy

17.3.1 Objectives

The Maastricht Treaty specifies that the main task of the Eurosystem is to deliver price stability, but the formulation is both vague and ambiguous:

> The primary objective of the ESCB shall be to maintain price stability. Without prejudice to the objective of price stability, the ESCB shall support the general economic policies in the Community with a view to contributing to the achievement of the objectives of the Community as laid down in Article 2.

> (Article 105)

The Treaty does not give an exact definition of price stability. The Eurosystem has chosen to interpret it first as follows: 'Price stability is defined as a year-on-year increase in the Harmonized Index of Consumer Prices (HICP)[8] for the Euro area of below 2 per cent. Price stability is to be maintained over the medium term.' In 2003, with fears of deflation rising, 'the Governing Council agreed that in the pursuit of price stability it will aim to maintain inflation rates close to 2 per cent over the medium term.'[9] Thus, while many central banks typically announce an admissible range for inflation, the Eurosystem only indicates an imprecise target. It does not specify either the meaning of 'the medium term'.

The Treaty considers price stability a 'primary objective'. Secondary objectives are described in Delphic terms, referring to Article 2 which states the objectives of the EU as including 'economic and social progress, and a high level of employment'. Price stability clearly takes precedence over these secondary objectives, but leaves the Eurosystem with quite some leeway to decide its

[8] The Harmonized Index of Consumer Prices is an area-wide consumer price index.
[9] *Monthly Bulletin*, ECB, May 2003, p. 8.

Changing the rules of the Eurosystem

Monetary policy choices are often delicate, with many pros and cons to be balanced. For this kind of decision, smaller committees are more efficient than larger ones. The expansion of the EU challenges the Eurosystem decision-making process as the size of the Governing Council could eventually grow to 30 or more members – a small parliament. The Nice Treaty of 2000 includes an enabling clause which calls upon the Eurosystem to make a recommendation to the Council on how to prevent an unwieldy situation. After long internal deliberations, the Eurosystem made its position known in December 2002. It suggests capping the number of NCB Governors exercising a voting right at 15. While all Council members will be attending the meetings,

NCB Governors will exercise a voting right on the basis of a rotation system. The frequency at which every NCB Governor will rotate will depend on the size of the financial market of his/her country, following a complex procedure.[1] This proposition, which will take its effect when the sixteenth member joins the euro area, has been approved by the EU Council. It was to be ratified by all EU member countries as part of the newly proposed Constitution. Rejection of the Constitution leaves the situation open.

[1] *For a complete description, see the May 2003 issue of the ECB's* Monthly Bulletin, *pp. 73–83 and the decision at* http://europa.eu.int/scadplus/leg/en/lvb/l25065.htm.

strategy. The Eurosystem has chosen to emphasize price stability and to discount the other aspects.

17.3.2 Instruments

Like most other central banks, the Eurosystem uses the short-term interest rate to conduct monetary policy. The reason is that very short-term assets – 24 hours or less – are very close to cash. As central banks have a monopoly on the supply of cash, they can control very short-term rates. On the other hand, longer-term financial instruments can be supplied by both the public and private sectors, making it nearly impossible for central banks to dominate the market and control the rate. In fact, longer-term rates incorporate market expectations of future inflation and future policy actions (Box 17.5 presents the expectations theory of interest rates). These expectations are beyond the control of the central bank, and therefore long-term interest rates cannot be steered with any degree of precision. By concentrating on short-term rates, central banks can achieve greater precision.

The problem is that central banks control the short maturity whereas it is the long-term interest rate that affects the economy because households and firms borrow for relatively long periods, typically from 1 to 20 years or more (see Box 17.5 for exceptions). Stock prices and exchange rates, which are the other channels

through which monetary policy affects the economy,[10] also incorporate longer-term expectations, similar to those that move the long-term interest rates. Thus central banks act indirectly on the economy. They affect the long-term interest rates through their influence on future short-term rates and inflation. Being clear about longer-run aims and intentions is part of the art of central banking.

The Eurosystem focuses on the overnight rate EONIA (European Over Night Index Average), a weighted average of overnight lending transactions in the euro area's interbank market). Control over EONIA is achieved in two ways:

★ The Eurosystem creates a ceiling and a floor for EONIA by maintaining open lending and deposit facilities at pre-announced interest rates. The marginal lending facility means that banks can always borrow directly from the ECB (more precisely, from the NCBs) at the corresponding rate; they would never pay more on the overnight market, so the marginal lending rate is in effect a ceiling. Similarly, since banks can always deposit cash at the ECB's deposit rate, they would never agree to lend at a lower rate, and this rate is the

[10] The channels of monetary policy are presented in Chapter 14.

Box 17.5

The expectations theory of interest rates

We consider periods of short duration to be one day or one week. The nominal interest over such a short period t is i_t. We also look at a very long period T, say five or ten years. We can borrow for the entire period T, at an interest I_T. Alternatively we can borrow for just one period, the coming one $t = 1$, at interest i_1, and then borrow again at rate i_2, and again and again until the end of the long period T. Since we can go either way, the cost should be the same.[1] But, while we know the interest rates i_1 and I_T on short- and long-term loans that are currently available, we do not know the interest rates on loans available in the future. In particular, i_t the short-term one-period rate for period t can only be guessed. We denote as $E[i_t]$ our best guess of the expected short-term rate; it is called the expected value of i_t.

The cost of the long-term loan is $(1 + I_T)$: we must reimburse the principal and the interest. The expected cost of the series of chained short-term loans is $(1 + i_1)(1 + E[i_2]) \ldots (1 + E[i_T])$. Equality is between the two expected costs:

$$(1 + I_T) = (1 + i_1)(1 + E[i_2]) \ldots (1 + E[i_T])$$

As time passes, the central bank will eventually control all the short-term rates $i_1, i_2, \ldots, i_T$, but it does not control today's expectations $E[i_2], E[i_3], \ldots, E[i_T]$. This is why it cannot control the long-term interest rate I_T. Since its actions will determine the future short-term rates $i_2, i_3, \ldots, i_T$, the markets try to guess future monetary policy when they set the long-term rate I_T.[2]

In most countries, the very short-term rates are only used by banks and other financial institutions when they deal with each other, and therefore do not affect households and firms. In some countries, such as Portugal and the UK, the long-term rates are indexed on the short-term rate: for example, when the short-term rate increases, so does the longer-term rate, according to a contractual formula. In this way, the central bank controls not only the short-term but also the longer-term interest rates.

[1] We consider a 'risk-free' rate, i.e. assuming that no one fears that the borrower will default and that we can freely borrow in each period.

[2] Implicitly, the interest rates are not written in annualized form as they are usually quoted. If the long period $T = 20$ years, the annualized interest rate is I_T, such that the total cost of the loan is $(1 + I_T)^{20}$. Similarly, if the short period is one week, the annualized interest rate i_t is such that the cost is $(1 + i_t)^{1/52}$. Then the formula is:

$$(1 + I_T)^{20} = (1 + i_1)^{1/52}(1 + E[i_2])^{1/52} \ldots (1 + E[i_T])^{1/52}$$

This does not affect the reasoning.

floor. Figure 17.4 shows that, indeed, EONIA moves within the corridor thus established.

★ The Eurosystem conducts, usually weekly, auctions at a rate that it chooses. These auctions, called main refinancing operations, are the means by which the ECB provides liquidity to the banking system and the chosen interest rate serves as a precise guide for EONIA.

How does liquidity flow from the Eurosystem to all the corners of the euro area banking system? As noted above, the Eurosystem organizes auctions on a regular basis. Each NCB collects bids from its commercial banks and passes the information to the ECB. The ECB then decides which proportion of bids will be accepted and instructs the NCBs accordingly. The commercial banks can then disseminate the liquidity on the interbank market. It does not matter where the initial injection is made: since there is a single interest rate throughout the euro area, the area-wide interbank market ensures that money is available where needed.

17.3.3 Strategy

How does the Eurosystem go about using its instrument (the short-term interest rate) to achieve its objective (inflation close to 2 per cent)? It announced its strategy

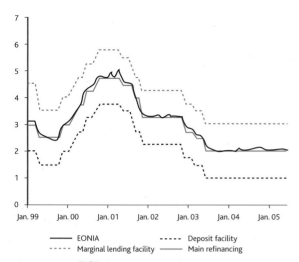

Figure 17.4: *ECB interest rates, January 1999–June 2005*

Source: *Monthly Bulletin*, ECB.

EONIA
Marginal lending facility
Deposit facility
Main refinancing

in October 1998, a few months before starting its operation. In spring 2003, it conducted a strategy review to take stock of the experience accumulated so far.[11] As stated, the strategy relies on three main elements: the definition of price stability, as presented in section 17.3.1, and two 'pillars' used to identify risks to price stability.

The first pillar is what the Eurosystem calls 'economic analysis'. It consists of a broad review of the recent evolution and likely prospects of economic conditions (including growth, employment, prices, exchange rates and foreign conditions). The second pillar, the 'monetary analysis', studies the evolution of monetary aggregates (M3, in particular) and credit which, in the medium to long term, affect inflation, in line with the neutrality principle developed in Chapter 14. In the Eurosystem's words, 'these two perspectives offer complementary analytical frameworks to support the Governing Council's overall assessment of risks to price stability. In this respect, the monetary analysis mainly serves as a means of cross-checking, from a medium- to long-term perspective, the short- to medium-term indications coming from economic analysis' (ECB, 2003).

What does this mean in practice? The Governing Council is presented by its Chief Economist with a broad analysis, including forecasts of inflation and growth. Monetary

[11] The initial strategy is presented in the ECB's *Monthly Bulletin*, January 1999. The strategy review is presented in the ECB's *Monthly Bulletin*, June 2003.

conditions are then used to qualify the forecasts and allow the Council to form a view of where inflation is heading. Then the real debate starts: What should happen to the interest rate? Should it be raised because inflation is perceived as excessive? How much weight should be attached to other considerations, such as growth and employment, or the exchange rate and stock markets? Officially, the Eurosystem is only dealing with inflation, but it has visibly adjusted its actions when it has felt the need to smooth the edges of what it considers to be secondary concerns. Importantly, the Eurosystem does not take any responsibility for the exchange rate, which is freely floating.

Is the Eurosystem's strategy special? Over the past decade, many central banks have adopted the inflation-targeting strategy. In Europe, this is the case of most non-monetary union member central banks (including the Czech Republic, Hungary, Norway, Poland, Sweden and the UK). Inflation targeting comprises announcing a target, publishing an inflation forecast at the relevant policy horizon (usually one to two years ahead), and adjusting the interest rate according to the difference between the forecast and the target. For example, if the forecast exceeds the target, the presumption is that monetary policy is tightened, i.e. that the interest rate is raised.

The Eurosystem has resisted this approach, along with the US Federal Reserve and the Bank of Japan. One reason is that the Eurosystem wants to claim the Bundesbank heritage, and the Bundesbank did not target inflation; it targeted money growth, which explains the second pillar. On the other hand, the Eurosystem's strategy resembles inflation targeting: there is an implicit target (the 2 per cent definition of price stability) and an inflation forecast is published twice a year. What the Eurosystem seems to reject is giving the impression that it acts mechanically.

17.4 Independence and accountability

Current wisdom is that a central bank should be primarily entrusted with the task of delivering price stability. To that effect, it must be free to pursue this task without outside interference. While, in principle, everyone approves of price stability, some important actors occasionally have second thoughts. As noted in section 17.1.2, financially stressed governments may come to see the printing press as the least bad option. Exporters like low exchange rates and are frequently asking their central banks to relax their policies, with the support of trade unions concerned with employment. Debtors like inflation for it erases the value of their (non-indexed) liabilities. Financial institutions often make larger profits when liquidity is plentiful. In any democracy, these are formidable coalitions, and this is why the modern trend of focusing monetary policy on price stability also argues in favour of central bank independence from all segments of society and, in particular, from the political powers.

On the other hand, monetary policy affects citizens of the monetary union in a number of ways. The interest rate directly impacts on the cost of borrowing and on the returns from saving; the exchange rate affects the competitiveness of firms and the purchasing power of citizens; and both of these factors indirectly influence wealth. In effect, by granting independence to their central bank, the citizens delegate a very important task to a group of individuals who are appointed, not elected, and who cannot be removed unless they commit grave illegal acts. In a democratic society, delegation to unelected officials needs to be counterbalanced by democratic accountability. This section examines how these two goals are dealt with in the EMU.

17.4.1 Independence

The Eurosystem is characterized by a great degree of independence; it is probably the world's most independent central bank. Both the ECB and the NCBs are strictly protected from political influence. Before joining the euro area, each country must adapt the statutes of its NCB to match a number of common requirements. In particular, the EU Treaty explicitly rules out any interference by national or European authorities in the deliberations of the Eurosystem:

> When exercising the powers and carrying out the tasks and duties conferred upon them by this Treaty and the Statute of the ESCB, neither the ECB, nor a national central bank, nor any member of their decision-making bodies shall seek or take instructions from Community institutions or bodies, from any government of a Member State or from any other body. The Community institutions and bodies and the governments of the Member States undertake to respect this principle and not to seek to influence the members of the decision-making bodies of the ECB or of the national central banks in the performance of their tasks.

(Article 108)

In addition, to guarantee their personal independence, the members of the Executive Board are appointed for a long period (eight years) and cannot be reappointed, which reduces the opportunity for pressures.[12] Similar conditions apply to the NCB governors, although they differ slightly from one country to another, but their mandates must be for a minimum of five years. No central bank official can be removed from office unless he or she becomes incapacitated or is found guilty of serious misconduct, with the Court of Justice of the European Communities competent to settle disputes.

The independence of the Eurosystem applies to the choice of both policy objectives and instruments. The Treaty sets the objectives in terms vague enough to allow the Eurosystem to decide what it tries to achieve, as explained in section 17.3.1. The Treaty further leaves the Eurosystem completely free to decide which instruments it uses, and how. Other central banks sometimes only have instrument independence. This is the case of the Bank of England which is instructed to pursue an inflation target set by the Chancellor of the Exchequer.

Finally, the ECB is financially independent. It has its own budget, independent from that of the EU. Its accounts are not audited by the European Court of Auditors, which monitors the European Commission, but by independent external auditors.

17.4.2 Accountability

Democratic accountability is typically exercised in two ways: reporting and transparency. Formally, the Eurosystem operates under the control of the European Parliament. Its statutes require that an annual report be sent to the Parliament, as well as to the Council and the Commission. This report is debated by the Parliament. In addition, the Parliament may request that the President of the ECB and the other members of the Executive Board testify to the Parliament's Economic and Monetary Affairs Committee. In practice, the President appears before the committee every quarter and the members of the Executive Board also do so quite often. In addition, the President of the EU Council and a member of the European Commission may participate in the meetings of the Governing Council without voting rights.

---

[12] In order to ensure a smooth rotation, the first members received mandates of staggered length, from four to eight years. Subsequent appointments are always for eight years.

Transparency contributes powerfully to accountability. By revealing the contents of its deliberations, a central bank conveys to the public (the media, the financial markets and independent observers) the rationale and difficulties of its decisions. The Eurosystem does not provide detailed reports of the meetings of its Governing Council. Instead the President of the ECB holds a press conference immediately after the monthly policy-setting meeting to present its decisions in highly standardized terms.

In this respect, the Eurosystem is probably less transparent than many other major central banks. Table 17.3 shows how major central banks reveal the work of their decision-making committee meetings. Several of them publish the committee meeting's minutes within a month, but since they can be heavily edited, minutes are not very informative. Very few (the US Federal Reserve and the Bank of Japan) publish extensive records of the discussion, but with very long delays, which makes the publication irrelevant except for historical purposes. Many central banks report on individual votes, which is a clear way of indicating how certain policy makers feel about their collective decisions. The Eurosystem is nearly alone in doing none of that. It considers that revealing individual votes could be interpreted in a nationalistic manner that does not, in fact, correspond to the thinking of members of the Governing Council.

17.5 The first years

17.5.1 Inflation and growth

During its early existence, the Eurosystem has faced a number of turbulences. In 2000, oil prices rose three-fold. An oil shock means both more inflation and less growth, a classic dilemma that all central banks fear. Simultaneously, stock markets fell worldwide, the end of a long-lasting financial bubble fed by unrealistic expectations of the impact of the information technology revolution. Within months, the US economy went into recession, and Europe's economy also slowed down. Then, the terrorist attacks of 11 September 2001 shook the world economy. The result has been a very poor economic performance, extending surprisingly far into 2005, when oil prices again reached unprecedented levels.

The result has been an inflation rate above the then-stated objective of keeping inflation below 2 per cent. Energy costs fuelled by the oil shock and rising import prices following a depreciation of the euro explain the resurgence of inflation in the euro area in 2001. Figure 17.5 shows that, from early 2000 until mid-2004, the Eurosystem has been in the embarrassing position of failing to deliver on its own definition of price stability. This may explain why, as part of its strategy review, the Eurosystem announced in May 2003 that it now aims at an inflation rate of 'close to 2 per cent'.

	Federal Reserve	ESCB	Bank of Japan	Bank of England	Bank of Canada	Swedish Riksbank
Interest-rate decision immediately announced	Yes (after 1994)	Yes	Yes	Yes	Yes	Yes
Supporting statement giving some rationale for a change	Yes	Yes	Yes	Sometimes	Yes	Yes
Release of minutes	5–8 weeks[a]	No	1 month	13 days	n.a.	2–4 weeks
Official minutes provide full details of:						
internal debate	Yes	No	Yes	Yes	n.a.	No
individuals' views						No
Verbatim records of MP meetings are kept	Yes	No	Yes	No	No	No
Verbatim records released to the public after:	5 years	n.a.	10 years	n.a.	n.a.	n.a.

[a] The minutes are released after the following FOMC meeting.

Source: Blinder *et al.* (2001).

Table 17.3: *Provision of information on monetary policy meetings*

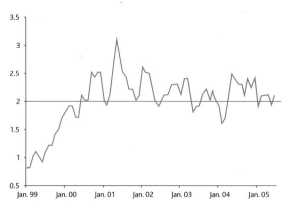

Figure 17.5: *Inflation in the euro area, January 1999–June 2005*

Source: *Monthly Bulletin*, ECB.

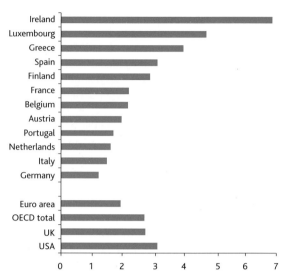

Figure 17.6: *Growth rate of GDP, 1999–2005*

Source: *Economic Outlook*, OECD.

It would be wrong to conclude that the ECB has failed to deliver price stability. Bad luck has brought a series of adverse shocks, especially oil shocks that create a serious policy dilemma. Should the central bank try to prevent inflation from rising, at the cost of a deeper and longer-lasting slowdown? Should it instead focus on limiting the contractionary effect of the oil shock and take the risk of missing its inflation objective? There is no simple answer to this question. Box 17.6 presents a simple – undoubtedly too simple – way of describing how a central bank trades off the conflicting objectives of price stability and adequate growth. The Eurosystem has established a clear hierarchy: price stability comes first, growth second (section 17.3.1). Overall, however, the Eurosystem has responded with a high degree of pragmatism. It has delivered an average inflation rate close to 2 per cent, which most people will recognize as suitably low.

Growth, on the other hand, has been slow, which has generated much criticism, including from member governments. The criticism may be unfair. To start with, growth has been slow on average, not in every euro area country. Some countries have grown very fast, as Fig. 17.6 shows. The overall eurozone's growth rate is low because some of the largest eurozone members – chiefly Germany and Italy, with France only slighter better – have achieved a disappointing performance. The Eurosystem has argued that the failure of some countries to grow faster is not due to an over-restrictive monetary policy stance. It has a point. The neutrality principle presented in Chapter 14 asserts that long-run growth is independent of monetary policy. Of course, six years may not be quite long enough to fully exonerate the Eurosystem, but the varied growth performance across the eurozone points to country-

specific features rather than to monetary policy. Indeed, the evidence presented in Chapter 8 relates the laggard countries to domestic rigidities.

17.5.2 The exchange rate

The Eurosystem has faced another vexing issue. Just when the euro was launched in early 1999, the dollar started to rise *vis-à-vis* all major currencies, including the euro and, to a lesser extent, the pound sterling. Given that the US dollar has long been the world's standard, the general interpretation was that the euro was weak. This left the impression that the Eurosystem was unable to deliver the strong currency that had been predicated upon its price-stability rhetoric. Then, from late 2002 onwards, the dollar has started to fall. Instead of praising the Eurosystem for having finally delivered a strong currency, critics complained that the euro was overvalued and hurting European exporters, lengthening the cyclical slowdown. Yet, as Fig. 17.8 shows, the movements of the dollar/euro exchange rate have not been particularly out of step with the past and the case for overvaluation is weak.

From the start, the Eurosystem has clearly announced that it would take no responsibility for the exchange rate. The discussion of exchange rate regimes in Chapter 14 suggests that very large and closed economies, like the eurozone, have little interest in stabilizing their exchange rates; the freely floating 'corner' is likely to be its best option, and this is where the Eurosystem has chosen to stand. 'Best option' does not mean that it does

Box 17.6

A Taylor rule for the ECB?

A simple way of describing the behaviour of central banks is to assume that they follow a Taylor rule, i.e. that they set the interest rate in reaction to deviations of both inflation and output from their desired levels.[1] Most central banks reject this interpretation as too mechanistic, but it is often amazing how well the rule fits actual behaviour. When this is the case, the Taylor rule reveals a central bank's preferences. In their overview of the ECB's actions, Begg et al. (2002) finds that the following Taylor rule is adequate:

$$i = i^* + a(\pi - \pi^*) + b(y - y^*)$$

where i^* is the equilibrium interest rate, π is the inflation rate and π^* the inflation objective, y is the GDP growth rate and y^* is the GDP growth trend. This formulation says that the central bank raises the interest rate above its equilibrium level, i.e. tightens up its policy stance, when inflation rises above its objective and/or during cyclical upturns, when growth exceeds its trend. Of special interest are the weights that represent the Eurosystem's relative dislike of inflation (parameter a) and cyclical fluctuations (parameter b). If $b = 0$, the central bank is a pure inflation-targeter; it pays no attention to the cyclical situation.[2] Using Fisher's principle (see note 2), the equilibrium interest rate can be written as $i^* = r^* + \pi^*$, where r^* is the equilibrium real interest rate. Begg et al. consider that the equilibrium real interest rate $r^* = 2$ per cent, that the inflation target is 2 per cent, and that the GDP growth trend is 1.2 per cent. They find that the weights that best repre-

sent the Eurosystem's relative dislike of inflation and cyclical fluctuations are $a = 2.0$ and $b = 0.8$, i.e. that the Eurosystem cares about both inflation and cyclical fluctuations, with a heavy weight on the former. Figure 17.7 provides a reasonable, yet far from perfect, interpretation of the actions of this rule over its short history. It suggests that the Eurosystem has kept interest rates pretty low, supporting rather than stunting growth.

[1] The rule is named after the Stanford economist John Taylor who first suggested this interpretation. See Taylor (1993).

[2] Things are never as simple as they look. The cyclical term $(y - y^*)$ can be used by a pure inflation-targeting central bank as a predictor of future inflation, so that $b > 0$ may indicate forward-looking behaviour.

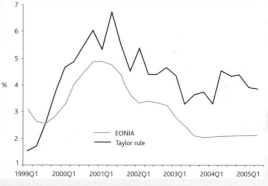

Figure 17.7: *The Eurosystem's Taylor rule*

not have some unpleasant implications, however, and critics have seized on these adverse effects to blame the Eurosystem. It is true that the Eurosystem has been unlucky. The euro weakness not only made a bad impression early on, but it also came at a time when oil prices were rising, thus worsening the shock. Then the euro appreciated when most of the developed economies were facing a slowdown following the 2000 stock market crash, thus hurting competitiveness just when the eurozone needed a boost. It is unclear whether the Eurosystem could have done something about these exchange rate movements. At the very least, it would have needed the cooperation of the USA. As the dollar

was moving in the 'right' direction, being strong during the oil shock and weak during the ensuing recession, it is pretty clear that the Federal Reserve was in no mood to provide a helping hand.

17.5.3 One money, one policy

Asymmetries

How about the much feared asymmetric shocks emphasized by the optimum currency area (OCA) theory? Sure enough, there is no lack of complaints that the Eurosystem does not pay attention to economic conditions in this or that country. The fact is that with

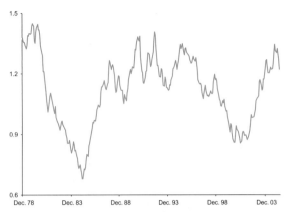

Figure 17.8: *The dollar/euro exchange rate, January 1979–June 2005*

Source: *Monthly Bulletin*, ECB.

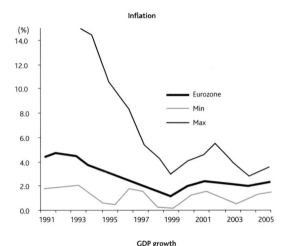

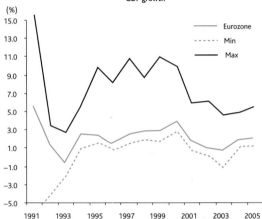

Figure 17.9: *Asymmetries in the euro area, 1991–2005*

Source: *Economic Outlook*, OECD.

one money there can exist only one central bank, and therefore one monetary policy. The Eurosystem can only deal with the eurozone as a whole. It would open a Pandora's box should it ever attempt to bend its policy to a particular country. After all, a key implication of the OCA theory, presented in Chapter 16, is that joining the monetary union implies the acceptance that member countries will occasionally have to bear some costs.

Figure 17.9 documents how different have economic conditions been throughout the eurozone, before and after monetary union (the figure displays the eurozone inflation and real GDP growth rates, along with the highest and lowest national rates each year). Inflation differences have narrowed dramatically during 1991–98, the Maastricht-mandated convergence years. In the aftermath of the 2000 oil shock, there has been a tendency towards some divergence but it has remained subdued. Real growth dispersion, too, has tended to narrow down and has stayed that way. So far, at least, there is no evidence of any dramatic asymmetric shocks. In fact, recent evidence indicates that inflation rates do not differ any more among the eurozone member countries than across broad regions in the USA.[13]

Lasting inflation differentials

That, in a given year, inflation is higher in one country than in the eurozone is normal. What matters is the possibility that, year after year, a particular country faces systematically higher (or lower) inflation. For instance, a country which faces continuously higher inflation than

others is bound to face a loss in competitiveness. If this process persists, the country would then have to undergo several years of lower inflation to restore competitiveness. As the Eurosystem strives to achieve and maintain price stability, this could require deflation – negative inflation – which is usually only achieved under severe pressure in the form of a protracted recession accompanied by high unemployment. This is an implication of the self-equilibrating mechanism of Hume. As explained in Chapter 13, high inflation results in an external deficit; the implied decline in the money supply acts as a contractionary monetary policy, which eventually dampens prices and wages. Conceivably, this ugly scenario could make leaving the eurozone an attractive option.[14]

[13] An article presented in the May 2005 issue of the *Monthly Bulletin* of the ECB (pp. 61–77) presents comparisons and discusses the causes and implications of inflation differences across a currency area.

[14] From 1991 to 2001, Argentina operated a currency board arrangement *vis-à-vis* the US dollar (see Chapter 14 for an explanation of currency boards). For many years, however, its inflation rate exceeded the US rate. Eventually inflation turned negative, but the pain of a deep recession triggered a popular revolt that led to the end of the currency board.

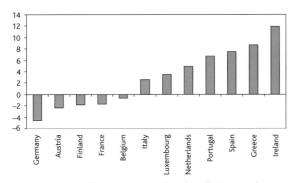

Figure 17.10: *Change in price levels relative to the eurozone, 1999–2005*

Source: *Economic Outlook*, OECD.

Figure 17.10 shows that, over the first six years of monetary union, lasting inflation differentials have occurred in several countries; inflation has been lower than average in Germany, Finland and France, and higher than average in Ireland, Spain, Portugal, the Netherlands and Italy. Why? The potential explanations are:

★ The Balassa–Samuelson effect. This effect, presented in Box 14.1, predicts that the real exchange rates of catching-up countries appreciate. Within a currency area, real appreciation can only be achieved through higher than average inflation.[15] This higher inflation rate does not imply a loss of competitiveness. Quite to the contrary, it is a consequence of rising productivity. This effect could be part of the explanation for the cases of Ireland, Spain and Portugal.

★ Wrong initial conversion rates. Each currency was converted into euros at the ERM parity that prevailed in 1998, but there was no certainty that these conversion rates were fully adequate. For instance, it is now generally accepted that Germany's conversion rate was overvalued; this may explain why, from 1999 to 2005, its consumer price index declined by 4.5 per cent relative to the eurozone's HICP.

★ Autonomous wage and price pressure. Wage negotiators should understand that wage increases in excess of labour productivity gains eat into competitiveness.[16] Wage agreements, however, are driven by other factors than economics. For example, minimum wages can be raised to reduce inequality; civil servants – who do not face directly

any foreign competition – may be well organized to extract wage increases; administered prices – electricity, transports – may be pushed up to avoid losses in state-owned companies. These increases filter down to all wages and prices as they raise production costs and the price level. These factors seem to have played a role in Greece, the Netherlands, Spain and Portugal.

★ Policy mistakes. Through excessively expansionary fiscal policies or public sector price and wage increases – mentioned above – governments may, temporarily at least, contribute to inflationary pressure.

★ Asymmetric shocks. This is the scenario that lies at the centre of the OCA theory. Over the first years, for instance, the oil shocks have not affected to the same extent all eurozone member countries. Many other factors may have played a role, even though none has been identified so far.

Asymmetric monetary policy effects

Different rates of inflation have another, more subtle effect. The single monetary policy implies a common nominal interest rate throughout the eurozone. Yet, monetary policy does not affect the economy through the nominal interest rate. What matters is the real interest rate, i.e. the nominal rate less expected inflation. Take the case of a country where inflation is, and is expected to remain, higher than average. Its real interest rate is lower than average, which means that monetary policy is comparatively expansionary. Conversely, a country with low growth and low inflation faces a relatively high real interest rate, which exerts a contractionary effect.

Is the single monetary policy systematically destabilizing, therefore? It all depends on the source of the inflation differential. If higher inflation is driven by productivity gains, e.g. the Balassa–Samuelson effect, the real exchange rate must appreciate through wage and price increases. In that case, the low real interest rate encourages investment, which is needed to implement the productivity gains, and its expansionary impact speeds up the rise of prices to their new equilibrium level.

If the higher inflation is due to national policy mistakes or unwarranted wage increases, possibly encouraged by a cyclical expansion, the low real interest rate adds fuel to an already overheated economy and monetary policy appears indeed to be destabilizing. How worrisome is this effect? One view is that there is no risk that things will get out of hand. Hume's mechanism ensures that excesses will eventually be corrected. Another view, however, is that the correction may be painful. As noted above, the

[15] One eurozone country's real exchange rate *vis-à-vis* the zone is EP/P^*. With a common currency the nominal exchange rate is $E = 1$, so the real exchange rate is P/P^*. A real appreciation requires that the domestic price level P increases faster than the foreign price level P^*.

[16] See Chapter 8 for an elaboration.

pain may one day lead a country caught in this process to reconsider its continuing monetary union membership. There is nothing that the Eurosystem can do about it. The only policy prescription is to avoid falling into the trap of inflation and, if it happens, to use a contractionary fiscal policy to try to contain the expansionary pressure.

17.5.4 Enlargement

The ten new EU members are expected, indeed required, to join the eurozone as soon as possible. To do so, they must meet the five convergence criteria described in section 17.1.2. The earliest that a country can become a eurozone member is two years after having joined the ERM. For the other criteria, satisfaction is indicated by colour shading in Table 17.4, which shows the state of play as of July 2005. On this basis, assuming that they maintain their latest performance, three countries are eligible for membership in late 2006: Estonia, Lithuania and Slovenia. A year later, Cyprus, Latvia, Malta and Slovakia will have been in ERM for two years but still have some way to go to fulfil the other criteria.

Should the new member countries indeed aim at early membership? By adopting the euro, they will reap the basic benefit of a currency area: a widely used currency. They will also gain from a credible central bank and the promise of price stability, which will immediately translate into lower interest rates. For those countries where the public debt is high, this will also mean a significant reduction in the cost of servicing that debt; Box 17.7 recalls how Italy benefited from this effect. Finally, trade with the eurozone is expected to increase.

On the other hand, they will also face the costs described in Chapter 16 if they do not fulfil the OCA criteria. On this issue, they share the characteristics of the current eurozone members. They are very open, and diversification is fast increasing. Labour mobility is low and the labour markets are generally characterized by classic European rigidity, although some countries seem to have more flexible and decentralized wage bargaining institutions and less restrictive employment protection legislation.[17]

Country	Inflation (%)	Long-term interest rate[a] (%)	ERM membership	Budget balance (%)	Public debt (%)
Cyprus	2.3	5.8	May 2005	−2.9	69.1
Czech Rep.	1.9	4.8		−4.5	36.4
Estonia	3.3	4.4	June 2004	0.9	4.3
Hungary	3.8	8.2		−3.9	57.8
Latvia	5.0	4.9	May 2005	−1.6	14.0
Lithuania	2.9	4.5	June 2004	−2.4	21.2
Malta	2.4	4.7	May 2005	−3.9	76.4
Poland	2.1	6.9		−4.4	46.8
Slovakia	3.7	5.0	November 2005	−3.8	44.2
Slovenia	2.6	4.7	June 2004	−2.2	30.2
Eurozone	1.9	4.0		−2.6	71.7
Convergence limit	3.4	6.0	Two years	−3.0	60.0

[a] Data for 2004.

Source: European Commission.

Table 17.4: *New EU members: the convergence criteria as of July 2005*

[17] There are few studies of the degree to which the new members satisfy the OCA criteria. For work concerning central and eastern Europe, see Fidrmuc (2004).

Box 17.7

Italy's windfall gain from eurozone membership

Italy has one of the largest public debts in Europe (see Fig. 17.2). At the time when the Maastricht Treaty was signed in December 1991, its government was spending on debt service some 12 per cent of GDP, about one-quarter of its total expenditures. Debt service is approximately equal to the product of the interest rate and the debt value (iB, where i is the interest rate and B the debt). This means that part of the debt burden was associated with a high interest rate. Why was the Italian interest rate high? Fisher parity provides the answer: when inflation is high and expected to remain high, the nominal interest rate is high.

Figure 17.11 shows how the Italian interest rate steadily declined in the years following the Maastricht agreement. The decline is explained by the disinflation process, as Italy strived to meet the convergence criteria. It is also explained by the credibility associated with eurozone membership and its price-stability-oriented central bank. The remarkable feature of this evolution is the parallel decline in debt service, which has declined to about 40 per cent of

what it used to be. Most of this huge windfall gain, worth 7.5 per cent of GDP, has been used by the Italian authorities to increase spending in many areas.

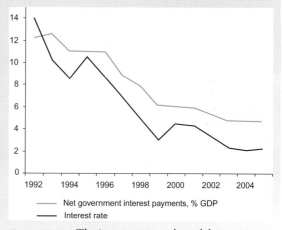

Figure 17.11: *The interest rate and net debt service as a percentage of GDP in Italy, 1992–2005*

Source: *Economic Outlook*, OECD.

Regarding the political criteria, a good indication is provided by the decision to join the ERM. The seven countries that did so soon after accession to the EU seem to exhibit strong popular support towards Europe. The three countries that did not join have become more sceptical. In general, a key issue is the two-year transition period of ERM membership; as explained in Chapter 15, this is a delicate

step where full capital mobility and an exchange peg may trigger speculative attacks. The best way to cross this period trouble-free is to make sure that all the other criteria are satisfied and, therefore, to convince the markets that adoption of the euro will come swiftly. Unsurprisingly, the three countries that have not yet joined the ERM are those where the budgets are in significant deficit.

17.6 Summary

The monetary union is an elaborate construction carefully mapped out in the Maastricht Treaty. The treaty was signed in 1991 and the single currency started to operate, as planned, in 1999, even though the new currency was not issued until 2002. This long process was part of a careful approach that recognized the unique nature of the undertaking. It rested on a number of provisions:

★ The adoption of a common currency had to be the end of a convergence process. All member countries would have to demonstrate their acceptance of price stability and of the discipline that goes with it.

★ Monetary union membership would not be automatic. Admission is to be assessed on the basis of five convergence criteria: low inflation, low long-term interest rates, ERM membership, low budget deficits and a declining public debt.

★ While all EU members are expected to join the currency area, two countries (Denmark and the UK) were given opt-out clauses. This was the first time that the possibility of a 'two-speed Europe' was accepted.

The monetary union implies the delegation of monetary policy to a single authority. Yet, the EU is not a federal system, so it was decided to maintain the national central banks. The resulting Eurosystem thus formally brings together the newly created ECB and the national central banks of all EU countries. Decisions are taken by the Governing Council, chaired by the President of the ECB, which includes the ECB's Executive Committee and the governors of the central banks of the countries that have adopted the euro. The size of the Governing Council is considered by outside observers to be excessive, a situation that will worsen when new members join the eurozone. A proposal has been advanced by the Governing Council; it caps the size of the Council by instituting a rotation of national central bank governors, taking into account the size of the country that they represent.

The Eurosystem has been given the primary goal of price stability, but it is free to decide what that means and how to go about it. It considers that price stability is achieved when the eurozone's inflation rate is close to 2 per cent over the 'medium term'. It has also adopted the common practice of steering the euro short-term interest rate through three channels: the marginal refinancing facility sets a ceiling, the deposit facility sets a floor, and the interest rate is kept close to the middle of that range through regular auctions that establish the main refinancing rate.

The logic of this procedure is that the short-term interest rate affects the economy through a number of channels that operate via credit availability and the money supply, the long-term real interest rate, asset prices and the exchange rate. Thus, the effect of monetary policy on the economy, and on inflation in particular, is indirect and the Eurosystem must factor in these various effects, all of which take time to produce results. This requires a strategy. The Eurosystem's approach is to rely on two pillars: economic analysis (the medium-term impact of current conditions on inflation) and monetary analysis (the longer-term impact of monetary aggregates on inflation). In addition, the strategy recognizes that in a monetary union, there can only be one monetary policy. This is why the Eurosystem explicitly cares only about the whole euro area, not about individual member countries. In addition, it takes no responsibility for the exchange rate that is freely floating.

The Eurosystem constitutionally enjoys considerable independence, both in defining its objectives and in deciding how to conduct monetary policy. It is not allowed to take instructions from any other authority, be it European or national. This independence is a condition for guaranteeing price stability, but it raises an important issue: in a democracy, every authority has to be accountable to its citizens for its actions. The solution adopted by the Maastricht Treaty is to make the Eurosystem formally accountable to the European Parliament. Accountability takes the form of an annual report and of regular hearings of the ECB Chairman and members of the Executive Board by the Parliament's Committee on Economic and Monetary Affairs. A number of observers feel that this is too weak a form of accountability and consider that the monetary union suffers from a 'democratic deficit'.

The Eurosystem has quickly established its reputation, in spite of several shocks that occurred during its first years of existence, fortunately with limited asymmetry. It has managed to keep inflation close to 2 per cent, even though its initial goal of keeping it below this limit has not been achieved, which led the Eurosystem to change slightly its definition of price stability. The Eurosystem is sometimes blamed for poor growth, but Europe's disappointing performance mainly concerns the larger eurozone member countries for purely domestic reasons. Two complicating factors remain. First, the exchange rate of the euro *vis-à-vis* the dollar has fluctuated widely, mostly worsening the impact of worldwide shocks (oil shocks, stock market crashes). This is as much a dollar as a euro issue, yet the Eurosystem has found itself criticized even though it has explicitly adopted a freely floating regime. The second complicating factor is the fact that the real interest rate is lower where fast growth fuels inflation and higher where a slowdown keeps inflation muted. A single monetary policy cannot avoid what looks like a destabilizing effect.

Self-assessment questions

1. What are the five convergence criteria and what is the logic behind each of them?

2. 'With one money there can exist only one central bank, and therefore one monetary policy.' What, then, is the role of national central banks in the EMU?

3. Why can inflation rates differ across the EMU member countries? What are the consequences?

4. Find data and assess how the countries of central and eastern Europe perform regarding the five convergence criteria.

5. What is the difference between objective and instrument independence?

6. What is the process of liquidity dissemination in the euro area? How do we know that every bank that needs liquidity will get it?

7. The Eurosystem sets the money supply in the euro area, but what drives the money stock in each country? How does this relate to Hume's mechanism and the gold standard (Chapter 13)?

8. What is the Eurosystem's definition of price stability? What would be your own definition?

9. Why can the Eurosystem not take responsibility for national inflation rates?

Essay questions

1. The Eurosystem asserts that, in its deliberations, it never pays attention to local (i.e. national) economic conditions. The reason is that there is a single monetary policy and that 'one size fits all'. Discuss this approach and imagine alternative approaches.

2. It is sometimes asserted that independence and accountability are substitutes, i.e. that more independence requires less accountability and vice versa. Discuss this assertion.

3. In the USA, monetary policy decisions are made by the Federal Open Market Committee which comprises the seven members of the Board – the equivalent of the ECB's Executive Board – the President of the Federal Reserve Bank of New York, who implements the Committee's decisions, and by annually rotating four of the remaining eleven regional Reserve Bank Presidents. Can this be a model for the Eurosystem?

4. Find on http://www.ecb.int the latest press conference on monetary policy decisions and interpret the text in the light of the stated strategy.

5. The Maastricht Treaty describes in minute detail the creation of the euro area but is silent on a possible break-up. Imagine that a country is suffering from a severe adverse shock. Could it leave? How? What could the other countries do to try to keep it in?

6. Box 17.4 presents the solution proposed by the Eurosystem to face the enlargement of the euro area. Evaluate this proposal and make your own suggestions.

7. Why are transparency and accountability so important for the Eurosystem? What kind of difficulties can you envision if the system is perceived as not sufficiently accountable? Not sufficiently transparent?

8. The convergence criteria are about nominal conditions (inflation, deficits and debts) but not about real conditions (GDP per capita, growth). This was understandable for the original founders but what does it mean for the upcoming wave of accession of the ten new EU members? Should the same criteria apply? Why or why not? Is the lack of real convergence problematic?

9. The last part of section 17.5.3 describes how the single monetary policy can be destabilizing, using the case of a country with higher than average inflation. Describe the opposite case of a country with lower than average inflation, explain the economic and political risks, and make policy suggestions.

10. Evaluate the costs and benefits for the new EU members of adopting the euro.

Further reading: the aficionado's corner

The Eurosystem's initial definition of its strategy can be found in Chapters 3 and 4 of the ECB's *The Monetary Policy of the ECB*, Frankfurt, 2001. The strategy review appears in the June 2003 issue of the ECB's *Monthly Bulletin*.

For presentations of the Eurosystem, see:
Mottiar, R. (1999) 'Monetary policy in the euro area: the role of national central banks', *Central Bank of Ireland Quarterly Bulletin*, Winter.
Padoa-Schioppa, T. (member of the Executive Board of the ECB) *An Institutional Glossary of the Eurosystem*. http://www.ecb.int/key/00/sp000308_1.htm.

On Taylor rules, see:
'Monetary policy in the euro area has been looser than critics think', *The Economist*, 14 July, 2005. http://www.economist.com/finance/displayStory.cfm?story_id=4174785.

For a debate among central bankers on accountability and transparency, see:
Buiter, W. (1999) *Alice in Euroland*, CEPR Policy Paper 1, Centre for Economic Policy Research, London.
Issing, O. (1999) *The Eurosystem: Transparent and Accountable or Willem in Euroland*, CEPR Policy Paper 2, Centre for Economic Policy Research, London.

On central bank independence, see:
Berger, H., J. de Haan and S. Eijffinger (2001) 'Central bank independence: an update of theory and evidence', *Journal of Economic Surveys*, 15(1): 3–40.

On diverging inflation rates in the eurozone, see:
ECB (2005) 'Monetary policy and inflation differentials in a heterogeneous currency area', *Monthly Bulletin*, May: 61–78.

On the decision of the new EU member countries to join the eurozone, see:
Schadler, S., P. Drummond, L. Kuijs, Z. Murgasova and R. van Elkan (2005) 'Adopting the euro in central Europe: challenges of the next step in European integration', Occasional Paper 234, IMF, New York.

Useful websites

The ECB website: http://www.ecb.int.

The Treaty of Maastricht: http://europa.eu.int/eur-lex/en/treaties/index.html.

Professor Giancarlo Corsetti's euro home page is the number one website on the euro area: http://www.iue.it/RSCAS/Research/Eurohomepage/.

The President of the ECB reports every quarter to the Committee of Economic and Monetary Affairs of the European Parliament. The transcripts of the meetings, gentlemanly called 'Monetary Dialogue', as well as background reports can be found at: http://www.europarl.eu.int/comparl/econ/emu/default_en.htm.

Public opinion on the euro: http://europa.eu.int/comm/dg10/epo/euro_en.html.

A website dedicated to EONIA and interest rates in the euro area: http://www.euribor.org/default.htm.

Annual reports on the ECB by academic observers, *'Monitoring the European Central Bank'*, published by the Centre for Economic Policy Research, can be found at http://www.cepr.org.

References

Begg, D., F. Canova, P. de Grauwe, A. Fatás and P. Lane (2002) *Surviving the Slowdown*: *Monitoring the European Central Bank*, 4, Centre for Economic Policy Research, London.

Blinder, A., C. Goodhart, P. Hildebrand, D. Lipton and C. Wyplosz (2001) *How Do Central Banks Talk?*, Geneva Reports on the World Economy 3, Centre for Economic Policy Research, London.

ECB (2003) 'The ECB's monetary policy strategy', Press Release, 8 May. http://www.ecb.int.

Fidrmuc, J. (2004) 'The endogeneity of the optimum currency area criteria, intra-industry trade and EMU enlargement', *Contemporary Economic Policy*, 22(1): 1–12.

Gros, D. and K. Lannoo (1999) *The Euro Capital Market*, John Wiley, Chichester.

Lane, P. (forthcoming) 'The real effects of EMU', *Journal of Economic Perspectives*.

Taylor, J. (1993) 'Discretion vs policy rules in practice', *Carnegie–Rochester Conference Series on Public Policy*, 39: 195–214.

Economic prosperity and the viability of the monetary union cannot be sustained without tackling past fiscal policy failures, i.e. a trend towards increasing government expenditure and taxation levels combined with high structural budget deficits and government debt accumulation.

European Commission (2001)

I know very well that the Stability Pact is stupid, like all decisions which are rigid.

Romano Prodi (EU Commission President), Le Monde, *17 October 2002*

18 Fiscal policy and the Stability Pact

18.1 Fiscal policy in the monetary union

18.1.1 An ever more important instrument?
18.1.2 Borrowing instead of transfers
18.1.3 Automatic stabilizers and discretionary policy actions

18.2 Fiscal policy externalities

18.2.1 Spillovers and coordination
18.2.2 Cyclical income spillovers
18.2.3 Borrowing cost spillovers
18.2.4 Excessive deficit and the no-bailout clause
18.2.5 Collective discipline

INTRODUCTION

The monetary union implies the loss of monetary policy as a macroeconomic stabilization instrument, which seems to enhance the role of fiscal policy. However, national fiscal policies affect other countries. Do these spillover effects also call for sharing the fiscal policy instrument? This chapter first reviews how fiscal policy operates across national boundaries and presents the principles that can help to decide whether some limits in national decisions are in order. This lays the ground for an understanding of the Stability and Growth Pact. The chapter next examines the pact's impact on policy choices and the controversies that have arisen in the early years of its implementation.

18.1 Fiscal policy in the monetary union

18.1.1 An ever more important instrument?

When joining a monetary union a country gives up one of its two macroeconomic instruments – monetary policy – but retains full control of the other – fiscal policy. Does this mean that fiscal policy has to do double work? In the simple Keynesian *IS–LM* world, monetary and fiscal policy are nearly substitute tools to stabilize output and employment fluctuations. It means that, in the euro area, fiscal policy becomes even more important. In the event of asymmetric shocks – identified by the optimum currency area theory in Chapter 16 as the main source of costs in a monetary union – fiscal policy is the only available macroeconomic instrument. This is a good departure point to keep in mind but, in practice, some important differences imply that the two instruments are not as easily substitutable as suggested by the *IS–LM* analysis. In particular, fiscal policy is more difficult to activate and less reliable than monetary policy.

A common problem with both instruments is that they affect spending largely through expectations. For monetary policy, as explained in Chapter 17, the central bank can only control very short-term interest rates while private spending is financed through long-term borrowing. For fiscal policy, changes in spending and/or taxes impact on the budget balance, which immediately raises the question of the financing of the public debt. Consider, for instance, a cut in income taxes that creates a budget deficit. The government will have to borrow and increase the public debt, but how will this new debt be reimbursed? If, as is plausible, taxes are eventually raised, the policy action is properly seen as the combination of a tax reduction today and a tax increase later. This is an action unlikely to wildly boost consumption.[1]

Fiscal policy faces a major additional drawback: it is very slow to implement. A central bank can decide to change the interest rate whenever it deems necessary, and can do so in a matter of seconds. Not so for fiscal policy. Establishing the budget is a long and complicated process. The government must first agree on the budget, with lots of heavy-handed negotiations among ministers. The budget must then be approved by the parliament, a time-consuming and highly political process. Then spending decisions must be enacted through the bureaucracy, and taxes can only be changed gradually as they are never retroactive. For example, income taxes can only affect future incomes, implying long delays. On the other hand, once implemented, fiscal policy actions tend to have a more rapid effect on the economy (6 to 12 months) than does monetary policy (12 to 24 months).

As a result, fiscal policy is like a tanker, it changes course very slowly. The delay may even be such that, when fiscal policy finally affects the economy, the problem that it was meant to solve has disappeared. In principle, macroeconomic policies are meant to be countercyclical, i.e. to slow down a booming economy or speed up a sagging economy. Fiscal policy has occasionally been found to be pro-cyclical: an expansionary action designed to deal with a recession hits the economy when it has already recovered. If this is the case, it actually speeds up the economy when it is already desirable to slow it down.

---

[1] The extreme case where consumers save all of the tax reduction to pay for future tax increases is called Ricardian equivalence. It is explained, and its empirical validity assessed in, for example, Burda and Wyplosz (2005), Chapter 6.

18.1.2 Borrowing instead of transfers

Another way of looking at fiscal policy is that the government borrows and pays back on behalf of its citizens. During a slowdown, the government opens up a budget deficit that is financed through public borrowing. In an upswing, the government runs a budget surplus which allows it to pay back its debt. A government that borrows to reduce taxes now and raises taxes later to pay back its debt is, in effect, lending to its citizens now and making them pay back later. Individual citizens and firms could, in principle, do it on their own, borrowing in bad years and paying back in good years. This would have the same stabilizing effect as fiscal policy. Is fiscal policy a futile exercise or, worse, a bad political trick? Not quite.

To start with, it is true that, in the previous example, the government simply acts as a bank *vis-à-vis* its citizens. The reason why it may make sense is that, when the economy slows down, lending becomes generally riskier and banks become very cautious. Many citizens and firms cannot borrow in bad times, or can only borrow at high cost. Indeed, workers who lose their jobs are considered by their banks as bad risk, and so are firms that face sagging profits or even losses. When governments are considered a good risk, which is generally the case in Europe, they can borrow at all times at reasonably low cost. This is why countercyclical fiscal policy can be effective.

An additional reason is related to one of the optimum currency area criteria examined in Chapter 16, the desirability of substantial inter-country transfers. In that dimension, Europe was found to do very poorly. Can this problem be alleviated? Fiscal policy is part of the answer. When a country faces an adverse asymmetric shock, its government can borrow from countries that are not affected by the shock. This is the equivalent of a transfer: instead of receiving a loan or a grant[2] from other eurozone governments or from 'Brussels', the adversely affected country's government borrows on international private markets. In this way fiscal policy makes up for the absence of 'federal' transfers in a monetary union. The transfers are inter-temporal instead of being inter-regional.

18.1.3 Automatic stabilizers and discretionary policy actions

Automatic stabilizers

Fiscal policy has one important advantage: it tends to be spontaneously countercyclical. When the economy slows down, individual incomes are disappointingly low, corporate profits decline and spending is rather weak. This all means that tax collection declines: income taxes, profit taxes, VAT, etc. are less than they would be in normal conditions. At the same time, spending on unemployment benefits and other subsidies rises. All in all, the budget worsens and fiscal policy is automatically expansionary. These various effects are called the automatic stabilizers of fiscal policy. Table 18.1, which displays estimates of the size of the stabilizers, shows that, on average, a 1 per cent decline in growth leads to a deterioration of the budget balance of about 0.5 per cent of GDP. There are some differences from one country to another, which reflect the structure of taxation and of welfare payments.[3]

Discretionary fiscal policy

The automatic stabilizers just happen. Discretionary fiscal policy, on the contrary, requires explicit decisions to change taxes or spending. As noted above, such decisions are slow to be made and implemented. This is why, in some countries, the budget law sets aside some funds that can be quickly mobilized by the government if discretionary action is needed. Even then, the amounts are small and their use is often politically controversial.

Because of the automatic stabilizers, the budget figures do not reveal what the government is doing with its fiscal policy. The budget can change for two reasons. It can improve, for example, because the government is cutting spending or raising taxes, or because the economy is booming. In order to disentangle these two factors, it is convenient to look at the cyclically adjusted budget. This procedure is based on the output gap concept.

The output gap is a measure of the country's cyclical position, the percentage difference between actual and potential GDP; a negative gap indicates that the economy is underperforming, it operates below its potential. The cyclically adjusted budget balance is an estimate of what the balance would be in a given year if

---

[2] A grant is not to be reimbursed, but a collective system of grants implies that any country is supposed to be alternatively giving and receiving, the total averaging zero over the long run. This is no different from long-term borrowing, receiving now, paying back later.

[3] For example, the more progressive are income taxes, the more tax collection declines during a slowdown, hence the greater the stabilization effect. Similarly, the automatic stabilizers are stronger the larger are the unemployment benefits.

Country	%	Country	%	Country	%	Country	%
Germany	0.5	Austria	−0.5	Greece	−0.6	Portugal	0.4
France	−0.5	Belgium	−0.5	Ireland	−0.4	Spain	−0.5
Italy	−0.4	Denmark	−0.7	Netherlands	−0.6	Sweden	−0.5
UK	−0.6	Finland	−0.5				

Source: OECD (1997).

Table 18.1: *Automatic stabilizers: sensitivity of government budget balances to a 1 per cent decline in economic growth*

the output gap were zero. The actual budget balance is lower than the cyclically adjusted budget balance when output is below potential, i.e. when the output gap is negative, and conversely when the output gap is positive. The difference between the evolution of the actual and cyclically adjusted budget balances is the footprint of the automatic stabilizers.

The cyclically adjusted budget balance is a reliable gauge of the stance of fiscal policy since it separates discretionary government actions from the cyclical effects of the automatic stabilizers. An improvement indicates that the government tightens fiscal policy whereas an expansionary fiscal policy worsens the cyclically adjusted budget balance. If the government would never change its fiscal policy, the cyclically adjusted budget balance would remain constant, at least to a first approximation.[4]

Figure 18.1 illustrates this point in the case of the Netherlands. The figure shows that the steady improvement in the budget that occurred during the convergence years 1995–99 is due partly to government efforts to meet the Maastricht conditions and partly to a rising output gap. It is also interesting to observe that the sharp deterioration of the budget over 2001–05 – which brought the Netherlands into violation of the Stability and Growth Pact – is the consequence of a serious slowdown, and occurred in spite of visible government efforts to avoid this outcome.

These two issues – the role of the automatic stabilizers and the distinction between the actual and cyclically adjusted budgets – play a crucial role in what follows.

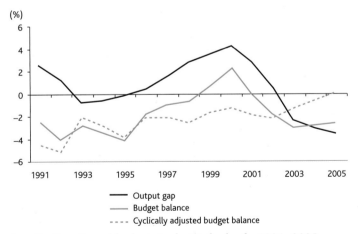

Figure 18.1: *Actual and cyclically adjusted budgets in the Netherlands, 1991–2005*

Source: *Economic Outlook*, OECD.

[4] Why to first approximation? Because as the economy grows, more people climb the income ladder and face higher tax rates. Also the structure of the economy changes, possible changing the way taxes are collected.

18.2 Fiscal policy externalities

18.2.1 Spillovers and coordination

So far, the discussion has concerned individual countries, but fiscal policy actions by one country may spill over to other countries through a variety of channels: income and spending, inflation, borrowing costs. Such spillovers, called externalities, mean that one country's fiscal policy actions can help or hurt other countries. In such a situation, when one country decides what to do, it cannot ignore the effect on its partners and, conversely, it also has to take into account policy decisions taken elsewhere. This implies that countries subject to each other's spillovers stand to benefit from coordinating their fiscal policies. In principle, all concerned countries could agree on each other's fiscal policy to achieve a situation that befits them all. This is what policy coordination is about.

While, formally, fiscal policy remains a national prerogative, it is natural to ask whether the deepening economic integration among eurozone countries calls for some degree of coordination. On the one hand, the setting up of a monetary union strengthens the case for fiscal policy coordination as it promotes economic integration. On the other hand, fiscal policy coordination requires binding agreements on who does what and when. Such detailed arrangements would limit each country's sovereignty, precisely at a time when the fiscal policy instrument assumes greater importance. The question is whether sharing the same currency increases the spillovers to the point where some new limits on sovereignty are desirable and justified. To answer this question, we review the channels through which

spillovers occur and examine what difference the eurozone makes.

18.2.2 Cyclical income spillovers

Business cycles are transmitted through exports and imports. When Germany enters an expansion phase, for instance, it imports more from its partner countries. For these partner countries, the German expansion means more exports and more incomes, and the expansion tends to be transmitted across borders. Figure 18.2, which displays output gaps in Germany and its three smaller neighbours, confirms that business cycles are highly synchronized. Quite obviously, the spillover is stronger the more the countries trade with each other, and the larger is the country taking action. This is one reason why Germany's fiscal policy is carefully watched everywhere else in Europe.

What does this mean for fiscal policy? Consider, first, the case when two monetary union member countries undergo synchronized cycles, for example both suffer from a recession. Each government will want to adopt an expansionary fiscal policy, but to what extent? If each government ignores the other's action, their combined action may be too strong as each economy pulls the other one from the recession – an effect of the Keynesian multiplier. If, instead, each government relies on the other to do most of the work, too little might be done. Consider next the case when the cycles are asynchronized. An expansionary fiscal policy in the country undergoing a slowdown stands to boost spending in the already booming country. Conversely, a contractionary fiscal policy move in the booming country stands to deepen the recession in the other country. The risk, in this case, is too much policy action.

18.2.3 Borrowing cost spillovers

A fiscal expansion increases public borrowing or reduces public saving. As the government is usually the country's biggest borrower, large budget deficits may push interest rates up. Once they share the same currency, eurozone member countries share the same interest rate. One country's deficits, especially if the country is large and its deficits sizeable, may impose higher interest rates throughout the euro area.[5] As high interest rates deter investment, they affect long-term growth. This is another spillover channel.

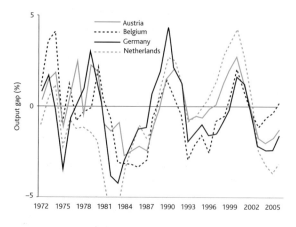

Figure 18.2: *Income spillovers, 1972–2005*

Source: *Economic Outlook*, OECD.

[5] Jürgen Stark, a high-level German official who was influential in designing the Stability and Growth Pact, writes: 'The state's absorption of resources which would otherwise have found their way into private investments results in higher long-term interest rates' (Stark, 2001, p. 79).

As stated, the argument is weak, however. Europe is fully integrated in the world's financial markets so any one country's borrowing is unlikely to make much of an impression on world and European interest rates. On the other hand, heavy borrowing may elicit capital inflows. This could result in an appreciation of the euro, which would hurt the area's competitiveness and cut into growth. Borrowing costs thus represent another channel for spillovers.

18.2.4 Excessive deficits and the no-bailout clause

The question of debt sustainability cannot be taken lightly in Europe in view of the near-tripling of public debts as a share of GDP since 1975, as Fig. 18.3 shows.[6] In the distant past, public debts have occasionally risen but only in difficult situations, and mostly during wars. The recent generalized debt build-up is partly related to the oil shocks of the 1970s and 1980s, but this is not the only reason. The figure illustrates what is sometimes called the 'deficit bias', a disquieting tendency for governments to run budget deficits for no other reason than political expediency. Does it call for a specific collective measure?

In principle, it is in each country's interest to resist the deficit bias, so fiscal discipline does not call for any collective measure unless spillovers can be identified. What happens when a public debt becomes unsustainable? As noted in Chapter 17, financially hard-pressed governments may be tempted to call upon the central bank to finance their deficits, the traditional route to inflation. Should the Eurosystem (the ECB and NCBs) oblige, inflation would rise throughout the euro area. This spillover door is explicitly closed by the Maastricht Treaty, which forbids the Eurosystem from providing direct support to governments.

Heavy public borrowing by one country is a sign of fiscal indiscipline that could trouble the international financial markets. If markets believe that one country's public debt is unsustainable, they could view the whole euro area with suspicion. The result would be sizeable capital outflows and euro weakness. This is another potential source of spillover.

There is still another potential spillover. If a government accumulates such a debt that it can no longer service it, it must default. The experience with such defaults is that the immediate reaction is a massive capital outflow, a collapse of the exchange rate and of the stock markets, and a prolonged crisis complete with a deep recession and skyrocketing unemployment. Too bad for the delinquent country, but being part of a monetary union changes things radically. It is now the common exchange rate that is the object of the market reaction. The spillover can further extend to stock markets throughout the whole monetary union.

The further fear is that the mere threat of one member country's default would so concern all other member governments that they would feel obliged to bail out the nearly bankrupt government.

In fact, this risk has been clearly identified in the Maastricht Treaty, which includes a no-bailout clause. This clause clearly states that no official credit can be extended to a distressed member government. In spite of the no-bailout clause, it remains that, in the midst of an emergency, some arrangement could still be found to bail out a bankrupt government. For example, the ECB could be 'informally' pressed to relax its monetary policy to make general credit more abundant at a lower cost, which would result in inflation. More generally, it is feared that a sovereign default would badly affect the euro area and undermine its credibility, with seriously adverse effects on the euro.

These spillovers do not rely on standard fiscal policy income effects but on the risk of excessive, and potentially unsustainable, deficits. They point to a catastrophic event. Defaults, however, do not occur in blue skies – it takes years to accumulate large debts. The implication is that a preventive procedure is required to avoid the need to deal with an emergency.

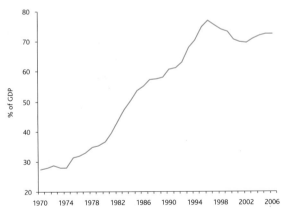

Figure 18.3: *Public debt of the eurozone, 1970–2006*

Source: *Economic Outlook*, OECD.

[6] This is the debt for the whole zone, but the situation differs from country to country. Two countries, Belgium and Italy, have a debt in excess of 100 per cent of GDP. These debts are seen as the weak elements of the chain.

Collective discipline

Why do governments seem to have a deficit bias, and why does this bias seem to differ from country to country, as can be seen in Table 18.2? Deficits allow governments to deliver goods and services today without facing the costs, passing the burden of debt service to future governments or even to future generations. It is tempting to do so, especially when elections are near; but adequate democratic accountability should prevent governments from indulging. Even though future generations are not here to weigh in, the current generation may reasonably expect to be called upon to service the debt, and anyway most people care about the next generation. So a debt build-up often reflects a failure of democratic control over governments. Why has this been happening in Europe's democracies?

Public spending often favours narrow interest groups (civil servants, the military, public road contractors, etc.), while the debt service is diffused and borne by an unstructured majority, and interest groups are well organized and influential with the government. The time of reckoning should come when elections are held, but the electoral process is not always effective at imposing budgetary discipline. Indeed, some political regimes – typically parliamentary regimes which involve large coalitions – seem to be doing less well in keeping deficits and debts in check.

Changing the democratic regime (the form of democracy, how elections are organized) could help, but it is a rather intractable endeavour. This is why some governments find it appealing to seek external restraint and to invoke

'Brussels' as a scapegoat that can be blamed when resisting interest groups and political friends. Collective discipline, even if not necessarily justified by spillovers, can be used as a substitute for adequate domestic institutions.

18.3 Principles

The existence of spillovers is one argument for sharing policy responsibilities among independent countries. It is not the only argument, however; and there are powerful counter-arguments. The broader question is, at which level of government – regional, national, supranational – should policies be conducted? The theory of fiscal federalism deals with this question. The principle of subsidiarity is another way of approaching the issue. Both approaches have been presented earlier (Chapter 3) and are briefly recalled in this section.

18.3.1 The theory of fiscal federalism

The theory of fiscal federalism asks how, in one country, fiscal responsibilities should be assigned between the various levels (national, regional, municipal) of government. It can be transposed to Europe's case, even though Europe is not a federation, by asking which tasks should remain in national – possibly regional in federal states – hands and which ones should be a shared responsibility, i.e. delegated to Brussels. There are two good reasons to transfer responsibility to Brussels and two good reasons to keep it at the national level. An additional concern is the quality of government at the national and supranational level.

Two arguments for sharing responsibilities: externalities and increasing returns to scale

As noted before, spillovers, also called externalities – when one country's actions affect other countries – lead to inefficient outcomes when each country is free to act as it wishes. Sometimes too much action is taken, sometimes not enough. This is the case of tariffs (see Chapter 4) and fiscal policy. The other argument is that some policies are more efficient when carried out on a large scale. Increasing returns to scale can be found in the use of money,[7] in the design of commercial law or in defence (army, weapons development and production), among others.

One solution is coordination, which preserves sovereignty but calls for repeated and often piecemeal negotiations, with no guarantee of success. Another solution is to give up sovereignty, partly or completely, and delegate a task

Country	% of GDP	Country	% of GDP
Austria	64.6	Latvia	16.1
Belgium	95.1	Lithuania	23.2
Cyprus	42.4	Luxembourg	5.2
Czech Rep.	76.9	Malta	75.9
Denmark	43.3	Netherlands	58.9
Estonia	5.3	Poland	50.8
Finland	46.5	Portugal	61.7
France	68.7	Slovakia	46.1
Germany	67.7	Slovenia	28.2
Greece	111.4	Spain	47.6
Hungary	57.6	Sweden	50.3
Ireland	26.9	UK	42.7
Italy	104.7	Eurozone	72.2

Source: *Economic Outlook*, OECD.

Table 18.2: *Public debts in Europe, 2005*

[7] Chapter 16 argues that this is a key benefit from a large currency area.

to a supranational institution. In Europe, some important tasks have already been delegated to the European Commission (the internal market and trade negotiations) and to the Eurosystem (monetary policy).

Two arguments for retaining sovereignty: heterogeneity of preferences and information asymmetries

Consider the example of common law concerning family life (marriages and divorces, raising children, dealing with ageing parents, etc.). Practices and traditions differ across countries, sometimes to a considerable extent. In this domain, preferences are heterogeneous and a supranational arrangement is bound to create much dissatisfaction.

Now consider the decisions of where to build roads, how large to make them, where to set up traffic lights, etc. These require a good understanding of how people move, or wish to move, in a geographic area: it is a case of information asymmetry, since it is likely that the information is more readily available at the local level than at a more global level.

Heterogeneity of preferences and information asymmetries imply that it would be inefficient to share competence at a supranational level. Much of the criticism levelled at 'Brussels' concerns cases where either heterogeneity or information asymmetries are important: deciding on the appropriate size of cheese or the way to brew beer are best left to national governments, or even local authorities, no matter how important the externalities or increasing returns to scale.

The quality of government

An implicit assumption so far is that governments always act in the best interest of their citizens. While this may generally be the case, there are numerous instances when governments either pursue their own agendas or are captured by interest groups. Indeed, like any institution, governments often wish to extend their domain of action, possibly in order to increase their own power or because they genuinely believe that they can deal with important problems. In addition, there is no such thing as 'the best interest of citizens': some citizens favour some actions, others do not. Governments exist in part to deal with such conflicts and do so under democratic control but, as noted in section 18.2.5, elections cannot sanction every one of the millions of decisions that favour well-connected interests. In spite of all the good things that can be said about democracy, it is not a perfect system, and it often fails.[8]

[8] Churchill is rumoured to have said: 'Democracy is the worst possible system, except for all others.'

Once this fact of life is recognized, the principles from the theory of fiscal federalism need to be amended. There is no general rule here, only the need to always keep in mind that a good solution may turn out to be bad if the government is misbehaving. In particular, the quality of government and of democratic control ought to be brought into the picture. The question here is whether Brussels performs better than the national governments.

18.3.2 The principle of subsidiarity

It should be clear by now that in most cases the four arguments for and against centralization at the EU level are unlikely to lead to clear-cut conclusions, and the warning about the quality of government further complicates the issue. In each case, one has to weigh the various arguments and trade off the pros and cons. This is often mission impossible, hence another question: where should the burden of proof lie?

The EU has taken the view that the burden of proof lies with those who argue in favour of sharing sovereign tasks. This is the principle of subsidiarity (presented in Chapter 3) and it is enshrined in the European Treaty:

> In areas which do not fall within its exclusive competence, the Community shall take action, in accordance with the principle of subsidiarity, only if and insofar as the objectives of the proposed action cannot be sufficiently achieved by the Member States and can therefore, by reason of the scale or effects of the proposed action, be better achieved by the Community.

(Article 5)

18.3.3 Implications for fiscal policy

A key distinction: micro vs macroeconomic aspects of fiscal policy

It is crucial to separate two aspects of fiscal policy. The first aspect is structural, that is, mainly microeconomic. It concerns the size of the budget, what public money is spent on, how taxes are raised, i.e. who pays what, and redistribution designed to reduce inequalities or to provide incentives to particular individuals or groups. The second aspect is macroeconomic. This is the income stabilization role of fiscal policy, the idea that it can be used as a countercyclical instrument.

Here, we focus on the macroeconomic stabilization component of fiscal policy, ignoring the structural aspects. To simplify, we look at the budget balance and ignore the size and structure of the budget and the resulting evolution of the public debt. We apply the principles of fiscal federalism to ask whether there is a case for limiting the free exercise of sovereignty on national budget balances and debts.

The case for collective restraint

Section 18.2 identified a number of spillovers: income flows, borrowing costs and the risk of difficulties in financing runaway deficits, possibly leading to debt default. Some of these spillovers can have serious effects across the euro area. In addition, some countries have not established political institutions that are conducive to fiscal discipline so it may be in their own best interest to use Brussels as an external agent of restraint. On the other hand, it is difficult to detect a scale economy.

These externalities call for some limits on national fiscal policies, and such limits can take various forms, ranging from coordination and peer pressure to mandatory limits on deficits and debts.

The case against collective restraint

Working in the opposite direction are important heterogeneities and information asymmetries. Macroeconomic heterogeneity occurs in the presence of asymmetric shocks. A common fiscal policy, on top of a common monetary policy, would leave each country without any countercyclical macroeconomic tool. Heterogeneity can also be the consequence of differences of opinions regarding the effectiveness of the instrument. Some countries (e.g. France and Italy) have long been active users of fiscal policy whereas others (e.g. Germany) have a tradition of scepticism towards Keynesian policies. Finally, national political processes are another source of heterogeneity. In some countries, the government has quite some leeway to adapt the budget to changing economic conditions whereas in others the process is cumbersome and politically difficult.

Information asymmetries chiefly concern the perception of the political implications of fiscal policies. Each government faces elections, and economics is often an important factor shaping voter preferences. Whether and how to use fiscal policy at a particular juncture is part of a complex political game, which makes national politics highly idiosyncratic. While governments have a lot of understanding for each other's electoral plight, they have a hard time absorbing all the fine details of foreign national politics.

Overall

It is therefore far from clear that the macroeconomic component of fiscal policy should be subject to external limits. Quite clearly, a single common fiscal policy is ruled out, but what about some degree of cooperation? The debate is ongoing and is unlikely to be settled in the near future. The subsidiarity principle implies that, as long as the case is not strong, fiscal policy should remain fully a national prerogative. On the other hand, the spillover that could result from *excessive* deficits is important, as it forms the logical basis for the Stability and Growth Pact.

18.3.4 Fiscal policy coordination

Traditional macroeconomic arguments also illuminate the issue of fiscal policy coordination. The open economy *IS–LM* apparatus – often referred to as the Mundell–Fleming model – leads to the important conclusions summarized in Table 14.3. When the exchange rate is fixed, the monetary policy instrument is lost because it must be dedicated to the exchange rate objective. To recover this instrument, the exchange rate must be allowed to float, but then the fiscal policy instrument becomes lost as its use is frustrated by movements in the exchange rate.

As a country joins the monetary union, it gives up monetary policy but retains the fiscal policy instrument. For the monetary union as a whole, in contrast, the fact that the euro is floating means that monetary policy is effective, hence the importance of the task attributed to the Eurosystem. On the other hand, the overall fiscal policy stance of the monetary union may matter for the euro's value, but it is likely to be ineffective as a collective instrument. This analysis suggests that fiscal policy should continue to be exerted at the national level (where the exchange rate is irremediably fixed) while there is little to be gained by aiming at a high level of coordination, beyond the spillover aspects studied in section 18.2.

18.3.5 What does it all mean for fiscal policy?

Applying the principles of fiscal federalism to the macroeconomic fiscal policy instrument leaves us with few uncontroversial conclusions. There are valid reasons for jointly imposing discipline and for policy coordination. There are equally valid arguments in the opposite direction. All in all, the case for further transfers of sovereignty is weak. This conclusion is challenged by some who attach much importance to spillovers and think that macroeconomic coordination is both promising and relatively easy to implement. It is also challenged from the opposite end of the spectrum by those who see coordination as a collusion of self-interested governments. Sceptics tend to conclude that, given the weakness of the case, subsidiarity should be applied and fiscal policy left entirely in national hands. The debate has been around for a decade and is not likely to disappear for some time.[9] For a while, it seemed to have been partly settled by the adoption of the Stability and Growth Pact, but the Pact itself has been highly controversial and has encountered serious difficulties.

18.4 The Stability and Growth Pact

18.4.1 From convergence to the quest for a permanent regime

As explained in Chapter 17, admission to the monetary union requires a budget deficit of less than 3 per cent of GDP and a public debt of less than 60 per cent of GDP, or declining toward this benchmark. But what about afterwards, in the permanent monetary union regime? Could countries achieve the two fiscal criteria, join the monetary union and then freely relapse in unbridled indiscipline? This would be against the spirit of the convergence criteria and it would raise the fears detailed in section 18.2.4. The founding fathers of the Maastricht Treaty were keenly aware of this risk and, indeed, Article 104 unambiguously states that 'Member States shall avoid excessive government deficits' and goes on to outline a detailed 'excessive deficit procedure'. The Treaty left the practical details of the procedure to be settled later – and this is the task fulfilled by the Stability and Growth Pact (SGP).[10]

As adopted in 1997, the SGP was meant to be strictly enforced. However, because fiscal policy remains a national competence, final word had to be given to ECOFIN, the council of Finance Ministers of the eurozone, acting on proposals from the Commission. The Commission has assumed the responsibility of 'tough cop', but ECOFIN has been loath to make decisions that would strongly antagonize its members, especially the Finance Ministers from the large countries. In November 2003, France and Germany were to be sanctioned. Under pressure from the French and German Finance Ministers, ECOFIN recanted and put the SGP 'in abeyance'. The

Commission took ECOFIN to the Court of Justice of the European Communities for violation of the Pact, an unprecedented action. In June 2004, the Court decided that ECOFIN had indeed breached the law but only because of the phrasing of its decision (the SGP cannot be put in abeyance). A new resolution quickly corrected the error, without changing the fact that France and Germany had not been sanctioned. This episode confirmed the view that the SGP was not well designed. Recognizing that it was too rigid to be enforceable, governments and the Commission prepared a reformulation of the Pact. The new version was adopted in June 2005.

The reasoning of section 18.3 explains the difficulties of the SGP. The benefits from coordination are limited, the collective need for discipline is high but collectively enforced discipline clashes with sovereignty. This conflict is unavoidable. Discipline cannot be enforced without the threat of sanctions. In the same spirit as nuclear deterrence – the cost of an attack would be so great that no attack will be undertaken – the initial version of the SGP sought to make sanctions automatic to avoid a situation where sanctions would be needed. Some small countries were put on the spot, as is explained further below, but the two largest countries called its bluff and the Pact caved in. The crisis exposed a latent rift between large and small countries, which complicated subsequent negotiations. The revised SGP does not solve the logical conflict that lies at its heart, as it keeps the principle of sanctions; instead it seeks to avoid a situation where sanctions have to be applied.

18.4.2 The Pact

The SGP consists of three elements:
★ A definition of what constitutes an 'excessive deficit'.
★ A preventive arm, designed to encourage governments to avoid excessive deficits.
★ A corrective arm, which prescribes how governments should react to a breach of the deficit limit and includes sanctions.

The SGP applies to all EU member countries but only the eurozone countries are subject to the corrective arm.

Excessive deficits

The SGP considers that deficits are excessive when they are above 3 per cent of GDP. In order to leave room for the automatic stabilizers to play their role, the Pact also stipulates that participants in the monetary union commit themselves to a medium-term budgetary stance

---

[9] Some references are provided in the further reading section at the end of this chapter.

[10] The initiative was taken by Germany in 1995 and the Pact adopted in June 1997 by the European Council. Informed by its own inter-war history, Germany was always concerned that fiscal indiscipline could lead to inflation. This is why it insisted on a clear and automatic procedure. It wanted to make full use of the provisions of the Maastricht Treaty, which allowed for fines in the case of excessive deficits. The other countries were less enthusiastic but Germany was holding the key to the eurozone. France, in particular, was unhappy with the German proposal. It obtained the symbolic addition of the word 'growth' to what Germany had initially called the Stability Pact.

'close to balance or in surplus'. The medium term is understood to represent about three years.

The SGP recognizes that serious recessions, beyond any government control, can quickly lead to deepening deficits. Trying to close down deficits during a recession implies adopting a contractionary policy, which may deepen the recession, with potentially disastrous consequences. Consequently, the pact defines exceptional circumstances when its provisions are automatically suspended. A deficit in excess of 3 per cent is considered exceptional if the country's GDP declines by at least 2 per cent in the year in question. The SGP also identifies an intermediate situation, when the real GDP declines by less than 2 per cent but by more than 0.75 per cent. In that case, if the country can demonstrate that its recession is exceptional in terms of its abruptness or in relation to past output trends, the situation can also be deemed exceptional. When output declines by less than 0.75 per cent, no exceptional circumstance can be claimed.

As could be expected from experience, these exceptional circumstances are truly exceptional, to the point of being unlikely to occur. The experience of 2001–03 has shown that shallower but longer-lasting slowdowns can gradually deepen the deficit, unless the automatic stabilizers are prevented from operating by tightening up the structurally adjusted budget. In that case, however, the risk is that a restrictive fiscal policy turns a shallow slowdown into a serious recession; this may allow a country to invoke an exceptional circumstance, but it is really no justification for the pain imposed by a pro-cyclical fiscal policy, i.e. a policy that deepens an ongoing recession.

This is why, in its revised version, the SGP introduces two elements of flexibility. First it admits that a negative growth rate or an accumulated loss of output during a protracted period of very low growth may be considered as exceptional. Second, it suggests taking account of 'all other relevant factors'. In contrast with the 3 per cent limit and the -2 and -0.75 per cent definition of exceptional circumstances, these new elements are vaguely specified. In particular, the notion of 'all other relevant factors', presented in Box 18.1, opens the door to a very flexible interpretation of the SGP.

Box 18.1   What are 'all the other factors'?

The definition of 'all of the other factors' pitted against each other those who wanted to keep the SGP unchanged and those who wished to make it more flexible.

One part concerns the definition of excessive deficits. A number of countries wanted some 'good' expenditures that particularly matter to them to be excluded from the deficit calculation. France was keen to spend more on research and obtained a reference to the Lisbon Strategy. Germany claimed that its unification with East Germany was still a drain on its budget and obtained a reference to 'the unification of Europe'. The UK is committed to providing aid to the poor countries and obtained a reference to 'fostering international solidarity'. The other countries' wishes were recognized through mention to 'achieving European policy goals'.

The other part concerns the preventive arm. The idea is that budget consolidation is easier in good times, when a restrictive fiscal policy is indeed countercyclical. The new SGP stipulates that judgement on whether a country is in an excessive deficit – no longer a simple matter given the vagueness of the definition of good spending – will take into account the efforts made in good times.

It will take time to see how this new concept is implemented. Clearly, the flexibility camp, which included most of the large countries, has won, and this has alarmed the ECB:

> The Governing Council of the ECB is seriously concerned about the proposed changes to the Stability and Growth Pact. It must be avoided that changes in the corrective arm undermine confidence in the fiscal framework of the European Union and the sustainability of public finances in the euro area Member States.

(ECB statement, 21 March 2005)

The preventive arm

The SGP's aim is to ensure that member countries will conduct disciplined fiscal policies. As explained in section 18.2.4, the premise is that governments exhibit a deficit bias because of domestic pressure and political expediency. The SGP can exert counterpressure in the form of peer pressure, called mutual surveillance. The preventive arm is designed to submit Finance Ministers to a collective discussion of each country's fiscal policy in the hope that this will be enough to deliver budgetary discipline. Prevention is meant to prevent the need for correction.

Formally, each eurozone government submits early each year a Stability Programme. The document presents the government's budget forecast for the current and next three years. If the deficit is expected to exceed 3 per cent of GDP, the programme also explains what actions will be taken to correct this violation of the SGP. The Commission examines each programme, including its detailed technical aspects, and submits its individual assessments to ECOFIN. Each assessment must include an evaluation of whether the planned budgets are consistent with the SGP and whether previous commitments have been honoured. The Commission may also point out technical errors, for instance overoptimistic forecasts.

ECOFIN then delivers an opinion, adopted by qualified majority. The opinion can only be approval, but it can also include recommendations that form the corrective arm. All these documents are made public.[11]

EU member countries that are not part of the eurozone must still submit Convergence Programmes. The content of these programmes and the procedure is the same as in the case of the Stability Programmes, with the difference that ECOFIN cannot impose sanctions, it can only issue recommendations. However, for the countries that are aiming to join the monetary union, failure to comply with the SGP implies a violation of the budgetary criteria.

The reformed SGP intends to strengthen the preventive arm. Previously, a country with a deficit of less than 3 per cent of GDP could not be blamed, unless it was

found that it did not deliver on the previous year's commitment – see the Irish case in Box 18.2. However, several countries ran into trouble in 2002–04 because of the impact of the automatic stabilizers during the economic slowdown. Had they achieved a better budget position during the preceding good years, close to balance or in surplus, they might have been able to keep their deficits above 3 per cent. This is why the new procedure intends also to blame countries that do not take advantage of favourable economic conditions to improve their budget positions.

The corrective arm

When a country does not meet the requirements of the SGP, ECOFIN is supposed to apply gradually increasing peer pressure. The process starts with an 'early warning'. Early warnings are issued when ECOFIN concludes that a country is likely to see its deficit become excessive. A country given an early warning is also presented with recommendations – which may or may not be made public – which it is expected to follow in order to prevent being in a situation of excessive deficit. An early warning can be seen as a political hand grenade.

The next step is the excessive deficit procedure (EDP). The procedure is triggered by an ECOFIN opinion stating that a country's budget is in excessive deficit, as defined above. ECOFIN simultaneously issues recommendations – following a recommendation from the Commission – which the country must follow. The country must soon present a set of prompt corrective measures, which are examined by the Commission. The Commission submits its assessment to ECOFIN, which may or may not be satisfied with the proposed measures. A mandatory recommendation can be seen as a political conventional bomb.

What follows is a set of evaluations of the measures taken by the delinquent country and of the budget outcome. More recommendations can be issued, increasingly pressing and tight. In the end, if the country remains in excessive deficit, sanctions are to be imposed by ECOFIN, as explained below. Whereas the initial SGP established a precise set of deadlines, the revised Pact allows for quite some flexibility, at the discretion of ECOFIN.

Sanctions

If a country fails to take corrective action and to bring its deficit below 3 per cent by the deadline set by the Council, it is sanctioned. A sanction can be seen as a political nuclear bomb. The sanction takes the form of a non-remunerated deposit at the Commission. The deposit starts at 0.2 per cent of GDP and rises by 0.1 of

---

[11] The programmes can be found at http://europa.eu.int/comm/ economy_finance/about/activities/sgp/scplist_en.htm. The Commission's assessments appear at http://europa.eu.int/comm/ economy_finance/about/activities/sgp/ca_en.htm. ECOFIN's opinions are at http://europa.eu.int/comm/economy_finance/ about/activities/sgp/co_en.htm.

Box 18.2

The Pact's scoreboard

Several countries have run foul of the SGP since it started to be implemented in January 1999, when the euro was adopted. This box briefly presents these cases in chronological order.[1]

2001 – Ireland: early warning issued
In early 2001, Ireland was the first country to be formally warned. This is an odd case. Its 2000 budget sported a surplus of 4.7 per cent of GDP and the Commission recognized that its debt level was low. The 2000 Stability Programme announced a budget surplus of 4.3 per cent for 2001, continuing high surpluses for the following years and a further decline in the debt ratio. Explanation: in 2001, the budget ended up with a surplus of 1.7 per cent, much lower than the commitment. ECOFIN detected this upcoming slippage and reacted with an early warning. The year 2001 was an election year and the outgoing government relaxed its virtuous stance. As Ireland was booming in 2000–01 (while growth in most of Europe was sluggish), the Council concluded that an expansionary fiscal policy was not adequate because it was pro-cyclical at a time when inflation was rising. The Irish government and citizens were infuriated and saw the heavy hand of Brussels invading their national sovereignty.

2002 – Portugal: early warning proposed, not issued
In its 2001 Stability Programme, Portugal announced a deficit of 1.1 per cent of GDP for 2001. The outcome was 2.2 per cent. When this figure became known, the Commission proposed to issue an early warning. ECOFIN decided not to follow this recommendation.

2002 – Portugal: excessive deficit declared
The new government, elected in 2002, revealed that the 2001 budget deficit actually stood at 4.1 per cent of GDP. This triggered the first excessive deficit procedure (EDP). The recommendations asked Portugal to bring its budget deficit to less than 3 per cent in 2003, which it did ahead of schedule in 2002.

2002 – Germany: early warning proposed, not issued
The Stability Programme presented by Germany at the end of 2000 anticipated a deficit of 1.5 per cent

of GDP for 2001; the final figure was 2.7 of GDP. Following pledges from the German government, ECOFIN decided not to follow the Commission's recommendation of an early warning.

2003 – Germany: excessive deficit declared
Contrary to the government's previous promises, the 2002 budget deficit stood at 3.8 per cent of GDP. The German government argued that this was the result of an unforeseeable exceptional event, floods in eastern Germany. This explanation did not cut much ice with the Commission and ECOFIN, and Germany, the promoter of the SGP, became the second country to be put under the EDP in January 2003. A long list of recommendations was issued, covering not just the budget but also the need for structural reforms.

2003 – France: early warning issued
For 2001, France had announced a deficit of 1.4 per cent of GDP, the outcome was 2.7. After many delaying tactics during 2002, when the deficit reached 3.2 per cent of GDP, the Commission anticipated a deficit in excess of 3 per cent of GDP for 2003 – against a very optimistic French projection of 2.6 per cent – and recommended issuing an early warning. In January 2003, ECOFIN followed this recommendation and asked France to cut its budget deficit by 0.5 per cent of GDP each year until 2006.

2003 – France: excessive deficit declared
By June 2003, the 2002 deficit in excess of 3 per cent became known and the forecasts for 2003 grew worse, partly because income taxes were reduced in both years following an election campaign promise by President Chirac. ECOFIN accepted the Commission recommendation to trigger the EDP and reiterated its recommendation that the deficit be cut by 0.5 per cent of GDP each year until 2006.

2003 – France and Germany: excessive deficit declared
2003 – France and Germany escape the SGP
By November 2003, it became clear that France and Germany were not heeding the recommendations

continued

made earlier by ECOFIN. Their 2003 deficits, not yet known, turned out to both reach 3.7 per cent of GDP, and forecasts for 2004 and 2005 did not envision a decline to below 3 per cent. The Commission wrote about Germany as follows:

> Despite the budgetary consolidation measures taken during 2003, Germany is therefore in non-compliance with the second Article 104(7) Council recommendation issued on 21 January 2003. Germany therefore will not put an end to the excessive deficit situation by 2004 as required by the Council. The Commission has an obligation under the rules laid down in the Treaty Article 104(8) and Regulation 1466/97 of the Stability and Growth Pact to inform the Council of this fact and recommend further steps to be taken according to Article 104(9) of the excessive deficit procedure.

This amounted to issuing a mandatory recommendation, the last step before sanctions. A similar recommendation concerned France.

After intense lobbying by France and Germany, ECOFIN decided by qualified majority to 'hold the excessive deficit procedure for France and Germany in abeyance for the time being'. This decision was subsequently annulled by the Court of Justice of the European Communities.

2004 – Italy: early warning proposed, not issued
Anticipating a deficit in excess of 3 per cent of GDP for 2004, the Commission recommended in May that an early warning be issued. In spite of a deficit of 3.2 per cent of GDP in 2003, an obviously dispirited ECOFIN decided not to follow the Commission.

2004 – The Netherlands: EDP declared
In 2003, the Dutch deficit stood at 3.2 per cent, the result of a long slowdown (see Fig.18.1). It was expected to fall below 3 per cent in 2004 and afterwards. Given previous decisions, no action should have been taken. But the Dutch government had led the resistance against the French and German whitewash in November 2003 and was keen to restore credibility to the SGP. In June 2004, it therefore asked to be put under the EDP, which was removed a year later.

2004 – Greece: EDP declared
The government newly elected in 2004 revealed that an auditing of the public finances showed that the 2003 budget had in fact exceeded 3 per cent of GDP, contrary to previously provided information. The government also announced that, due to the costs of the Olympic Games, the 2004 budget would also exceed the 3 per cent limit. ECOFIN had no choice but to declare the EDP in July.

2004 – Six new EU members meet the EDP
Six new EU members (Czech Republic, Cyprus, Hungary, Malta, Poland and Slovakia) were found with deficits in excess of 3 per cent of GDP. With nice words for 'special circumstances', the EDP was declared for all them.

[1] *For details, see* http://europa.eu.int/scadplus/leg/en/lvb/l25057.htm.

---

the excess deficit up to a maximum of 0.5 per cent of GDP, as shown in Table 18.3. Deposits are imposed each year until the excessive deficit is corrected. If the excess is not corrected within two years, the deposit is converted into a fine, otherwise it is returned.

Several aspects of the SGP are noteworthy. First, formally, it does not remove fiscal policy sovereignty. Governments are in full control; they only agree to bear the consequences of their actions. Second, the intent is clearly pre-emptive since there is a lengthy procedure between the time a deficit is deemed excessive and the time when a deposit is imposed, with two more years before the deposit is transformed into a fine. Third, while a fine is politically a nuclear bombshell,

the declaration that a country is in violation of the Pact is a more conventional bombshell, meant to elicit prompt corrective action. Finally, all decisions are in the hands of

Size of deficit (% of GDP)	Amount of fine (% of GDP)
3	0.2
4	0.3
5	0.4
6+	0.5

Table 18.3: *Schedule of fines*

the Council, a highly political body that can exploit many of the 'ifs' included in the Pact.[12]

18.4.3 The Pact and countercyclical fiscal policies: how much room to manoeuvre?

Early experience with the Stability and Growth Pact has revealed some problems, as Box 18.2 recalls. These early difficulties raise the question of whether the Pact leaves enough room for countercyclical fiscal policies. The answer requires consideration of the two aspects of fiscal policy mentioned in section 18.1.3: the automatic stabilizers and discretionary policy.

The automatic stabilizers

The automatic response of budget balances to cyclical fluctuations is a source of difficulty for the SGP. The Pact's strategy is that, in normal years, budgets should be balanced to leave enough room for the automatic stabilizers in bad years. A simple example illustrates the idea. Table 18.1 shows that, on average, a 1 per cent decline in GDP growth tends to worsen the budget deficit by 0.5 per cent of GDP. Using this rough estimate, the left-hand panel of Fig. 18.4 shows how much, depending on the initial budget position, the GDP can decline before the automatic stabilizers bring the budget to a deficit of 3 per cent. Obviously, if the budget is already at the 3 per cent limit (the leftmost point on the horizontal axis), there is no room available and the stabilizers must be blocked – fiscal policy becomes pro-cyclical – independently of the size of the slowdown (the zero on the vertical axis). If, instead, the budget is initially balanced (the zero on the horizontal axis), it would take a fall of 6 per cent of GDP (read off the vertical axis) to

reach a deficit of 3 per cent. In comparison, the GDP decline that has led France and Germany to breach the limit in 2003 was about 2 per cent.

Discretionary policy

This reasoning assumes that countercyclical fiscal policy – the use of the budget to cushion business cycles – relies only on the automatic stabilizers. However, having abandoned the monetary policy instruments, governments may consider that it is not enough to rely only on the automatic stabilizers when the economic situation worsens. Forsaking discretionary fiscal policy can prove to be politically unacceptable for real-life governments, especially if they face elections.

The promoters of the SGP have an easy response. Governments can avail themselves of much more room to carry out discretionary policy by running a budget surplus, possibly a large one, in normal years. This idea is illustrated in Fig. 18.4. The right-hand panel asks the following question: Suppose that the GDP declines by 2 per cent of GDP, what is left for a further discretionary fiscal expansion over and above the automatic stabilizers? Using the same rule of thumb as in the left-hand panel, we know that the stabilizers worsen the budget by 1 per cent of GDP. The remaining room for manoeuvre depends again on the initial budget position. The graph shows that if the budget was, for instance, in a surplus of 1 per cent (to be read on the horizontal axis), the government can voluntarily increase spending, or cut taxes, to the tune of 3 per cent of GDP (the top reading on the vertical axis).

Bringing budgets to the safe zone? Staying there?

Thus the SGP intentionally provides a strong incentive to bring the budget to a position of balance, or even surplus.

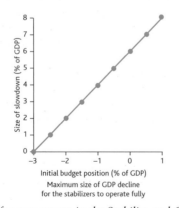

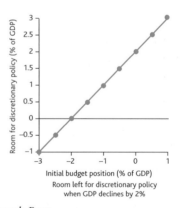

Figure 18.4: *Room for manoeuvre in the Stability and Growth Pact*

[12] For details, see http://europa.eu.int/scadplus/leg/en/lvb/l25057.htm.

According to their promoters, when this is achieved, monetary union member countries will have recovered almost all the required room for manoeuvre. Only deep recessions will prevent the countercyclical use of fiscal policy, and deep recessions will qualify as exceptional. The main challenge, therefore, lies in the early years, when a number of countries still run deficits. It is bad luck, in this view, that the early years have been characterized by a protracted slowdown, thus delaying the time when all budgets are in balance or surplus. There is no reason to give up, especially as some countries have now fully adjusted. Figure 18.5 shows the situation in 2005.

To this, the SGP critics make two objections. Maybe, they say, Europe's poor economic performance since 1999 is partly due to the SGP, which has prevented a more dynamic countercyclical use of fiscal policies. Figure 18.1 shows how the Dutch government, an ardent supporter of the SGP, has exercised a countercyclical fiscal policy from 2001 onwards. Not only may this policy have deepened and prolonged the slowdown, it did not even prevent the Netherlands from being (self) declared in breach of the SGP (see Box 18.2). This is like shooting yourself in the foot.

In addition, SGP critics observe that if the budget is in surplus in normal years, it means small deficits in bad years and big surpluses in good years. On average, therefore, the budget will be in surplus. This may sound good, but what does it mean for the public debt? Surpluses, year in and year out, imply that the public debt will be on a declining trend. Looking at Fig.18.3 and Table 18.2, this seems exactly what Europe needs. But there remains a question: How far will the debt decline? As long as the budget remains on average in surplus, the debt will decline, so one day it will be zero. And after? The debt will become negative, which means that the government will start lending to the private sector, at home or abroad. Put differently, the government will raise taxes to make loans, competing with private banks. This makes little sense, critics argue.

Of course, the promoters of the SGP have answers to these counterarguments, and the debate is raging. The SGP has been and will remain controversial. The next section takes a step backwards and looks at the principles presented in section 18.2 that lie behind the debate.

18.4.4 Limits of the Pact

The SGP is meant to serve two main useful purposes: to counteract the deficit bias and to reduce the odds of a debt default within the monetary union which, as noted in section 18.2.4, could result in highly painful spillover effects. Yet, it does not come without a number of weaknesses as its tumultuous history illustrates. The economic rationale is weak and the political conditions of its implementation are bound to be contentious.

Economic issues

The 3 per cent limit is artificial. In the face of economic and political difficulties – rising unemployment, for instance – governments may find it hard to justify a particular number. Those who stand to suffer from a rigorous application of the Pact may ask: Why 3 per cent and not 2 or 3.5 per cent? In addition, targeting the budget balance is like shooting at a moving duck: it changes all the time as economic conditions evolve, and it is therefore beyond government control. This opens the door to endless discussions on whether a government should be blamed, possibly even sanctioned, for an excessive deficit.

One frequently made suggestion is to target the cyclically adjusted budget balance since it captures discretionary actions. Requiring, for instance, that the cyclically adjusted budget always be in balance allows the full use of the automatic stabilizers. Allowing it to be balanced on average over a business cycle additionally

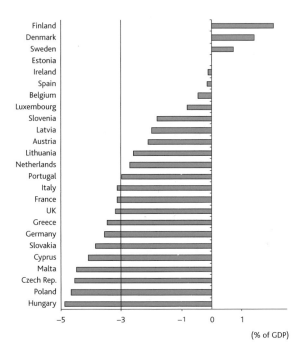

Figure 18.5: *Bringing budgets to the safe zone: forecasts for 2005*

Source: *Economic Outlook*, OECD.

permits the countercyclical discretionary use of fiscal policy. This makes good economic sense. There is a serious difficulty, however. If the SGP is to have any influence on governments subject to the deficit bias, it must be backed by credible sanctions. If sanctions are imposed, the conditions under which they are triggered must be clear and uncontroversial. The problem is that computing the cyclically adjusted budget balance is more art than science. There exist many methods to do so, each of which leads to different results. It is easy to foresee a country threatened with sanctions produce its own cyclically adjusted estimates, which cannot be dismissed.

Is there a better measure than fiscal discipline? Yes, there is, and it is rooted in good economics. Why do we care about fiscal discipline in the first place? Section 18.2.4 provides the answer: because lack of discipline eventually leads to a debt default. The natural implication is that the SGP should target the debt-to-GDP ratio. As long as it declines or remains at a moderate level, there is no threat of default. The EDP, as described in the Maastricht Treaty, refers to both the annual deficit (limit set at 3 per cent of GDP) and to the public debt (limit set at 60 per cent of GDP). The SGP makes a passing reference to the debt but chose instead to focus on the deficit figure. One possible reason is that the 60 per cent reference is unrealistic given the situation of many countries. Instead of jettisoning this other arbitrary number, the SGP de-emphasized the debt. The Commission has proposed to reintroduce it, but has not been followed by ECOFIN. Yet such a step would dispose of most of the controversies that currently plague the Pact. Targeting the public debt over the medium term – not the budget balance year after year – would leave governments free to use fiscal policy as they see fit in the short term, while anchoring their actions to the need to pay back previous borrowing.

Political issues

Imposing fiscal discipline from outside has the obvious advantage of protecting governments from domestic interest groups. On the other hand, using Brussels as a scapegoat may be good politics in the short term but, if invoked too often, it can undermine general support for European integration. In particular, the imposition of fines could be met with popular rejection. But, without fines, the SGP is unlikely to have enough teeth and could be overlooked when it is politically convenient to do so, which in effect means that there is no pact.

When the SGP was under discussion, one view was that it should be entirely automatic, with each step, including sanctions, to be decided by the Commission on the basis of a transparent and unambiguous roadmap. The opposite camp pointed out that fiscal policy remains an element of national sovereignty. In every country, budgets are set by the government and the parliament in a procedure that has a deep justification. In every democracy, deciding who will pay taxes and how much, and how the public money is to be spent, is in the hands of elected officials. An automatic application of the SGP, including detailed mandatory recommendations, would clearly violate this basic principle of democracy. This is why, in the end, the final say on whether to issue an early warning, on the imposition of the EDP and its associated recommendations, and of course on sanctions, is in the hands of ECOFIN, which brings together representatives of democratically elected governments. Yet, seen from the angle of a particular country, ECOFIN is not an institution which enjoys domestic democratic legitimacy. This feature perhaps helps explain why the SGP could not be applied to France and Germany once their governments strenuously objected.

Yet, leaving the final decision in the hands of ECOFIN has a serious drawback. Finance Ministers are, by definition, politicians. As such, they make elaborate calculations involving tactical considerations often far away from the principles discussed here. This has been made clear by the surprising early warning addressed to small Ireland, while France and Germany were spared the rigour of the EDP (see Box 18.2).

We face a serious contradiction. The budget is firmly identified as a sovereign prerogative, and time-honoured democratic principles vest the budget with democratically elected officials. On the other hand, domestic politics often give rise to a deficit bias and all eurozone countries have an interest in preventing fiscal indiscipline in any of its members. The SGP tries to deal with this contradiction, but the magic formula remains to be found.

18.5 Summary

The loss of national monetary policy leaves fiscal policy as the only macroeconomic instrument. Budgets can be seen as a substitute for the absence of intra-eurozone transfers, one of the OCA criteria not satisfied in Europe.

Fiscal policy operates in two ways. The automatic stabilizers come into play without any policy action because deficits increase when the economy slows down, and decline or turn into surpluses when growth is rapid. Discretionary policy results from willing actions taken by the government.

The main arguments in favour of some collective influence on national fiscal policies are:

★ The presence of spillovers, the fact that one country's fiscal policy affects economic conditions in other eurozone countries. The main spillover channels are: income flows via exports and imports; and the cost of borrowing as there is a single interest rate.

★ The fear that a default by a government on its public debt would badly affect the common exchange rate and generally hurt the union's credibility.

The theory of fiscal federalism provides arguments for and against the sharing of policy instruments. The presence of spillovers and of increasing returns to scale argues for policy sharing. The existence of national differences in economic conditions and preferences, and of asymmetries of information, argues against policy sharing. Finally, the quality of government matters.

The Stability and Growth Pact (SGP) reflects the view that excessive deficits are a matter of common concern in a monetary union. It aims at making permanent the fiscal convergence criteria. It is an application of the excessive deficit procedure envisioned in the Maastricht Treaty.

The SGP is based on three organizing principles:

★ A definition of excessive deficits. In principle, deficits should not exceed 3 per cent of GDP. Special circumstances correspond to deep recessions. The 2005 revision allows for a number of 'other factors', a step designed to introduce flexibility, but the list is so vague that it remains to be seen how it will be implemented.

★ A preventive arm, which is designed to encourage, through peer pressure, governments to resist the deficit bias. Prevention rests on annual Stability Programmes. These programmes are evaluated by the Commission, which issues a recommendation to ECOFIN. ECOFIN, in turn, expresses an opinion.

★ A corrective arm, which is triggered when a country is found to have an excessive deficit. This triggers a procedure which takes the form of increasingly binding recommendations by ECOFIN, based on suggestions from the Commission. A milder procedure, called early warning, can be triggered when ECOFIN determines, on the basis of a recommendation from the Commission, that a country may soon run an excessive deficit. When a country has not followed the recommendations and remains in excessive deficit, sanctions may apply. Sanctions take the form of fines.

The SGP limits the countercyclical use of fiscal policy – including the full working of the automatic stabilizers – when the budget is not initially in the safe zone of balance or surplus. This provides an incentive to achieve such a position as soon as possible.

The implementation of the SGP has revealed many cracks. The most dramatic event occurred in 2003 when ECOFIN rejected a recommendation from the Commission to declare France and Germany in a situation of excessive deficit. Instead, ECOFIN decided, by a narrow qualified majority, to put the application of SGP to France and Germany 'in abeyance'. The Court of Justice of the European Communities subsequently nullified this decision.

This has led to a revision of the SGP in 2005. Without affecting the SGP's basic structure, the revision has sought to introduce more flexibility. This affects the definition of an excessive deficit and the schedule of graduated pressure that follows.

The difficulties encountered in the implementation of the SGP can be traced to both economic and political considerations:

★ From an economic viewpoint, targeting the annual budget deficit can lead to pro-cyclical policies, i.e. policies that reinforce either a slowdown or a boom. Imposing an arbitrary ceiling makes it difficult to justify fiscal policy tightening during a slowdown. The revised SGP intends to encourage counter-cyclical policies in good times, i.e. to encourage budget consolidation during the upswing phase of business cycles.

★ From a political viewpoint, the SGP faces a formidable contradiction. Fiscal policy is a matter of national sovereignty, in the hands of democratically elected governments and parliaments. At the same time, fiscal policy is recognized as a matter of common concern. The chosen solution, to leave the final decision on the application of the SGP in the hands of ECOFIN, has the merit of involving democratically elected governments. On the other side, the injunctions of ECOFIN do not have much democratic legitimacy at the national level.

Self-assessment questions

1. What is the difference between actual and cyclically adjusted budgets? Why are discretionary actions visible only in changes of the cyclically adjusted budget balance?

2. In Fig. 18.1 identify years when fiscal policy is pro-cyclical, and years when it is counter-cyclical.

3. What are externalities or spillovers? How do they operate in the case of fiscal policy?

4. Explain the no-bailout clause.

5. Why is heterogeneity of preferences an argument against moving policy decisions from a lower to a higher level of government?

6. What is the intended purpose of the Stability and Growth Pact?

7. Why is fiscal policy useful at the country level in the monetary union and not at the overall EU level?

8. When is a deficit of 5 per cent automatically seen as exceptional by the Stability and Growth Pact? When can it be non-automatically seen as exceptional?

9. When can ECOFIN impose fines in the framework of the Stability and Growth Pact?

10. If the Pact required the cyclically adjusted budget to be balanced every year, explain why fiscal policy would be strictly confined to the automatic stabilizers. What difference would it make if the cyclically adjusted budget would have to be balanced on average over business cycles?

11. Why are fines under the Stability and Growth Pact sometimes described as pro-cyclical fiscal policy?

12. What difference does it make whether a country target annual budget balances or the debt-to-GDP ratio?

13. Why is there a contradiction between the Stability and Growth Pact and sovereignty in the matter of budgets?

Essay questions

1. Apply the principles of fiscal federalism to the EU in the following areas: education, internal security, migration and foreign affairs.

2. How would you reform the Stability and Growth Pact?

3. Imagine that a eurozone member country is running budget deficits and accumulating a large public debt. What scenario can you envision when financial markets refuse to further finance the deficits? In your story, consider the reaction of domestic citizens as well as that of the Commission and ECOFIN.

4. How would you rate your own government as a benevolent protector of the interests of its citizens?

5. Explain how the Stability and Growth Pact could work if the criterion could be cyclically adjusted rather than actual budget deficits.

6. When the Stability and Growth Pact was being negotiated, some countries wanted it to be a fully automatic procedure, others wanted decisions to be interpreted by the Finance Ministers. Why is this distinction important? How does the agreed-upon pact reflect this difference of opinions?

7. Some countries have argued that the monetary union needs a common fiscal policy to match the common monetary policy. Evaluate this view.

8. With the Stability and Growth Pact and its limits on fiscal policy, what is left for governments to do in the monetary union?

9. As part of its decision on whether to join the euro area, the UK Treasury has studied the Stability and Growth Pact and states:

   Where debt is low and there is a high degree of long-term fiscal sustainability, the case for adopting a tighter fiscal stance to allow room for governments to use fiscal policy more actively is not convincing. Provided that arrangements are put in place to ensure that discretionary policy is conducted symmetrically, then long-term sustainability would not in any way be put at risk.

   (*Fiscal Stabilization and Eurozone*, HM Treasury, May 2003)

   Interpret and comment.

Further reading: the aficionado's corner

An excellent collection of readings is Part III in:
De Grauwe, P. (ed.) (2001) *The Political Economy of Monetary Union*, Edward Elgar, Cheltenham.

For a presentation and a defence of the Stability and Growth Pact, see:
Brunila, A., M. Buti and D. Franco (eds) (2001) *The Stability and Growth Pact*, Palgrave, Basingstoke.

For a detailed and critical presentation of the Stability and Growth Pact, see:
Eichengreen, B. and C. Wyplosz (1998) 'The Stability Pact: more than a minor nuisance?', *Economic Policy*, 26: 65–104.

On the tendency of governments not to always serve their citizens' interests and what it means for the EU, see:
Persson, T. and G. Tabellini (2000) *Political Economics*, MIT Press, Cambridge, Mass.
Vaubel, R. (1997) 'The constitutional reform of the European Union', *European Economic Review*, 41(3–5): 443–50.

Fiscal policy
On the cyclical behaviour of fiscal policy, see:
European Commission (2001) 'Fiscal policy and cyclical stabilization in Eurozone', *European Economy*, 3: 57–80.
Hallerberg, M. and R. Strauch (2002) 'On the cyclicality of public finances in Europe', *Empirica*, 29: 183–207.
Melitz, J. (2000) 'Some cross-country evidence about fiscal policy behaviour and consequences for Eurozone', *European Economy*, 2: 3–21.

The case for fiscal policy coordination is developed in:
Coeuré, B. and J. Pisani-Ferry (2003) 'A sustainability pact for the eurozone', available at http://www.pisani-ferry.net.

For analyses on the politico-economic aspects of fiscal policy, see:

Alesina, A. and R. Perotti (1995) 'The political economy of budget deficits', *IMF Staff Papers*, 42(1): 1–37.
Persson, T., G. Roland and G. Tabellini (2000) 'Comparative politics and public finance', *Journal of Political Economy*, 108(6): 1121–61.
von Hagen, J. and I.J. Harden (1994) 'National budget processes and fiscal performance', *European Economy Reports and Studies*, 3: 311–408.

For an introduction to the theory of fiscal federalism, see:
Oates, W. (1999) 'An essay in fiscal federalism', *Journal of Economic Literature*, 37(3): 1120–49.

Reform of the Stability and Growth Pact
Buiter, W. (2003) 'How to reform the Stability and Growth Pact', http://www.nber.org/~wbuiter/banker.pdf.
Wyplosz, C. (2002) http://www.cepr.org/Pubs/new-dps/dplist.asp?dpno=3238.

Useful websites

The official texts can be found on the Commission's website at http://europa.eu.int/comm/economy_finance/about/activities/sgp/sgp_en.htm.

The Commission's proposal on the reform of the SGP may be found at http://europa.eu.int/comm/economy_finance/publications/sgp_en.htm.

Euractiv's overview of the SGP, with many references, is at http://www.euractiv.com/Article?tcmuri=tcm:29-133199-16&type=LinksDossier.

References

Burda, M. and C. Wyplosz (2005) *Macroeconomics*, 4th edn, Oxford University Press, Oxford.

European Commission (2001) *Communication from the Commission to the Council and the European Parliament*, ECFIN/581/02-EN rev.3, 21.11.2001.

Stark, J. (2001) 'Genesis of a pact', in A. Brunila, M. Buti and D. Franco (eds) *The Stability and Growth Pact*, Palgrave, Basingstoke.

The big payoff on the Euro is, of course, in the capital markets. [...]
It will move from the dull bank-based financing structure to big-time debt markets and markets for corporate equities that offer transparency for the mismanaged or sleepy European companies. Capital markets are good at kicking butt.

Rudi Dornbusch (2000), p. 242

Chapter

19 The financial markets and the euro

19.1 The capital markets

19.1.1 What are financial markets and institutions?
19.1.2 What do financial markets do?
19.1.3 Characteristics of financial markets

19.2 Microeconomics of capital market integration

19.2.1 EU policy on capital market integration
19.2.2 Economics of capital mobility: allocation efficiency
19.2.3 Economics of capital mobility: the diversification effect
19.2.4 Effects of a single currency on financial markets

19.3 Financial institutions and markets

19.3.1 Banking
19.3.2 Bond markets
19.3.3 Stock markets
19.3.4 Regulation and supervision
19.3.5 Channels of monetary policy

INTRODUCTION

This chapter looks at the integration of European financial markets. Following the single market, adoption of the euro is expected to encourage further integration of Europe's capital markets, providing savers and borrowers alike with more and better opportunities. This, in turn, is expected to improve the overall productivity of the European economy and could also affect the way monetary policy works.

The chapter starts by outlining what is special about the financial services industry, distinguishing between banks and financial markets. It shows that financial markets can be at the same time very efficient and yet subject to some important failures. The next section, 19.2, presents the microeconomic analysis of capital market integration. It establishes the basic result that capital market integration raises economic efficiency and welfare. Yet, some gain and some lose from capital market integration, which explains why it is controversial.

Section 19.3 provides a review of the situation before and after the adoption of the single currency. An important aspect of this evolution is that financial institutions and markets have been shaped by centuries of national traditions. The single market (presented in Chapter 4) has already deeply modified the financial markets, but important differences remain. The single currency might well usher in a new era of transformation, exposing many limitations of the single market and calling for further actions, which are examined here. This leads to an evaluation of the unfinished business of adapting the national regulation and supervision of financial activities to the new challenges of the common currency.

Finally comes the question whether the euro will become a currency used worldwide alongside the US dollar, why it matters and what has happened so far.

19.1 The capital markets

19.1.1 What are financial institutions and markets?

Because they support the accumulation of capital, the capital markets are central to long-term growth, as explained in Chapter 7. Their task is to collect savings and to provide producers with the financial means that they need to invest in productive equipment and new operations. There are many different forms of capital market and institutions that cater to different customers with varied and sometimes complex requirements. At a very general level, the capital market performs three main functions:

★ *It transforms maturity.* Savers typically do not like to part with their 'money' – we call it their assets, because money is just one type of asset – for too long. Borrowers, on the other hand, typically prefer to obtain stable resources. The markets therefore mostly borrow short and lend long.

★ *It performs intermediation.* Savers and borrowers do not meet face to face. Savers deposit their funds in financial institutions that re-lend them to borrowers. The trip may be long, going through many financial institutions and across many national borders.

★ *It deals with inherent risk.* A loan implies giving out money against the promise of future repayment. In the meantime, the borrower may face difficulties that make repayment partly or totally impossible, and some borrowers may simply be dishonest.

The best-known financial institutions are banks: they receive deposits, in effect borrowing from their customers; they offer loans; and they often provide assistance for managing portfolios. In contrast to these universal banks, investment banks specialize in managing portfolios; they do not even accept deposits and sometimes cater only to wealthy customers. Many fund management firms do not even deal with individuals; they offer 'wholesale' services to banks and insurance companies. Insurance companies are also considered to be financial institutions. Part of their activity is to provide insurance, which, strictly speaking, is not a financial service. Yet, in order to face potentially high payments, they accumulate large reserves, which they want to manage in order to obtain returns as high as possible. In effect, they take 'deposits' – the insurance premia paid by their customers – that they use to 'make loans' as they invest in financial assets. In addition, many insurance companies propose pension schemes and life insurance, which can be seen as deposits with very long maturities. In fact, recent years have seen the emergence of financial conglomerates that combine classic universal banking, investment banking and insurance.

The bond and stock markets represent the other component of the financial system. Like banks, they are designed to collect savings and lend them back to borrowers, with the crucial difference that the end users – lenders and borrowers – 'meet' each other on the markets. Bonds are debts issued by firms and governments for a set maturity at an explicit interest rate, which can be indexed and therefore variable. Stocks (also called shares) are ownership titles to firms: they have no maturity since they last as long as the firm itself and the returns are determined by the firm's performance. Lenders (also called investors), usually operate though intermediaries – brokers, investment banks – which they instruct to buy or sell assets on their behalf on the markets. Most small investors, and many large ones too, in fact purchase funds, which are ready-made baskets of shares and bonds managed by financial intermediaries. Each fund has particular characteristics: the relative importance of bonds and stocks, the industry or country where they invest, the degree of risk and associated guarantees, as explained in the next section.

Financial institutions come in all shapes and sizes. A few huge international banks coexist with small, strictly local ones. Some financial markets attract lenders and borrowers from all over the world (New York's Wall Street and the City of London are the two largest), whereas others deal in a very narrow range of local assets. As will be explained below, financial markets are more efficient the larger they are.

19.1.2 What do financial markets do?

Matching lending and borrowing needs: maturity

The function of financial markets is to make savers and borrowers meet and to offer each saver and each borrower the best possible deal. This not only includes returns but also the available menu of size and maturity of assets, as well as the ability to sell or buy any amount at any time.

Imagine an individual who wants to put aside a given amount. She can always deposit this amount with her bank on a chequing account and withdraw whenever she wants whatever she wants, but the interest rate offered is quite low. She can do better by choosing term deposits; in that case she will have to pay a penalty if she needs to withdraw before the maturity is reached. On the other hand, term deposits offer more attractive interest, which grows with the maturity. The bank thus encourages its customers to choose longer-term deposits. Why? Because the bank will re-lend the deposit to another customer who will be ready to pay a higher interest for loans of longer maturity. Time has a value, and the market sets its price.

Bank deposits are not the only way to save. She could buy bonds, with various maturities, or stocks, which are of unlimited duration. In that case, she would lend directly – albeit via her broker and the market – to the borrowers who issue bonds and stocks. The returns will be higher than bank deposits of the same maturity because these bonds and stocks are riskier than bank deposits. Risk is another issue that we now examine.

Matching lending and borrowing needs: risk

Bonds are issued by governments, banks and firms. Their maturities range from the very short term – 24 hours or less – to the very long term – 10, 20 years or more. Stocks are issued by firms; the holder owns a share of the firm and is entitled to the corresponding portion of profits. Bonds and shares are risky: if the issuer goes bankrupt, they are probably worth nothing, at best a fraction of their face value.[1] How do financial markets deal with risk?

Consider the return to investing in a particular project, say a new factory. When the investment is made, there is usually no way of knowing for certain whether the project will yield profits. And even if the venture proves profitable, the future profit level is uncertain. Tastes, exchange rates, prices and the level of competition can all change unexpectedly, thereby altering profits. Of course, one can make a reasonable guess as to what the profit will be, i.e. calculate what the profit should be, on average, but in deciding whether to invest, the best-guess average is not enough. The owner of the investment must also consider uncertainty. If two projects have the same average return (i.e. expected value), but the profit flow is more variable (i.e. riskier) for one than the other, then savers should judge the riskier project to be worth less. 'A bird in the hand is worth two in the bush' is the colloquial way of expressing the commonsense principle

---

[1] Bonds issued by solid governments are in essence riskless.

that people tend to discount the expected value of a risky project more than that of a risk-free project.

But what has this to do with financial markets? Bonds and shares are issued by firms that plan new investments. Bondholders and shareholders thus bear the investment risk. For them to be willing to buy a risky asset, there must be a reward. This is why the rate of return is adjusted for risk by incorporating a risk premium. The premium is set so that borrowers can convince savers to bear the risk. Savers obviously prefer no or little risk, but they may be attracted by a higher return. They face a trade-off between return and risk. This is why the risk-adjusted return typically rises with the risk of the asset, as shown in Fig. 19.1. Depending on her appetite for risk and return, the saver will choose where on the curve she would like to be.

Different savers will pick different points on the risk–return trade-off schedule because they have different degrees of aversion to risk. Financial markets allow every saver to find an asset that meets its preference and therefore every borrower to find the resources that he needs.[2] Markets balance demand and supply by setting the risk premium. Put differently, the markets put a price tag on risk and all assets nicely fit on the same risk–return schedule shown in Fig. 19.1. The risk–return schedule reveals the price of risk, and financial markets allow everyone to trade off a higher return for more risk, or the converse, depending on personal preferences.

Diversification

Markets do not just price risk, they also allow for diversification. The basic issue can be illustrated by an example. Ask yourself, 'How risky is it to bet on red at the roulette table?' You might answer that you win almost half the time since on a roulette wheel all numbers, except 0 and 00, are either red or black. This is the correct answer if you consider the bet-on-red 'project' in isolation. But there is a more complete answer. For instance, suppose you add a bet-on-black 'project' to your 'portfolio' of projects. That is, in addition to betting on red with each roll of the ball, you also bet on black with each roll. Now the effective risk of this betting venture is much reduced. You always win and always lose, except for when the ball lands on 0 or 00, in which case you lose both bets to the house.[3]

The point to note here is that the average loss from either 'portfolio' – the only-on-red portfolio and the both-red-and-black portfolio – is the same. In both cases, you lose on average 2 out of every 38 rolls of the ball (there are 38 numbers on the wheel – 18 red numbers, 18 black and the two zeros). However, the more 'diversified' portfolio (the both-red-and-black portfolio) provides less variation because one element of the portfolio does well when the other does badly. Clearly, the both-red-and-black betting strategy would take all the fun out of betting, but when we apply the same reasoning to a more serious investment – say a worker's pension fund – then the reduced volatility is highly valued.

The lesson to be learned from this example is that the risk of a particular project must be evaluated from the perspective of the investor's total portfolio of projects. Typically, some projects will do well when others do badly, so the average return to the portfolio is less risky than any individual project. Or, to put it in terms of the 'risk-adjusted rate of return' phraseology, the risk-adjusted return on a diversified portfolio is higher than that on an undiversified portfolio of investment projects.

Financial markets can offer almost unbounded possibilities of diversification, the more so the bigger they are. By increasing the variety of projects, i.e. assets, large financial markets allow savers to hold relatively riskless portfolios composed of very risky assets. Both savers and borrowers stand to benefit from the situation. Because the portfolios bear little risk, the risk premium is reduced and this reduction is shared among savers, who receive higher returns, and borrowers who face lower borrowing costs.

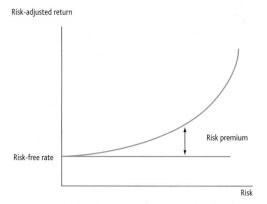

Figure 19.1: *Risk-adjusted returns*

[2] Well, not every borrower. Very risky borrowers are usually unable to raise funds.

[3] In finance jargon, the red and black 'projects' are perfectly negatively correlated (their correlation coefficient is −1). More generally, risk diversification is higher the more negatively correlated are the assets that make up a portfolio.

19.1.3 Characteristics of financial markets

Financial markets are shaped to deal with the functions previously described, that is, matching the needs and preferences of borrowers and lenders, pricing risk and allowing for risk diversification. A number of characteristics follow.

Scale economies

Matching and risk diversification are both easier when there is a large number of borrowers and lenders. The finance industry is subject to massive scale economies which affect banks and financial markets. Where small banks and markets survive, it is not difficult to find some barriers to competition. The existence of different currencies is one such barrier. Indeed, before the advent of the euro, an Irish saver who purchased Portuguese assets faced currency risk in addition to the normal lending risk, and this made Irish assets more attractive to her. The creation of a single currency removes this particular barrier to competition.

Networks

One response to scale economies is the emergence of large financial institutions and markets. Another response, which goes hand in hand with the first, is the building of networks. When a financial firm receives funds from a saver, it needs to re-lend these funds as soon as possible since 'time is money'. With some luck, it will find among its customers a borrower with matching needs and preferences, but more often not. The solution is to re-lend the saver's money to another financial firm which may have spotted a borrower or identified another financial firm which may have spotted a borrower, etc. This is why financial markets operate as networks. Indeed, money passes quickly from firm to firm until it finds a house – a suitable borrower – somewhere in the network, and quite possibly in a very different corner of the world.

A financial firm is like a telephone hook-up: if you are the only one with a hook-up, it is of no use. A telephone is more useful the more people are connected to the network. This effect is called a network externality. A financial firm can offer better deals when it is in contact with a large number of other firms which deal with many customers, savers and borrowers alike. Network externalities exploit increasing returns to scale: the larger the network, the better it works. The best network could well be the whole world, hence the tendency towards the globalization of financial services.

Asymmetric information

A fundamental characteristic of financial activities is that the borrower always knows more about his own riskiness than the lender. This information asymmetry carries profound implications. Borrowers may intentionally attempt to conceal some damning information for the sake of obtaining a badly needed loan. As a consequence, lenders are very careful, not to say suspicious. They may simply refuse to lend rather than take unbounded risks. Alternatively, they may set the price of risk very high, i.e. they ask for very large risk premia. This, in turn, may discourage low-risk borrowers who cannot convincingly signal their true riskiness, while desperate borrowers are willing to pay any premium. If this process goes unchecked, only bad risks are present in the market and, knowing that, lenders withdraw.[4] At best, the price of risk is excessive, at worst the financial market dries up.

Asymmetric information is unavoidable and it tends to undermine the development of financial institutions and markets. This phenomenon explains many features of the financial services industry presented below. One general response is regulation, i.e. legislative measures that aim at reducing the overall riskiness.

19.2 Microeconomics of capital market integration

19.2.1 EU policy on capital market integration

Until the 1986 Single European Act and the 1988 directive that ruled out all remaining restrictions on capital movements among EU residents, EU capital markets were not very integrated. Although the free movement of capital is in the Treaty of Rome, the Treaty provided several large loopholes that EU members eagerly exploited. The basic problem was that, until recently, EU nations just did not believe that unrestricted capital mobility was a good idea, and Box 19.1 explains why.

The main goal of EU capital market liberalization prior to the 1980s was to facilitate real business activities. For example, national policies should not hinder a company based in one Member State from setting up business in another Member State. This so-called right of

---

[4] This phenomenon is called adverse selection. Borrowing in a desperate situation is sometimes called 'gambling for resurrection'.

Fear of capital mobility

As recalled in Chapter 13, throughout the first half of the twentieth century, but especially in the first three decades, international capital flows were widely held responsible for repeated balance-of-payment crises and banking crises. In light of that experience, policy makers, including the founders of that bastion of global capitalism, the International Monetary Fund (IMF), were reluctant to promote the free movement of capital. When its rules were established in 1945, the IMF allowed members to control capital flows in whatever way they saw fit. Indeed, economists at the time, including John Maynard Keynes, argued forcefully against liberalizing international capital movements.

Given the intellectual climate in the 1950s, it is not surprising that the Treaty of Rome imposed no formal requirements concerning capital market liberalization. The only stricture was a general one against capital restrictions that inhibited the proper functioning of the Common Market. The European Commission advanced capital flow liberalization only modestly, with directives in 1960 and 1962. These promoted partial liberalization but included numerous opt-out and safeguard clauses, which were in fact extensively used by EU members.

establishment covered international transfers of capital that may be necessary to set up business. Likewise, national policies were not supposed to hinder the repatriation of profits or wages among Member States to the extent that such hindrances act as restrictions on the free movement of goods and workers.

Chapter 1 explains that the Single European Act 1986 instituted the principle that all forms of capital mobility should be allowed inside the EU. The actual liberalization was implemented by a series of directives which ended with the 1988 directive that ruled out all remaining restrictions on capital movements among EU residents. The resulting integration was raised to the level of a Treaty commitment by Article 56 of the Maastricht Treaty. This banned all national restrictions on the movement of capital except those required for law enforcement and national security reasons.[5]

The costs of international capital mobility are macroeconomic. The impossible trinity principle introduced in Chapter 15 explains the necessity to give up monetary policy independence while keeping exchange rates fixed and the associated risk of financial instability. The benefits of allowing capital to move across national boundaries are microeconomic. They fall into two categories: allocation efficiency and diversification, which we consider in turn.

[5] Details on current EU policy and its evolution are available on http://www.europarl.eu.int/factsheets/3_2_4_en.htm, one of the European Parliament's excellent internet factsheets.

19.2.2 Economics of capital mobility: allocation efficiency

The normal functioning of a market economy requires capital to be invested in the activities that yield the highest rewards. To the extent that capital market barriers inhibit this efficient allocation, capital controls lower the allocative efficiency of the European economy. To understand this point, we start with the simplest analytic framework that allows us to organize our thinking about the economic consequences of capital market integration. Specifically, we suppose that there are only two nations (Home and Foreign) and that, initially, capital flows are not allowed between them. We also assume that these nations initially have different returns to capital. To keep things simple, we suppose that there is only one good and it is produced by both nations using capital and labour.

The framework can be depicted with the diagram shown in Fig. 19.2. This will eventually allow us to look at the international distribution of capital and impact of capital flows, but to get started we focus on Home, ignoring capital mobility. The *MPK* curve in the diagram shows how the 'marginal product of capital' (the amount of output produced by an extra unit of capital) declines as the total amount of capital employed increases. The marginal product of capital is declining in this diagram for exactly the same reason that the GDP/*L* curve was convex in Fig. 7.2. Holding constant the amount of

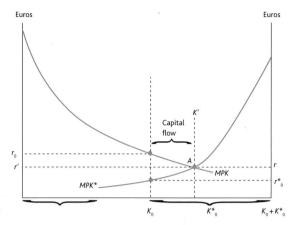

Figure 19.2: *Simple economics of capital market integration*

labour employed in Home, the addition of more capital increases the overall output, but each additional unit of capital adds less output than the previous one.

If the capital stock in Home is given by K_0, then the equilibrium marginal product of capital in Home will be r_0, assuming that the capital market is competitive. The idea is that firms competing for Home's capital supply force the 'price' of capital, r, up to the point where the price they pay for capital just equals its marginal product. By the usual logic of competition, the outcome is that competitive firms pay r_0 and all capital is employed.

Next consider the situation in the other nation, Foreign. To keep everything in one diagram, we add the Foreign capital stock to that of Home's to get the total two-nation supply of capital. This is shown as $K_0 + K_0^*$ on the horizontal axis. We also draw the marginal product curve for foreign capital, but we reverse it since we measure the amount of capital employed in Foreign from right-to-left (Home employment of capital is measured from left-to-right). Following the same competitive logic as for Home, we see that the foreign return to capital will be r_0^* since this is the MPK^* where all of the capital is employed in Foreign. (This way of depicting the Home plus Foreign capital stock makes it easy to study partitions of the total between the two nations; each point on the horizontal axis between zero and $K_0 + K_0^*$ shows a different partition.)

Analysis of capital market integration

As the diagram is drawn, capital earns a higher return in Home than it does in Foreign. If we now allow international capital flows and, for the sake of simplicity,

assume that such flows are costless, it is clear that capital will leave Foreign and move to Home in search of a higher reward. Such capital flows raise the level of capital employed in Home and lower it in Foreign, thus narrowing the gap between r_0 and r_0^*. Indeed, under our assumption that capital flows are costless, capital moves from Foreign to Home until the returns are equalized. This occurs at point A, where the two MPK curves intersect. The resulting capital flow and the common reward, r', are illustrated in the diagram. Notice that the capital movement has raised the return in the sending nation and lowered it in the receiving nation.

Winners, losers and net welfare effects

Who wins and who loses from this capital movement? What are the overall effects on native workers and capital owners?

To answer these questions, we need to show how one determines the impact of capital movements on the earnings of labour (we have already seen the impact on the reward to capital). Looking at Fig. 19.3, we note that the area under the MPK curve gives total Home output. The reason follows directly from the definition of the marginal product of capital. The first unit of capital employed produces output equal to the height of the MPK curve at the point where $K = 1$. The amount produced by the second unit of capital is given by the level of MPK at the point where $K = 2$, and so on. Adding up all the heights of the MPK curve at each point yields the area under the curve.

The total earnings of Home capital is just the equilibrium reward, r_0, times the amount of capital, K_0. And, since we are assuming that capital and labour are the only two

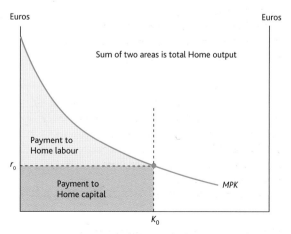

Figure 19.3: *Division of output between capital and labour*

factors of production in this simple world, labour receives all the output that is not paid to capital. Graphically, this means that capital's income is the grey rectangle shown in the diagram, while labour's income is the blue area between the MPK curve and the r_0 line. With this in hand, we turn now to the welfare effects of capital flows.

In our simple, no-capital-mobility-to-free-capital-mobility policy experiment, the 'native' capital owners in Home lose since their reward has fallen from r_0 to r' (see Fig. 19.2). The amount of the loss is measured by the rectangle A in Fig. 19.4 (the A in this diagram is unrelated to the A in Fig. 19.2). Home labour increases its earnings by area A plus the triangle B. Thus the total economic impact on Home citizens is positive and equal to the triangle B. Another way of seeing that Home gains from capital mobility is to note that the extra capital that flows in raises total output in Home by the areas B + C + D + E, but the payments to the new capital only equal the areas C + D + E (i.e. r' times the capital flow).

Correspondingly, Foreign output drops by D + E, while the capital remaining in Foreign sees its reward rise from r_0^* to r'. The size of this gain is shown by rectangle F, which is the change in r times the amount of capital left in Foreign after the integration (this is illustrated by point A). Foreign labour sees its earnings drop by D + F. Combining all these losses and gains, the Foreign factors of production that remain in Foreign lose overall by an amount measured by triangle D. However, if we count the welfare of Foreign factor owners, including the capital that is now working in Home, the conclusion is reversed. Total gains to Foreign capital are C + D + F, while the loss to Foreign labour is D + F. Foreign gains from the capital outflow by an amount equal to the triangle C.

In short, while capital flows create winners and losers in both nations, collectively both nations gain from the movement of capital. The deep reason for this has to do with efficiency. Without capital mobility, the allocation of productive factors was inefficient. For example, on the margin, Foreign capital was producing r_0^*, while it could have been producing r_0 in Home. The capital flow thus improves the overall efficiency of the EU economy and the gains from this are split between Home and Foreign. Foreign gets area C; Home gets area B.

The result that both countries benefit from capital market integration is the basis for the single market and the Commission directive. It underpins the view that, by further encouraging capital mobility, adoption of the euro will raise economic efficiency and welfare.[6] It is important, however, to remember the assumptions that were made in reaching this result, in particular that the capital market itself is functioning perfectly well. This assumption is not warranted. Section 19.1.3 explains the many specificities of this market, including asymmetric information, which makes it difficult to deal with inherent risk, and network externalities, which skew competition. When the perfect market assumption is removed, the result no longer holds: capital market integration may or may not be beneficial; it all depends on the details of the deviations from perfection and on a host of other features.

Does it mean that capital market integration is a bad idea? Probably not. The presumption is that, as long as competition is strong enough, integration is beneficial. Yet, things can go wrong and this is why the authorities have to be vigilant and, when needed – and only when needed – regulate the markets to ensure that the expected benefits from integration are reaped. This issue is taken up in section 19.3.4.

19.2.3 Economics of capital mobility: the diversification effect

Section 19.1.3 explains how financial markets facilitate investment by matching borrowers and savers and by pricing risk. Capital market integration (and the exchange rate stability that comes with the euro – see next section) reduce the risk premium and therefore lower the borrowing costs of firms while offering better returns to savers. This makes Europe a better place to invest. In this way, financial market integration can raise the investment rate and growth as explained in Chapter 7.

[6] It is also the rationale for financial globalization, but that is another story.

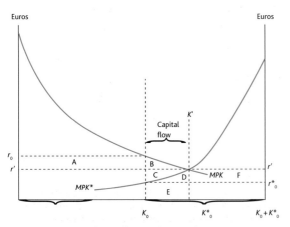

Figure 19.4: *Welfare effects of capital 'migration'*

Since European integration is rather gradual and since many things affect the risk-adjusted rate of return, it can be difficult to figure out exactly how financial market integration affects the investment climate in Europe as a whole. The same logic, however, applies to individual nations joining the EU. Since the financial markets in some nations – for example, a small nation like Estonia – are relatively undeveloped, getting access to the European financial markets by joining may have a big impact on their risk-adjusted rate of return and thus a big impact on their investment rate.

19.2.4 Effects of the single currency on financial markets

The adoption of the euro eliminates the currency risk within the euro area. In principle, therefore, savers do not have to worry about where the asset is issued as long as it is denominated in euros, and borrowers can tap the whole area by taking on euro-denominated debt. There is no longer any reason for financial markets to be Finnish, Greek or German.

A single financial market first means more competition as national currencies that used to act as non-tariff barriers are eliminated.[7] Rents associated with dominating positions should disappear and the need to retain and attract new customers should push financial institutions to constantly improve their performance. A unified financial market should also allow a better exploitation of scale economies, with the emergence of large financial institutions and markets. Table 19.1 shows that only three euro area banks are in the top ten league (until recently, US banks were hamstrung by legislation that prevented them from operating in more than one state).[8] Similarly the euro area stock markets (Frankfurt,

Paris, Milan, etc.) are small in comparison with Wall Street and the City of London.

One possible negative aspect, however, is that the potential for diversification shrinks. Before the advent of the euro, a Belgian saver could diversify her portfolio by acquiring German, Italian and other European assets. Now these assets are less diverse as they all share the same currency and as cyclical conditions become more homogeneous (as shown in Chapter 17). To achieve a high degree of diversification, these assets may have to move further, to less well-known parts of the world.[9] All in all, however, the positive effects of scale economies in a wider unified market are likely to outweigh the negative effects of reduced diversification.

Finally, the fact that the US dollar is a world currency gives US citizens and firms some advantages. The potential emergence of the euro as another world currency, and the expected benefits, are examined in section 19.4.

19.3 Financial institutions and markets

19.3.1 Banking

What is special about banking?

The banking industry is special in three respects. First, banks are naturally fragile, and bank failures can be systemic, as explained in section 19.3.4 below. As a consequence, banks are highly regulated and supervised. Second, the information asymmetry problem is acute since banks earn profits primarily from their lending

Rank	Bank	Country	Rank	Bank	Country
1	UBS	Switzerland	6	BNP Paribas	France
2	Citigroup	USA	7	JP Morgan Chase	USA
3	Mizuho	Japan	8	Deutsche Bank	Germany
4	HSBC	UK	9	Royal Bank of Scotland	UK
5	Crédit Agricole	France	10	Bank of America	USA

Source: *The Banker*, July 2005.

Table 19.1: *The top ten commercial banks in 2005*

[7] Chapter 3 presents non-tariff barriers, i.e. restrictions to trade that are designed to protect local firms by such means as specific regulation, standards, administrative authorizations and controls, etc.

[8] The situation was the same in the first edition of this book; in 2002, there were one French and two German banks in the top league.

[9] This is not a serious concern. As globalization develops, so do the possibilities of diversification. Over the past few years, Chinese and Indian assets have joined Brazilian and Korean assets in well-diversified portfolios.

activities. Banking does not conform to the perfect market model.

One implication is that long-term relationships are important as they provide banks with track records of their customers and help to build up confidence, breaking somewhat the information asymmetry. The downside is that well-established customers have little incentive to quit their banks. While this attachment alleviates the information asymmetry problem, it also reduces competition.

That aspect is further reinforced by the fact that it is plainly painful to change bank. Many payment orders are automated, some payments and receipts are always under way, and so it is never the right time to shift to another bank. Proximity of the branch also often discourages switching. For these reasons, most banking relationships tend to be long-lasting, much longer than in most other service industries, and competition is less severe.

The starting point

These features explain why banks started to develop at the local level, which allowed them to know their customers reasonably well, thus minimizing information asymmetries. Scale economies next led to a process of growth and mergers as banks sought to become ever bigger, but so far this process has generally taken place within national boundaries. Figure 19.5 shows that the number of banks has declined in the euro area recently, and a large part of this decline is explained by mergers and acquisitions. However, Fig. 19.6 indicates that a vast majority (77 per cent for the euro area as a whole) of these mergers and acquisitions take place within countries. The figure also reveals that there are big differences

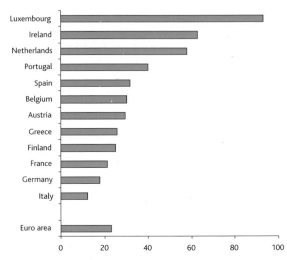

Figure 19.6: *Percentage of mergers and acquisitions of EU banks carried out across countries within the euro area, 1995–2004*

Source: *Monthly Bulletin*, ECB, May 2005.

across countries. Quite clearly, mergers and acquisitions in the big countries are predominantly conducted internally.

There exists further evidence that the euro has not led banks to operate at the euro area level. For instance, loans by euro-area-based banks to customers located elsewhere in the area, remain a small (6 per cent) and unchanged proportion of total bank loans.

National or pan-European concentration

The fact that each country had its own currency – in Europe the exception being the Belgium–Luxembourg currency union – and that many restrictions to capital movements were in place until the late 1980s, explains why the concentration process initially took place within, and not across, countries. The advent of the euro could change all that, but little has happened so far. Several reasons have been advanced to explain the continuing apparent parochialism of banks in contrast with other industries.

First, local regulations still differ. This has long been recognized and has led to a succession of harmonization efforts, described in Box 19.2. In addition, while in theory a 'single banking market' is now in place, several non-regulatory hurdles remain. They operate like non-tariff barriers and are used by national authorities to protect home-grown banks and, in effect, stifle competition.

Second, cultural differences remain prevalent. For several centuries, banks have developed along diverse lines.

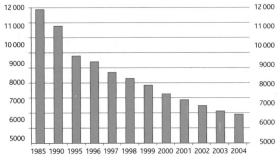

Figure 19.5: *Number of credit institutions in the euro area, 1985–2004*

Source: *Monthly Bulletin*, ECB, May 2005.

Box 19.2

Harmonization of banking regulation in Europe

Efforts at building a unified banking market in Europe go far back in history. The main steps are as follows:

★ In 1973, a directive on the Abolition of Restrictions on Freedom of Establishment and Freedom to Provide Services for self-employed Activities of Banks and other Financial Institutions established the principle of national treatment. All banks operating in one country are subject to the same non-discriminatory regulations and supervision as local banks. Yet, widespread capital controls limited competition and, in the absence of any coordination of banking supervision, banks were deterred from operating in different countries.

★ In 1977, the First Banking Directive on the Co-ordination of Laws, Regulations and Administrative Provisions Relating to the Taking Up and Pursuit of Credit Institutions established a gradual phasing in of the principle of home country control. Under this principle, it is the home country of the parent bank that is responsible for supervising the bank's activities in other EU countries. The directive left open a number of loopholes, including the need to obtain authorization from the local supervision authorities to establish subsidiaries and continuing restrictions on capital movements.

★ In 1989, the Second Banking Directive was designed to apply to the banking industry the provisions of the Single European Act 1986, which mandated the elimination of capital controls. The directive stipulates that any bank licensed in a EU country can establish branches or supply cross-border financial services in the other countries of the EU without further authorization. It can also open a subsidiary on the same conditions as nationals of the host state. The parent bank must now consolidate all its accounts for supervision by its own authority. Yet, the host country can impose specific regulations if they are deemed to be 'in the public interest'.

★ Facing a lack of progress, a Financial Services Action Plan (FSAP) was adopted in 1999. The stated aim is to achieve full integration of banking and capital markets by 2005. The Plan outlines four objectives: (i) a single EU wholesale market; (ii) open and secure retail banking and insurance markets; (iii) the development of state-of-the-art prudential rules and supervision; (iv) wider conditions (essential fiscal rules) for an optimal single financial market.

The 'single banking market' is not limited to the EU members. When the EFTA countries, with the exception of Switzerland, joined the European Economic Area (EEA) in 1992, they accepted the European banking legislation.

Source: Dermine (2003).

Traditions in banking differ significantly from one country to another. While acquiring a foreign bank could be the easiest way of adjusting to that country's culture, problems with integrating personnel seem to deter mergers and acquisitions.

Third, the tax treatment of savings differs from country to country. Thus the choice of where to bank may be driven by tax purposes rather than by the quality of banking services. Tax evasion may well have become as strong an incentive to scout the European banking scene as the search for better service or risk diversification, thus undermining the very purpose of financial integration. In 2005, a new agreement came into effect to combat tax evasion; all EU-based banks must now report their foreign customers to their tax authorities.

Finally, protectionism is suspected. The fact that mergers and acquisitions in the large countries are predominantly within-borders (see Fig.19.6) may simply be a size effect, but it may also be the result of protectionism. For instance, in 2005, the Governor of the Bank of Italy was officially warned by the EU Commission not to interfere in attempted purchases of two large Italian banks by a Spanish and a Dutch bank; yet, these attempts failed and the matter has been sent to the courts.

The evidence so far is that, through mergers and acquisitions, banks have been consolidating at the national level. Their strategy seems to be, first, to reach a size that is large enough to enable them to engage in foreign purchases. Meanwhile, as banks merge at the national level, concentration increases (Fig. 19.7), which may result in less, not more, competition. Thus, in contrast with the effects expected from the Single European Act as laid out in Chapter 3, it could be that the early impact of the monetary union is to reduce competition. This could be the perverse effect of combining partial integrative measures with continuing NTB protectionism. There is some recent evidence, though, that competition has not declined. More optimistically, we may just be at the eve of a wave of pan-European mergers and acquisitions that will eventually make the single banking market a reality.

Trade in services

While banks do not consolidate at the pan-European level, they could still offer services across borders. This form of competition is exactly what the Second Banking Directive was meant to promote, and the elimination of exchange risk should reinforce it. They can open new branches and move close to their customers to circumvent the information asymmetry. Figure 19.8 shows the percentage of local branches of banks from the European Economic Area.[10] With few exceptions,

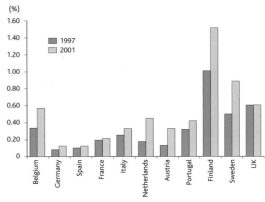

Figure 19.8: *Share of branches of foreign EEA banks in 1997 and 2001*

Source: *Structural Analysis of the EU Banking Sector*, ECB, November 2002.

there is not yet any sign of a powerful euro effect that would prompt banks to move into other countries. They may expect that it will be very hard to win away customers because of the large fixed costs involved in changing banks. The limited extent of cross-border competition is further confirmed by bank charges for bank transfers from one eurozone country to another, which have been kept so high (some €17 on average for a €100 transfer in 2000, about ten times the cost of a domestic transfer) that the Commission stepped in and imposed a new regulation which prohibits banks from charging a different fee for within-eurozone transfers from the one they apply to domestic transfers.

19.3.2 Bond markets

We first look at the market for bonds issued by national governments. Most governments are believed to be highly trustworthy, financially at least. This is why interest rates on public debts are often considered risk-free and therefore directly comparable, without having to adjust for risk.

Figure 19.9 shows the evolution of interest rates on government short-term bonds. For decades, interest was lowest on German bonds. Since the other currencies were perceived as being weaker than the Deutschmark, other governments had to pay higher rates to compensate for currency risk.[11] This is called the currency risk. As the date of launching the single currency drew nearer and more certain, the currency risk

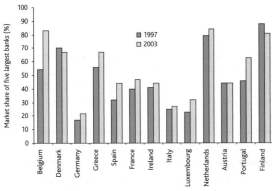

Figure 19.7: *Concentration in national banking, 1997 and 2003*

Source: Walkner and Raes (2005).

[10] The EEA includes the old EU15 member countries as well as Iceland, Liechtenstein and Norway which have accepted the European banking legislation.

[11] This is the interest parity principle, which can be stated as: Interest rate in Italy − Interest rate in Germany = Expected depreciation of the lira *vis-à-vis* the Deutschmark.

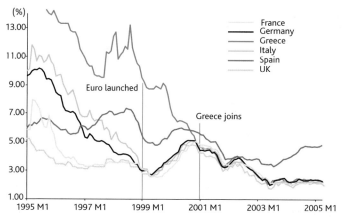

Figure 19.9: *Interbank (3 months) interest rates, January 1995–April 2005*

Source: IMF.

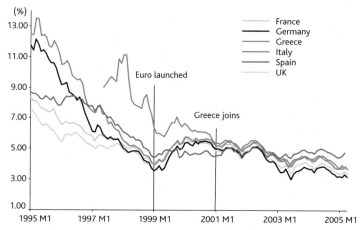

Figure 19.10: *Interest rates on long-term government bonds, January 1995–April 2005*

Source: IMF.

declined and gradually became irrelevant. The figure shows an impressive convergence of the French and Italian rates towards the German level by January 1999. The convergence becomes complete as time passes, an indication that the short-term compartment of the bond market is fully integrated. Note the evolution of the Greek interest rate since Greece joined the euro area in January 2001; this is when convergence occurs. It is also interesting to observe that the UK rate does not converge since the UK has decided not to adopt the euro.

The long-term compartment of the bond market is examined in Fig. 9.10. The picture is broadly similar, with two differences. The convergence occurs earlier, before the launch of the euro. This is logical. Long-term rates can be seen as the average of current and future short-term rates, all the way to maturity. If markets expect the

short-term rates to converge in the future, the weight of the not-yet converged short-term rates declines as time passes by. The early convergence therefore reveals that the financial markets have been convinced ahead of time that the monetary union would start as planned. Yet a keen eye will detect that convergence is not complete. This may reflect differences in the perceived quality of governments as borrowers,[12] or less than full integration because of remaining institutional differences in this market segment. Most observers conclude that full integration has been achieved on the interbank market, not on the government bond market, and much less on

[12] This could reflect different public debt size or varying degrees of compliance with the Stability and Growth Pact (Chapter 18). The fact that interest rates on the German debt remain the lowest while Germany's deficit is excessive suggests that this is not the explanation.

the market for private bonds issued by large corporations.

19.3.3 Stock markets

The stock market is where large – and some medium-sized – firms raise the financial resources that they need to acquire capital and generally develop their activities. They issue shares which are held by individuals or by large institutional investors, such as pension funds and insurance companies. Increasingly, individuals buy shares from collective funds designed to offer good risk–return trade-offs through extensive diversification, as explained in section 19.1.2. Yet, for all the hype about globalization, it is striking that stock markets are characterized by a strong home bias: borrowers and savers alike tend to deal mostly on domestic markets and to hold domestic assets.

One reason for the home bias is information asymmetry: investors know more about domestic firms. This is unlikely to change. Another reason is currency risk. This obstacle to capital mobility has been eliminated within the euro area, so we would expect less of a home bias. Is it happening? Apparently, yes. The continuous line in Fig. 19.11 shows that the proportion of assets held by eurozone-based investing funds that report pursuing a Europe-wide strategy has sharply increased following the adoption of the euro in 1999. Could it just be part of the globalization trend? The dotted line, which shows the proportion of the same funds that have followed worldwide investment strategy, confirms the plausibility of a euro effect.

Another piece of evidence is provided by the evolution of stock exchanges, the marketplace where shares are traded. Most European countries long had one stock exchange, or more. This was natural when currency risk was segmenting the various national markets. Will things change with the advent of the euro? In the USA, which is similar to the euro area in economic and geographic size, there are fifteen stock exchanges, but only two or three significant ones, all dominated by the New York Stock Exchange (NYSE). Because stock exchanges display strong scale economies, the perception is that the euro area is evolving in this direction, towards one major centre and a handful of secondary exchanges. The question is where will they be? Each country seems to be keen to retain its stock exchange, for reasons of prestige and because it can be a major activity.

Table 19.2 displays the sizes of the European exchanges as well as those of the NYSE and Tokyo, measured by market capitalization, i.e. the total valuation of all the firms listed on the exchange. In comparison with the NYSE, European exchanges remain small, and therefore likely to suffer from limited scale economies. London dominates, and seems to have taken advantage of the creation of the euro by attracting many corporations from the euro area. For a while it was thought that Frankfurt would benefit from the location of the ECB, but this has not happened. In fact, London and Frankfurt tried to merge in 1998, but this attempt failed for reasons explained in Box 19.3. In order to challenge both London and Frankfurt, a number of exchanges have merged. Euronext was created in 2000 by the exchanges of Paris, Brussels and Amsterdam, keeping physical operations in each city. In 2003, Stockholm and Helsinki merged into OMX, which has since linked up with Copenhagen and the Baltic states (Riga, Tallinn and Vilnius), also keeping physical operations in each of these cities. The process of consolidation is slowly under way.

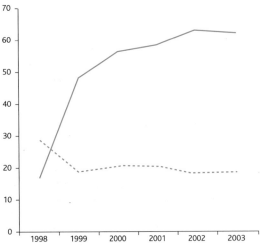

Figure 19.11: *Asset share of Europe-wide funds, 1998–2003*

Source: ECB (2004).

19.3.4 Regulation and supervision

The rationale

Section 19.1 identified a number of characteristics specific to financial markets: these markets display important scale economies, they operate as networks and they suffer from information asymmetries. These

Exchange	€ bn	% GDP	Exchange	€ bn	% GDP	Exchange	€ bn	% GDP
New York	10 729	112.7	OMX	593	90.6	Luxembourg	40	145.3
Tokyo	2 850	76.5	Milan	592	42.0	Budapest	26	28.8
London	2 284	131.3	Oslo	134	58.9	Prague	25	27.4
Euronext	1 910	78.0	Athens	100	57.5	Cyprus	4	35.7
Frankfurt	936	42.1	Vienna	93	37.9	Bratislava	4	11.3
Madrid	769	91.8	Dublin	89	55.7	Malta	2	56.7
Zurich	667	221.5	Warsaw	57	25.7			

Note: Euronext is Paris, Brussels and Amsterdam; OMX is Copenhagen, Helsinki, Stockholm, Tallinn, Riga and Vilnius.

Source: European centres: Federation of European Securities Exchanges; New York and Tokyo: NYSE; GDP estimates from *Economic Outlook*, OECD and IMF.

Table 19.2: *Size of stock markets (total capitalization), June 2005*

characteristics imply that financial markets suffer from 'market failures', i.e. deviations from the textbook description of perfect markets. In the presence of failures, markets may malfunction, which justifies interventions by the authorities. Indeed, in every country, financial markets are regulated and the financial institutions are closely supervised.

The presence of scale economies implies that a few large firms eventually dominate the market. The tendency for competition to become monopolistic challenges the perfect competition assumption.[13] It also means that financial markets are vulnerable to difficulties suffered by one or two of these important players. This vulnerability is sharpened by the two other characteristics. The network feature means that all large financial institutions are continuously dealing with each other, and routinely borrowing and lending huge amounts among each other. If one of these institutions fails, all the others may be pulled down. Failures tend to be systemic.

The third characteristic, the presence of information asymmetries, means that all financial firms routinely take risks. Every asset represents the right to receive payments in the future, be it 24 hours or 15 years. It is trivial to observe that the future is unknown, but this feature has deep implications for financial markets. Today's value of an asset represents the best collective judgement by financial market participants of the likely payments that the asset holder may expect to receive upon maturity. But one thing is sure: the future will differ from today's expectations. The asset may yield better returns than expected, but can also be revealed as catastrophic and its value can deeply deteriorate. When this happens, asset holders see their wealth decline, and the decline is typically sudden. This is why financial systems are inherently fragile and prone to panics and crises.

As the financial institutions are central to modern economies, systemic failures immediately provoke severe disruptions that leave no firm or citizen unharmed. When declines in asset values are widespread, those who hold large amounts of assets can become insolvent. Many financial institutions (banks, pension funds, insurance companies) that hold large amounts of assets may then fail, spreading the hardship to the whole economy as numerous examples – from the Wall Street crash of 1929 to Korea in 1998 or Argentina in 2002 – remind us.

Regulation and supervision

To reduce the incidence of such catastrophic events, and possibly even eliminate them, financial institutions are regulated. Over the years, regulation has changed and become more sophisticated. The general thrust is to ensure that financial institutions adopt prudent strategies. This is done by requiring them to hold enough high-quality assets, for example bonds issued by respectable governments or by solid corporations.

Regulation, in turn, requires supervision. It is not enough to pass down good rules, it is essential to make sure that they are respected. Since financial conditions can quickly deteriorate, supervision must be continuous. Given the complexity of modern finance, and the possibility of hiding emerging problems, supervisors must be as sophisticated as the financiers themselves, and they need to exercise their duties with great diligence and firmness.

[13] As explained in Chapter 6, monopolistic competition describes the situation where a small number of large firms dominate the market.

Box 19.3

Consolidation of stock markets

Some consolidation is taking place among traditional stock markets. The most noticeable example has been the creation of Euronext in September 2000, the result of a merger of the Amsterdam, Brussels and Paris stock exchanges. Euronext is subject to Dutch legislation and has a subsidiary in each of the participating countries. Each subsidiary holds a local stock market licence that gives access to trading in all the participating countries. Euronext achieved consistency in some, but not all, of the institutional characteristics of its predecessor markets. Single quotation and a common order book are guaranteed as well as price dissemination systems, a unified trading platform and one clearing and settlement system, Euroclear. Nevertheless, the local markets are not legally merged, which implies, for example, that the regulatory body in each of the participating countries retains its prerogatives. From the beginning, Euronext was not intended to be a closed structure and was eager to finalize agreements with other stock exchanges. In 2001, this resulted in the acquisition of Liffe, the London derivatives trading platform, and the agreement to integrate also the Portuguese exchanges of Lisbon and Porto.

Before Euronext, another, even larger merger between stock exchanges was tried. In 1998, the Deutsche Börse (DB) and the London Stock Exchange (LSE) were planning to merge in an attempt to gain a leadership position in Europe. The creation of iX ('international Exchange') was officially announced on May 2000. The DB and the LSE planned to participate in equal measure as shareholders of the new exchange, which would be subject to British legislation. It was envis-aged to quote the 'blue chips' of both exchanges in London and the technology stocks in Frankfurt. The trading system would have been the German one (Xetra), considered to be the more modern and reliable. While the negotiations between the two stock exchanges were still in process, the OM Gruppen, owner of the Stockholm stock exchange, made an unexpected public offer and tried to take over the LSE. This event critically affected the projected merger between DB and LSE, which was subsequently rejected by the LSE board.

Several reasons led to the failure of the merger. In general, there were some doubts that the merger would create value added and would consistently exploit economies of scale. First, contrary to Euronext, where companies belonging to the same sector retained the freedom to choose the location of their listing, iX required the 'blue chips' to be traded in London and the technology stocks in Frankfurt. This solution would have implied costs for both exchanges. Second, some of the companies would have had to move from one exchange to the other and deal with the change in regulations and supervisory authorities. Finally, the new entity did not include the creation of a common clearing and settlement system, hence it would have failed to provide lower settlement costs.

In 2005, there were again rumours of a possible purchase of the LSE by DB.

Source: Adapted from Hartmann *et al.* (2003).

The current situation

Regulation – the establishment of rules – is largely designed at the EU level[14] whereas supervision – the implementation and enforcement of regulation – continues to be carried out at the national level. This assignment of

tasks is understandable. The EU's central aim is often described as 'the four freedoms': free mobility of goods, services, assets and people. For financial services to move freely, financial institutions need to be allowed to operate throughout the EU if they so wish. If national regulations differed, financial institutions would have to register in each and every country where they wished to operate. This would greatly hamper the mobility of financial services. Savers, unsure about the quality of foreign regulations, would prefer to keep their money at home.

[14] More precisely, EU-level regulation sets minimum standards, leaving individual countries free to establish more stringent – but not more lenient – rules. Within this principle, national-level rules are subject to the principle of mutual recognition, i.e. foreign rules are recognized as substitutes for domestic ones.

What about supervision? One argument for keeping supervision at the national level is the existence of another kind of information asymmetry, this time between supervisor and supervisee. Obviously each financial firm knows more about its business, and the risks that it is taking, than its supervisor. Quite likely, most firms wish to hide their difficulties, especially if their disclosure would lead to fines or outright closure. It is argued that these information asymmetries are lower at the national than at the union level. National supervisors know their financial institutions well, and over the years have developed a relationship that allows for a smooth process. Another argument is subsidiarity: unless proved impossible or inefficient, supervision should remain at the national level. So far, in the absence of any major shake-up, it is impossible to prove that national-level supervision is inadequate. Yet most observers believe that this is the case and that the true reason for retaining national-level supervision is a lack of interest. After all, this is also about jobs in Amsterdam, Helsinki and Madrid, and old, possibly cosy, links between supervisors and supervisees.

Adapting regulation and supervision to the single currency

National supervisors differ in important ways. Their legal briefs vary and their level of expertise is not uniform. This can be problematic if and when financial crises suddenly occur, because, at that stage, in an effort to stunt systemic effects, prompt reaction is of the essence. The authorities must decide whether to bail out – at taxpayers' expense – failing institutions or let them fail. Given the networking among financial institutions, the bailout decision is unlikely to concern a single country.[15] A proper reaction therefore calls for instantaneous and extensive sharing of information, based on an intimate knowledge of the institutions and their managers.

The current solution relies on cooperation among national supervisors, but there is no presumption that all can be told quickly enough. More ominously, national supervisors may be sensitive to the interests of their national financial institutions and wish to protect them. Proximity may reduce information asymmetries but it can also nurture nationalistic sentiments. If that is the case, cooperation is unlikely to develop into a fully trusted partnership. Finally, the national agencies in charge of supervision have an obvious interest in not being closed down. Some of them are actually part of

the national central banks which have already lost their monetary policy-making role and are highly reluctant to be deprived of their last important function, supervision.

Even if an agreement to establish Europe-wide supervision could be reached, should it be carried out by the ECB or by a separate agency? Currently, as Table 19.3 shows, the responsibility for supervising financial institutions rests with central banks in some countries, and with specialized agencies in others. Sweden and the UK have opted for a single independent supervisor. Technical discussions are under way, but 'turf' considerations are present.

19.3.5 Channels of monetary policy

The link between a financial system and monetary policy is tight. Monetary conditions deeply affect the daily functioning of financial markets. Financial systems cannot blossom unless the currency is reasonably stable and monetary policy cannot operate without a well-functioning financial market. Because most of what we call money is in the form of bank deposits, the good functioning of the banking and financial systems is crucial to the trust that underwrites any money. This is one reason why central banks have a direct interest in the quality of the financial system.

Another reason is that monetary policy decisions are transmitted via financial markets through the availability and cost of credit. The financial system is the channel through which monetary policy affects the economy, its growth and its inflation rates. The fact that the euro is the currency of different countries, each with its own financial system, creates a novel situation.

The main question is whether a given policy decision can have different and unwanted effects in different countries. There are many reasons why this can be the case:

★ The ECB sets the short-term interest rate (EONIA) as described in Chapter 17. In most countries, loans depend on longer-term interest rates, which typically move less than short-term rates and whose movements depend on the reaction of the financial market. In these countries, the effect of central bank actions is both muted and somewhat uncertain. In some countries, however, the interest rate that applies to loans is indexed on the short-term rate and central bank actions have a stronger impact.

★ The effect of the interest rate largely depends on the importance of bank credit. In some countries,

---

[15] Small banks are typically not operating internationally, so the problem concerns larger banks, precisely those that are important for systemic contagion.

bank credit is the main source of financing for most firms and households, but in other countries, firms make more important use of stock markets. Monetary policy will have a more direct effect in the first group of countries than in the latter, where the evolution of share prices will become an important, yet uncertain, channel.

★ Monetary policy also operates through the exchange rate. With a common exchange rate, those countries that have a higher share of external trade with the non-eurozone countries stand to be more strongly affected.

EMU countries differ on all these dimensions, which raises the possibility that monetary policy could be a source of asymmetric shocks, precisely what the OCA theory suggests is the main drawback of a monetary union (see Chapter 16). Whether all these differences add up to a serious problem, however, is another question, so far with no clear answer. A further issue is whether, over time, the existing structural differences will fade away. Early indications are that it is the case.[16]

19.4 The international role of the euro

The classic attributes of money apply to its international role. Externally, a currency can be a medium of exchange used for international trade, a unit of account used to price other currencies or widely traded commodities, and a store of value used by foreign individuals and authorities. Domestically, these attributes are underpinned by the legal status of money; internationally they have to be earned.

In the nineteenth century, sterling was the undisputed international currency. It was displaced by the US dollar in the twentieth century. Clearly, only large economies can expect their currency to achieve an international status, a condition that the euro area fulfils. Currently, some 305 million people live in the euro area, and new membership could eventually bring this number to 470 million, to be compared with 280 million people living in the USA. The EU's GDP is 75 per cent of that of the USA. Another condition is that the currency must be stable. The Eurosystem's commitment to price stability further suggests that, eventually, the euro can aspire to having a

---

[16] The ECB and the NCBs have conducted a detailed investigation of the channels of monetary policy. A summary of the results is in the ECB's *Monthly Bulletin*, October 2002.

large international role. Will it, and if so, when? Would it be a good thing? These are the issues that we consider in this final section.

19.4.1 Medium of exchange: trade invoicing

Whenever an export takes place, there must be an agreement on the currency that will be used to set the price and then carry out the payment. Will it be the exporter's, the importer's, or a third currency? Each side of the trade would rather use its own currency to avoid exchange costs and uncertainty. In that sense, the euro area stands to benefit from a wider acceptability of its currency.

There is some evidence that European firms are increasingly able to invoice trade in euros, as shown in Fig. 19.12. Yet the bulk of primary commodities (oil, gas, raw materials) are priced in US dollars in specialized markets, and this is unlikely to change in the foreseeable future. Even if European firms can now more often avoid exposure to currency risk by using the euro, the dollar is and will remain the currency of choice among countries which are in neither the USA nor the euro currency areas. The exception seems to be countries on the periphery of the EU, mostly those in Europe that will join the EU in the coming years.

19.4.2 Unit of account: vehicle currencies on foreign exchange markets

The foreign exchange market is a network of financial institutions that trade currencies among themselves. This is a huge market where, on any average day, some US$1000 billion worth of exchanges take place (this amounts to more than one month of activity in the whole of the US economy). Each transaction must

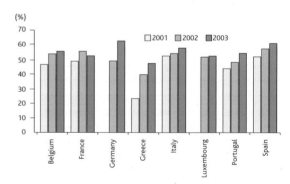

Figure 19.12: *Share of extra-eurozone exports invoiced in euro, 2001–03*

Source: ECB (2005).

| | | | Form of central bank involvement in banking supervision | | | |
| | | | Central bank is not the banking supervisor | | | |
Country	Number of public institutions responsible for supervision	Central bank is involved in banking supervision[a]	Central bank is the banking supervisor	Central bank is involved in the management of the banking supervisor[b]	Central bank specific tasks in banking supervision[c]	Central bank and banking supervisor share resources
Belgium	2[d]	Yes	No	Yes	No	No[e]
Denmark	1	No	No	No	No	No
Germany	1	Yes	No	No	Yes	Yes
Greece	3	Yes	Yes			
Spain	3	Yes	Yes			
France	6[f]	Yes	No	Yes	No	Yes
Ireland	1[g]	Yes	No	No	No	Yes
Italy	3	Yes	Yes			
Luxembourg	2	No	No	No	No	No
Netherlands	3[h]	Yes	Yes			
Austria	1	Yes	No	Yes	Yes	No
Portugal	3	Yes	Yes			
Finland	2	Yes	No	Yes	No	Yes
Sweden	1	Yes	No	Yes	No	No[i]
United Kingdom	1	Yes	No	Yes	No	No[j]

[a] The central bank is involved in banking supervision when it is the banking supervisor itself or, where this is not the case, is involved in the management/oversight of the banking supervisor, contributes to supervisory policy-shaping, carries out tasks in line supervision, processes supervisory reporting or shares resources with the supervisory agency.

[b] The central bank is involved in the management of the banking supervisor if the former is represented in the management (e.g. management committee, secretary-general and chairman) or in the supervisory or oversight board of the latter.

[c] The central bank carries out off- and on-site monitoring in specific areas.

[d] The two existing supervisors will merge on 1 January 2004 into one institution.

[e] The law foresees a pooling of resources between the *Commission Bancaire et Financière Commissie voor het Bank- en Financiewezen* (Banking and Finance Commission – CBF), the *Office de Contrôle des Assurances/Centrale dienst voor verzekeringen* (Insurance Control Office – OCA/CDV) and the central bank, the Banque Nationale de Belgique/Nationale Bank van België (BNB/NBB).

[f] A variety of institutions and bodies are involved in the supervisory framework. The number given (six) includes the *Commission Bancaire* (Banking Commission), the *Comité des Etablissements de Crédit et des Entreprises d'Investissement* (Committee for the Establishment of Credit Institutions and Investment Companies – CECEI), the *Autorité des Marchés Financiers* (Financial Market Authority – FMA), the *Commission de Contrôle des Assurances* (Insurance Supervision Commission – CCA) and the Ministry of Economic Affairs and Finance. The *Conseil Nationale due Crédit et des Titres* (National Credit and Securities Council – CNCT), the *Collège des Autorités de Contrôle des Entreprises du Secteur Financier* (Board of Financial Sector Authorities – CACESF) and the new committees envisaged in the future, i.e. the *Comité Consultatif de la Législation et de la Réglementation Financière* (Advisory Committee on Financial Legislation and Regulation – CCLRF) are not included.

[g] The single supervisory authority (IFSRA) is a constituent but autonomous part of the central bank and is responsible for the day-to-day supervision of all areas of financial services. The governor of the central bank retains the right to appoint officers to inspect financial institutions if he so wishes. Information technology and other resources are shared between the constituent parts of the CBFSAI.

[h] There will be only two institutions in January 2005 (at the latest), as a result of the planned integration of the Nederlandsche Bank and the *Pensioen- en Verzekeringskamer* (Pensions and Insurance Supervisory Authority).

[i] The Swedish Finansinspektionen (SFSA) and Sveriges Ribsbank have concluded a Memorandum of Understanding, which includes similar features to that between the UK authorities (see next footnote), apart from explicit arrangements for the secondment of staff.

[j] The Bank of England (BoE) and the Financial Services Authority (FSA) are obliged to share information. Under a specific Memorandum of Understanding, the avoidance of duplication of labour is stated, while an agreement on the collecting institution and on data communication is foreseen to be reached in cases where the FSA and the BoE need the same information. The BoE and the FSA occasionally second staff to each other, which might be viewed as a form of sharing resources.

Source: ECB.

Table 19.3: *Financial supervision in the EU Member States as of July 2003*

involve two currencies. Since there exist more than 180 currencies in the world, there are about 16 000 bilateral exchange rates.[17] If all these bilateral rates were traded, most of them (think of the exchange rate between the Samoan tala and the Honduran lempira) would involve very few trades, resulting in a host of shallow, hence inefficient and volatile, markets. This is why foreign exchange markets use the property of triangular arbitrage to considerably reduce the number of currency pairs that are traded.

The idea is simple and illustrated in Fig. 19.13. Consider two currencies, A and B, and their bilateral exchange rate, e_{AB}. Currency A has an exchange rate *vis-à-vis* the dollar, $e_{A\$}$, and so does currency B, $e_{B\$}$. Once these two rates are known, the bilateral rate can be found as $e_{AB} = e_{A\$}/e_{B\$}$. In this example, the dollar is used as a currency vehicle and the implied bilateral rate e_{AB} is called a cross-rate.

In practice, cross-rates are rarely traded; the bulk of transactions involve a vehicle currency. Table 19.4 reports the percentage of trades that involve, on one side or another, the three main world currencies (the sum for all currencies would be 200 per cent since each transaction involves a pair of currencies). The share of the euro in 2001 is much smaller than the sum of the shares of its constituent currencies. This simply reflects the elimination of exchange rate transactions among the currencies that joined the euro area. Overall, the table reveals considerable stability. The pre-eminence of the dollar remains unchallenged.

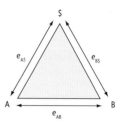

Figure 19.13: *Triangular arbitrage*

enormous market. Figure 19.14 shows that the share of bonds issued in euros has taken off following the launch of the euro. This is not very surprising when we look at Figs 19.9 and 19.10. The national bond markets have been promptly unified into a single euro market whose depth does not differ markedly from that of the dollar bond market. As a result, Europe can now claim its fair share of the market, and is increasingly doing so. Interestingly, the City of London has become the leading marketplace for this instrument whereas New York seems disinterested.

19.4.4 Store of value: international reserves

All national central banks hold foreign exchange reserves to underpin trust in their currencies and, if need be, to intervene on foreign exchange markets. Currencies appropriate for this role as a store of value must be widely traded and be perceived as having long-term stability. Figure 19.15 and Table 19.5 show that the euro has made some modest progress since its creation, but the dollar seems firmly entrenched as the leading currency.

European countries at the periphery of the euro area (including the UK) are gradually replacing dollars with

19.4.3 Store of value: bond markets

Large firms and governments borrow on the international markets by issuing long-term debt, bonds. This is an

	US dollar	Euro	Yen	Deutschmark	French franc	ECU and other EMS currencies	Pound sterling	Swiss franc
1992	82.0		23.4	39.6	3.8	11.8	13.6	8.4
1995	83.3		24.1	36.1	7.9	15.7	9.4	7.3
1998	87.3		20.2	30.1	5.1	17.3	11.0	7.1
2001	90.3	37.6	22.7				13.2	6.1
2004	88.7	37.2	20.3				16.9	6.1

Note: If all currencies were listed, the sum would be 200 per cent since each exchange involves two currencies.

Source: Bank for International Settlements Annual Report 2004.

Table 19.4: *Currency composition of exchange trading volume (%)*

[17] With *n* currencies, there exist $n(n - 1)/2$ bilateral exchange rates. Here 16 110 = (180 × 179)/2.

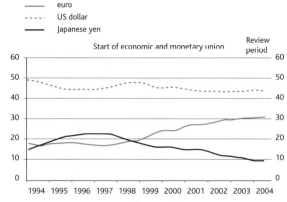

euro
US dollar
Japanese yen

Start of economic and monetary union   Review period

Figure 19.14: *Currency shares of international bonds, 1994–2004*

Source: ECB (2005).

euros. A number of developing countries have also announced their intention to do so, largely for political reasons. Recently, various Asian authorities, which accumulated vast reserves in dollars, have signalled that they could be diversifying into the euro. This would be an important step.

Why should the euro eat into the dollar's market share? Besides politics, central banks are traditionally unwilling to change the currency composition of their reserves. In particular, large-scale sales of dollars could precipitate a depreciation of the US currency with two adverse effects: the depreciation would alter international competition in trade and it would create losses for dollar-holders, including for the central banks themselves. This is why, even if the euro may be an attractive store of value, a major shift would require a serious deterioration in the dollar's own quality as a store of value. For example, Fig. 19.15 shows that the dollar's share dropped in the late 1970s when inflation rose in the USA.

19.4.5 The euro as an anchor

When a country does not let its exchange rate float freely, it must adopt an anchor, a foreign currency to which its own currency is more or less rigidly tied. The anchor, which works as a unit of account, can be a single currency or a basket of currencies. The link can be deliberately vague – known as a managed float – or quite explicit, ranging from wide crawling bands to the wholesale adoption of a foreign currency (for details, see Chapter 14).

In 2005, out of some 150 currencies not classified as freely floating, 40 used the euro as an anchor in one

way or another. Table 19.6 shows that, for 35 of these cases, the euro is the only anchor; elsewhere, it is part of a basket. Most of the countries that use the euro as an anchor are geographically close to the euro area (central and eastern Europe, northern Africa) or have historical ties to one of its constituent legacy currencies (e.g. French-speaking Africa). Two former members of the Yugoslav Federation, Kosovo and Montenegro, have 'euroized', i.e. they have unilaterally adopted the euro as their own currency but are not part of the Eurosystem. Four countries operate a currency board tied to the euro.

19.4.6 Parallel currencies

Foreign currencies are also sometimes used alongside the domestic currency, fulfilling all three functions of means of payment, unit of account and store of value. Parallel currencies, as the phenomenon is called, emerge in troubled countries where the value of domestic currency is eroded by very rapid inflation or political instability. In most cases, the parallel currency circulates in cash form, but a number of countries also allow bank deposits.

The dollar is the universal parallel currency of choice, but the Deutschmark has also been used in central and eastern Europe and in Turkey, and the French franc used to circulate widely in northern Africa and parts of Sub-Saharan Africa. In all these countries the euro has replaced the Deutschmark and the franc. In Russia, the euro's role remains modest but seems to be spreading. During the first six months following the introduction of euro notes in 2002, the ECB has shipped about 8 per cent of the total euros in circulation to outside the euro area. No doubt, more has leaked.[18]

19.4.7 Does it matter?

In the minds of some Europeans, launching the euro also means challenging the supremacy of the dollar. Indeed, the dollar reigns supreme: it is the currency of choice for international trade; it is the first foreign currency that is held by individuals, corporations and central banks; and it is also the currency most widely used to denominate financial assets. The wish to displace the dollar is no doubt driven by political sentiment, but what about the economic advantages?

When international trade is invoiced in a foreign currency, importers and exporters face an exchange risk. Between the time a commercial contract is undertaken

---

[18] For detailed information, see ECB (2005).

US dollar	Japanese yen	Euro	Deutschmark	ECUs
1965	56.1		0.1	
1966	56.5		0.2	
1967	58		0.3	
1968	55.3		0.4	
1969	54.4		0.5	
1970	71		1.6	
1971	64.5		2.5	
1972	68.2	0.1	3.8	
1973	64.5	0.1	5.5	
1974	69.9	0.1	4.9	
1975	78.9	1.8	8.8	
1976	78.1	2.3	9.5	
1977	79.2	2.2	9.3	
1978	76.6	3.1	11.1	
1979	63.3	3.2	11.5	13.3
1980	56.9	3.7	12.9	16.5
1981	57.9	3.7	11.9	15.1
1982	57.9	4.1	11.6	13.8
1983	58.4	4.2	10.7	14.2
1984	58.6	4.8	11.2	11.5
1985	53.5	6.8	13.2	11.6
1986	54.7	6.9	13.4	12.5
1987	53.9	6.8	13.8	13.6
1988	53	7	15	11.7
1989	49.5	7.2	18.6	10.7
1990	45.9	7.8	17.4	9.7
1991	45.9	8.4	16.1	10.2
1992	48.9	7.4	14	9.7
1993	53.3	7.6	14.7	8.2
1994	53.1	7.8	15.3	7.7
1995	53.4	6.7	14.7	6.8
1996	56.8	6	14	5.9
1997	59.1	5.1	13.7	5
1998	62.6	5.4	13.1	0.8
1999	64.9	5.4	13.5	
2000	66.6	6.2	16.3	
2001	66.9	5.5	16.7	
2002	63.5	5.2	19.3	
2003	63.8	4.8	19.7	
2004				

Table 19.5: *Foreign exchange reserves: share of main currencies*

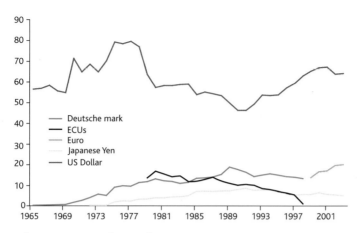

Figure 19.15: *Foreign exchange reserves: shares of main currencies*

Source: Chinn and Frankel (2005).

and payment is made, many months can elapse. In the intervening period, the exchange rate may change, imposing a risk on traders. They can purchase insurance (in the form of forward exchange contracts), but at cost. US firms, which mostly carry international transactions in dollars, thus enjoy some advantage.

In addition, 'greenbacks' are conspicuous all over the world. It is estimated that half of the dollars printed by the USA circulate outside its borders. Paper money is virtually costless to produce but, of course, it is not freely provided, being exchanged against goods, services or assets. The profit earned by the central bank, known as seigniorage, is a form of tax. When it is levied on

residents, it is just one form of domestic taxation, but when levied on foreigners, it represents a real transfer of resources. The value of expatriate dollars is about 3 per cent of the US GDP – a nice sum. However, once we realize that it has been accumulated over several decades, it is not really a significant source of revenue.

All in all, the economic benefits of having a world currency are quite modest. This explains why the ECB considers that a possible international role for the euro is something that it should neither encourage nor discourage. Beyond some legitimate pride, it does not really care.

ERM 2	Peg to euro	Peg to basket involving euro	Managed floating with euro as reference currency	Euro-based currency boards	Unilateral euroization
Cyprus	CFA Franc Zone	Botswana	Croatia	Bulgaria	European micro states
Denmark		Israel	Czech Rep.	Bosnia-Herzegovina	Kosovo
Malta		Morocco	Hungary	Estonia	Montenegro
Latvia		Russia	Macedonia	Lithuania	
Slovenia		Seychelles	Romania		
Slovakia		Tunisia	Serbia		
		Vanuatu			

Table 19.6: *Countries using the euro as an anchor*

19.5 Summary

Financial markets allow savers and borrowers to 'meet' to their mutual benefit. They also set a price on risk and offer ways to reduce exposure to risk via diversification. The presumption is that market integration improves the allocation of saving and borrowing, thus raising the overall economic performance. Not all factors of production benefit from capital market integration, however.

The financial markets are special. They are subject to economies of scale, they operate as networks and they face important information asymmetries. As a consequence, they do not conform to the perfect market assumption. In particular, they are prone to systemic instability.

This instability, as well as other market failures, explains why financial systems are regulated and supervised. For the most part, regulation has been fully harmonized throughout the EU but supervision remains at the national level. This is unlikely to be a lasting solution, but further centralization faces stiff opposition.

Banks share these characteristics, which explains why competition does not take the form implied by the perfect market assumption. In particular, large switching costs and information asymmetries explain why the adoption of the euro has not been followed by a deep restructuring of the banking industry. So far, bank mergers and acquisitions have occurred mostly at the national level; only a few banks have succeeded in expanding across borders. Differences in national regulations and some degree of protectionism on the part of supervisors also seem to limit changes. Plans have been drawn up to break this logjam.

The effects of the launch of the euro are still under way, and depend on which market segment is considered. Bond markets have been promptly unified. Stock markets, on the other hand, remain small. Some consolidation is taking place, but the largest European exchanges, including Europe's largest – London – remain undersized relative to New York or Tokyo.

The euro has the potential for challenging the US dollar as an international currency, but old habits die hard and, despite some changes, the dollar's supremacy has not been seriously dented. The euro has made some progress in trade invoicing and bond issuance. At the periphery of the euro area, it plays a dominant role as anchor for local currencies and parallel currency. Little change is reported regarding its function as a vehicle currency or foreign exchange reserves holding.

Self-assessment questions

1. What is depth in financial markets? What is breadth? What are network externalities?

2. What is the phenomenon of inflation asymmetry? How can it explain why banks refuse credit to some customers? How can it contribute to systemic risk in financial markets?

3. List the reasons why banks are subject to increasing returns to scale. Why do fixed switching costs matter for competition among banks?

4. How do we know that bond markets have been unified in the euro area upon the launch of the euro? Why has this not happened for stock markets?

5. Explain the home bias in equity holdings.

6. Explain how the three functions of money apply at the international level.

7. What is the phenomenon of gambling for resurrection? Why can it be lethal to financial markets?

8. Why is the ECB concerned with financial market integration?

9. How are banks responding to the introduction of the euro?

10. What is the difference between regulation and supervision? What are the dangers of decentralized supervision in the euro area? Why is centralization resisted?

11. What is the difference between a parallel and a vehicle currency?

12. Where is the euro used as a parallel currency?

Essay questions

1. Banks can expand through either organic growth (winning new customers) or mergers and acquisitions. How does this distinction matter for the single European banking market?

2. Imagine how financial markets could operate in the euro area if regulation had not been harmonized.

3. Write the cases for and against bank regulation and supervision to be carried out inside the central bank. (Recently the UK has set up an independent agency, the Financial Services Authority, to regulate and supervise *all* financial institutions. Its website, http://www.fsa.gov.uk/, provides a justification for this set-up.)

4. In which ways can the existence of different national financial systems complicate monetary policy in the euro area? What kinds of measures could help the ECB?

5. The largest dollar banknote denomination is $100, the largest euro denomination is €500. This has led some to suspect that Europe wants to capture the market of currencies used for illegal transactions. What is your view of this motive?

6. How do you foresee the European banking system twenty years from now? Describe the number of major banks, their ownership structure and the way they compete.

7. What, in your view, can reduce the home bias in equity holdings across Europe?

8. As several countries from central and eastern Europe join the EU and then the euro area, what can be the effects on their financial markets and on the financial markets in the rest of the euro area?

9. Comment on the quote from Rudi Dornbusch at the head of this chapter.

10. Finance is a major industry in the UK, accounting for some 5 per cent of its GDP. Does this characteristic make membership to the euro area rather more or rather less appealing?

Further reading: the aficionado's corner

General texts on financial markets and the euro:
Dermine, J. and P. Hillion (eds) (1999) *European Capital Markets with a Single Currency*, Oxford University Press, Oxford.
Gaspar, V., P. Hartmann and O. Sleijpen (eds) (2003) *The Transformation of the European Financial System*, European Central Bank, Frankfurt.
Gros, D. and K. Lannoo (1999) *The Euro Capital Market*, John Wiley, Chichester.
Ingo, W. and R.C. Smith (2000) *High Finance in the Euro-zone*, Financial Times/Prentice Hall, London.

On the structure of the European banking system, see:
Structural Analysis of the EU Banking Sector, ECB, November 2002. Available at http://www.ecb.int.

On financial integration, see:
Cabral, I., F. Dierick and J. Vesala (2002) *Banking Integration in the Euro Area*, Occasional Paper No. 6, European Central Bank, Frankfurt.

On bank mergers and acquisitions, see:
Bush, C. and G. DeLong (2003) 'Determinants of cross-border bank mergers: is Europe different?', in H. Herrmann and R.E. Lipsey (eds) *Foreign Direct Investment in the Real and Financial Sector of Industrial Countries*, Springer Verlag, New York.
Dermine, J. (2003) 'European banking, past, present, and future', in V. Gaspar, P. Hartmann and O. Sleijpen (eds) *The Transformation of the European Financial System*, European Central Bank, Frankfurt.
Mergers and Acquisitions Involving the EU Banking Industry – Facts and Implications, ECB, December 2000. Available at http://www.ecb.int.
Walkner, C. and J.P. Raes (2005) 'Integration and consolidation in EU banking – an unfinished business', Economic Papers 226, *European Economy*. Available at http://europa.eu.int/comm/economy_finance/publications/economic_papers/2005/ecp226en.pdf.

On integration of European financial markets, see:
Adjaouté, K. and J.-P. Danthine (2003) 'European financial integration and equity returns: a theory-based assessment', in V. Gaspar, P. Hartmann and O. Sleijpen (eds) *The Transformation of the European Financial System*, European Central Bank, Frankfurt.
Gaspar, V. and P. Hartmann (2005) 'The Euro and money markets: lessons for European financial integration', in A. Posen (ed.) *The Euro at Five: Ready for a Global Role?*, Institute for International Economics, Washington, DC.

Hartmann, P., A. Maddaloni and S. Manganelli (2003) 'The Euro area financial system: structure, integration and policy initiatives', *Oxford Review of Economic Policy*, 19(1): 180 213.
Klaus, A., T. Jappelli, A. Menichini, M. Padula and M. Pagano (2002) *Analyse, Compare and Apply Alternative Indicators and Monitoring Methodologies to Measure the Evolution of Capital Market Integration in the European Union*, Report for the European Commission.
The Lamfalussy Report (a 2001 report on measures to take to support further integration of European financial markets). Available at http://europa.eu.int/comm/internal_market/en/finances/general/lamfalussyen.pdf.

On the international role of the euro, see:
Chinn, M. and J. Frankel (2005) 'Will the euro eventually surpass the dollar as leading international reserve currency?', NBER Working Paper 11510. Available at http://www.nber.org/papers/w11510.
Detken, C. and P. Hartmann (2002) 'Features of the Euro's role in international financial markets', *Economic Policy*, 35 (October): 555–69.
ECB (2005) *Review of the International Role of the Euro*. Available at http://www.ecb.int/pub/pdf/other/euro-international-role2005en.pdf.
Rey, H. (2005) 'The impact of a five year old euro on financial markets', pp. 111–16, in A. Posen (ed.) *The Euro at Five: Ready for a Global Role?*, Institute for International Economics, Washington, DC.

On stock markets in the accessing countries, see:
Claessens, S., R. Lee and J. Zechner (2003) *The Future of Stock Exchanges in European Union Accession Countries*, Centre for Economic Policy Research, London. Available at http://www.cepr.org.

Useful websites

Websites concerned with regulation and supervision:
The Basel Committee on Banking Supervision: http://www.bis.org/bcbs/aboutbcbs.htm.
Financial Stability Institute (FSI): http://www.bis.org/fsi/index.htm.
The ECB–CFS research network: http://www.eu-financial-system.org.
The Euro Homepage on the website of Giancarlo Corsetti: http://www.econ.yale.edu/~corsetti/euro/.
The Financial Services Action Plan website, full or reports and legal texts: http://europa.eu.int/comm/internal_market/en/finances/actionplan/.

References

Chinn, M. and J. Frankel (2005) 'Will the euro eventually surpass the dollar as leading international reserve currency?', NBER Working Paper 11510. Available at http://www.nber.org/papers/w11510.

Dermine, J. (2003) 'European banking, past, present, and future', in V. Gaspar, P. Hartmann and O. Sleijpen (eds) *The Transformation of the European Financial System*, European Central Bank, Frankfurt.

Dornbusch, R. (2000) *Keys to Prosperity, Free Markets, Sound Money and a Bit of Luck*, MIT Press, Cambridge, Mass.

ECB (2004) *Measuring Financial Integration in the Euro Area*, Occasional Paper No.14, April.

ECB (2005) *Review of the International Role of the Euro*, European Central Bank, Frankfurt. Available at http://www.ecb.int/pub/pdf/other/euro-international-role2005en.pdf.

Hartmann, P., A. Maddaloni and S. Manganelli (2003) 'The Euro area financial system: structure, integration and policy initiatives', *Oxford Review of Economic Policy*, 19(1): 180–213.

Walkner, C. and J.P. Raes (2005) 'Integration and consolidation in EU banking – an unfinished business', Economic Papers 226, *European Economy*. Available at http://europa.eu.int/comm/economy_finance/publications/economic_papers/2005/ecp226en.pdf.

Index